BBC

Bitesize

Bitesize AQA GCSE (9–1) COMBINED SCIENCE TRILOGY

REVISION GUIDE

FOUNDATION

Series Consultant:
Harry Smith

Authors:
Karen Bailey
Kieron Nixon

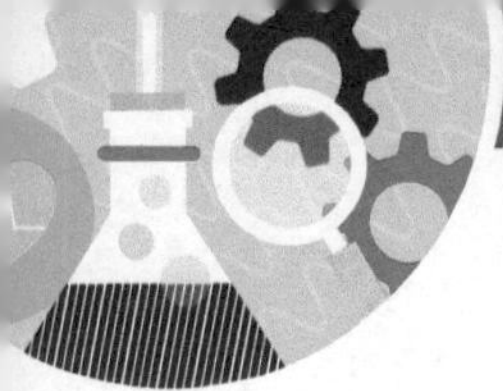

Contents

How to use this book iv
Your Science GCSE v
Multiple choice questions vi
Short-answer questions vii
Extended-response questions viii

Biology

Cell biology

- Levels of organisation 1
- Prokaryotic and eukaryotic cells 2
- Animal and plant cells 3
- Microscopy 4
- Using microscopes 5
- Specialised cells 6
- Cell differentiation 7
- Chromosomes, mitosis and the cell cycle 8
- Stem cells 9
- Diffusion 10
- Osmosis 11
- Investigating osmosis 12
- Active transport 13

Organisation

- Plant tissues 14
- Plant transport 15
- Digestion in humans 16
- Food tests 17
- Investigating enzymes 18
- The blood 19
- The heart and lungs 20
- Health issues 21
- Coronary heart disease 22
- Risk factors in disease 23
- Cancer 24

Infection and disease

- Communicable diseases 25
- Viral diseases 26
- Bacterial and fungal diseases 27
- Protist diseases 28
- Human defence systems 29
- Vaccination 30
- Antibiotics and painkillers 31
- Development of drugs 32

Bioenergetics

- Photosynthesis 33
- Rate of photosynthesis 34
- Uses of photosynthesis 35
- Investigating photosynthesis 36
- Aerobic and anaerobic respiration 37
- Response to exercise 38
- Metabolism 39

Response

- The human nervous system 40
- Reaction times 41
- Homeostasis 42
- Human endocrine system 43
- Control of blood glucose 44
- Hormones in reproduction 45
- Contraception 46

Inheritance, variation and evolution

- Asexual and sexual reproduction 47
- Meiosis 48
- DNA and the genome 49
- Genetic inheritance 50
- Inherited disorders 51
- Variation and mutation 52
- Sex determination 53
- Evolution 54
- Selective breeding 55
- Genetic engineering 56
- Fossils 57
- Extinction 58
- Resistant bacteria 59
- Classification 60

Ecology

- Communities 61
- Abiotic factors 62
- Biotic factors 63
- Adaptations 64
- Organisation of an ecosystem 65
- Investigating population size 66
- Using a transect 67
- Cycling materials 68
- Biodiversity 69
- Waste management 70
- Land use 71
- Deforestation 72
- Global warming 73
- Maintaining biodiversity 74

Chemistry

Atomic structure and the periodic table

- Atoms, elements and compounds 75
- Mixtures 76
- The model of the atom 77
- Subatomic particles 78
- Size and mass of atoms 79
- Isotopes and relative atomic mass 80
- Electronic structure 81
- The periodic table 82
- Developing the periodic table 83
- Metals and non-metals 84
- Group 0 85
- Group 1 86
- Group 7 87

Structure, bonding and properties of substances

- Chemical bonds 88
- Ionic bonding 89
- Ionic compounds 90
- Covalent bonding 91
- Metallic bonding 92
- States of matter 93
- Properties of ionic compounds 94
- Properties of small molecules 95
- Polymers 96
- Giant covalent structures 97
- Properties of metals and alloys 98
- Metals as conductors 99
- Diamond 100
- Graphite 101
- Graphene and fullerenes 102

Quantitative chemistry

- Conservation of mass 103
- Relative formula mass 104
- Balancing equations 105
- Mass changes 106
- Chemical measurements 107
- Concentrations of solutions 108

Chemical changes

- Metal oxides 109
- The reactivity series 110
- Extraction of metals and reduction 111
- Reactions of acids with metals 112
- Salt production 113
- Soluble salts 114
- Making salts 115
- The pH scale and neutralisation 116
- Electrolysis 117
- Electrolysis to extract metals 118
- Electrolysis of aqueous solutions 119
- Electrolysis of copper(II) chloride 120
- Exothermic and endothermic reactions 121
- Temperature changes 122
- Reaction profiles 123

Rate of reaction

- Calculating rate of reaction 124
- Factors affecting rate of reaction 125
- Rate of reaction 126
- Catalysts 127

- Reversible reactions 128
- Energy changes in reversible reactions 129

Organic chemistry
- Crude oil, hydrocarbons and alkanes 130
- Fractional distillation 131
- Hydrocarbons 132
- Cracking and alkenes 133

Chemical analysis
- Pure substances 134
- Formulations 135
- Chromatography 136
- Paper chromatography 137
- Testing for gases 138

The Earth's atmosphere
- Gases in the atmosphere 139
- Earth's early atmosphere 140
- Oxygen and carbon dioxide levels 141
- Greenhouse gases 142
- Human contribution to greenhouse gases 143
- Global climate change 144
- The carbon footprint 145
- Atmospheric pollutants 146

The Earth's resources
- Earth's resources 147
- Potable water 148
- Purifying water 149
- Waste water treatment 150
- Life cycle assessment 151
- Reducing the use of resources 152

Physics

Energy
- Energy transfers in a system 153
- Gravitational potential energy 154
- Kinetic energy 155
- Energy in a spring 156
- Using energy equations 157
- Power 158
- Efficiency 159
- Renewable energy resources 160
- Non-renewable energy resources 161

Electricity
- Circuit diagrams 162
- Current, resistance and potential difference 163
- Electrical charge 164
- Resistance 165
- Resistors 166
- Series and parallel circuits 167
- *I*-*V* characteristics 168
- Mains electricity 169
- Energy transfers in appliances 170
- Electrical power 171
- Transformers and the National Grid 172

Particle model of matter
- Density 173
- Density of materials 174
- State changes 175
- Specific heat capacity 176
- Specific heat capacity (practical) 177
- Specific latent heat 178
- Particle motion in gases 179

Atomic structure
- The structure of an atom 180
- Mass number, atomic number and isotopes 181
- Development of the atomic model 182
- Radioactive decay and nuclear radiation 183
- Half-lives 184
- Nuclear equations 185
- Radioactive contamination 186

Forces
- Scalar and vector quantities 187
- Forces 188
- Gravity 189
- Resultant forces 190
- Work done and energy transfer 191
- Forces and elasticity 192
- Force and extension 193
- Distance and displacement 194
- Speed and velocity 195
- Distance–time relationships 196
- Uniform acceleration 197
- Velocity–time graphs 198
- Newton's laws of motion 199
- Newton's second law 200
- Investigating acceleration 201
- Stopping distance 202
- Braking distance 203

Waves
- Types of wave 204
- Properties of waves 205
- Investigating waves 206
- Types of electromagnetic wave 207
- Properties of electromagnetic waves 208
- Infrared radiation 209
- Applications of EM waves 210
- Magnetic fields 211
- Electromagnetism 212

Exam skills
- Equations 213
- Converting units 214
- Making estimations 215
- Interpreting data 216
- Using charts and graphs 217
- Using diagrams 218
- Planning practicals 219
- Comparing data 220
- Evaluating data 221
- Working scientifically 222

Answers 223
Periodic table 240
Physics Equation Sheet 241

☑ Tick off each topic as you go.

Grades have been assigned to most questions in this revision guide. These are intended to show you the level of challenge of those questions, and to help you track your progress. In your exam, your grade will be based on your overall mark, and not on your responses to individual questions.

How to use this book

Use the features in this book to focus your revision, track your progress through the topics and practise your exam skills.

Features to help you revise

Each bite-sized chunk has a **timer** to indicate how long it will take. Use them to plan your revision sessions.

Complete **worked examples** demonstrate how to approach exam-style questions.

Test yourself with **exam-style practice questions** at the end of each page and check your answers at the back of the book.

Tick boxes allow you to track the sections you've revised. Revisit each page to embed your knowledge.

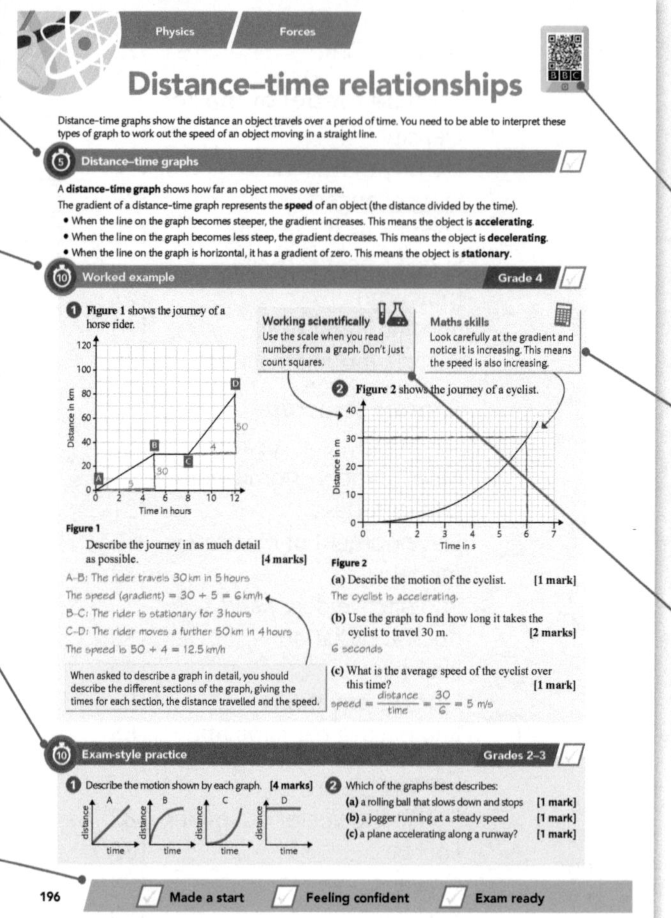

Physics | Forces

Distance–time relationships

Distance–time graphs show the distance an object travels over a period of time. You need to be able to interpret these types of graph to work out the speed of an object moving in a straight line.

5 Distance–time graphs

A **distance–time graph** shows how far an object moves over time.

The gradient of a distance–time graph represents the **speed** of an object (the distance divided by the time).

- When the line on the graph becomes steeper, the gradient increases. This means the object is **accelerating**.
- When the line on the graph becomes less steep, the gradient decreases. This means the object is **decelerating**.
- When the line on the graph is horizontal, it has a gradient of zero. This means the object is **stationary**.

10 Worked example — Grade 4

1 **Figure 1** shows the journey of a horse rider.

Working scientifically: Use the scale when you read numbers from a graph. Don't just count squares.

Maths skills: Look carefully at the gradient and notice it is increasing. This means the speed is also increasing.

Figure 1

Describe the journey in as much detail as possible. [4 marks]

A–B: The rider travels 30 km in 5 hours

The speed (gradient) = 30 ÷ 5 = 6 km/h

B–C: The rider is stationary for 3 hours

C–D: The rider moves a further 50 km in 4 hours

The speed is 50 ÷ 4 = 12.5 km/h

When asked to describe a graph in detail, you should describe the different sections of the graph, giving the times for each section, the distance travelled and the speed.

2 **Figure 2** shows the journey of a cyclist.

Figure 2

(a) Describe the motion of the cyclist. [1 mark]

The cyclist is accelerating.

(b) Use the graph to find how long it takes the cyclist to travel 30 m. [2 marks]

6 seconds

(c) What is the average speed of the cyclist over this time? [1 mark]

speed = $\frac{\text{distance}}{\text{time}} = \frac{30}{6} = 5$ m/s

10 Exam-style practice — Grades 2–3

1 Describe the motion shown by each graph. [4 marks]

2 Which of the graphs best describes:

(a) a rolling ball that slows down and stops [1 mark]

(b) a jogger running at a steady speed [1 mark]

(c) a plane accelerating along a runway? [1 mark]

196 Made a start | Feeling confident | Exam ready

Scan the **QR codes** to visit the BBC Bitesize website. It will link straight through to more revision resources on that subject.

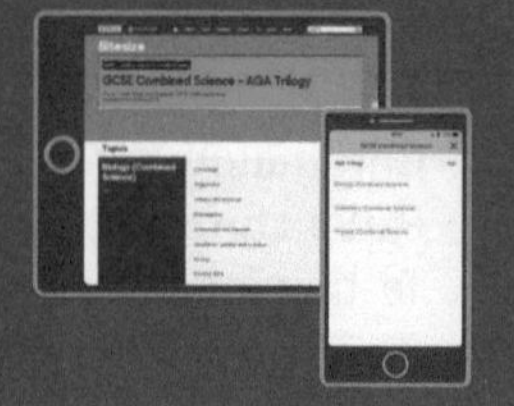

Questions that test **maths skills** are explained in callouts and in the *Exam skills* section at the back of the book.

Topics that are related to **working scientifically** are explained in callouts throughout the book.

Exam focus features

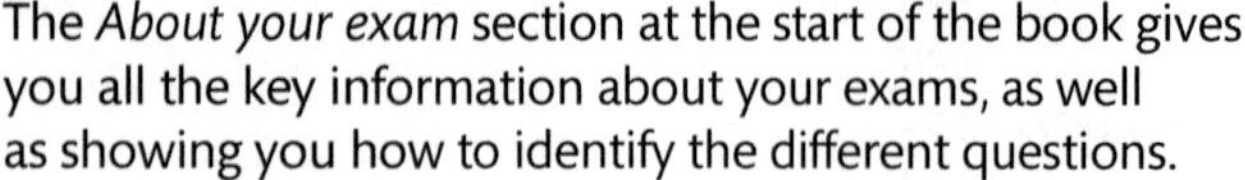

The *About your exam* section at the start of the book gives you all the key information about your exams, as well as showing you how to identify the different questions.

You will also find green *Exam skills* pages and purple *Practical* pages. These work through an extended exam-style question and provide further opportunities to practise your skills.

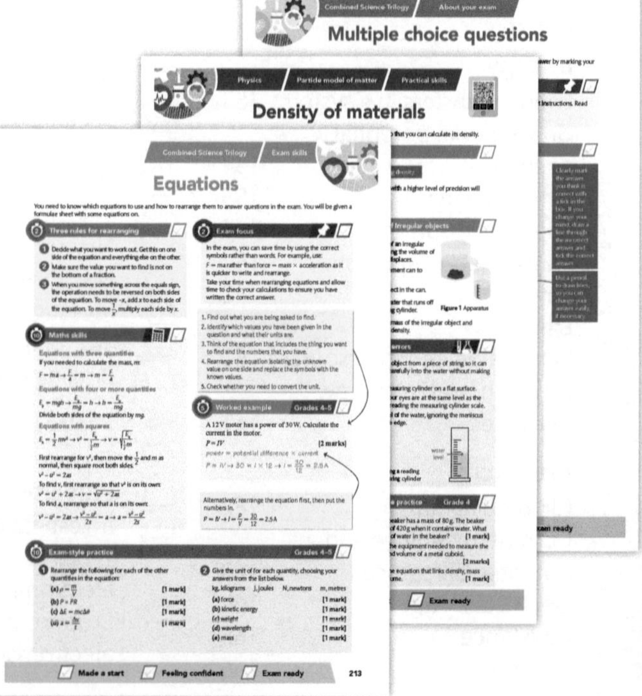

ActiveBook and app

This Revision Guide comes with a **free online edition**. Follow the instructions from inside the front cover to access your ActiveBook.

You can also download the **free BBC Bitesize app** to access revision flash cards and quizzes.

If you do not have a QR code scanner, you can access all the links in this book from your ActiveBook or visit **www.pearsonschools.co.uk/BBCBitesizeLinks**.

Your Science GCSE

This page will tell you everything you need to know about the structure of your upcoming AQA GCSE Combined Science: Trilogy (Foundation Tier) exams.

About the exam papers

You will have to take **six** papers as part of your AQA GCSE Combined Science: Trilogy (Foundation Tier) qualification: **two biology, two chemistry** and **two physics**. The papers will test your knowledge and understanding of different topic areas and your ability to work scientifically.

Paper 1	Paper 2	Paper 3	Paper 4	Paper 5	Paper 6
Biology 1	Biology 2	Chemistry 1	Chemistry 2	Physics 1	Physics 2
1 hour 15 minutes	1 hour 15 minutes	1 hour 15 minutes	1 hour 15 minutes	1 hour 15 minutes	1 hour 15 minutes
70 marks in total	70 marks in total	70 marks in total	70 marks in total	70 marks in total	70 marks in total
		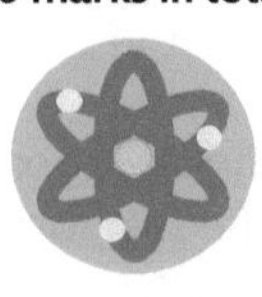			

Exam topics

- **Paper 1 Biology 1** (16.7%): Topics include: cell biology; organisation; infection and response; bioenergetics
- **Paper 2 Biology 2** (16.7%): Topics include: homeostasis and response; inheritance; variation and evolution; ecology
- **Paper 3 Chemistry 1** (16.7%): Topics include: atomic structure and the periodic table; bonding, structure and the properties of matter; quantitative chemistry; chemical changes; energy changes
- **Paper 4 Chemistry 2** (16.7%): Topics include: the rate and extent of chemical change; organic chemistry; chemical analysis; using resources; chemistry of the atmosphere
- **Paper 5 Physics 1** (16.7%): Topics include: energy; electricity; particle model of matter; atomic structure
- **Paper 6 Physics 2** (16.7%): Topics include: forces; waves; magnetism and electromagnetism

Maths skills

You will be required to demonstrate the following mathematical skills in your GCSE Science exams:

- rearranging equations
- interpreting data from graphs and tables, including finding a gradient
- converting units
- using standard form
- using ratios, fractions and percentages
- calculating mean, mode and median
- using geometry (volumes, areas, angles, working out sides of triangles).

Working scientifically

There are 21 required practical activities you will carry out throughout your GCSE Science course.

Practical activities are an opportunity for you to apply your knowledge and understanding, while developing relevant practical skills and techniques.

You need to know how to:

- plan and carry out an investigation
- use apparatus correctly and safely
- take accurate measurements and record data appropriately
- analyse your findings
- evaluate your investigation.

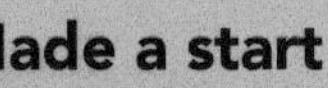

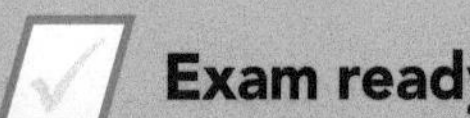

Made a start | Feeling confident | Exam ready

Multiple choice questions

Multiple choice questions give you several options to choose from. You must indicate the correct answer by marking your choice clearly.

1 Types of multiple choice question

- tick box
- linking boxes
- sentence completion

1 Exam focus

Bold words usually give important instructions. Read them carefully.

e.g. Tick **one** box.

5 Exam explainer

A cricket ball is hit by a bat. The bat and ball exert a force on each other. Choose the correct statement about the two forces. Tick **one** box.

[1 mark]

- **A** the force on the bat and the force on the ball are in the same direction ☐
- **B** the bat has a larger mass so it exerts a larger force on the ball ☐
- **C** the two forces are equal ✓
- **D** the two forces give the bat and ball equal accelerations ☐

If you are unsure of the answer, use what you know to rule out the incorrect options.

Clearly mark the answer you think is correct with a tick in the box. If you change your mind, draw a line through the incorrect answer and tick the correct answer.

Draw **one** line from each diagram to the name of the cell.

[2 marks]

Diagram	Name of cell
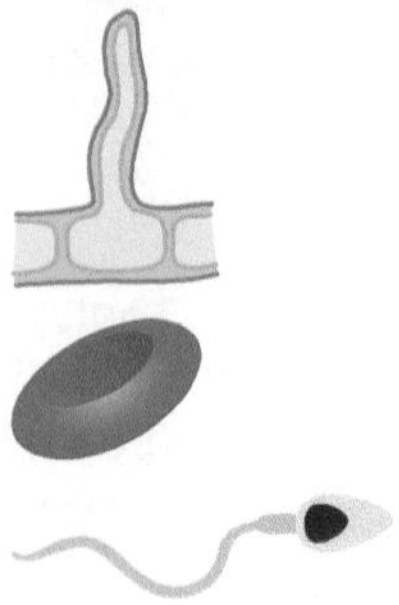	red blood cell
	sperm cell
	root hair cell

Use a pencil to draw lines, so you can change your answer easily, if necessary.

The pH scale is a measure of the acidity or alkalinity of a solution.

Use words from the box to complete the sentences.

[2 marks]

neutral	acidic	alkaline

A solution with a pH value of 5 is ____________.

A solution with a pH value of 7 is ____________.

A solution with a pH value of 13 is ____________.

Read the question carefully. Here, you are instructed to only use words from the box provided. You would not be awarded marks for using similar words.

Short-answer questions

Short-answer questions come in a variety of forms and are the most common type of questions.

Exam explainer

Underline key information, such as numbers and units. Make sure you include the correct units in your answer.

A power station has an efficiency of 0.45. Its energy comes from burning coal, which it uses at a rate of 300 MW.

(a) Calculate the useful output of electrical power. **[2 marks]**

(b) Describe the advantages and disadvantages of this type of power station compared to a wind turbine. **[3 marks]**

It is important to show your working when answering a calculation question. If done correctly, you will get method marks even if the final answer is wrong.

For a sketch question, you only need to draw approximately. You should only use a ruler if it helps you to make your answer clear.

Sketch a reaction profile for an endothermic reaction. **[3 marks]**

A student investigated the rate of reaction between calcium carbonate and hydrochloric acid.

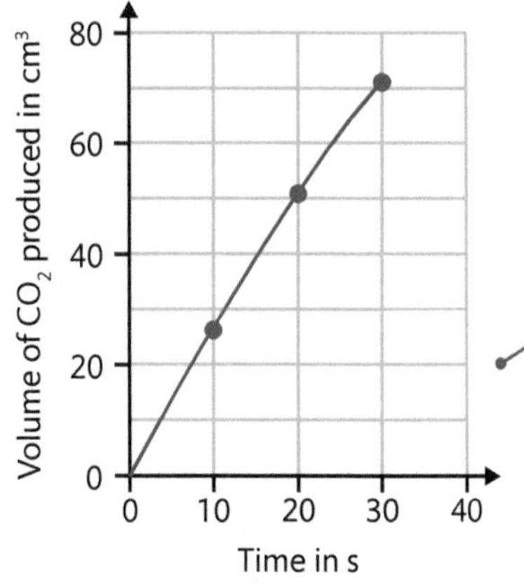

Figure 1 The student's results for one concentration of hydrochloric acid.

You will need to be able to interpret information from a graph, photo, table or image in your exam papers.

The table shows the student's results when the concentration was two times greater than the results shown in **Figure 1**.

Time in s	Volume of CO_2 in cm^3
0	0
10	41
20	62
30	71

(a) Plot the results shown in the table on the grid in **Figure 1**. Draw a line of best fit. **[3 marks]**

(b) Give **one** conclusion about how the rate of reaction changed when the concentration of hydrochloric acid was changed. **[1 mark]**

Extended-response questions

Some questions require a longer written response or a multi-step calculation. They are typically worth 4, 5 or 6 marks. You should give a clear and logical line of reasoning in your answer.

Command words

- explain – set out purposes or reasons
- evaluate – consider evidence for and against and conclude
- calculate – use numbers provided to work out the answer
- compare – identify similarities and/or differences
- describe – recall some facts, events or processes

Structure your answers

1. Make a **point** – for example: *Embryo screening is an expensive procedure.*
2. **Develop** your point – for example: *This means that the procedure is available only to people who can afford it.*
3. **Link** your point back to the question – for example: *This is a socio-economic issue because the procedure is not accessible to everyone.*

Exam explainer

4 mark questions have **two** levels:

1. basic
2. clear.

A clear answer interprets, evaluates or analyses scientific information or resources.

Aluminium can be extracted from its ore by electrolysis.

Explain how aluminium is extracted from aluminium oxide by electrolysis.

[4 marks]

For this question, you are expected to use your knowledge of electrolysis to explain how the process can be used to extract aluminium from aluminium oxide. You need to include references to ions, electrodes and reduction in your answer.

For this type of question, you should provide specific examples for each of the issues mentioned, interpreting them in an objective way, and finishing with a reasoned conclusion.

Evaluate the use of embryo screening for cystic fibrosis. In your answer discuss the economic, social and ethical issues.

[6 marks]

6 mark questions have **three** levels:

1. basic
2. clear
3. detailed.

A detailed answer shows understanding of scientific topics and knowledge of specific information. It is presented in a clear and balanced way.

When asked to calculate something, always show your working. There are often some marks available for method and it also helps you to check your answer.

Calculate the mass of calcium carbonate needed to produce 56 g of calcium oxide during thermal decomposition.

[5 marks]

Made a start

Feeling confident
Exam ready

Levels of organisation

You need to understand the principles of organisation within living organisms.

Organisation

Cells are the fundamental building blocks of all living things. Simple organisms, such as bacteria, are just one single cell (they are **unicellular**). **Multicellular** organisms have various levels of organisation within them, ranging from the individual cell to the entire organism. The levels of organisation range in complexity, from simplest to most complex, and in size, from very small to large.

Cells contain **organelles**, also known as sub-cellular structures, which perform specific functions within the cell. Individual cells can perform specific functions (page 6). Groups of specialised cells, which all have a similar structure and function, are called **tissues**. Groups of tissues that perform specific jobs are known as **organs**. Groups of organs form **organ systems**.

Cells are very small. You need a microscope to be able to examine them. Go to pages 4 and 5 to revise microscopy.

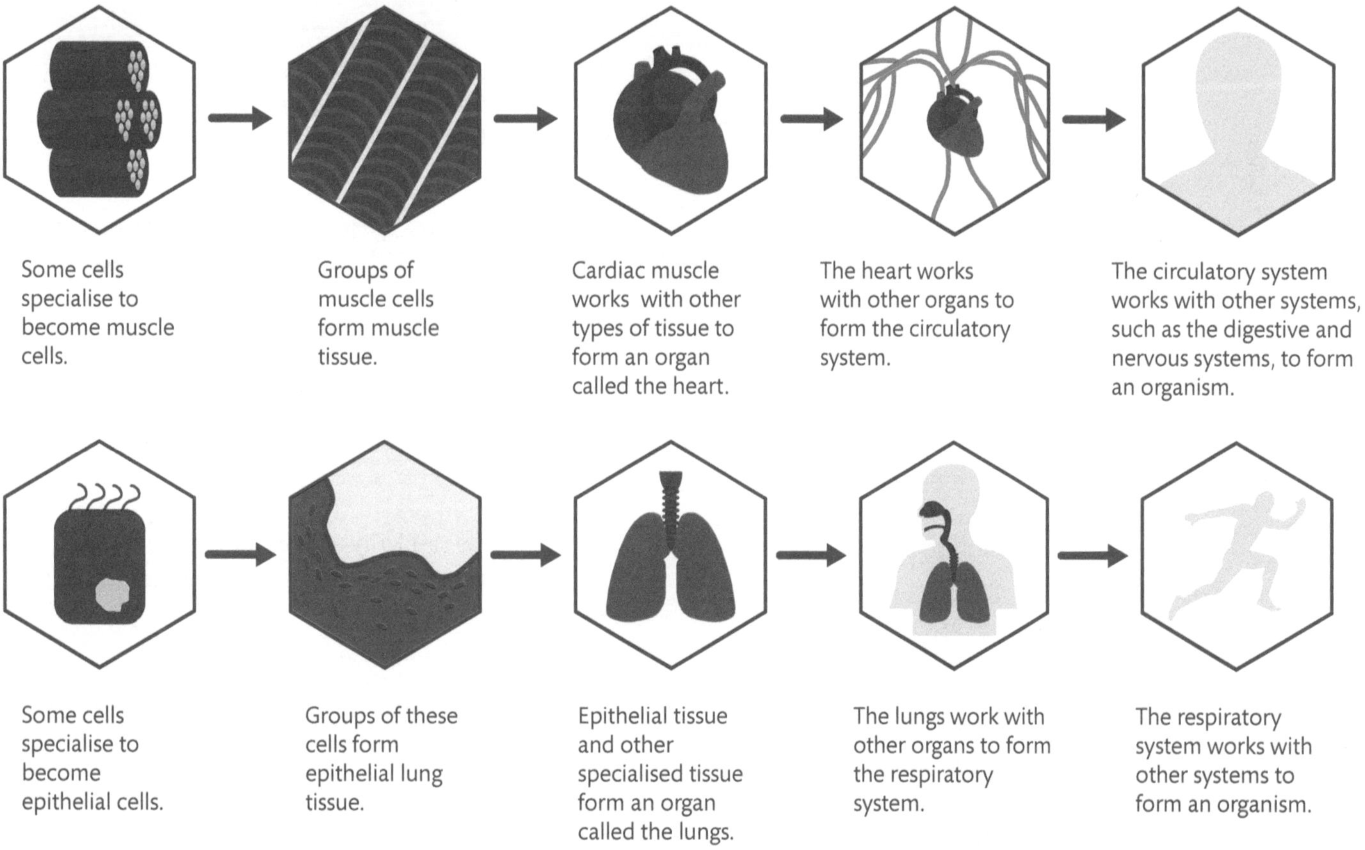

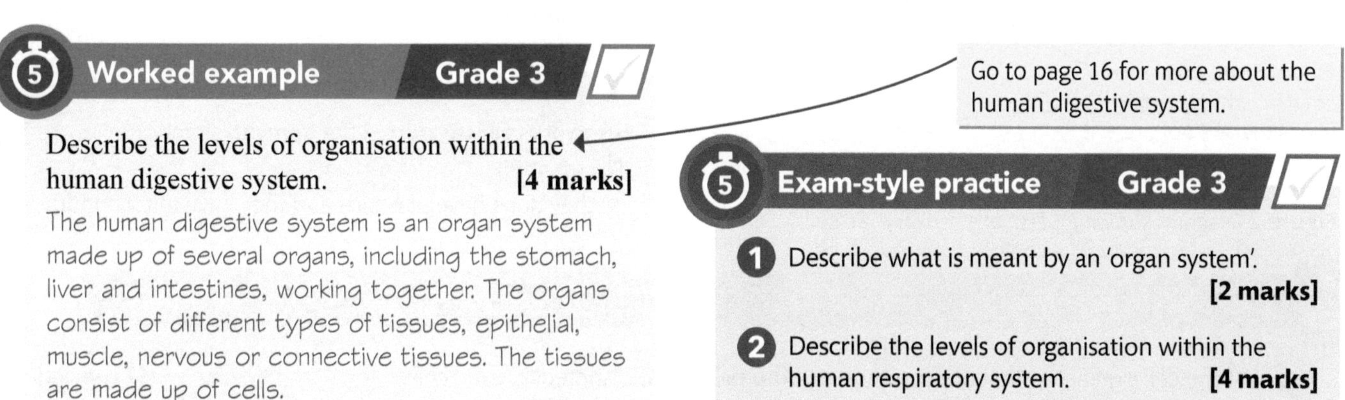

Some cells specialise to become muscle cells.
Groups of muscle cells form muscle tissue.
Cardiac muscle works with other types of tissue to form an organ called the heart.
The heart works with other organs to form the circulatory system.
The circulatory system works with other systems, such as the digestive and nervous systems, to form an organism.
Some cells specialise to become epithelial cells.
Groups of these cells form epithelial lung tissue.
Epithelial tissue and other specialised tissue form an organ called the lungs.
The lungs work with other organs to form the respiratory system.
The respiratory system works with other systems to form an organism.

Figure 1 The levels of organisation within the circulatory system (top) and the respiratory system (below)

Worked example — Grade 3

Describe the levels of organisation within the human digestive system. **[4 marks]**

The human digestive system is an organ system made up of several organs, including the stomach, liver and intestines, working together. The organs consist of different types of tissues, epithelial, muscle, nervous or connective tissues. The tissues are made up of cells.

Go to page 16 for more about the human digestive system.

Exam-style practice — Grade 3

1. Describe what is meant by an 'organ system'. **[2 marks]**
2. Describe the levels of organisation within the human respiratory system. **[4 marks]**

See page 20 for more about the respiratory system.

Prokaryotic and eukaryotic cells

You need to know the differences in structure and function of prokaryotic and eukaryotic cells.

10 Prokaryotes and eukaryotes

Cells can be classified as either **prokaryotic cells** (prokaryotes) or **eukaryotic cells** (eukaryotes). Animals and plants are made of eukaryotic cells. Bacteria are prokaryotic cells. Eukaryotic cells are larger and more complex than prokaryotic cells.

Ribosomes are tiny structures where proteins are made.

Cytoplasm is a jelly-like substance where chemical reactions take place.

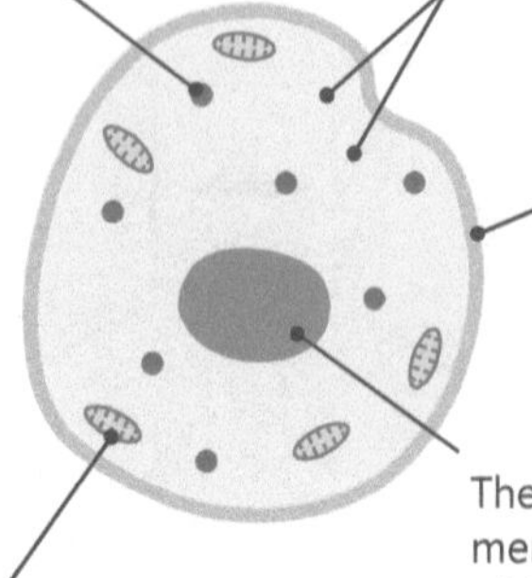

The **cell membrane** controls the movement of substances into and out of the cell.

Mitochondria release energy for cell processes. The energy is a product of respiration.

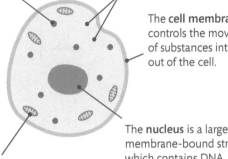

The **nucleus** is a large membrane-bound structure which contains DNA. DNA controls the growth and development of every living thing.

Figure 1 Diagram showing the parts of a eukaryotic cell

Genetic material is in a **single loop of DNA** not contained within a nucleus.

cytoplasm

cell membrane

A **cell wall** protects the cell.

ribosome

Plasmids are small rings of DNA, which contain genes that are not present in the chromosome.

Flagella enable the cell to move.

Figure 2 Diagram showing parts of a prokaryotic cell

1 Working scientifically

Most cells are microscopic. You need to understand the scale and size of cells and use the correct prefixes.

The following are compared to one metre.

centimetre (cm) = one hundredth or 10^{-2} m

millimetre (mm) = one thousandth or 10^{-3} m

micrometre (μm) = one millionth or 10^{-6} m

nanometre (nm) = one billionth or 10^{-9} m

Remember, prokaryote means 'before nucleus'. Prokaryotic cells do not have a nucleus. They contain a single DNA loop and small rings of DNA called plasmids.

5 Worked example — Grades 3–4

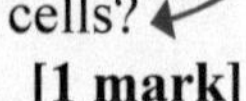

1 Where is DNA found in prokaryotic cells? **[1 mark]**

Prokaryotic cells contain a single DNA loop and small rings of DNA called plasmids. The DNA is not enclosed in a nucleus.

2 Give **one** similarity and **one** difference between the structure of prokaryotic and eukaryotic cells. **[2 marks]**

Similarity: They both have a cell membrane.

Difference: Eukaryotic cells have DNA contained within a nucleus. Prokaryotic cells do not have DNA in a nucleus.

Eukaryotic cells and prokaryotic cells are similar in that they both have:

- a cell membrane
- cytoplasm.

Eukaryotic cell structures differ from prokaryotic cells because:

- they don't have plasmids and they have mitochondria.

5 Exam-style practice — Grade 3

1 List the cell organelles that are common to both prokaryotic and eukaryotic cells. **[2 marks]**

2 Describe the structure of DNA within a prokaryotic cell. **[2 marks]**

 Made a start  Feeling confident  Exam ready

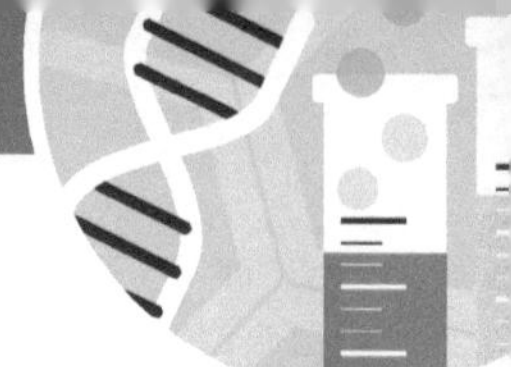

Animal and plant cells

You need to be able to describe and explain the differences in the structure of animal and plant cells.

Animal and plant cell structures

Although both animal and plant cells are eukaryotic, there are important structural differences between them. Plants stay in the same place and photosynthesise. They produce their own food. Animals move around in search of an external supply of food. These differences are the main reasons animal and plant cell structures differ.

Algal cells have a similar structure to plant cells. They also have a cellulose cell wall that strengthens the cell.

Go to page 1 to revise the functions of organelles.

Organelle	Plant cell	Animal cell
nucleus	✓	✓
cytoplasm	✓	✓
cell membrane	✓	✓
cell wall	✓	×
mitochondria	✓	✓
ribosomes	✓	✓
chloroplasts	✓	×
permanent vacuole	✓	×

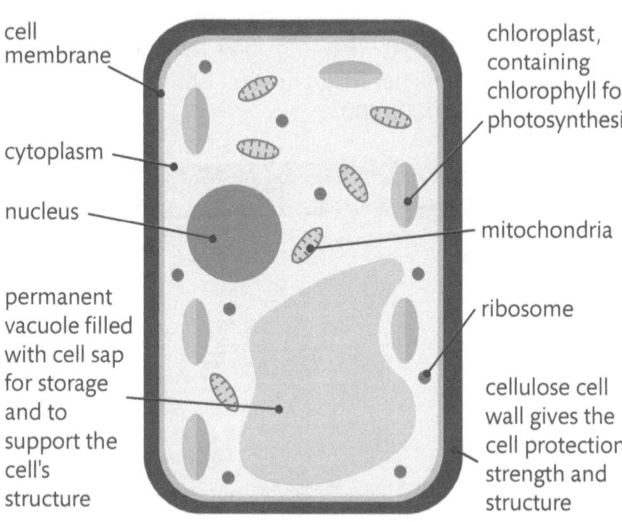

Figure 1 Diagram of a plant cell

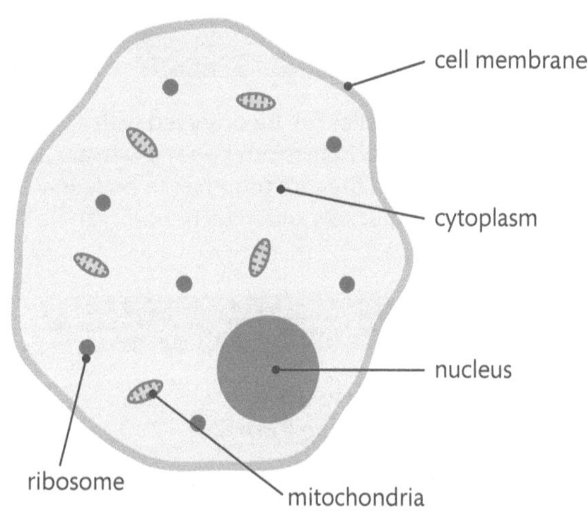

Figure 2 Diagram of an animal cell

Worked example — Grade 5

Name **two** structures within plant cells and for each give its function. **[4 marks]**

Structure is often related to function. Think of how animals and plants are different from one another.

(a) Name: Chloroplast

Function: Contains chlorophyll, which uses energy from sunlight to convert water and carbon dioxide into glucose and oxygen (photosynthesis).

(b) Name: Cellulose cell wall

Function: Makes the cell much more rigid, helping to support the plant.

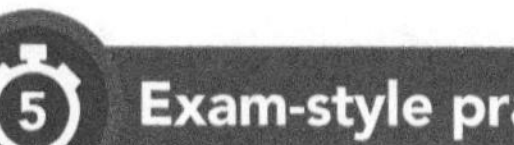

Exam-style practice — Grade 3

1. List the features found only in a plant cell. **[3 marks]**
2. Describe **three** differences between animal and plant cell structures. **[3 marks]**

 Made a start 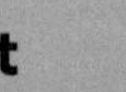 Feeling confident 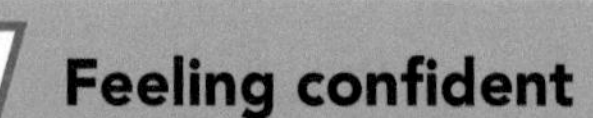  Exam ready

Microscopy

You need to know how microscopes have developed. Scientists can now study very small structures within cells.

Types of microscope

Microscopes are used to study cells. Over time, different kinds of microscope have been developed. The first light microscope, which could be used to observe simple cell structures, was invented about 350 years ago. This was gradually improved upon and refined to give the compound light microscopes that we use today. These can view complex cell structures. The electron microscope was invented in the 1930s.

Figure 1 Tiny cell organelles can be observed with an electron microscope. Ribosomes can be seen with an electron microscope but they are too small to be seen with a light microscope. The nucleus and mitochondria can be seen with a light microscope.

Maths skills

You need to know how to work out magnification using the formula:

$$\text{magnification} = \frac{\text{size of image}}{\text{size of real object}}$$

size of image

magnification | size of real object

Using a formula triangle can help you rearrange an equation.

Use a ruler to measure the size of the image.

Maths skills

Standard form is an efficient way of writing very big or very small numbers. For example: 35 000 000 can be written as:

$3.5 \times 10 \times 10 \times 10 \times 10 \times 10 \times 10 \times 10$

or 3.5×10^7 in standard form.

The number before the multiplication sign, 3.5 in this example, is a number greater than or equal to 1 and less than 10. The superscript above the 10 is the power of 10.

Numbers greater than 1 have a positive power of 10.

$920\,000 = 9.2 \times 10^5$

Numbers less than 1 have a negative power of 10.

$0.007\,03 = 7.03 \times 10^{-3}$

Magnification and resolution

Magnification is the measure of how many times bigger the image is than the object.

If a microscope has an eyepiece lens of ×10 and an objective lens of ×50, the image looks 10 × 50 times bigger, that is 500 times bigger.

Light microscopes use light to see an image. They can only magnify up to about ×1200, before resolution becomes a problem.

Resolution is the measure of how well a microscope can distinguish between two very close objects.

Above ×1200, light microscopes cannot distinguish between two close objects. This limit is due to the wavelength of light.

Electron microscopes use electrons rather than light. Electrons have a much shorter wavelength than light. This means they can distinguish between or resolve two very close objects at a much higher magnification, some even reaching up to ×10 000 000.

Worked example — Grades 4–5

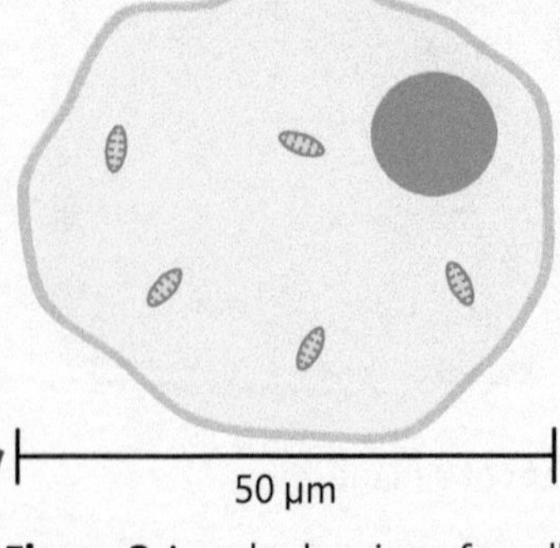

Figure 2 A scale drawing of a cell

Calculate the magnification of the image in **Figure 2**. **[3 marks]**

diameter of image = 5 cm

5 cm = 50 000 µm ← Convert units to those in the image.

diameter of real cell = 50 µm ← from scale bar

$$\text{magnification} = \frac{50\,000}{50} = \times 1000$$

Exam-style practice — Grade 5

1. A cell has a width of 100 µm. A scale drawing of the same cell has a width of 2 cm.
   Calculate the magnification of the drawing. Write your answer in standard form. **[3 marks]**
2. Give 357 800 in standard form. **[1 mark]**

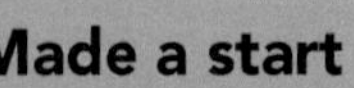

Made a start — Feeling confident — Exam ready

Using microscopes

You need to know how to set up and use a microscope to look at cells. You also need to be able to draw and label cells from a micrograph.

5 Using a microscope

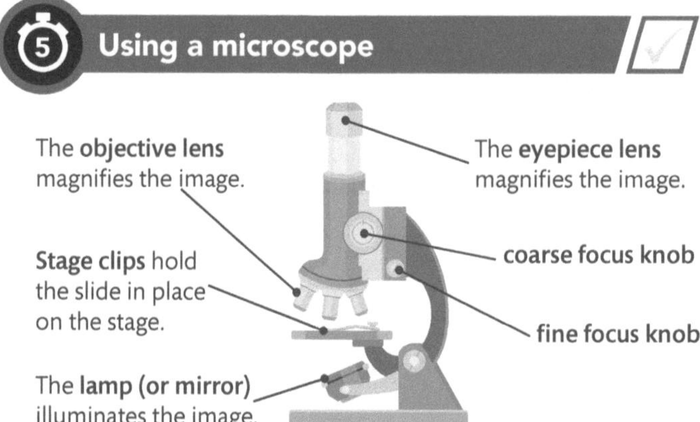

Figure 1 A light microscope

2 Working scientifically

You need to be able to use appropriate measurements when answering questions about the size of microscopic cells.

centimetre (cm) = one tenth of a metre
millimetre (mm) = one thousandth of a metre
micrometre (μm) = one millionth of a metre
nanometre (nm) = one billionth of a metre

10 Worked example — Grade 4

(a) Describe how you would prepare a slide of onion epidermal tissue. Use the diagram to help you. **[4 marks]**

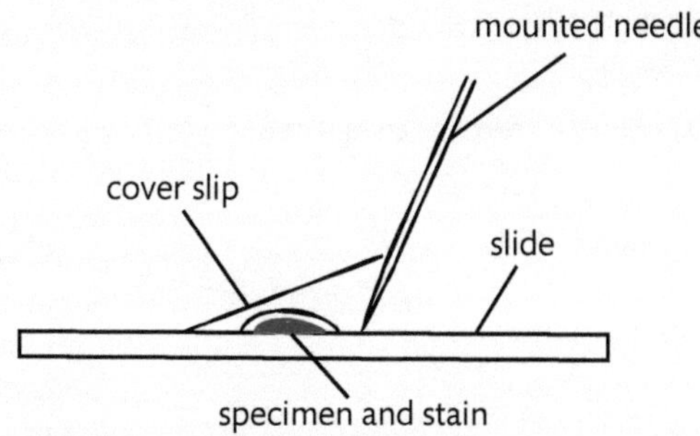

Drop a spot of water on a glass slide. Peel off a one-cell thick layer of cells and place on a glass slide. Add one drop of stain to the tissue. Use a mounted needle to lower the cover slip slowly and carefully to avoid trapping any air bubbles.

Tissue samples are stained to add contrast because most cells are colourless. Samples should be one cell thick so that cells can be seen clearly without different layers overlapping.

(b) Explain how you would view the slide under a microscope. **[4 marks]**

Place the prepared slide under the stage clips of the microscope. Use the coarse focus knob to lower the low power objective lens to just above the slide. Look through the eyepiece lens and raise the lens until the image is nearly in focus. Use the fine focus knob to get a clear sharp image.

(c) Look at **Figure 2**. Draw a labelled diagram of the cell. **[2 marks]**

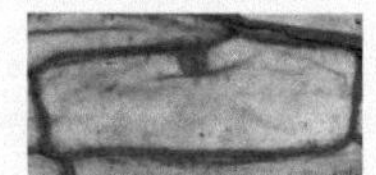

Figure 2 An onion cell

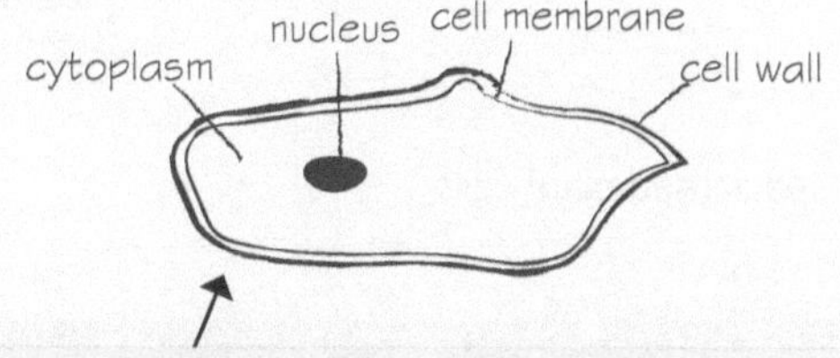

- You should only draw the things that you can see and not the things that you think should be there.
- Do not use shading.
- Keep the labels simple and clearly identify the structures.

5 Exam-style practice — Grade 4

1. Suggest why tissue samples must be very thin to be viewed with a microscope. **[1 mark]**
2. Suggest why scientists often stain tissue samples before viewing them with a microscope. **[2 marks]**

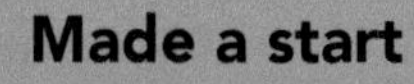

Made a start | Feeling confident | Exam ready

Specialised cells

Multicellular organisms are large organisms, like animals, made up of more than one type of cell. You need to know how the structures of specialised cells are adapted so that they can perform specific functions.

Specialised plant cells

You need to know how the following plant cells are specialised to carry out particular functions.

Xylem cells transport water and dissolved mineral ions from the roots to the rest of the plant. Go to page 14 to revise the functions of the plant organs in more detail.

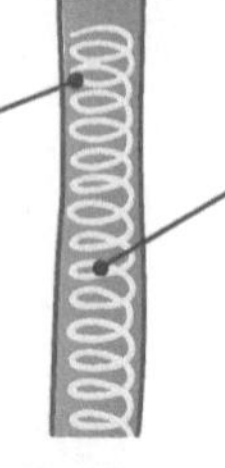

Lignin walls provide extra strength and support.
Hollow centre (lumen) allows water and dissolved mineral ions to flow easily through the plant.

Root hair cells absorb water and mineral ions from the soil.

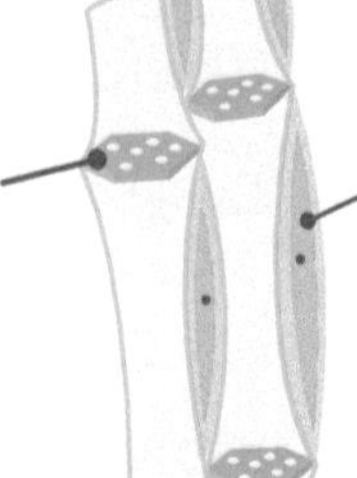

Large vacuole increases the rate of osmosis (page 11) into the cell from the soil.
A large surface area maximises the rate of osmosis and active transport.
Many mitochondria provide energy from respiration for the active transport of mineral ions into the cell from the soil.

Phloem cells transport dissolved sugars from the leaves to the roots, where they are stored.

Sieve plates allow solutions to move from cell to cell.

Companion cells contain many mitochondria to provide energy for active transport.

Figure 1 Specialised plant cells

Worked example — Grades 4–5

1 Describe **two** ways nerve cells are adapted for their function. **[2 marks]**

Nerve cells have long axons so they are able to transmit nerve impulses between distant parts of the body. They also have branched endings called dendrites that connect with other nerve cells.

2 Why do muscle cells contain many mitochondria? **[1 mark]**

Mitochondria produce the energy needed for muscles to contract.

Specialised animal cells

You need to know how the following animal cells are specialised to carry out a particular function.

Nerve cells carry electrical impulses around the organism.

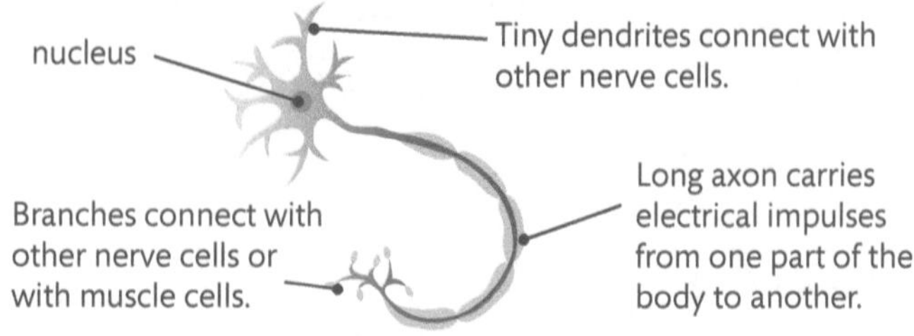

Muscle cells move, causing the muscle to contract (shorten).

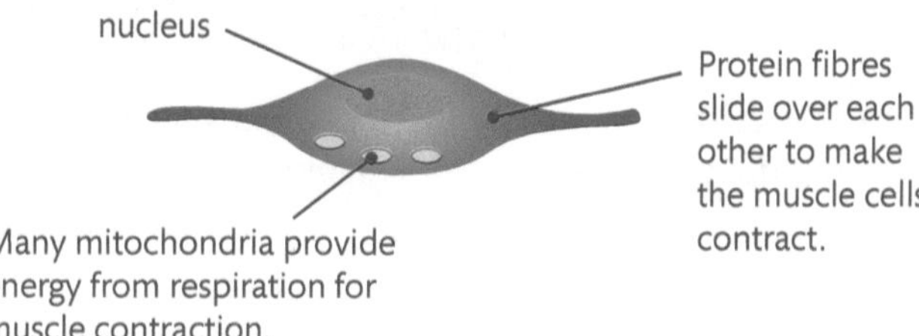

Protein fibres slide over each other to make the muscle cells contract.

Sperm cells swim and fertilise an egg cell.

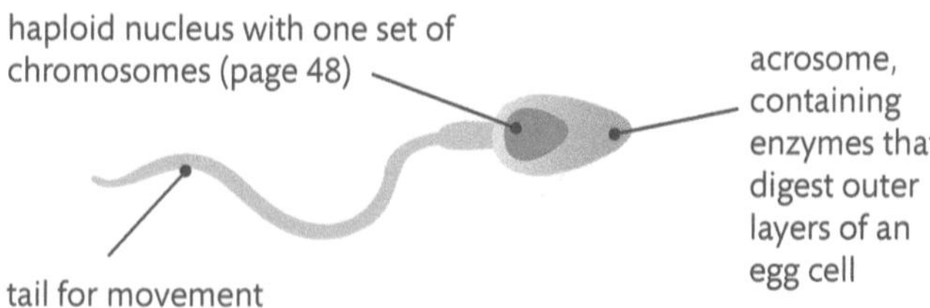

haploid nucleus with one set of chromosomes (page 48)

tail for movement

Ciliated cells, such as those in the trachea, move substances in a particular direction.

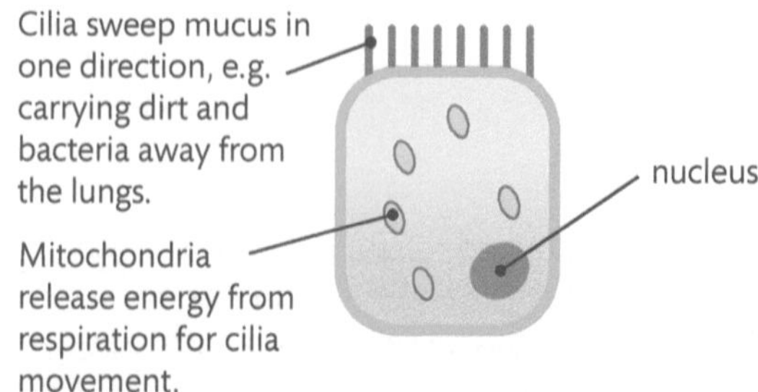

Cilia sweep mucus in one direction, e.g. carrying dirt and bacteria away from the lungs.

Figure 2 Specialised animal cells

Red blood cells are another type of specialised cell. Go to page 19 to revise the functions and adaptations of red blood cells.

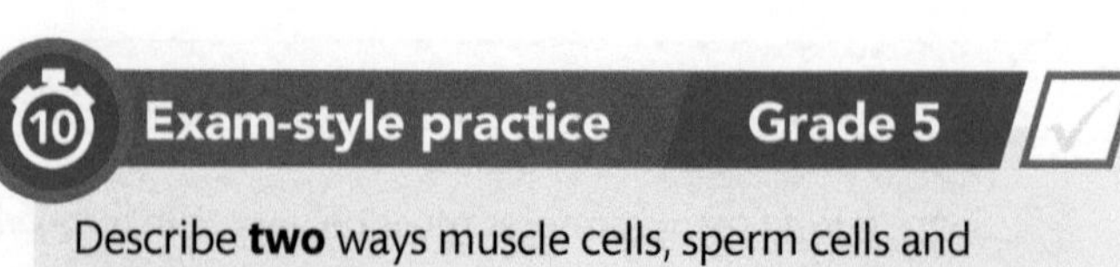

Exam-style practice — Grade 5

Describe **two** ways muscle cells, sperm cells and phloem are each specialised to perform their functions. **[6 marks]**

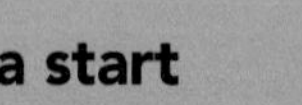

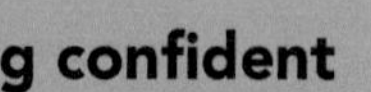

Made a start · Feeling confident · Exam ready

Cell differentiation

You need to understand the importance of cell differentiation in plants and animals.

Cell differentiation

As an organism develops, cells divide and differentiate to form different types of specialised cells. When a cell differentiates, it acquires different sub-cellular structures and sometimes a different form to help it to perform specific functions well.

- Muscle cells need to contract to cause movement.
- Nerve cells need to transmit electrical impulses to allow rapid communication between different parts of the organism.
- Root hair cells need a large surface area to absorb water and dissolved mineral ions from the soil.

Go to page 6 to revise how some cells have become specialised to perform their function.

Stem cells can differentiate into any kind of cell. Animal stem cells can come from embryos or from differentiated tissue such as bone marrow. Go to page 9 to revise stem cells.

Differentiation in animal cells

Most types of animal cell differentiate at an early stage in the life of an organism. In mature animals, cell division and differentiation are restricted mainly to repair and replacement, such as generating new blood cells, healing skin cuts, hair and fingernail growth, and healing broken bones.

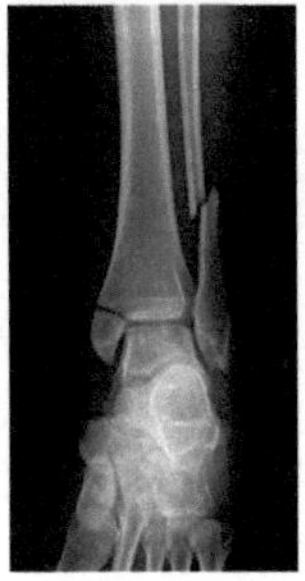

Figure 1 An X-ray of a broken ankle

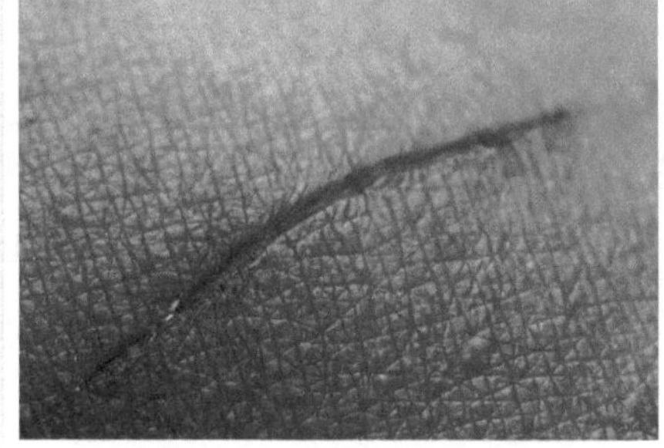

Figure 2 A healing cut

Differentiation in plant cells

Many types of plant cell can differentiate throughout the life of the organism, producing new leaves, flowers, branches, xylem and phloem. This is why plants can regrow branches that are cut or broken off. Cells in meristems (page 14) in plants can differentiate into any type of plant cell throughout the life of the plant.

Worked example — Grade 2

1 Which **two** functions is cell division restricted to in mature animals?
Tick **two** boxes. **[2 marks]**

fertilisation	☐
replacement	✓
diffusion	☐
contracting muscles	☐
repair	✓

2 Explain the role of cell differentiation in healing cuts in adults. **[2 marks]**

Cells can differentiate to regrow skin.
This is used to heal cuts.

Exam-style practice — Grade 3

1 The production of red blood cells is an example of replacement in humans. Give **two** other examples of cell repair and replacement in humans. **[2 marks]**

2 In plants, cells of the meristem can differentiate to produce different types of specialised plant cells.
Name **two** types of specialised cell found in a plant. **[2 marks]**

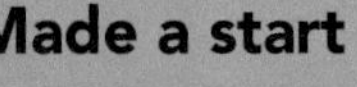

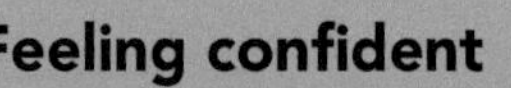
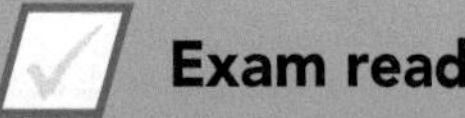

Chromosomes, mitosis and the cell cycle

Multicellular organisms grow and develop using a type of cell division called mitosis. You need to know how this occurs.

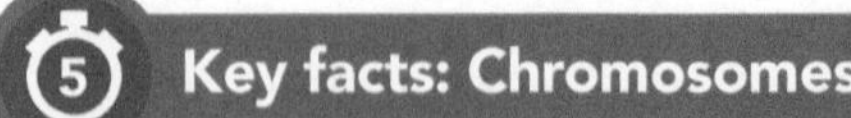

5 Key facts: Chromosomes

- Chromosomes are found in the nucleus of nearly all types of cell.
- There are two copies of each chromosome in nearly all body cells. In humans, there are 23 pairs of chromosomes, giving a total of 46 chromosomes in each cell (but not in the sex cells - see page 53 to revise how gender is determined.).
- Chromosomes consist of long strands of DNA coiled up.
- Each chromosome carries many **genes**. These are sections of DNA which control our characteristics.

5 Mitosis

Mitosis is the process of cell division involved in asexual reproduction. The products of mitosis are genetically identical clone cells produced for growth, repair and replacement of damaged body cells.

Before a cell can divide, it needs to grow and increase its number of sub-cellular structures such as ribosomes and mitochondria.

During the cell cycle the genetic material is doubled and then divided into two identical cells. Mitosis takes place after the cell contents have been replicated.

Mitosis produces **diploid** cells, cells with two versions of each chromosome.

10 Stages in the cell cycle

The cell cycle consists of **three stages** that lead to the production of two daughter cells from one parent cell.

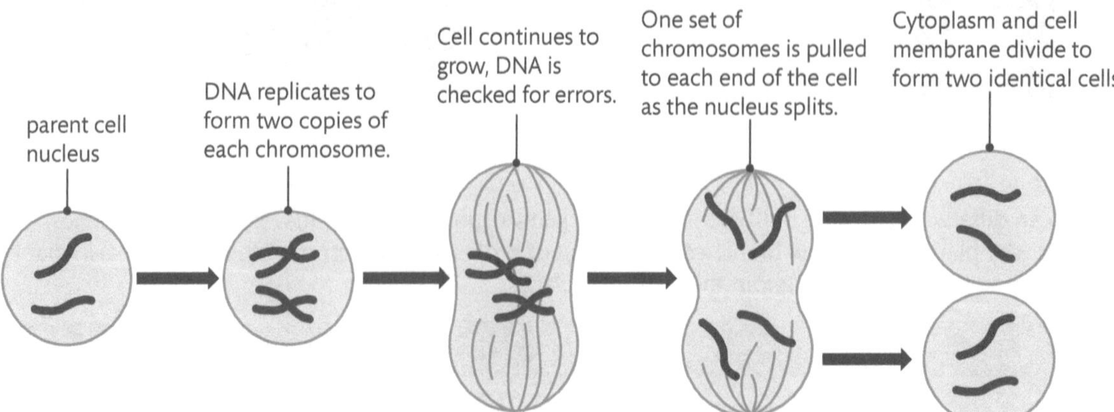

Figure 1 The cell cycle

10 Worked example — Grade 5

Figure 2 shows a cell during the cell cycle.

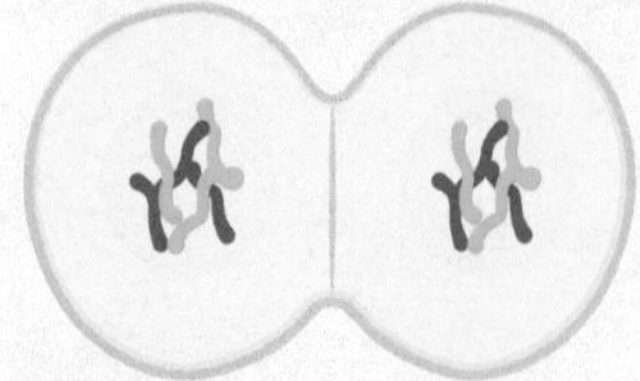

Figure 2

Describe what is happening in **Figure 2**. **[3 marks]**

The chromosomes have been pulled apart to opposite ends of the cell and two separate nuclei have formed. A cell membrane has formed between the two halves of the cell.

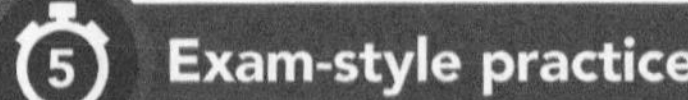

5 Exam-style practice — Grade 3

1. Describe **two** changes that happen inside a cell before it divides by mitosis. **[2 marks]**
2. Describe stages of the cell cycle. **[3 marks]**

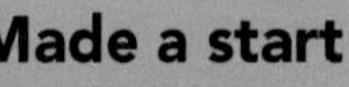
Made a start

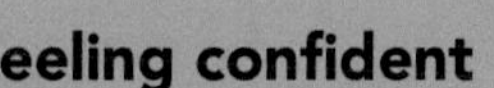
Feeling confident
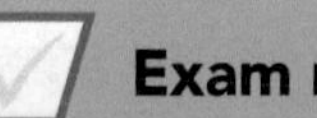
Exam ready

Stem cells

A stem cell is an undifferentiated cell of an organism, which is capable of giving rise to many more cells of the same type. Other types of cells can arise from stem cells when they differentiate.

2 Stem cells

Stem cells may one day be used to cure diseases by replacing faulty cells. They could cure diseases such as diabetes, paralysis, hearing and vision loss, and Parkinson's disease.

5 Adult stem cells

Adult stem cells are undifferentiated cells found within differentiated tissues, such as bone marrow or brain tissue.

Adult stem cells can form many, but not all, types of cells, as they are used in the body for repair and replacement of cells.

Adult stem cells are useful in the treatment of some conditions. For example, adult stem cells that are found in bone marrow, can form new red blood cells or white blood cells. They are used to treat people suffering blood disorders.

An advantage of using adult stem cells is that donation of adult stem cells is a choice and no life is destroyed. However, it can be a painful procedure.

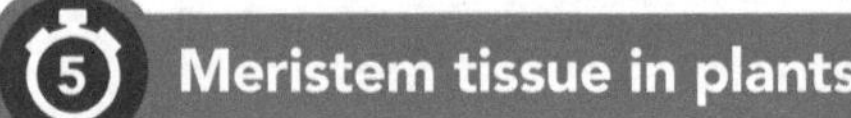

5 Meristem tissue in plants

Stem cells in the meristems (areas of growth in plants) can differentiate into any type of plant cell throughout the life of the plant. They can be used to quickly and cheaply produce **cloned** plants by taking cuttings. They are useful for growing rare species of plants to protect them from extinction. They can be used to grow lots of identical crops exhibiting desired traits, such as disease resistance.

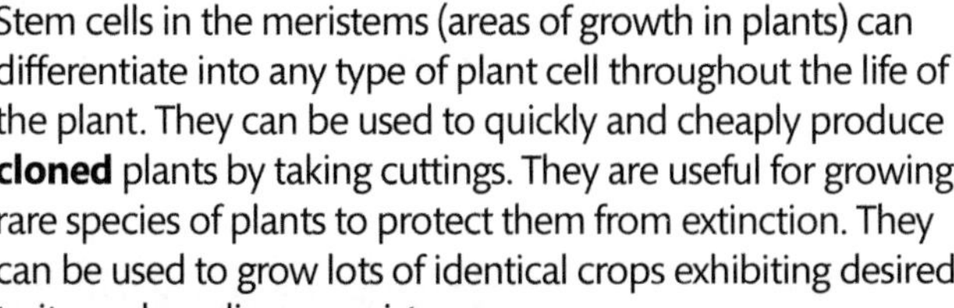

A clone is an organism that is genetically identical to another organism.

1 Working scientifically

Some people have ethical and religious objections to stem cell research and the use of stem cells. They say it is wrong to destroy human embryos. There is also a risk that cultured stem cells could be contaminated with viruses which would be transferred to a patient. Other people believe the advantage of using stem cells to cure diseases or injured people outweighs the rights of an embryo.

1 Exam focus

You don't need to know details about stem cell techniques for the exam, but you are expected to be able to evaluate the risks and benefits. You also need to know about the social and ethical issues involved in the use of stem cells in medical research.

5 Embryonic stem cells

Stem cells from embryos can be cloned and made to differentiate into most types of human cells when given the right treatment. These cells are currently used for research and might in the future be used to replace damaged cells.

However, embryos cannot choose to donate and they are destroyed in the process. Unwanted embryos from fertility clinics are often used.

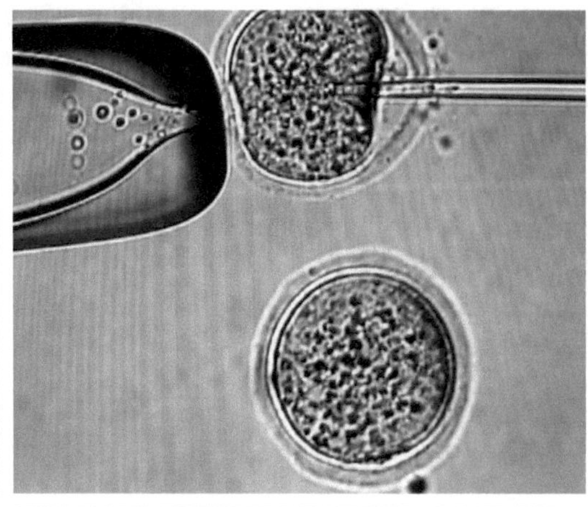

Figure 1 Stem cell research – an adult cell nucleus being injected into an egg cell

10 Worked example — Grade 4

1 Name the tissue in plants where stem cells can be found. **[1 mark]**

Meristem tissue

2 Describe the difference between embryonic and adult stem cells in a human. **[4 mark]**

Embryonic stem cells are found in human embryos and can differentiate into any kind of cell.

Adult stem cells are only found in certain places, such as bone marrow. They can only differentiate into certain types of cell. For example, stem cells in bone marrow can become blood cells.

10 Exam-style practice — Grade 4

1 Give **one** advantage for commercial growers using cloned plants. **[1 mark]**

2 Many groups are against the use of embryonic stem cells. Give **two** arguments against their use. **[2 marks]**

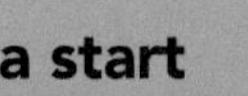

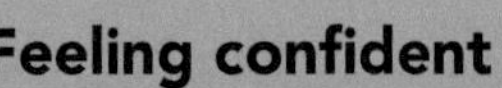
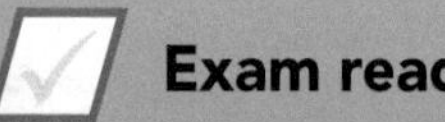

Made a start Feeling confident Exam ready

Diffusion

You need to know how certain factors affect the rate of diffusion, and how multicellular organisms are adapted for the effective exchange of substances.

Diffusion

Diffusion is the **net movement** of particles of gas or particles in solution, down a **concentration gradient**, from an area of their higher concentration to an area of their lower concentration. Individual particles move randomly in all directions, but because there are more of them in the area of high concentration, more of them move away from that area than into it. Diffusion is important in both plants and animals for the exchange of substances with the environment. Useful substances such as oxygen and glucose diffuse into cells. Waste products diffuse out of cells. Carbon dioxide is a waste product of respiration. It passes out of the organism to the environment, during gas exchange in fish gills, leaf cells and the lungs. Urea is a waste product that diffuses out of cells into the blood plasma and is then excreted in the kidney.

Factors affecting the rate of diffusion include:

- **difference in concentrations** – the greater the concentration gradient, the faster the rate of diffusion
- **temperature** – as temperature increases, the rate of diffusion increases because molecules move faster
- **surface area of the membrane** – as surface area increases, the rate of diffusion increases, see below.

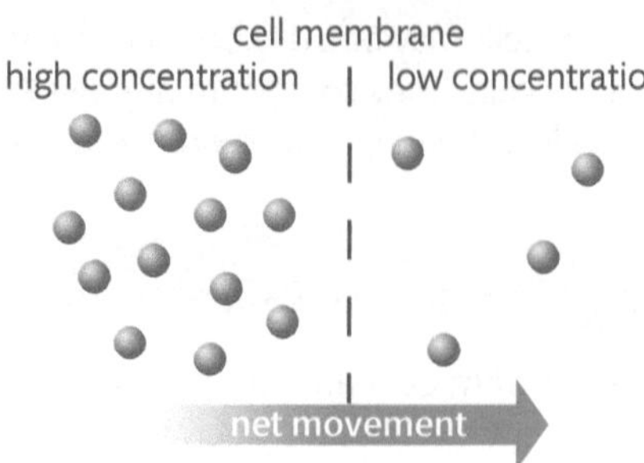

Figure 1 More molecules pass through the cell membrane from left to right than from right to left. So there is net movement to the right until there is the same concentration on both sides. The concentration gradient is the difference between the concentrations on either side.

Specialised plant cells

Diffusion can happen fast enough in small organisms (such as single cells) to exchange all they need with their environment. Multicellular organisms have specialised exchange surfaces that maximise the rate of diffusion by having:

- a large surface area
- a thin membrane for a short diffusion path
- a transport system (e.g. blood system) and ventilation (breathing) to maintain a high concentration gradient. This is important for efficient gaseous exchange of oxygen and carbon dioxide.

Examples of specialised exchange surfaces include:

- air sacs in the lungs and filaments in fish gills, for exchanging gases with the environment. Go to page 20 for more about adaptations within the lungs.
- villi in the small intestine, for absorbing digested food molecules. Go to page 16 for more about digestion in humans.
- leaf shape and structure, for gas exchange with the air. Go to page 14 to revise the adaptations of leaf cells and tissues.

Another answer is the thickness of the membrane.

Maths skills

Surface area to volume ratio

The rate of diffusion is faster when the surface area is larger.

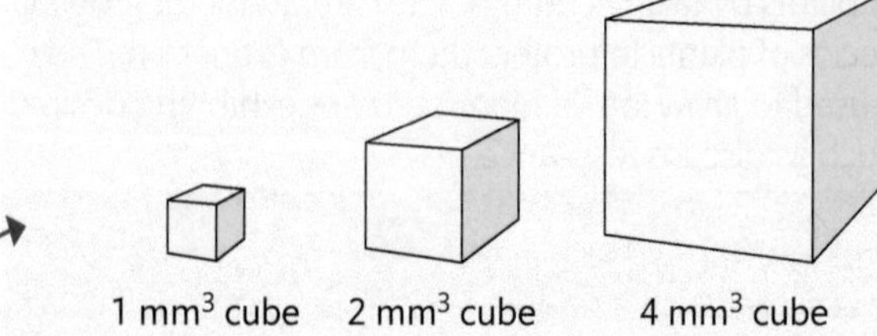

The ratio of surface area to volume is larger in the 1 mm cube than it is in the 2 mm cube.

Worked example — Grades 4–5

Give **three** factors that affect the rate of diffusion into and out of cells. **[3 marks]**

The difference in concentrations between two areas (i.e. the concentration gradient), the temperature and the surface area of the membrane.

Exam-style practice — Grade 5

1. State what is meant by diffusion. **[2 marks]**
2. Air sacs in the lungs have a large surface area. Explain the effect this has on the rate of gas exchange. **[2 marks]**

 Made a start  Feeling confident  Exam ready

Osmosis

You need to understand the process of osmosis and be able to draw and interpret labelled diagrams that model the diffusion of water molecules.

Diffusion of water molecules

Osmosis is the diffusion of water molecules, from a **dilute solution** to a **concentrated solution**, through a **partially permeable membrane**.

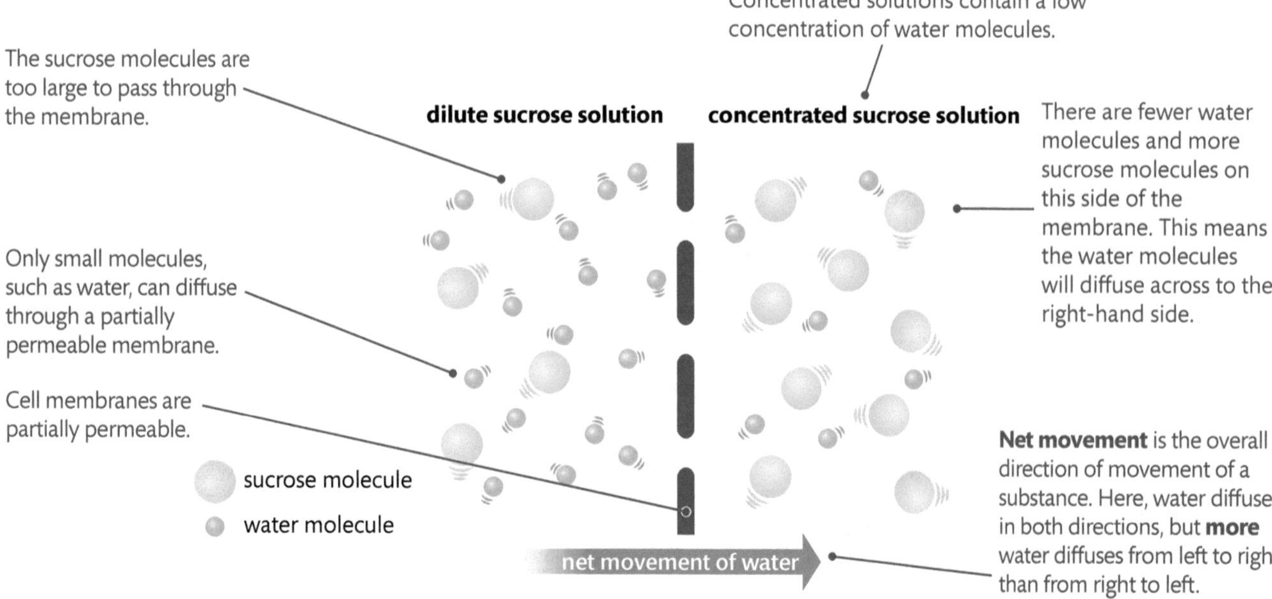

Concentrated solutions contain a low concentration of water molecules.
The sucrose molecules are too large to pass through the membrane.
dilute sucrose solution
concentrated sucrose solution
There are fewer water molecules and more sucrose molecules on this side of the membrane. This means the water molecules will diffuse across to the right-hand side.
Only small molecules, such as water, can diffuse through a partially permeable membrane.
Cell membranes are partially permeable.
sucrose molecule
water molecule
net movement of water
Net movement is the overall direction of movement of a substance. Here, water diffuses in both directions, but more water diffuses from left to right than from right to left.

Figure 1 Osmosis model

Worked example

Grade 4

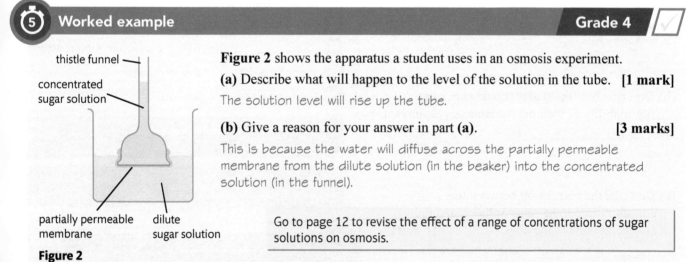

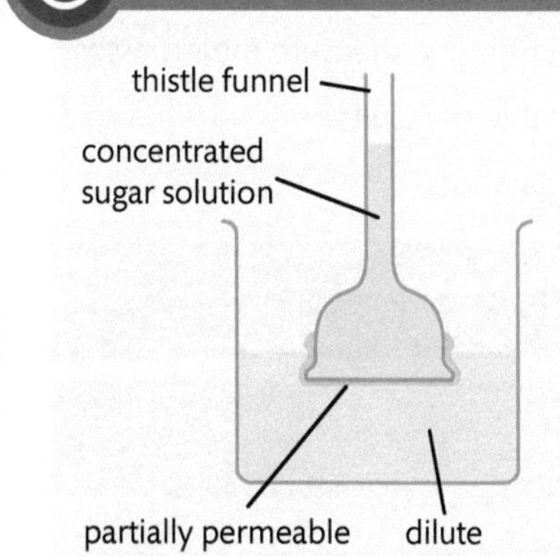

Figure 2

Figure 2 shows the apparatus a student uses in an osmosis experiment.

(a) Describe what will happen to the level of the solution in the tube. **[1 mark]**

The solution level will rise up the tube.

(b) Give a reason for your answer in part **(a)**. **[3 marks]**

This is because the water will diffuse across the partially permeable membrane from the dilute solution (in the beaker) into the concentrated solution (in the funnel).

Go to page 12 to revise the effect of a range of concentrations of sugar solutions on osmosis.

Exam-style practice

Grades 3–5

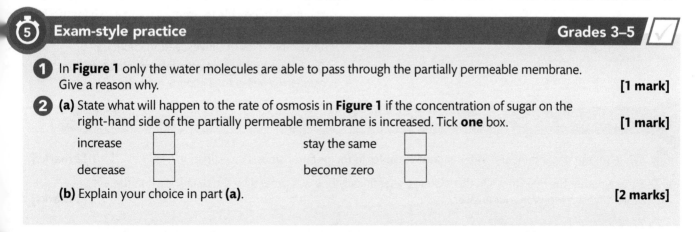

1 In **Figure 1** only the water molecules are able to pass through the partially permeable membrane. Give a reason why. **[1 mark]**

2 **(a)** State what will happen to the rate of osmosis in **Figure 1** if the concentration of sugar on the right-hand side of the partially permeable membrane is increased. Tick **one** box. **[1 mark]**

increase ☐ stay the same ☐

decrease ☐ become zero ☐

(b) Explain your choice in part **(a)**. **[2 marks]**

Investigating osmosis

You need to know how to produce a hypothesis and investigate the effect of different concentrations of sugar solution on osmosis.

Worked example — Grades 4–5

A student placed equal-sized raw potato chips in different concentrations of sugar solution for two hours. The table shows the change in mass of each of the potato chips. If the mass goes up it's a positive change and a negative change if it goes down.

Sugar solution concentration in g/dm^3	Initial mass of chip in g	Final mass of chip in g	Percentage change in mass
0	2.50	2.95	+18
80	2.51	2.46	−2
160	2.49	2.22	
240	2.7	2.07	−18
320	2.5	1.98	−21

(a) Percentage change is calculated using this equation:

$$\text{percentage change} = \frac{\text{increase in mass}}{\text{original mass}} \times 100\%$$

Use the equation to calculate the missing value in the table. **[2 marks]**

Increase in mass = 2.22 − 2.49 = −0.27g

$$\text{Percentage change} = \frac{-0.27}{2.49} \times 100\% = -10.8\%$$

Percentage change = −11%

(b) Describe how the student could check the repeatability of their measurements. **[2 marks]**

The student could repeat the investigation several more times under the same conditions to see whether the results are similar.

(c) Describe the correlation between the concentration of the sugar solution and the change in mass of the chip. **[1 mark]**

As the concentration of sugar solution increases, the mass of the chip decreases.

Apparatus

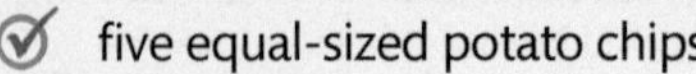

- five equal-sized potato chips
- five different concentrations of sugar solution:
  - 0 g/dm^3
  - 80 g/dm^3
  - 160 g/dm^3
  - 240 g/dm^3
  - 320 g/dm^3
- ruler
- balance

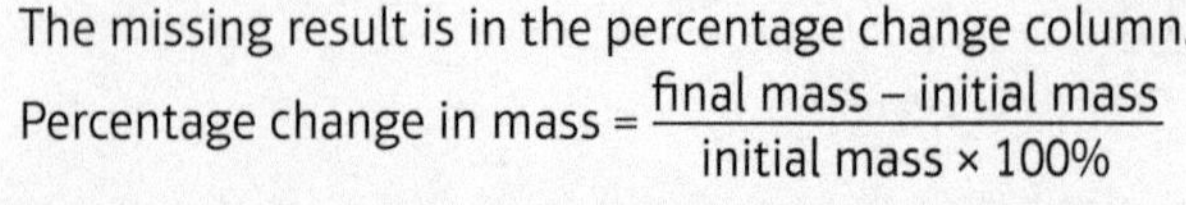

Maths skills

The missing result is in the percentage change column.

$$\text{Percentage change in mass} = \frac{\text{final mass} - \text{initial mass}}{\text{initial mass} \times 100\%}$$

Method

1. Using the balance, measure accurately five **equal-sized** potato chips.
2. Place each potato chip in a different concentration of sugar solution.
3. Leave the chips for several hours.
4. Remove each of the chips and measure their masses.
5. Record the data in a table of results.
6. Calculate percentage gain/loss.

The mass of the potato chips is the dependent variable that you measure.

The concentration of the sugar solution is the independent variable that you change.

Working scientifically

You need to be able to produce a suitable hypothesis based on your understanding of osmosis. For example, a hypothesis for this investigation could be:

The higher the concentration of sugar solution, the greater the percentage change in mass.

Exam-style practice — Grade 5

1. What are the dependent and independent variables in the potato osmosis investigation? **[2 marks]**
2. State whether the hypothesis in the Working scientifically box was proved by the data shown in the table. Give a reason for your answer. **[2 marks]**

 Made a start  Feeling confident 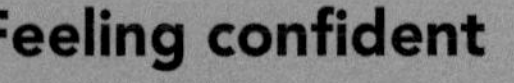  Exam ready

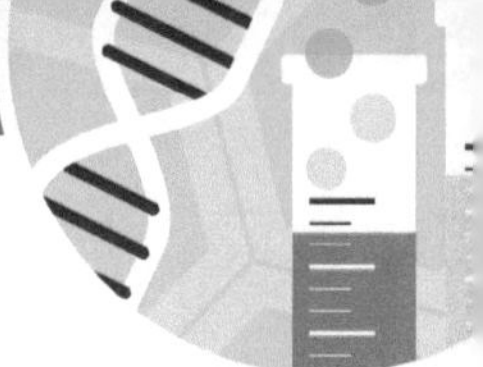

Active transport

You need to understand how substances are transported by active transport and be able to describe how it differs from osmosis and diffusion.

Active transport

Active transport is the movement of a substance from a dilute solution to a more concentrated solution against the **concentration gradient**. This process requires energy from respiration.

Root hair cells absorb mineral ions from the soil, where their concentration is much lower than inside the root cells. So the cells use active transport to move mineral ions from the soil across their cell membrane into the cell. Go to page 6 for more about adaptations of root hair cells.

In humans, active transport helps glucose to be absorbed quickly through the wall of the small intestine during digestion. The concentration of glucose is often higher in the blood than in the gut wall, so the glucose cannot be absorbed by diffusion. The glucose is then used in cells for respiration.

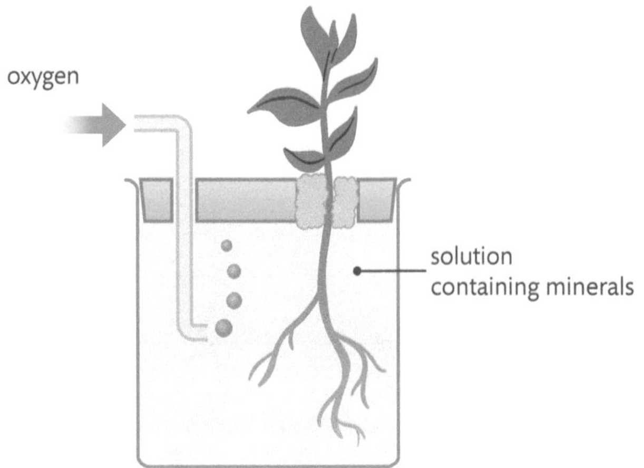

Figure 1 The apparatus shows a plant growing in a solution of mineral ions. Oxygen is bubbled through the solution.

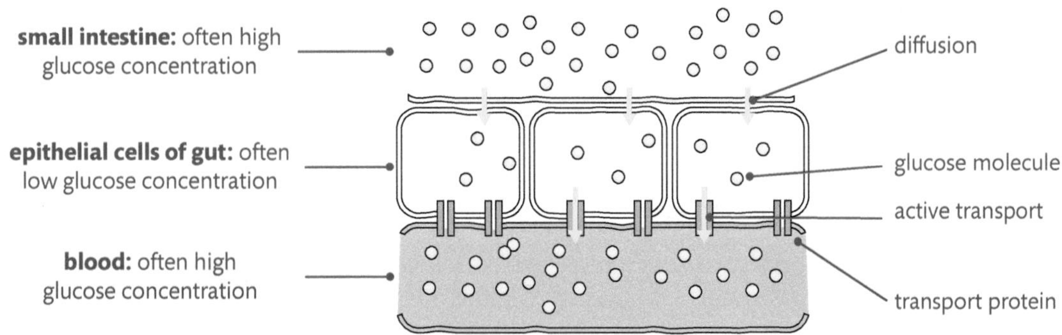

Figure 2 Active transport in the human gut. Glucose molecules move across the membrane against the concentration gradient. Mitochondria supply energy for active transport.

Worked example

Grade 5

Explain why plants use active transport to take up mineral ions from the solution in **Figure 1**. **[2 marks]**

Because the concentration of mineral ions inside the root hair cells is higher than the solution surrounding the root hair cell, therefore the plant cannot rely on diffusion.

Exam focus

You could be asked about the differences between diffusion and active transport in the exam. Unlike diffusion, active transport involves substances moving against the concentration gradient and requires energy.

Exam-style practice

Grade 4

1. Describe **two** differences between diffusion and active transport. **[3 marks]**
2. Describe **two** different examples of active transport in living organisms. **[2 marks]**

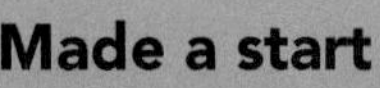

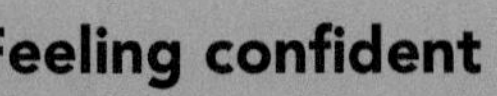
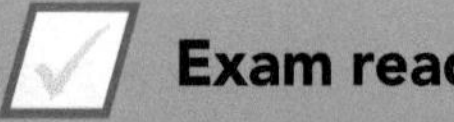

Plant tissues

You need to know how the structures of plant tissues work together and how they are related to their functions.

Plant tissues in the leaf

A tissue is a group of similar cells. Groups of different types of tissue working together can form an organ, such as a plant leaf.

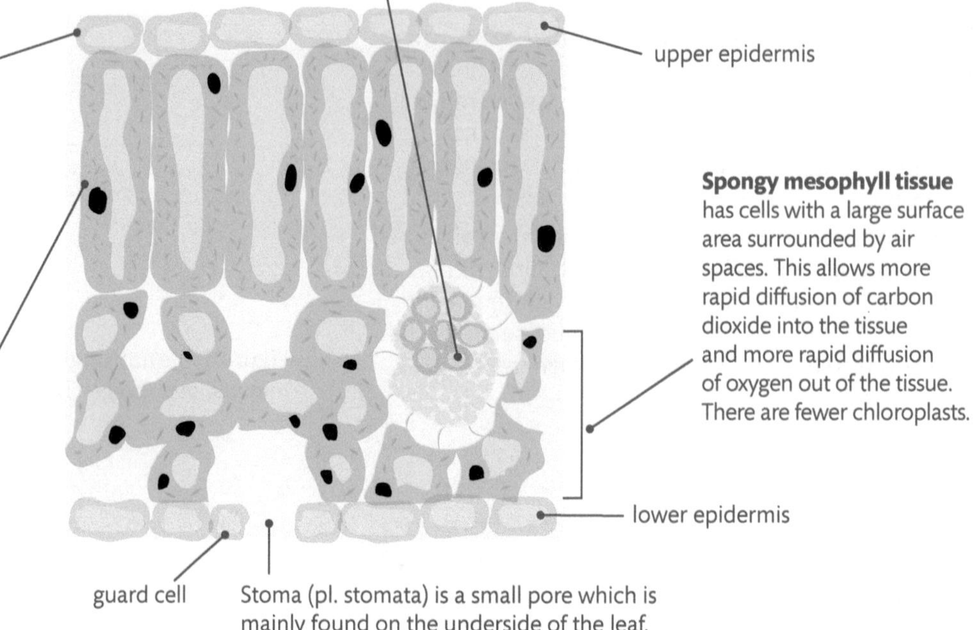

Figure 1 Cross-section through a leaf showing the different tissues

Meristems

Plant growth occurs by cell division and differentiation in certain areas called **meristems**. Meristems consist of stem cells, which are cells that can differentiate to form any type of plant cell, such as xylem and phloem cells. Meristems are found, for example, at the tips of shoots and roots.

Meristems can produce new cells throughout the life of the plant.

Guard cells in a leaf

The stomata also control the loss of water through transpiration. (You can revise this on page 15.)
Plants cannot photosynthesise at night, so guard cells (specialised cells in epidermal tissue) close the stomata. This prevents valuable water from evaporating from the leaf. Stomata are closed at night.

Worked example — Grade 4

1 Explain why chloroplasts are found mostly near the upper surface of a leaf. **[2 marks]**

Because the upper surface of the leaf is where most light hits the leaf so there are lots of chloroplasts in this area to absorb the light for photosynthesis.

2 The lower surface of a leaf contains many tiny holes called stomata. Describe the function of the stomata. **[2 marks]**

To allow carbon dioxide to diffuse into the leaf and oxygen to diffuse out.

Exam-style practice — Grade 4

1 Name the leaf tissue where most photosynthesis occurs. **[1 mark]**

2 The spongy mesophyll tissue has a large surface area. Explain why this is important for photosynthesis. **[2 marks]**

 Made a start  Feeling confident  Exam ready

Plant transport

You need to know how the roots, stem and leaves of a plant are adapted to transport water and dissolved mineral ions by transpiration, and food molecules by translocation.

Transport in plants

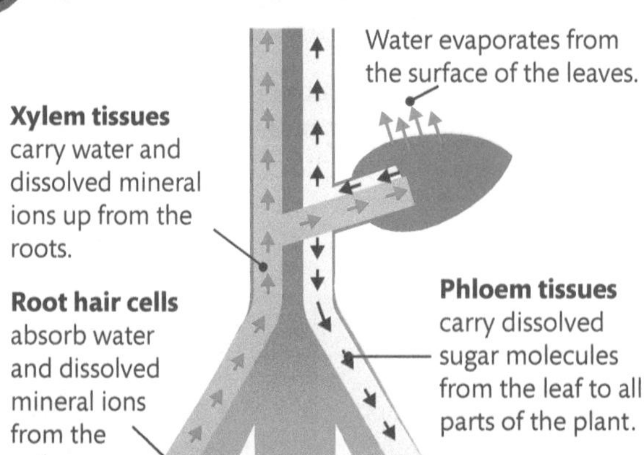

Figure 1 Transport of substances in plants

Phloem

The movement of food molecules through phloem tissue is called **translocation**. Phloem tubes are elongated cells. The ends of each tube have a sieve plate with pores. Cell sap moves through the pores carrying dissolved sugars.

Xylem

Xylem tissue transports water and dissolved minerals. It is made of hollow tubes strengthened by lignin. Pits (thin areas) in the tubes allow water and ions to move between xylem tubes.

Root hair cells

Root hair cells have a large surface area to absorb water and mineral ions, as well as a large vacuole to increase the rate of absorption of water by osmosis, and many mitochondria to provide the energy needed for active transport.

Worked example — Grade 5

B

A

Rate of transpiration

Light intensity

Figure 2

Describe the relationship between rate of transpiration and light intensity on the part of **Figure 2**:

(a) labelled **A** **[3 marks]**

As the light intensity increases so does the rate of transpiration.

(b) labelled **B.** **[1 mark]**

As the light intensity increases the rate of transpiration stays the same.

(c) Light affects the opening of stomata. In dim, or no light, the stomata are closed. As the light intensity increases, the stomata open up more, up to a maximum width. Use this information to explain the shape of the graph. **[4 marks]**

As the light intensity increases, so does the width of the stomata so more water can diffuse out, meaning the rate of transpiration increases.
At a certain light intensity, the stomata opening reaches maximum width and so the rate of diffusion of water out of the stomata cannot increase anymore, so the rate of transpiration levels off.

Transpiration

Transpiration is the movement of water through a plant from the roots to the leaves. Water evaporates from the surface of mesophyll cells in the leaves and diffuses out through open stomata. This causes more water to be drawn up xylem cells through the plant. More water is absorbed from the soil by osmosis in root hair cells.

Factors affecting the rate of transpiration

- **Temperature** – As temperature increases, water molecules move faster. This means evaporation from the leaf increases, so transpiration is faster at higher temperatures.
- **Humidity** – As air humidity increases, the concentration gradient between the water vapour inside the air spaces of the leaf and the outside air decreases. This causes the rate of diffusion to decrease, slowing the rate of transpiration.
- **Air movement** – As wind speed increases, the water molecules, which have just left the stomata, get blown away. This maintains a greater concentration gradient so water molecules diffuse out of the leaf more rapidly, increasing the rate of transpiration.
- **Light intensity** – At night, the guard cells close the stomata to retain valuable water resources, so transpiration stops. In bright light, the stomata open wider to allow more carbon dioxide to enter the leaf for photosynthesis, so the rate of transpiration increases.

Exam-style practice — Grade 4

1. Describe the passage of water through plants from the root hairs to the stomata. **[3 marks]**
2. List the **two** main ways in which root hair cells are adapted to their function. **[2 marks]**

 Made a start  Feeling confident 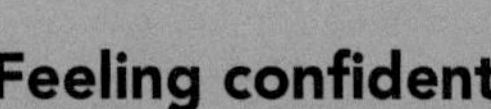  Exam ready

Digestion in humans

Digestion occurs when enzymes break down large food molecules into smaller molecules so that they can be absorbed into the bloodstream. The molecule that the enzyme acts upon is the substrate. The molecules that result from the enzyme action are the products. Enzymes are catalysts. They speed up chemical reactions without changing themselves, so they can be used again.

2 Lock and key model

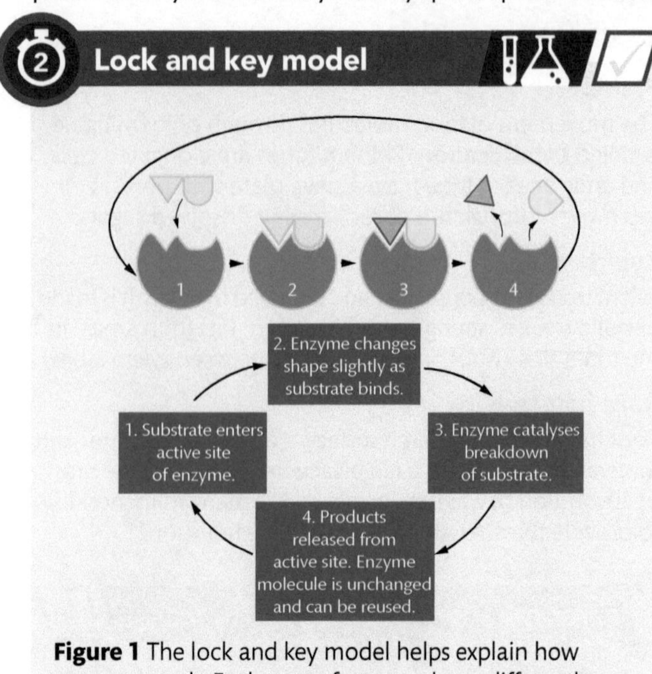

Figure 1 The lock and key model helps explain how enzymes work. Each type of enzyme has a differently shaped active site so can only work with a specific shape of molecule.

5 Factors that affect enzymes

Different enzymes digest different substrates. Each reaction has a specific enzyme which catalyses it. Each enzyme has a certain temperature and pH that it works best at. High temperatures and a different pH can change the shape of the active site of the enzyme, so it is no longer effective.

5 Worked example — Grade 5

The following statements describe how enzymes work. Give the correct order of the statements by writing 1, 2 or 3 in the box beside each statement. **[2 marks]**

Enzyme catalyses the breakdown of substrate. 2

Products are released from enzyme. 3

Substrate binds to active site of enzyme. 1

10 Enzymes and digestion

The products of digestion are used to build up new proteins, carbohydrates and fats in our body. Some of the glucose produced is used for respiration and the release of energy.

Protease enzymes

- Proteases, such as pepsin, break down proteins into amino acids in the stomach and small intestine.
- Proteases are produced in the stomach, small intestine and pancreas.

Carbohydrase enzymes

- Carbohydrases, such as amylase break down carbohydrates into sugars.
- Amylase is produced in the salivary glands, small intestine and pancreas. Amylase breaks down starch in the mouth and small intestine.

Lipase enzymes

- Lipases break down fats and oils into fatty acids and glycerol in the small intestine.
- They are produced in the pancreas and the small intestine.
- They work best in alkaline conditions.

protein molecule
protease
amino acids

starch molecule
amylase
maltose molecules

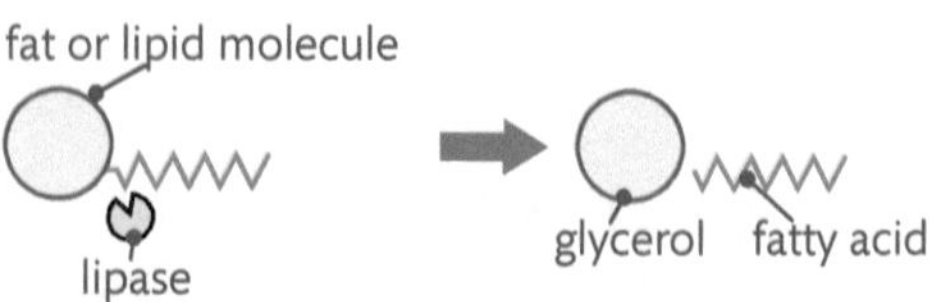

Figure 2 Enzymes in digestion

Bile

Bile is produced by the liver, stored in the gall bladder, and released into the small intestine. Bile is alkaline, so it neutralises hydrochloric acid from the stomach. It also emulsifies fats, which means that it breaks them into smaller droplets. The droplets have a larger surface area, so the enzyme can reach fat molecules more easily to digest them.

2 Exam-style practice — Grade 5

Bile is an alkaline substance that is released into the small intestine.

Describe **two** functions of bile. **[2 marks]**

 Made a start  Feeling confident  Exam ready

Food tests

You need to know how food can be tested to see whether it contains carbohydrates, lipids or proteins.

10 Testing for carbohydrates, lipids and proteins

Type of food	Reagent used	Method	Positive result
starch	iodine solution	Drop iodine solution onto the sample.	turns from amber to black
simple sugars	Benedict's solution	1. Add Benedict's solution to the sample. 2. Boil in a water bath for two minutes.	turns red-orange or green depending on the amount of sugar present
lipids (fats)	ethanol	1. Add ethanol to the sample. 2. Shake the mixture. 3. Add a few drops of water to the mixture.	forms a milky white emulsion
proteins	biuret reagent – sodium hydroxide and copper sulfate solution	1. Add dilute sodium hydroxide to the sample. 2. Add copper sulfate solution to the mixture.	turns purple/violet

Working scientifically

These tests are **qualitative**. They indicate whether the type of food is present, but they do not indicate how much is present.

5 Worked example — Grade 4

A student carries out food tests on an unknown sample of food.

Table 1

Test	Result
iodine solution	turns black
Benedict's solution	no change

(a) Name the food type that is tested for using iodine. **[1 mark]**

Starch

(b) What does Benedict's solution test for? Tick **one** box. **[1 mark]**

protein ☐ simple sugars ☑

lipids ☐ starch ☐

(c) What conclusion can the student draw based on the results of the food tests? **[1 mark]**

That the sample contains starch, but not simple sugars.

5 Exam-style practice — Grade 4

A student carries out a test of a sample of food. They mix some of the food with ethanol, then add a few drops of the mixture to water.

(a) What does this test identify? Tick **one** box. **[1 mark]**

starch ☐ lipids ☐

simple sugars ☐ proteins ☐

(b) Describe what a positive result would look like for this test. **[1 mark]**

Investigating enzymes

You need to know how to investigate the effect of pH on the rate of reaction of an enzyme. Most enzymes will only work efficiently within a narrow pH range.

Apparatus

- three beakers containing the same volume of water
- three test tubes containing starch solution
- three test tubes containing amylase solution in buffer solutions at different pH's
- water bath at 25 °C
- spotting tile
- iodine solution
- thermometer
- three pipettes
- stirrers

Working scientifically

You must control temperature during this investigation, as it affects the behaviour of enzymes.

Worked example — Grade 5

1. Why is amylase a good choice of enzyme to investigate when investigating the effect of pH on enzyme activity? Tick **two** boxes. **[2 marks]**

because amylase works best at a specific temperature	☐
because amylase works best at a specific pH	✓
because amylase is harmful	☐
because the effect of amylase can be observed	✓

2. Look at **Figure 1**. At which pH condition do the drops go from black to brown first? **[1 mark]**

pH 7

3. A student measures how long it takes amylase to break down starch at different pH values. The results are shown in the table. **[1 mark]**

pH	Time taken for starch to disappear in s	Rate of reaction per second
4	474	0.0021
6	110	0.0091
8	272	0.0037

Calculate the rate of reaction at pH 6 and 8. Give your answers to two significant figures. The rate of reaction per second is calculated using this equation: **[2 marks]**

$$\text{rate} = \frac{1}{\text{time in seconds}}$$

For pH 6:

$$\text{rate} = \frac{1}{110} = 0.0091$$

For pH 8:

$$\text{rate} = \frac{1}{272} = 0.0037$$

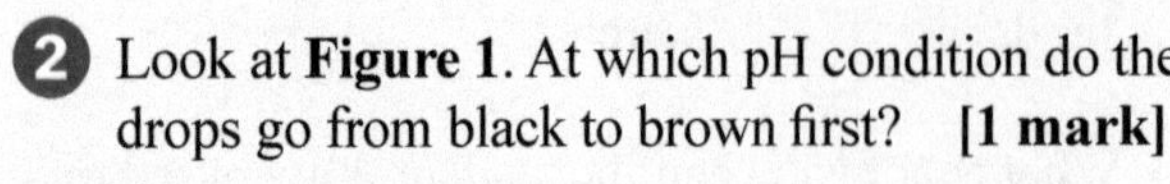

Method

1. Add one drop of iodine solution to each well in the spotting tile.
2. Make up three beakers of water, each containing a test tube of starch solution and a test tube of amylase solution in a buffer solution. Each buffer solution should be at a different pH, for example: pH 7, pH 8 and pH 9.
3. Place the beakers in the water bath, and leave long enough to reach the temperature of the water.
4. Pour one test tube of amylase solution into each test tube of starch solution. Stir thoroughly to mix.
5. Starting at 0 seconds, take a drop from each test tube every 30 seconds and add it to the iodine using a separate pipette for each solution.

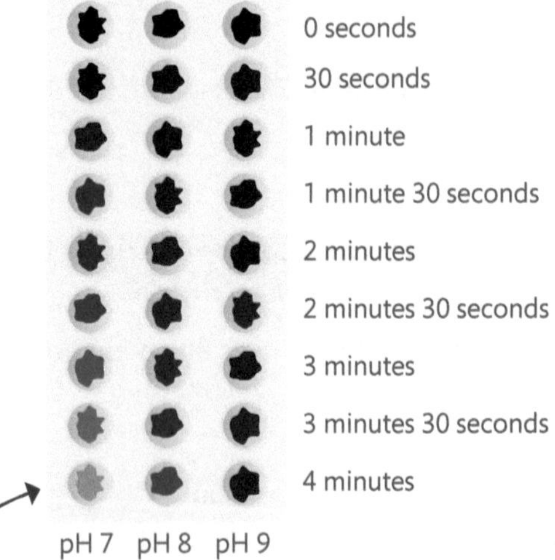

Figure 1 Results

Working scientifically

Iodine solution turns from yellow to black in the presence of starch. When the spots on the tile no longer turn black, all the starch has been broken down by the amylase. You need to judge when this happens, as shown by pH 7 at 4 minutes.

Maths skills

You need to know how to calculate the rate of a reaction. The rate of a reaction is inversely proportional to the time taken to complete.

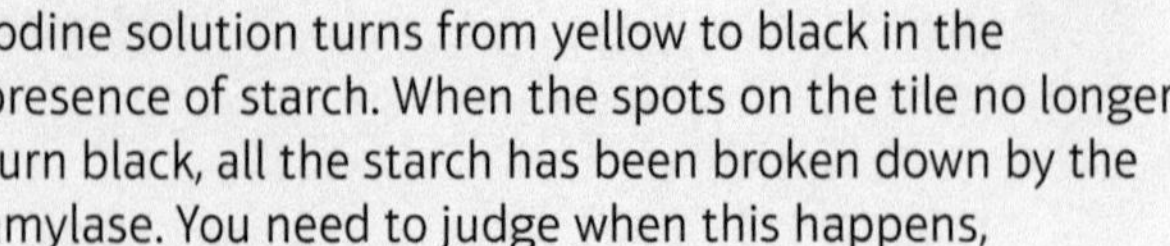

Exam-style practice — Grade 5

1. Explain why the beakers containing the test tubes are placed in the water bath. **[3 marks]**
2. Suggest **one** way that the student could check the repeatability of these results. **[1 mark]**

 Made a start  Feeling confident  Exam ready

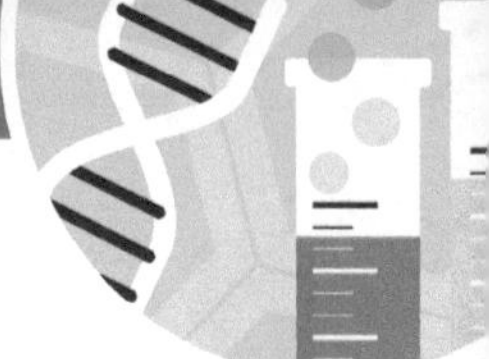

The blood

You need to be able to recognise the different components of blood and describe their functions. You also need to know how blood is transported around the body by three different types of blood vessel.

Key components of the blood

Blood is a tissue. It consists of a fluid called plasma in which red blood cells, white blood cells and platelets are suspended. **Platelets** help blood to clot.

Plasma

Plasma distributes heat and transports many substances, including carbon dioxide, water, dissolved food molecules, urea and hormones, around the body.

Red blood cells

Red blood cells absorb oxygen from the lungs and carry it to muscles and tissue around the body. They are adapted for this function in several ways.

- They have no nucleus, which increases the space available for haemoglobin.
- They have a biconcave shape (curved inwards on both sides) to increase their surface area to volume ratio, so oxygen can diffuse in and out more rapidly.
- They are small and can bend, which allows them to pass easily through the smallest capillaries.

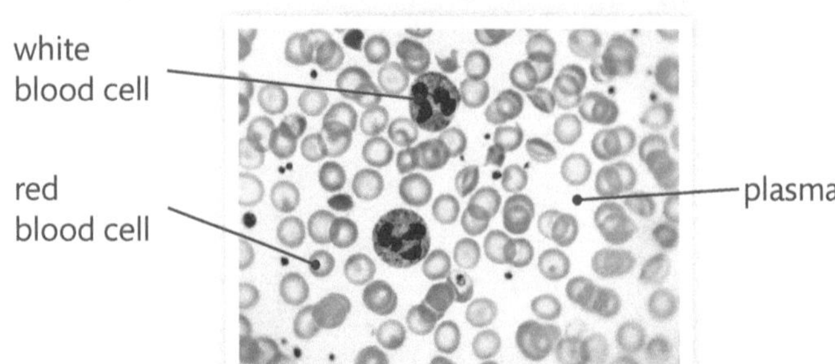

Figure 1 Blood viewed through a light microscope.

White blood cells

White blood cells help protect us from disease:

- Some white blood cells are **phagocytes**, which ingest or surround and destroy pathogens (phagocytosis).
- Some white blood cells produce **antibodies** in response to an **antigen**. Antigens are substances that are markers on the outside of cells. White blood cells use them to determine if the cell is harmful or not. Antibodies are specialised proteins that cause the immune system to attack cells that are not from the body.
- Some white blood cells produce **antitoxins**, which neutralise harmful substances produced by infectious microorganisms. Antitoxins neutralise specific toxins. See page 29 to learn about human defence systems.

5 Worked example — Grade 3

1 Describe the function of plasma. **[2 marks]**

It transports heat, carbon dioxide, water, dissolved food molecules, urea and hormones around the body.

2 Draw three lines to link each type of vessel with the correct description. **[2 marks]**

Name of vessel	Description
artery	Carries blood to the heart. Contain valves.
vein	Has thin walls that are only one cell thick.
capillary	Carries blood away from heart towards the organs. Walls are strong and elastic.

Working scientifically

Health care workers often come into contact with blood and products related to blood. It is important that they evaluate the risks of working with them. Risks include using sharp objects such as syringe needles and scalpels, and infection from contaminated blood.

Exam-style practice — Grade 4

1 Name **four** components found in blood. **[4 marks]**

2 The rate of blood flow can be calculated using this equation:

$$\text{rate of blood flow} = \frac{\text{volume of blood}}{\text{number of minutes}}$$

1560 ml of blood passed through a particular point in a vein in 5 minutes. Use the equation to calculate the rate of blood flow in the vein in ml/min. **[2 marks]**

The heart and lungs

You need to know how the structures of the heart and lungs are adapted to their functions within the circulatory system.

The double circulatory system

'Double' means there is one circulation between heart and lungs and one between heart and body.

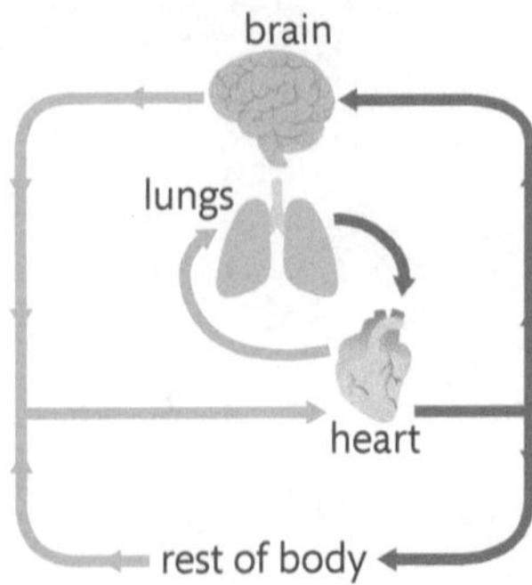

Figure 1 The double circulatory system

The regular beat of the heart is controlled by a group of cells in the wall of the right atrium called the **pacemaker**. An artificial pacemaker is an electrical device. It may be installed when the heartbeat becomes irregular.

The heart

The blood enters the right and left atria, which contract, forcing blood into the ventricles. The left and right ventricles contract, forcing blood into the arteries. The coronary arteries supply **oxygenated blood** to the heart.

The **pulmonary artery** carries **deoxygenated blood** from the heart to the lungs.

The **aorta** carries **oxygenated blood** away from the heart to the body.

The **vena cava** carries deoxygenated blood from the body to the heart.

The **pulmonary vein** carries oxygenated blood from the lungs to the heart.

left atrium

pacemaker

right atrium

The **right ventricle** pumps blood to the lungs

The **left ventricle** has a thicker muscle wall than the right ventricle because it pumps blood all around the body.

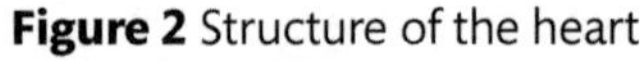

⋯▸ deoxygenated (low-oxygen concentration) blood → oxygenated (high-oxygen concentration) blood

Figure 2 Structure of the heart

The lungs

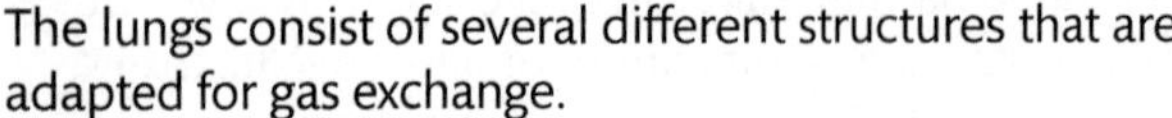

The lungs consist of several different structures that are adapted for gas exchange.

1. Air enters the lungs via the **trachea** (the windpipe). The trachea contains rings of cartilage in its walls, which hold it open, allowing air to pass through.
2. The cells lining the trachea and bronchus are covered in **cilia**, see page 6. Cilia are hair-like structures that move dust and microorganisms up and out of the lungs.
3. The trachea leads from the nose to the two **bronchi**. Bronchi branch into **bronchioles** and at the end of each bronchiole are **alveoli**.
4. Alveoli are small air sacs. They have thin membranes to allow gases to diffuse quickly between air in alveoli and blood in capillaries. Millions of alveoli produce a very large surface area for exchange.
5. A capillary network provides a good blood supply to transport the gases to and from the rest of the body and maintains the concentration gradient.

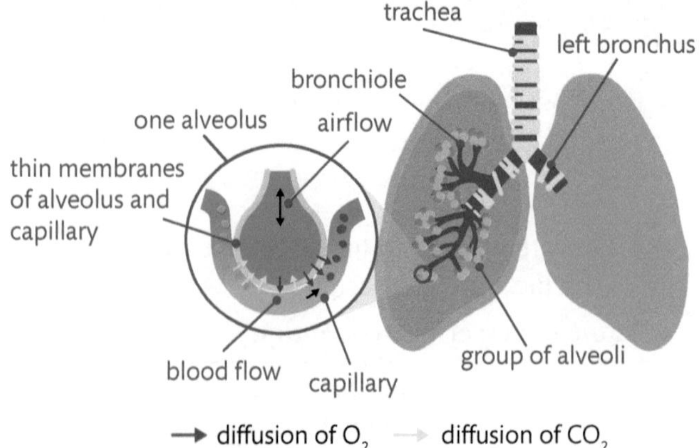

Figure 3 The lungs

Worked example — Grade 5

Describe the path taken by a red blood cell from the left ventricle to the left atrium. **[4 marks]**

Left ventricle, into aorta, around body, to vena cava, into right atrium and then right ventricle, into pulmonary artery, to the lungs and then to left atrium.

Exam-style practice — Grade 5

The alveoli are small air sacs in the lungs where gas exchange happens.

Describe **three** features of the alveoli that make them well adapted for exchanging gas. **[3 marks]**

 Made a start 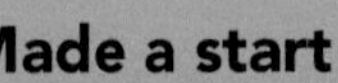  Feeling confident  Exam ready

Health issues

Health is the state of physical and mental wellbeing, including being free from disease. Disease is a disorder that has specific symptoms and is not caused by injury. You need to know about factors that can cause ill health.

Types of disease

Some diseases are communicable and some are not.

Communicable diseases

Communicable diseases are diseases that can be spread from one person to another. They are often called infectious diseases. They are caused by pathogens – microorganisms that cause disease. Examples of pathogens are:

- bacteria
- viruses
- fungi
- protists.

Examples include flu, measles and food poisoning.

Non-communicable diseases

Non-communicable diseases are diseases that cannot be passed on from one person to another.

Examples include cardiovascular diseases, some cancers and diabetes.

They are usually caused by lifestyle factors, such as diet, stress, drinking and smoking, and/or failures within the body's own systems, such as autoimmune diseases and old age.

Worked example — Grade 4

The table shows some data on the number of cases of a disease called Ebola in an African country over a 6-week period.

Week	1	2	3	4	5	6
Number of cases of Ebola	50	72	124	181	293	598

(a) Which statement best describes the trend caused by the data?
Tick **one** box. **[1 mark]**

- [ ] There was no change in the number of Ebola case over the 6 weeks.
- [ ] The number of Ebola cases increased slightly between week 1 and 6.
- [x] The number of Ebola cases increased considerably between week 1 and 6.
- [ ] The number of Ebola cases decreased between week 1 and 6.

(b) Explain whether the disease is communicable or non-communicable **[2 marks]**

It is communicable, because it spreads by contact between people.

Disease interaction

Some diseases may be caused by more than one factor.

- Defects in the immune system mean a person is more likely to suffer from infectious diseases.
- Viruses living inside cells can sometimes trigger cancer. Cancer is the result of changes in cells that lead to uncontrolled growth and division.
- Immune reactions initially caused by a pathogen can trigger allergies such as skin rashes and asthma.
- Severe illnesses can lead to mental illnesses, including depression.

Exam focus

In the exam, you could be expected to interpret data from a table, graph or chart. Before answering any questions, make sure you know what the data are, what the units are, and if there are any trends.

Exam-style practice — Grade 5

1. State what is meant by a 'pathogen'. **[1 mark]**
2. Give **two** examples of pathogens. **[2 marks]**
3. The influenza virus can be carried in droplets in the air. Suggest how an infected person could infect someone else sitting nearby. **[2 marks]**

Coronary heart disease

Cardiovascular disease (CVD) involves the heart or blood vessels. It includes coronary heart disease (CHD). You need to know how different diseases of the heart occur and how they can be treated.

Diseases of the heart

Blocked coronary arteries

The coronary arteries supply the heart muscle cells with blood containing oxygen and glucose.

The build-up of fatty deposits in the coronary arteries is related to high blood cholesterol levels. The deposits can narrow or even block arteries, starving the heart muscle of oxygen. This can cause a heart attack, when the heart stops beating.

Faulty valves

The valves in the heart prevent blood from flowing backwards when the muscles of the heart contract. Sometimes the valves in the heart become faulty, preventing the valve from opening fully, or the valve may develop a leak. This makes it harder for the heart to pump blood around the body.

Heart failure

Heart failure occurs when the heart is unable to pump blood around the body properly.

Go to page 20 for more about the heart.

Treatment

Treating blocked coronary arteries

- Stents can be inserted into the artery to keep the artery open.
- Drugs such as statins can be used to lower blood cholesterol concentration.

Treating faulty valves

- Biological or mechanical valves are used to replace a faulty valve, using surgery.

Treating heart failure

- Heart or heart and lung transplants can replace damaged organs with healthy ones.
- An artificial heart may be used to keep a patient alive while they are waiting for a heart transplant. An artificial heart can also help a damaged heart rest to help it recover.

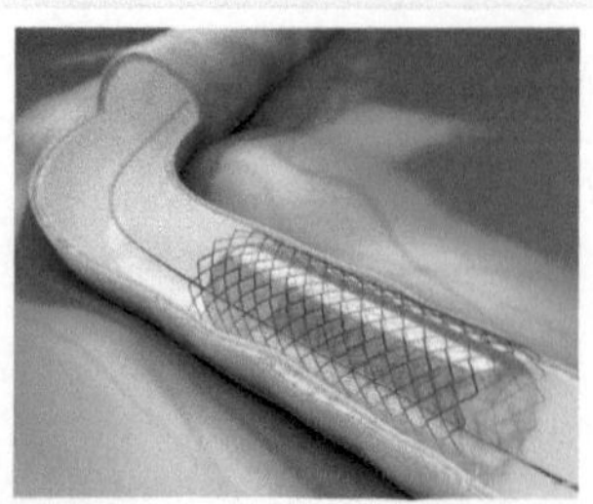

Figure 1 A stent is used to keep arteries open

Evaluation of treatments

- Heart surgery is serious and there is a risk of death. Also, surgery is not always successful.
- The patient's body may reject the new heart or valve.
- Artificial hearts need a source of power, such as batteries, to make them work so are inconvenient.
- Treatment using drugs, such as statins, may have harmful side effects in some people.
- Mechanical replacement valves can wear out.
- There is a slight risk of a blood clot forming at the site of the stent or valve.

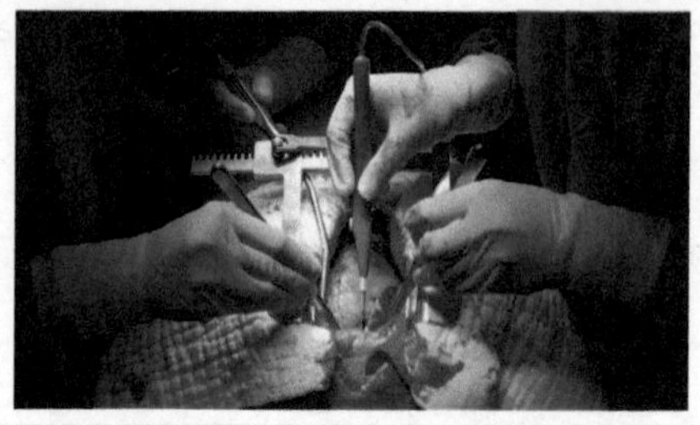

Figure 2 Heart surgery

Worked example — Grade 4

Give **two** advantages of using stents to treat coronary heart disease. **[2 marks]**

They lower the risk of a heart attack and therefore prolong life for someone with coronary heart disease.

They are effective for a long time.

Exam-style practice — Grade 4

Statins are drugs that can reduce blood cholesterol. The list below gives information about statins.

Statins:

- reduce the risk of coronary heart disease
- are a long-term drug that must be taken regularly
- reduce blood pressure which can reduce risk of other diseases
- may cause unwanted side effects such as liver damage.

Using the information given in the box:

(a) give **two** advantages of statins **[2 marks]**

(b) give **two** disadvantages of statins. **[2 marks]**

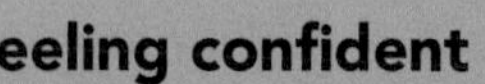

Risk factors in disease

You need to know how lifestyle and environment can affect whether or not people develop some non-communicable diseases.

Risk factors

Lifestyle risk factors

- Smokers are more likely than non-smokers to develop lung cancer and CVD.
- Heavy drinkers are more likely to suffer damage to the brain and liver than less heavy drinkers.
- Smoking and drinking during pregnancy increase the risk of poor growth and development in unborn babies.
- Obese people are more likely to develop Type 2 diabetes than people with a healthy weight. Body mass index is a measure of obesity.
- Lack of exercise and eating a lot of fatty food can increase the risk of developing coronary heart disease, see page 22.

Environmental risk factors

- People who live in houses in areas affected by radioactive radon gas are more likely to develop cancer, see page 24.

Impact on non-communicable disease

Interaction of risk factors

Many risk factors interact to increase the risk of non-communicable diseases. For example the chances of getting coronary heart disease increase dramatically for someone who smokes, drinks heavily, is obese and takes little exercise.

Impact of lifestyle

Having a poor lifestyle can affect an individual, their family and the wider community.

Cost implications

Local and national authorities must plan their spending on new hospitals, doctors and surgeries.

Non-communicable diseases, which lifestyle factors contribute to, affect the government's spending on the National Health Service.

Worked example — Grade 5

1 Describe the relationship between body mass index (BMI) and blood cholesterol concentration, shown in **Figure 1**. **[2 marks]**

As the BMI increases so does the blood cholesterol concentration

2 Blood cholesterol concentration is a risk factor for heart disease.

Use **Figure 1** to explain why a doctor would encourage an obese patient to reduce their body mass index. **[2 marks]**

The graph shows the higher the BMI, the higher the blood cholesterol concentration, which increases the chances of the patient developing heart disease. Therefore, if the obese patient reduced their BMI (lost weight) they could reduce their chance of getting heart disease.

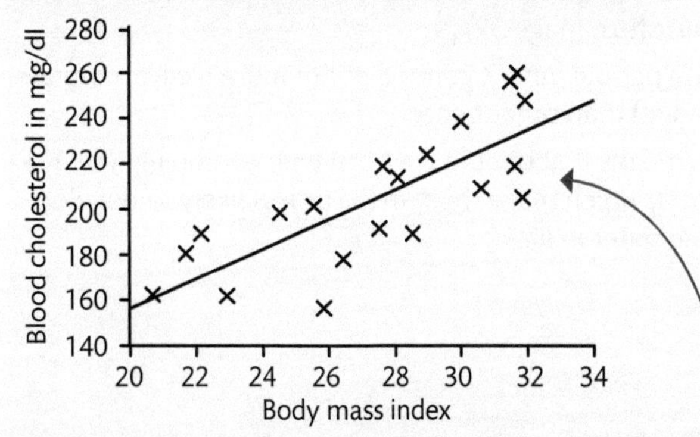

Figure 1 Scatter diagram showing the correlation between body mass index and blood cholesterol concentration

Maths skills

A scatter diagram is a graph where the values of two variables are plotted against each other. The pattern of the plots might show a correlation between them.

Causal mechanisms

A causal mechanism is a process that explains how a risk factor can cause a particular disease. For example, it is the carcinogens in tobacco smoke that cause lung cancer. For many years it was thought that smoking caused lung cancer but no one had found a causal mechanism to link the two together. However, people know now that carcinogenic substances in tobacco smoke can cause cells to become cancerous.

Exam-style practice — Grades 3–4

1 Name **one** disease that smoking is a risk factor for. **[1 mark]**

2 A patient has been diagnosed with Type 2 diabetes. Inactivity is one risk factor for developing Type 2 diabetes. List **one** other risk factor. **[1 mark]**

3 Describe a personal cost and a national cost of Type 2 diabetes. **[2 marks]**

Cancer

Cancer is caused by changes inside cells that lead to uncontrolled cell division and tissue growth. You need to know the lifestyle and genetic risk factors linked to some cancers.

Types of tumour

Benign tumours are growths of abnormal cells. They usually grow slowly and in one area, often surrounded by a membrane. They are not cancerous and usually do not invade other parts of the body.

Malignant tumours are growths of abnormal cells called cancers. They often grow rapidly, invading neighbouring tissues in the body. Cancerous cells can break free from the tumour and get carried by the blood to other parts of the body. These cells continue to divide, producing secondary tumours.

Worked example — Grade 5

Give **two** reasons why benign tumours are easier to treat than malignant tumours. **[2 marks]**

Benign tumours are often contained in a membrane, malignant tumours spread into nearby tissues.

Genetic risk factors

Cancer is caused by changes to genes in the DNA that control cell growth. A change in the DNA of a cell is called a **mutation** (page 52).

Some people inherit genes that are more likely to mutate (change) than other genes.

This means that people are born with certain genetic risk factors, which make them more or less likely to develop cancer later in life.

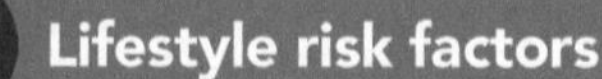

Lifestyle risk factors

Carcinogens are substances or agents that are risk factors for some cancers.

- **UV radiation in sunlight** – risk factor for skin cancer
- **smoking** – risk factor for lung cancer
- **alcohol** (drinking) – risk factor for liver and other cancers
- **asbestos** (found in some building materials) – risk factor for lung and other cancers
- **radon** (from rocks below houses in some areas) – risk factor for many cancers

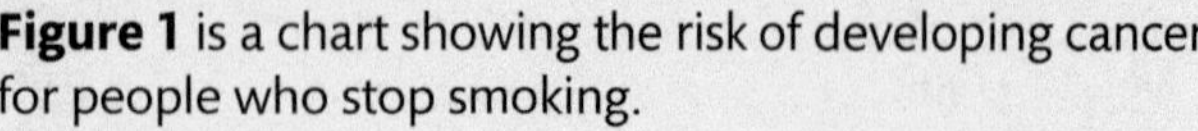

Exam-style practice — Grade 5

Figure 1 is a chart showing the risk of developing cancer for people who stop smoking.

(a) Explain what is meant by <30 on the *x*-axis. **[1 mark]**

(b) Describe the relationship between the factors shown in the chart. **[1 mark]**

(c) Suggest **one** reason why people might be at risk of lung cancer when they have never smoked. **[1 mark]**

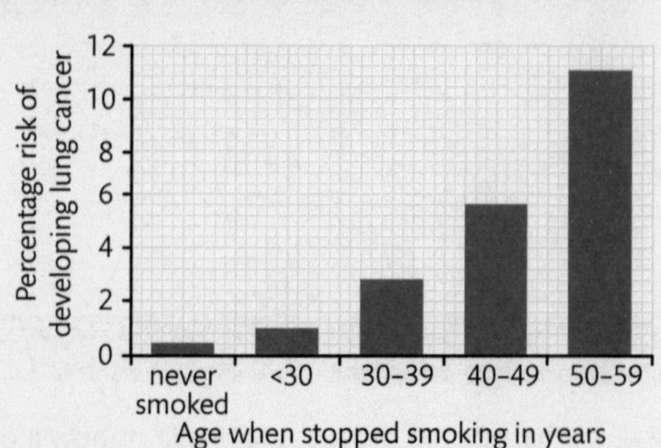

Figure 1

 Made a start  Feeling confident  Exam ready

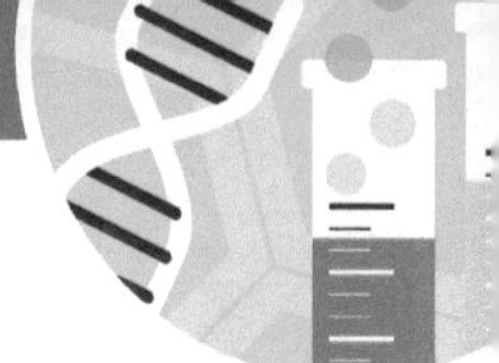

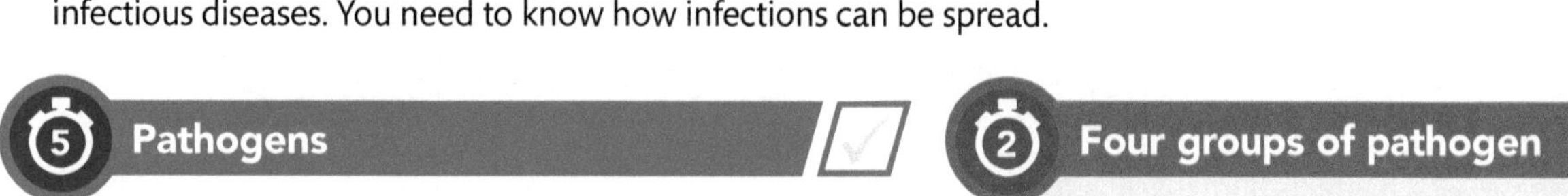

Communicable diseases

Communicable diseases are diseases that can be spread from one person to another. They are sometimes called infectious diseases. You need to know how infections can be spread.

5 Pathogens

Pathogens are microorganisms that cause infectious diseases. Once inside the body they may reproduce rapidly.

- Viruses enter cells and force them to make more copies of the virus.

  The cells are damaged when they break open to release the new viruses, which then invade other cells.
- Bacteria produce poisonous waste products called toxins. These toxins damage tissue and can make you feel ill.

Go to page 27 to revise bacterial diseases.

2 Four groups of pathogen

Pathogens can belong to one of these types of organism:

1. viruses
2. bacteria
3. fungi
4. protists.

Go to page 26 to revise viral diseases.

5 Spread of communicable diseases

Communicable diseases can be spread by:

1. **direct contact**, which involves touching or coming into contact with the diseased person, plant or animal
2. **indirect contact**, which involves touching objects that have been contaminated with the disease-causing organism, breathing in airborne disease-causing organisms, or eating or drinking contaminated food or water.

The spread of communicable diseases can be reduced or prevented by:

- reducing contact with the microorganism that causes the disease
- using physical barriers, such as surgical masks
- using the immune system to destroy the pathogen
- using drugs, such as antibiotics to destroy bacteria
- vaccination.

Go to page 29 to revise human defence systems.

10 Worked example

Grade 5

(a) Describe how bacteria make a person feel ill. **[2 marks]**

The bacteria produce poisonous waste products called toxins.

These toxins damage tissue.

(b) Cholera is a bacterial infection that is spread by drinking water contaminated with the diarrhoea of somebody who is infected with cholera.

Suggest **one** method of preventing the spread of cholera. **[1 mark]**

Only drink clean or treated water.

5 Exam-style practice

Grade 4

1. Chicken pox is an infectious disease caused by a virus. Describe what is meant by the term 'infectious'. **[1 mark]**
2. The chicken pox virus is spread by touching or breathing in the virus particles that come from the blisters on an infected person.

   Suggest **one** method of preventing the spread of the chicken pox virus. **[1 mark]**

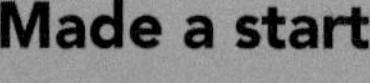

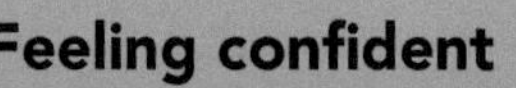

Viral diseases

A virus is an infective agent that is too small to be seen using a light microscope. You need to know about some viral diseases.

Measles

Measles is a viral disease, which affects humans. It is spread by breathing in airborne droplets from sneezes and coughs.

Symptoms include a fever, sore eyes and a red skin rash. Most people recover from the disease but fatal complications can sometimes arise. These complications include swelling of the brain, called encephalitis, and ear and eye infections. This is why most young children are vaccinated against measles.

For more about vaccinations see page 30.

Figure 1 Measles is usually accompanied by a fever and a red skin rash.

Human Immunodeficiency Virus (HIV)

HIV causes flu-like symptoms when it first infects the body. The virus attacks the human immune system, which is why the body cannot destroy the virus.

In late-stage HIV infection, the immune system is so damaged it can no longer protect the body from other pathogens or cancers. This stage is called Acquired Immune Deficiency Syndrome (AIDS). The infected person will develop other diseases. It is these diseases that normally kill a person with HIV.

People infected with HIV can take antiviral drugs to prevent the virus from damaging their immune system.

HIV is spread by sexual contact or other exchanges of bodily fluids, such as blood when drug users share needles.

Tobacco Mosaic Virus (TMV)

Tobacco Mosaic Virus is a disease which commonly affects some types of plants, such as tomato plants.

It produces a characteristic mosaic pattern on the leaves. The TMV-affected leaves can no longer photosynthesise. This causes the plant to die because it can no longer manufacture its own food.

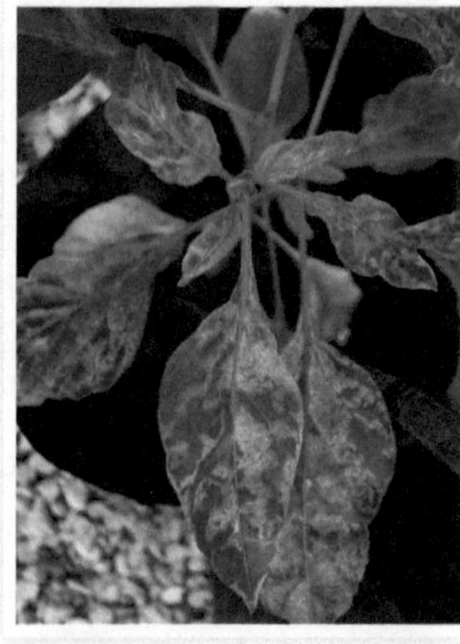

Figure 2 Plant leaves with TMV

Worked example — Grade 5

Compare how HIV and the measles virus are spread. **[2 marks]**

HIV can only be passed from one person to another through the transfer of body fluids. Measles can be spread by droplets coughed or sneezed out by an infectious person.

Exam-style practice — Grade 3

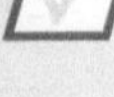

1. State **one** method of preventing children developing the measles virus. **[1 mark]**
2. Name **one** type of plant that can be infected by the Tobacco Mosaic Virus. **[1 mark]**

Bacterial and fungal diseases

You need to know about two kinds of bacterial disease that affect humans and one fungal disease that affects plants.

Bacterial diseases

Food poisoning

Salmonella is a bacterium that is spread through contaminated food, such as chicken and eggs.

It can be spread through a lack of proper food hygiene, particularly through food not being cooked thoroughly. *Salmonella* then can cause food poisoning. Symptoms include vomiting, diarrhoea, fever and abdominal cramps, caused by the toxins (poisons) that the bacteria produce.

In the UK, chickens are vaccinated against *Salmonella* to help control the spread of the disease.

Gonorrhoea

Gonorrhoea is a sexually transmitted disease (STD). Symptoms include a thick yellow or green discharge from the penis or vagina and pain when urinating.

The disease used to be treated using the antibiotic penicillin. However, new strains of gonorrhoea have appeared, which are resistant to penicillin so new types of antibiotic now have to be used.

The spread of the disease can also be reduced by using a barrier method of contraception such as a condom.

Rose black spot

Rose black spot is a fungus which infects rose plants. It produces purple or black spots on the rose's leaves.

The leaves then turn yellow and fall from the plant. This slows the plant's growth as it has fewer leaves that photosynthesise and produce food for growth.

Rose black spot is spread by water or wind. It can be treated by removing the affected leaves and burning or burying them. It can also be treated by spraying the plant with a fungicide, a substance that kills the fungus.

Figure 1 Rose black spot

Worked example — Grades 4–5

Figure 2 shows the cases of gonorrhoea in Canada during 2008. Look at **Figure 2**.

(a) Compare the number of cases of gonorrhoea in males and females before and after the age of 25. **[2 marks]**

Before the age of 25, more females have gonorrhoea than males. After the age of 25, more males have gonorrhoea than females.

(b) Suggest why there are more cases of gonorrhoea in 15–24 year olds than in people over 60 years old. **[2 marks]**

People aged 15–24 may have more different sexual partners, so they are more likely to get gonorrhoea.

Number of cases per 100 000 (0–200)
Age group in years: 15-19, 20-24, 25-29, 30-39, 40-59, 60+
male / female

Figure 2

(c) Gonorrhoea is a sexually transmitted disease.
Explain how this knowledge could be used to reduce the incidence of the disease. **[2 marks]**

The disease can be transmitted from one person to another by sexual intercourse. Therefore, barrier methods of contraception can reduce the spread of the disease.

Exam-style practice — Grade 2

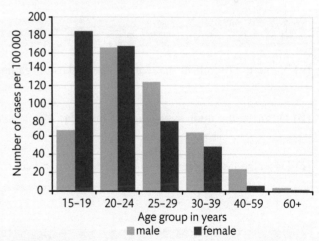

1. State how *Salmonella* bacteria cause the symptoms of food poisoning. **[1 mark]**
2. Describe **one** method for preventing the spread of gonorrhoea. **[1 mark]**

Protist diseases

Protists are a group of organisms that are usually unicellular (made of just one cell). Some protists cause disease in humans. Protist diseases like malaria are spread by vectors. Vectors are carriers.

10 Malaria

Malaria is spread from person to person by mosquitoes. If left untreated, malaria can be fatal. Millions of people die each year from malaria.

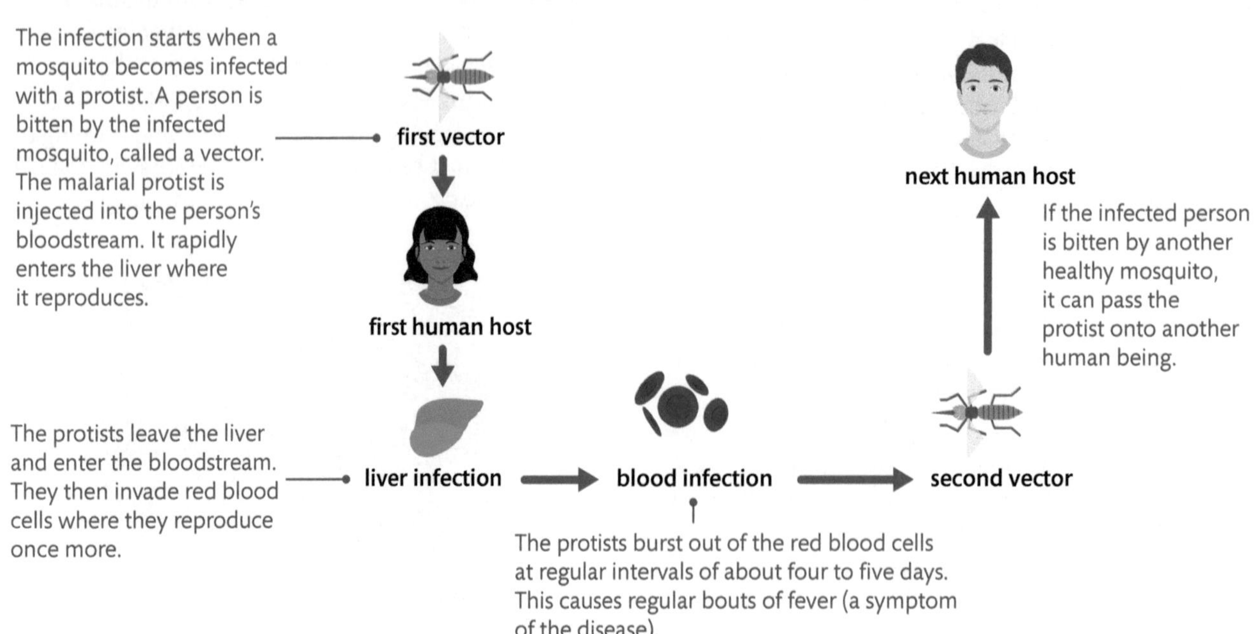

The infection starts when a mosquito becomes infected with a protist. A person is bitten by the infected mosquito, called a vector. The malarial protist is injected into the person's bloodstream. It rapidly enters the liver where it reproduces.
first vector
first human host
next human host
If the infected person is bitten by another healthy mosquito, it can pass the protist onto another human being.
The protists leave the liver and enter the bloodstream. They then invade red blood cells where they reproduce once more.
liver infection
blood infection
second vector
The protists burst out of the red blood cells at regular intervals of about four to five days. This causes regular bouts of fever (a symptom of the disease).

Figure 1 The life cycle of the malarial protist

The spread of malaria can be controlled by preventing mosquitoes from breeding and by people using nets to avoid being bitten.

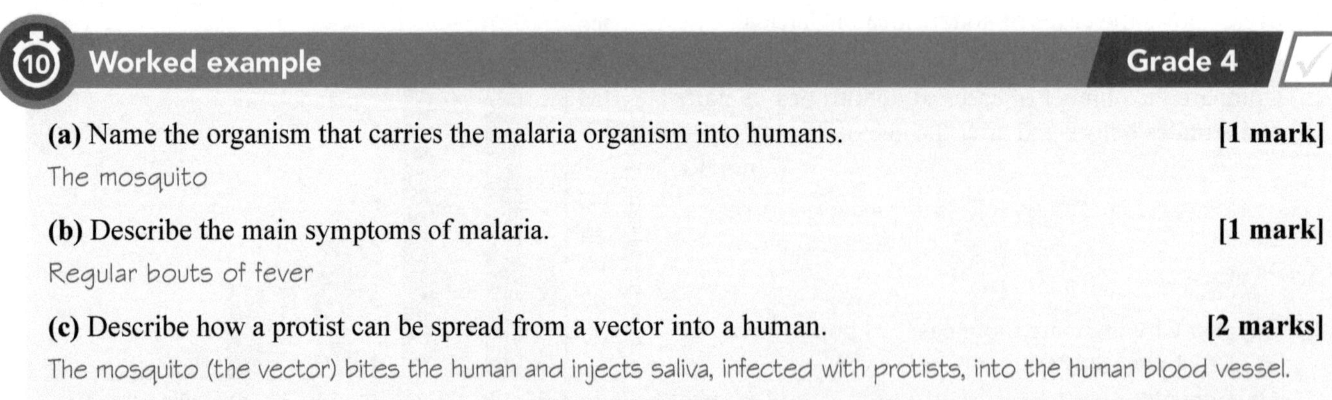

10 Worked example — Grade 4

(a) Name the organism that carries the malaria organism into humans. **[1 mark]**

The mosquito

(b) Describe the main symptoms of malaria. **[1 mark]**

Regular bouts of fever

(c) Describe how a protist can be spread from a vector into a human. **[2 marks]**

The mosquito (the vector) bites the human and injects saliva, infected with protists, into the human blood vessel.

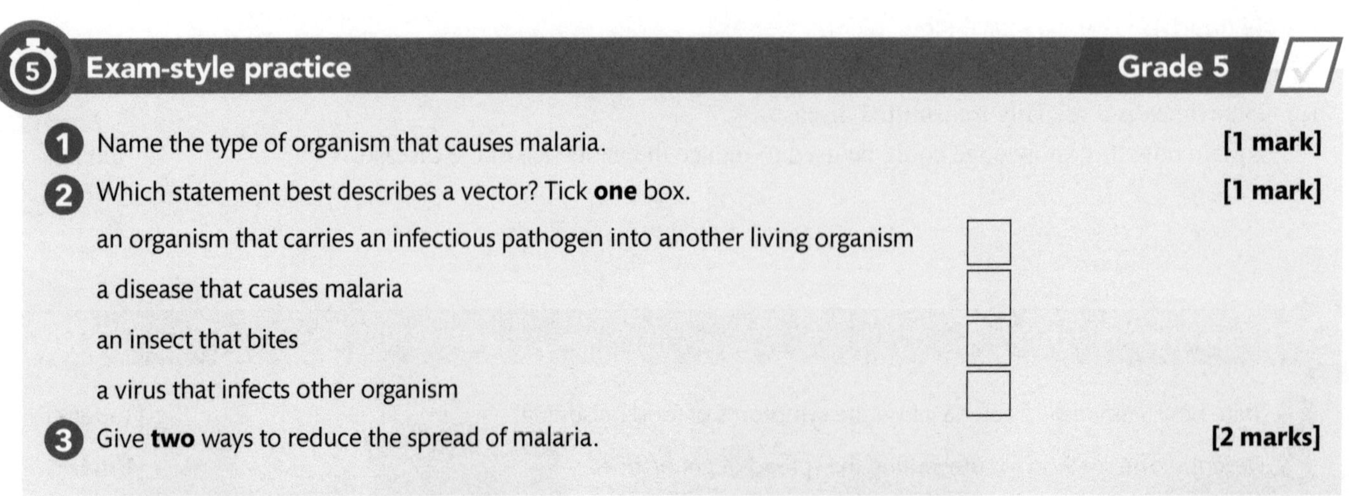

5 Exam-style practice — Grade 5

1. Name the type of organism that causes malaria. **[1 mark]**
2. Which statement best describes a vector? Tick **one** box. **[1 mark]**
   - an organism that carries an infectious pathogen into another living organism ☐
   - a disease that causes malaria ☐
   - an insect that bites ☐
   - a virus that infects other organism ☐
3. Give **two** ways to reduce the spread of malaria. **[2 marks]**

Human defence systems

You need to know about the human body's defence mechanisms and how they protect us from invading pathogens.

Physical defences

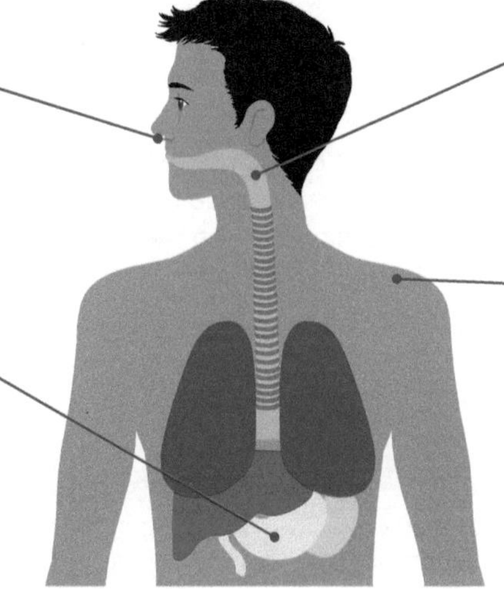

The nose is lined with hairs and mucus to trap pathogens to stop them getting to the lungs.
Sticky mucus in the trachea and bronchi traps pathogens. Cilia on the cells lining these passages move mucus and trapped pathogens out of the lungs towards the back of the throat where they are swallowed.
The stomach produces hydrochloric acid to help kill any pathogens in food.
The skin is a barrier that pathogens have difficulty getting through. The skin also secretes substances that can kill pathogenic bacteria or inhibit their growth. Scabs form over damaged skin, keeping pathogens out while the skin repairs itself.

Figure 1 The body's non-specific defences make it difficult for pathogens to enter the body.

The immune system

When a pathogen enters the body the **immune system** tries to destroy it. There are several ways it does this:

- **phagocytosis** – some white blood cells engulf the pathogen and digest it.
- **antibody production** – some white blood cells produce antibodies. Antibodies are proteins that recognise and target specific antigens on the pathogen and destroy it.
- **antitoxin production** – some white blood cells produce **antitoxins**. Antitoxins are proteins that attach to the poisonous toxins produced by pathogens and **neutralise** them.

Worked example — Grade 4

1. Describe how the stomach can defend the body against invading pathogens. **[1 mark]**

   It produces hydrochloric acid, which kills any pathogens that are swallowed.

2. Give **two** ways the skin can protect a human from invading pathogens. **[2 marks]**

   It acts as a barrier to pathogens. It also secretes substances that kill pathogens or stop their growth.

3. Smoking can damage the cilia in the trachea and bronchi. Suggest why a smoker is more at risk of diseases caused by pathogens in the lungs. **[3 marks]**

   The cilia waft mucus that traps pathogens to the top of the throat where it can be swallowed. If the cilia are damaged they can't do this and so pathogens are more likely to get into the lungs and cause disease.

Exam-style practice — Grade 5

1. Explain how the nose helps prevent pathogens entering the body. **[2 marks]**
2. Describe **three** ways in which white blood cells help defend the body against disease. **[3 marks]**

 Made a start  Feeling confident 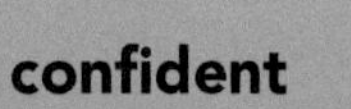  Exam ready

Vaccination

You need to know how a vaccination can prevent infection by a particular pathogen.

5 Vaccination

Vaccination is the process of using dead or inactive pathogens to stimulate the immune system to recognise and quickly respond to the live pathogen if the person becomes infected with the disease.

1. Dead or inactive pathogens are injected into the body.
2. The white blood cells respond by producing antibodies specific to the pathogen as well as memory cells.
3. If the live pathogen infects the body in the future, cells in the blood rapidly produce large quantities of antibodies to destroy the pathogen.

2 Working scientifically

To prevent a disease from spreading, not everyone in the population needs to be vaccinated although this is preferable.

This is because the more people that are vaccinated, the less chance there is of an infected person meeting and passing on the infection to someone who has not been vaccinated.

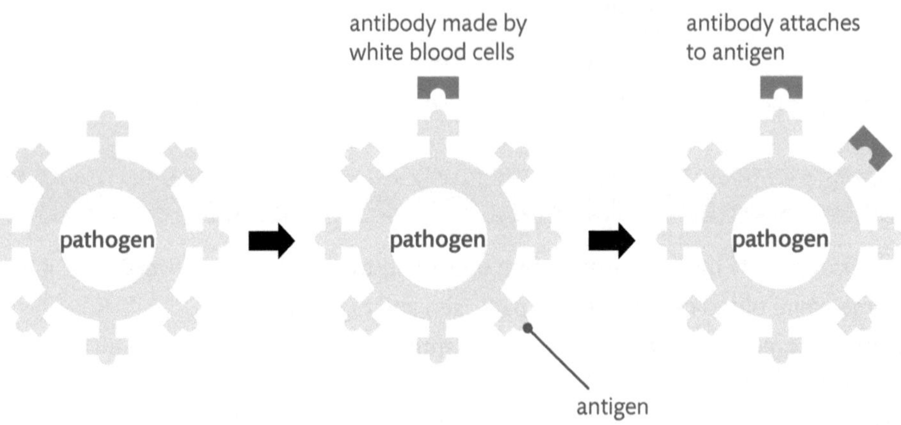

Figure 1 How antibodies attack pathogens

Go to page 29 for more about antibodies.

10 Worked example — Grade 5

In some countries, the MMR vaccine is offered to all children. The vaccine protects against the viruses that cause mumps, measles and rubella.

(a) Give **two** advantages of giving the MMR vaccine to as many children around the world as possible.

It helps prevent children developing mumps, measles or rubella. Giving it to as many children as possible also helps control the spread of mumps, measles and rubella and makes an epidemic much less likely.

(b) Give **two** disadvantages of giving the MMR vaccine to as many children as possible in the UK.

A very few children might have a bad reaction to the vaccine. It is also expensive.

10 Exam-style practice — Grade 4

1. State what is injected into the body when a vaccination is given. **[1 mark]**
2. Describe how white blood cells respond when a vaccination is given. **[1 mark]**
3. A student is travelling to a country where there has recently been an outbreak of the communicable disease 'yellow fever'. Give **one** advantage and **one** disadvantage of the student having the vaccination before entering the country. **[2 marks]**

The advantages and disadvantages of vaccination are the same whatever the disease. Look at the worked example to help with this question.

 Made a start  Feeling confident Exam ready

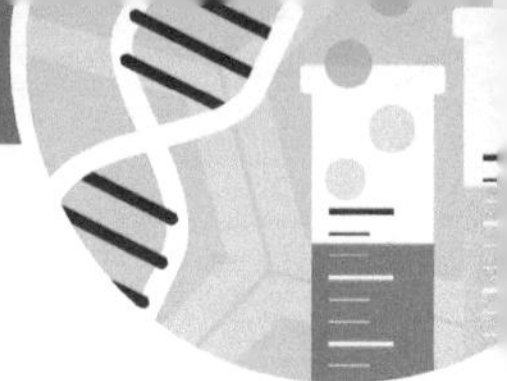

Antibiotics and painkillers

Since the 1940s a range of antibiotics have been developed which have proved successful against a number of lethal diseases caused by bacteria. You need to know how drugs (medicines) can be used to treat diseases and reduce symptoms.

2 Antibiotics: Key facts

- Antibiotics are medicines that kill bacteria.
- Specific bacteria can only be treated using specific antibiotics.
- Antibiotics do not destroy viruses.
- Antibiotics have significantly reduced the number of deaths from infectious bacterial diseases since their discovery.
- However, many strains of bacteria are now evolving, which are resistant to antibiotics. This has serious implications for treating bacterial diseases.

1 Working scientifically

At present, the majority of new drugs are synthesised by scientists in laboratories. However, some drugs and substances are still extracted from natural sources, such as plants.

One drug extracted from plants is digitalis. It comes from foxgloves and is used for treating heart conditions.

Find out more about drug development on page 32.

2 Other medicines

Painkillers are medicines that relieve pain. Painkillers do not affect pathogens and so do not cure the disease. They only treat the symptoms of disease, such as pain. Other medicines treat other symptoms, such as high body temperature (fever) caused by infection.

There are drugs used to treat diseases caused by viruses. They are called antivirals. Viruses enter cells, making it very difficult to kill the viruses without also killing the cells. This is why there are not many antiviral drugs. New antiviral drugs are being developed to help destroy the virus which causes AIDS, HIV.

10 Worked example — Grade 5

Penicillin was the first antibiotic to be discovered.

The discovery was made by Alexander Fleming.

Fleming was growing bacteria in a Petri dish, shown in **Figure 1**.

The Petri dish was contaminated by the mould *Penicillium*.

Fleming noticed that around the patch of mould there were few or no bacteria.

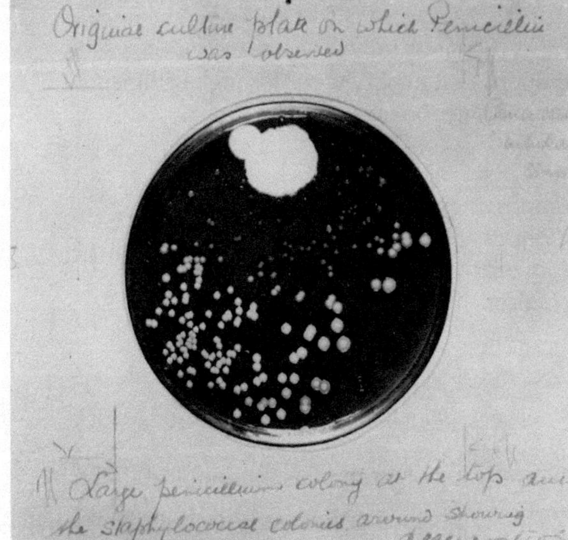

Figure 1

Explain how this observation led to Fleming discovering penicillin. **[3 marks]**

Fleming realised that the mould must be producing a substance that killed bacteria because very few or no bacteria were growing around it. He discovered the mould naturally produces penicillin, which became the first antibiotic.

10 Exam-style practice — Grade 4

1. Which **two** of the following are symptoms? Tick **two** boxes. **[2 marks]**

   fever ☐ headache ☐ antibiotic ☐ painkiller ☐

2. An ear infection is often caused by bacteria. Antibiotics can be used to treat ear infections. What other type of drug is used to ease the symptoms of an ear infection? **[1 mark]**

3. Influenza, also known as 'flu', is caused by a virus. Explain why antibiotics cannot be used to treat influenza. **[1 mark]**

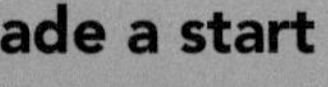

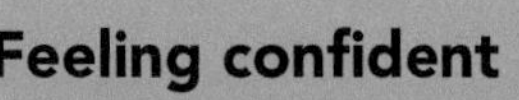
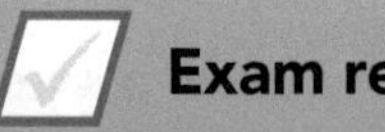

Development of drugs

You need to know how drugs are discovered and tested over time.

10 Timescale for drug development

Research & development 3–6 years	Pre-clinical studies 1 year	Clinical trials 4–7 years	Review & approval 1–2 years
This is when potential new drugs are made or discovered.	This is when the drug is tested in the laboratory.	This is when the drug is tested on healthy human volunteers, starting with very low doses for toxicity and efficacy.	This is when new drugs are approved to be used on patients.
Scientists first decide what drugs are needed.	*In vitro* ('in glass') tests on cells and tissues (the drug is tested in Petri dishes and test tubes).	**Phase 1** It is tested on about 50 people to check for side effects and to see how quickly the body breaks down the drug.	If the drug is effective it is sent to regulating bodies for approval.
Scientists then look for compounds that might do the job they are looking for.	Testing in animals.	**Phase 2** It is tested on about 200 patients with the condition.	The governing body fast-tracks drugs that are desperately needed. If the benefits outweigh the risks it is approved.
Thousands of chemical compounds are then tested or modified to improve their action.	Testing in mammals.	**Phase 3** If the drug is found to be safe, it is tested on about 2000 people to see how well the drug works and its optimum dose.	When the drug is available for doctors to use it is monitored for side effects indefinitely.

5 Worked example — Grades 3–4

New drugs may be tested using double-blind trials and placebos.

(a) Which of these statements best describes a double-blind trial?
Tick **one** box. **[1 mark]**

- [ ] Only the doctor knows if the patient is getting the drug or a placebo.
- [ ] Only the patient knows if they are getting the drug or a placebo.
- [ ] Both the patient and the doctor know if they are getting the drug or a placebo.
- [x] Neither the patient nor the doctor know if they are getting the drug or a placebo. ✓

(b) Explain why a placebo may be used. **[2 marks]**

A placebo is a substance that does not contain the drug. It is used to show that any changes in people taking the drug are caused by the drug and nothing else.

A placebo is exactly like the new drug in how it looks and how it is used, but contains none of the drug.

2 Working scientifically

All the results from testing and trialling new drugs should be published. Other scientists then peer-review the data. This means they check the results and the theories suggested. They may also carry out further tests to check the results. Peer review helps to ensure that the results of the trials of new drugs can be trusted.

5 Exam-style practice — Grade 3

1. Explain what is meant by 'peer review'. **[2 marks]**
2. Preclinical testing of drugs is carried out on which **two** of the following? Tick **two** boxes. **[2 marks]**

patients in hospital ☐ live animals ☐

cell and tissue samples ☐ dead animals ☐

 Made a start  Feeling confident  Exam ready

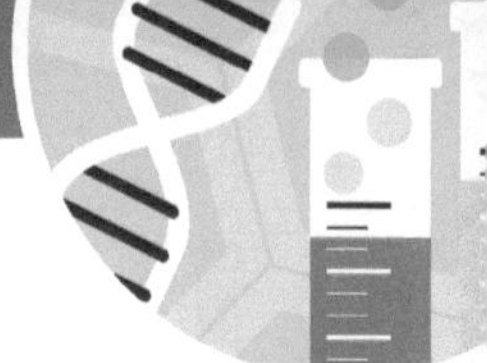

Photosynthesis

You need to understand the process of photosynthesis, including the chemical equation for the reaction.

5 Photosynthesis

Plants transfer energy from sunlight to chlorophyll molecules in chloroplasts inside some of their cells. This energy is then transferred to the reaction of photosynthesis in which carbon dioxide reacts with water to produce glucose and oxygen.

The chemical equation for photosynthesis

Water for the whole plant is absorbed by root hair cells.

Go to page 15 for more about how this happens.

Go to page 35 to read about the uses of glucose in plants.

$$\text{carbon dioxide} + \text{water} \xrightarrow[\text{chlorophyll in green leaves}]{\text{light from the Sun}} \text{glucose} + \text{oxygen}$$

$$6CO_2 + 6H_2O \xrightarrow[\text{chlorophyll in green leaves}]{\text{light from the Sun}} C_6H_{12}O_6 + 6O_2$$

Go to page 10 to revise diffusion.

Carbon dioxide diffuses from the air into the cell. Oxygen diffuses from the cell into the air.

Energy is transferred by light to chloroplasts in plant cells.

5 Endothermic reactions

Photosynthesis is an **endothermic reaction**. This means that more energy is absorbed than given out.

The energy transferred by the photosynthesis reaction is light energy.

Most of the endothermic reactions you meet in your chemistry course involve thermal energy being transferred to chemical energy. See page 121.

The plant transfers this light energy to chemical energy, building glucose, and then larger molecules from glucose. Later, the plant can use this chemical energy for other processes. This is why plants kept in the dark will eventually die: they cannot make the complex molecules or store the energy that they need.

Figure 1 Cress seeds grown in the light (left) and in the dark (right). Most plants need a source of light to be healthy.

Go to page 14 to revise the structure of plant tissues.

10 Worked example — Grade 3

1 **(a)** Name the organelle responsible for photosynthesis in plants. **[1 mark]**

chloroplasts

(b) What is the name of the chemical compound that is found in these organelles? **[1 mark]**

chlorophyll

2 Most chloroplasts are found in cells towards the upper surface of a leaf. Suggest why. **[1 mark]**

More light reaches the upper surface of the leaf for photosynthesis.

2 Exam-style practice — Grade 3

Name **two** products of photosynthesis. **[2 marks]**

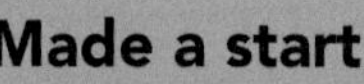

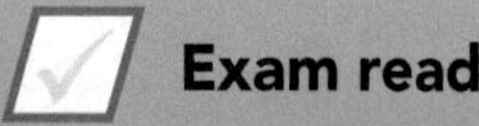

Rate of photosynthesis

The rate of photosynthesis is determined by four factors: temperature, light intensity, carbon dioxide concentration and the amount of chlorophyll. You need to know how each of these factors affects the rate of photosynthesis.

10 Graphs of limiting factors

Limiting factors are environmental conditions that can limit the rate of a process. There are four factors that affect the rate of photosynthesis. Three of them are shown in the graphs below.

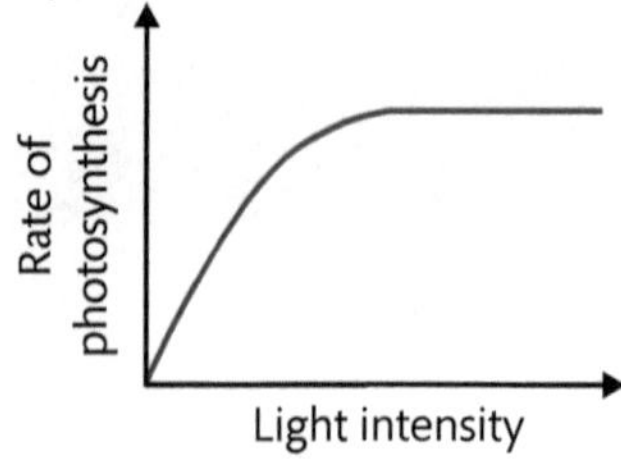

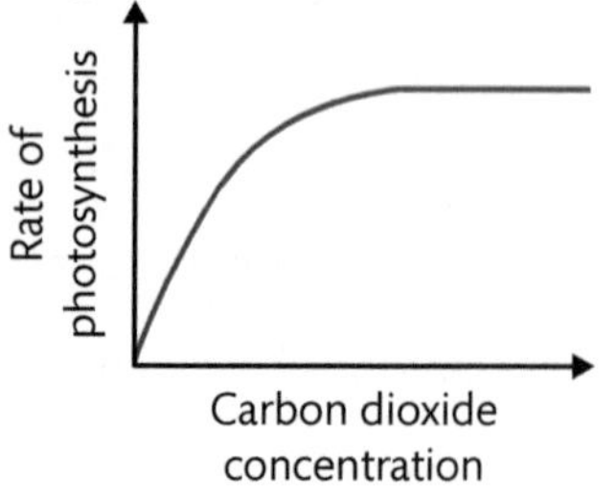

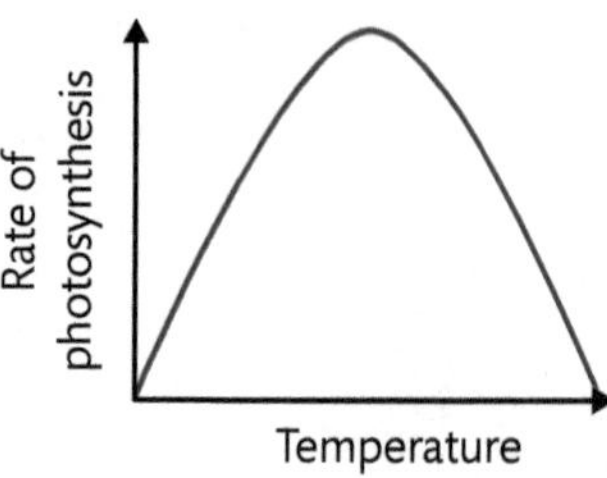

Figure 1 Graphs showing three limiting factors of photosynthesis

Light

When light intensity is low, the rate of photosynthesis is slow as it is limited by the lack of light. As light intensity increases, the rate of photosynthesis increases until it reaches a maximum level when any further increase in light intensity has no effect. This suggests that there must be another factor that is now limiting the rate of photosynthesis.

Carbon dioxide

Carbon dioxide is a common limiting factor affecting the rate of photosynthesis because it is at a low level in the atmosphere. The level of carbon dioxide can be increased by burning a fuel like oil or gas if plants are grown in a greenhouse.

Temperature

As temperature increases, the rate of photosynthesis increases until it reaches a maximum because enzyme activity increases, and then begins to decrease until it reaches zero. This is because at high temperatures the enzymes that control photosynthesis are denatured.

Amount of chlorophyll

Not all plant cells contain chlorophyll, and so this affects where photosynthesis takes place in a plant.

10 Worked example — Grade 5

A scientist carried out an experiment to investigate the effects of light intensity on the rate of photosynthesis. The results were plotted on the graph shown in **Figure 2**.

Describe what happens to the rate of photosynthesis:

(a) as the light intensity increases from 0 to 3 arbitrary units **[1 mark]**

It increases.

(b) as the light intensity increases from 3 to 6 arbitrary units. **[1 mark]**

It stops increasing and stays at the same rate.

(c) At a certain point, light no longer limits the rate of photosynthesis. State **two** factors that could be limiting the rate of photosynthesis at this point. **[2 marks]**

carbon dioxide concentration or temperature

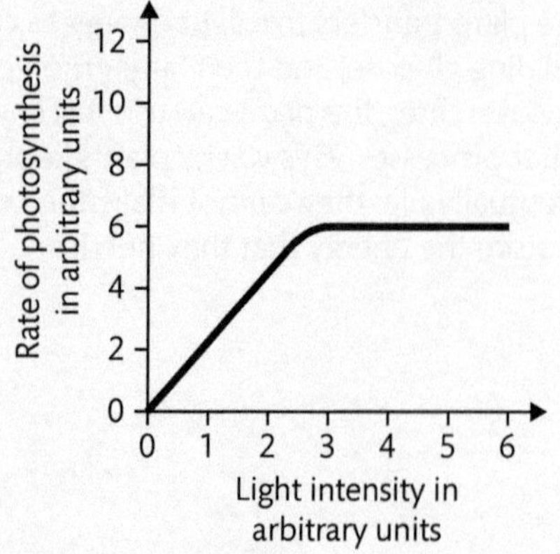

Figure 2

5 Exam-style practice — Grade 4

1. Name **four** factors that can affect the rate of photosynthesis. **[4 marks]**
2. How does the amount of chlorophyll affect the rate of photosynthesis? **[1 mark]**

 Made a start  Feeling confident  Exam ready

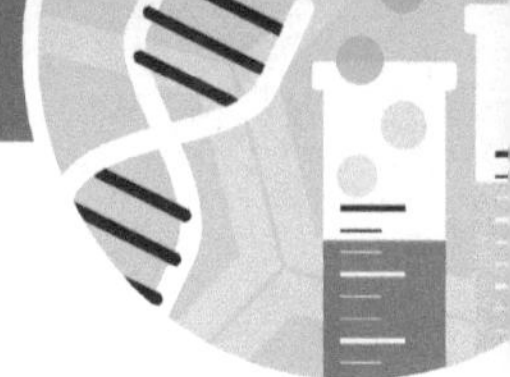

Uses of photosynthesis

You need to know how the glucose produced by photosynthesis is used by plants.

5 Uses of glucose

Glucose is a soluble sugar. It is produced by photosynthesis and transported around the plant in a solution. Glucose has several different uses in a plant.

It is used to make cellulose, a structural carbohydrate, which forms cell walls, giving strength and support to the plant.

Along with nitrate ions that are absorbed from the soil, glucose is used to make proteins for growth and repair.

It is also used in respiration to release energy required for plant cells.

The oxygen produced by photosynthesis is a waste product. Any glucose made by the plant that isn't required immediately can be converted and stored as:

- insoluble starch
- fat or oil.

Wheat plants store glucose as starch, while oilseed rape plants store glucose as rapeseed oil.

5 Worked example — Grade 5

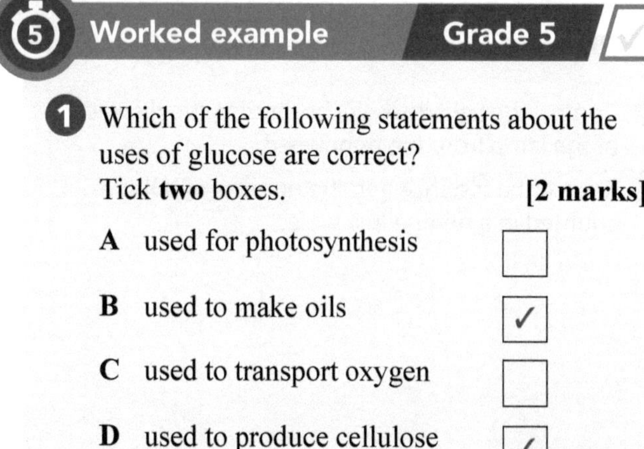

1 Which of the following statements about the uses of glucose are correct? Tick **two** boxes. **[2 marks]**

A used for photosynthesis ☐

B used to make oils ☑

C used to transport oxygen ☐

D used to produce cellulose ☑

E used to absorb light ☐

2 Give the role of cellulose in plants. **[2 marks]**

It is used to make cell walls to support the plant.

10 Respiration

One of the uses of glucose is respiration (page 37). Plants respire all the time, whereas they can only photosynthesise during daylight hours. At night, there is no sunlight so plants cannot photosynthesise, but they still need to respire so oxygen is taken in and carbon dioxide is given out.

In dim light, the rate of photosynthesis is equal to the rate of respiration so neither gas is taken in or given out, as they cancel each other out.

The maximum rate of photosynthesis occurs around midday, when sunlight is brightest. The rate of photosynthesis is greater than the rate of respiration so carbon dioxide is taken in and oxygen is given out.

During the day, plants make more glucose than they use.

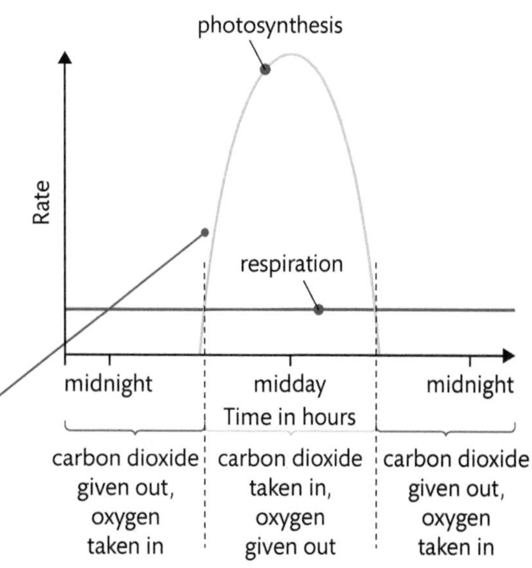

Figure 1 The graph shows that the rate of respiration stays constant over a 24-hour period but the rate of photosynthesis varies.

Go to page 15 to revise transport and storage in plants.

5 Exam-style practice — Grade 3

1 Explain why it is important that plants can store glucose made during the day. **[1 mark]**

2 Glucose can be stored as starch. Name another substance into which glucose can be converted for storage. **[1 mark]**

3 In a potato plant, glucose is converted to starch. Suggest where the starch is stored. **[1 mark]**

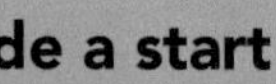

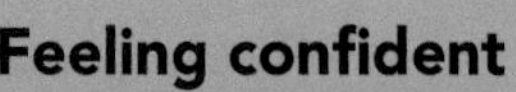

Investigating photosynthesis

You need to know how to investigate the effect of light intensity on the rate of photosynthesis.

Method

1. Control the light intensity by altering the distance of the lamp from the pondweed.
2. Record the distance and the number of bubbles counted in a minute in a table.

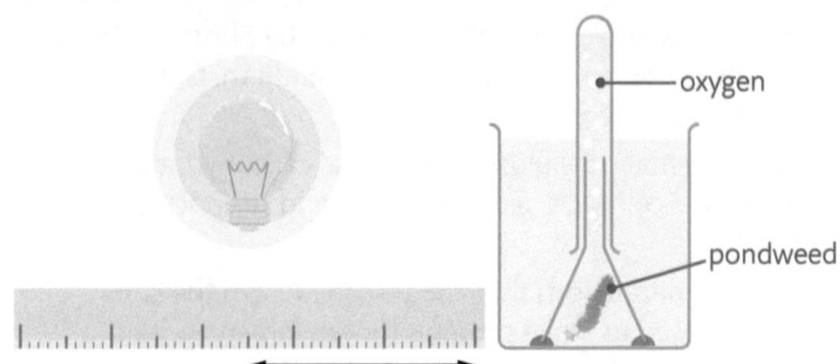

Figure 1 Investigating light intensity

Worked example — Grade 4

A student investigates how light intensity affects the rate of photosynthesis in pondweed. The student's results are shown in the table below.

Distance from lamp in cm	Number of bubbles produced in one minute
10	60
20	25
30	8
40	2
50	0

(a) Draw a graph to show the student's results. **[4 marks]**

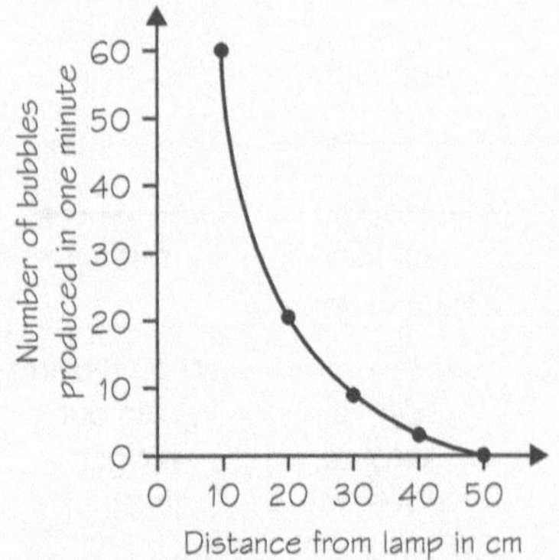

(b) Use the graph you have drawn to estimate the number of bubbles produced in one minute if the lamp was positioned at 35 cm from the pondweed. **[1 mark]**

5 bubbles

(c) Explain how this investigation could be improved. **[2 marks]**

Repeat it several times and calculate a mean.

Variables

This practical investigates the effect of light intensity on the rate of photosynthesis. This means that light intensity is the **independent variable**. You change the independent variable to see what effect it has on the dependent variable.

The rate of photosynthesis is determined by counting the number of oxygen bubbles produced in a given period of time. This is the **dependent variable**. This variable depends on the variable you are changing, so this is the one you measure. Everything else must be kept constant, for example, temperature because it affects the rate of photosynthesis.

Key experimental skills

- Use of correct apparatus to record measurements accurately.
- Safe use of hot devices, such as a lamp.
- Consider ethical issues by removing any small invertebrates on the pondweed before starting the investigation.
- Use appropriate apparatus and techniques to observe and measure change.
- Measure rate of photosynthesis by counting oxygen bubbles.

Exam-style practice — Grade 5

1. Use the graph from the Worked example to describe the effect of light intensity on the rate of photosynthesis. **[1 mark]**
2. Explain why light intensity affects the rate of photosynthesis. **[2 marks]**

 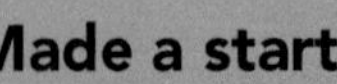 Made a start  Feeling confident  Exam ready

Aerobic and anaerobic respiration

Respiration is a chemical reaction that takes place inside all living things cells. It transfers energy to the body to carry out other processes. You need to know about two types of respiration - aerobic and anaerobic.

Respiration

Respiration is an **exothermic reaction** because it gives out more energy than it takes in during the reaction.

The energy released by respiration is transferred to many other processes:

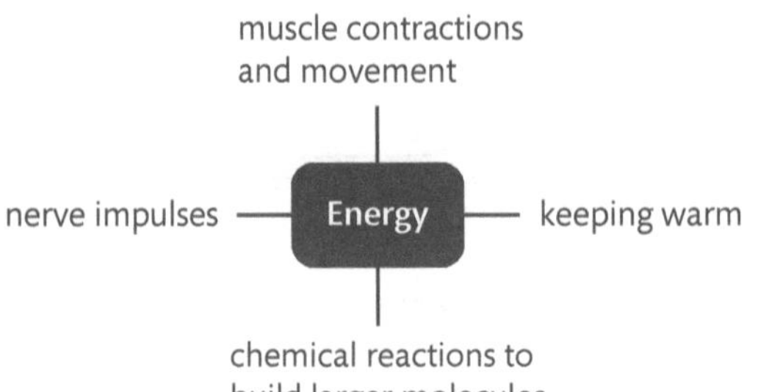

Anaerobic respiration

Anaerobic respiration is like aerobic respiration in transferring energy from glucose.

Differences from aerobic respiration:

- Anaerobic respiration does not need oxygen.
- Less energy is transferred in anaerobic respiration.
- Anaerobic respiration in muscles breaks down glucose to lactic acid.
- Anaerobic respiration in plant and yeast cells breaks down glucose to ethanol and carbon dioxide. This is also called fermentation. It is used in making bread and alcoholic drinks.

Aerobic respiration

Aerobic respiration requires oxygen.

glucose + oxygen → carbon dioxide + water

$C_6H_{12}O_6 + 6O_2 \rightarrow 6CO_2 + 6H_2O$

Most of the reactions involving aerobic respiration happen inside mitochondria in cells.

The rate of aerobic respiration can be measured by how much oxygen is used over a given time.

Worked example — Grade 4

1 What does the term 'aerobic respiration' mean? **[1 mark]**

In aerobic respiration, glucose reacts with oxygen to produce carbon dioxide and water and transfer energy.

> **Exam focus**
> You will be expected to recall the definitions of certain key terms in the exam. Make sure you know the meaning of all the terms used in this revision guide.

2 Give the word equation to show aerobic respiration. **[1 mark]**

glucose + oxygen → carbon dioxide + water

> The equation for aerobic respiration is the reverse of the equation for photosynthesis.

3 Suggest when our bodies may need to respire anaerobically. **[1 mark]**

When we cannot get enough oxygen, such as during hard exercise.

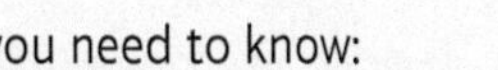

> **Exam focus**
> For the exam, you need to know:
> - the word equations for aerobic and anaerobic respiration
> - the chemical symbols for glucose, water, oxygen and carbon dioxide.

Exam-style practice — Grade 3

Give **two** similarities and **two** differences between aerobic and anaerobic respiration in animals. **[4 marks]**

 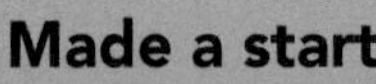 Made a start  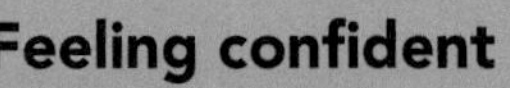 Feeling confident  Exam ready

Response to exercise

You need to know how the human body responds to the increased demand for energy during exercise.

Three responses

During exercise the human body responds to the increased demand for energy in three ways:

1. The rate of breathing increases.
2. Breaths are deeper so the volume of each breath increases.
3. The heart rate increases.

These changes supply glucose and oxygen more rapidly to muscle cells for respiration, and remove carbon dioxide faster from the body.

Investigating the effects

You can investigate the effect of exercise on the human body by:

- counting the number of breaths per minute before and immediately after exercise
- measuring the volume of each breath, using a device called a spirometer, before and immediately after exercise
- measuring the heart rate by counting the pulse rate in the wrist before, during and after exercise.

Oxygen debt

There is a level of exercise when aerobic respiration can no longer transfer energy fast enough to muscle cells. Beyond this point the additional energy is transferred from anaerobic respiration.

During long periods of vigorous activity muscles become fatigued and stop contracting efficiently.

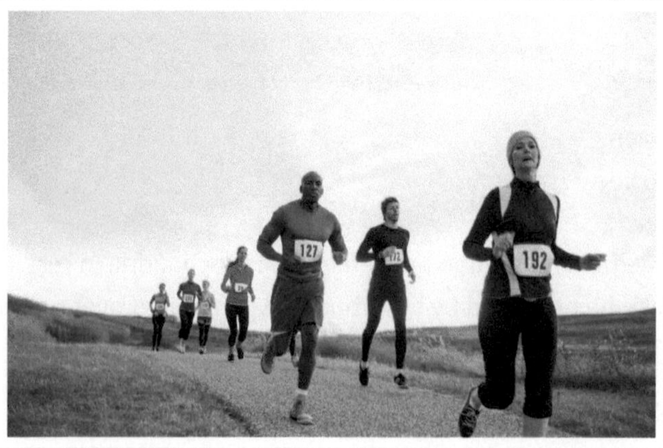

Figure 1 Runners continue to breathe deeply and rapidly after exercise because of an 'oxygen debt'.

Worked example — Grade 4

1. During vigorous exercise, anaerobic respiration takes place. Describe **three** other ways in which the body responds to the increased demand for energy during vigorous exercise. **[3 marks]**

   1. Breathing rate increases.
   2. Breaths are deeper so the volume of each breath increases.
   3. The heart rate increases.

2. Give **one** benefit of anaerobic respiration taking place during vigorous exercise. **[1 mark]**

   It means energy can still be released and available to meet the demands of the muscles, even in the absence of oxygen.

During vigorous physical activity the heart cannot pump enough oxygenated blood to the muscles. In this situation, anaerobic respiration will occur.

When breathing is faster and deeper, the gas transfer of oxygen and carbon dioxide by diffusion in the lungs will be faster.

Exam-style practice — Grade 5

1. Some athletes run a 100 m race without taking any breaths. This is because once all the oxygen has been used by the body another type of respiration will take place. State the name of the type of respiration that takes place in the absence of oxygen. **[1 mark]**
2. During a game of football, the players' breathing rate increases. Explain why. **[3 marks]**

 Made a start  Feeling confident  Exam ready

Metabolism

Metabolism is the sum of all of the reactions, in which molecules are made or broken down, happening in a cell or organism.

10 Forming new molecules

Some of the energy that is transferred during respiration is used by organisms to synthesise new, larger molecules. These processes are controlled and catalysed by enzymes. Metabolism includes:

Converting glucose

Glucose can react in different ways to form:

- starch for storage in plants
- cellulose to strengthen plant cell walls
- glycogen for storage in muscle cells and liver cells.

Amylase breaks down starch to form glucose. Go to page 16 to revise digestive enzymes.

Breakdown of glucose in respiration

Glucose is broken down in both aerobic and anaerobic respiration.

Go to page 37 to revise respiration.

glucose + oxygen → carbon dioxide + water (aerobic)

glucose → lactic acid (anaerobic in muscle cells)

glucose → ethanol + carbon dioxide (anaerobic respiration in plant and fungal cells (fermentation))

Lipid molecules consist of a glycerol molecule joined to three fatty acids.

Forming lipids

Lipids are fats and oils. They are used for storage in plants and animals, and for insulation in animals.

Each lipid molecule is formed from three fatty acid molecules joined to one glycerol molecule.

Forming amino acids and proteins

Plants absorb nitrate ions through their roots. These ions combine with glucose to form amino acids in the reaction:
glucose + nitrate ions → amino acids

Different amino acids join together to form different proteins. Proteins include enzymes, collagen and keratin. In animals, excess proteins are broken down to form urea, which is then excreted by the kidney in urine.

5 Worked example — Grade 4

1 Which of these statements is the correct definition of metabolism?
Tick **one** box. **[1 mark]**

- [ ] the synthesis of compounds in a cell
- [x] all of the reactions in a cell or organism
- [ ] the movement of substances through the membranes in a cell
- [ ] the breakdown of substances in a cell or organism

2 Some metabolic reactions convert glucose molecules into other molecules.
Name a molecule made from glucose in:
animals glycogen plants starch **[2 marks]**

3 Name the molecules that are joined together to form proteins. **[1 mark]**

amino acids

5 Exam-style practice — Grade 5

1 The reactions that take place in metabolism need to be carefully controlled. What is responsible for controlling these reactions? Tick **one** box. **[1 mark]**

☐ nuclei ☐ enzymes ☐ lipids ☐ hormones

2 Describe where the energy for metabolism comes from. **[2 marks]**

The human nervous system

The nervous system senses a stimulus (a change in the body or environment) and coordinates the body's response. You need to know the structure and function of the human nervous system.

Coordination

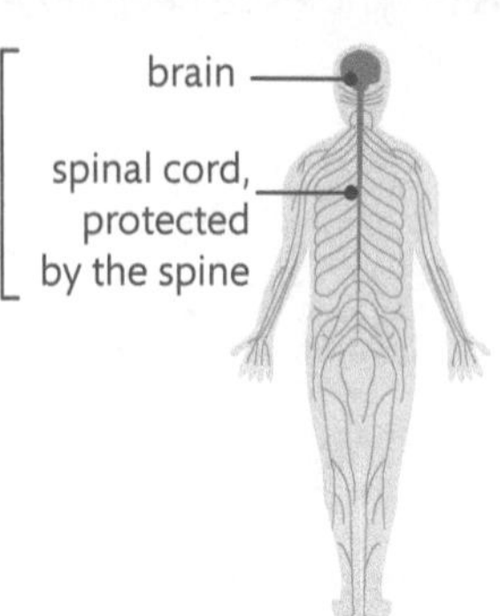

Figure 1 The nervous system

When receptors, such as those on your fingertips, are stimulated, information in the form of electrical impulses is passed from the receptor along a sensory neurone to the central nervous system (CNS).

The CNS coordinates the information and passes instructions along motor neurones to an effector such as a muscle or gland to cause a response such as a muscle moving.

stimulus → receptor → coordinator → effector → response

Examples include: touch, substances in food, temperature and light.

Worked example — Grade 5

Figure 3 shows a synapse.

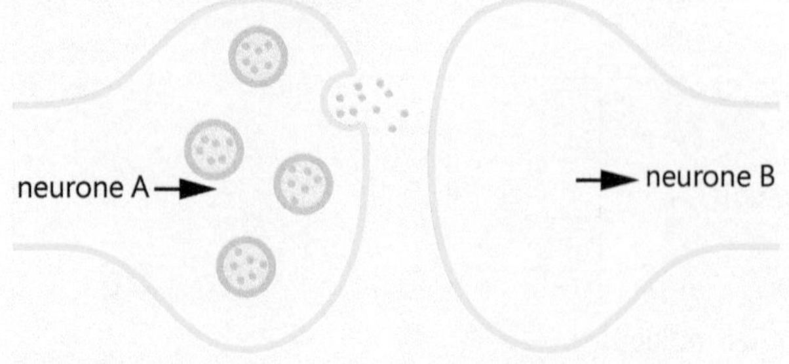

Figure 3

(a) Describe how an electrical impulse in neurone **A** can cause an electrical impulse in neurone **B**. **[2 marks]**

Neurotransmitter is released from neurone A into the gap between the neurones.
The neurotransmitter diffuses across the gap to neurone B and triggers an electrical impulse.

(b) Describe **one** advantage of synapses in the nervous system. **[1 mark]**

It makes sure information only passes in one direction through the system.

Types of neurone

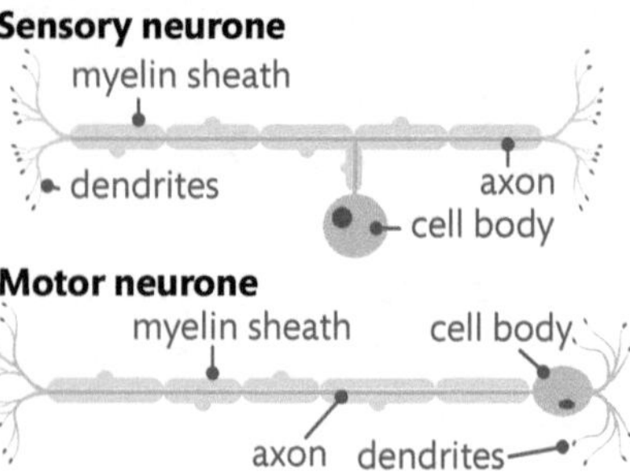

Figure 2 Neurones

Neurones are cells in the nervous system that carry electrical impulses.

- **Sensory neurones** carry information from a receptor, such as light receptors in the retina and touch receptors in the skin, to the CNS.
- **Motor neurones** carry instructions from the CNS to an effector, such as a muscle or a gland.
- **Relay neurones** in the spinal cord and brain (the CNS) carry impulses from sensory neurones to motor neurones.
- **Synapses** are gaps between each neurone where chemical messengers called **neurotransmitters** diffuse from one neurone to the next.

Reflex arcs

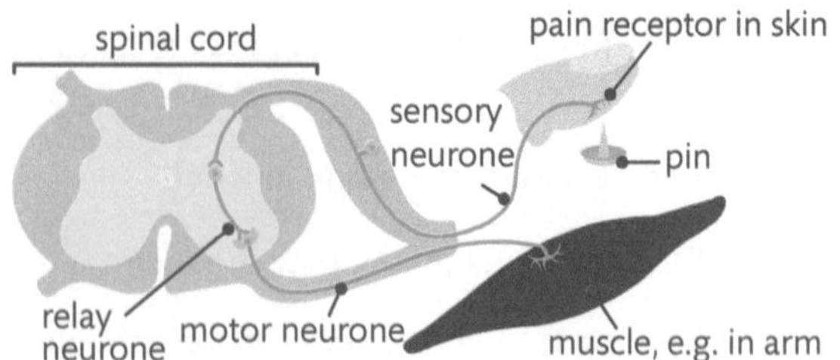

Figure 4 A reflex arc

The impulse in a sensory neurone passes to a relay neurone in the spinal cord and then to a motor neurone. This makes the response much faster than when the brain is involved.

receptor → sensory neurone → relay neurone → motor neurone → effector

Reflex arcs are a sequence of neurones that respond to a simulus but do not involve the brain. They are important to survival because they speed up reaction times where thinking slows down the response and could cause harm, such as when touching something hot.

Exam-style practice — Grade 4

Give **two** examples of each of the following:

(a) a receptor **[2 marks]**

(b) an effector. **[2 marks]**

 Made a start  Feeling confident Exam ready

Reaction times

You need to know how to plan and carry out an investigation into factors that affect human reaction times.

5 Method

This method requires two students: one who is doing the testing (student **A**) and one who is being tested (student **B**).

1. Student **B** rests their elbow on a table so that their hand extends over the side.
2. Student **A** holds a metre ruler vertically between student **B**'s thumb and index finger, but not touching. The zero mark on the ruler is lined up with student **B**'s fingers.
3. Student **B** indicates that they are ready.
4. Without warning, student **A** releases the ruler and lets it drop.
5. Student **B** catches it as quickly as possible.
6. Record the distance the ruler falls.
7. Repeat three times and calculate the mean score by adding the scores together and dividing by three.
8. Repeat the test again, but with student **B** performing a task, such as counting to 100 or saying the alphabet backwards.

2 Factors affecting reaction times

There are many factors that can affect human reaction time. Reaction time is the length of time taken for a person to respond to a given stimulus.

Factors known to affect reaction times include: distraction, physical fitness and fatigue.

2 Working scientifically

You could repeat this investigation to test how a range of factors affect reaction time. For example, have student **B** do physical exercise (the effect of fatigue) before the second test.

5 Exam-style practice Grade 4–5

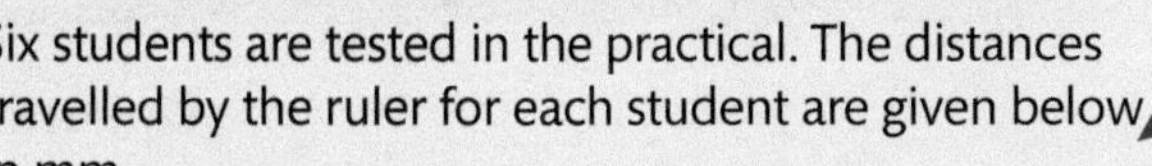

Six students are tested in the practical. The distances travelled by the ruler for each student are given below in mm.

103 110 113 101 121 113

(a) Calculate the mean distance travelled by the ruler. **[1 mark]**

(b) The results shown above were collected early in the morning. A second set of results were collected in the last lesson of the day. Predict how collecting the results in the last lesson of the day is likely to affect the reaction times. Give a reason for your answer. **[2 marks]**

10 Worked example Grade 4

1 State the equipment needed to perform this investigation. **[1 mark]**

A metre ruler

2 The method says to repeat the test three times and calculate the mean score. Explain why this is better than taking the measurement from only one test. **[1 mark]**

It increases the repeatability of the results.

3 Step **8** of the method states to repeat the test again, but with student **B** performing a task, such as counting to 100 or saying the alphabet backwards. Write a prediction to say how counting to 100 during the test would affect the reaction time. **[1 mark]**

Counting to 100 during the test will increase the time taken to react.

4 Explain your prediction. **[2 marks]**

Counting will be a distraction which will affect concentration and slow down the reaction time.

5 **Figure 1** is a graph showing the effect of age on reaction time.

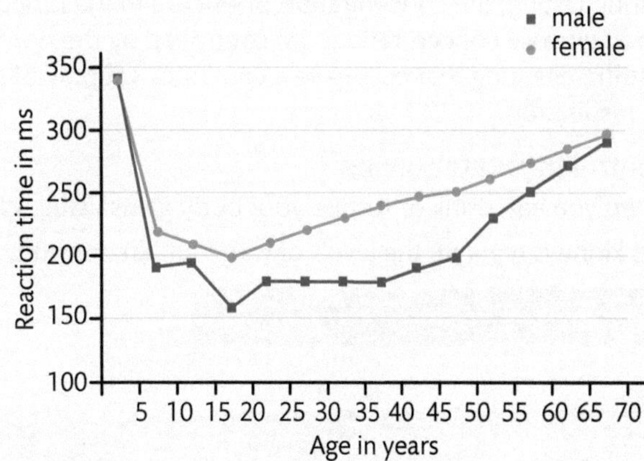

Figure 1

(a) How much slower is the female reaction time than male reaction time at age 47? Show your working. **[2 marks]**

250 – 200 = 50 ms

(b) At what age do males have the fastest mean reaction time? **[1 mark]**

17 years old

Go to page 216 to revise handling data.

Homeostasis

You need to know how homeostasis regulates the internal conditions of a cell or an organism to maintain a constant internal environment.

Homeostasis

Homeostasis is the regulation of conditions inside the body, such as temperature, to maintain optimum conditions for enzymes and all cell functions.

Enzymes in human cells only work within very specific conditions. Many need a constant temperature of about 37 °C. Cell cytoplasm and blood plasma need the right amount of water to carry out their functions well.

See page 16 about factors that affect enzyme action.

Homeostatic control systems

Homeostatic control systems are either electrical (the nervous system) or chemical (hormones).

All control systems use:

- a receptor which detects a stimulus, such as a change in temperature in the body or surrounding environment
- a coordination centre (such as the brain) or a gland (such as the pancreas), which receives and processes information from receptors
- an effector (such as a muscle or a gland that releases a hormone), which brings about a response that restores conditions to a normal optimum level.

Regulating temperature, blood glucose and water

Temperature control

When you are too hot, your body responds to transfer more energy to the surroundings by heating.

When you are too cold, your body responds to lose heat more slowly, as shown.

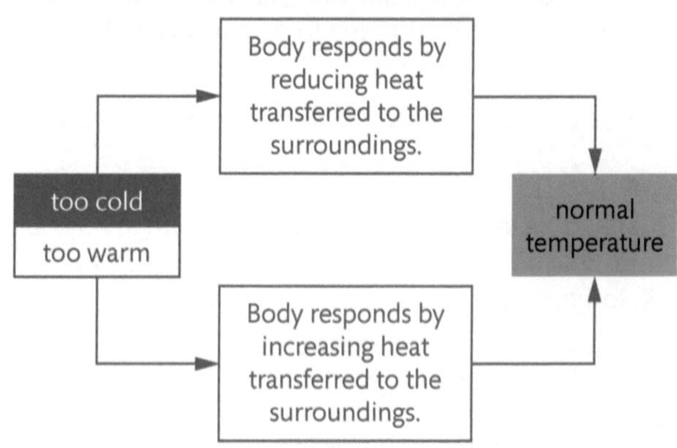

Figure 1 How the body responds to the environment to control temperature

Maintaining glucose concentration

Glucose is produced by the digestion of carbohydrates in food. Soon after a meal, the concentration of glucose in the blood rises. During fasting, the concentration of glucose in the blood falls. Blood glucose concentrations are controlled by the hormone **insulin**, ensuring that cells have a continuous supply of glucose for respiration.

Controlling water levels

When you eat, drink or respire your body gains water. When you sweat, breathe or urinate your body loses water.

The kidneys regulate the levels of water within our body by adjusting how much water is lost in urine.

Go to page 44 for more about insulin.

Worked example — Grade 3

Name the **two** types of homeostatic control system. **[2 marks]**

Nervous and hormonal

Exam-style practice — Grade 5

1. Describe what is meant by 'homeostasis'. **[2 marks]**
2. Explain why the body needs to maintain a constant body temperature. **[2 marks]**

 Made a start 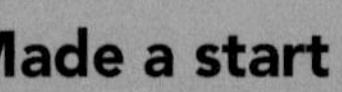 Feeling confident 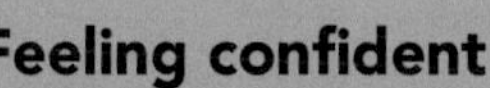 Exam ready 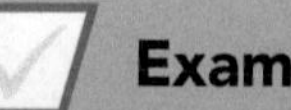

Human endocrine system

You need to know how the release and distribution of hormones is controlled by the human endocrine system.

Hormones

Hormones are sometimes called chemical messengers. They are secreted by glands and released directly into the blood. The blood carries the hormone to a target organ where the hormone produces an effect. The effects of the hormone system are much slower than the nervous system as it takes time for hormones to be transported around the body by the blood. The effects of the hormone last longer than an impulse sent by the nervous system.

Hormonal glands

See page 45 about hormones in reproduction.

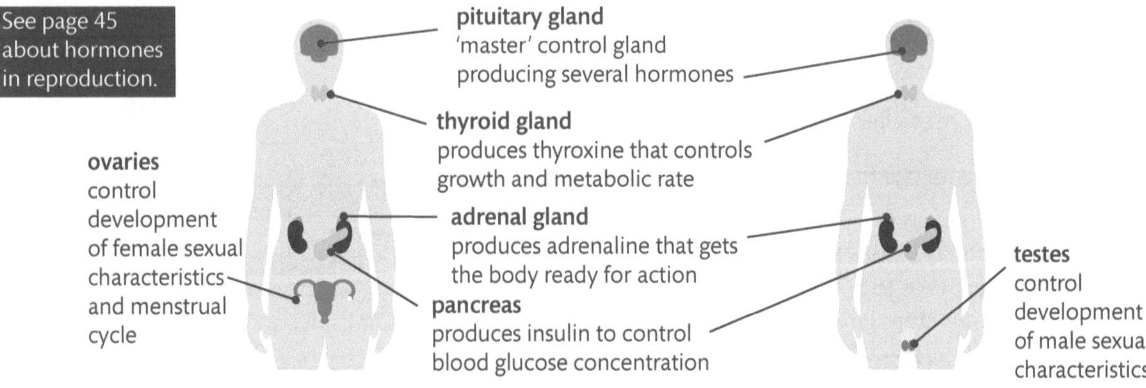

Figure 1 Glands that produce hormones

The pituitary gland

The pituitary gland is sometimes called the 'master gland'. It secretes several different hormones that control other hormonal glands by stimulating them to release their own hormone. The pituitary does this when the concentration of the hormone from the gland begins to fall.

Worked example — Grade 4

1 **Figure 2** is a graph showing the concentration of serum cortisol (a hormone) in the blood. State at what time of the day the level of serum cortisol is: **[2 marks]**

highest 8 am

lowest 10 pm

2 Complete the table to show the differences between the endocrine system and the nervous system. **[3 marks]**

	Endocrine system	Nervous system
Type of message	chemical (hormone)	electrical
Time taken for response	slow	fast
Duration of effects	long term	short term

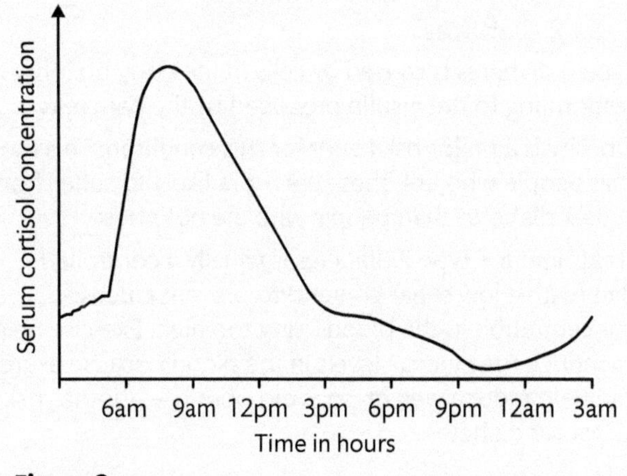

Figure 2

Exam-style practice — Grade 3

Complete the table to show the major glands, the hormones they produce and their effects on the body. **[3 marks]**

Name of gland	Hormone produced	Effect on body
thyroid		controls growth and metabolic rate
	adrenaline	gets the body ready for action
pancreas	insulin	

 Made a start  Feeling confident  Exam ready

Control of blood glucose

Controlling the concentration of glucose in the blood is very important as glucose is needed for respiration. You need to know how glucose concentration is controlled in the human body.

Blood glucose

After a meal, carbohydrates are digested into simple sugars, such as glucose, which are absorbed into the blood. Blood glucose concentration falls as glucose is taken into cells for respiration, but can be too high which is harmful.

Go to page 37 to revise the role of glucose in respiration.

The role of insulin

1. Blood glucose concentration rises after a meal.
2. This stimulates the pancreas to release the hormone insulin.
3. Insulin causes cells to take glucose from the blood. It also causes muscle and liver cells to convert excess glucose into glycogen, which is stored in the cells.

This ensures that blood glucose concentration remains at a safe level.

Diabetes

Type 1 diabetes

Type 1 diabetes is caused by the pancreas not producing insulin. This means that after a meal, the concentration of glucose in the blood may rise dangerously high. Injections of insulin into the blood help to control blood glucose concentration.

Type 2 diabetes

Type 2 diabetes is caused by cells in the body no longer responding to the insulin produced by the pancreas.

Obesity is a major risk factor for this condition. This means that people who are obese are more likely to suffer from Type 2 diabetes than people who are not obese.

Treatment for Type 2 diabetes is usually a controlled diet (with a low sugar content) to prevent glucose concentration in the blood rising too high. Exercise helps to reduce the glucose levels in the blood because exercise can help reduce weight, so avoid obesity – another risk factor for diabetes.

Worked example — Grade 5

Figure 1 shows the results of a study into the relationship between weight and percentage of people with diabetes.

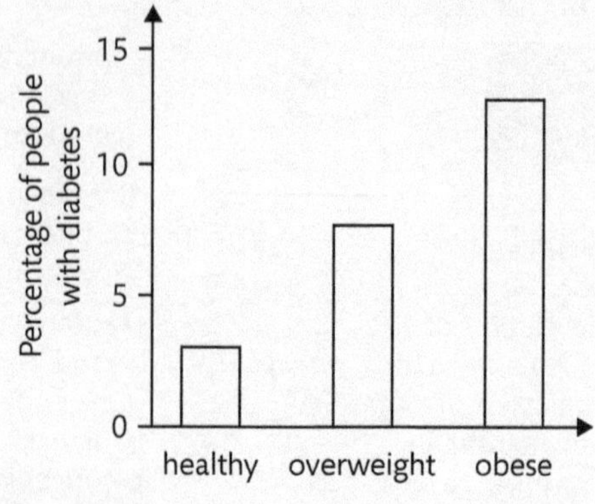

Figure 1

(a) State the percentage of obese people that had diabetes. **[1 mark]**

13%

(b) Describe the relationship shown by the bar chart. **[1 mark]**

The chart shows that as the weight category increases so does the percentage of people with diabetes.

(c) Which of the following conclusions can be drawn from the data in the bar chart.
Tick **one** box. **[1 mark]**

- being obese increases your risk of developing diabetes ✓
- all overweight people develop diabetes ☐
- people with a healthy weight never develop diabetes ☐
- being diabetic causes obesity ☐

Exam-style practice — Grade 5

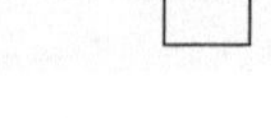

1. Describe **three** of the differences between Type 1 and Type 2 diabetes. **[3 marks]**
2. Explain why a low-sugar diet and exercise can help people with Type 2 diabetes. **[2 marks]**
3. The hormone insulin is a protein. Suggest why people with Type 1 diabetes need to inject themselves with insulin rather than take insulin tablets. **[2 marks]**

 Made a start  Feeling confident Exam ready

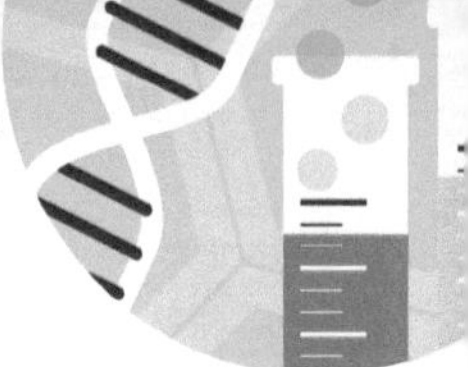

Hormones in reproduction

During puberty, reproductive hormones control the production of secondary sexual characteristics in males and females, and the menstrual cycle in females. You need to know the roles of different hormones in the menstrual cycle.

Male characteristics

The main reproductive hormone in men is testosterone, which is produced in the testes. Testosterone levels increase during puberty and cause male secondary sexual characteristics to develop:

- voice breaks and gets deeper
- growth of facial and pubic hair
- muscle growth
- production of sperm in testes.

Female characteristics

One of the main reproductive hormones in women is oestrogen, which is produced in the ovaries. Oestrogen levels increase during puberty and cause female secondary sexual characteristics to develop:

- growth of pubic hair
- breast development
- start of menstruation. This happens about once a month. It is when the lining of the uterus is lost.

The menstrual cycle

The **menstrual cycle** continues about every month, until a woman reaches the menopause at about 50 years, apart from when she is pregnant when the uterus lining is prepared for pregnancy. Several hormones are involved in this cycle.

Follicle-stimulating hormone (FSH) causes an egg to mature.

Oestrogen is secreted by the ovaries and causes only one egg to mature during each monthly cycle.

Luteinising hormone (LH) triggers **ovulation**, the release of the mature egg from the ovary.

Progesterone builds up and maintains the uterus lining during the middle part of the cycle and pregnancy.

Worked example — Grade 4

The statements below describe four stages of the menstrual cycle. Add numbers to show the correct order in which they happen. The first one has been done for you. **[2 marks]**

The uterus lining breaks down and menstruation begins.	1
The lining of the uterus is maintained for about 14 days.	4
An egg is released from the ovary.	3
The lining of the uterus builds up.	2

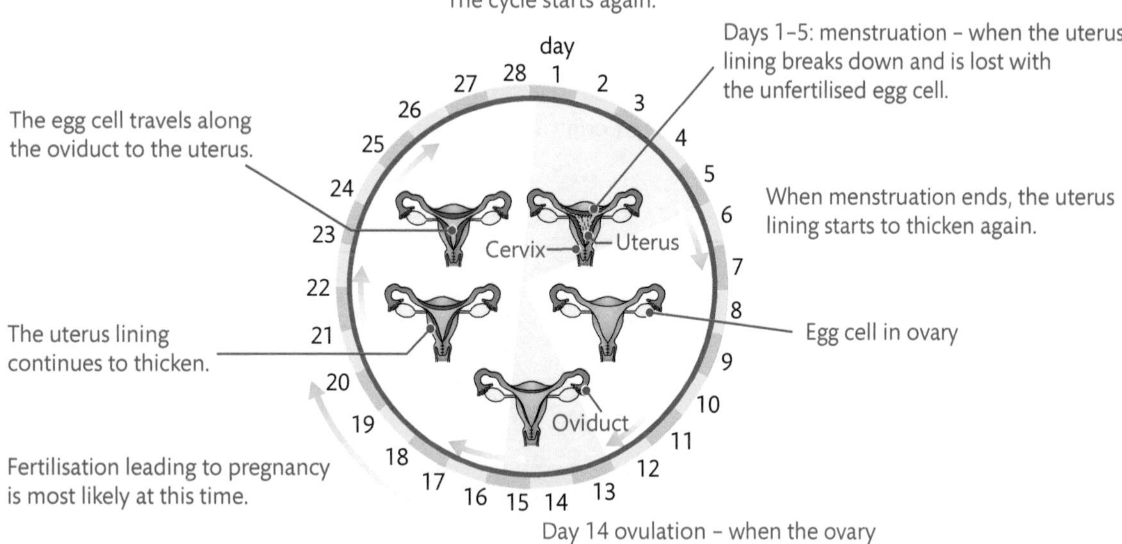
The cycle starts again.
day
28 1 2 3 4 5 6 7 8 9 10 11 12 13 14 15 16 17 18 19 20 21 22 23 24 25 26 27
Days 1–5: menstruation – when the uterus lining breaks down and is lost with the unfertilised egg cell.
When menstruation ends, the uterus lining starts to thicken again.
Egg cell in ovary
Day 14 ovulation – when the ovary releases the egg cell into the oviduct.
Fertilisation leading to pregnancy is most likely at this time.
The uterus lining continues to thicken.
The egg cell travels along the oviduct to the uterus.
Cervix
Uterus
Oviduct

Figure 1 One menstrual cycle

Exam-style question — Grade 3

Give the function of follicle stimulating hormone (FSH). **[1 mark]**

 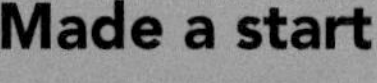  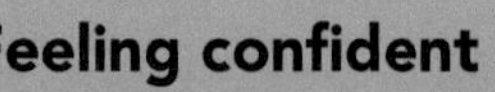 

Made a start | Feeling confident | Exam ready

Contraception

You need to know how both hormonal and non-hormonal methods of contraception can be used to prevent pregnancy.

Methods of contraception

Hormonal

- Oral contraceptives such as 'the pill' contain hormones that inhibit or prevent FSH production. This stops eggs maturing and being released ready for fertilisation.
- Injections, skin patches or implants contain slow-release progesterone. This prevents the maturation and release of eggs for months or years.

Non-hormonal

- Barrier methods such as the condom and diaphragm act as a physical barrier so that sperm cannot reach the egg.
- Intrauterine devices (IUDs) prevent the fertilised egg from implanting or attaching and growing in the uterus. IUDs may also release a hormone.
- Spermicides kill or disable sperm.
- Avoiding intercourse during the time in the menstrual cycle when an egg could be fertilised. This is sometimes called the rhythm method.
- Male and female sterilisation are surgical methods of preventing conception.

Working scientifically

Ethics

Science can answer some questions such as: 'How can you stop a sperm fertilising an egg?'

There are some questions that science cannot answer, such as: 'Should we stop a sperm from fertilising an egg?'

Individuals have to decide whether or not to use contraception to prevent pregnancy. They also have to decide which method of contraception to use.

Science can provide data to help you decide which methods are the most successful and understand the advantages and disadvantages of each method.

However, some people think that contraception is wrong, for reasons such as religion.

Each person should evaluate personal, social, economic and religious implications, and make a decision about contraception based on evidence and argument.

Worked example

Grade 5

The table summarises different methods of contraception.

	The contraceptive pill	Diaphragm	Rhythm method	Sterilisation
Reliability	very reliable	reliable	not very reliable	very reliable
Level of risk to health	some risk	little risk	no risk	some risk
Are effects reversible?	reversible	reversible	reversible	may not be reversible

A young married couple decide they do not want to have children until they are older.
Use the data in the table to identify **two** methods of contraception that would **not** be suitable.
Explain your answer. **[4 marks]**

The rhythm method is unsuitable because it is unreliable and may fail over the next ten years. Sterilisation is unsuitable because it may not be reversible so the couple may not be able to have children in the future.

Exam focus

Always read exam questions carefully. This question asks which contraceptive methods are **not** suitable.

You could also comment on the health risk associated with different methods of contraception. The contraceptive pill and sterilisation are less suitable because they pose some risk to health.

Exam-style practice

Grade 4

Draw **four** lines to link the type of contraception with its method of prevention. **[4 marks]**

Contraception
The oral contraceptive pill
Condom
The contraceptive implant
Diaphragm

Method of prevention
Hormonal
Non-hormonal

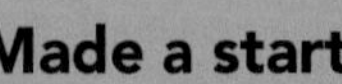

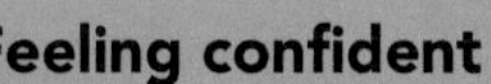

Exam ready

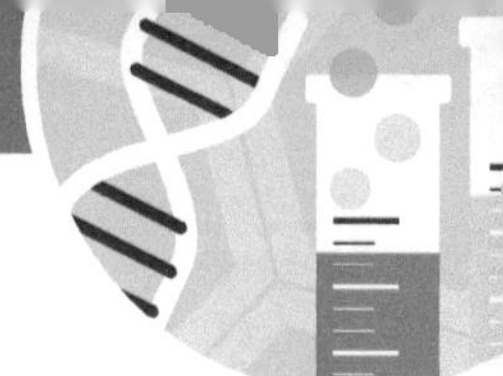

Asexual and sexual reproduction

You need to know how living organisms can reproduce by either asexual reproduction or sexual reproduction.

Sexual reproduction

Sexual reproduction requires male (sperm) and female (ova or egg) gametes. A **gamete** is a sex cell which contains genetic information. Gametes in reproductive organs are produced by a type of cell division called meiosis (page 48).

During fertilisation, the nuclei of the male and female gametes fuse together to make a fertilised egg cell called a **zygote**. The zygote divides many times by a type of cell division called mitosis (page 8), eventually forming an embryo.

In sexual reproduction, genetic information from the male and the female parent is mixed together. This causes variation in the offspring, so some offspring may be better adapted to their environment than the parents.

Nuclei is the plural of nucleus.

Go to page 52 to revise variation.

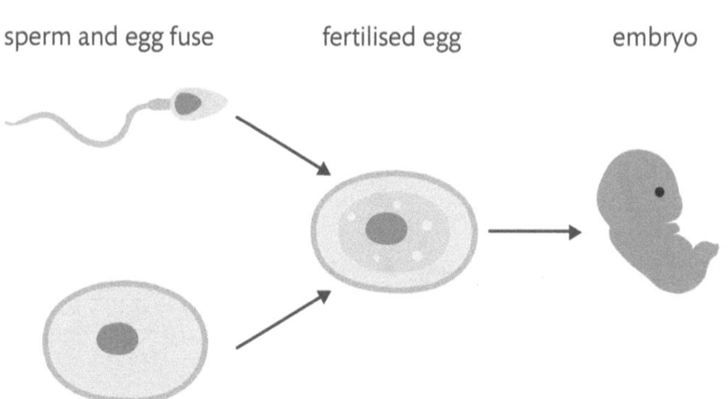

Figure 1 Fertilisation

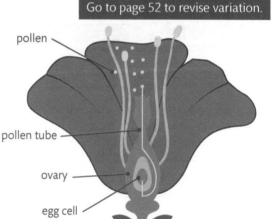

pollen
pollen tube
ovary
egg cell

Figure 2 In plants, a pollen grain contains the male nucleus that fertilises the egg cell in the ovary.

Asexual reproduction

Asexual reproduction involves only one parent. There is no fusion of male and female gametes.

This means that there is no mixing of genetic information, so when the cells divide, all the offspring are genetically identical to the parent. These offspring are called clones.

The type of cell division involved in asexual reproduction is called mitosis. Organisms which can reproduce asexually include bacteria, and plants such as fungi, potatoes and daffodils.

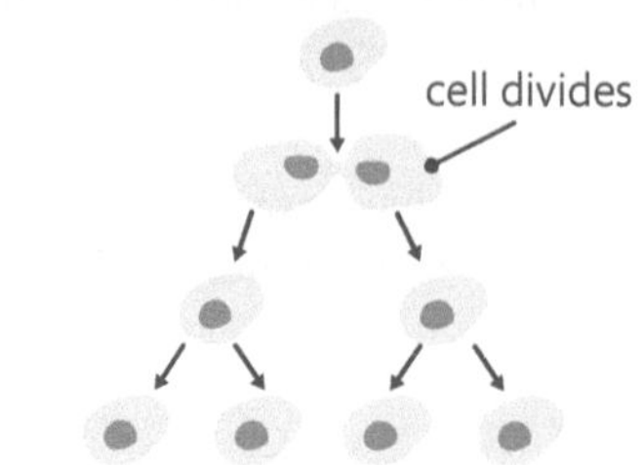

Figure 3 Asexual reproduction involves only mitosis.

Worked example — Grade 4

Compare sexual and asexual reproduction. In your answer you should refer to:

- the number of parents needed
- the amount of variety seen in the offspring produced. **[4 marks]**

Sexual reproduction involves two parent cells, whereas asexual reproduction involves one parent cell.

Sexual reproduction produces variety in offspring but asexual reproduction leads to genetically identical offspring.

Exam skills

You could be asked to compare sexual and asexual reproduction in the exam. Make sure you know the differences between the two types of cell division.

Exam-style practice — Grades 3–4

1. Define the term 'gamete'. **[1 mark]**
2. Describe **one** difference between asexual and sexual reproduction. **[2 marks]**

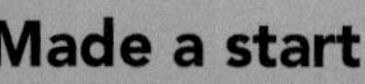

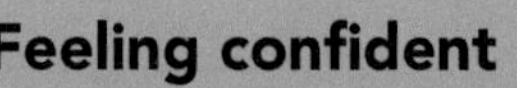

Made a start | Feeling confident | Exam ready

BBC

Meiosis

You need to know how meiosis produces gametes for sexual reproduction. This occurs in the reproductive organs. For animals, these are the testes and ovaries.

The stages of meiosis

Meiosis results in sperm and egg cells (**gametes**).

Although similar to mitosis, it is a two-stage cell division process, resulting in the production of four cells, each haploid (containing a single set of chromosomes rather than two sets as in a normal cell.)

The final stage of division during meiosis will always produce cells containing half the number of chromosomes in the parent cell.

Fertilisation

The gametes produced by meiosis are genetically different from each other (see **Figure 1**).

Later, during fertilisation, one male gamete and one female gamete join up to form a cell with the typical number of chromosomes in a body cell. (For example, in humans, 46 chromosomes arranged in 23 pairs.)

This cell will then divide by mitosis as the embryo develops. As the embryo develops, cells differentiate.

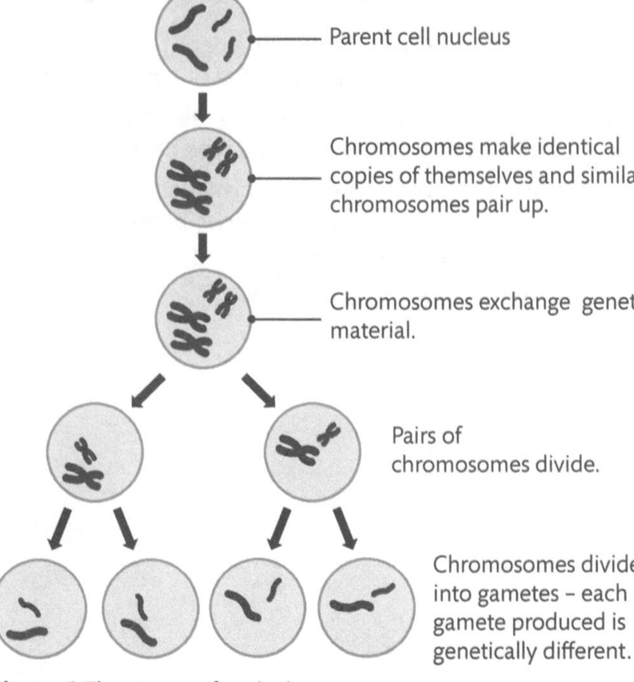
Parent cell nucleus
Chromosomes make identical copies of themselves and similar chromosomes pair up.
Chromosomes exchange genetic material.
Pairs of chromosomes divide.
Chromosomes divide into gametes – each gamete produced is genetically different.

Figure 1 The stages of meiosis

Worked example

Grade 4–5

1 Where does meiosis take place? **[1 mark]**

In the reproductive organs.

2 State what happens to the chromosomes at the start of meiosis before the first division. **[2 marks]**

The chromosomes make identical copies of themselves and similar chromosomes pair up.

3 How many times does a cell divide in meiosis? **[1 mark]**

two

Exam focus

You need to know the differences between meiosis and mitosis (page 8) for the exam.

Key terms

- **gametes** – sex cells: sperm and egg cells
- **diploid** – a cell containing two sets of chromosomes
- **haploid** – a cell containing a single set of unpaired chromosomes

Exam-style practice — Grade 4

1 Name the male and female gametes in animals. **[2 marks]**

2 Human body cells contain 46 chromosomes.

(a) State how many chromosomes there are in human gametes. **[1 mark]**

(b) Give a reason for your answer to part **(a)**. **[1 mark]**

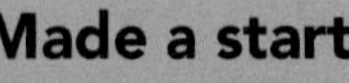
Made a start

Feeling confident
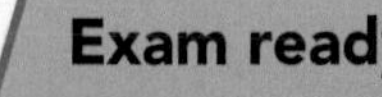
Exam ready

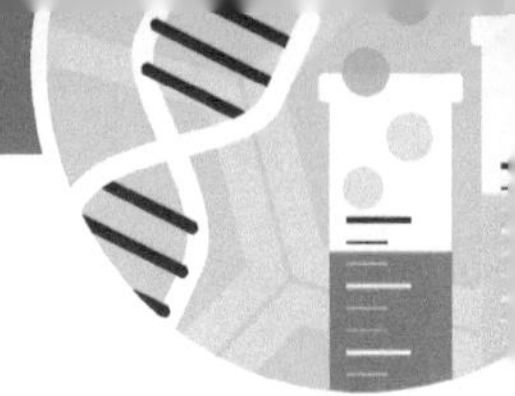

DNA and the genome

The whole genetic material of an organism is called its genome. You need to know about the substance that makes up all genetic material, DNA - deoxyribonucleic acid. DNA is a polymer, which means it is a long chain made up of repeating units.

The structure of DNA

The total genetic material of an organism is called its genome.

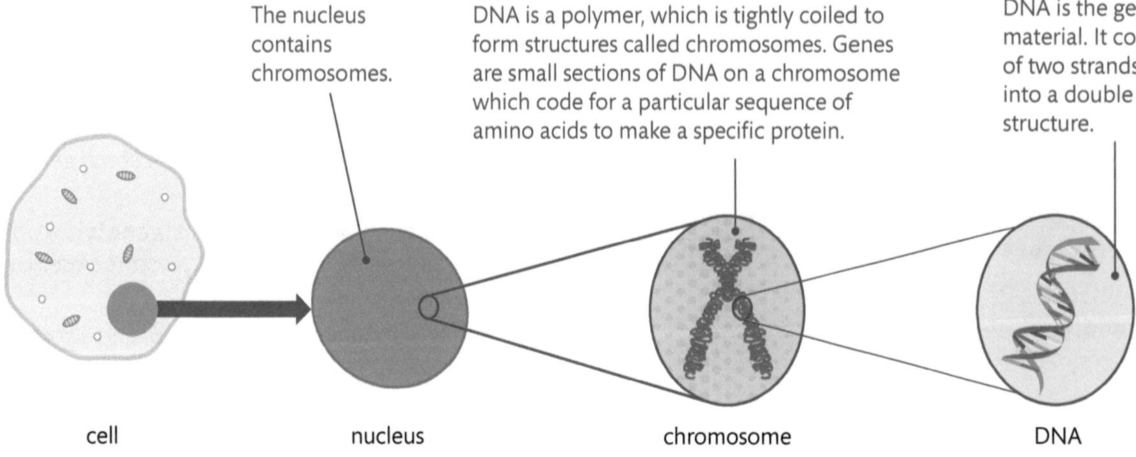

The nucleus contains chromosomes.
DNA is a polymer, which is tightly coiled to form structures called chromosomes. Genes are small sections of DNA on a chromosome which code for a particular sequence of amino acids to make a specific protein.
DNA is the genetic material. It consists of two strands coiled into a double helix structure.
cell
nucleus
chromosome
DNA

Figure 1 DNA in a cell

Understanding the human genome

The whole human genome has now been mapped.

This is important for:

- searching for genes linked to different types of disease
- understanding and treatment of inherited genetic disorders
- tracing human migration patterns from the past, using differences between genome of people from different areas.

Worked example — Grade 5

Genetic markers are areas in the sequence of DNA that vary between individuals. These genetic markers support the idea that modern humans left Africa around 50 000 years ago, migrating to different parts of the world.

Suggest how genetic markers were used to trace human migration. **[2 marks]**

Mapping the occurrence of these markers around the world can show the movement of human populations. As humans have migrated, their genome has mutated, showing small variations for different populations in different areas.

Exam-style practice — Grade 4

1. Define the term 'genome'. **[1 mark]**
2. Ali's genome shows he has a gene that means he might develop a genetic disease in the future. Suggest one way that Ali's doctor could use this information to help Ali. **[1 mark]**
3. What is the human genome useful for? **[3 marks]**

 **Made a start**  **Feeling confident**  **Exam ready**

Genetic inheritance

Many of our characteristics are controlled by the genes on the chromosomes we inherit. We have two of each chromosome, and two of each gene. You need to know how alleles, the different forms of each gene, cause variation between individuals.

5 Key terms

- **gene** – a short section of DNA which codes for a protein
- **allele** – one version of a gene
- **dominant** – only one dominant allele is needed for a characteristic to be expressed
- **recessive** – two recessive alleles are needed for the characteristic to be expressed
- **homozygous** – both alleles for a gene are identical
- **heterozygous** – the alleles for a gene are different
- **genotype** – the alleles present for a gene
- **phenotype** – the physical characteristics, determined by the alleles

10 Worked example Grade 5

1 Describe the difference between a genotype and a phenotype. **[2 marks]**

A genotype refers to the alleles in an organism, whereas the phenotype is the physical appearance resulting from the alleles.

2 The recessive allele **m** causes a rare blood-linked condition. Two parents produce offspring. Parent A has the alleles **Mm** and parent B has the alleles **mm**.

Complete the Punnett square to calculate the percentage chance of their offspring inheriting the gene. **[3 marks]**

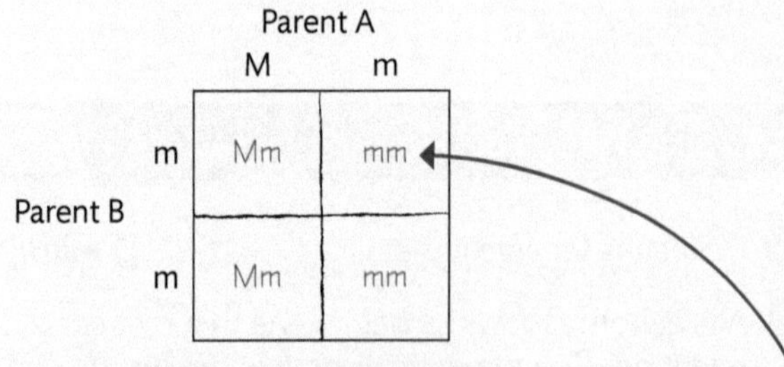

- possible 2 Mm and 2 mm
- only mm causes disease
- so chance of a child inheriting disease is 1 out of 2 = 50%

Dominant alleles are represented by a capital letter, while recessive alleles are shown by a lowercase letter.

5 Genes

Some characteristics are controlled by a single **gene**, such as red-green colour blindness in humans.

Most characteristics are controlled by multiple genes interacting, such as multiple genes affecting eye and skin colour.

Body cells have two copies of each chromosome. So they have two copies of each gene (except some genes on the sex chromosomes).

The combination of alleles present (**genotype**) operates at a molecular level to develop a person's observable characteristics (**phenotype**).

A gene has a dominant form (allele) **B**, and a recessive allele **b**. There are three possible genotypes: **BB**, **Bb** and **bb**.

Individuals with the genotype **BB** or **Bb** will look the same (because **B** is dominant to **b**).

Individuals with the genotype **bb** will have a different phenotype.

2 Exam focus

In the exam, you are expected to know how to complete genetic cross diagrams and make predictions about the probability of inheriting a particular genotype or phenotype from the genotypes of the parents. The results of genetic crosses are usually represented as either a ratio or a percentage.

10 Exam-style practice Grade 5

Polydactyly is an inherited condition which causes the sufferer to have extra fingers or toes. It is caused by a dominant allele, **D**. A mother has a genotype **DD**, the father has the genotype **dd**.

(a) Complete the Punnett square to show the possible genotypes of the offspring. **[3 marks]**

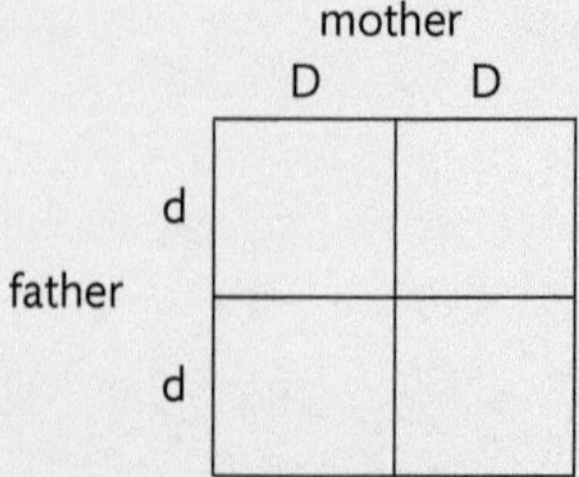

(b) Calculate the percentage of the offspring that will inherit polydactyly. **[1 mark]**

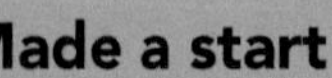

Feeling confident

Exam ready

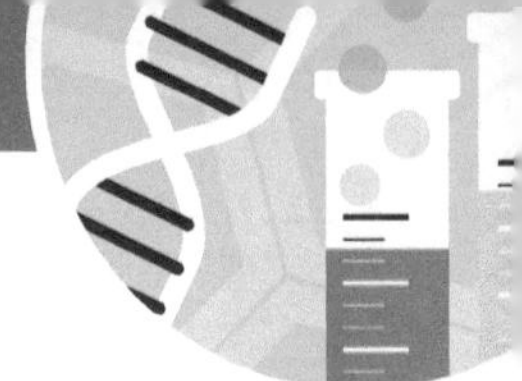

Inherited disorders

You need to know how genetic disorders like polydactyly and cystic fibrosis are inherited.

Polydactyly and cystic fibrosis

Polydactyly is a disorder in which the person has extra fingers or toes. It is caused by a dominant allele.

Cystic fibrosis is a disorder of the cell membranes that causes the production of a thick sticky mucus which affects organs, particularly the lungs. It is caused by a recessive allele.

This means that people will only have cystic fibrosis if they inherit two copies of the recessive allele. Go to page 50 for more about alleles.

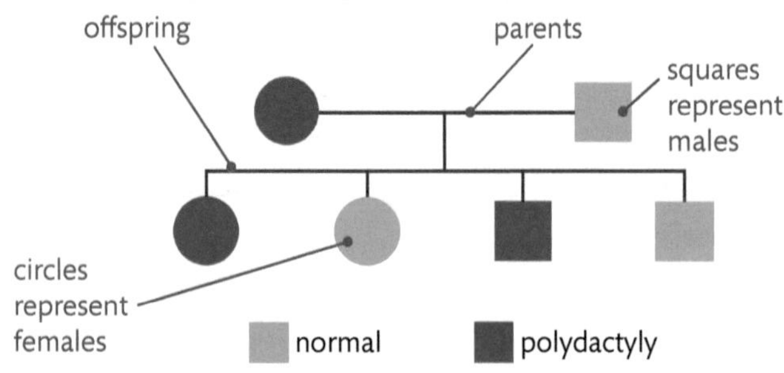

Figure 1 This family tree shows the inheritance of polydactyly within a family.

Worked example — Grade 5

1 What percentage of the offspring in **Figure 1** have polydactyly? **[1 mark]**

2 out of 4 offspring have polydactyly.

$\frac{2}{4} \times 100 = 50\%$

2 The allele for polydactyly is dominant. Show that the parent with polydactyly is heterozygous for the allele. **[3 marks]**

	Mother (polydactyl)		
		P	p
Father (normal)	p	Pp	pp
	p	Pp	pp

If the mother was homozygous PP, all offspring would be polydactyl, but 50% are polydactyl so the mother is heterozygous Pp.

Working scientifically

Embryo screening can be used to identify whether an unborn child has inherited a genetic condition from its parents. Embryo screening cannot be used to treat the problem but it will allow parents to make an informed decision as to whether it is fair to have the child if the condition causes a lot of pain.

Embryo screening

There are economic, ethical and social issues around embryo screening for inherited disorders.

Economic issues relating to the use of embryo screening include the fact that it is a very expensive procedure. However, the cost of bringing up a child with cystic fibrosis could be much more expensive.

Social issues include the possibility that the embryo might be damaged during the testing, causing social issues when born. Wider social issues include the possibility that testing for genetic disorders may cause people to become prejudiced against anyone with a disorder, but by using embryo screening the child is more likely to be born healthy and is unlikely to pass on the CF gene to its offspring.

Ethical issues related to embryo screening include the fact that some people believe it is wrong to kill an embryo as it is a living thing. However, it may mean that a child won't be born who would have to suffer a life-limiting illness.

Exam-style practice — Grade 5

Cystic fibrosis is caused by a recessive allele.

(a) Complete the Punnett square to show the cross between a heterozygous woman and man. Use 'f' to represent the recessive allele for cystic fibrosis and 'F' the dominant allele. **[4 marks]**

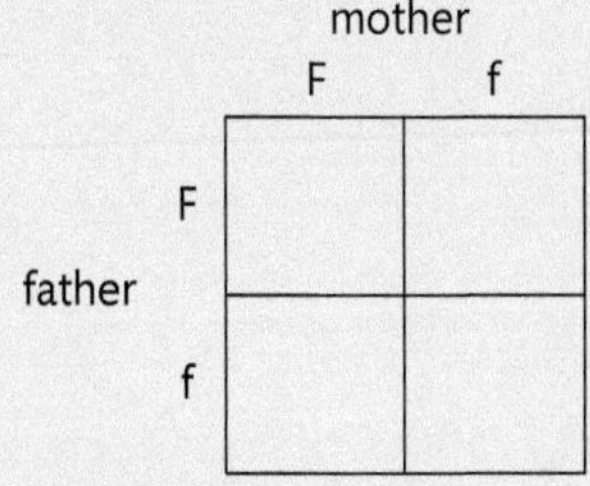

(b) Describe the phenotypes of the:

(i) mother **[1 mark]**

(ii) father. **[1 mark]**

(c) If a person has the genotype **ff**, what is their phenotype? **[1 mark]**

(d) Describe the symptoms of cystic fibrosis. **[2 marks]**

(e) Give **one** advantage of screening an embryo for cystic fibrosis. **[1 mark]**

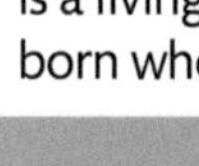

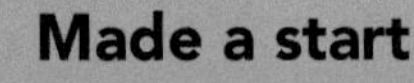

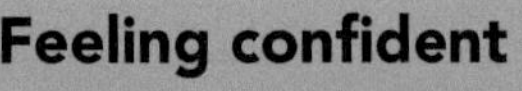

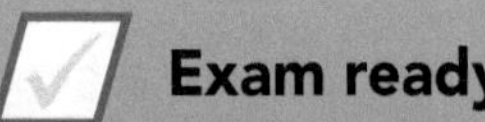

Variation and mutation

You need to know how variation in a species is affected by genes and the enivornment.

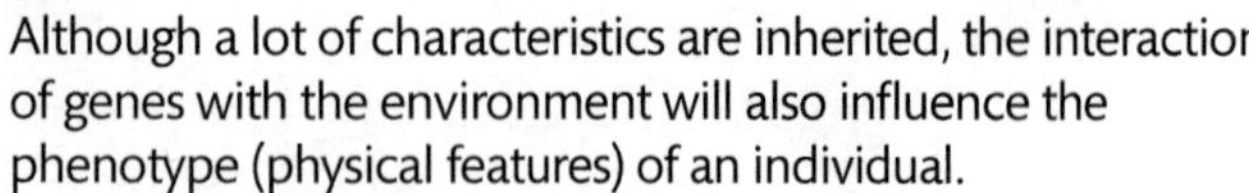

5 Causes of variation

Although a lot of characteristics are inherited, the interaction of genes with the environment will also influence the phenotype (physical features) of an individual.

Variation between individuals occurs due to differences in:

- inherited genes
- the environment in which the individual grew up
- the interaction of genes with the environment.

Some characteristics brought about by genetic variation include Down's syndrome, blood group and eye colour.

Some characteristics brought about by environmental variation include weight and language spoken.

Many kinds of variation are influenced by both environmental and genetic factors. For example, a person may have the potential to be tall, but an unhealthy diet can cause poor growth.

There is usually a lot of genetic variation within a population of a species.

5 Mutations: key facts

- A mutation is a change in genetic material (DNA).
- Mutations occur naturally and continuously.
- Genetic variation is caused by mutations.
- Most mutations will have no effect on the phenotype; only rarely do mutations lead to a new phenotype.
- If the new phenotype is better suited to an environmental change it can lead to a relatively rapid change in the species.

Mutations can have positive or negative effects:

- improve chances of survival
- increase genetic diversity
- can lead to diseases, such as cancer (page 24)
- can lead to genetic disorders (page 51).

10 Worked example — Grades 2–5

1 Use the correct words from the box to complete the sentences to explain how extensive variation occurs within a species. **[4 marks]**

phenotype	rapid	variation	mutations

Differences in the characteristics of individuals in a population are called variation. Differences arise as mutations that occur continuously. Only rarely does a mutation change the phenotype but if the change increases the chance of survival then it can lead to a rapid change in the species as individuals with the mutation have more offspring.

2 Identical twins are individuals who developed from a single fertilised egg cell. So they have identical DNA. Explain why identical twins may not look identical when they reach adulthood. **[2 marks]**

Phenotype is controlled by genetic inheritance, environmental factors and the interaction between them. However, environmental factors such as their diet will also affect their phenotype so their appearance could be different.

Remember, the phenotype (appearance) is determined by a combination of genetic and environmental factors.

5 Exam-style practice — Grade 3

1 Give **one** example of genetic variation and **one** example of environmental variation. **[2 marks]**

2 Give **one** way in which a mutation can be beneficial. **[1 mark]**

 Made a start  Feeling confident  Exam ready

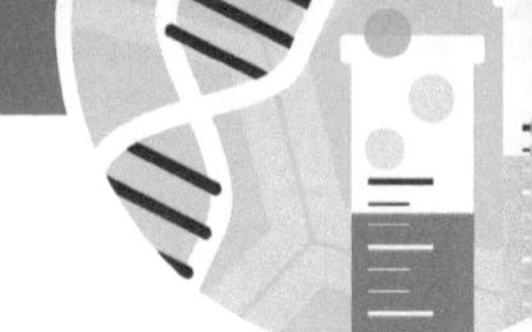

Sex determination

You need to know how sex is determined by chromosomes.

Formation of sex chromosomes

Human body cells each contain 23 pairs of chromosomes, which control a person's characteristics.

The 23rd pair also carry the genes that determine whether a person is male or female. These are called the sex chromosomes.

In humans, the female sex chromosomes are XX. The male sex chromosomes are XY.

Female sex cells (gametes) contain only an X chromosome. The male sex cells (gametes) can contain either an X or a Y, depending on how the sex chromosome pair separated during meiosis. Therefore an X chromosome is always inherited from the egg but there is a 50% chance of inheriting an X or a Y chromosome from the sperm, which determines the sex of the offspring.

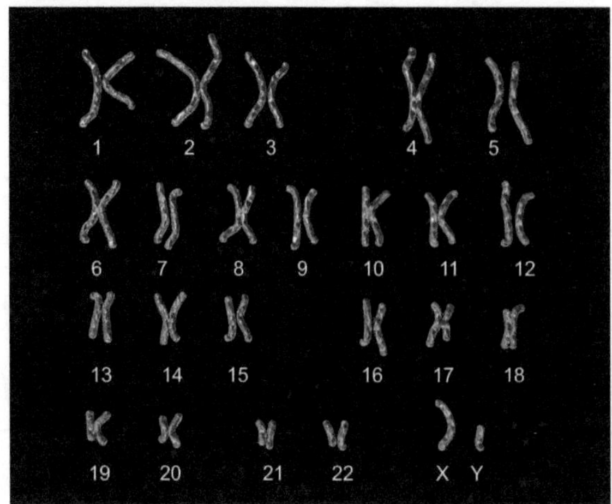

Figure 1 Humans have 22 chromosome pairs and two sex chromosomes. What is the sex of the person whose chromosomes these are?

Genetic cross diagrams

A genetic cross diagram can be used to determine the sex of offspring.

1. To construct a genetic diagram, the phenotype of each parent must be given on the top line.
2. The next line shows the genotype for each parent, underneath their phenotype.
3. The next line shows the genotype of all the gametes which can be passed on to the offspring.
4. The final stage in the genetic cross diagram is to show all of the combinations of gametes which could occur, which gives the different genotypes possible.

Exam focus

You are expected to know the genotype for a male and a female:

- In males, the two sex chromosomes are different. They are XY.
- In females, the two sex chromosomes are the same. They are XX.

Worked example — Grade 4

There is a 1:1 chance of a child being a boy or a girl. Complete the diagram below to explain this. **[4 marks]**

		Male	
	Gametes	X	Y
Female	X	XX	XY
	X	XX	XY

The diagram shows that there is a 2 : 2 chance of female : male offspring which equates to a 1 : 1 ratio or 50% female, 50% male.

Exam-style practice — Grade 4

Humans have two different sex chromosomes: X and Y.

(a) Give the genotype of a female. **[1 mark]**

(b) Give the probability of having a male child. Explain your answer. **[2 marks]**

(c) A couple have three daughters. Give a reason why the probability of their next child being a girl is the same as it being a boy. **[2 marks]**

 Made a start  Feeling confident  Exam ready

Evolution

The theory of evolution states that all species of living things have evolved from simple life forms that started to develop over three billion years ago.

Natural selection

Evolution is a word used to describe a change in the inherited characteristics of a population over time. It happens through a process called natural selection.

Natural selection is when organisms that are the best suited to their environment are most likely to survive and reproduce. Their offspring will inherit genes that give rise to phenotypes suited to the environment. This can cause changes to the population over time, which is known as evolution.

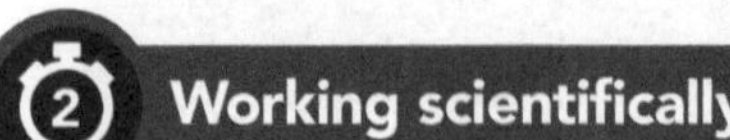

Working scientifically

The theory of evolution by natural selection explains how the modern giraffe species has developed a longer neck than its ancient ancestors.

1. Giraffes within ancient populations had slightly longer necks than others.
2. Giraffes with longer necks were better suited to the environment because they could reach the leaves high up in trees so they were better nourished and more likely to survive and have lots of offspring.
3. The alleles for the longer neck are passed down to the next generation so all the offspring have longer necks.
4. Over time, the gene for the longer neck becomes more common in the population. Over a long time, the giraffe species changes from having a shorter neck to a longer neck.

Worked example — Grade 4

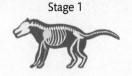

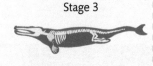

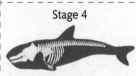

Stage 1 | Stage 2 | Stage 3 | Stage 4

Figure 2

Figure 2 shows how the whale is thought to have evolved from its early ancestors.

Give **two** ways in which the whale has adapted since Stage 1. **[2 marks]**

The early ancestor had four limbs, and the whale alive today doesn't.

The whale has a fin on its back unlike its ancestors.

Evidence of evolution

Evidence for the theory of evolution by natural selection comes from a study of fossil records and evolution of antibiotic resistance in bacteria. The theory is now widely accepted.

You can find out more about the fossil record on page 57 and resistant bacteria on page 59.

Example of evidence of evolution

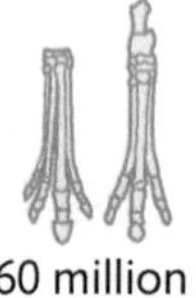
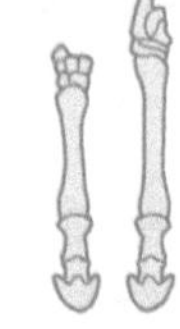

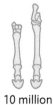

Figure 1 Fossil evidence of changes in the legs and feet of the horse.

Scientists have used the theory of evolution by natural selection to explain how horse legs and feet have changed over millions of years, as in **Figure 1**. Ancient horses had shorter legs and three toes. They lived in forested areas. Modern horses live in open grassland where they can easily be spotted by predators. They have longer legs and hooves, which are thought to have been an advantage. They enable the horse to gallop faster and move away from predators easily.

You are not expected to recall evolutionary stages in the development of species; you need to use the information provided in the question.

New species can form when the genes of individuals within a species become so different that their phenotype changes and they can no longer interbreed to form fertile offspring. This is known as **speciation**.

Exam-style question — Grade 5

The deer mouse is a mouse found in many parts of North America. Normally deer mice have a dark fur coat, which enables them to blend in with dark soils and avoid being seen by predators such as owls and hawks.

Deer mice found in sandhills, where the ground is a lighter colour, have been found with a pale coloured fur.

The pale-coloured mice have a mutated Agouti gene which causes the lighter fur colour.

Use the theory of evolution by natural selection to explain why the mice found in the sandhills have a lighter fur colour. **[3 marks]**

Selective breeding

You need to know about the effects of selective breeding on plants and animals, and the positive and negative impacts.

Positive and negative impacts

Selective breeding is like natural selection (page 54), but humans choose the desired characteristics to produce the best offspring. Humans have been doing this for thousands of years.

Selective breeding is also called artificial selection. It involves selecting and breeding together parents with the desired (useful) characteristic from a mixed population. Those offspring that have the desired characteristic are then bred together. This is repeated for many generations, until all the offspring show the desired characteristic.

Impacts of selective breeding

Positive (useful characteristics selected for)	Negative effects of selective breeding
plants crop plants produce more food for us more resistant to disease large or unusual flowers. **animals** increased milk production each animal produces more milk sociable domesticated animals.	Inbreeding can lead to inherited defects. Reduction in the variety of alleles in the population restricts the ability to produce new varieties in the future. None of the organisms in a species may be resistant to a new disease and they could all die.

wild cabbage plant (*Brassica oleracea*)

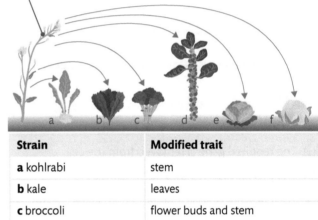

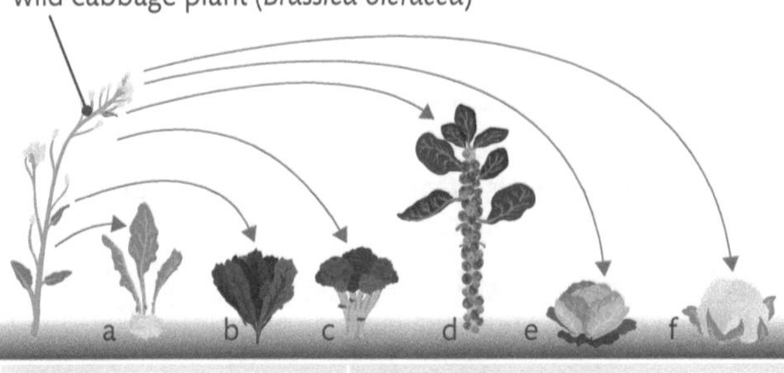

Strain	Modified trait
a kohlrabi	stem
b kale	leaves
c broccoli	flower buds and stem
d Brussels sprouts	lateral leaf buds
e cabbage	terminal leaf bud
f cauliflower	flower buds

Figure 1 Example of the effects of artificial selection on wild cabbage

Worked example — Grade 5

1 Describe **two** advantages of selectively breeding plant crops. **[2 marks]**

To obtain plants that produce higher crop yield or have better resistance to diseases.

2 Selective breeding often results in a population of animals with very similar genes. Give **one** disadvantage of having a population of chickens with similar genes. **[1 mark]**

Similar genetics means that the population will have the same strengths but also the same weaknesses e.g. being prone to the same diseases.

Exam-style practice — Grade 3–4

1 Number the following statements to describe the correct order of the steps in selectively breeding sheep for the best wool. The first one has been done for you. **[2 marks]**

From existing stock, identify sheep which have the best wool.	1
Continue to breed the sheep with the best wool over several generations until all the offspring have the desired wool.	
Breed sheep with the best wool together.	
Offspring with the best wool are bred together.	

2 Suggest **one** reason a pig farmer might use selective breeding. **[1 mark]**

Made a start | Feeling confident | Exam ready

Genetic engineering

You need to know how genetic engineering is used to change the genome of an organism.

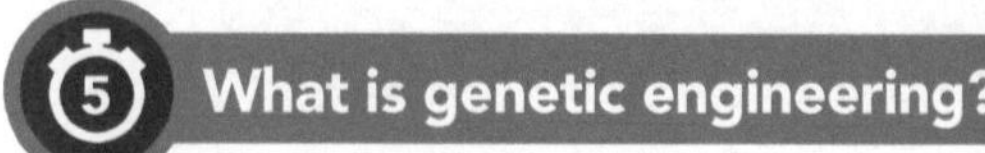

5 What is genetic engineering?

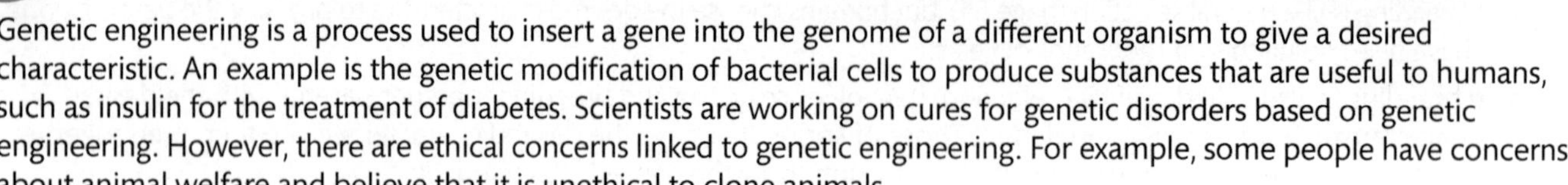

Genetic engineering is a process used to insert a gene into the genome of a different organism to give a desired characteristic. An example is the genetic modification of bacterial cells to produce substances that are useful to humans, such as insulin for the treatment of diabetes. Scientists are working on cures for genetic disorders based on genetic engineering. However, there are ethical concerns linked to genetic engineering. For example, some people have concerns about animal welfare and believe that it is unethical to clone animals.

Genetically modified (GM) crops

GM crops are crops that have had genes inserted into them to alter their characteristics.

Plant crops have been genetically engineered to produce higher quality and increased yield, and be disease-, herbicide- and insect-resistant. Crops can also be engineered to produce added nutrients. An example is Golden Rice, which has higher levels of vitamin A. This is useful for countries where vitamin deficiencies are common.

5 Stages in genetic engineering

1. The required gene is removed from the cell.
2. The gene is inserted into bacterial DNA.
3. The bacterial DNA is then put into the cells of the desired organism (animal, plant or microorganism) at an early stage of their development.
4. The organism develops exhibiting the desired characteristics.

5 Worked example — Grade 5

1. Give **two** reasons why people are against the growth of GM crops. **[2 marks]**

They might cross pollinate with wild plants and may pass on their herbicide resistance to wild plants or weeds. We don't know if there are potential health risks for humans.

2. Give **one** advantage to growing herbicide resistant crops. **[1 mark]**

Farmers can spray the crops with herbicide as the crops won't be harmed (only the weeds).

5 Risks and benefits

Benefits of genetic modification:

- crop plants with increased yields, pest and disease resistance
- nutritional value or drought tolerance
- new medical treatments for humans with inherited disorders
- bacteria able to produce medical drugs cheaply or synthesise fuel or useful chemicals
- animals with more desirable characteristics.

Risks of genetic modification:

- Monocultures (all one type of crop) are more likely to all die of new diseases.
- Some people fear that genes from GM crops may harm wildlife or cross into wild plants, for example, transfer herbicide resistance.
- Some people fear that large companies may control stocks of all popular seeds.
- Some people think not enough research has been done on the effects of eating GM food.

This answer could also be developed to include concerns about the effect of GM crops on the ecosystem and how insects feeding off the crops might be affected.

5 Exam-style practice — Grade 4

1. **(a)** What is meant by 'genetic modification'? **[1 mark]**
   (b) Name a disease that can be treated with the help of genetically modified bacteria. **[1 mark]**
2. Give **two** ethical issues associated with GM crops being herbicide-resistant. **[2 marks]**

 Made a start  Feeling confident  Exam ready

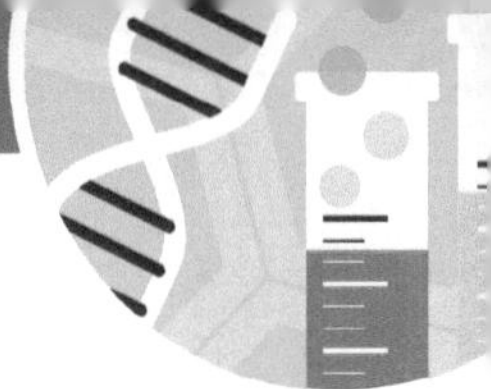

Fossils

A fossil is the preserved remains of an organism that lived millions of years ago. You need to know how fossils form and how they are used as evidence for evolution.

Formation of fossils

Fossils are found preserved in rocks, amber (hardened tree resin), ice, acidic peat bogs and tar pits. Fossils can be formed in a number of ways.

- Parts of the organism have not decayed (usually hard parts of an organism such as bone, shells and claws do not decay easily. The majority of fossils tend to be of species with hard skeletons.
- Parts are replaced by minerals as they decay.
- Traces of organisms may be preserved. These include footprints, burrows, droppings and rootlet traces.

Conditions needed for decay include no oxygen or moisture present, toxic gases, acidic environment, or too cold.

Figure 1 A fossil of a fish preserved in rock

Worked example — Grade 5

1 The fish fossil shown in **Figure 1** was found in mudstone rock. Suggest **two** reasons the fish did not decay. **[2 marks]**

There might not have been enough oxygen or enough moisture in the mudstone rock for decay to occur.

2 A fossilised baby mammoth was found in frozen ground in Siberia. Explain how the mammoth fossil was formed. **[2 marks]**

The baby mammoth must have died and frozen quickly before it was eaten by other animals. It was too cold for microorganisms to decompose the mammoth, so it was preserved intact, in ice as a 'frozen fossil'.

3 The fossil record has been used to construct a hypothesis about how life first began on Earth. Suggest **one** reason why scientists can't be certain about how life began on Earth. **[2 marks]**

Soft-bodied organisms tend to decay without forming fossils so the fossil record is incomplete.

If the fossilised mammoth thawed it would decompose rapidly unless preserved by other means.

Working scientifically

There are gaps in the fossil record because:

- Fossilisation itself is a rare occurrence. The organism has to die and lie undisturbed in just the right conditions.
- Many fossils have just not been found yet.
- Many have been formed but have been destroyed by erosion and other geological changes.

Exam-style practice — Grade 4

1 Which statement best describes a fossil?
Tick **one** box. **[1 mark]**

- the remains of an organism from many years ago, found in rocks ☐
- the remains of an organism that recently died ☐
- the DNA fingerprint of an organism ☐
- the bones of an organism found in rock ☐

2 A fossil of a reptile was found in some rock. Explain how the skeleton of a reptile can become fossilised. **[2 marks]**

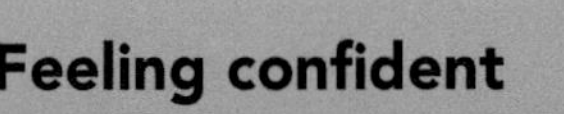

Extinction

Extinction of a plant or animal species occurs when there are no more individuals of that species alive and the loss of the species is permanent. You need to know how and why species can become extinct.

5 Key factors contributing to extinction

- **New predators** – if a new species is introduced or a predator moves into the territory, it may wipe out a species which isn't adapted to protecting itself.
- **New diseases** – if a species' defences against pathogens (e.g. immune system in mammals) cannot protect it against a viral or bacterial disease, it could become extinct.
- **Mutations** – if another species evolves as a result of mutation, it could become a more successful competitor.
- **Temperature change** – global warming is causing changes in habitats, which could leave species without shelter or food.
- **Environmental change** – destruction of habitat can leave organisms without food or shelter.
- **Catastrophic event** – an asteroid colliding with Earth, a comet strike or a tsunami could wipe out an entire community.
- **Speciation** – a species evolves and the original species dies out.

10 Human influence

The following human activities have a major effect on extinction:

- hunting
- increasing levels of pollution
- destruction of habitats.

The fossil record shows species that have become extinct.

The dodo is thought to have become extinct because of new competitors being introduced to the island where it lived and because it was hunted by humans.

Many animals are critically endangered, including the giant panda and Sumatran tiger.

Figure 1 The golden toad became extinct in 1989. Scientists believe global warming was instrumental in its extinction.

5 Worked example Grade 4

1. Give **two** physical factors and **two** biological factors that may have caused a species to become extinct. **[4 marks]**

Physical factors – volcanoes and earthquakes

Biological factors – lack of food and mates

You could also suggest an ice age, climate change or an asteroid collision for physical factors.

You could suggest disease, speciation or lack of habitat for biological factors.

2. Why do scientists not always know what extinct species looked like, even though they have fossils of the species? **[1 mark]**

Only their bones or fossils remain so it is difficult to guess what their appearance may have been.

You could also say that nobody has ever seen one.

5 Exam-style practice Grade 2

1. Give **two** strategies which can be used to try to prevent the extinction of a species. **[2 marks]**
2. Describe how an ice age could lead to the extinction of a species. **[2 marks]**

 Made a start  Feeling confident Exam ready

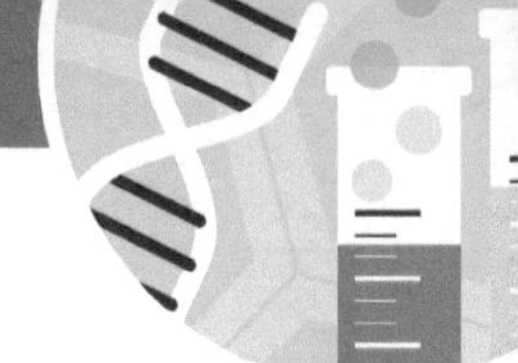

Resistant bacteria

More and more strains of bacteria are developing resistance to antibiotics. You need to know the effects this has on the treatment of bacterial diseases.

Bacterial resistance to antibiotics

Bacteria can develop resistance to antibiotics by evolution and natural selection (page 54).

- Some bacteria have mutations which make them more resistant to an antibiotic.
- Bacteria that do not have that mutation are killed when the antibiotic is used.
- Bacteria that have the mutation survive longer and reproduce more.
- Bacteria can reproduce very rapidly, so soon all the surviving bacteria are resistant to the antibiotic.
- Resistant strains can then spread because people are not immune to them and there are no effective treatments.

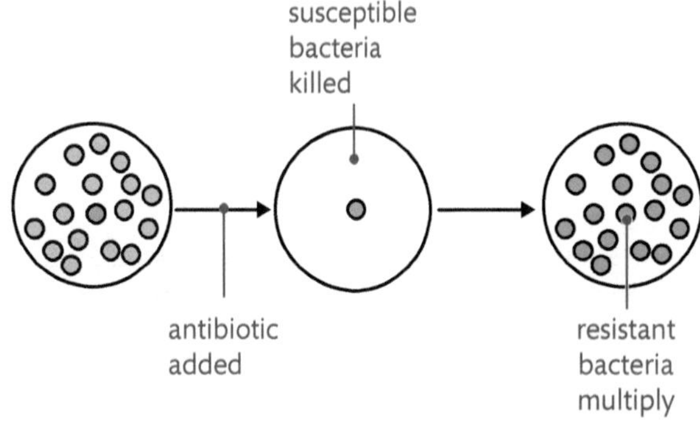

Figure 1 Bacteria developing resistance to an antibiotic

MRSA

MRSA is a strain of bacteria that is resistant to many known antibiotics and is therefore difficult to treat.

To reduce the chances of other bacteria developing antibiotic resistance:

- Doctors should not prescribe antibiotics for diseases caused by pathogens that are not bacteria, e.g. viruses.
- Doctors should not prescribe antibiotics for non-serious diseases that the immune system will clear up without help.
- A patient should complete their course of antibiotics to reduce the chances of any bacteria surviving and forming a resistant strain.
- The use of antibiotics in agriculture to increase growth rates in healthy animals should be restricted.

Antibiotics are often prescribed, inappropriately, for minor viral infections. This misuse of antibiotics means that bacteria meet antibiotics more often and so the evolution of antibiotic resistance happens faster, resulting in some commonly used antibiotics becoming ineffective.

The future of antibiotics

Producing new drugs is very expensive and slow.

Because microorganisms can evolve so rapidly it is unlikely that the discovery and production of new antibiotics will keep up with the emergence of new resistant strains of bacteria.

Go to page 32 for more about developing new drugs.

Worked example — Grade 4

Describe **two** ways doctors and patients can slow the development of bacterial resistance to new drugs. **[2 marks]**

They should only use antibiotics when necessary, and patients should make sure they finish their course of treatment.

Exam-style practice — Grade 5

1. What is meant by 'antibiotic-resistant bacteria'? **[1 mark]**
2. Bacteria can become resistant to an antibiotic very quickly. Explain why. **[2 marks]**

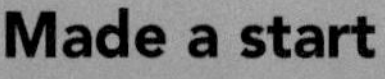

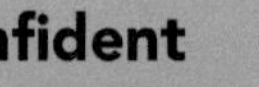
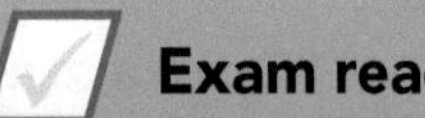

Made a start | Feeling confident | Exam ready

Classification

Classification is the way we arrange living organisms into groups, based on their similar structures and characteristics. You need to know how species are classified and how the process of classification has changed over time.

15 Classifying organisms

In the 18th century, Carl Linnaeus introduced a hierarchical system for classifying living organisms and giving them scientific names. Linnaeus divided all living things into large **kingdoms** according to the features of organisms' cells. Then he divided them into smaller and smaller groups, as shown in **Figure 1**.

You need to know about five kingdoms:

1. Animals **2.** Plants **3.** Fungi
4. Prokaryotes **5.** Protists.

As the classification groups get smaller, the organisms have more characteristics in common.

Naming species

A unique scientific name allows scientists to identify and refer to individual species quickly and accurately. The scientific name of an organism is its genus and species. This double name is called the **binomial system** of naming.

Kingdom	animal
Phylum	chordate
Class	mammal
Order	primate
Family	hominid
Genus	*Pongo*
Species	*albelii*

Figure 1 Classification of a Sumatran orangutan

2 Working scientifically

Over time, scientists' understanding of biochemistry and cell structure has changed as scientific equipment and techniques have developed. Advances such as more powerful microscopes and DNA analysis and sequencing have led to new classification systems.

In 1977, Carl Woese proposed that all living organisms be divided into **three domains**:

- **archaea** – primitive bacteria that live in extreme environments
- **bacteria** – true bacteria
- **eukaryota** – protists, fungi, plants and animals.

1 Exam focus

This mnemonic can help you remember the Linnaean classification system.

King **P**hilip **c**ame **o**ver **f**rom **g**reat **S**pain

5 Worked example — Grade 5

Figure 3 below shows a model of how different organisms A–E are related.

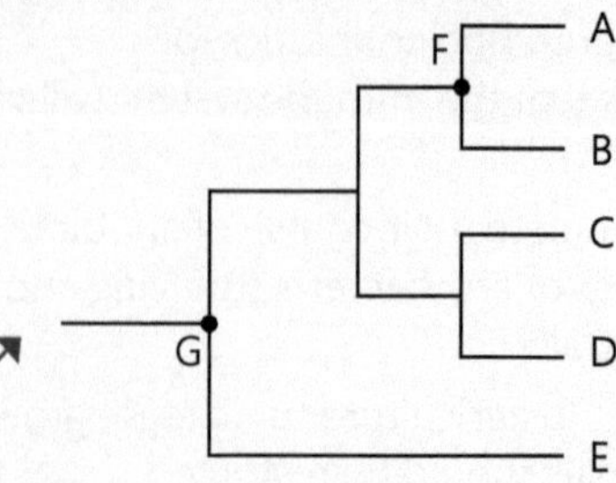

Figure 3

(a) Which letter shows the most common ancestor of **C** and **D**?

G

(b) Which letter represents the species most distantly related to **A**?

E

Branching occurs where **speciation** has taken place. A group of organisms has evolved into a new species from its common ancestor.

5 Evolutionary trees

Evolutionary trees show how scientists think organisms are related to one another. The evidence for evolutionary trees comes from classification data for living organisms and the fossil record for extinct organisms.

The evolutionary tree in **Figure 2** shows that these organisms all have a common ancestor. A common ancestor is an ancestor which two or more species have descended from. An ancestral species is a species that the species has evolved from.

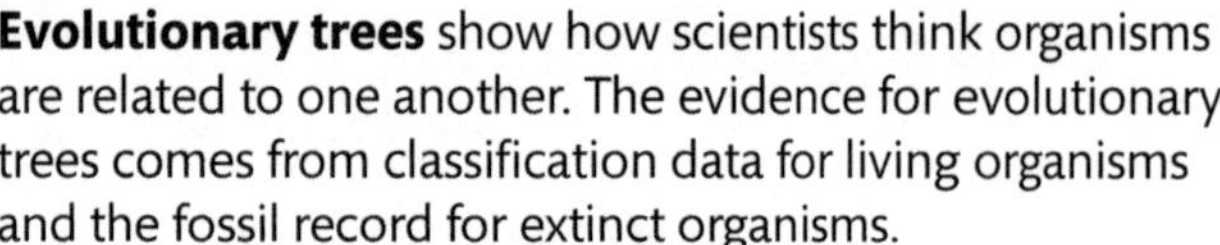

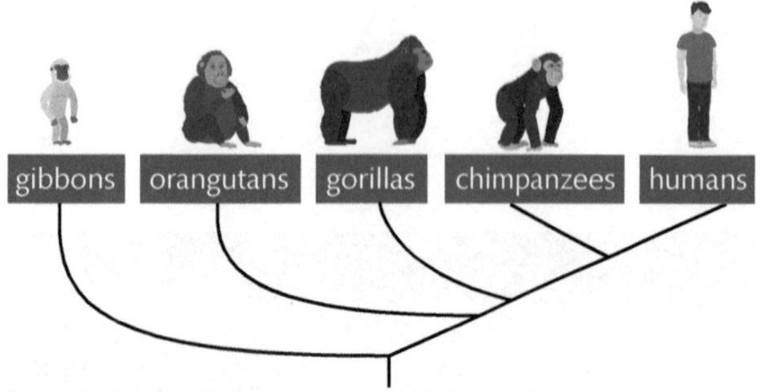

Figure 2 An evolutionary tree of gibbons, the great apes and humans. Gorillas and chimpanzees are the most closely related to humans.

5 Exam-style practice — Grade 5

Use **Figure 1** to identify the scientific name for the Sumatran orangutan. **[1 mark]**

 Made a start  Feeling confident  Exam ready

Communities

A community is all the populations of living organisms within an ecosystem. You need to know how the organisms within a community depend on one another.

Features of an ecosystem

A **population** is all the **organisms** of one species within an ecosystem.

A **community** consists of all the populations of different species living in the same habitat. A **habitat** is the environment where an organism lives.

An **ecosystem** is the interaction of a community of all the living organisms (**biotic factors**, page 63) with the non-living (**abiotic factors**, page 62) parts of their environment.

Plants in a community may compete for the following abiotic factors, if there is a limited supply:

- light
- space
- water
- mineral ions.

Animals in a community may compete for:

- food
- water
- a mate
- territory.

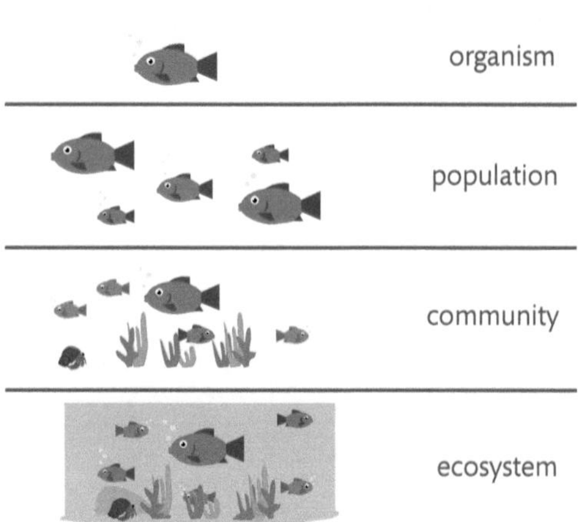

Figure 1 The different levels of organisation in an ecosystem

Interdependence and competition

Within a community, each species depends upon other species for the things they need, including food, shelter, pollination and seed dispersal. This is known as **interdependence**. Flowering plants depend on insects for pollination. Some plants depend on animals to disperse their seeds.

If a change occurs, such as the removal of a species, then the whole community could be affected. If all the species and environmental factors in a community are in balance, then the community is stable so that the size of populations remains fairly constant.

Worked example — Grade 3

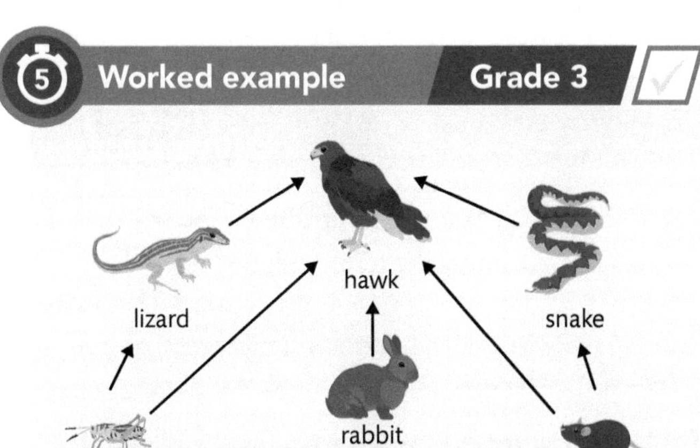

Figure 2

Figure 2 shows a food web for a grassland ecosystem.

(a) Give **one** reason why **Figure 2** shows interdependence between the organisms in a grassland ecosystem. **[1 mark]**

It shows how organisms in the ecosystem depend on each other for food.

(b) Name **three** organisms that are competing for grass as a source of food. **[3 marks]**

Grasshopper, rabbit and mouse

Exam-style practice — Grade 4

Snails and algae live in the same area. The snails eat the algae.

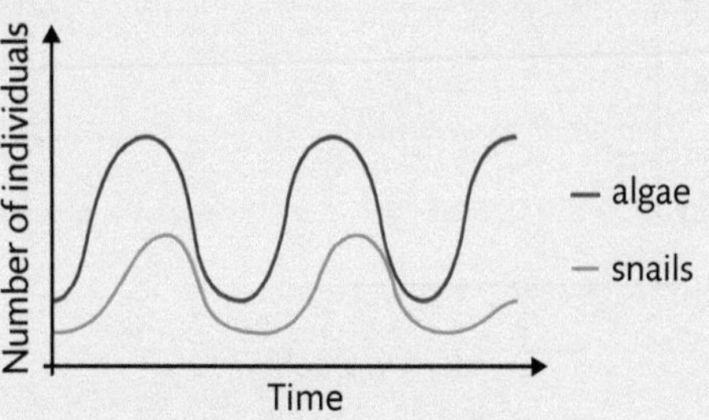

Figure 3

Figure 3 shows how the population sizes of snails and algae in an area changes over time.

(a) Look at **Figure 3** and explain how a drop in the population size of algae affects the population of snails. **[2 marks]**

(b) Suggest how the population of algae would alter if a new predator that eats the snails was introduced to the ecosystem. Explain your answer. **[2 marks]**

 Made a start  Feeling confident  Exam ready

Abiotic factors

You need to know how abiotic (non-living) factors can affect a community and its survival.

Abiotic factors

Abiotic factors are non-living factors, including:

- temperature
- pH and mineral content of soil
- wind intensity and direction
- light intensity
- carbon dioxide levels (mainly affects plants)
- oxygen levels (for aquatic animals)
- moisture levels.

Figure 1 Changes in abiotic factors, such as temperature, can have a serious impact on the environment. Rising temperatures are causing sea ice in the Arctic to melt. This is reducing numbers of polar bears, which are adapted to hunt and breed on ice.

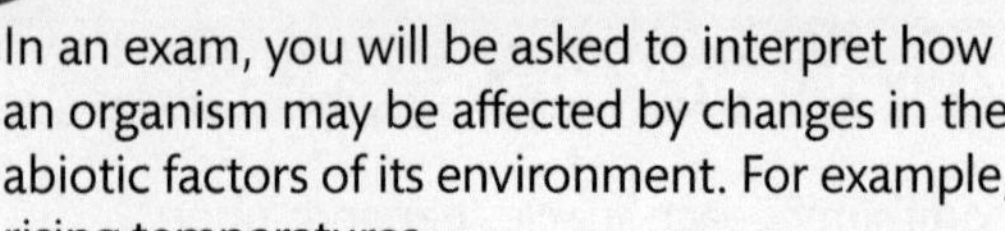

Exam focus

In an exam, you will be asked to interpret how an organism may be affected by changes in the abiotic factors of its environment. For example, rising temperatures.

Worked example

Grade 4

Figure 2 shows the results of a study on the growth of ivy plants in different habitats and its relationship to the pH of the soil.

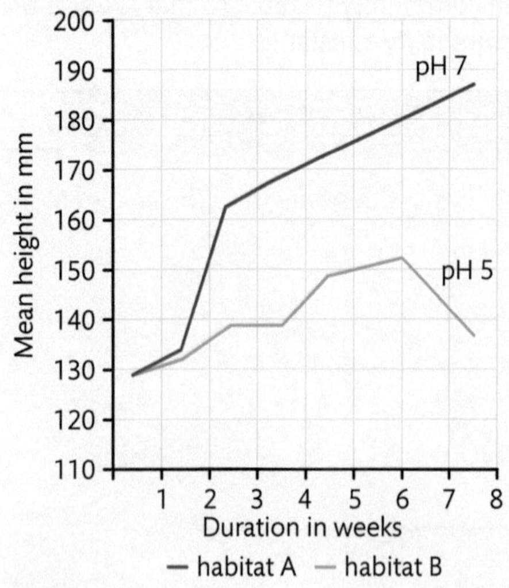

Figure 2

(a) Soil pH is an example of an abiotic factor.

What is meant by the term 'abiotic factor'? **[1 mark]**

Abiotic factors are the non-living factors that can affect a community.

(b) Using **Figure 2**, how tall were the ivy plants in the pH 7 soil after 6 weeks? **[1 mark]**

180 mm

(c) How much did the plants in the pH 5 soil grow in the first 6 weeks? Show your working. **[2 marks]**

At pH 5, ivy plants were 129 mm at the start of the study and at 6 weeks 151 mm, so they had grown:

151–129 = 22 mm

(d) Write a suitable conclusion for the results shown in the graph. **[2 marks]**

The plants grew 51 mm at pH 7 and only 22 mm at pH 5, so ivy plants grow better in soil that is pH 7 rather than pH 5.

When you are asked to 'use data' you will need to refer to specific data from a chart or table and explain the pattern it shows.

Exam-style practice

Grade 3

Give **three** abiotic factors in the rainforest. **[3 marks]**

 Made a start  Feeling confident  Exam ready

Biotic factors

You need to know how biotic (living) factors can affect a community.

Types of biotic factors

Biotic factors are living factors, including:

- availability of food
- new predators arriving
- pathogens
- competition for food, mates and territory.

You can find out more about pathogens on pages 26–28.

Worked example — Grade 4

1 Figure 2 shows changes in the population size of a species of rabbit between 2004 and 2010.

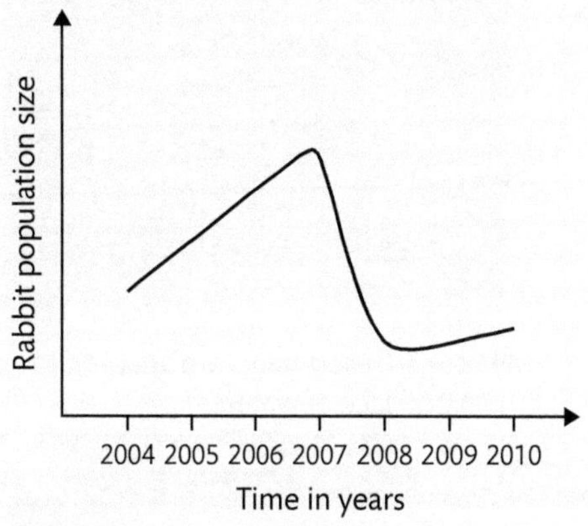

Figure 2

(a) Describe what happened to the population size of rabbits between 2007 and 2008. **[1 mark]**

It rapidly decreased.

(b) Suggest **two** biotic factors that could explain the change in population size between 2007 and 2008. **[2 marks]**

A pathogen and a new predator arriving

2 Deforestation removes habitat for insects and small organisms.

Explain how a decline in the number of insects and small organisms could affect the number of birds living in a forest. **[2 marks]**

A decline in the number of insects and small organisms would mean a decline in food for birds, so the bird population could decrease.

Example of biotic factors

In the 1870s, American grey squirrels were introduced to Britain. The grey squirrels ate the same food as native red squirrels and lived in similar habitats. However, grey squirrels were able to outcompete the native red squirrels for **food**. There was less food available for the native red squirrels and so the population size decreased.

The grey squirrels also carry the squirrel pox virus, a type of **pathogen**. This virus causes death in red squirrels but can be carried by grey squirrels without causing any harm. Many red squirrels died from the squirrel pox virus, but the grey squirrels survived.

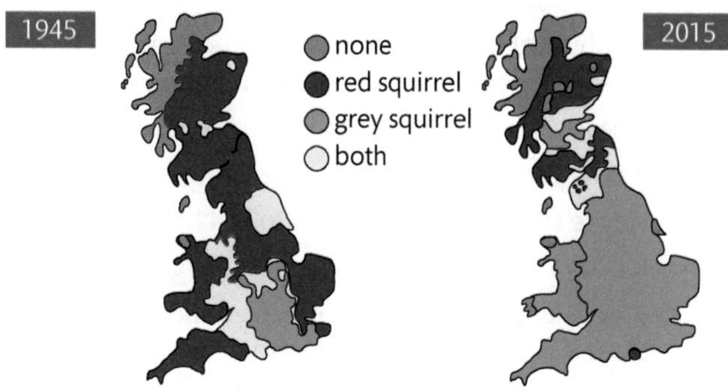

Figure 1 Showing the change in the population of red squirrels between 1945 and 2015

Exam-style practice — Grade 3

The table shows how the population of badgers changed in an area over five years.

Year	2013	2014	2015	2016	2017
Number of badgers	800	1110	850	400	190

(a) Calculate the percentage change in the population of badgers between 2014 and 2017. **[2 marks]**

(b) Which of the following are **biotic** factors that could have caused the change in the badger population. Tick **two** boxes. **[2 marks]**

- temperature ☐
- hunting by humans ☐
- moisture level of soil ☐
- competition for territory ☐

Adaptations

Organisms are adapted to enable them to survive the conditions of their natural environment. An adaptation is a feature that helps an organism grow well and reproduce in its habitat. You should be able to interpret information about a habitat and its features and explain why the adaptations improve chances of survival and reproduction.

Types of adaptation

Organisms are adapted to abiotic and biotic factors that affect the environment they live in, including:

- high and low temperatures
- lack of water
- lack of sunlight
- predators.

These adaptations enable them to survive. Adaptations can be classed as structural, behavioural or functional.

Structural adaptations

These are physical features, for example, polar bears have structural adaptations to living and hunting on ice.

- They have a thick layer of fat to keep them warm.
- Their paw pads have special bumps to help grip ice.
- They have sharp teeth and claws to catch prey.

Structural adaptations of desert hares (see **Figure 1**):

- They have large ears to provide a large surface area for heat loss. This is an adaptation to their environment because over heating is dangerous for cells.

Behavioural adaptations

These are ways in which an organism's behaviour is adapted for survival:

- Polar bears can dig deep into the snow to gain shelter, and they move slowly to prevent overheating.
- Desert hares are active at dawn and dusk to avoid the hot sun during the day.

Functional adaptations

These are functions that an organism carries out to survive. Functional adaptations of polar bears include:

- They have an incredible sense of smell to detect prey over long distances.
- They have good long sight vision to spot prey.

Functional adaptations of desert hares:

- They produce only small amounts of urine and sweat to conserve water, because there is little water in the desert.

Figure 1 Desert hares are adapted to heat and lack of water.

Exam focus

You will be given information about an organism and be expected to explain how the organism is adapted to its environment.

Extremophiles

Some organisms have adaptations that allow them to survive in different extreme conditions.

These organisms are known as **extremophiles**.

Many bacteria are examples of extremophiles.

Examples of extreme conditions are:

- high temperatures in hot-water springs and deserts and pressure in deep sea vents
- areas with high acid, alkali or salt concentration, such as hot springs and salt marshes.

Worked example — Grade 3–4

Cacti are plants that live in hot dry desert conditions. Cacti have spines rather than leaves, and swollen stems.

Suggest how these features allow the cacti to survive in desert conditions. **[2 marks]**

The spines have a small surface area, which reduces water lost through transpiration and protects them from predators. The swollen stem can store water for when the plant needs it.

The roots of the cactus are located near the surface of the ground to quickly collect any surface water.

Exam-style practice — Grade 3–4

Some British birds migrate to other countries in the British winter.

State what type of adaptation migration is classed as. **[1 mark]**

Organisation of an ecosystem

You need to know about some of the feeding relationships that exist within an ecosystem.

5 Food chains

Feeding relationships within an ecosystem can be represented by food chains.

Experimental methods, including transects and quadrats, can be used to determine the population size and distribution of different species within an ecosystem.

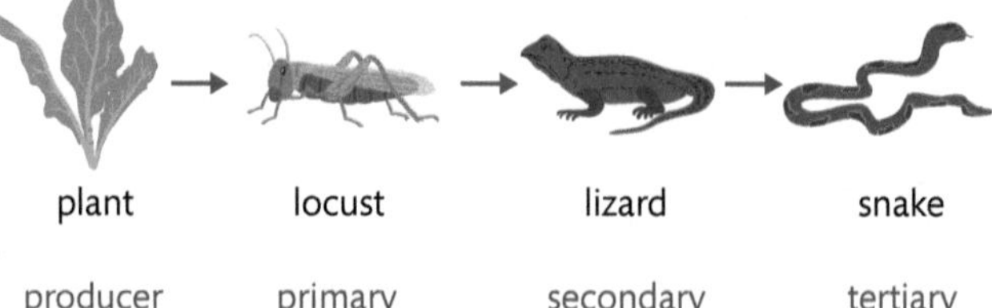

Figure 1 A simple food chain

All food chains must begin with a producer, as producers photosynthesise and produce biomass that is eaten by other organisms.

5 Key terms

- **biomass** – the mass of living material
- **producer** – usually a green plant or alga, which makes glucose during photosynthesis
- **consumer** – an organism which cannot make its own food; eats producers or other consumers
- **primary consumer** – eats producers; the first consumer in the food chain
- **secondary consumer** – eats the primary consumer; the second consumer in the food chain
- **tertiary consumer** – eats the secondary consumer; the third consumer in the food chain
- **predator** – kills and eats other animals
- **prey** – animal that is hunted and killed by a predator

5 Worked example — Grade 4–5

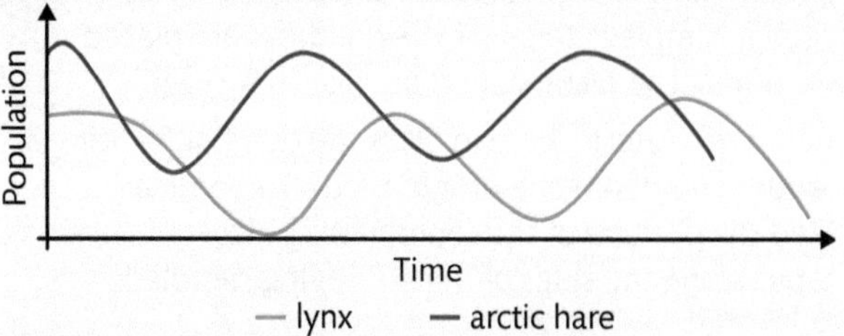

Figure 2

The Arctic hare is the main food of the lynx. Scientists have monitored the population sizes of the Arctic hare and the lynx over many years. This has enabled scientists to develop a model graph to show how the population sizes of these two species are linked over time.

Figure 2 shows this graph.

(a) What happens to the number of lynx after the number of hares decreases? **[1 mark]**

The number decreases.

(b) Suggest a reason for this. **[2 marks]**

There is less food available so some of the lynx starve and die.

Besides stating that the lynx die of starvation, you could also explain that they do not have enough food to enable them to breed successfully and that is why numbers are decreasing.

5 Exam-style practice — Grade 3

1 What type of organism must a producer be? Tick **one** box. **[1 mark]**

- one which cannot make its own food ☐
- one which kills and eats other animals ☐
- one which eats the primary consumer ☐
- one which makes its own food, by photosynthesis ☐

2 Give **one** reason why the first organism in a food chain is a producer. **[1 mark]**

3 State what is meant by the term 'tertiary consumer'. **[1 mark]**

Investigating population size

Quadrats can be used to measure the population size and distribution of a common species in a habitat.

5 Using quadrats

A quadrat can be used to estimate the population size of a species such as dandelions in a given area.

Method:

1. Place a quadrat on the ground at a **randomly selected** point.
2. Count and record the number of dandelions in each quadrat.
3. Repeat steps **1** and **2**. The number of repeats will depend on the size of the area being sampled. The **validity** and **reproducibility** will increase the more samples that are taken.

This method can be used to compare the distribution of a species in two different areas. For example, the number of dandelions in an area of lawn with no shade compared to an area of lawn with shade from trees.

10 Worked example — Grade 4

The table shows the number of dandelions found in five different randomly placed quadrats in a habitat.

Quadrat	1	2	3	4	5
Number of dandelions	2	4	5	1	3

(a) Calculate the mean number of dandelions per quadrat.

The mean = $\frac{\text{Total number of dandelions}}{\text{Number of quadrats}}$

$2 + 4 + 5 + 1 + 3 = 15$ (total number of dandelions)

So $\frac{15}{5} = 3$ dandelions per quadrat

(b) Using your answer from **(a)**, estimate the population of dandelions in the field. One quadrat has an area of $0.5\,m^2$ and the field has an area of $125\,m^2$.

The total area of a quadrat is $0.5\,m^2$

The total area of the habitat being sampled is $125\,m^2$

The total number of quadrats that could fit into the area being sampled can be worked out using:

$$\frac{\text{total area of habitat}}{\text{area of one quadrat}} = \frac{125}{0.5} = 250$$

The estimated total number of dandelions in the area sampled is

$3 \times 250 = 750$

1 Key terms

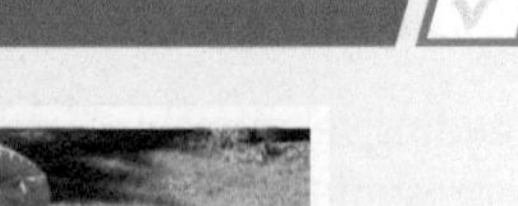

Figure 1 A **quadrat** is a square frame used to sample the distribution of plants or animals.

Working scientifically

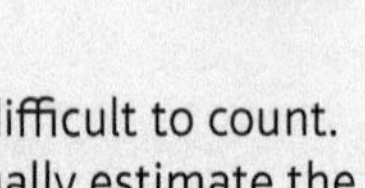

Percentage cover

Organisms such as moss or grass are difficult to count. For these organisms, it is easier to visually estimate the percentage of the quadrat covered by the species.

Working scientifically

Ideally every place within the area being sampled should have an equal chance of being sampled each time a sample is taken. If the quadrats are placed randomly the results are more like to be valid.

Randomly select where to place the quadrat by using a random number generator to produce coordinates. Find the position of the coordinates by laying measuring tapes along the sides of the area being sampled.

5 Maths skills

You are expected to understand the terms:

- **mean** – the average of all the values
- **mode** – the most commonly occurring value
- **median** – middle value when put in value order.

5 Exam-style practice — Grade 4

A student placed a quadrat randomly in eight positions in a field and counted the number of daisy plants in each quadrat. The quadrat measured $1\,m^2$; the field was $2000\,m^2$. The table shows the results.

Quadrat	1	2	3	4	5	6	7	8
Number of plants	3	5	3	1	3	5	2	2

(a) Calculate the mean number of daisy plants per quadrat. **[1 mark]**

(b) Estimate the number of daisy plants in the field. **[1 mark]**

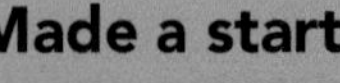

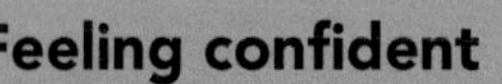

Made a start   Feeling confident   Exam ready

Using a transect

Sometimes ecologists want to see if the number of species changes within an area. This can be done using a transect.

Using a transect

Figure 1 A **transect** is a line across a habitat or part of a habitat.

A transect is usually used to investigate a gradual change in the distribution of species across a habitat. Changes in distribution of a species may be caused by abiotic factors such as soil moisture or light.

For example, the distribution of grass could be measured at regular intervals from a tree to find out the effect of the tree canopy blocking light.

Find out about abiotic factors on page 62.

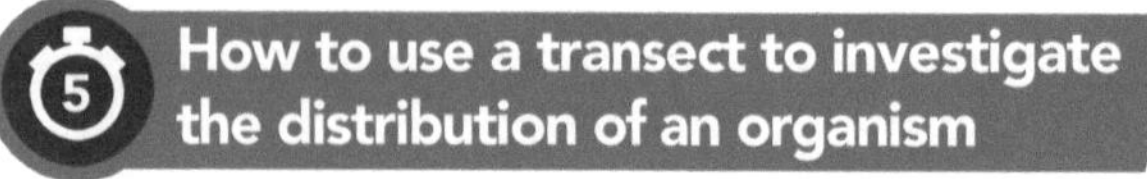

How to use a transect to investigate the distribution of an organism

1. Lay a tape or rope marked at set intervals across the area being studied.
2. Place a quadrat next to the 0 m mark on the line. Record the number or percentage cover of your chosen species.
3. Move the quadrat a set distance along the tape and repeat step **2**. Continue to repeat measurements of the species until the end of the line is reached.

Kite diagrams

The data collected from a transect can be presented in a type of chart called a kite diagram. **Figure 2** shows how the number of dandelions and grasses changes at different distances along a transect.

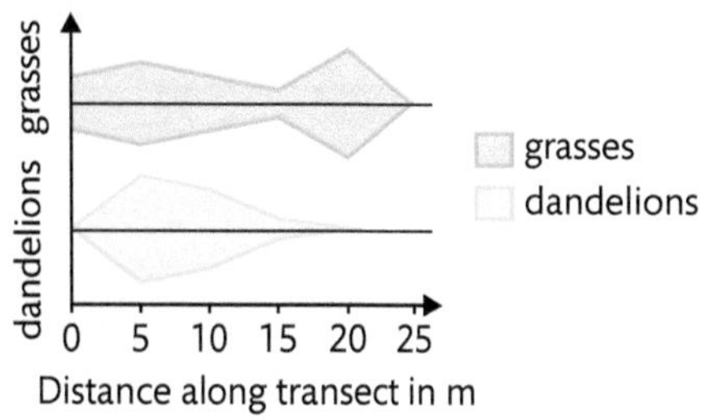

Figure 2 Kite diagram

Figure 2 shows how the number of dandelions increases between 0 m and 5 m and then decreases gradually between 5 m to 20 m. This change in the number of dandelions along the transect can happen because of a gradual change in an abiotic factor such as light or soil conditions.

Worked example — Grade 5

1. Describe what happens to the number of grasses between 5 and 15 metres in **Figure 2**. **[1 mark]**

   The number of grasses gradually decreases.

2. The number of grasses was highest at 20 m along the transect. Which of the following statements describes an abiotic factor likely to explain why the most grass was found at 20 m?
   Tick **one** box. **[1 mark]**

The soil contained no minerals.	☐	There was no light.	☐
The soil was moist.	✓	The soil was dry.	☐

3. Suggest **two** reasons why no dandelions or grasses were found at 25 m. **[2 marks]**

   There might not have been enough light or the soil might have been too dry.

Exam-style practice — Grade 4

A student is asked to investigate how the distribution of buttercup plants changes in a grassy area of land at the edge of a woodland. The student wants to find out if there will be fewer buttercups growing in the grass closest to the woodland.

Describe a method the student could use to find out if the number of buttercups changes at different distances from the woodland. **[4 marks]**

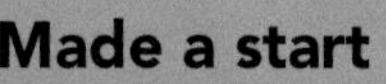

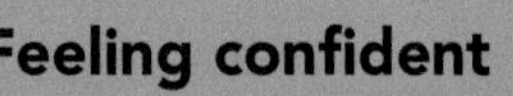

Cycling materials

You need to know that different materials cycle through the biotic and abiotic parts of an ecosystem, to provide the building blocks for future organisms. You also need to explain the importance of the carbon cycle and the water cycle for living organisms.

5 The carbon cycle

Carbon, in the form of carbon dioxide (CO_2), is removed from the atmosphere by photosynthesis in plants and algae. Carbon is stored as carbon compounds in fossil fuels and in animals and plants, for example, as glucose, carbohydrate, protein and fat. CO_2 is released into the atmosphere by animals, plants and microorganisms respiring.

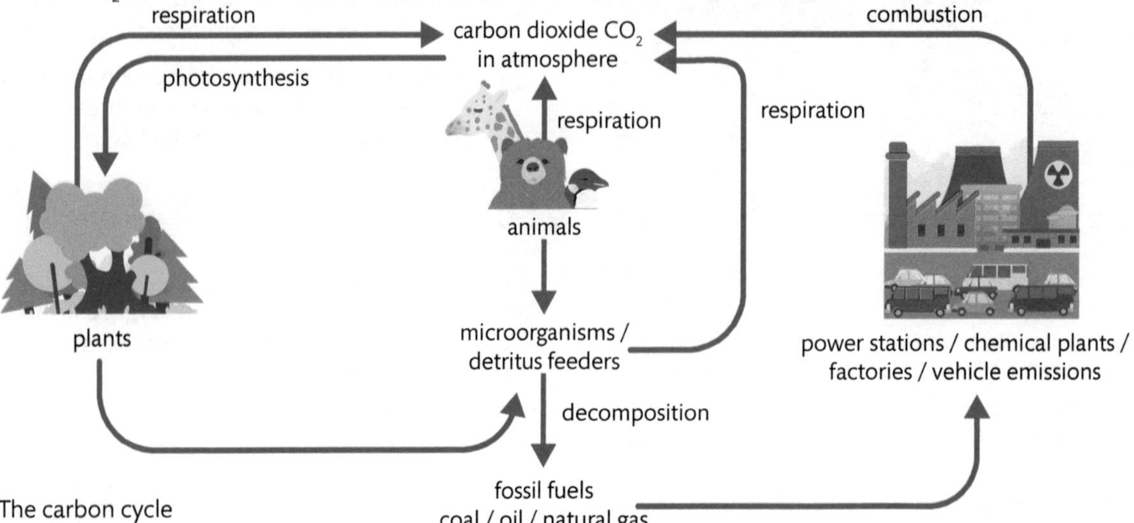

Figure 1 The carbon cycle

5 The water cycle

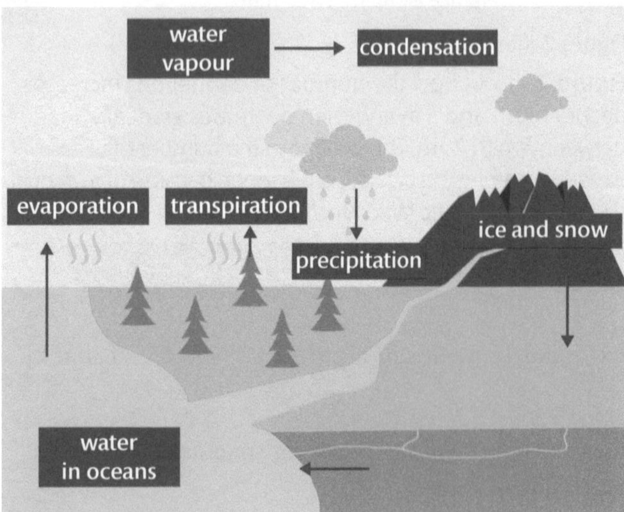

Figure 2 The water cycle

Without water, all living organisms would die very quickly. The water cycle recycles water and nutrients, providing fresh water on land. There are four main stages to the water cycle.

1. **Evaporation** – the (heat) energy from the Sun causes water in the oceans, lakes and rivers to evaporate, forming water vapour in the atmosphere.
2. **Condensation** – as the water vapour cools high up in the atmosphere it condenses to form clouds.
3. **Precipitation** – as the clouds become more condensed water falls as rain, snow, ice or hail.
4. **Collection** – the water may fall into rivers, lakes and oceans where the process begins again, or it may be absorbed into the soil and taken up by plants to eventually evaporate from the leaves (by **transpiration**). Water that isn't absorbed (surface run-off) flows over the ground until it reaches an area of water.

5 Worked example — Grade 4

Describe how microorganisms help to cycle materials through an ecosystem by decomposing dead plants. **[3 marks]**

Microorganisms feed on dead plant matter.

As they break down the plant waste they return mineral ions to the soil and release carbon dioxide to the atmosphere through respiration.

10 Exam-style practice — Grade 4

1. Explain how a water particle in the ocean can end up in a cloud. **[4 marks]**
2. Name the process that removes carbon from the atmosphere. **[1 mark]**

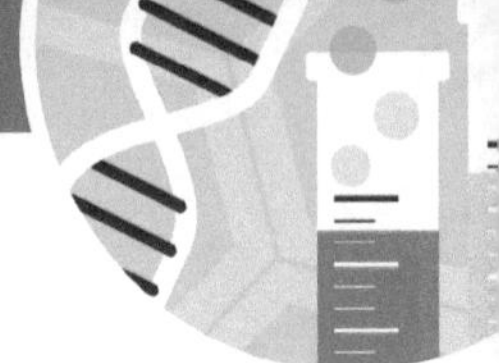

Biodiversity

Biodiversity is the variety of species within an ecosystem. You need to be able to discuss the benefits of and threats to biodiversity.

5 Advantages of biodiversity

An ecosystem with high biodiversity is generally more stable than an ecosystem with low biodiversity. This is because a wider variety of species in an ecosystem reduces the dependence of one species on another for food or shelter. A wider variety of species also buffers ecosystems from environmental stresses, like changes in climate.

For example, an increase in temperatures could change the number of insects able to survive in an area. This might then cause insect-eating birds to starve or move to other areas. Fewer birds might mean predators of birds would also starve and decrease in numbers. Together, these changes would reduce the biodiversity in the area. If there are more species of insects in the area (greater biodiversity) before the increase in temperature then the effects would not be as catastrophic.

2 Key threats to biodiversity

Many human activities are reducing biodiversity such as:

- deforestation
- pollution
- climate change due to global warming
- landfill waste.

Measures have been taken to try to stop this reduction only recently.

Deforestation is the destruction of forests. Go to page 72 for more about deforestation and the impacts it has on biodiversity.

See page 74 on maintaining biodiversity.

10 Worked example — Grade 4–5

In Borneo, large areas of rainforest are being destroyed to make space for oil palm plantations. A group of scientists studied the impacts of deforestation on the population size of native frog species. The study found that there was a higher number of frog species in rainforest areas compared to oil palm plantation sites.

(a) Suggest **two** reasons why more native frog species can survive in the rainforest compared to an oil palm plantation. **[2 marks]**

They have more sources of food and more shelter.

(b) Suggest **one** method of maintaining the biodiversity of frogs in Borneo. **[1 mark]**

Protect the rainforest from deforestation for other land uses like oil palm plantations

Working scientifically

The rainforest areas have a higher biodiversity than the oil palm plantations because there are more species living there.

Larger holes in nets allow small young cod to return to the sea and breed.

10 Exam-style practice — Grade 3–4

Figure 1 shows the change in the size of the cod population in an area of the North Sea between 1963 and 1999.

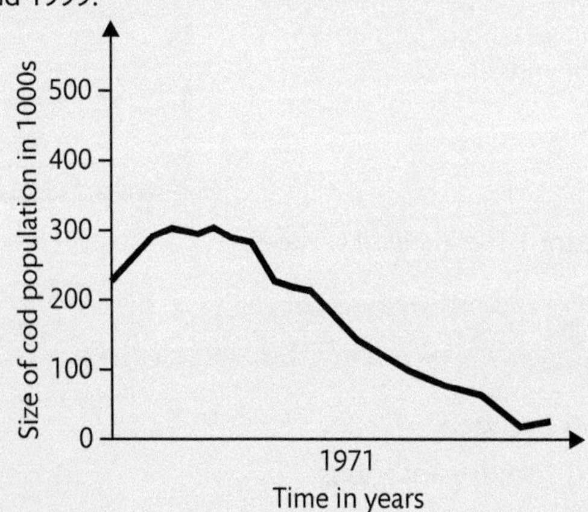

Figure 1

(a) Describe the change in the population of North Sea cod between 1971 and 1999. **[1 mark]**

(b) Suggest how an increasing human population could have caused the change in the size of the cod population between 1971 and 1999. **[1 mark]**

(c) Which of the following would be most effective in helping the population of cod to increase? Tick **two** boxes. **[2 marks]**

- using nets with bigger holes ☐
- allowing more fishing in the North Sea ☐
- protect other endangered species of fish ☐
- limiting how many fish can be caught in any given period of time ☐

Waste management

You need to know how human population growth is causing an increase in waste production. This causes pollution.

Pollution

Pollution is something added to the environment that causes harm to living organisms. Pollution created by humans can occur in water (e.g. from fertiliser), in the air (e.g. from smoke) and on land (e.g. from landfill).

Pollution destroys habitats, and kills animals and plants. A reduction in the numbers of animals and plants leads to a reduction in biodiversity. A reduction in biodiversity will cause further species to become extinct and could lead to food shortages. Handling waste and chemical materials properly will reduce pollution.

An increase in the human population is leading to more water pollution from sewage, fertilisers and substances from industry and farming entering water supplies. This has a negative effect on aquatic life.

Air pollution, such as smoke and toxic gases, is being produced from burning fossil fuels and other substances. This is causing global warming, acid rain and smog.

Why is there an increase in the waste that humans are producing?

Find out more about air pollution on page 146.

Landfill and toxic substances are polluting land, making it uninhabitable for plants and animals.

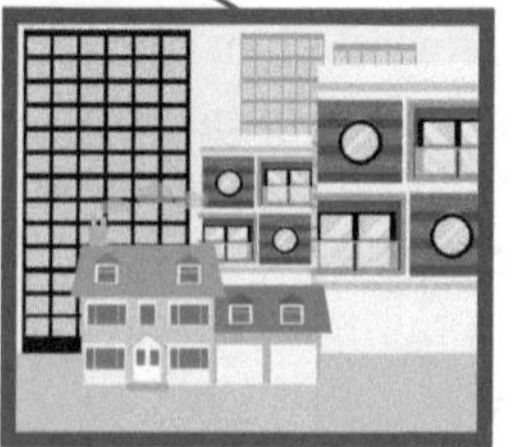

An increase in the standard of human living means more resources are being used, which in turn, produces more waste.

Figure 1 The increase in waste

Key terms: waste substances

- sewage
- smoke and gases
- herbicides, pesticides and fertilisers
- paper and cardboard
- plastic
- waste electricals
- scrap metals
- organic waste

Worked example — Grade 5

Give **two** reasons why the mass of household waste is increasing. **[2 marks]**

The global population is increasing in size. Increases in the standard of living are resulting in more resources being used and waste being produced.

Exam-style practice — Grade 4

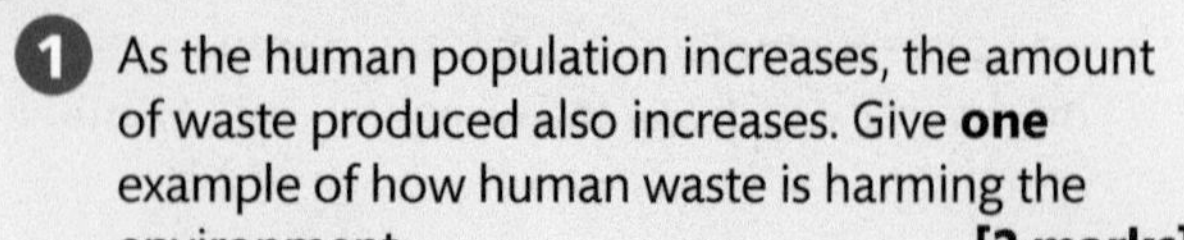

1. As the human population increases, the amount of waste produced also increases. Give **one** example of how human waste is harming the environment. **[2 marks]**
2. **Figure 2** shows what happens to the domestic waste we produce in the UK.

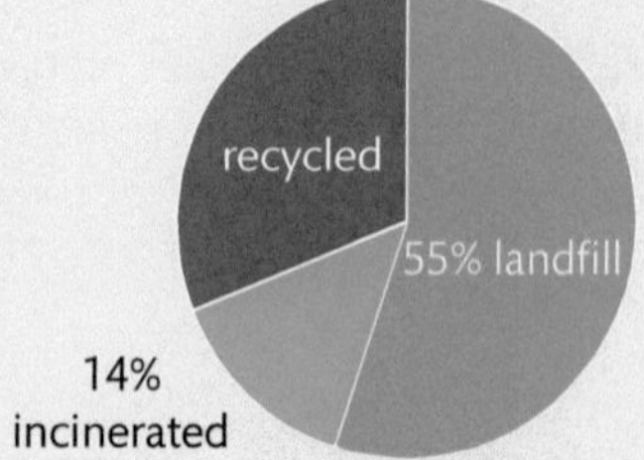

Figure 2

(a) Calculate what percentage of the domestic waste in the UK is recycled. **[1 mark]**

(b) Suggest **one** reason why it is important to recycle products such as plastic bottles. **[1 mark]**

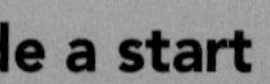

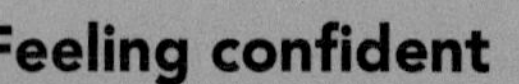

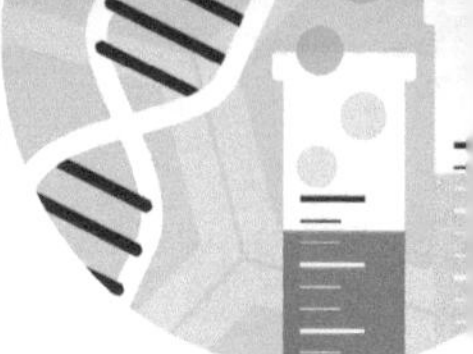

Land use

You need to know how the use of land by humans is reducing the habitats available for plants and animals.

Examples of land use

Human activity is having significant effects on the environment and on biodiversity (page 69). As the world's population continues to grow rapidly, these effects are increasing in severity and becoming more widespread.

Human land use

Farming
As the human population increases, more people need more food so more land is used for agriculture.

Building
As our population increases, more land is needed for houses, shops, roads and factories.

Landfill
Landfill sites are areas of land where household and industrial waste is dumped and eventually buried. Disposal of waste in landfill sites has a negative effect on the environment. Poisonous chemicals leak into the environment and they take up space.

Quarrying
A quarry is where rock and minerals are dug out of the ground. There is a huge demand for the products of quarrying, such as limestone. This can destroy wildlife habitats and it creates pollution.

Peat bogs

Peat is an important store of carbon. Humans are destroying peat bogs to produce compost. Compost is then used on gardens to increase plant growth, including food production. This reduces areas of peat-bog habitat for plants, animals and microorganisms, which decreases biodiversity in these habitats.

Peat dries out and starts to decay when it is dug from the ground. When peat decays or is burned, carbon dioxide is released into the atmosphere, leading to increased greenhouse gas emissions and contributing to global warming.

Figure 1 Peat drying out after being cut from a peat bog.

Worked example — Grade 4

Marshlands provide habitats for a wide range of species. Some areas of marshland surrounding the River Thames have been converted to farmland to graze cattle.

(a) Explain how changing land use from marshland to farmland is likely to affect biodiversity of the area. **[2 marks]**

The biodiversity of the farmland will be much less than the marshland because farmland for grazing cattle is not a diverse habitat and can only support a limited number of species.

(b) Suggest **one** other land use that threatens natural areas such as the Thames marshlands. **[1 mark]**

Building new homes

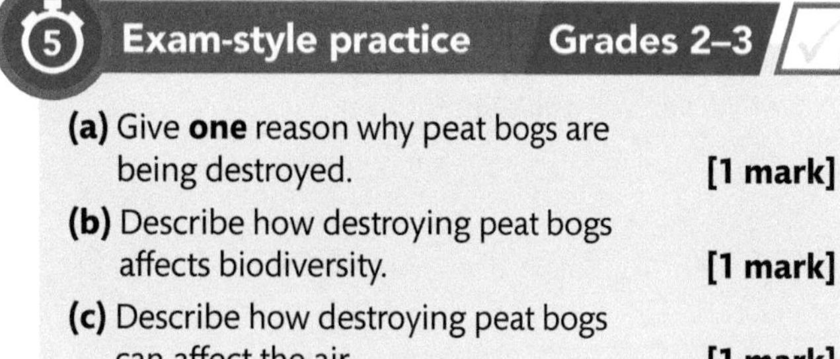

Exam-style practice — Grades 2–3

(a) Give **one** reason why peat bogs are being destroyed. **[1 mark]**

(b) Describe how destroying peat bogs affects biodiversity. **[1 mark]**

(c) Describe how destroying peat bogs can affect the air. **[1 mark]**

 Made a start  Feeling confident  Exam ready

Deforestation

You need to know how deforestation (forest destruction) on a large scale in tropical areas is causing harm to the environment.

2 Reasons for deforestation

Vast areas of forest are being destroyed to:

- provide land for cattle and rice fields
- provide land for the growth of crops for biofuels
- create fuel, furniture and paper
- clear land to produce palm oil and coffee
- clear land for housing.

Biofuels mostly come from plant materials, for example, oily crops for biodiesel and sugar-rich crops for bioethanol.

Figure 1 Deforestation destroys large areas of native forest, reducing biodiversity and the ability to 'lock-up' carbon dioxide in the future.

10 Impacts of deforestation

Deforestation has a series of negative effects on the environment:

- **Flooding** – trees absorb the rain, releasing it back into the atmosphere as water vapour. Fewer trees will absorb less water, leading to flooding.
- **Climate change** – trees absorb carbon dioxide for photosynthesis. Fewer trees means more carbon dioxide in the atmosphere. Trees also affect the levels of water vapour in the atmosphere, which contributes to global warming.
- **Loss of species** – the more trees that are destroyed, the less habitat there is available for other species to live in, so some species may gradually become extinct.
- **Soil erosion** – tree roots anchor soil. Without them, the soil can be eroded quickly making it difficult to grow crops.
- **Water pollution** – soil erosion can lead to silt entering water sources, which decreases the quality of the water and can affect human health.

There is a conflict between the need for deforestation to increase the land available for food production and the need to conserve forests to prevent the impacts listed above.

5 Worked example — Grade 5

Explain how deforestation could lead to the extinction of species. **[2 marks]**

Without trees photosynthesising, levels of carbon dioxide increase, leading to an increase in the temperature of the planet. This could wipe out species of plants or animals that cannot cope with increasing temperatures.

Deforestation also means that not as much water is taken up by trees through transpiration. Flooding is a risk, which can wipe out habitats.

5 Exam-style practice — Grade 5

Trees need to be cleared quickly to provide land for the growth of crops such as rice.

(a) Name a technique used to clear the trees. **[1 mark]**

(b) Why do farmers not need to use fertilisers when using this technique? **[1 mark]**

(c) What gas has increased in the air due to increased numbers of cattle and rice growth? Tick **one** box. **[1 mark]**

- oxygen ☐
- carbon dioxide ☐
- nitrogen ☐
- methane ☐

(d) What effect can deforestation have on soil? **[1 mark]**

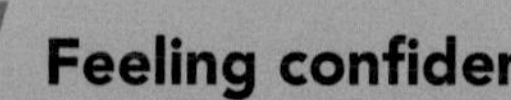

Made a start | Feeling confident | Exam ready

Global warming

Global warming is the upward trend in temperature across the entire Earth since the early 20th century. Increased levels of the greenhouse gases, carbon dioxide and methane, in the atmosphere contribute to global warming. You need to be able to describe how global warming affects living things in their environments.

Climate change

Climate change results from the increasing average global temperature. This includes changes in rainfall patterns, more heatwaves and other extreme weather, such as hurricanes.

Figure 1 The changes to the Earth that result from global warming

Biological effects of global warming

Biological effects of global warming result in reduced biodiversity because they threaten populations of plant and animal species.

Rising sea levels cause habitat loss

As global temperature increases, ice begins to melt. This flows into the oceans making the sea level rise.

Water also expands as it gets warmer so as the temperature of the ocean goes up the ocean expands and the sea level rise. Rising sea levels cause flooding of low-lying places and loss of habitats.

Increase in ocean temperature affect coral reefs

There is less oxygen dissolved in warm water compared to cold water. The lack of oxygen causes coral to lose its colour and eventually die.

Rainfall pattern changes affect plant and animal distribution

Rising global temperatures affect rainfall patterns in some areas. For example, rhinos living in Nepal rely on the annual monsoon to bring rain, so the plants they feed on grow. Climate change disrupts the annual monsoon and causes droughts.

Average temperature changes affect plant and animal distribution

Species that need warmer temperatures may spread as the warmer conditions they need exist in a wider area. Species needing cooler temperatures may become less widely distributed as cooler conditions are found in a smaller area.

Weather pattern changes affect plant and animal reproduction

Climate changes may cause earlier frosts than normal in some areas, harming early-flowering plants.

Local climate changes affect migration patterns

Warmer temperatures are causing some birds to arrive at their summer breeding grounds too early, when there may not be enough food resources available.

Warmer temperatures increase pests and disease

Pests and disease can survive in warmer conditions, particularly pests that are normally killed off by winter frosts.

Worked example — Grade 5

Scientists predict that low-lying areas of the UK could be permanently flooded if global warming continues. Explain how a rise in global temperatures could lead to flooding of areas of land. **[2 marks]**

Higher air temperatures cause seawater to expand and more ice to melt both of which would cause the sea level to rise.

Exam-style practice — Grade 5

A species of butterfly that used to only be found in England is now found in Scotland. Explain how global warming could cause a species of butterfly to change its distribution. **[3 marks]**

Maintaining biodiversity

The growing human population is damaging biodiversity in many ecosystems. You need to know the methods used to maintain biodiversity and the difficulties involved.

Maintaining biodiversity

Breeding programmes to help endangered species

Endangered species are at serious risk of extinction. A species may become endangered if its habitat is destroyed. For example, the mountain gorilla in Uganda is endangered because its habitat, the cloud forest, is being destroyed. Breeding programmes are used to help protect wild animals from becoming extinct. Wild animals are bred in zoos or wildlife reserves to boost population numbers. Some animals are then released back into the wild. This is one way of helping maintain biodiversity of wild animals.

Reducing carbon dioxide emissions

Some governments have introduced carbon dioxide emission regulations to limit the amount of carbon dioxide being released into the atmosphere by businesses. Keeping carbon dioxide levels in the atmosphere as low as possible will reduce global warming and changes in local climates. Change in local climates could reduce biodiversity because many species are adapted to survive in a particular climate.

Recycling waste

This reduces the amount of landfill and reduces the number of ecosystems destroyed by being used for landfill, therefore, helping maintain biodiversity.

Protecting and regenerating rare habitats

Rare habitats are uncommon, such as wetlands or coral reef. If rare habitats are protected, it helps prevent species that are adapted to that habitat dying out completely.

Figure 1 A giant panda, born and raised in a captive breeding programme, being released into the wild

Reintroducing field margins and hedgerows

Field margins and hedgerows provide a habitat for many species and so increase biodiversity in these areas.

Reducing the rate of deforestation

This would reduce damage to forest habitats and help protect the species living in forests. If forest habitats are maintained, so is the biodiversity found living within them.

Forests are important in combating global warming. See pages 73 (global warming) and 33 (photosynthesis)

Worked example — Grade 5

Farmers are being encouraged to plant more hedgerows and have wide field margins.

(a) Explain why farmers are being encouraged to plant more hedgerows and have wide field margins. **[2 marks]**

Because the hedgerows and field margins provide habitats and sources of food, so they can support a wider variety of organisms compared to the single crop habitat.

(b) Some farmers are reluctant to plant more hedges and have wide field margins. Suggest **two** reasons why. **[2 marks]**

Because planting more hedges costs time and money and takes up space that could be used to grow crops. Wide field margins also reduce the farmer's profit because it means less area of land is used for growing crops.

Exam-style practice — Grades 3–4

1 A government bans deforestation in a large area of rainforest. The local people living in the rainforest depend on this area of forest to grow food crops and raise cattle to sell. Some locals are also employed by tree felling companies that previously cut down the trees to sell the timber.

Give **two** reasons why locals that live in this area might not agree with the ban. **[2 marks]**

2 **(a)** Which area of land is likely to support the most biodiversity? Tick **one** box. **[1 mark]**

- an area of rainforest that is protected ☐
- an area of land that has been deforested to provide timber for a company ☐

(b) Explain your answer. **[1 mark]**

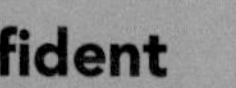

Atoms, elements and compounds

You need to be able to apply your knowledge of atoms, elements and compounds to name substances and write balanced chemical equations.

Elements and compounds

Everything, whatever its state of matter, is made of atoms. An **atom** is the smallest part of an **element** that can exist. Go to page 78 to revise the structure of the atom.

Elements

There are over 100 different elements, which are shown in the **periodic table**. Each element is made of atoms that have the same atomic number (number of protons). Each type of atom can be represented by an atomic symbol. For example, 'Na' for an atom of sodium.

An element is a pure substance that cannot be chemically broken down into anything simpler. The atoms of a particular element are chemically identical to each other.

Compounds

Compounds form when two or more elements chemically combine in fixed proportions. The name or symbol of a compound is derived from the elements reacting. For example, sodium and chlorine form sodium chloride.

Compounds can only be separated into elements by chemical reactions. Chemical reactions always involve the formation of new substances. The reactions also often involve an energy change.

If only a metal element and a non-metal element react, the compound name ends in **-ide**.

If a compound also contains oxygen, its name will end in **-ate**.

Key skills

- Use the names and symbols of the first 20 elements in the periodic table, and the elements in Groups 1 and 7.
- Name compounds from given formulae or symbol equations.
- Write word equations and produce balanced chemical equations for given reactions.

Go to page 79 to find out about protons and atomic number.

Atoms do not have the same properties as molecular substances.

Worked example — Grade 3

1 Name the compounds formed by the combination of the following elements.

(a) Cu and F **[1 mark]**

Copper fluoride

(b) Cu, O and F **[1 mark]**

Copper fluorate

2 Write a word equation for the reaction between magnesium and oxygen. **[1 mark]**

magnesium + oxygen → magnesium oxide

Exam-style practice — Grade 3

1 Use **one** word from the box to complete the sentence. **[1 mark]**

compound	atom	molecule	metal

Aluminium is an element because it is made of only one type of ______________.

2 Give the atomic symbol for aluminium. **[1 mark]**

3 Look at **Figure 1**, a section of the periodic table.

(a) Give the name of the labelled element in Group 1. **[1 mark]**

(b) (i) Give the name and symbol of the element in the blue box. **[1 mark]**

(ii) Write a word equation showing this element reacting with chlorine. **[1 mark]**

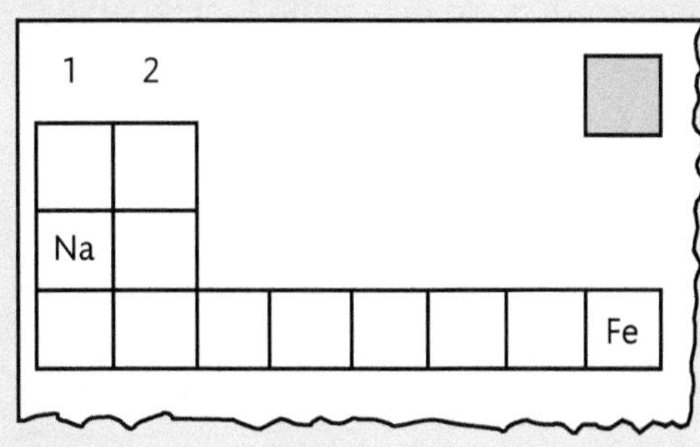

Figure 1

Mixtures

You need to know the different types of mixture and how they can be separated using physical methods.

Separating mixtures

A mixture contains two or more substances that are not chemically bonded together. This means they can be separated by physical methods. The chemical properties of the substances in the mixture are unchanged as they haven't reacted with each other.

- **Filtration** separates an insoluble solid from a liquid. A mixture is passed through filter paper in a filter funnel. The liquid can pass through the gaps in the filter paper but the solid cannot.
- **Simple distillation** separates a solvent from a solution. A mixture is heated and the liquid evaporates, re-condenses and is collected.
- **Fractional distillation** separates a mixture of liquids. It is covered in more detail on page 131.
- **Crystallisation** separates a soluble solid from a liquid. A mixture is heated until the solvent evaporates, leaving a crystallised solid behind.
- **Chromatography** separates a mixture of several liquids. It is covered in more detail on page 136.

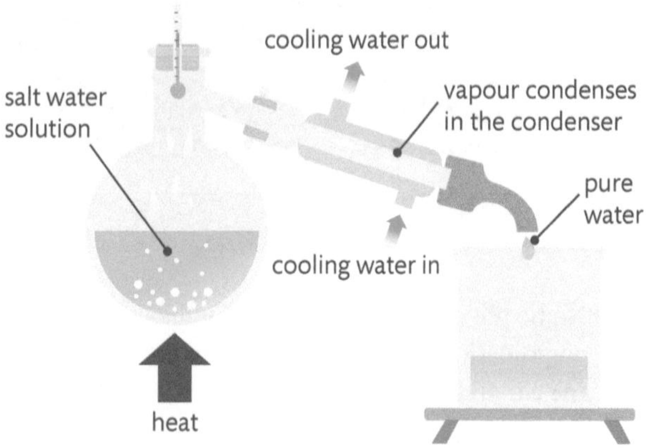

Figure 1 Simple distillation

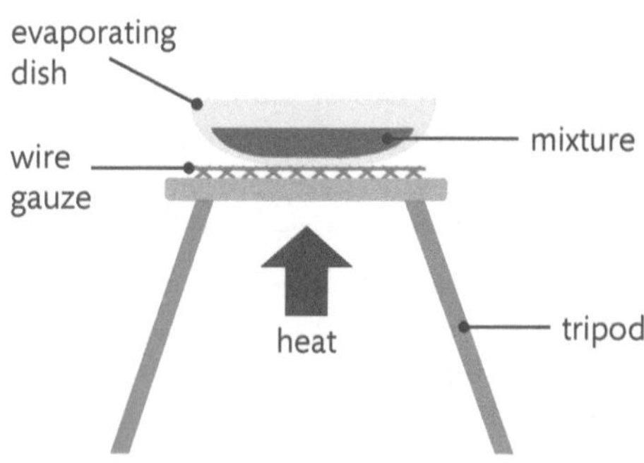

Figure 2 Crystallisation

Worked example — Grade 4

A student is given a mixture containing a liquid that evaporates at 65 °C, a soluble solid and a second liquid that evaporates at 98 °C. Describe the steps the student should follow to separate the soluble solid. **[4 marks]**

Step 1: The two liquids can be separated by fractional distillation. The liquid with a boiling point of 65 °C will evaporate first and can be collected in a beaker.

Step 2: The remaining mixture should be heated in an evaporating dish to evaporate the liquid. It should then be left to cool to allow crystals to form.

Exam-style practice — Grades 2–3

1 Match the mixtures to the methods of separation. **[3 marks]**

Mixture
ink and water
sand and water
crude oil
sugar and water

Separation method
filtration
simple distillation
evaporation
fractional distillation

2 Name the apparatus labelled **W**, **X** and **Y** in **Figure 3**. **[3 marks]**

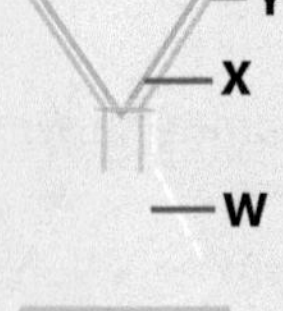

Figure 3

 Made a start  Feeling confident  Exam ready

The model of the atom

The work of many scientists has led to our current model of the atom. The models developed over time as scientific techniques improved and more evidence became available.

Developing the model of the atom

1. Before electrons were discovered, it was thought that atoms were tiny spheres, which could not be divided into anything else.

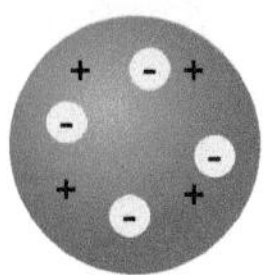

2. The **plum pudding model** was proposed by scientists who thought that the atom was like a positively charged 'pudding', with electrons like 'plums' embedded in it.

3. Ernest Rutherford tested the plum pudding model by aiming a beam of positively charged alpha particles at a very thin sheet of gold foil. This is called the scattering experiment. Some of the alpha particles were repelled by positively charged particles that were concentrated in the centre of the atom (the nucleus). Most alpha particles passed through unaffected, showing that the nucleus was only a very small part of the atom. This evidence gave rise to the **nuclear model**.

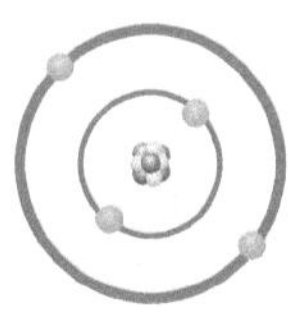

4. Niels Bohr adapted the nuclear model. Using theoretical calculations and experimental observations, Bohr suggested that electrons travel in circular orbits around the nucleus. Further research showed that the nucleus was composed of smaller particles with equal amounts of positive charge. These became known as protons. Approximately 20 years after the nuclear model became accepted, James Chadwick discovered that neutrons existed in the nucleus.

Working scientifically

You need to know how scientific theories develop over time. New experimental evidence may lead to a scientific model being changed or replaced. The **scientific method** is a systematic, logical approach used to make scientific discoveries. It is used to gather experimental and theoretical evidence and observations to solve a problem.

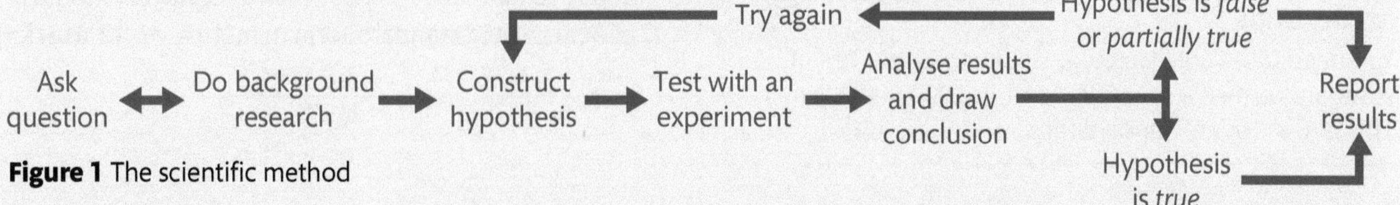

Figure 1 The scientific method

Worked example

Grade 5

In Rutherford's experiment, positively charged alpha particles were aimed at thin gold foil.

(a) Give a reason why most of these particles passed straight through the foil. **[1 mark]**

Most of a gold atom is empty space.

(b) Give a reason why some alpha particles were deflected as they passed through the foil. **[1 mark]**

They were repelled by positively charged particles in the gold foil.

(c) Give a reason why a very small number of alpha particles were deflected through a large angle. **[1 mark]**

There must be a very small positively charged particle in a gold atom.

See page 182 for more about Rutherford's scattering experiment.

Exam-style practice

Grade 3

Give **three** differences between the plum pudding model and the nuclear model of the atom. **[3 marks]**

Subatomic particles

You need to know about the size and structure of atoms.

Structure of an atom

Everything is made of atoms. Atoms contain subatomic particles, some of which are charged.

Within the atom, there is a central **nucleus** that contains the protons and neutrons. As the number of protons (the atomic number) identifies the element, all atoms of the same element must have the same number of protons.

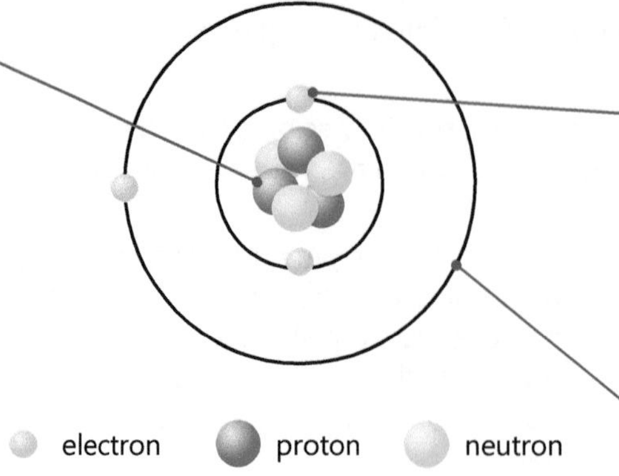

The tiny negatively charged electrons are found in electron shells surrounding the nucleus. They are attracted to the positively charged protons.

The **atomic number** is the number of protons the atom contains. The number of electrons in an atom is equal to the number of protons in its nucleus.

Atoms are electrically neutral as they have an equal number of protons (+) and electrons (−) and neutrons are not charged.

Figure 1 The nuclear model of the atom

Size of an atom

The atom is the smallest part of an element. Atoms have a radius of about 0.1 nanometres (nm), which is equivalent to one tenth of a billionth of a metre (1×10^{-10} m). The nucleus of an atom has a radius of about 0.000 01 nm (1×10^{-14} m).

Go to page 79 for more about the size of an atom.

Maths skills

You need to be able to recognise numbers written in standard form. For example, 1 nm = 0.000 000 001 m. This is 1×10^{-9} in standard form.

Worked example — Grade 5

The radius of an atom is about 0.1 nm, which is 1×10^{-10} m in standard form. The radius of a nucleus is about 10 000 times smaller than this. Give the radius of a nucleus in standard form in metres, m. **[2 marks]**

$$\text{radius of nucleus} = \frac{1 \times 10^{-10}}{10\,000} = 1 \times 10^{-14}\ \text{m}$$

Exam-style practice — Grade 4

1 **(a)** Give the radius of an atom in nm. **[1 mark]**

(b) How many times greater is the radius of an atom compared to the radius of a nucleus? Tick **one** box. **[1 mark]**

100	☐	1000	☐
10 000	☐	100 000	☐

2 Give the electrical charge of the nucleus of an atom. **[1 mark]**

3 Name the subatomic particles found in the nucleus of an atom. **[2 marks]**

4 Look at **Figure 2**, a diagram of a helium atom.

(a) Give the atomic number of helium. **[1 mark]**

(b) Explain why an atom of helium has no overall charge. **[2 marks]**

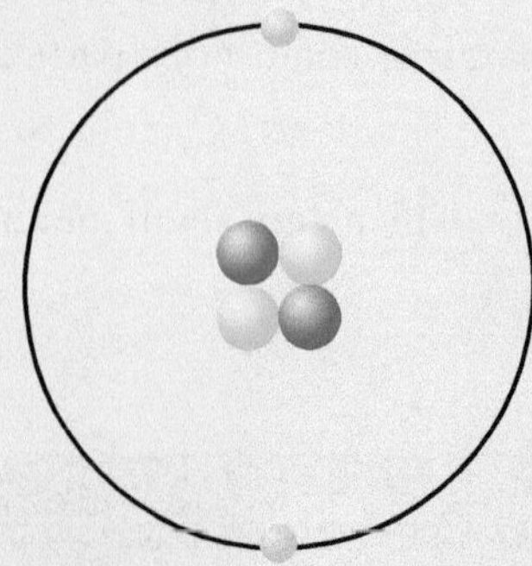

Figure 2

 Made a start  Feeling confident  Exam ready

Size and mass of atoms

The number of particles in an atom can be calculated from its atomic number and mass number.

5 Representing atoms

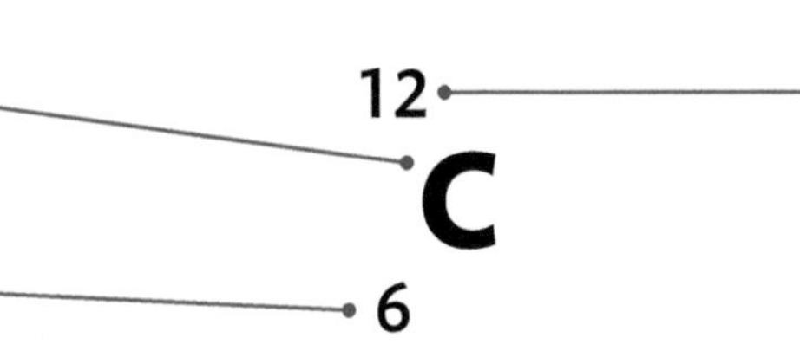

The **atomic symbol** is the short-hand name for the element.

The **atomic number** is the number of protons in an atom. Atoms contain the same number of protons and electrons.

The **mass number** is the number of protons and neutrons in an atom. Almost all the mass of an atom is in the nucleus.

$^{12}_{6}C$

10 Worked example — Grades 4–5

1 Give the relative charge and relative mass of a proton, neutron and electron. **[3 marks]**

Protons have a relative mass of 1 and a charge of +1.
Electrons have a very small relative mass and a charge of –1.
Neutrons have a relative mass of 1 and a charge of 0.

2 An atom of carbon has the symbol $^{14}_{6}C$.

(a) Determine the number of protons in the nucleus of this atom. **[1 mark]**

6

(b) Calculate the number of neutrons in this atom. **[1 mark]**

14 – 6 = 8

(c) Use your answer to part (a) to give the number of electrons in a carbon atom. **[1 mark]**

6

mass number – atomic number

3 The atomic number of oxygen is 8. An oxygen atom gains two electrons when it forms an oxide ion, O^{2-}. Calculate the number of electrons in an oxide ion. **[2 marks]**

Number of electrons = 8 + 2 = 10

In an atom, the number of electrons is equal to the number of protons. In a negatively charged ion, there are more electrons than protons. In a positively charged ion, there are more protons than electrons. In this case, there are two more electrons than protons.

1 Maths skills

You need to know how to use mass number and atomic number to work out the number of protons, neutrons and electrons.

For aluminium (mass number 27, atomic number 13):

number of protons = atomic number = 13

number of electrons = number of protons = 13

number of neutrons = mass number – atomic number
= 27 – 13 = 14

15 Exam-style practice — Grade 5

(a) Atoms have different atomic numbers and mass numbers. In terms of subatomic particles, describe the differences between an atom's atomic number and its mass number. **[2 marks]**

(b) Complete the table. **[6 marks]**

Subatomic particle	Relative mass	Relative charge
	$\frac{1}{1840}$	
neutron		
	1	

(c) Determine the number of protons, neutrons and electrons in a $^{19}_{9}F$ atom. **[3 marks]**

Isotopes and relative atomic mass

Isotopes are atoms of the same element that have different numbers of neutrons. You need to be able to calculate relative atomic mass given the percentage abundance.

Isotopes

Isotopes have the same atomic number but different mass numbers. This means they have the same number of protons and electrons but a different number of neutrons. Most elements have two or more isotopes. Isotopes of an element have the same chemical properties. Isotopes of the same element are usually specifically identified by their mass number, e.g. hydrogen-3.

Isotopes of hydrogen

	hydrogen-1 $^{1}_{1}H$	hydrogen-2 $^{2}_{1}H$	hydrogen-3 $^{3}_{1}H$
Number of protons	1	1	1
Number of electrons	1	1	1
Number of neutrons	0	1	2

Atoms can be represented in this way. The top number is the mass number. The bottom number is the atomic number.

Radioactive isotopes

Some radioactive isotopes have useful applications. For example, cobalt-60 is used in cancer treatment. Fluorine-18 is used as a tracer for detecting cancers and in cardiac and brain imaging.

Worked example — Grade 5

1 Explain why $^{7}_{3}$Li and $^{8}_{3}$Li are isotopes of lithium. **[3 marks]**

The atoms have the same atomic number but different mass numbers. Both atoms have 3 protons, but one atom has 4 neutrons and the other has 5 neutrons.

2 In a sample of chlorine, 75% of the atoms were $^{35}_{17}$Cl and 25% were $^{37}_{17}$Cl. Calculate the relative atomic mass of chlorine. **[3 marks]**

$$A_r = \frac{(35 \times 75) + (37 \times 25)}{100}$$

$$A_r = \frac{2625 + 925}{100} = 35.5$$

Relative atomic mass

The relative atomic mass (A_r) is the average mass of one atom of an element compared with $\frac{1}{12}$ of a carbon-12 atom. The relative atomic mass of an element is the average value of the mass of all isotopes of the element, taking into account their abundance.

The percentage abundance of an element's isotopes is needed to calculate the A_r.

Maths skills

To calculate the relative atomic mass (A_r):

1. Multiply the atomic mass of each isotope by its percentage abundance.

2. Add these values together and divide by 100.

Isotopes of the same element have the same atomic number.

Exam-style practice — Grade 5

1 Look at the atomic symbols below. They represent isotopes of the same element. The letters are not the symbols for these elements. Give **two** reasons why these symbols show **R** and **S** are isotopes of the same element. **[2 marks]**

$^{6}_{3}$R $^{7}_{3}$S

2 Complete the following sentences by choosing the correct words provided in the box below. **[3 marks]**

atomic	isotopes	element	average	atom

The relative ____________ mass of an element is the ____________ value of the mass of all ____________ of the element.

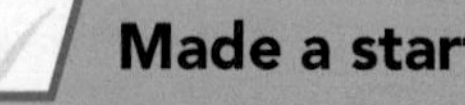

Electronic structure

You need to be able to recognise and represent the electronic structures of the first 20 elements of the periodic table.

Electronic structure

Negatively charged electrons are held in electron shells surrounding the positively charged nucleus of an atom. Electron shells are also referred to as energy levels.

Electrons occupy the lowest energy level first; this is the innermost electron shell. This electron shell is very small and can hold only two electrons. Each subsequent shell can hold up to eight electrons.

The electronic structure of an atom can be represented by a diagram or by listing the number of electrons in each shell, starting with the innermost shell.

- The atomic number gives you the number of electrons in an atom.
- The number of electrons in the outermost electron shell is the same as the element's group number in the periodic table. The exception to this is elements in Group 0 which have complete outer shells.
- The number of electron shells is the same as the element's period number in the periodic table.

Examples of electronic structures

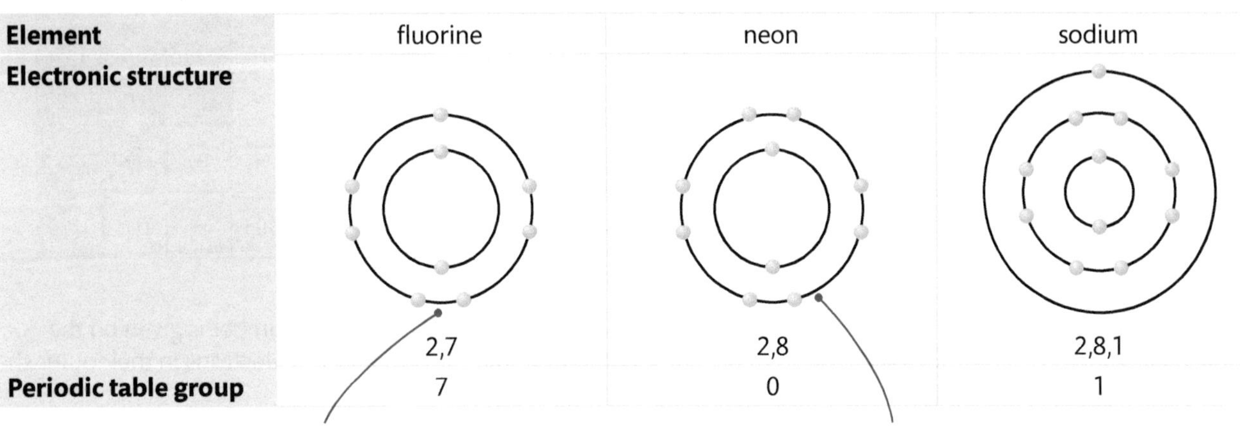

Element	fluorine	neon	sodium
Electronic structure	2,7	2,8	2,8,1
Periodic table group	7	0	1

It is helpful to pair the electrons so you can clearly see how many are in each shell.

Go to page 78 for more about the properties of electrons.

Worked example

Grade 5

(a) Nitrogen has the atomic number 7. Write the electronic structure of nitrogen. **[1 mark]**

2,5

Nitrogen is in Group 5 so it has five electrons in its outer electron shell. Use the periodic table to see which group an element is in.

(b) Complete the diagram to show the electronic structure of nitrogen. **[2 marks]**

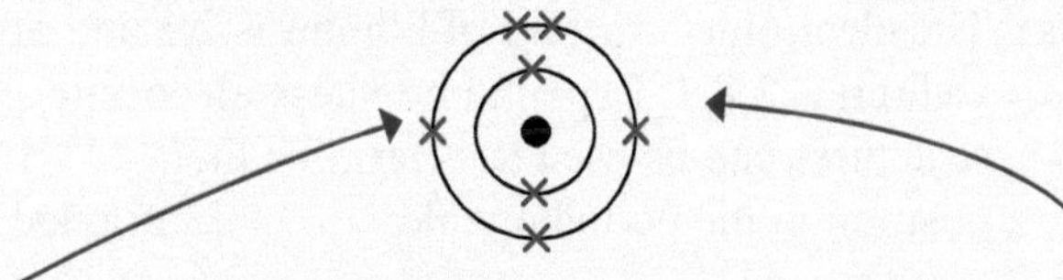

The inner shell is filled first with two electrons, then any further electrons are added to the second shell until it contains eight electrons.

The number of electron shells is equal to the period the element is in, which is 2. The number of electrons in the outer shell is equal to the group, which is 5.

Exam-style practice

Grade 5

The electronic structures of three elements are: **A** 2,5 **B** 2,7 **C** 2,8,8

Use the periodic table to answer these questions.

Identify which element, **A**, **B**, or **C**:

(a) is a Group 0 gas **(b)** is fluorine **(c)** is in Period 3. **[3 marks]**

The periodic table

The periodic table contains all known elements arranged in order of their atomic number. You will be given a copy of the periodic table in your exam.

10 Groups and periods

The periodic table is so-called because elements with similar properties occur at regular intervals. An element's position in the periodic table indicates how it reacts and how reactive it is likely to be.

alkali metals (Group 1)

Hydrogen atoms have one electron in their outer shells, just like alkali metal atoms. However, hydrogen is a non-metal gas and is difficult to place.

halogens (Group 7)

noble gases (Group 0)

The zigzag line divides the metals and the non-metals, with the metals to the left of the line.

1	2											3	4	5	6	7	0
							1 H 1										4 He 2
7 Li 3	9 Be 4											11 B 5	12 C 6	14 N 7	16 O 8	19 F 9	20 Ne 10
23 Na 11	24 Mg 12											27 Al 13	28 Si 14	31 P 15	32 S 16	35.5 Cl 17	40 Ar 18
39 K 19	40 Ca 20	45 Sc 21	48 Ti 22	51 V 23	52 Cr 24	55 Mn 25	56 Fe 26	59 Co 27	59 Ni 28	63.5 Cu 29	65 Zn 30	70 Ga 31	73 Ge 32	75 As 33	79 Se 34	80 Br 35	84 Kr 36
85 Rb 37	88 Sr 38	89 Y 39	91 Zr 40	93 Nb 41	96 Mo 42	98 Tc 43	101 Ru 44	103 Rh 45	106 Pd 46	108 Ag 47	112 Cd 48	115 In 49	119 Sn 50	122 Sb 51	128 Te 52	127 I 53	131 Xe 54
133 Cs 55	137 Ba 56	139 La 57	178 Hf 72	181 Ta 73	184 W 74	186 Re 75	190 Os 76	192 Ir 77	195 Pt 78	197 Au 79	201 Hg 80	204 Tl 81	207 Pb 82	209 Bi 83	[210] Po 84	[210] At 85	[222] Rn 86
[223] Fr 87	[226] Ra 88	[227] Ac 89	[261] Rf 104	[262] Db 105	[266] Sg 106	[264] Bh 107	[277] Hs 108	[268] Mt 109	[271] Ds 110	[272] Rg 111	[285] Cn 112	[286] Uut 113	[289] Fl 114	[289] Uup 115	[293] Lv 116	[294] Uus 117	[294] Uuo 118

Groups

Elements with similar properties are found in vertical columns known as **groups**. The group number is given on the periodic table above each column. All elements in the same group have the same number of electrons in their outer shell, for example, oxygen is in Group 6 and has six electrons in its outer shell (2,6).

Periods

Rows of elements are called **periods**. All elements in the same period have the same number of occupied electron shells. For example, sodium is in Period 3 and has three occupied electron shells. Across a period, the number of electrons in the outer shell increases by 1. For example, lithium (Period 2) has the electronic structure 2,1. The next element in the period, beryllium, has the electronic structure 2,2 and so on.

Worked example — Grades 4–5

(a) The electronic structure of lithium is 2,1 and of sodium is 2,8,1. Explain how these electronic structures can be used to determine their position in the periodic table. **[3 marks]**

The number of electrons in an element's outer shell is the same as its group number, so both lithium and sodium must be in Group 1.

The number of occupied shells is the same as an element's period number, so lithium must be in Period 2 and sodium must be in Period 3.

(b) When lithium metal is added to water it fizzes, producing lithium hydroxide and hydrogen gas. Predict the reaction between sodium and water. Name the products formed. **[2 marks]**

Sodium would fizz more violently and produce sodium hydroxide and hydrogen.

Find sodium and lithium in the periodic table above and compare their positions with the answer. When counting rows, remember that the first row or period only contains two elements, H and He.

10 Exam-style practice — Grades 4–5

1 An element has the electronic structure 2,8,5.

(a) Give the group this element is in. **[1 mark]**

(b) Give the period this element is in. **[1 mark]**

(c) Name another element that would react in a similar way to this element. **[1 mark]**

2 Describe how the elements are arranged in the periodic table. **[3 marks]**

3 Explain why elements in Group 7 have similar chemical properties. You should answer in terms of their electronic structure. **[2 marks]**

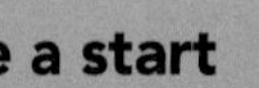

Made a start

Feeling confident

Exam ready

Developing the periodic table

You need to be able to describe the development of the periodic table over time.

Early periodic tables

In the 19th century, scientists attempted to classify elements using a system based on the knowledge available at the time. In the early 1800s, Johann Döbereiner noticed similar properties in small groups of elements – **the law of triads**.

In 1864, John Newlands arranged the elements in order of their atomic weight (similar to relative atomic mass). He proposed **the law of octaves** – every eighth element had similar properties.

Early periodic tables were incomplete and some atomic weights had been calculated incorrectly. This meant that some elements were placed in the wrong groups.

Later discoveries and knowledge of isotopes explained why it was not possible to arrange atoms solely according to their atomic weight.

Group						
1	2	3	4	5	6	7
H	Li	Be	B	C	N	O
F	Na	Mg	Al	Si	P	S
Cl	K	Ca				

Figure 1 Part of Newlands' table

Worked example — Grade 2

In the 19th century, many scientists developed systems to classify the elements.

(a) Draw a line from each scientist to their classification system. **[2 marks]**

Scientist	Classification system
Johann Döbereiner	Periodic table
John Newlands	Law of octaves
Dmitri Mendeleev	Law of triads

(b) Why did Newlands group lithium, sodium and potassium together? **[1 mark]**

They had similar properties.

(c) How did Mendeleev arrange his table of elements? **[1 mark]**

atomic mass

(d) How is the modern periodic table arranged? **[1 mark]**

atomic number

Mendeleev's periodic table

In 1869, Mendeleev correctly identified trends between elements and grouped them accordingly. Mendeleev arranged his table in order of increasing relative atomic mass. Mendeleev realised there was a link between relative atomic mass and how elements reacted. In some cases, he changed the order of the elements to fit the trend better. He also left gaps for elements that had not yet been discovered.

Over the next 20 years more elements were discovered and their properties were found to match Mendeleev's predictions.

Row	Group							
	1	2	3	4	5	6	7	8
1	H	–	–	–	–	–	–	–
2	Li	Be	B	C	N	O	F	–
3	Na	Mg	Al	Si	P	S	Cl	–
4	K	Ca	?	Ti	V	Cr	Mn	Fe, Co, Ni, Cu
5	(Cu)	Zn	?	?	As	So	Br	–
6	Rb	Sr	Yt	Zr	Nb	Mo	?	Fe, Co, Ni, Cu

Figure 2 Part of the early periodic table developed by Dmitri Mendeleev

Working scientifically

To develop new scientific ideas, predictions need to be tested. If the evidence supports the prediction, a scientific idea will start to be accepted.

The development of the periodic table is an example of how scientific ideas develop. Many scientists suggested possible arrangements of the elements but others rejected them as they weren't supported by evidence.

Exam-style practice — Grade 4

1. Look at **Figure 1**. Name **one** element that Newlands put into his Group 4. **[1 mark]**

2. **(a)** Which property did Mendeleev first use to arrange the elements in his periodic table? Tick **one** box. **[1 mark]**

atomic mass ☐ atomic number ☐
atomic size ☐ atomic reactivity ☐

(b) Give a reason why Mendeleev left gaps in his periodic table. **[1 mark]**

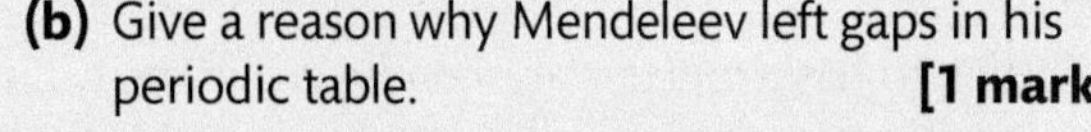

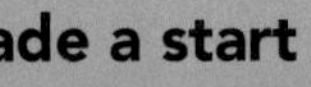

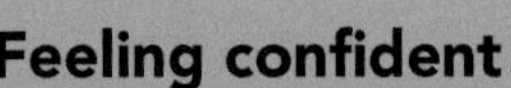

Made a start | Feeling confident | Exam ready

Metals and non-metals

You need to know about the electronic structure, reactivity and properties of metals and non-metals.

Differences between metals and non-metals

An element can be classified as a metal or a non-metal based on the electronic structure of its atoms.

- Metals lose electrons when they react, forming positive ions. Go to pages 89 and 94 to revise ionic bonding and ionic compounds.
- Non-metals gain electrons when they react, forming negative ions (page 89). They can also share electrons, forming molecules (page 91).

As you go across a period (from left to right) the number of outer electrons in an atom increases. The atoms become more likely to gain electrons or to share them, so they become less metallic. The elements to the left of a period are metals, and the elements to the right are non-metals.

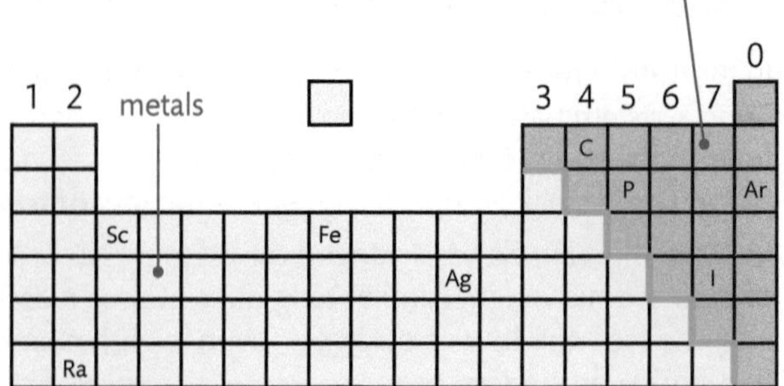

Figure 1 Metals are on the left of the periodic table and non-metals are on the right.

Properties of metals and non-metals

	Metals	Non-metals
State	Solid at room temperature (except mercury)	• Usually liquids or gases at room temperature • Some non-metals have giant structures so are solid at room temperature
Conduction of heat and electricity	Good conductors	• Usually poor conductors • Some forms of carbon conduct electricity
Strength	Strong	Weak
Melting point	High	Usually low
Appearance	Shiny when cut	Dull
Malleability	Malleable (can be hammered into shape)	Brittle

Worked example

Grade 2

1. On which side of the periodic table are the non-metals found? **[1 mark]**

   On the right

2. Which of the following statements describe what happens when a metal reacts? Tick **two** boxes. **[2 marks]**

   lose electrons ✓
   gain electrons ☐
   form neutral molecules ☐
   form positive ions ✓
   share electrons ☐

3. When a metal reacts with a non-metal a compound is formed. Name the bonding which takes place between a metal and a non-metal. **[1 mark]**

   Ionic

4. The statements below describe the properties of metals and non-metals. For each statement state whether the property relates to metals or non-metals. **[5 marks]**

   High melting point metal
   Poor conductor non-metal
   Brittle non-metal
   Shiny when cut metal
   Gas at room temperature non-metal

Exam-style practice

Grade 4

Aluminium has a low density, conducts electricity and is resistant to corrosion. Identify **one** of these properties that makes aluminium suitable to use as kitchen foil. Give a reason for your answer. **[2 marks]**

Group 0

You need to know the electronic structures of Group 0 elements, such as helium and argon, and the trends in their physical properties.

10 Electronic structure

The elements in Group 0 are known as the **noble** or **inert gases** due to their characteristic lack of reactivity. This is due to their stable electron arrangement. They all have eight electrons in their outermost energy level, except helium which has two. They do not easily form molecules but exist as **monatomic** (single) atoms.

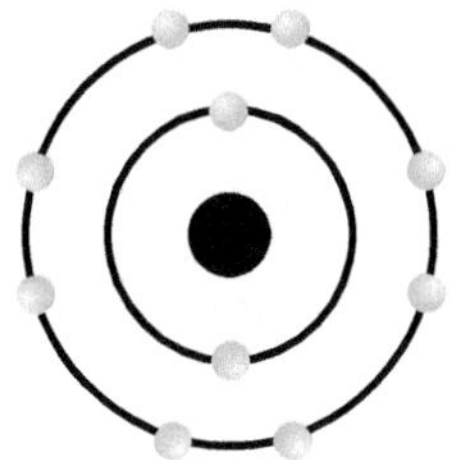

Figure 1 Neon has the electronic structure 2,8.

2 Physical and chemical trends

Trends are observed in the properties of Group 0 elements.

Helium (He)	Going down the group, the **atomic number** and **relative atomic mass** increase.
Neon (Ne)	
Argon (Ar)	The number of occupied electron shells increases, so the **size of the atoms** increases.
Kryton (Kr)	The **boiling point** increases as the strength of intermolecular forces between atoms increases.
Xenon (Xe)	

10 Worked example — Grade 5

1 Explain why the noble gases are unreactive. **[2 marks]**

Their outer shell is full so they do not need to gain or lose any electrons. Therefore, they do not react with any other atoms.

Go to page 81 to revise electronic structure.

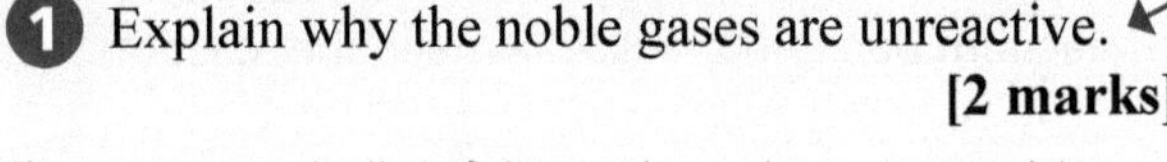

2 **(a)** Describe how the boiling point of Group 0 elements changes down the group. **[1 mark]**

It increases.

(b) Explain why the boiling points change in this way. **[2 marks]**

Going down the group, the relative atomic mass increases, so the strength of the forces between atoms increases.

3 The radius of a neon atom is 154 pm. Predict whether the radius of a xenon atom will be larger or smaller than that of a neon atom. Justify your answer. **[2 marks]**

The radius of a xenon atom will be larger than the radius of a neon atom, because xenon has 3 more occupied electron shells than neon.

1 Exam focus

Make sure you know the trends in **Group 0** and **Group 1** of the periodic table. You need to be able to predict the properties of the elements in these groups.

5 Exam-style practice — Grades 2–4

1 Choose the correct answer from the box to complete each sentence.

(a) Noble gases are in Group:

0	1	7

(b) Noble gases are: ______________________

slightly reactive	unreactive	very reactive

2 **(a)** Explain why relative atomic mass increases down Group 0. **[2 marks]**

(b) Give a reason why the noble gases are unreactive. **[1 mark]**

3 Draw the electronic structure of an argon atom. **[2 marks]**

Group 1

You need to know the electronic structures of Group 1 elements, such as sodium and potassium, and the trends in their chemical properties.

Properties of Group 1 elements

Group 1 elements are called the **alkali metals** because they form alkaline solutions when they react with water.

The atoms of all Group 1 elements have one outer electron. When they react, they lose this electron and form a positively charged ion.

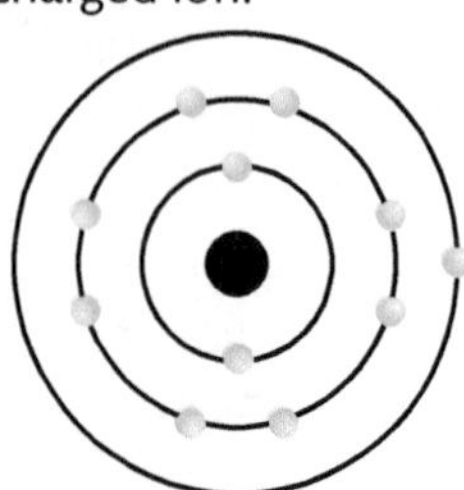

Figure 1 Sodium has the electronic structure 2,8,1.

Oxygen, chlorine and water

The first three Group 1 metals are lithium, sodium and potassium. The following table shows how these metals react with oxygen, chlorine and water.

Element	Oxygen	Chlorine	Water
Li	red flame	red flame, white powder	fizzes
Na	yellow-orange flame	yellow flame, white powder	fizzes rapidly, may ignite
K	lilac flame	lilac flame, white powder	ignites, may be a small explosion

Reactivity of Group 1 elements

Going down the group, the alkali metals become more reactive. This is because as the size of their atoms increases, the outer electron becomes further from the nucleus and so is more easily lost in reactions.

Lithium, sodium and potassium float on water and react with it. The reactions transfer energy to the surroundings, mainly by heat. Fizzing is seen when lithium and sodium react with water. Potassium bursts into a lilac flame in the reaction:

potassium + water → potassium hydroxide + hydrogen

Worked example — Grade 5

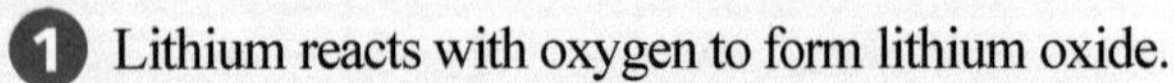

1 Lithium reacts with oxygen to form lithium oxide.

(a) Write a word equation for this reaction. **[1 mark]**

lithium + oxygen → lithium oxide

All Group 1 elements react with oxygen to form an oxide layer on their surface.

(b) Balance the equation for this reaction.

$\underline{4}\ Li + O_2 \rightarrow \underline{2}\ Li_2O$ **[1 mark]**

2 Sodium reacts with water in a similar way to potassium. Write a word equation for the reaction of sodium with water. **[2 marks]**

sodium + water → sodium hydroxide + hydrogen

Alkali metals react vigorously with water to produce an alkaline solution containing a metal hydroxide that turns universal indicator purple. Hydrogen gas is also produced. You should know the test for hydrogen – a lit splint produces a squeaky pop.

3 Sodium reacts with chlorine to produce a salt.

(a) Write a word equation for the reaction. **[1 mark]**

sodium + chlorine → sodium chloride

This reaction is vigorous, producing a metal chloride salt, a white crystalline solid. NaCl is the salt used in cooking.

(b) Balance this equation. **[1 mark]**

$\underline{2}\ Na + Cl_2 \rightarrow \underline{2}\ NaCl$

Exam-style practice — Grade 5

1 Explain why there is an increase in reactivity of elements down Group 1. **[4 marks]**

2 Lithium reacts with water. Give **one** reason why bubbles of gas are seen. **[1 mark]**

Group 7

You need to know the electronic structures of Group 7 elements, such as chlorine, and their physical properties and reactivity.

Bonding

Group 7 elements, also known as the **halogens**, have seven outer electrons. It would take too much energy to try to remove such a large number of electrons. Therefore halogens either gain electrons by reacting with a metal, forming an ionic compound, or they share electrons with non-metals, forming a covalent bond.

The halogens exist as **diatomic molecules** (pairs of atoms), sharing electrons in a covalent bond (see page 91).

Properties

Group 7 elements share similar properties, including:

- non-metals
- low melting and boiling points
- brittle when solid
- poor conductors of heat and electricity
- coloured vapours
- molecules each contain two atoms (diatomic).

Worked example — Grade 5

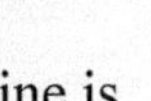

1 Explain, in terms of electrons, why fluorine is the most reactive halogen. **[3 marks]**

Fluorine is the most reactive halogen because its outer electron shell is closest to its nucleus. This makes it easier for fluorine to attract electrons. The easier it is to gain an electron, the more reactive the halogen is.

2 Explain why the boiling points of the halogens change down the group from fluorine to iodine. **[2 marks]**

The boiling points increase down Group 7 because as the atoms get larger there are greater intermolecular forces to overcome.

3 (a) Chlorine dissolves in water to form an aqueous solution. This chlorine solution can displace bromine from an aqueous solution of potassium bromide. Write a word equation for this reaction. **[2 marks]**

chlorine + potassium bromide → potassium chloride + bromine

(b) Balance this equation for the reaction. **[1 mark]**

$Cl_2 + \underline{2}\ KBr \rightarrow \underline{2}\ KCl + Br_2$

Reactivity

Halogens react vigorously with metals to form halide ions with a charge of −1. They react with non-metals to form small molecules (page 95).

As you go down Group 7:

Fluorine (F) reactivity decreases
Chlorine (Cl) relative molecular mass increases
Bromine (Br) melting and boiling points increase
Iodine (I)

Displacement reactions

A more reactive halogen will displace (push out) a less reactive halogen from an aqueous solution of its salt.

Chlorine is more reactive than iodine, so chlorine will displace iodine from an aqueous solution of an iodide salt.

chlorine + magnesium iodide → magnesium chloride + iodine

Bromine is less reactive than chlorine, so bromine cannot displace chlorine – no reaction takes place.

bromine + sodium chloride → no reaction

The table shows the results of the reactions between halogens and aqueous solutions of halide salts.

	Chloride	Bromide	Iodide
Chlorine	**no reaction**	bromine forms (turns orange)	iodine forms (turns brown)
Bromine	**no reaction**	**no reaction**	iodine forms (turns brown)
Iodine	**no reaction**	**no reaction**	**no reaction**

Exam-style practice — Grade 4

1 Give **one** reason why chlorine displaces iodine from silver iodide. **[1 mark]**

2 Suggest which halogen produces bromine when it reacts with lithium bromide. **[1 mark]**

3 At room temperature, fluorine and chlorine are gases, bromine is liquid and iodine is solid. Give a reason that explains this. **[2 marks]**

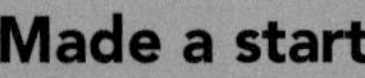

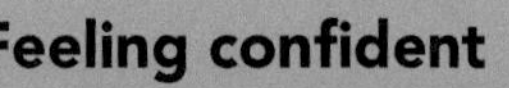

Chemical bonds

You need to be able to apply knowledge about the types of chemical bonds to the physical and chemical properties of substances.

Types of bonding

You need to know about three types of chemical bond: ionic (page 89), covalent (page 91) and metallic (page 92).

Chemical bonding occurs because atoms need a full outer shell of electrons to become stable.

Atoms can join together by **transferring** electrons or by **sharing** electrons.

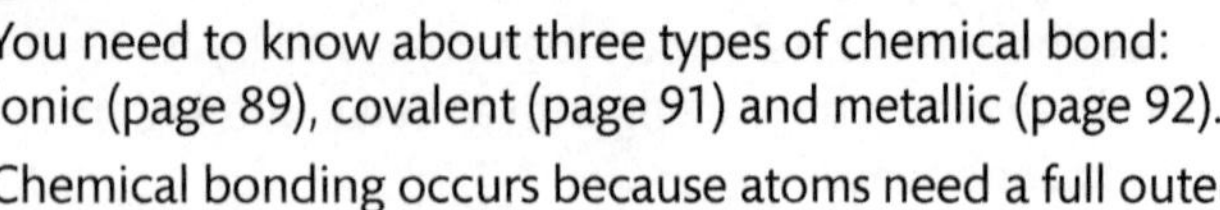

Technology

Technology is science put into practical use to solve problems or invent useful materials or tools.

Scientists have engineered new materials with useful properties using their understanding of structure and bonding.

Comparing types of bonding

Type of bonding	ionic bonding	covalent bonding	metallic bonding
Occurs between	metals and non-metals	non-metallic elements and compounds of non-metals	metallic elements
Diagram	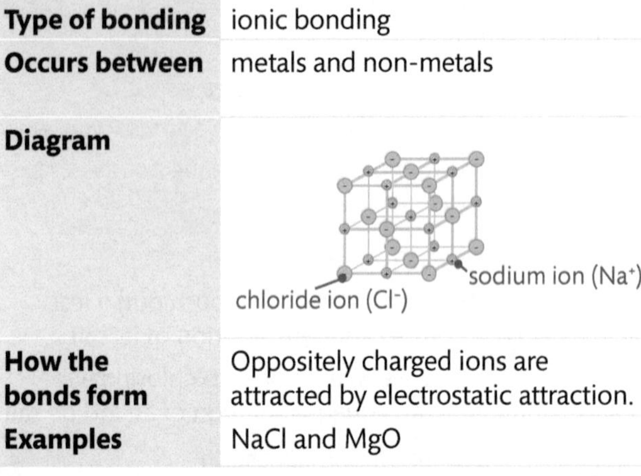	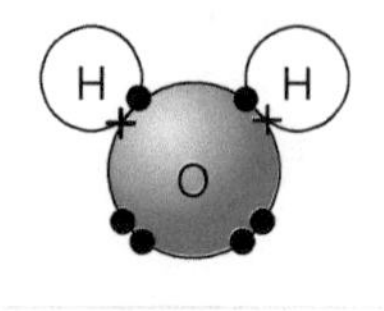	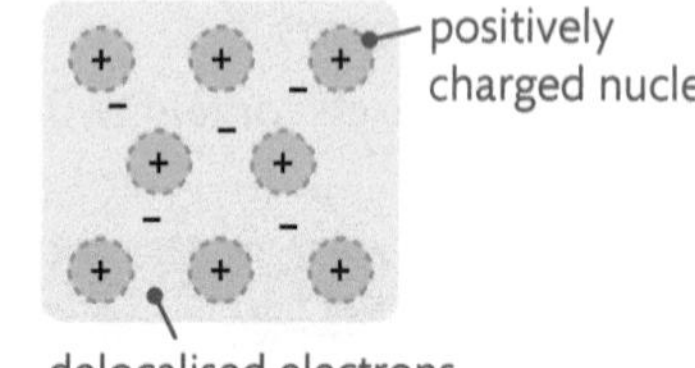
How the bonds form	Oppositely charged ions are attracted by electrostatic attraction.	Atoms share a pair of electrons.	Metal atoms share delocalised electrons.
Examples	NaCl and MgO	CO_2 and H_2O	Cu and Al

Worked example

Grade 2

1 Give a reason why atoms form chemical bonds. **[1 mark]**

To gain a full outer shell

You could also say 'to increase their stability'.

2 This question is about types of bonding. For each type of substance listed, name the type of bonding that occurs.

(a) Compounds formed by a metal and a non-metal. **[1 mark]**

ionic bonding

(b) Molecules formed by non-metal elements. **[1 mark]**

covalent bonding

(c) Metal elements **[1 mark]**

metallic bonding

3 Draw **one** line from each type of bonding to describe how the bonds form. **[2 marks]**

Type of bonding	How the bonds form
Ionic	atoms share pairs of electrons
Covalent	giant structure of atoms sharing delocalised electrons
Metallic	electrostatic attraction between oppositely charged ions

Exam-style practice

Grade 2

(a) Explain the term 'delocalised electrons'. **[1 mark]**

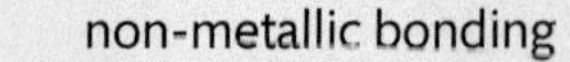

(b) Which type of bonding involves delocalised electrons? Tick **one** box. **[1 mark]**

ionic bonding ☐ covalent bonding ☐ metallic bonding ☐ non-metallic bonding ☐

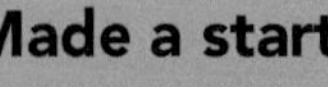 Made a start

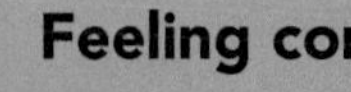 Feeling confident

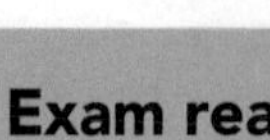 Exam ready

Ionic bonding

You need to know how to describe ionic bonding and represent it using dot and cross diagrams.

Ionic bonding

Ionic bonding occurs in compounds formed from positive and negative ions. Metal atoms lose electrons to form positively charged ions, such as Na^+. Non-metal atoms gain electrons to form negatively charged ions, such as Cl^-.

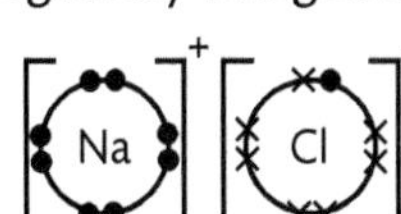

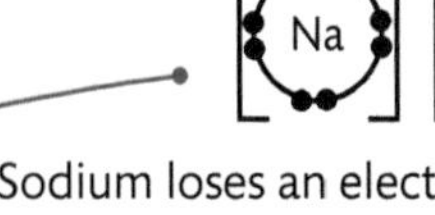

Figure 1 Sodium loses an electron to become a positive ion and chlorine gains an electron to become a negative ion.

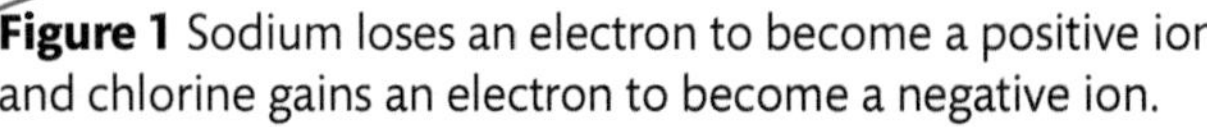

Sometimes, only the bonding electrons in the outer shell are displayed in dot and cross diagrams.

The ions that form the metals in Groups 1 and 2 and the non-metals in Groups 6 and 7 have the electronic structure of a Group 0 element.

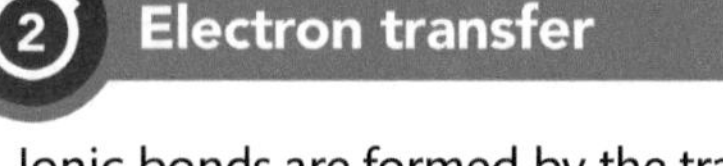

Electron transfer

Ionic bonds are formed by the transfer of electrons from metal atoms to non-metal atoms, so both gain a stable arrangement of electrons. Electron transfer is represented by dot and cross diagrams.

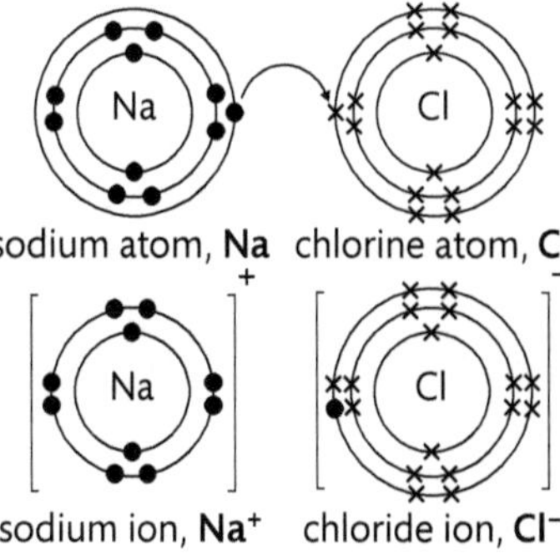

Figure 2 The dot and cross diagrams show the formation of sodium chloride, an ionic compound. Go to page 90 to revise ionic compounds.

Worked example — Grade 3

1 Name the type of diagram used to show ionic bonding. **[1 mark]**

dot and cross

2 When ions form, electrons are lost from metal atoms. Identify the shell involved in this. **[1 mark]**

The outer shell

3 Describe how the sodium atom and fluorine atom in **Figure 3** form sodium fluoride. You should give the charge on each ion formed. **[4 marks]**

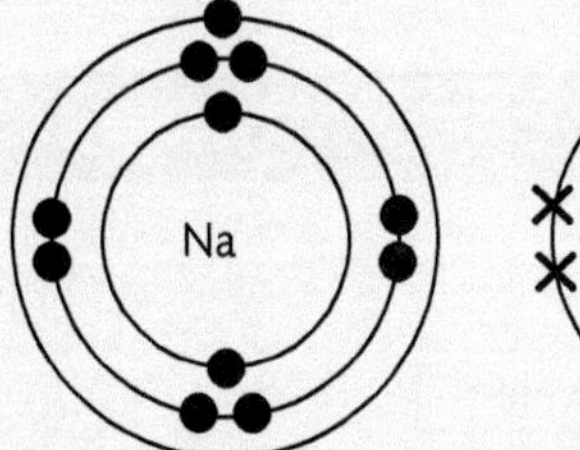

Figure 3

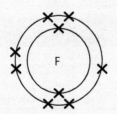

The sodium atom loses its outer electron to form an Na^+ ion. This electron is gained by a fluorine atom to form an F^- ion.

Sodium is in Group 1 so it has one electron in its outer shell. When sodium reacts, it needs to lose this outer electron to have a full outer shell. When sodium loses its negatively charged electron, the sodium ion becomes positively charged.

Exam focus

In the exam, you could be asked to draw dot and cross diagrams for ionic compounds formed between metals in Groups 1 and 2 and non-metals in Groups 6 and 7. Make sure you know the charge of the ions formed.

Group	Charge of ion formed
1	1+
2	2+
6	2−
7	1−

Fluorine is in Group 7 so it needs to gain one electron to have a full outer shell. Because fluorine gains an electron the fluoride ion is negatively charged.

Exam-style practice — Grade 4

1 Identify the group of elements that has the same electronic configurations as ions produced by metal and non-metal elements. **[1 mark]**

2 Magnesium reacts with oxygen. Complete the dot and cross diagrams in **Figure 4** to show the transfer of electrons and charges on the ions produced in this reaction. **[3 marks]**

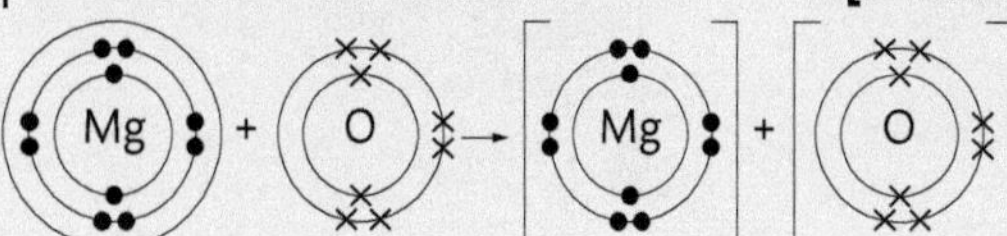

Figure 4

Made a start | Feeling confident | Exam ready

Ionic compounds

You need to be able to identify ionic compounds and work out their empirical formulae from different types of diagram.

5 Giant ionic structures

Ionic compounds are made up of many ions, which are held together by strong electrostatic forces of attraction. Ionic compounds form giant structures called **lattices**. The **electrostatic forces of attraction** between the ions are strong due to the attraction between the oppositely charged ions.

Ionic lattices are three-dimensional structures. The forces of attraction act in all directions throughout the lattice. Ionic compounds can be represented in several ways:

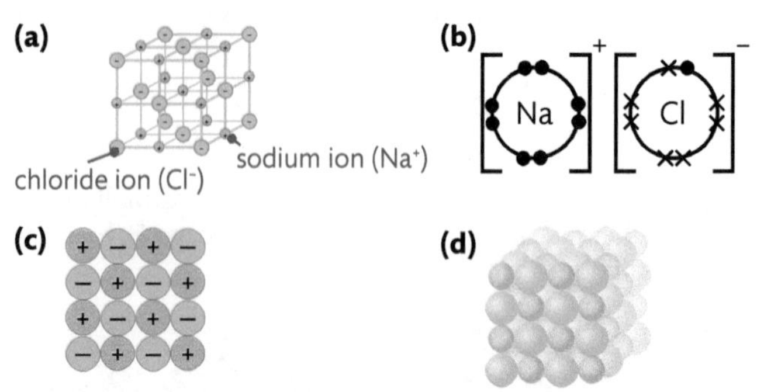

Figure 1 Ionic compounds can be represented in several ways: (a) ball and stick diagram; (b) dot and cross diagram; (c) two-dimensional diagram; (d) three-dimensional diagram.

The empirical formula is the simplest whole number ratio of atoms in an ionic compound.

You can use the structure in **Figure 1(a)** to count how many atoms of each element are present. Although the ratio may not be exact, it should be clear what the empirical formula is.

The diagram shows 14 × Cl^- ions and 13 × Na^+ ions. The ratio is very close to 1 : 1.

10 Worked example — Grade 5

1 Give the limitations of each of the following models for representing ionic compounds.

(a) Ball and stick diagram **[2 marks]**

Ball and stick diagrams are a three-dimensional representation of the ions and the bonds between the ions. However, these diagrams are not to scale (so the size of the ions is incorrect) and they do not show the electronic structure of the ions.

(b) Dot and cross diagram **[2 marks]**

Dot and cross diagrams only give a two-dimensional representation of the ions in a single formula unit; they do not show the arrangement of the ions.

(c) Two-dimensional diagram **[2 marks]**

Two-dimensional diagrams don't show the electronic structure of the ions or the arrangement of giant structures.

(d) Three-dimensional diagram **[2 marks]**

Three-dimensional diagrams show the size of the ions and give a more realistic idea of the position of the ions; however, they do not show the bonds or the electronic structure.

2 Suggest the empirical formula for sodium chloride, based on **Figure 1**. **[1 mark]**

There are 13 Na^+

There are 14 Cl^-

13 : 14 = 0.9 : 1.0

The formula is NaCl

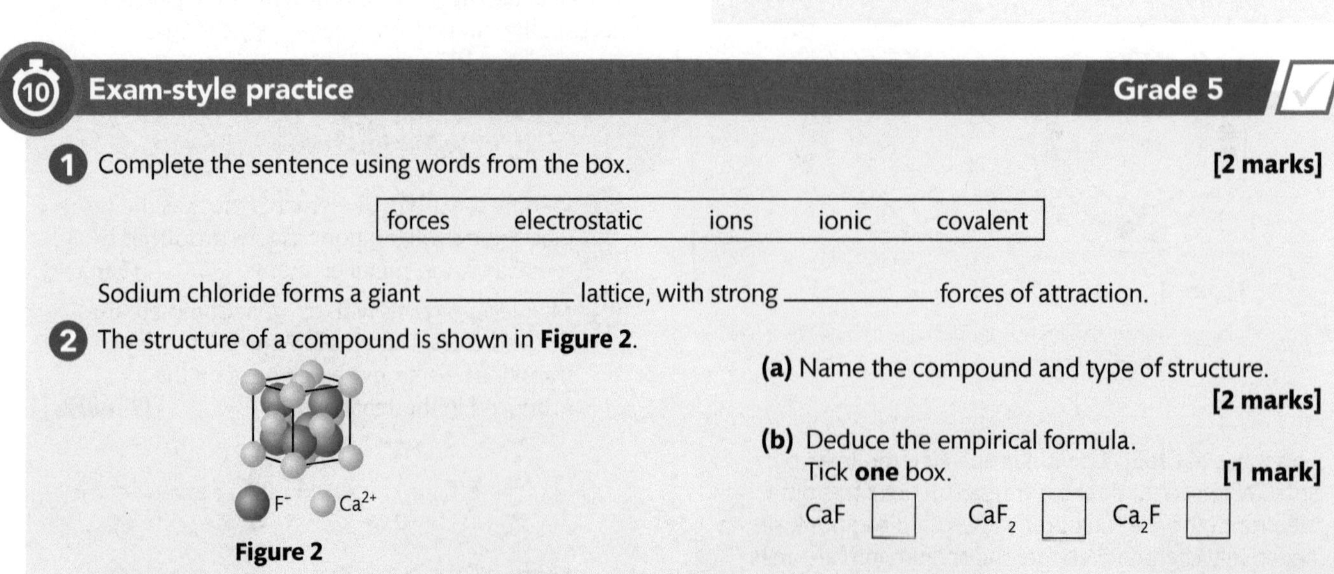

10 Exam-style practice — Grade 5

1 Complete the sentence using words from the box. **[2 marks]**

forces	electrostatic	ions	ionic	covalent

Sodium chloride forms a giant __________ lattice, with strong __________ forces of attraction.

2 The structure of a compound is shown in **Figure 2**.

Figure 2

(a) Name the compound and type of structure. **[2 marks]**

(b) Deduce the empirical formula. Tick **one** box. **[1 mark]**

CaF ☐ CaF_2 ☐ Ca_2F ☐

 Made a start  Feeling confident  Exam ready

Covalent bonding

You need to be able to identify and draw covalent bonds for small molecules, polymers and giant covalent structures.

5 Forming covalent bonds

A covalent bond is a shared pair of electrons. These electrons are shared between two atoms to form a strong bond. Covalent bonds are found in small molecules (page 95), polymers (page 96) and giant covalent structures (page 97).

Covalent bonds form between non-metal atoms, which join together by sharing outer shell electrons. The shared pair of electrons holds the two atoms together. When atoms bond in this way, they form a molecule.

Go to page 90 to revise the advantages and disadvantages of the different types of diagram.

Only the electrons in the outermost shell can be shared.

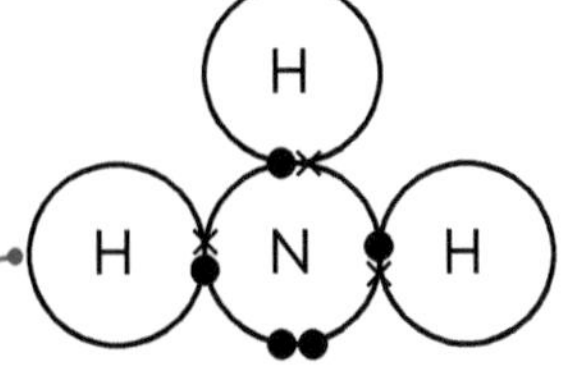

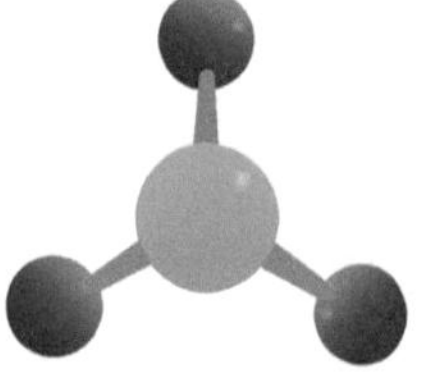

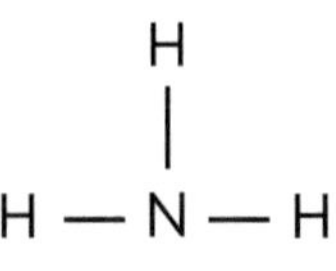

Figure 1 The covalent bonding in ammonia can be displayed in different ways.

5 Worked example — Grade 5

Complete the dot and cross diagram in **Figure 2** to show the bonding in methane, CH_4.

[4 marks]

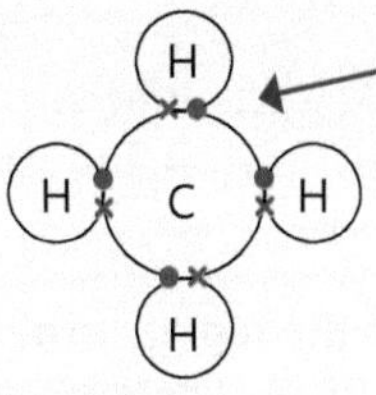

H, H, C, H, H

Figure 2

A hydrogen atom has one electron in its outer shell. Carbon has four electrons in its outer shell.

The bond must clearly show a **shared pair** of electrons, one being a dot and one being a cross.

The covalent compound must show each atom correctly bonded with a full outer shell.

Look at **Figure 4** and count how many shared pairs of electrons there are.

Alternatively, look at the periodic table. Nitrogen is in Group 5 so it is three electrons short of a full outer shell.

1 Exam focus

In the exam, you will need to be able to recognise small molecules, polymers or giant structures from diagrams showing their bonding.

2 Exam checklist

For the exam, you need to know how to:

- draw dot and cross diagrams for H_2, Cl_2, O_2, N_2, HCl, H_2O, NH_3 and CH_4
- show a single covalent bond as a line between two atoms
- describe the limitations of dot and cross, ball and stick, 2D and 3D models to represent covalent molecules and giant structures
- deduce the molecular formula of a substance from a given diagram.

10 Exam-style practice — Grade 5

1. Each of the lines in **Figure 3** represents a covalent bond. Describe a covalent bond. **[2 marks]**

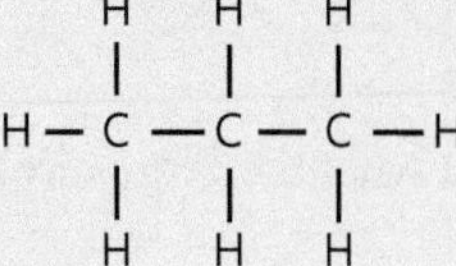

Figure 3

2. **Figure 4** shows a molecule of N_2. State how many bonds there are between the atoms. **[1 mark]**

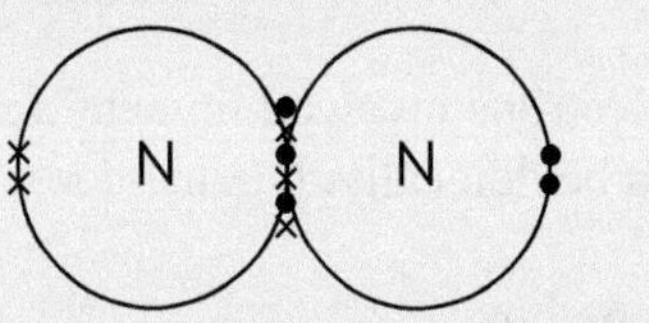

Figure 4

3. Draw a dot and cross diagram to show the bonding in chlorine, Cl_2. **[2 marks]**

 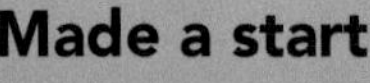 Made a start  Feeling confident  Exam ready

Metallic bonding

Metals have very strong bonds due to the presence of free electrons. You need to be able to recall the structure and arrangement of metal particles.

Structure of metals

Most metals (excluding the transition metals) have between one and three electrons in their outer shell. These electrons are said to be 'delocalised', which means they are not in fixed positions. Instead they are free to move throughout the metal structure.

As the electrons can move, they are shared within the structure, giving rise to strong metallic bonds.

The metallic bonds are formed from the strong attraction between positively charged nuclei and the negatively charged electrons.

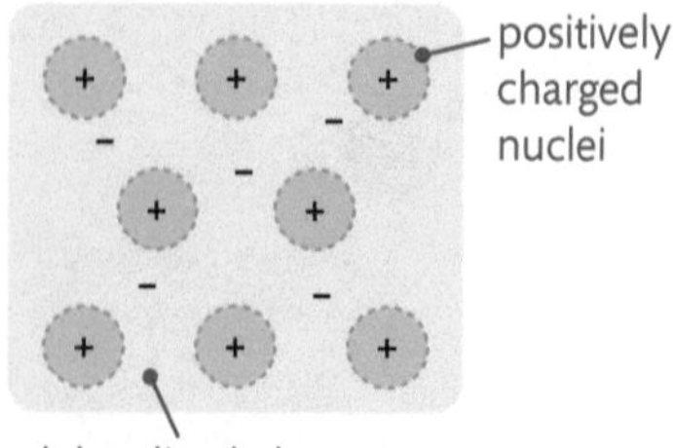

Figure 1 The arrangement of metal ions and electrons in metallic bonding

Figure 2 Metals, such as copper, are used to make saucepans because of their high strength and thermal conductivity.

Worked example Grade 3

1 Describe the structure of a metal. **[3 marks]**

Metals consist of giant structures of metal ions arranged in a regular pattern, with delocalised electrons.

2 **Figure 3** shows the arrangement of particles in a metal.

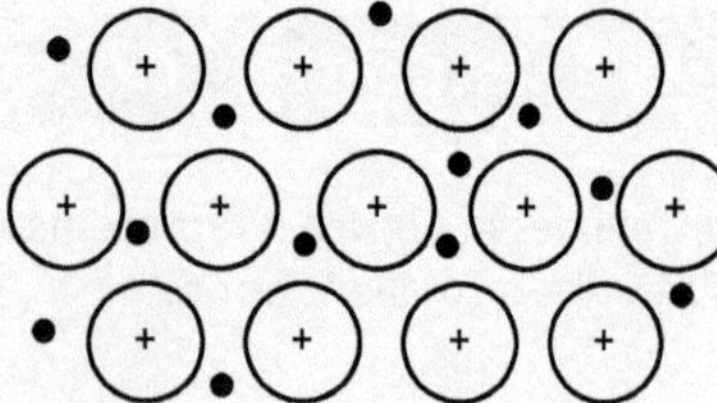

Figure 3

(a) Describe what the large circles represent. **[1 mark]**

Metal ions

(b) Describe what the dots represent. **[1 mark]**

Electrons

3 The electrons involved in metallic bonding are said to be delocalised. What does 'delocalised' mean?
Tick **one** box. **[1 mark]**

- The electrons are in fixed positions. ☐
- The electrons combine with positive ions. ☐
- The electrons are free to move. ☑

Exam focus

Make sure you use key scientific terminology, such as delocalised electrons, in your answer.

This diagram shows the regular arrangement of the metal atoms as positively charged particles surrounded by negative electrons.

Exam-style practice Grade 3

1 Which of these statements best describes metallic bonding? Tick **one** box. **[1 mark]**

- transfer of electrons ☐
- sharing electrons ☐
- attraction between positive nuclei and electrons ☐
- atoms form hexagonal rings ☐

2 The structure of metals allows metallic bonds to form. Complete the sentences below to explain how metallic bonds form. **[4 marks]**

Use words from the box.

metallic	move	electrons	sharing
ions	covalent	attraction	

The ________ in the outer shell of metal atoms are delocalised and so are free to ________ through the whole structure. The ________ to delocalised electrons gives rise to strong ________ bonds.

Made a start Feeling confident  Exam ready

States of matter

You need to be able to predict the states of substances at different temperatures and explain changes of state using the particle model.

Changing state

The three states of matter, solid, liquid and gas, can be explained by the **particle model**. In this model, the particles are shown as small solid spheres. The particle model can be used to show how particles are arranged in solids, liquids and gases. It can also help to explain melting, boiling, freezing and condensing. When substances are heated or cooled the forces **between** particles change. The density, arrangement and motion of particles change when a substance changes state.

Particles in a substance **gain energy** when the substance turns from a solid to a liquid (**melting**) or from a liquid to a gas (**boiling**).

- The distance between particles increases.
- The strength of the forces between particles decreases.
- The particles have more energy so move faster.

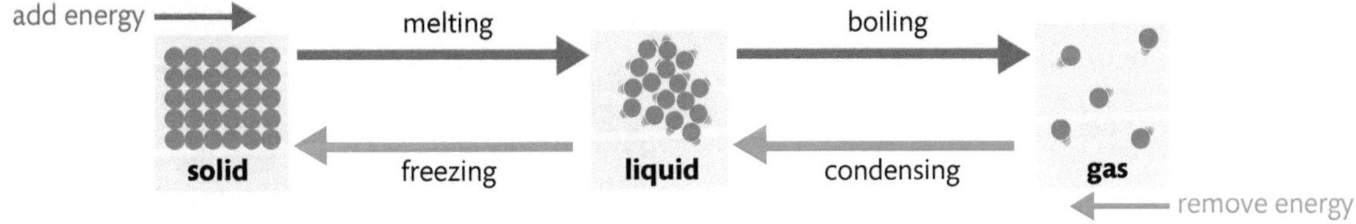

Figure 1 The particle model of states of matter

Particles in a substance **lose energy** when the substance turns from a gas to a liquid (**condensing**) and from a liquid to a solid (**freezing**).

- The distance between particles decreases.
- The strength of the forces between particles increases.
- The particles have less energy so move more slowly.

The amount of energy needed to change state from a solid to a liquid and from a liquid to a gas varies depending on the substance. The energy must be great enough to overcome the forces of attraction **between** the particles. The strength of the forces varies according to the type of bonding and the structure of the substance. The stronger the forces between the particles, the higher the **melting point** and **boiling point** of the substance.

State symbols

Symbols are used in a chemical equation to represent states of matter and if a substance is in solution:

- (s) for solids, e.g. ice
- (l) for liquids, e.g. water
- (g) for gases, e.g. steam
- (aq) for aqueous solutions, e.g. NaCl in water.

For example: $2Na(s) + 2H_2O(l) \rightarrow 2NaOH(aq) + H_2(g)$

Worked example Grades 4–5

Explain why more energy is required to change the state of a solid than to change the state of a liquid. **[2 marks]**

The forces of attraction are much greater in a solid due to the regular lattice arrangement. The particles in a solid are much closer together than in a liquid so the forces of attraction are greater and more difficult to overcome.

Exam-style practice Grade 3

1 Draw **one** line from each substance to the symbol which represents the state of matter at room temperature. **[2 marks]**

carbon dioxide	(s)
water	(g)
lead	(l)

2 Name the change of state taking place when water turns into steam. **[1 mark]**

3 When a substance is cooled the arrangement and motion of the particles change, causing the substance to change state.

Complete the sentences. Use words from the box. **[2 marks]**

increases	strength	energy	decreases

As a substance cools it loses __________.

The distance between the particles __________.

 Made a start 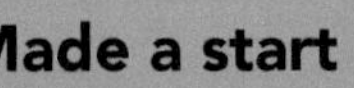  Feeling confident 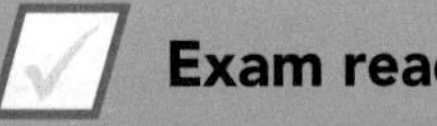 Exam ready

Properties of ionic compounds

You can use the structure and type of bonding in an ionic compound to determine its properties.

Properties of ionic compounds

Go to pages 89 and 90 to revise ionic bonding and the structure of ionic compounds.

Structure	giant lattices
Melting point	generally high
Boiling point	generally high
Electrical conductivity	good conductors when molten or dissolved in water
Solubility in water	generally soluble

Ionic compounds have high melting and boiling points because a large amount of energy is required to break the strong electrostatic forces that hold the oppositely charged ions together in all directions within the giant lattice structure.
Go to page 93 for more about state changes.

Ionic compounds can conduct electricity when melted (molten) or dissolved in water (aqueous) because the ions are free to move, allowing charge to flow.

Worked example — Grade 3

Ionic compounds, such as sodium chloride, cannot conduct electricity when solid. Complete the sentences. Use words from the box. **[4 marks]**

weak	ions	strong	fixed	move

To conduct electricity, ions need to be free to move allowing the charge to flow. When solid, sodium ions and chloride ions are in fixed positions, held by strong ionic bonds, and so cannot conduct electricity.

Exam focus

In your exam, you will only need to know about the structure of sodium chloride. However, you may be asked to apply your knowledge about this structure to explain the properties of other ionic compounds.

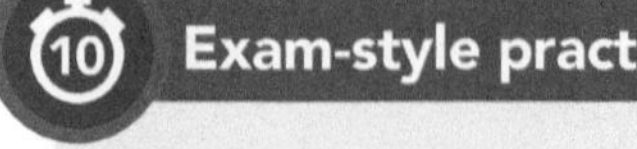

Exam-style practice — Grade 3

1 Ionic compounds have common properties. Complete the sentences. Use words from the box. You can use words more than once. **[3 marks]**

low	high	soluble	conduct

Ionic compounds have ________ melting points and ________ boiling points.

They ________ electricity when molten.

2 Magnesium oxide has a similar structure to sodium chloride. Use your understanding of ionic compounds to answer the following questions about magnesium oxide.

(a) Describe the structure of magnesium oxide. You may use a diagram. **[2 marks]**

(b) Give **one** reason that explains why magnesium oxide can conduct electricity when molten. **[1 mark]**

(c) Give **one** reason that explains why magnesium oxide has a high melting point. **[2 marks]**

 Made a start  Feeling confident  Exam ready

Properties of small molecules

Small molecules, such as carbon dioxide and water, consist of two or three atoms bonded together. You need to use your knowledge of forces and bonding to predict the properties of small molecules.

Structure and properties of small molecules

Structure	Two or three atoms joined together by strong covalent bonds as shown in **Figure 1**	Between molecules are weak intermolecular forces. The intermolecular forces increase with the size of the molecules, so larger molecules have greater intermolecular forces.
Melting point	Generally low	Small molecules are usually liquids or gases at room temperature. This is because the weak intermolecular forces need little energy to break.
Boiling point	Generally low	Larger molecules have higher melting and boiling points because there are greater intermolecular forces to overcome.
Electrical conductivity	Do not conduct electricity	There are no charged particles or free electrons to carry an electrical current.

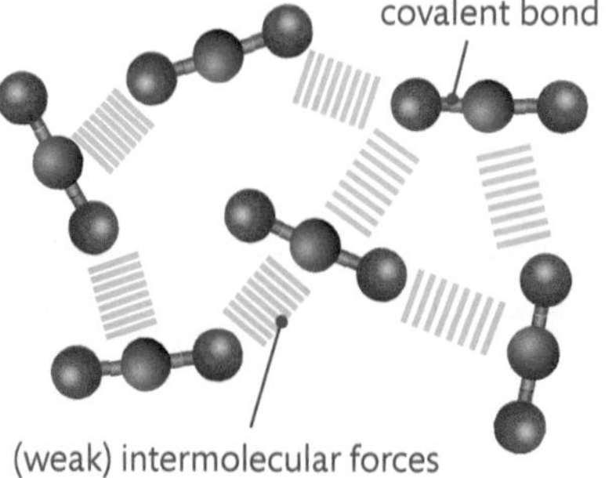

Figure 1 Carbon dioxide is a simple covalent molecule.

Worked example — Grade 5

1 Chlorine, Cl_2, is a small, covalently bonded molecule with a relatively low boiling point (−34 °C). Explain this fact in terms of structure and intermolecular forces. **[3 marks]**

Only the intermolecular forces between the Cl_2 molecules need to be overcome to boil chlorine, not the strong covalent bonds between the atoms.

Intermolecular forces between small molecules are very weak, so only a small amount of energy is needed to overcome them.

2 **Figure 2** shows the molecular structures of two alkane molecules, methane and pentane.

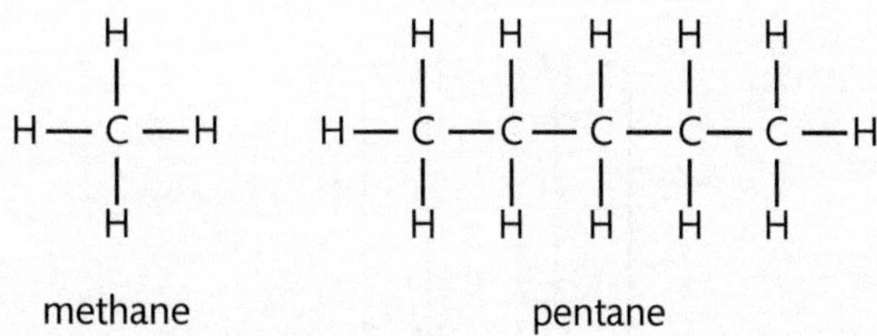

Figure 2

Using ideas about intermolecular forces, explain which alkane has the higher boiling point. **[2 marks]**

Intermolecular forces increase with the size of molecules. As pentane has larger molecules it will have a higher boiling point.

Exam-style practice — Grade 5

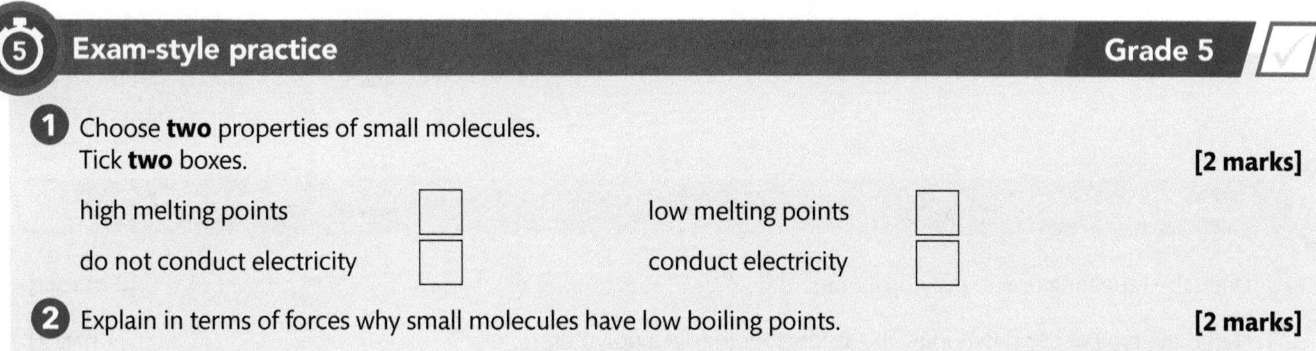

1 Choose **two** properties of small molecules.
Tick **two** boxes. **[2 marks]**

- high melting points ☐
- low melting points ☐
- do not conduct electricity ☐
- conduct electricity ☐

2 Explain in terms of forces why small molecules have low boiling points. **[2 marks]**

Polymers

You need to be able to identify polymers and describe their structure and bonding.

Polymers

Polymers are very large molecules. The atoms in a polymer molecule are joined together by strong covalent bonds in long chains. There are variable numbers of atoms in the chains of a particular polymer. One example of a polymer is poly(ethene).

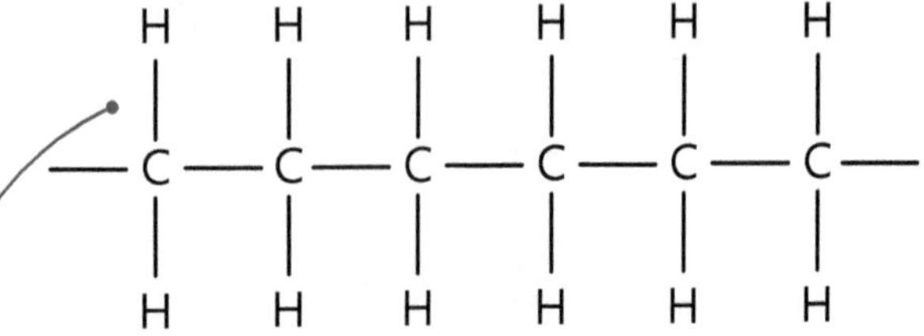

Figure 1 Part of a poly(ethene) molecule

Go to page 91 for more about covalent bonds.

The intermolecular forces between polymer molecules are strong compared to the intermolecular forces between small molecules, so polymers melt at higher temperatures. Polymers are solids at room temperature.

Repeating unit

Polymer molecules consist of lots of identical, repeating units in a chain.

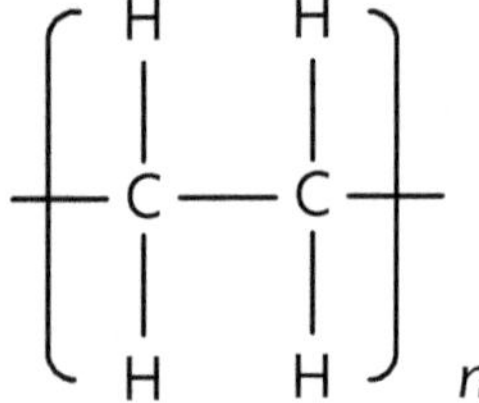

Figure 2 The repeating unit of poly(ethene)

The word poly means 'many' so poly(ethene) is made from many ethene molecules joined together.

A repeating unit will always include two of the carbon atoms joined together in the chain and any other atoms attached to the carbon atoms (that are not part of the carbon chain).

Worked example — Grade 5

1. **Figure 3** shows the structure of the polymer poly(propene).

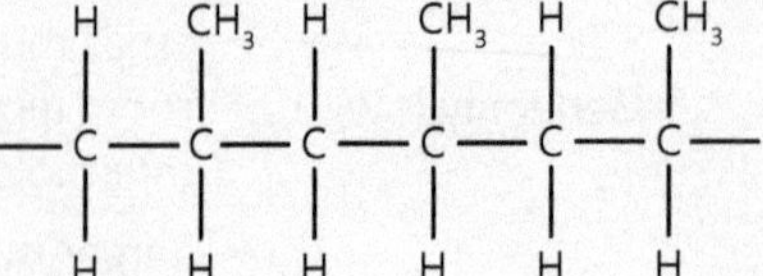

Figure 3

Use **Figure 3** to draw the repeating unit of poly(propene). **[2 marks]**

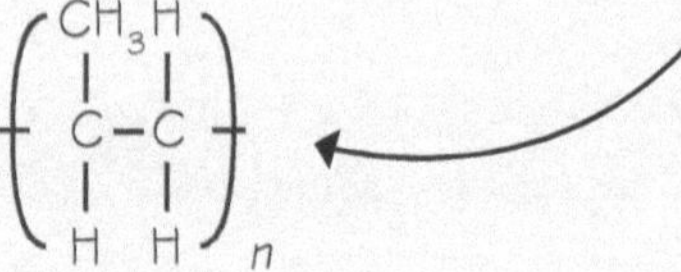

2. Polymers are usually solids and not liquids at room temperature. Suggest why. **[1 mark]**

Because they have relatively strong intermolecular forces between the molecules

3. **Figure 4** shows the repeating unit of poly(butene). Explain how you can tell that **Figure 4** represents a polymer. **[3 marks]**

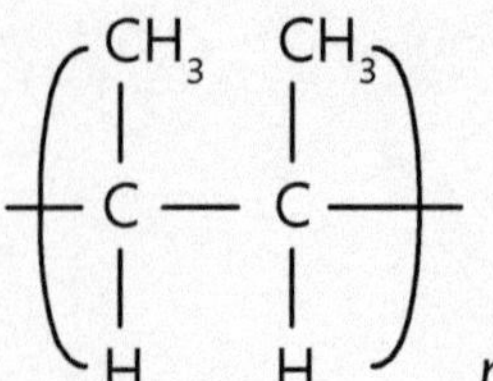

Figure 4

Polymers are made from many smaller molecules joined together to form very large molecules. Because polymer molecules are so large, they are shown as repeating units in large brackets rather than the whole molecule. The *n* shows it repeats *n* times.

Exam-style practice — Grade 4

1. Draw the repeating unit of poly(propene). **[2 marks]**
2. Name the type of bond that joins the atoms together in a polymer molecule. **[1 mark]**

 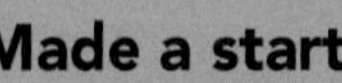 Made a start  Feeling confident  Exam ready

Giant covalent structures

You need to be able to recognise a giant covalent structure from a diagram that shows its structure and bonding.

Three types of giant covalent structure

Giant covalent structures are covalently bonded solids. They contain many atoms. The atoms are usually arranged in lattices. Examples of giant covalent structures include graphite, diamond and silicon dioxide.

Each carbon atom in graphite forms three covalent bonds. Each carbon atom in diamond forms four covalent bonds. Silicon dioxide has a similar structure to diamond, but it contains silicon and oxygen atoms instead of carbon.

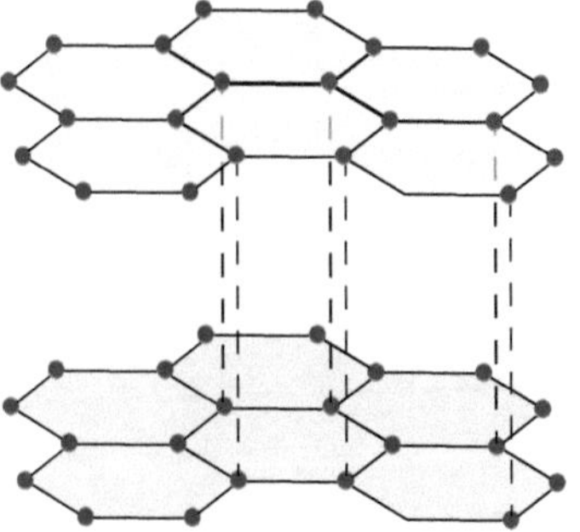

Figure 1 Graphite (page 101)

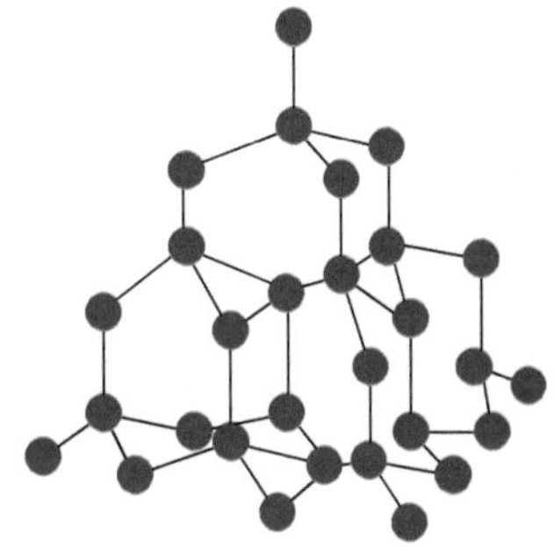

Figure 2 Diamond (page 100)

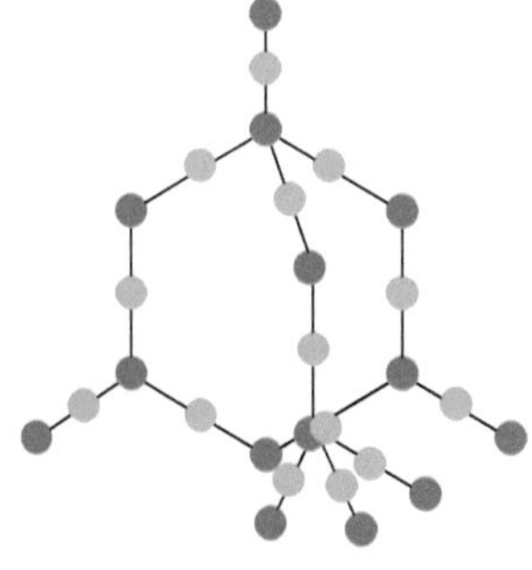

Figure 3 Silicon dioxide (silica)

Properties of giant covalent structures

Structure	Many atoms arranged in lattices and joined by strong covalent bonds
Melting point	Generally very high
Boiling point	Generally very high
Electrical conductivity	Some giant covalent structures can conduct electricity (for example, graphite) and others cannot (for example, diamond and silica)

A lot of energy is required to break the many strong covalent bonds.

Larger molecules have higher melting and boiling points because there are greater intermolecular forces to overcome.

Electrical conductivity depends on whether there are charged particles that are free to move. Graphite contains charged particles, so can conduct electricity. This is because each carbon atom has only three covalent bonds.

Worked example — Grade 5

Figures 1 and **2** show the structures of two forms of carbon. Use **Figures 1** and **2** and your knowledge of structure and bonding to give reasons why:

(a) graphite is very soft **[2 marks]**

The layers of graphite can break off easily as they are not bonded together.

(b) diamond is very hard. **[2 marks]**

The atoms in diamond are bonded together in a three-dimensional structure, so the structure is harder to break.

Graphite is soft as the layers can slide. This is because they are only held together by weak forces of attraction.

All the carbon atoms in diamond are held together by strong covalent bonds, which require a large amount of energy to break.

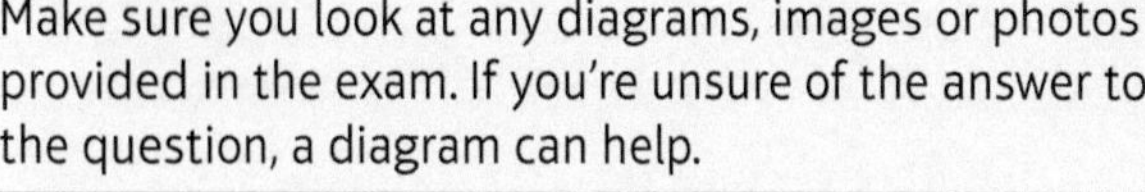

Exam focus

Make sure you look at any diagrams, images or photos provided in the exam. If you're unsure of the answer to the question, a diagram can help.

Exam-style practice — Grade 5

1. Give the number of bonds each carbon atom forms in graphite. **[1 mark]**
2. Give the number of bonds each carbon atom forms in diamond. **[1 mark]**
3. Name the type of bonding that occurs in diamond and graphite. **[1 mark]**
4. **Figure 3** shows the structure of silicon dioxide, SiO_2.
   (a) Name the type of structure formed by silicon dioxide. **[1 mark]**
   (b) Explain why silicon dioxide has a very high melting point. **[2 marks]**

 Made a start  Feeling confident 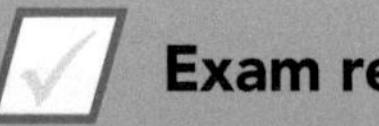 Exam ready

Properties of metals and alloys

You need to know how the properties of metals are linked to their bonding and structure.

Properties of metals

Metals form giant structures in which electrons in the outer shells of the metal atoms are free to move. This gives them the following properties. Go to page 92 to revise the structure of metals.

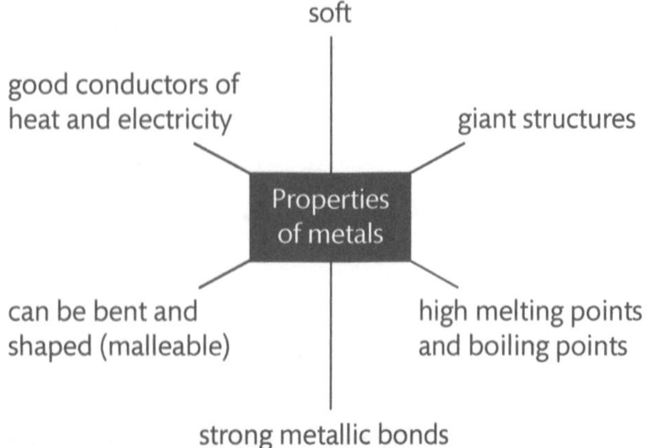

Figure 1 The atoms in a metal are arranged in layers; the layers can slip, which allows metals to be bent and shaped.

Properties of alloys

An alloy is a mixture of two or more elements. At least one element is a metal. Different metals and elements are mixed together to form a material with specific properties, such as high strength.

The strength of an alloy is based on its structure. Each element in the alloy has a different-sized atom. The different sizes of the atoms distort the structure of the layers and so prevent the layers sliding over each other when a force is applied.

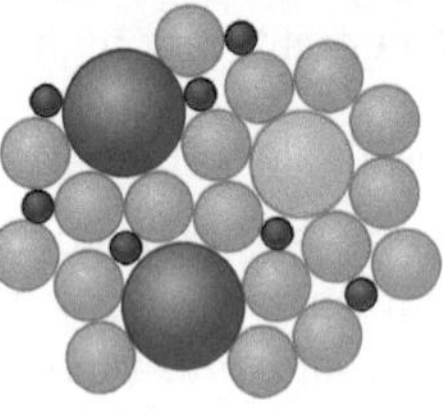

Figure 2 Alloys are harder than metals because they have different elements mixed in with the metal.

Worked example — Grade 5

(a) Describe how the structure of an alloy is different from the structure of a pure metal. **[2 marks]**

A pure metal contains atoms of only one element. All the atoms are the same size and are arranged in regular layers. An alloy is a mixture of two or more elements. At least one element is a metal. Each element in the alloy has different-sized atoms, so the layers in the alloy are distorted.

(b) Explain how the structure of an alloy makes it harder than a pure metal. **[2 marks]**

The layers in alloys are distorted by the different sizes of atoms. This means the layers cannot slide over each other when a force is applied.

Exam focus

Sometimes it is easier to answer this type of question with diagrams, as long as they are correctly labelled.

Be careful with use of language – alloys are **mixtures** not **compounds**.

Metals are malleable because their atoms are in layers which can slide easily over each other; this makes them easy to bend and shape. This is not the case for the distorted layers in alloys.

Exam-style practice — Grade 5

This question is about alloys.

(a) Describe what is meant by an 'alloy'. **[1 mark]**

(b) Alloys are often stronger than pure metals. Give a reason why. **[1 mark]**

Made a start   Feeling confident   Exam ready

Metals as conductors

You need to be able to explain the electrical and thermal conductivity of metals.

Electrons and conductivity

Metals are good conductors of both heat and electricity because they have delocalised electrons within their metallic structure.

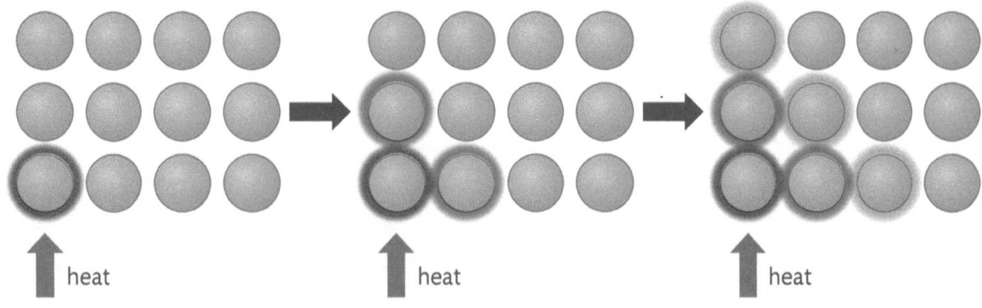

Figure 1 When heat is applied to one part of a metal, the metal ions vibrate more vigorously, transferring thermal energy as they collide with neighbouring particles. Metals have many free electrons, which move around randomly. These also transfer heat from one part of the metal to another.

Figure 2 Copper is used for electrical wiring because it has very good electrical conductivity.

Worked example — Grade 5

1. Iron is a metal. Explain why iron is a good electrical conductor. **[2 marks]**

The electrons in the outer shell are delocalised, so they are free to move and carry a current.

Remember, it is only the electrons in the outer shell (highest energy level) that are free to move throughout the metallic structure.

2. Explain how thermal energy is transferred along a copper rod. **[4 marks]**

Delocalised electrons gain energy and move quickly through the metal. When the electrons collide with other electrons, or metal atoms, thermal energy is transferred. Metal ions also vibrate more vigorously and transfer thermal energy to neighbouring particles when they collide.

Although thermal energy, and electrical charge, are transferred by metal ions, it is the presence of free electrons within a metal that enables them to be such efficient conductors.

Exam-style practice — Grade 5

1. Give the term used to describe a material that allows energy transfer to take place within the material. **[1 mark]**
2. Give **one** reason why metals are better thermal conductors than non-metals. **[1 mark]**
3. Describe how thermal energy is transferred through a metal. **[3 marks]**

 Made a start  Feeling confident  Exam ready

Diamond

Diamond is a rare and expensive form of carbon. You need to know the properties of diamond, and how they can be explained in terms of structure and bonding.

Structure of diamond

The unique structure and properties of carbon make it suitable for many different uses.

Diamond has a giant covalent structure, consisting of carbon atoms held in a regular lattice.
Each carbon atom is bonded to four other carbon atoms.
There are strong covalent bonds between each of the atoms.

Figure 1 Molecular structure of diamond

Properties and uses of diamond

The properties of diamond, such as high melting point, are related to its giant covalent structure.

State at room temperature	solid
Melting and boiling points	very high
Hardness	very hard
Electrical conductivity	does not conduct
Appearance at room temperature	transparent

There are strong covalent bonds between carbon atoms in diamond. Each carbon atom forms four bonds and all of the bonds must be broken to melt diamond. A large amount of energy is required to break the large number of strong covalent bonds. Therefore diamond has a very high melting point.

Diamond cannot conduct electricity as all of the outer electrons are involved in covalent bonding, meaning there are no charged particles free to move.

Worked example — Grade 3

1. Explain why diamond has a high melting point. **[2 marks]**

There are many strong covalent bonds which must be broken.

2. The properties of diamond make it suitable to be used in cutting tools. Which **two** properties of diamond make it suitable for this purpose? Tick **two** boxes. **[2 marks]**

- [x] hard
- [x] high melting point
- [ ] high boiling point
- [ ] transparent

Although all of the properties listed are related to diamond, only the properties that make it suitable for use in cutting tools must be identified.

Exam focus

In the exam, you need to be able to explain the properties of diamond in terms of its structure and bonding.

Exam-style practice — Grade 4

1. Name the type of structure formed by diamond. **[1 mark]**
2. Diamond is formed from a single element. Name this element. **[1 mark]**
3. Give the number of bonds each atom forms in diamond. **[1 mark]**
4. Diamonds have many uses related to their properties.
   (a) Give **one** reason why diamonds are used in jewellery. **[1 mark]**
   (b) Give **one** reason why diamond is not used in electrical circuits. **[1 mark]**

 Made a start  Feeling confident  Exam ready

Graphite

Graphite is another form of carbon. It is a non-metal but can conduct electricity due to its structure. You need to know about the properties of graphite and how they can be explained in terms of structure and bonding.

5 Structure of graphite

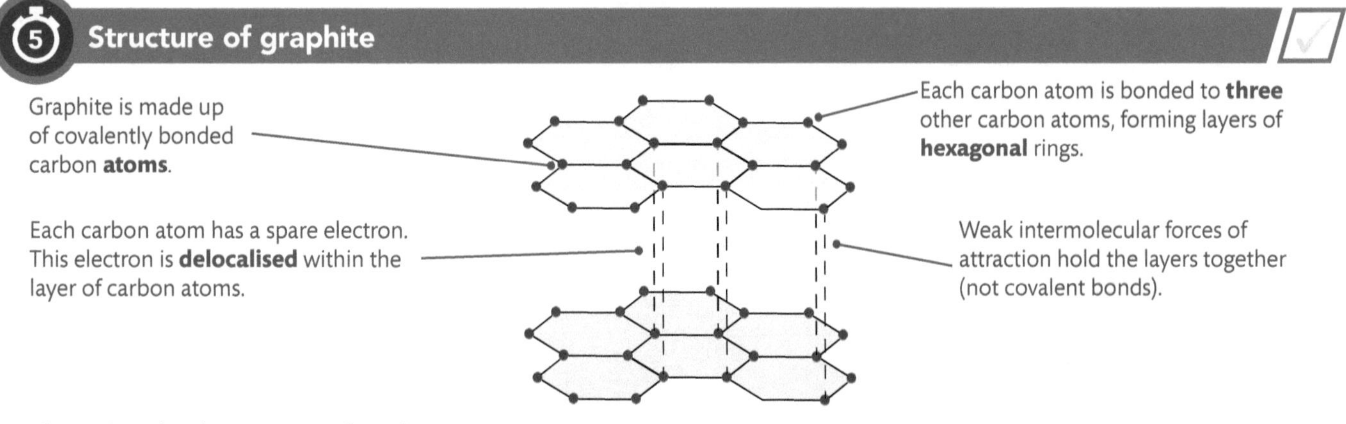

Graphite is made up of covalently bonded carbon **atoms**.
Each carbon atom is bonded to **three** other carbon atoms, forming layers of **hexagonal** rings.
Each carbon atom has a spare electron. This electron is **delocalised** within the layer of carbon atoms.
Weak intermolecular forces of attraction hold the layers together (not covalent bonds).

Figure 1 Molecular structure of graphite

5 Properties and uses of graphite

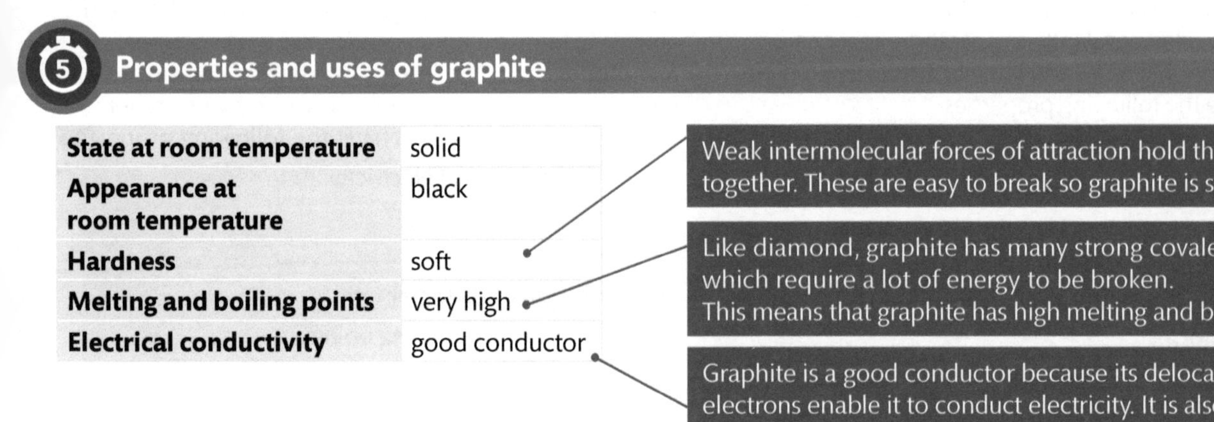

Property	
State at room temperature	solid
Appearance at room temperature	black
Hardness	soft
Melting and boiling points	very high
Electrical conductivity	good conductor

5 Worked example — Grade 5

Use your knowledge and understanding of the structure of graphite to suggest why graphite can be used:

(a) as an electrical conductor **[2 marks]**

Graphite is a good conductor of electricity as there are delocalised electrons free to move within its structure.

(b) as the 'lead' in a pencil. **[3 marks]**

Graphite is made of layers of carbon atoms. The layers are held together by weak forces of attraction. The layers can easily slide over each other. When graphite is moved over a piece of paper, a layer can be rubbed off, marking the paper.

10 Exam-style practice — Grade 3

(a) Graphite can be used as electrodes in electrolysis. Which **two** properties make graphite suitable for this purpose?
Tick **two** boxes. **[2 marks]**

- high melting point ☐
- conducts thermal energy ☐
- soft ☐
- conducts electricity ☐

(b) Complete the following statement:
Each carbon atom in graphite is joined to three other carbon atoms by ________ bonds. **[1 mark]**

(c) Why is graphite slippery and soft?
Tick **one** box. **[1 mark]**

- It is made of layers. ☐
- It is an ionic compound. ☐
- It is made of small molecules. ☐

Graphene and fullerenes

Graphene and fullerenes are carbon structures based on covalently bonded rings of carbon atoms. You need to know about the structure and properties of graphene and fullerenes and how they relate to their uses.

Graphene

Structure and properties

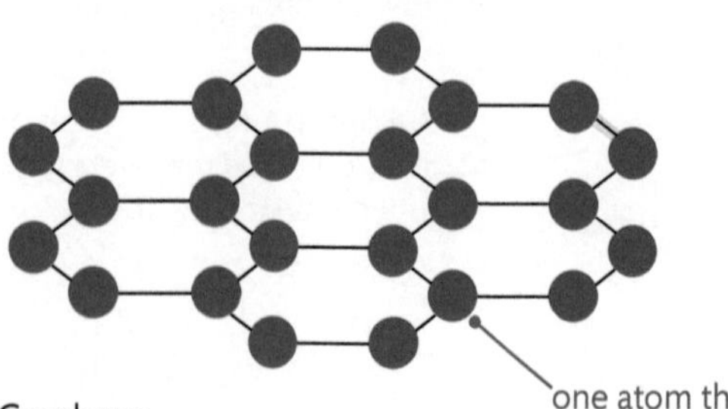

Figure 1 Graphene

Graphene is a single layer of graphite formed from carbon atoms, each bonded covalently to only three other carbon atoms in a hexagonal ring arrangement. This arrangement gives graphene the following properties:

- good conductor of electricity
- strong
- lightweight
- flexible
- transparent, as only one atom thick.

Uses of graphene

Potential uses of graphene include: display screens, electric circuits, solar cells. It can also be used in medical, chemical and industrial processes. Graphene is a relatively recent discovery and scientists are learning more about its uses each day.

Worked example Grade 5

(a) Describe the properties of graphene that make it suitable for use in flexible touch screens. **[2 marks]**

It is almost transparent and conducts electricity.

You could also say it is flexible.

(b) Explain why graphene shows the properties you gave in **(a)**. **[2 marks]**

1. Graphene is transparent because its layers are only one atom thick.

2. Graphene conducts electricity because graphene bonds with three other carbon atoms and the fourth electron pair are non-bonding and are free to move.

Use scientific terminology to show your understanding.

Graphene is very flexible (and strong) because it contains many covalent bonds.

Fullerenes

Structure and properties

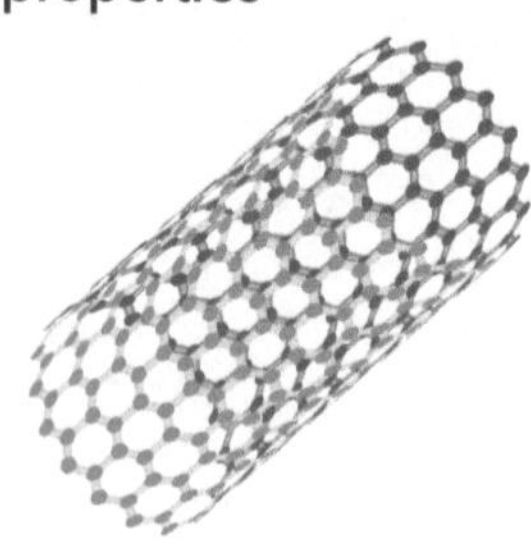

Figure 2 Fullerene

Fullerenes are hollow cages or tubes made of carbon atoms. Cylindrical fullerenes (**carbon nanotubes**) form tubes based on hexagonal rings of carbon. Fullerenes may also include rings with five or seven carbon atoms. Fullerenes have the following properties:

- good conductor of electricity
- strong
- high tensile strength
- high length to diameter ratio
- high melting and boiling points.

Uses of fullerenes

Fullerenes may be used for transporting drugs within the body because of their hollow structure.

The first fullerene to be discovered was **buckminsterfullerene**, a sphere containing 60 carbon atoms.

Fullerenes are useful for nanotechnology, electronics and in drug delivery systems for fighting cancers. Tube fullerenes (nanotubes) are used for reinforcing structures, for example tennis racket frames, as they are very light but very strong.

Exam-style practice Grade 5

1. Name the element common to diamond, graphite, fullerenes and graphene. **[1 mark]**
2. Give **two** similarities and **one** difference between the structure of carbon nanotubes and graphite. **[3 marks]**

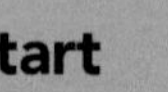 Made a start  Feeling confident  Exam ready

Conservation of mass

The law of conservation of mass enables scientists to make predictions about chemical reactions before carrying them out.

Conservation of mass and balanced chemical equations

You need to know the law of conservation of mass:

> In a closed system, the mass of the products equals the mass of the reactants.

This means that no atoms are lost or made during a chemical reaction – only their arrangement changes. For example, hydrogen and oxygen react to form water (**Figure 1**). The total number of hydrogen and oxygen atoms is unchanged in the reaction. There are four hydrogen atoms and two oxygen atoms before the arrow (reactants) and after the arrow (products).

To be able to measure the conservation of mass, the reaction must take place in a **closed system** where none of the reactants or products can escape.

You can write the law as an equation and use it to find missing masses in chemical reactions:

mass of A + mass of B → mass of AB

total mass of reactants = total mass of products

The law of conservation of mass applies to changes of state (page 93). This includes sublimation. **Sublimation** is the process by which a solid turns directly into a gas.

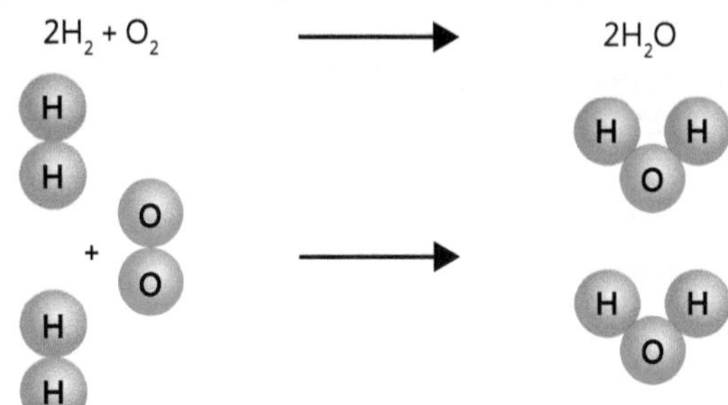

Figure 1 Hydrogen reacts with oxygen to form water in a balanced chemical equation.

Worked example

Grade 5

1 112 g of iron reacts with oxygen to produce 160 g of iron oxide. Calculate the mass of oxygen used in this reaction. **[2 marks]**

iron + oxygen → iron oxide

112 g + ? = 160 g

160 – 112 = 48 g of oxygen

2 Magnesium and chlorine react to produce magnesium chloride in the following reaction.

$Mg + Cl_2 \rightarrow MgCl_2$

Show that mass is conserved in this reaction.

(Relative masses: $Mg = 24$, $Cl_2 = 71$, $MgCl_2 = 95$) **[3 marks]**

$Mg + Cl_2 \rightarrow MgCl_2$

$24 + 71 \rightarrow 95$

$95 \rightarrow 95$

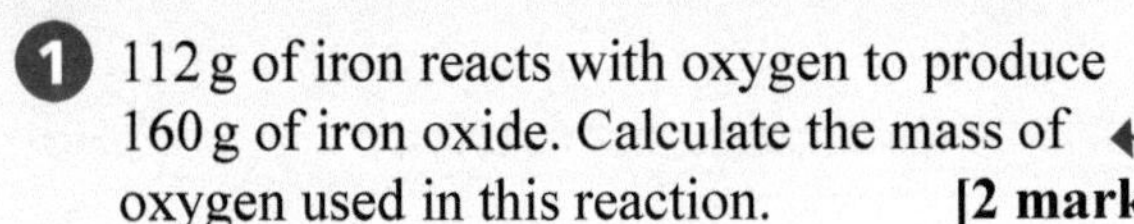

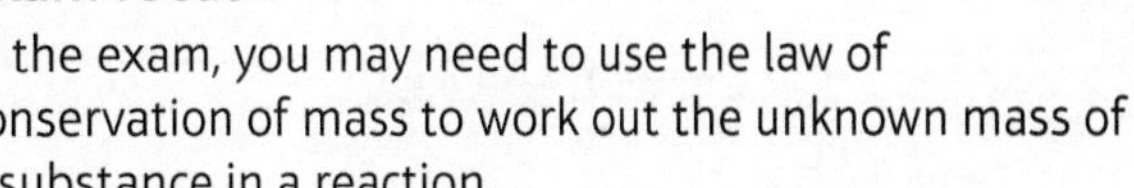

Exam focus

In the exam, you may need to use the law of conservation of mass to work out the unknown mass of a substance in a reaction.

1. Write the word equation for the reaction.
2. Write the masses provided in the question under the correct substances.
3. Rearrange the masses to calculate the missing mass. Don't forget to include units in your answer.

You can show conservation of mass by adding up the relative atomic masses (see pages 80 and 104) of the atoms on either side of a balanced symbol equation. The total mass of the atoms on the left-hand side (the reactants) always equals the total mass of the atoms on the right-hand side, in a balanced equation.

Exam-style practice

Grade 4

1 When 5 g of iodine crystals are heated, they sublime completely to form iodine vapour. Give the mass of iodine vapour formed. **[1 mark]**

2 **(a)** When heated, magnesium carbonate thermally decomposes, producing magnesium oxide and carbon dioxide. Write the word equation for this reaction. **[1 mark]**

(b) When 84 g of magnesium carbonate is heated, 40 g of magnesium oxide is produced. Calculate the mass of carbon dioxide produced in the reaction. **[2 marks]**

Relative formula mass

The relative formula mass of a compound is found by adding together the relative atomic masses of all the atoms in the compound.

5 Relative formula mass

Relative formula mass (M_r) is the sum of the relative atomic masses of all the atoms in a compound. For example, to find the M_r of sodium hydroxide (NaOH), you add together the A_r values of all the atoms in its formula:

A_r of Na is 23

A_r of O is 16

A_r of H is 1

so the M_r of NaOH is 23 + 16 + 1 = 40.

In a balanced equation, the sum of the M_r of the reactants is equal to the sum of the M_r of the products.

10 Worked example — Grade 4

1 Calculate the relative formula mass of carbon dioxide. **[2 marks]**

$CO_2 = C + (2 \times O)$
$= 12 + (2 \times 16)$
$= 44$

Go to page 80 to revise relative atomic mass.

Look at the periodic table to find the relative atomic mass of each atom.

The relative formula mass has no units.

2 The balanced equation below shows the reaction which takes place when calcium reacts with chlorine.

$$Ca + Cl_2 \rightarrow CaCl_2$$

Relative atomic masses (A_r): Cl = 35.5; Ca = 40

(a) Calculate the relative formula mass of the product calcium chloride. **[2 marks]**

$CaCl_2 = Ca + 2 \times Cl$
$= 40 + (2 \times 35.5)$
$= 111$

Remember the products are the substances made during the reaction and appear to the right of the arrow.

(b) In a reaction, how does the relative formula mass of the reactants compare to that of the products? **[1 mark]**

The sum of the relative formula masses of all the reactants is the same as the sum of the relative formula masses of all the products.

In a balanced chemical equation, the sum of the relative formula masses of the reactants in the quantities shown equals the sum of the relative formula masses of the products in the quantities shown.

10 Exam-style practice — Grade 5

1 Calculate the relative formula masses of the following substances. (Relative atomic masses: H = 1, N = 14, O = 16)

(a) O_2 **[1 mark]**

(b) H_2O **[1 mark]**

(c) NH_3 **[1 mark]**

(d) NH_4NO_3 **[1 mark]**

2 Calculate the relative formula mass of aluminium sulfate. The formula for aluminium sulfate is $Al_2(SO_4)_3$.
(A_r values: Al = 27; S = 32; O = 16) **[2 marks]**

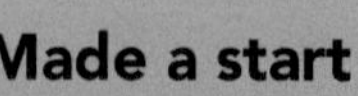

Made a start

Feeling confident

Exam ready

Balancing equations

You need to be able to balance a chemical equation given the masses of the reactants and the products, using the law of conservation of mass.

Balancing equations

Chemical reactions can be represented by balanced symbol equations. In a balanced chemical equation, there must always be the same number of each element on either side of the arrow. This is because no atoms are lost or made in a chemical reaction.

Chemical equations can only be balanced by putting multipliers in front of the formulae of elements or compounds. You cannot change the formulae of elements or compounds to balance an equation.

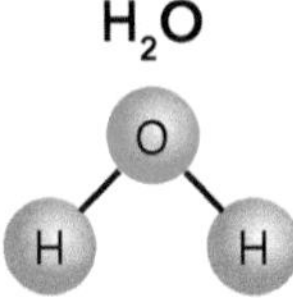

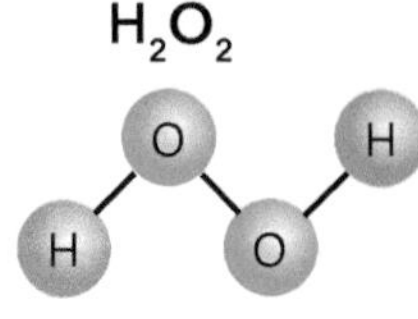

Figure 1 H_2O is a molecule with one oxygen atom and two hydrogen atoms. Hydrogen peroxide, H_2O_2 has two hydrogen atoms and two oxygen atoms.

If you tried to balance an equation by adding a 2 to the end of the formula for water, you would end up with a new substance – hydrogen peroxide H_2O_2.

Worked example — Grade 5

Balance the following equations.

Symbol equations show the balanced chemical formulae of reactants and products. Word equations show names of the reactants and products but are not balanced.

(a) $CH_4 + \underline{2}O_2 \rightarrow CO_2 + \underline{2}H_2O$ **[1 mark]**

Carbon atoms: 1 → 1

Oxygen atoms: 2 → 3

Hydrogen atoms: 4 → 2

Work out how many atoms of each element are present on each side of the equation.

Adding a 2 before H_2O balances the hydrogen atoms. There are now 4 oxygen atoms on the right side of the reaction and 2 on the left. Adding a 2 before O_2 balances the oxygen atoms.

(b) $\underline{2}Na + \underline{2}H_2O \rightarrow \underline{2}NaOH + H_2$ **[1 mark]**

Oxygen atoms: 1 → 1

Hydrogen atoms: 2 → 3

Sodium atoms: 1 → 1

- There is one more hydrogen atom on the right than on the left, so increase the number of water molecules to two.
- Now there is more hydrogen on the left, so double the sodium hydroxide to give four H atoms on each side.
- You need to double the sodium atoms on the left to give two on each side.
- Finally, check that the number of oxygen atoms is balanced.

Checking balanced equations

You can check that an equation is balanced using the law of conservation of mass. For example, aluminium reacts with bromine to create aluminium bromide in the equation:

$$2Al + 3Br_2 \rightarrow 2AlBr_3$$

To check that the equation is balanced, use relative formula mass (M_r) to find the total mass of the reactants and products.

Reactants		
2Al	2 × 27	= 54
$3Br_2$	3 × (80 × 2)	= 480
$2Al + 3Br_2$	54 + 480	= 534

Products		
$AlBr_3$	27 + (3 × 80)	= 267
$2AlBr_3$	2 × 267	= 534

The total masses for the reactants and products are equal, so the equation is balanced.

Go to page 103 for more about the law of conservation of mass.

Exam-style practice — Grade 4

1 Chemical reactions can be represented by balanced equations. Give **one** reason why a balanced chemical equation provides more useful information than a word equation. **[1 mark]**

2 Which **two** equations shown below represent balanced equations? Tick **two** boxes. **[2 marks]**

- $2Ca + Br_2 \rightarrow CaBr_2$ ☐
- $4K + O_2 \rightarrow 2K_2O$ ☐
- $NaOH + HCl \rightarrow NaCl + H_2O$ ☐
- $2Be + Cl_2 \rightarrow 2BeCl_2$ ☐

Mass changes

Some chemical reactions seem to involve a change in mass. This is usually because one of the reactants or products is a gas.

5 Change in mass

If a reactant or a product is a gas, its mass is often not included in calculations. This occurs when a reaction does not take place in a closed system. There are two possibilities:

1. A gaseous product escapes while the reaction takes place. The product mass will be lower than the reactant mass.
2. Gases from the air enter a reaction. They have not been measured with the reactants so the mass will appear to increase.

Change in mass can be calculated using the law of conservation of mass (page 103). For example, after heating 6.2 g of copper carbonate (**Figure 1**), the product (copper oxide) had a mass of 4 g. This means that 2.2 g of gas was produced and lost to the atmosphere during the reaction.

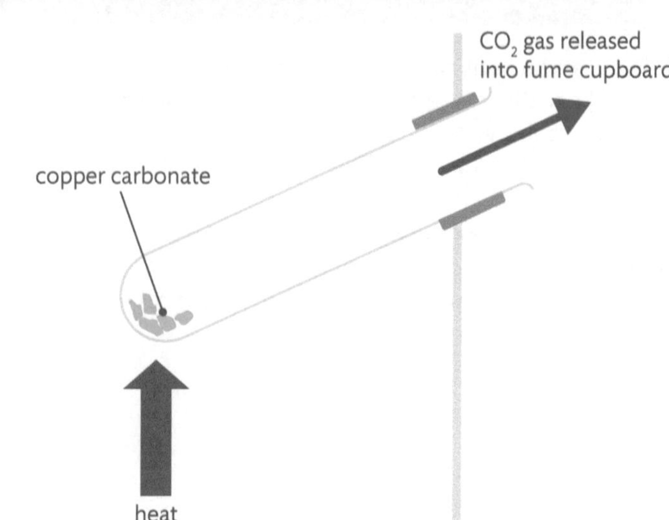

Figure 1 Heating copper carbonate will cause it to decompose and release carbon dioxide. If the gas is not collected, there will appear to be a loss in mass during the reaction.

Go to page 138 to revise the tests for different gases.

5 Worked example — Grade 4

For each of the following reactions, explain how and why the mass may appear to change during the reaction.

(a) magnesium + oxygen → magnesium oxide **[2 marks]**

The mass appears to increase because oxygen from the air is gained in the reaction.

> When a metal is heated, it may react with oxygen from the air. The mass of the magnesium oxide will be greater than the mass of the magnesium.

(b) calcium carbonate → calcium oxide + carbon dioxide **[2 marks]**

The mass appears to decrease because carbon dioxide is given off in the reaction.

> When a substance undergoes thermal decomposition, the mass of the products may appear to be less than the mass of the reactants, as the gas produced can escape, leaving only the metal oxide as the product.

> Think about the conditions required for the law of conservation of mass (page 103).

10 Exam-style practice — Grade 5

1. When heated, zinc carbonate decomposes to produce zinc oxide and carbon dioxide.
   - **(a)** Give the word equation for this reaction. **[1 mark]**
   - **(b)** A student heated 50 g of zinc carbonate in an unsealed container. After the reaction, there was only 32 g of product. Give **one** reason why. **[1 mark]**
   - **(c)** Explain how a closed system could be used to improve accuracy when measuring the mass of the products. **[2 marks]**
2. When ethanol, C_2H_5OH, burns it reacts with oxygen from the air. Carbon dioxide and water are produced.
   - **(a)** Complete the equation below to give a balanced symbol equation to show the reaction. **[2 marks]**

     $C_2H_5OH + \_O_2 \rightarrow \_CO_2 + \_H_2O$
   - **(b)** Explain why the mass appears to decrease during the reaction, when it happens in an open container. **[1 mark]**

Chemical measurements

You need to know the factors that affect the uncertainty of measurements and be able to make estimations about uncertainty.

Uncertainty of measurements

All measurements have a degree of uncertainty regardless of the **precision** and **accuracy** involved.

Precision: Measurements are precise if they are very similar to each other.

Accuracy: The accuracy of a set of results is a measure of how close they are to the true value. Accuracy of measurements can be improved by taking averages of a series of trials.

Uncertainty: There are three main factors affecting uncertainty:

- the limitation of the measuring instrument
- the skill of the experimenter taking the measurements
- changes in the environment, e.g. temperature.

Go to page 219 to revise planning practicals and choosing suitable apparatus.

Human error in measurement is not classed as a factor.

Anomalous results are results that do not fit the trend; they should be ignored when taking the mean of a set of results.

Systematic error

- If a measuring cylinder measures 9.8 cm^3 at the 10 cm^3 mark, every measurement will be out by about 0.2 cm^3.
- Taking the mean value is unlikely to give a more accurate value as each measurement will have the same error.
- The error is reproducible.

Random error

- Random errors are variable; they could fall either side of the true value.
- Taking a series of readings and then finding the mean of these results will increase the accuracy of the value.
- The error is not reproducible.

Worked example — Grade 3

A student measures the volume of gas produced in 30 seconds. The results are shown in the table below.

Trial	1	2	3
Volume of gas produced in cm^3	55.2	48.4	58.4

(a) Calculate the mean volume of gas produced by the three trials. **[1 mark]**

$$\text{mean} = \frac{(55.2 + 48.4 + 58.4)}{3} = 54.0\ cm^3$$

(b) Calculate the range of the three trials. **[1 mark]**

range = 58.4 – 48.4 = 10.0 cm^3

(c) Calculate the uncertainty of the results. **[1 mark]**

$$\text{uncertainty} = \frac{10}{2} = 5.0\ cm^3$$

the uncertainty of the mean is 54.0 ± 5.0 cm^3

Working scientifically

- To calculate the mean, add up the results for each trial and divide by how many trials there are.
- To calculate the range, find the difference between the highest and the lowest values.
- To calculate uncertainty, divide the range by two.

Exam-style practice — Grade 3

The table shows the time it takes magnesium ribbon to disappear in its reaction with dilute hydrochloric acid. **[5 marks]**

Trial number	1	2	3	4
Time taken to dissolve in s	62	65	77	68

(a) Calculate the mean time taken for the magnesium to disappear, using suitable results from the table above. **[2 marks]**

(b) Calculate the range of the results used in part **(a)**. **[1 mark]**

(c) Use your answer from part **(b)** to calculate the uncertainty of the results. **[2 marks]**

Concentrations of solutions

Many chemical reactions take place in solutions. The concentration of a solution depends on the mass of solute and the volume of solution.

Calculating concentrations

A solution is prepared by dissolving a solute (solid) in a solvent (liquid).
The concentration of a solution is how much solute is dissolved into the solvent.

Concentration can be calculated using the formula given below:

$$\text{concentration (g/dm}^3\text{)} = \frac{\text{mass (g)}}{\text{volume (dm}^3\text{)}}$$

If the mass of solute is increased but the volume of solvent stays the same, the concentration of the solution will increase.

If the volume of solvent is increased but the mass of solute stays the same, the concentration of the solution will decrease.

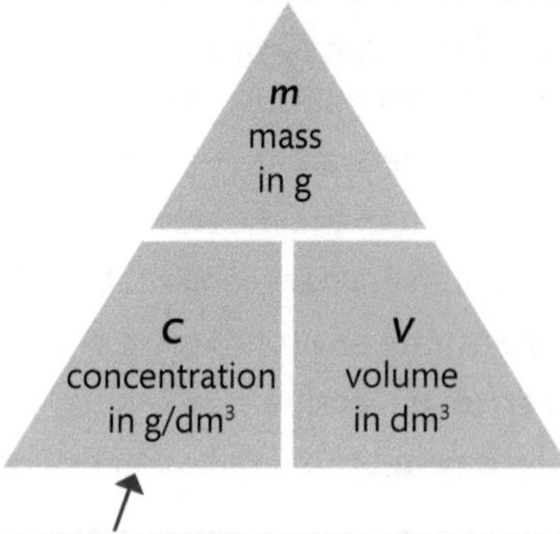

Exam focus
Use formula triangles to help you rearrange an equation, but always write the equation in an answer.

Worked example — Grade 5

1 37 g of sodium carbonate is dissolved in water to produce 4.25 dm^3 of solution. Calculate the concentration of this solution. **[2 marks]**

$$\text{concentration} = \frac{\text{mass}}{\text{volume}}$$

$$\text{concentration in g/dm}^3 = \frac{37\text{ g}}{4.25\text{ dm}^3}$$

$$= 8.705882353$$

$$= 8.7\text{ g/dm}^3$$

Give your answer to no more than the lowest number of significant figures in the values given to you.

2 Calculate the mass of solute that must be dissolved in water to produce 1.5 dm^3 of a solution with a concentration of 3 g/dm^3. **[2 marks]**

You can use the units as a clue to work out the formula. The units of concentration are g/dm^3. This tells you that concentration = mass ÷ volume.

$$\text{concentration} = \frac{\text{mass}}{\text{volume}}$$

$$3\text{ g/dm}^3 = \frac{\text{mass in g}}{1.5\text{ dm}^3}$$

$$\text{mass} = 3 \times 1.5 = 4.5\text{ g}$$

3 58 g of sodium hydroxide was dissolved in water to produce a solution with a concentration of 16.11 g/dm^3. Calculate the volume of this solution. **[2 marks]**

$$\text{concentration} = \frac{\text{mass}}{\text{volume}}$$

$$16.11\text{ g/dm}^3 = \frac{58\text{ g}}{\text{volume in dm}^3}$$

$$\text{volume} = \frac{58}{16.11}$$

$$= 3.6\text{ dm}^3$$

Remember to give the correct units.

Maths skills

You need to know how to convert units from cm^3 to dm^3 and vice versa.

$1\text{ dm}^3 = 1000\text{ cm}^3$ (multiply by 1000)

$1\text{ cm}^3 = 0.001\text{ dm}^3$ (divide by 1000)

Exam-style practice — Grade 4

1 A student dissolves 60 g of sodium chloride in 1.5 dm^3 of water.
Calculate the concentration of the solution of sodium chloride produced. **[2 marks]**

2 Calculate the mass of calcium chloride needed to produce a solution with a concentration of 10 g/dm^3 when dissolved into 5 dm^3 of water. **[3 marks]**

3 State how adding more solute to a fixed volume of solution affects the concentration of the solution produced. **[1 mark]**

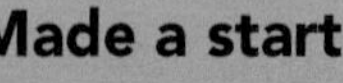
Made a start

Feeling confident

Exam ready

Metal oxides

You need to be able to state the properties of metal oxides and give equations for their formation.

Formation of metal oxides

Metal oxides are formed when a metal reacts with oxygen.

metal + oxygen → metal oxide

Metal oxides are examples of a giant ionic lattice structure. They are usually solid at room temperature. They generally have high melting and boiling points.

Naming metal oxides

When metals react to form oxides, they gain oxygen so they are **oxidised**.

- copper + oxygen → copper oxide
- calcium + oxygen → calcium oxide
- iron + oxygen → iron(III) oxide (iron present as Fe^{3+} ions)
- lead + oxygen → lead oxide

When copper oxidises it forms black copper oxide. This reacts with substances in rain and atmospheric gases to form a green layer. Many old buildings have copper roofs that have oxidised over time, which is why a lot of old buildings have green roofs.

Worked example

Grade 3

1 A student investigates magnesium oxide, a metal oxide.

(a) Name the type of bonding present in the magnesium oxide. **[1 mark]**

ionic bonding

(b) Magnesium oxide is formed when magnesium reacts with oxygen.

What type of reaction is this?

Tick **one** box. **[1 mark]**

- reduction ☐
- displacement ☐
- oxidation ☑
- decomposition ☐

(c) The equation for this reaction is:

$2Mg + O_2 \rightarrow 2MgO$

Use the equation to explain which element is oxidised. **[2 marks]**

Magnesium is oxidised because it gains oxygen.

2 When heated, powdered aluminium reacts with oxygen to form a metal oxide. Write a word equation to show this reaction. **[1 mark]**

aluminium + oxygen → aluminium oxide

When a substance gains oxygen it is called **oxidation**. If a substance loses oxygen it is called **reduction**.

The metal oxide produced is named by first giving the full name of the reacting metal and then changing oxygen to oxide.

Exam-style practice

Grade 3

Write a word equation to identify the product formed in the reaction of zinc and oxygen. **[1 mark]**

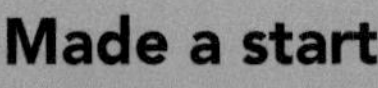

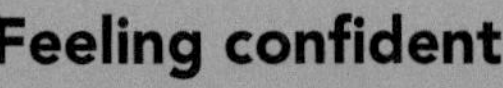

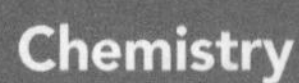

The reactivity series

Metals can be arranged in order of their reactivity. You need to understand how the reactivity of metals with water or dilute acids is related to the tendency of the metal to form its positive ion and be able to deduce an order of reactivity of metals based on experimental results.

Reactivity of metals

When metals react, they lose their outer shell of electrons to form positive ions. The more readily a metal loses its outer electrons the more reactive it is.

The reactivity series places metals in order from the most reactive to the least reactive metal. Hydrogen is often included in the reactivity series, although it isn't a metal. This is because when hydrogen reacts it loses an electron in the same way that metals do.

A more reactive metal will displace a less reactive metal from a compound of the less reactive metal.

The reactivity of metals can be compared using their reactions with water and dilute acids.

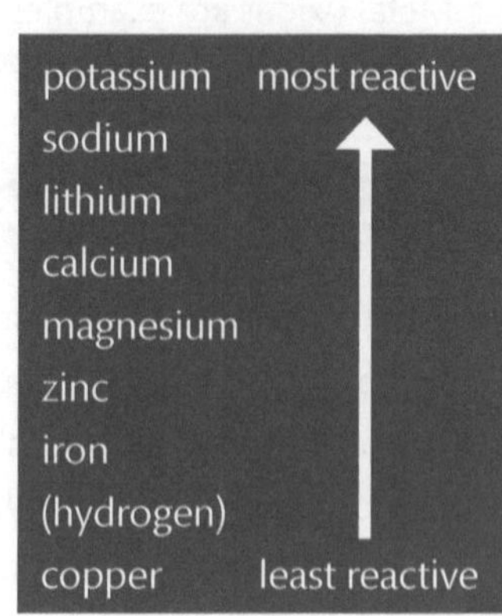

Reactions of metals with acids and water

The alkali metals, potassium, sodium and lithium, all react vigorously with cold water (see page 86). Calcium and magnesium have less vigorous reactions with water. Less reactive metals, such as zinc and iron, are further down the reactivity series because they need dilute acids to react. Copper does not react with dilute acids because it is less reactive than hydrogen. The more vigorous the reaction, the more reactive the metal.

Worked example — Grade 4

A student uses displacement reactions to investigate the reactivity of four different metals. The table shows the student's observations.

	Cu	Mg	Zn	Ag
$CuSO_4$	no reaction	**colour change**	**colour change**	no reaction
Ag_2SO_4	**colour change**	**colour change**	**colour change**	no reaction
$ZnSO_4$	no reaction	**colour change**	no reaction	no reaction
$MgSO_4$	no reaction	no reaction	no reaction	no reaction

Table 1

When given the results of reactivity experiments, you should be able to deduce the order of reactivity of the metals either by how many reactions they took part in or by how vigorous their reactions were.

(a) Use the results shown in the table to place zinc, copper and magnesium in order of reactivity. **[1 mark]**

magnesium (most reactive) zinc copper (least reactive)

(b) Describe what the results show about the reactivity of silver. **[1 mark]**

It is the least reactive of the four metals tested.

(c) Write a word equation for the reaction between magnesium and copper sulfate. **[2 marks]**

magnesium + copper sulfate → magnesium sulfate + copper

Exam-style practice — Grade 5

1. Name **one** metal that does not react with dilute acids. **[1 mark]**
2. **Figure 1** shows four metals reacting with dilute hydrochloric acid. The four metals used are magnesium, iron, copper and calcium. Use your knowledge of reactivity to identify metals **A**, **B**, **C** and **D**. **[2 marks]**
3. Explain how a metal's reactivity is determined by the tendency of the metal to form a positive ion. **[2 marks]**

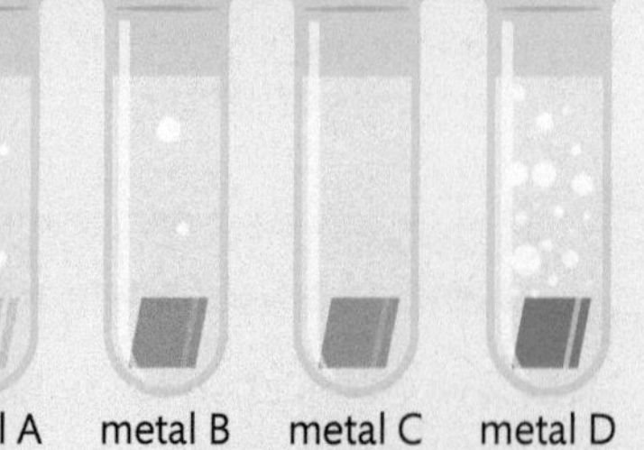

Figure 1

Made a start

Feeling confident
Exam ready

Extraction of metals and reduction

You need to know how carbon is used to extract metals from their ore. Ores are naturally occurring rocks that contain a metal or metal compound in sufficient amounts to make it worth extracting.

The reactivity series

Different methods of extraction are used depending on how reactive a metal is.
This is shown in **Figure 1**.

	Metal	
	potassium	most reactive
	sodium	
	lithium	
	calcium	
	magnesium	
must be extracted using electrolysis	aluminium	
	(carbon)	
can be extracted by heating with carbon	zinc	
can be extracted by heating with carbon	iron	
can be extracted by heating with carbon	copper	
found in pure form	gold	least reactive

Figure 1 The reactivity series

Worked example — Grade 5

1 Iron can be extracted from its oxide.

(a) Name the type of reaction involved in this process. **[1 mark]**

Reduction

> The iron loses the oxygen it is combined with and is **reduced**.

> Reduction is when oxygen is given up from a compound.

(b) Describe how oxygen can be removed from iron oxide to make iron. **[2 marks]**

Heat the iron oxide with carbon to reduce the iron and remove the oxygen.

> Only metals below carbon in the reactivity series can be extracted from their oxides using this process. As aluminium is further up the reactivity series than carbon, a different process is required.

(c) Explain why this process cannot be used to extract aluminium from its oxide. **[2 marks]**

Aluminium is above carbon in the reactivity series so carbon cannot remove oxygen from aluminium oxide.

2 The following equation is an example of a reduction reaction used to extract a metal from its ore.

$2CuO + C \rightarrow 2Cu + CO_2$

(a) Write the word equation for the reaction taking place. **[1 mark]**

copper oxide + carbon → copper + carbon dioxide

(b) Explain why this reduction reaction can take place. **[1 mark]**

Because copper is less reactive than carbon

Exam-style practice — Grade 5

1 Lead oxide reacts with carbon to form the products lead and carbon dioxide.

(a) Write a word equation to show the reduction of lead oxide using carbon. **[1 mark]**

(b) Give the name of the type of reaction occurring between carbon and oxygen. **[1 mark]**

(c) Lead oxide has the formula PbO_2. Write a balanced symbol equation for the reaction. **[2 marks]**

2 Calcium cannot be reduced from calcium oxide using carbon. Explain why. **[2 marks]**

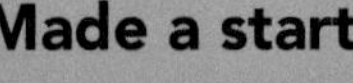
Made a start

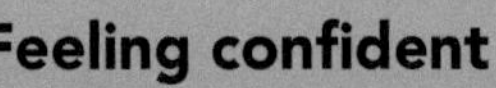
Feeling confident

Exam ready

Reactions of acids with metals

When acids and some metals react, a salt and hydrogen gas are produced. You need to know the reactions of acids with metals.

5 Reactions of metals with sulfuric acid

If the acid is sulfuric acid, the metal salt will be a metal sulfate.

$Mg + H_2SO_4 \rightarrow MgSO_4 + H_2$ $Zn + H_2SO_4 \rightarrow ZnSO_4 + H_2$ $Fe + H_2SO_4 \rightarrow FeSO_4 + H_2$

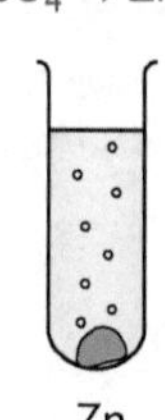

Figure 1 Reactions of dilute sulfuric acid and metals to make a metal sulfate

Metal	Salt
magnesium	magnesium sulfate
zinc	zinc sulfate
iron	iron sulfate

5 Reactions of metals with hydrochloric acid

If the acid is hydrochloric acid, the metal salt will be a metal chloride.

$Mg + 2HCl \rightarrow MgCl_2 + H_2$ $Zn + 2HCl \rightarrow ZnCl_2 + H_2$ $Fe + 2HCl \rightarrow FeCl_2 + H_2$

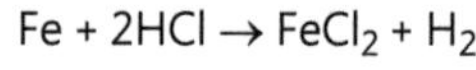

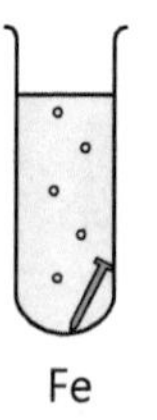

Figure 2 Reactions of dilute hydrochloric acid and metals to make a metal chloride

Metal	Salt
magnesium	magnesium chloride
zinc	zinc chloride
iron	iron chloride

5 Worked example — Grade 5

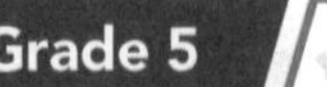

Write balanced symbol equations for the following reactions.

(a) magnesium + sulfuric acid **[1 mark]**

$Mg + H_2SO_4 \rightarrow MgSO_4 + H_2$

(b) hydrochloric acid + iron **[1 mark]**

$2HCl + Fe \rightarrow FeCl_2 + H_2$

(c) zinc + sulfuric acid **[1 mark]**

$Zn + H_2SO_4 \rightarrow ZnSO_4 + H_2$

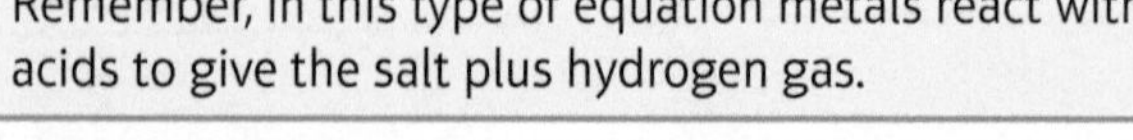

Remember, in this type of equation metals react with acids to give the salt plus hydrogen gas.

Remember the charges on the ions. The hydrogen ion has one positive charge, but iron forms Fe^{2+}, so it will form a salt with two chloride ions, Cl^-. Think carefully about how to balance the equation so that there is the same number of each type of atom on each side.

Working scientifically

When hydrogen gas is released, the reaction mixture will bubble or fizz. You can confirm that the gas is hydrogen using a lighted splint (page 138) because hydrogen is flammable in air.

2 Exam focus

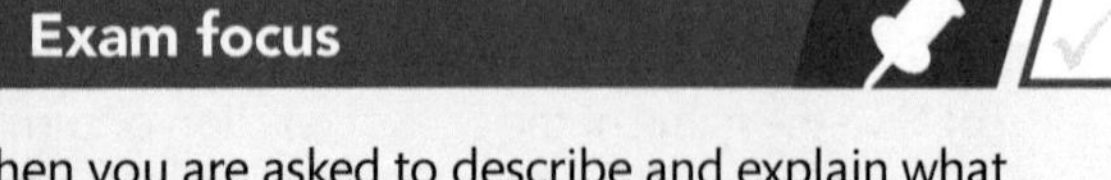

When you are asked to describe and explain what will happen in a reaction, you should state what you observe (for example, fizzing or bubbling) **and** explain why (for example, because hydrogen gas is released from the solution).

5 Exam-style practice — Grade 5

A piece of zinc metal falls into a jar of hydrochloric acid used for cleaning in a workshop.

(a) Describe and explain what would be observed. **[2 marks]**

(b) Explain any safety precautions that people in the workshop should take. **[2 marks]**

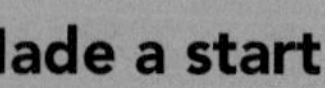

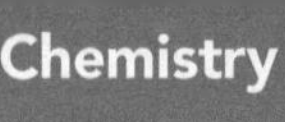

Salt production

You need to know how salts are formed and the conventions used for naming them.

Forming salts

Salts are produced by the reaction between an acid and an alkali. When an acid is neutralised by an alkali, such as a soluble metal hydroxide, or by a base, the products are always a salt and water.

acid + metal oxide → salt + water

acid + metal hydroxide → salt + water

So, magnesium hydroxide and sulfuric acid would produce a salt called magnesium sulfate (and water).

If a metal carbonate is neutralised, then carbon dioxide is also produced.

acid + metal carbonate → salt + water + carbon dioxide

If magnesium carbonate reacted with nitric acid, then magnesium nitrate would be produced (with water and carbon dioxide).

Naming salts

A salt has a name with two parts; the first part is just the name of the metal reacting.

For example, if the base is magnesium hydroxide, the first part of the name of the salt is magnesium.

The second part comes from the type of acid reacting:

Acid reacting	Second part of salt name
sulfuric	sulfate
nitric	nitrate
hydrochloric	chloride

Worked example — Grade 5

(a) Calcium oxide is added to hydrochloric acid; a neutralisation reaction occurs. Give a word equation for the reaction. **[1 mark]**

calcium oxide + hydrochloric acid → calcium chloride + water

(b) Give the balanced symbol equation for the reaction. **[2 marks]**

$CaO + 2HCl \rightarrow CaCl_2 + H_2O$

1. Identify the metal reacting. It is calcium.
2. Work out the salt name ending from the acid. The acid is hydrochloric acid, so the second part of the name of the salt is chloride.
3. Name the salt. It is calcium chloride.
4. Complete the equation.

Working scientifically

When producing a balanced symbol equation, you will need to work out the formula of the salt produced. The overall charge on a compound of the salt is zero, so any charges must be balanced.

This table shows the charges on some common ions:

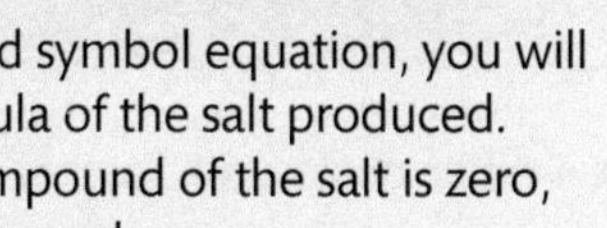

Ion	Charge
carbonate	CO_3^{2-}
sulfate	SO_4^{2-}
nitrate	NO_3^{-}
chloride	Cl^{-}

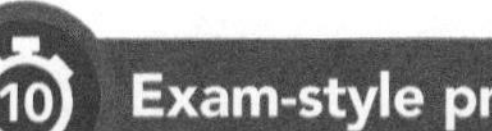

Exam-style practice — Grade 3

1. Name the salt produced in the reaction between potassium hydroxide and nitric acid. **[1 mark]**
2. Give the name of the type of reaction that produces a salt. **[1 mark]**
3. Name the acid reactant used to produce the salt copper chloride. **[1 mark]**
4. Give the formula for each of the following salts.

   (a) lithium sulfate, Li ____ **[1 mark]**

   (b) magnesium chloride, Mg ____ **[1 mark]**

   (c) calcium nitrate, Ca ____ **[2 marks]**

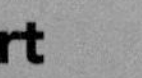
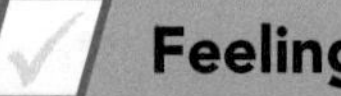

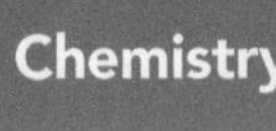

Soluble salts

You need to be able to describe the preparation of a soluble salt.

Making a soluble salt

A soluble salt can be produced by reacting an acid with solid insoluble substances, such as metals, metal oxides, hydroxides or carbonates.

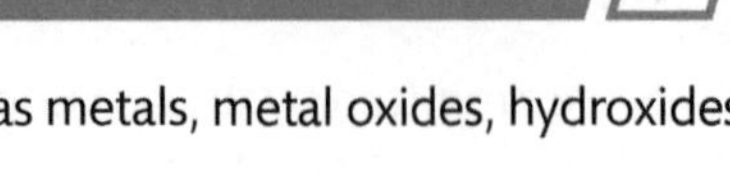

1. Add solid, e.g. metal oxide, to the acid until no more reaction takes place.

2. Filter to remove excess solid.

3. Heat gently, then leave to crystallise into a solid salt.

Working scientifically

When using a Bunsen burner you should take the following precautions:

- Wear eye protection.
- Stand at a reasonable distance away from the flame.
- Place the Bunsen burner on a heat-resistant mat.

Remember, add the solid to the acid in excess until the reaction is complete. Then remove the excess solid by filtering.

Different types of reactants

Some metals are too reactive, or not reactive enough, to produce soluble salts. This is why metal oxides, hydroxides or carbonates are used.

- Sodium chloride – sodium is too reactive, so sodium hydroxide or sodium carbonate is used instead.
- Copper chloride – copper does not react with dilute hydrochloric acid so copper oxide or copper carbonate is used instead.

Crystallisation is a separation technique used to separate solids from liquids by evaporating the solvent. See page 76 for more information on separation techniques.

Worked example — Grade 3

1. A student reacts magnesium carbonate with dilute sulfuric acid.

   Describe how the student could ensure that all of the acid has completely reacted. **[2 marks]**

   Keep adding magnesium carbonate until the fizzing stops.

2. Name the process used to produce a sample of solid salt from a solution of soluble salt. **[1 mark]**

   Crystallisation

Exam-style practice — Grade 3

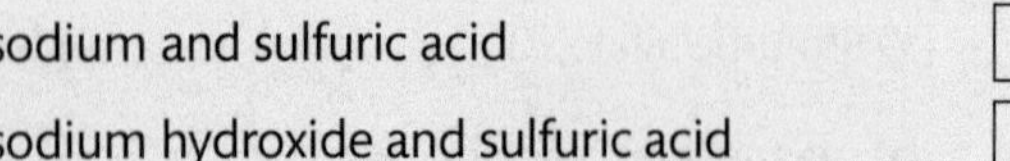

1. A soluble salt is made by reacting an excess of an insoluble base with a dilute acid. Suggest a method that could be used to remove the unreacted base. **[1 mark]**
2. Identify the reactants used to safely produce sodium sulfate. Tick **one** box. **[1 mark]**

   sodium hydroxide and hydrochloric acid ☐

   sodium and sulfuric acid ☐

   sodium hydroxide and sulfuric acid ☐
3. Name the soluble salt produced when copper oxide reacts with nitric acid. **[1 mark]**
4. Describe what is meant by the term 'soluble'. **[1 mark]**

 Made a start  Feeling confident  Exam ready

Making salts

You need to know how to prepare a sample of a pure, dry soluble salt from an insoluble oxide or carbonate.

Making a salt

1. Pour 200 cm^3 sulfuric acid into a beaker and warm.
2. Stir in copper oxide powder until no more reacts. The liquid will turn blue.

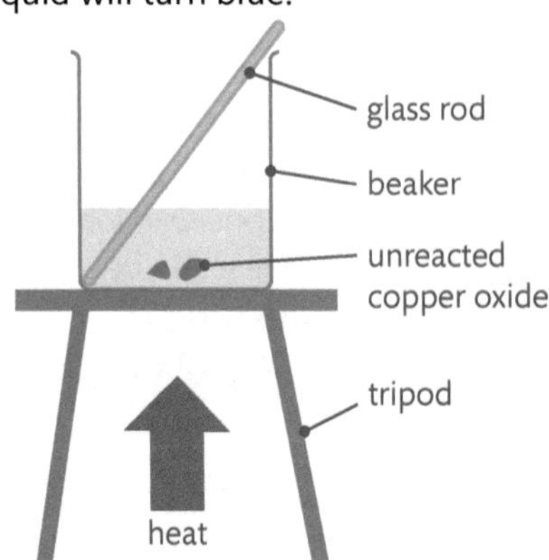

Figure 1 Adding copper oxide to sulfuric acid

3. Allow the apparatus to cool.
4. Set up the funnel and filter paper apparatus.
5. Filter the solution.

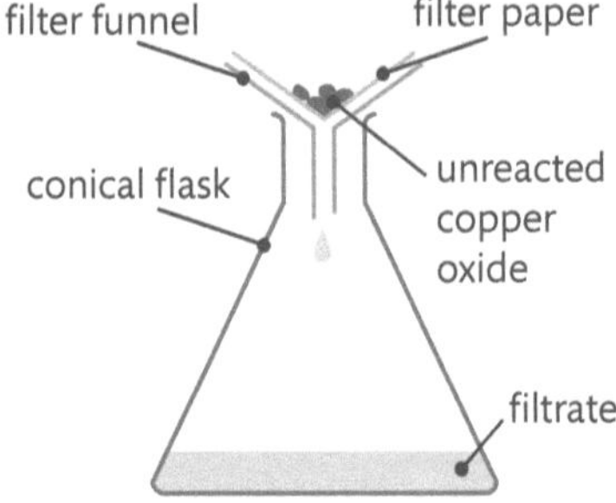

Figure 2 Filtration

6. Collect the filtrate in a conical flask.
7. Gently heat the filtrate, so that it evaporates and crystals begin to form.
8. Pour the filtrate into an evaporating dish and leave to crystallise for 24 hours.
9. Remove crystals from evaporating dish, put onto filter paper and pat dry. The crystals can then be weighed if required.

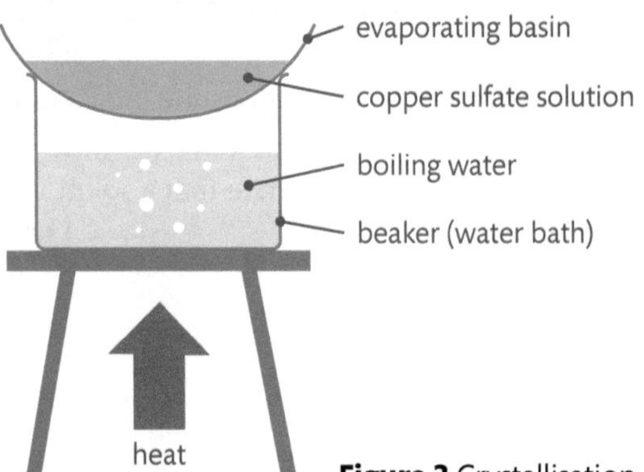

Figure 3 Crystallisation

Worked example — Grade 4

1. A salt can be made by reacting an acid and an alkali. Name this type of reaction. **[1 mark]**

Neutralisation

2. (a) Write a word equation for the reaction between copper oxide and dilute sulfuric acid. **[2 marks]**

copper oxide + sulfuric acid → copper sulfate + water

(b) Explain why the following steps are important in the production of the salt copper sulfate. **[4 marks]**

Warming the acid:

speeds up the reaction

Adding excess copper oxide:

ensures all the acid reacts

Filtering the mixture:

collects any excess copper oxide

Heating the filtrate to begin evaporation:

encourages the formation of crystals

(c) Explain how the observations for a reaction between sulfuric acid and copper carbonate would differ from the reaction between copper oxide and sulfuric acid. **[2 marks]**

The reaction with copper carbonate would bubble because carbon dioxide gas is being produced. The reaction with copper oxide would not bubble.

Describe the observation and say why it is occurring.

Exam-style practice — Grade 4

Sort the following statements into the correct order, to describe how to prepare a salt. Write numbers 1–5 in the boxes. **[2 marks]**

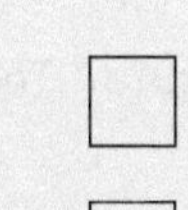

Leave to cool so more crystals will form. ☐

Heat the solution until most of the water has evaporated and crystals start to form. ☐

Warm dilute sulfuric acid and add excess zinc hydroxide. ☐

Dry the crystals obtained. ☐

Filter the solution. ☐

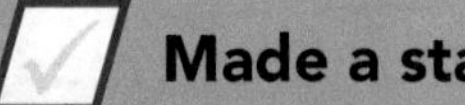

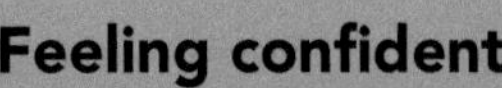
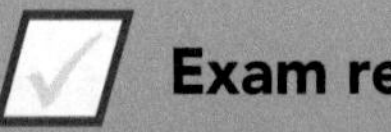

The pH scale and neutralisation

You need to know how to use the pH scale to measure how acidic or alkaline a solution is.

Acids, bases and alkalis

Acids

An **acid** is a substance that produces hydrogen (H^+) ions when dissolved in water.

Acids have a pH of less than 7.

The lower the pH number, the stronger the acid.

Bases and alkalis

Bases react with acids and neutralise them to make a salt and water. They are usually metal oxides or metal hydroxides.

Alkalis are bases that are dissolved in water. Copper oxide is a base but not an alkali, whereas sodium hydroxide is an alkali and a base because it dissolves in water.

An alkali produces hydroxide (OH^-) ions when dissolved in water.

Aqueous solutions of alkalis have a pH greater than 7.

The higher the pH number, the stronger the alkali.

Neutralisation reactions

A solution with pH 7 is neutral. When **acids** and **alkalis** react, a neutralisation reaction occurs.

The hydrogen ions react with the hydroxide ions to produce water:

$$H^+(aq) + OH^-(aq) \rightarrow H_2O(l)$$

Acids react with **metal carbonates** to give a salt, water and carbon dioxide gas.

metal carbonate + acid → salt + water + carbon dioxide

$$CaCO_3 + 2HNO_3 \rightarrow Ca(NO_3)_2 + H_2O + CO_2$$

Indicators, such as universal indicator, are used to measure the approximate pH of a solution. Universal indicator changes colour to show the pH of a substance. pH can also be measured using a pH probe.

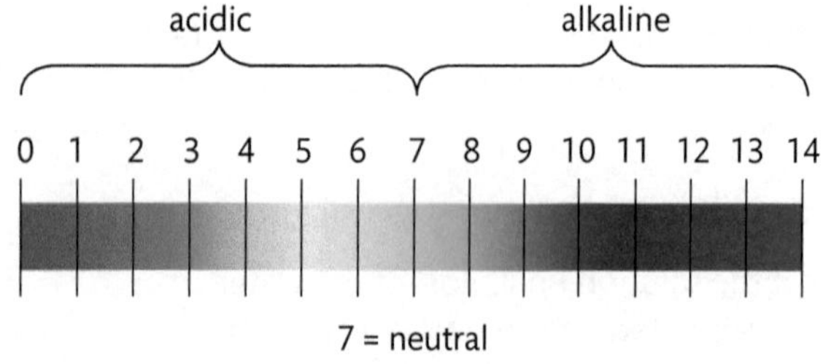

Figure 1 The pH scale

Working scientifically

When an acid and an alkali react in solution, the acid provides hydrogen ions and the alkali provides hydroxide ions. The neutralisation reaction between the two produces water.

When balancing neutralisation reactions, remember that the alkali has to provide one OH^- ion for every H^+ ion from the acid. So the reaction between NaOH (one OH^-) and sulfuric acid (two H^+) is:

$$H_2SO_4(aq) + \mathbf{2}NaOH(aq) \rightarrow 2H_2O(l) + Na_2SO_4(aq)$$

Worked example — Grade 5

Vinegar has a pH of about 2.5.

(a) Describe what pH shows about a solution. **[1 mark]**

How acidic or alkaline the solution is

(b) From the pH value of vinegar, what type of substance is vinegar? Explain your answer. **[2 marks]**

Its pH is lower than 7 so vinegar is an acid.

(c) Identify the ion responsible for the pH at 2.5. **[1 mark]**

H^+

Exam-style practice — Grade 5

1. Write a word equation for the neutralisation reaction between hydrochloric acid and sodium hydroxide. **[2 marks]**
2. An unknown solution is tested using universal indicator. The indicator changes to a deep blue colour.
   (a) Identify the type of solution being tested. **[1 mark]**
   (b) Identify the ion that causes the indicator to change to blue. **[1 mark]**
3. Suggest how you could prove that a solution has a neutral pH. **[1 mark]**

 Made a start  Feeling confident Exam ready

Electrolysis

You need to understand what electrolysis is and how it works.

Electrolytes

Liquids and solutions that are able to conduct electricity are called **electrolytes**.

Electrolytes consist of ionic compounds, either melted or dissolved in water. The ions in ionic compounds must be free to move so that electrolysis can happen. Ions are free to move in:

- molten (liquid) ionic compounds
- ionic compounds dissolved in water.

Ions are held in fixed positions in solid ionic compounds. The ions there cannot move about, so solid ionic compounds cannot conduct electricity and are not electrolytes.

Conducting electricity

An electric current needs a potential difference (voltage), and charged particles that can move.

A potential difference can be supplied by:

- a battery, or
- a power pack.

A direct current (dc) flows if a battery is used. Power packs can be set to produce dc at different voltages.

Electrons are the charged particles that move in electrical wires and cables, and in electrodes. However, **ions** are the charged particles that move in the electrolyte during electrolysis.

Worked example — Grade 3

Figure 1 shows an electrolysis cell.

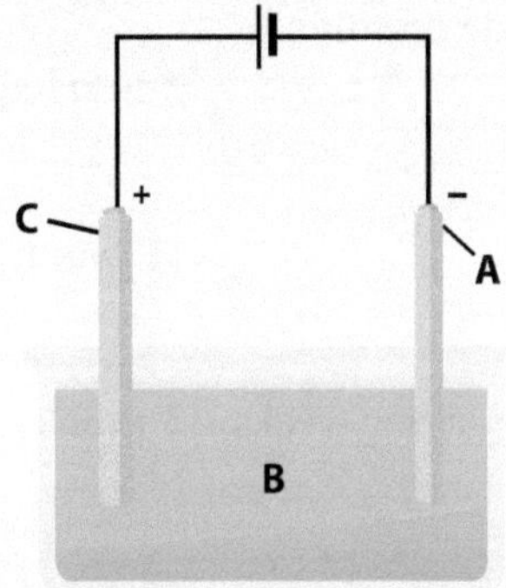

Figure 1

(a) Identify the parts **A**, **B** and **C** in **Figure 1**. **[3 marks]**

A: cathode (negative electrode)

B: electrolyte in a container

C: anode (positive electrode)

(b) Describe what happens during electrolysis. **[4 marks]**

Positive ions are attracted to the negative electrode (the cathode). Negative ions are attracted to the positive electrode (the anode). When the ions reach the electrodes, they are discharged and produce elements.

Opposite charges attract each other. Ions are discharged when they gain or lose electrons at an electrode.

The process of electrolysis

Electrolysis is the breaking down of an electrolyte to produce elements. It needs two **electrodes** to conduct electricity into the electrolyte:

- a **cathode**, a negatively charged electrode
- an **anode**, a positively charged electrode.

It may help to remember: Anode Add (+).

Electrodes are usually made from graphite, or from an unreactive metal, such as platinum.

Exam-style practice — Grade 3

1 Draw one line from each part to its description. **[3 marks]**

Part	Description
electrolyte	positively charged electrode
electrode	negatively charged electrode
anode	solid electrical conductor
cathode	liquid that conducts electricity

2 Give a reason why electrodes are needed in electrolysis. **[1 mark]**

3 Metals form positive ions. Name the electrode that metal ions will move towards. Give a reason for your answer. **[1 mark]**

 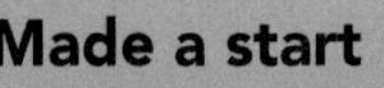 

Electrolysis to extract metals

You need to know how reactive metals can be extracted from their compounds using electrolysis.

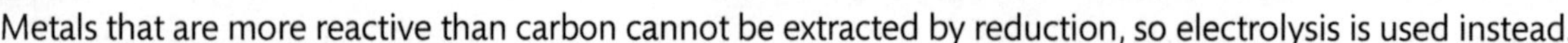

5 Reactive metals

Metals that are more reactive than carbon cannot be extracted by reduction, so electrolysis is used instead.

The electrolysis of metals involves large amounts of energy. This is because metal compounds have high melting points and must be kept in a molten state. Energy is also needed to produce the necessary electrical current.

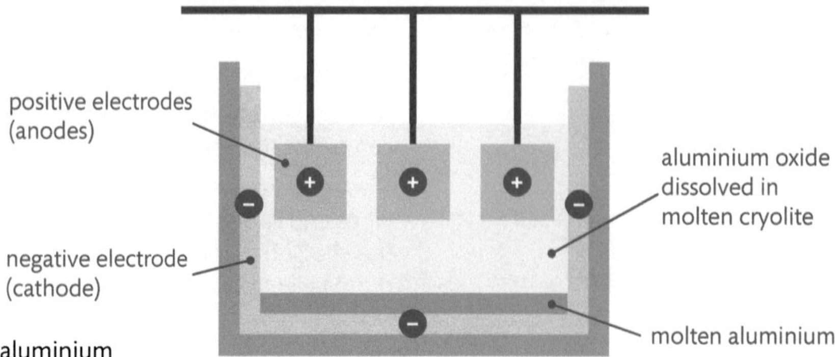

Figure 1 Electrolysis of aluminium

10 Worked example — Grades 4–5

(a) The electrolyte for electrolysis of aluminium is a molten mixture of aluminium oxide dissolved in cryolite. Explain why. **[2 marks]**

Cryolite melts at a lower temperature than aluminium oxide, so less energy is needed to form the electrolyte.

(b) Name the substance used for the electrodes in the electrolysis of aluminium. **[1 mark]**

Graphite (a form of carbon)

(c) Oxygen is produced at the anode. Suggest a reason why the anode needs replacing after a few weeks. **[2 marks]**

The oxygen produced reacts with the carbon electrode to produce carbon dioxide. This results in the electrode gradually wearing away.

(d) Explain why aluminium forms at the negative electrode. **[3 marks]**

Aluminium ions are positive, therefore they are attracted to the negative electrode (the cathode) where they gain electrons and are discharged as the metal.

10 Exam-style practice — Grade 4

1 **Figure 2** shows how magnesium can be produced from magnesium chloride using electrolysis.

Explain why large amounts of energy are used in the extraction process. **[2 marks]**

cathode (−ve) anode (+ve)

Mg^{2+} Cl^-

Figure 2

2 The melting point of aluminium oxide is over 2000 °C. Name the substance used to produce an electrolyte at a lower temperature. **[1 mark]**

3 Metals can be extracted from their ores either by reduction with carbon or by electrolysis.

(a) Give the property that the choice of method used is based on. **[1 mark]**

(b) Give a reason why some metals cannot be extracted from their ores using carbon. **[1 mark]**

(c) Give **one** reason why electrolysis is expensive. **[1 mark]**

(d) Give the state in which the metal compound must be for electrolysis to happen. **[1 mark]**

Electrolysis of aqueous solutions

You need to be able to predict what will happen to aqueous solutions during electrolysis.

At the cathode

Positively charged ions are discharged at the cathode (the negatively charged electrode).

An aqueous solution always contains hydrogen ions, H^+. This is because a tiny number of water molecules naturally break down into ions.

An aqueous solution may also contain positively charged metal ions from the dissolved ionic compound. For example, silver nitrate produces silver ions, Ag^+, when it dissolves.

Rules

Hydrogen is produced if the metal is more reactive than hydrogen.

The metal is produced if the metal is less reactive than hydrogen, like silver.

For example:

- hydrogen is produced from sodium sulfate
- copper is produced from copper sulfate.

You can find out about the reactivity series of metals on page 110.

At the anode

Negatively charged ions are discharged at the anode (the positively charged electrode).

An aqueous solution always contains hydroxide ions, OH^-. This is because a tiny number of water molecules naturally break down into ions.

An aqueous solution usually also contains negatively charged ions from the dissolved ionic compound. For example, copper sulfate produces sulfate ions, SO_4^{2-}, when it dissolves.

Rules

Oxygen is produced, unless the solution contains halide ions. In this case, the halogen is produced:

- chloride ions produce chlorine
- bromide ions produce bromine
- iodide ions produce iodine.

For example:

- oxygen is produced from sodium sulfate
- chlorine is produced from sodium chloride.

Worked example

Grade 5

1 **Figure 1** shows a method for the electrolysis of sodium chloride solution.

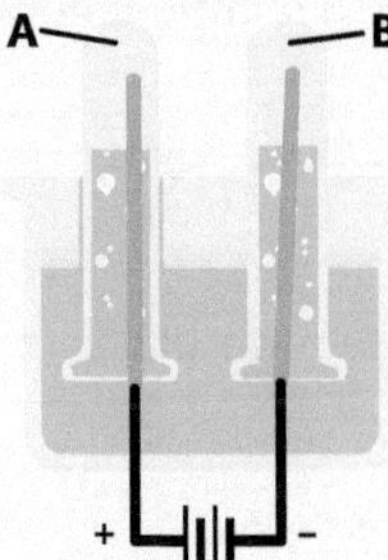

Figure 1

Name gases **A** and **B**. **[2 marks]**

Gas A: chlorine Gas B: hydrogen

2 Predict the element produced at the positive electrode during the electrolysis of:

(a) dilute sulfuric acid, H_2SO_4(aq) **[1 mark]**

oxygen

Copper would be produced at the negative electrode if copper chloride was used instead. This is because copper is less reactive than hydrogen.

(b) dilute hydrochloric acid, HCl(aq). **[1 mark]**

chlorine

Dilute nitric acid, HNO_3(aq), would also produce oxygen. Oxygen is always produced unless halide ions (F^-, Br^- or Cl^-) are present.

Exam-style practice

Grade 5

Predict the element formed at each electrode during the electrolysis of the following electrolytes.

(a) potassium iodide solution **[2 marks]**

(b) silver nitrate solution. **[2 marks]**

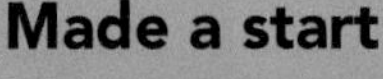

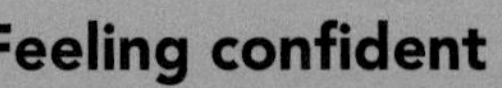

Electrolysis of copper(II) chloride

You need to know what happens when aqueous solutions are electrolysed using inert electrodes. This page covers the electrolysis of copper(II) chloride.

2 Apparatus

- 50 cm^3 copper(II) chloride solution
- 100 cm^3 beaker
- Petri dish lid with two holes
- two carbon rod electrodes
- two crocodile/4 mm plug leads
- low-voltage power supply
- blue litmus paper
- tweezers

5 Electrolysis of copper(II) chloride

1. Pour copper(II) chloride solution into the beaker to about 50 cm^3.
2. Add the Petri dish lid and insert carbon rods through the holes. **The rods must not touch each other**. Attach crocodile leads to the rods. Connect the rods to the **dc (red and black)** terminals of a low-voltage power supply.
3. Switch on the power supply (4 V).
4. Look at both electrodes. Is there bubbling at neither, one or both of the electrodes?
5. Use tweezers to hold a piece of blue litmus paper in the solution next to the positive electrode.
6. Record your observations.

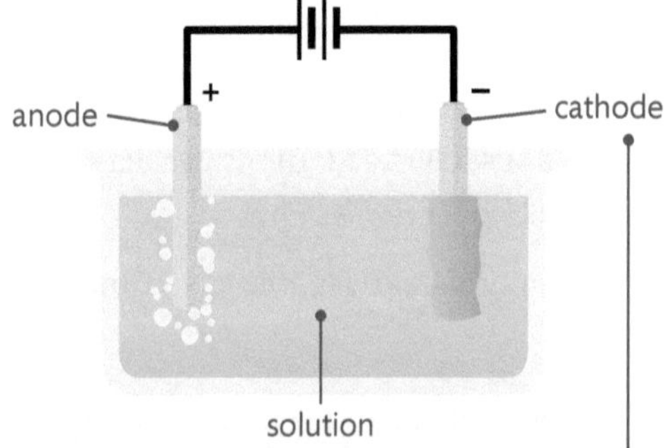

Figure 2 Electrolysis apparatus

The products of electrolysis are reactive, so it is important to use inert (unreactive) materials for the electrodes.

10 Worked example — Grade 5

Figure 1 shows the apparatus for the electrolysis of copper(II) sulfate solution.

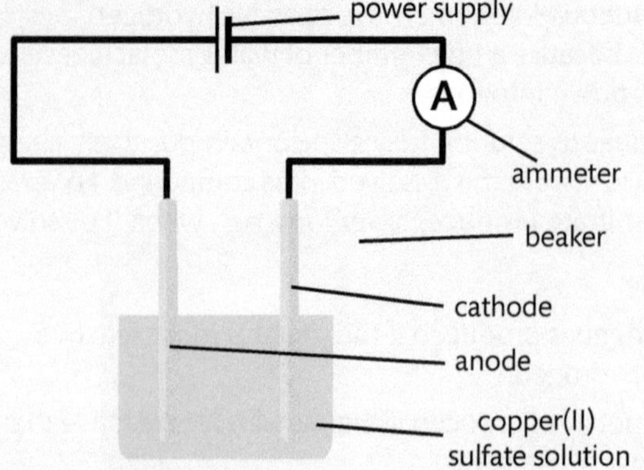

Figure 1

(a) Use your knowledge and understanding to predict the product at each electrode. **[2 marks]**

Copper metal at the cathode and oxygen gas at the anode.

(b) Describe what you should see at each electrode if your hypothesis is correct. **[2 marks]**

Red-brown deposit (copper metal) at the cathode and bubbling at the anode.

(c) Describe how you could identify **one** of the products using a simple laboratory test. **[2 marks]**

The oxygen gas should relight a glowing splint.

For testing gases see page 138.

Working scientifically
When you are asked to predict you are being asked to make a hypothesis. A hypothesis is an idea you can test based on knowledge and understanding, rather than a guess.

10 Exam-style practice — Grade 5

(a) Name the products of the reaction when sodium chloride solution is electrolysed. **[2 marks]**

(b) Explain which product is formed at the positive electrode and which product is formed at the negative electrode when sodium chloride solution is electrolysed. **[4 marks]**

 Made a start  Feeling confident  Exam ready

Exothermic and endothermic reactions

You need to know the difference between endothermic and exothermic reactions and be able to identify the type of reaction when given details about temperature changes.

Classifying reactions

During a reaction, energy is transferred from the reactants to the surroundings, or from the surroundings to the reactants. **Exothermic** reactions **release** energy (usually as thermal energy) to the surroundings. The temperature of the surroundings **increases**. Examples include: oxidation, metal displacement, neutralisation and combustion.

Endothermic reactions **take in** energy from the surroundings. The temperature of the surroundings **decreases**. Examples include: thermal decomposition, photosynthesis, electrolysis and citric acid reacting with sodium hydrogencarbonate.

In an exothermic reaction, heat exits the reaction mixture. In an endothermic reaction, heat enters the reaction mixture.

Worked example

Grade 5

1 A student investigates the energy change in the reaction between sodium carbonate and ethanoic acid. He measures the temperature at the start and end of the reaction.

Starting temperature: 46 °C Final temperature: 25 °C

What type of reaction took place? Explain your answer. **[2 marks]**

An endothermic reaction – this is evident because the temperature decreased.

2 Exothermic and endothermic reactions can be used for everyday purposes.

Name the type of reaction used by cooling pads and sports injury packs. **[1 mark]**

Endothermic

3 A student wants to identify the best reaction to use in a hand warmer. She investigates three different reactions (**A**, **B** and **C**). The table shows her results, and how much it would cost to use each reaction in a hand warmer.

Reaction	Temperature change in °C	Cost in £
A	+6	3.50
B	–3	2.00
C	+17	25.00

(a) Explain why reaction **B** is unsuitable for a hand warmer. **[2 marks]**

Hand warmers should get warm, but this reaction gives a decrease in temperature.

(b) Identify the reaction that produced the greatest change in temperature. **[1 mark]**

Reaction C

(c) The student calculates the cost per °C change in temperature for reaction **A**:

3.50/6 = £0.58/°C

Calculate the cost per °C of reaction **C**. **[1 mark]**

25.00/17 = £1.47/°C

(d) Use your answers to parts **(b)** and **(c)** to identify the most suitable reaction for a hand warmer. Give a reason for your answer. **[1 mark]**

Reaction A because it would be the cheapest way to warm up the hand warmer.

Exam-style practice

Grade 5

A student reacts two substances and measures the temperature change during the reaction. This shows that the products have less energy than the reactants. Give the name of this type of reaction. **[1 mark]**

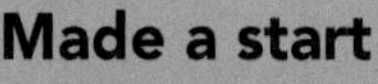

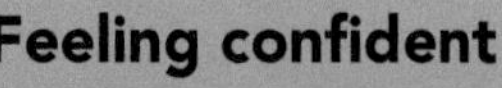

Temperature changes

You need to know how to investigate variables that affect temperature changes in reacting solutions, e.g. acid with metals or carbonates, neutralisation reactions and displacement of metals.

2 Apparatus

- dilute hydrochloric acid
- sodium hydroxide solution
- expanded polystyrene cup and lid
- 250 cm³ beaker
- measuring cylinder
- thermometer

5 Maths skills

You may need to plot a graph of your results.

You will need to draw a line of best fit. This is a line that shows the trend or correlation in the points plotted on a graph. The line should be drawn so that the points are evenly distributed each side of the line.

2 Working scientifically

Control variables are the factors you need to keep the same during the experiment, to ensure it is a fair test. In this reaction, the concentration and volume of hydrochloric acid must be kept the same.

10 Method

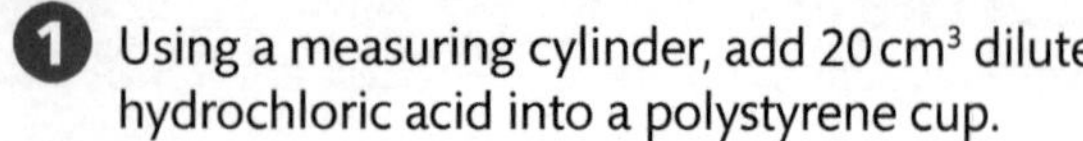

1. Using a measuring cylinder, add 20 cm³ dilute hydrochloric acid into a polystyrene cup.
2. Stand the cup inside a beaker. This will make it more stable and will insulate it.
3. Use a thermometer to measure the temperature of the acid. Record the temperature.
4. Measure 10 cm³ of sodium hydroxide solution.
5. Pour the sodium hydroxide solution into the cup. Loosely fit the lid and gently stir the mixture with the thermometer through the hole. When the reading on the thermometer remains constant, record the temperature in your table.
6. Repeat steps **4** and **5** two more times, adding 5 cm³ more of sodium hydroxide solution each time.
7. Repeat steps **1–6** of this experiment two more times and record the findings as below.

Total volume of NaOH added in cm³	Increase in temperature in °C			
	1	2	3	mean
10	8	6	5	6.3
15	17	19	19	18.3
20	24	25	26	25.0

5 Worked example — Grade 5

A student uses the apparatus in **Figure 1** to measure the temperature change when sulfuric acid reacts with calcium carbonate.

(a) Describe how the apparatus can be altered to reduce heat loss to the surroundings. **[2 marks]**

Use a polystyrene cup instead of the beaker and loosely place a lid on top of the cup.

(b) Give **one** observation the student will see if the reaction is exothermic. **[1 mark]**

The reading on the thermometer will increase.

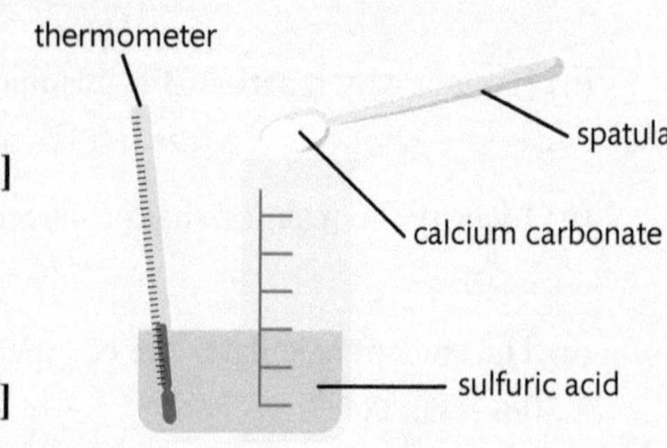

Figure 1

5 Exam-style practice — Grade 5

A student measures the temperature change when water is added to anhydrous cobalt chloride. Calculate the mean temperature change and identify the type of reaction that took place. **[3 marks]**

	Trial 1	Trial 2	Trial 3	Mean
Temperature change in °C	−6	−8	−5	

 Made a start  Feeling confident  Exam ready

Reaction profiles

You need to know about reaction profiles. They are used to compare the energy of reactants and products to determine the type of reaction taking place.

A reaction profile

A reaction profile (also called an energy level diagram) provides information about:

- the energy of the reactants
- the energy of the products
- the amount of **activation energy** needed for the reaction. Activation energy is the minimum amount of energy required for a reaction to take place.
- whether the reaction is exothermic or endothermic.

Go to page 121 for more information about endothermic and exothermic reactions.

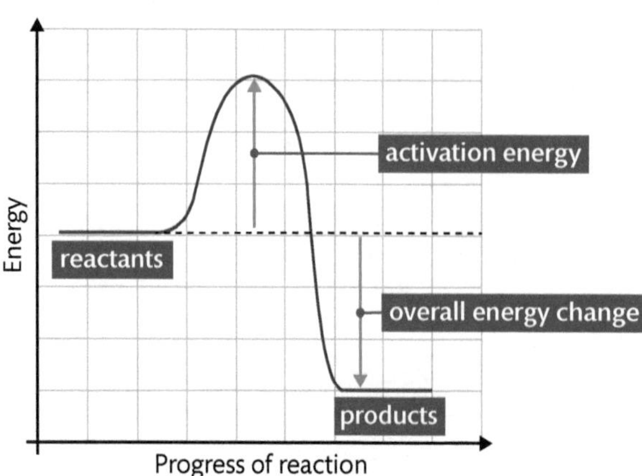

Figure 1 A reaction profile for an exothermic reaction

Worked example — Grade 5

The reaction between ammonium chloride and water is endothermic. Complete the reaction profile to show this reaction. Label the activation energy and the overall energy change. **[4 marks]**

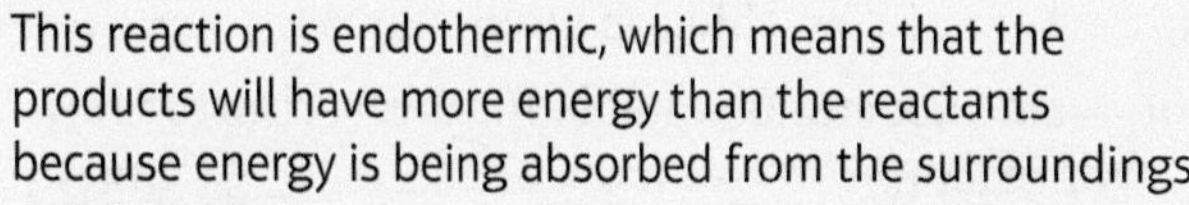

This reaction is endothermic, which means that the products will have more energy than the reactants because energy is being absorbed from the surroundings.

Energy

activation energy

overall energy change

Progress of reaction

The activation energy is the increase in energy from the energy level of the reactants to the top of the curve. This is true for exothermic reactions as well as endothermic reactions.

The curve is drawn from the reactants to the products. The peak of the curve must be higher than the energy level of the products to show the activation energy required by the reaction (for both exothermic and endothermic reactions).

The energy change is the difference between the energy level of the products and the energy level of the reactants.

Exam focus

In the exam, you could be asked to do the following:

- Draw energy level diagrams for exothermic and endothermic reactions.
- Label the activation energy and the overall energy change of a reaction.
- Use energy level diagrams provided to identify the type of reaction taking place.

Exam-style practice — Grade 5

The diagram below shows the reaction profile for the combustion of methane.

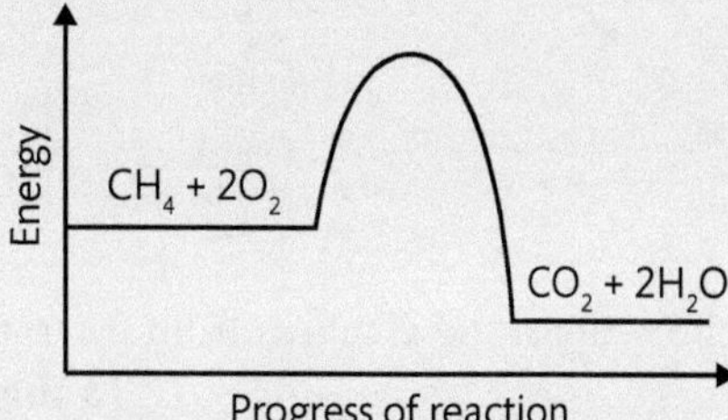

(a) Using the diagram, explain what type of reaction is taking place. **[2 marks]**

(b) Label the activation energy of the reaction on the diagram. **[1 mark]**

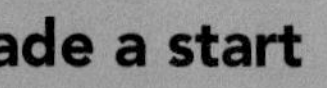

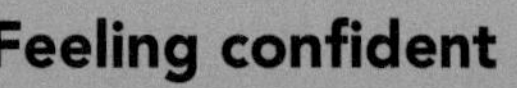

Exam ready

Calculating rate of reaction

You need to be able to calculate the rate of a reaction using formulae or by drawing a tangent to a graph.

Determining a value

The rate of reaction measures how much product is made per second in a particular reaction.

The rate of a reaction can be found by measuring the mass of a solid or volume of a gas, produced over a fixed period of time during a reaction. Alternatively, it may be found by measuring the quantity of the reactant used over time.

$$\text{mean rate of reaction} = \frac{\text{quantity of reactant used OR product formed}}{\text{time taken}}$$

If mass is measured (in grams), the unit for rate is g/s.

If volume is measured, the unit for rate is cm^3/s.

Time measured in seconds.

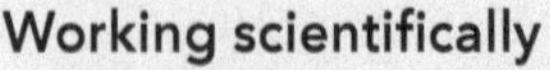

Working scientifically

Rates of chemical reactions are affected by many variables. In industry, chemists use these variables to control the rate of a reaction and the amount of product produced in the reaction (the yield).

Worked example — Grade 5

A student investigates the reaction between zinc powder and hydrochloric acid. Hydrogen and a solution of zinc chloride are produced.

Consider the reaction being described; it is worth writing out an equation to see what reaction is taking place.

(a) Name apparatus suitable for measuring the rate of reaction. **[1 mark]**

gas syringe

(b) The table shows the results of the experiment. Calculate the mean rate of the reaction using the data in the table. **[2 marks]**

Time in s	0	10	20	30	40	50	60
Volume of gas in cm^3	0	20	40	58	72	80	80

$$\text{mean rate} = \frac{\text{volume of gas}}{\text{time}} = \frac{80}{50} = 1.6\,cm^3/s$$

The rate of reaction is usually quickest at the start and slows down as the reactants are used up. The results show that the reaction had finished by 50 seconds as no more gas was produced. Therefore the amount of gas produced at 50 s can be used to calculate the mean.

(c) Plot the results on a graph. **[3 marks]**

Make sure you choose suitable intervals on your graph.

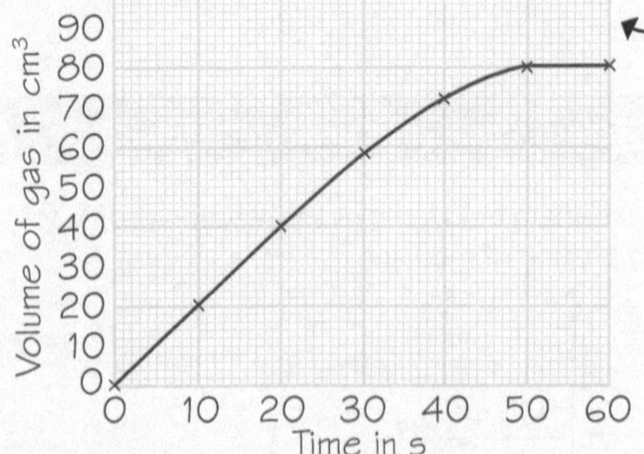

(d) Explain how the slope changes from 0 s to 60 s. **[3 marks]**

The slope gets gradually less steep until it's horizontal. This is because the rate of reaction decreases as the reaction proceeds, until it becomes zero at 50 s when the reactions stops.

Exam-style practice — Grade 4

Figure 1 is a graph showing rate of reaction.

Look at **Figure 1**.

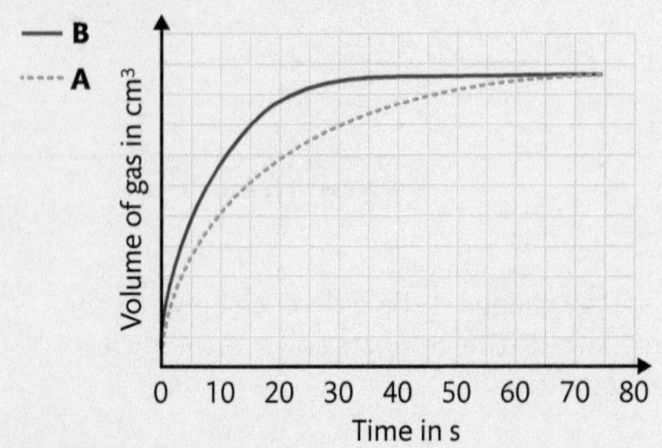

Figure 1

(a) Identify the line (**A** or **B**) that shows the faster rate of reaction. **[1 mark]**

(b) Determine how long it took for the reaction shown by line **A** to end. **[1 mark]**

(c) Both lines were produced from the same reaction. A catalyst was used in one of the reactions. Identify the line, **A** or **B**, which represents the catalysed reaction. Give a reason for your answer. **[1 mark]**

 Made a start  Feeling confident  Exam ready

Factors affecting rate of reaction

Chemical reactions can occur at different rates. You need to know about five main factors that can affect the rate of a reaction.

5 Measuring the rate

Depending on the type of reaction taking place, the rate of reaction can be measured by:

- measuring how long the reaction takes
- collecting the gas given off during a reaction (with a gas syringe or upturned measuring cylinder)
- mass change (with a balance)
- colour change (disappearing cross).

2 Working scientifically

You need to know how to vary the conditions of an experiment to alter the reaction rate. You can control conditions to ensure that a reaction occurs within a reasonable timeframe.

5 Factors affecting rate of reaction

Factors affecting rate of reaction

Pressure of reacting gases
Increasing pressure gives a higher rate of reaction. Gas particles are more likely to collide as they are being squashed into a smaller volume, so the rate of collision increases.

Surface area to volume ratio of solid reactants
A larger surface area on a solid gives a higher rate of reaction. Reactions take place on the surface of a solid, so a greater surface area to volume ratio means there is a greater rate of collision.

Concentration of reactants in solution
The higher the concentration, the higher the rate of reaction; there are more particles present in the reaction mixture, so a greater rate of collision.

Temperature
As the temperature increases, the particles move faster. They collide more frequently and with more energy, so the rate of reaction increases.

Catalysts
Catalysts increase the rate of a reaction. They reduce the amount of energy needed for the reaction by providing an alternative pathway which has a lower activation energy.

5 Worked example — Grade 5

1 Which of the following correctly describes particles and reaction rate?
Tick **one** box. **[1 mark]**

- [ ] The more collisions there are, the greater the rate.
- [x] The more frequent the collisions are, the greater the rate.
- [ ] Reactions only happen when particles pass by each other.
- [ ] The more energetic the collisions, the lower the rate of reaction.

2 Explain why increasing the temperature increases the rate of reaction. **[3 marks]**

As the temperature increases, the particles gain energy and their collisions become more energetic. The particles also move more quickly, so they collide more often.

10 Exam-style practice — Grade 5

A student investigates the reaction between marble chips and hydrochloric acid.

Figure 1 is a graph showing rate of reaction.

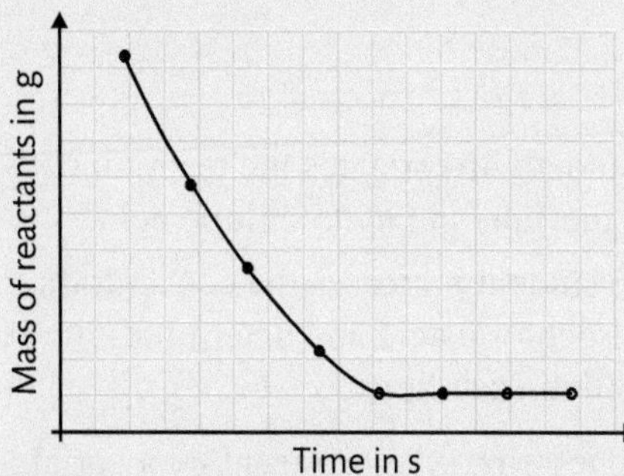

Figure 1

(a) Using **Figure 1**, describe how the student knew that the reaction was complete. **[1 mark]**

(b) Sketch the curve to show the results if the experiment was repeated at a higher temperature. **[2 marks]**

(c) Suggest another way of increasing the rate of the reaction other than changing the temperature. **[1 mark]**

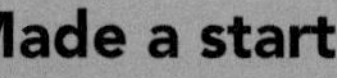

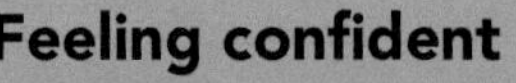
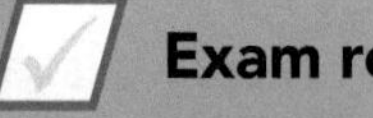

Rate of reaction

You need to know how to investigate the way changes in concentration affect the rates of reactions. This includes methods of measuring the volume of a gas produced and the change in colour.

Apparatus

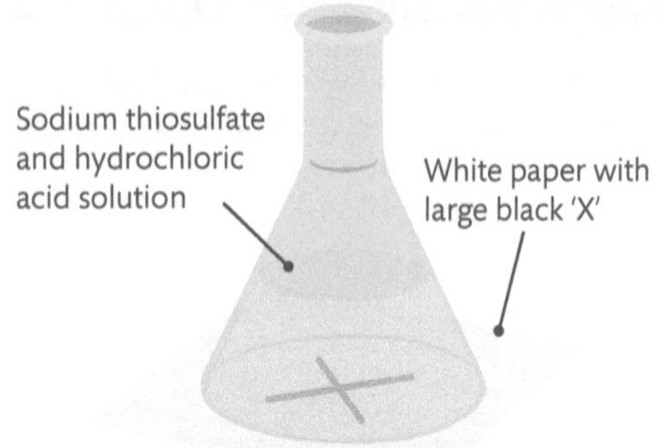

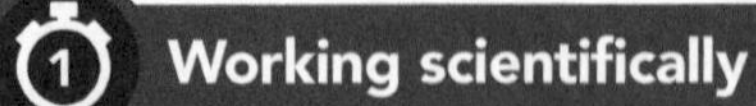

Working scientifically

Make sure you use a fume cupboard to avoid breathing in any sulfur dioxide fumes when carrying out this experiment.

Worked example — Grade 3

1. Describe when the student should stop timing in the experiment above. **[1 mark]**

When the cross can no longer be seen

2. Suggest a suitable piece of equipment to use to measure the hydrochloric acid. **[1 mark]**

A measuring cylinder

3. Suggest how the reliability of the results can be increased. **[3 marks]**

Repeat the experiment and calculate mean values, ignoring any anomalous results.

4. A student investigates the reaction between magnesium and hydrochloric acid.
   The student increases the concentration of the hydrochloric acid and determines the rate of reaction each time.

   (a) Describe what is meant by a variable. **[2 marks]**

   A factor that can be measured, controlled or changed

   (b) Give **two** variables that must be controlled in this experiment. **[2 marks]**

   The temperature of the acid and the surface area of the magnesium

Method

Sulfur is produced when sodium thiosulfate reacts with hydrochloric acid. The longer it takes for the sulfur to hide a cross under the flask, the slower the reaction. This method can be used to investigate the effect of varying the concentration of one of the reactants.

1. Prepare the sodium thiosulfate solution in a conical flask. Use a measuring cylinder to add water.
2. Place the conical flask on top of the printed black cross.
3. Use a measuring cylinder to measure the dilute hydrochloric acid.
4. Pour the acid into the conical flask. At the same time, swirl the flask gently and start the stop clock.
5. Look down through the top of the flask. Stop the clock when you can no longer see the cross. Record the time in seconds.
6. For reliability, repeat this process three times for each concentration of sodium thiosulfate. Calculate the mean time taken for each concentration.

Increased concentration means there are more thiosulfate particles present so more chance of successful collisions. As a result, the rate of the reaction increases as the concentration increases.

More accurate equipment could be used – pipette or burette – but is not necessary.

You could also say the volume of the acid or the mass of the magnesium.

Exam-style practice — Grades 4–5

The rate of the reaction between sodium thiosulfate and hydrochloric acid increases as the concentration of hydrochloric acid is increased.

(a) Explain why this happens. **[2 marks]**

(b) Give the independent variable, dependent variable and control variables you would use in this investigation. **[3 marks]**

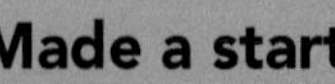

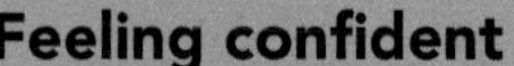

Exam ready

Catalysts

You need to know what a catalyst is and how it affects the rate of a chemical reaction.

Reaction pathways

A **catalyst** is a substance that can change the rate of a chemical reaction but is not used up during the reaction. Catalysts increase the rate of reaction by providing a different pathway for the reaction. The pathway provided has a lower activation energy. This means that more of the collisions between reactant particles occur with enough energy (activation energy) to react, so the reaction is faster. Different catalysts are needed for different reactions. Enzymes are biological catalysts.

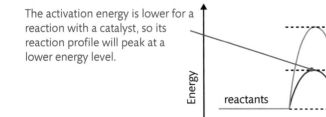

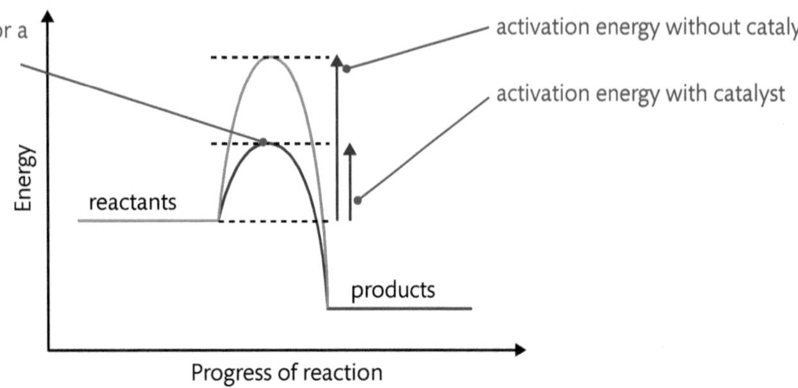

Figure 1 A reaction profile diagram showing the effect of a catalyst

Worked example — Grade 5

1 Hydrogen peroxide decomposes **slowly** to produce water and oxygen.

$2H_2O_2 \rightarrow 2H_2O + O_2$

Using **Figure 2**, draw and label the reaction profile for the reaction with a catalyst added. **[2 marks]**

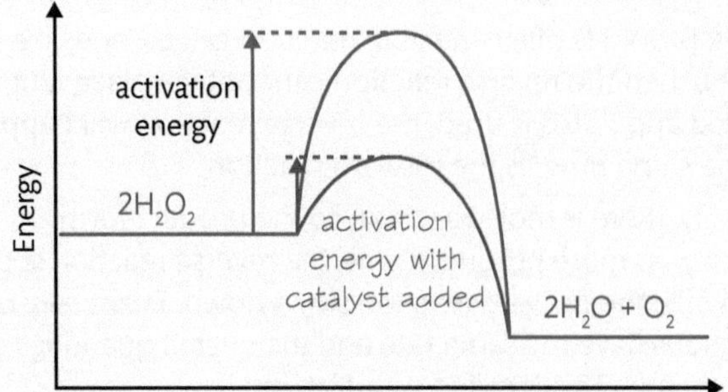

Figure 2

2 Explain how catalysts work. Refer to their effect on the activation energy of a reaction. **[4 marks]**

A catalyst provides an alternative pathway for the reaction, which has a lower activation energy. This makes more of the collisions successful, therefore increasing the rate of reaction.

3 Name the catalyst in the reaction below.

hydrogen + nitrogen $\xrightarrow{\text{iron}}$ ammonia **[1 mark]**

iron

You can identify a catalyst in a reaction in a few different ways:

- the catalyst is written above the arrow
- if a substance is the same on both sides of the reaction, i.e. it is not part of the reaction
- if you are told a reaction speeds up, but the same reaction occurs, when a substance is added.

Exam-style practice — Grade 5

1 **(a)** Draw a reaction profile for an exothermic reaction. Label the activation energy on your diagram. **[4 marks]**

(b) On your diagram, draw and label the activation energy for the reaction with a catalyst. **[1 mark]**

2 Name the catalysts found in biological systems. **[1 mark]**

Reversible reactions

Many reactions, such as burning fuel, are irreversible - they go to completion and cannot be reversed easily. Some reactions are reversible. With a change of conditions, the products can react to form the original reactants.

Reversible reaction equations

A **reversible reaction** is indicated by a split arrow ($\rightleftharpoons$). This symbol means that the reaction can proceed in either direction.

A reversible reaction can be shown as:

$A + B \rightleftharpoons C + D$

An **irreversible reaction** is shown by

$X + Y \rightarrow W + Z$

The products, W and Z, do not react to form the reactants, X and Y.

Anhydrous means without water.

A reversible reaction

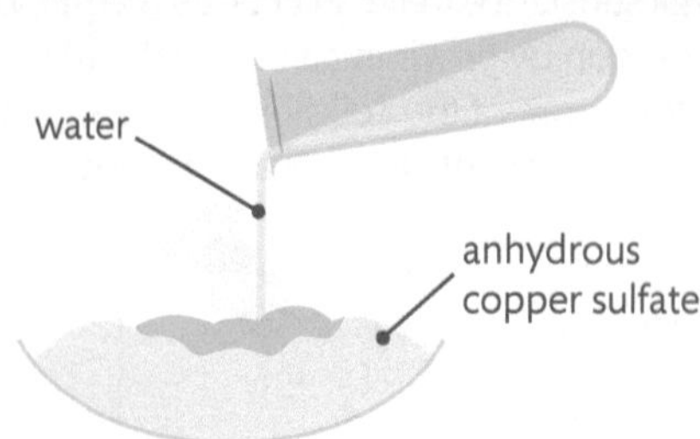

Figure 1 When water is added to white **anhydrous** copper sulfate, blue hydrated copper sulfate forms. When hydrated copper sulfate is heated, it loses water and anhydrous copper sulfate forms.

The reaction between anhydrous copper sulfate and water is reversible.

hydrated copper sulfate $\rightleftharpoons$ anhydrous copper sulfate + water

Direction

The direction of a reversible reaction can be altered by changing the conditions, such as temperature, concentration and, if gases are involved in the reaction, pressure.

Some reactions involve a colour change or a change of state.

Equilibrium

If the products of a reversible reaction can escape, like gases, then the reverse reaction cannot take place. But if closed apparatus is used, the reverse reaction will happen at the same time as the forward reaction.

Initially, there is more reactant, so the product forms quickly. As more product forms, the reverse reaction speeds up, while the forward reaction slows down. Eventually both reactions have the same rate and the overall quantities do not change. This is called **equilibrium**.

Worked example — Grade 5

1. Complete the word equation below, producing sulfur trioxide, to show that the reaction is reversible. **[1 mark]**

   sulfur dioxide + oxygen $\rightleftharpoons$ sulfur trioxide

2. Explain why equilibrium is only reached in a closed system. **[2 marks]**

   In an open system gaseous products can escape. If the system is closed, the gaseous products remain and can react to form the reactants.

3. The thermal decomposition of white ammonium chloride, into ammonia and hydrogen chloride, is reversible. Write a word equation to show the reaction. **[2 marks]**

   ammonium chloride $\rightleftharpoons$ ammonia + hydrogen chloride

4. When water is added to a sample of blue anhydrous cobalt chloride, pink hydrated cobalt chloride forms.

   (a) Write a word equation to show the reaction which takes place. **[1 mark]**

   anhydrous cobalt chloride + water $\rightleftharpoons$ hydrated cobalt chloride

   (b) Suggest how you could prove that this reaction is reversible. **[2 marks]**

   Heat the hydrated cobalt chloride to drive off the water. The cobalt chloride will change colour back to blue showing that the reaction has reversed.

Exam-style practice — Grade 5

1. The reaction between hydrogen and nitrogen is reversible. Define 'reversible'. **[2 marks]**

2. When hydrated copper sulfate is heated it changes colour from blue to white, producing anhydrous copper sulfate. When water is added, hydrated copper sulfate is reformed.

   (a) Describe how you can tell that the reaction is reversible. **[1 mark]**

   (b) Write a word equation to show the reaction taking place. **[1 mark]**

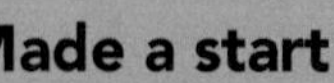

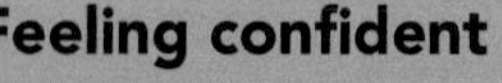

Energy changes in reversible reactions

In a reversible reaction, the amount of energy released if the reaction goes in one direction is equal to the amount of energy absorbed if it goes in the opposite direction.

Energy changes in reversible reactions

In a reversible reaction, energy needs to be supplied to drive the reaction in one direction. This is an **endothermic** reaction. When the reaction occurs in the opposite direction, energy will be released, usually as thermal energy. This is an **exothermic** reaction. The amount of energy released in one direction is equal to the amount of energy absorbed in the opposite direction. Go to page 121 for more about endothermic and exothermic reactions.

For example, when copper sulfate is dehydrated, energy must be supplied because it is an endothermic reaction. Energy is supplied in the form of thermal energy to drive out the water. When water is added to anhydrous copper sulfate, the reaction is exothermic and the water can be seen to bubble and spit due to the thermal energy being released.

hydrated copper sulfate ⇌ anhydrous copper sulfate + water

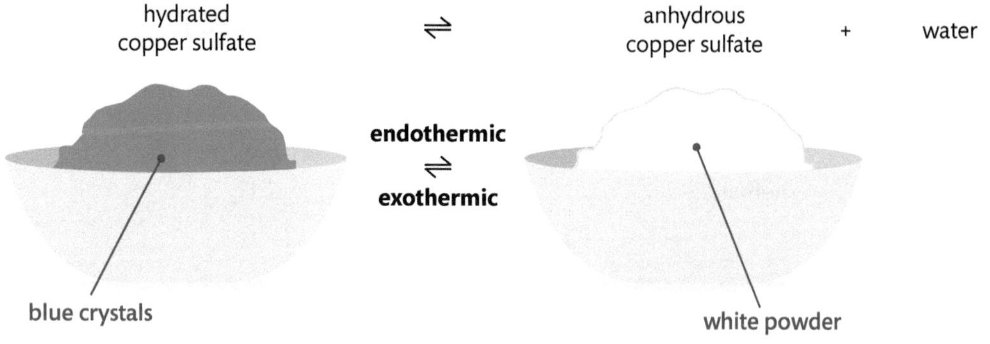

Worked example — Grade 5

The following word equation shows the reaction between anhydrous cobalt chloride and water, producing hydrated cobalt chloride:

anhydrous cobalt chloride + water ⇌ hydrated cobalt chloride

(a) Describe what sort of reaction the word equation shows. **[1 mark]**

Reversible reaction

(b) When a student adds water to the anhydrous cobalt chloride, a reaction takes place. Suggest **one** change the student will see. **[2 marks]**

The blue cobalt chloride will turn pink.

(c) The student repeats the reaction. During the reaction, the student measures the temperature with a thermometer. Explain why the temperature increases. **[2 marks]**

The forward reaction is when the student adds water. This must be an exothermic change where energy is transferred to the surroundings.

Working scientifically

You can find out whether a reaction is exothermic and energy is transferred to the surroundings by using a thermometer to measure the temperature change.

Think about the cobalt chloride paper you use to test for water, and how it changes colour. Remember to state the appearance of the reactant at the start as well as how it appears after the reaction has taken place.

Exam-style practice — Grade 5

1. Give **one** reason why the temperature of the surroundings can decrease during an endothermic reaction. **[1 mark]**
2. A reversible reaction is exothermic in one direction, and endothermic in the opposite direction. Describe how the amounts of energy transferred in each direction compare. **[1 mark]**
3. If a reaction releases 256 kJ/g of energy in the forward reaction for a certain quantity of reactants, determine how much energy will be needed for the reverse reaction of the same quantity of reactants to occur. **[1 mark]**

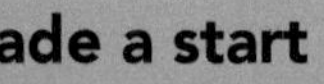

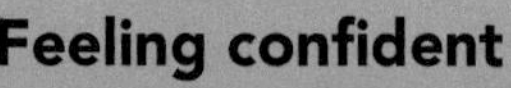

Made a start | Feeling confident | Exam ready

Crude oil, hydrocarbons and alkanes

Organic chemistry is the study of the structure, properties and reactions of the large variety of compounds that contain carbon. The main sources of these organic compounds are living or once-living organisms. You need to know the general formula for alkanes, as well as the names of the first four members of the alkane series.

Crude oil

Crude oil is a mixture of a very large number of compounds. It formed millions of years ago from the remains of biomass (mainly plankton) buried in mud. Crude oil can be found in rocks and trapped under the seabed of oceans.

Crude oil is a finite resource. It is made extremely slowly, so it will run out if we keep using it.

Most of the compounds in crude oil are hydrocarbons – compounds consisting of hydrogen and carbon only. Most of these hydrocarbons belong to a homologous series called the alkanes.

Alkanes

Alkanes share the general formula C_nH_{2n+2} where *n* is equal to the number of carbon atoms in the compound.

To name the first four alkanes, remember the mnemonic:
Mary
Eats
Peanut
Butter.

Name	Displayed formula	Molecular formula
methane	H | H—C—H | H	CH_4
ethane	H H | | H—C—C—H | | H H	C_2H_6
propane	H H H | | | H—C—C—C—H | | | H H H	C_3H_8
butane	H H H H | | | | H—C—C—C—C—H | | | | H H H H	C_4H_{10}

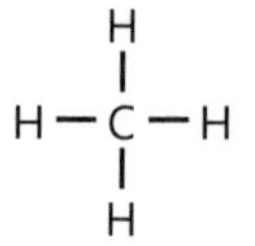

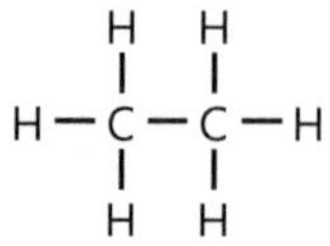

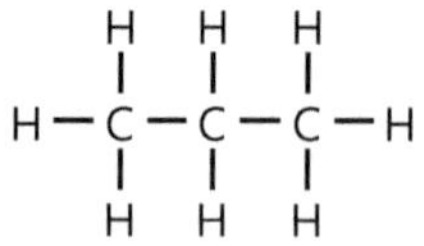

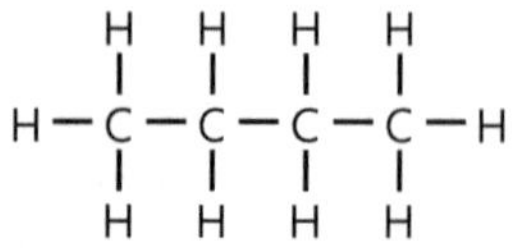

The size of a hydrocarbon depends on the number of carbon atoms, so the smallest hydrocarbon will have only one carbon atom.

Each carbon atom needs to make four covalent bonds to be stable.

Worked example — Grade 5

1 Predict the molecular formula for an alkane with eight carbons. **[2 marks]**

C_8H_{18}

Using the general formula C_nH_{2n+2}
If C = 8
H = (2 × 8) + 2
= 16 + 2 = 18
The formula can also be applied to question **2** to work out the number of hydrogen atoms to draw.

2 Pentane has five carbons. Draw the displayed formula for pentane. **[2 marks]**

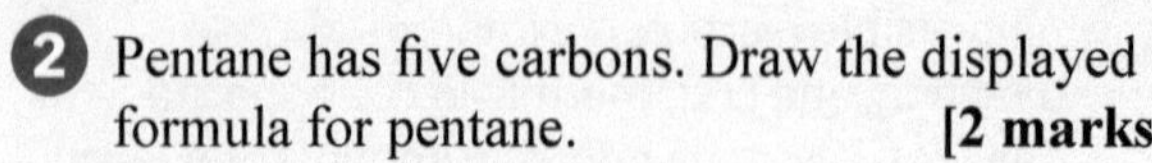

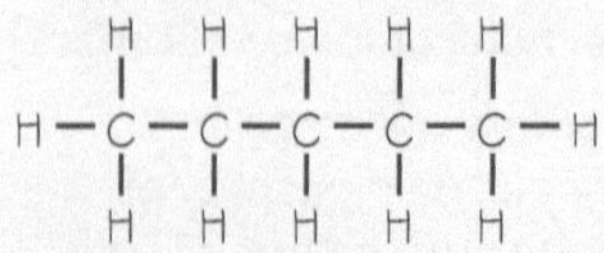

3 Give the meaning of the term 'hydrocarbon'. **[1 mark]**

A compound that contains only hydrogen and carbon

Exam-style practice — Grade 4

1 Crude oil is a finite resource. Describe what is meant by 'finite'. **[1 mark]**

2 Use the general formula for alkanes to show that the molecular formula of hexane is C_6H_{14}. **[1 mark]**

Fractional distillation

You need to know how fractional distillation is used to separate mixtures of several liquids, such as crude oil.

Fractions

Crude oil is a mixture of substances, which can be separated into fractions. Each fraction contains hydrocarbon molecules with a similar number of carbon atoms.

The fractions are then processed to produce fuels such as petrol, kerosene, diesel oil, heavy fuel oil and liquefied petroleum gases (LPG).

The fractions are also processed to be used as the raw materials for the petrochemical industry to produce an array of products, such as lubricants, solvents, detergents and polymers.

Gases rise, cool and condense at different levels according to their boiling point. The separated liquids are collected.

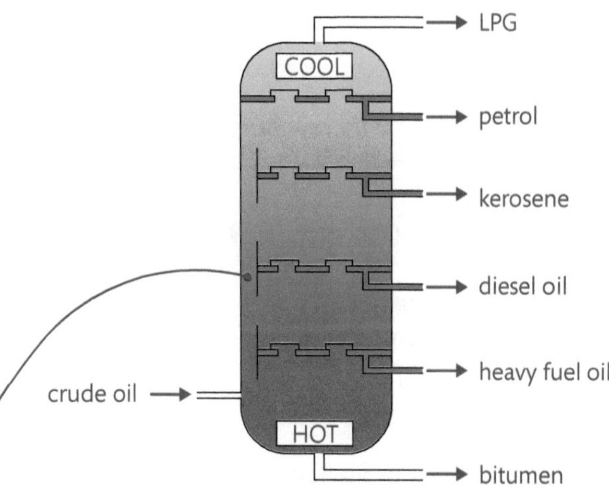

Figure 1 The fractional distillation column used to separate crude oil

The fractionating column has a **temperature gradient**. This means there is a difference in temperature between the top (cool) and the bottom (hot).

Worked example — Grade 5

1. Complete the sentence. **[1 mark]**

   Crude oil can be separated into fractions because the fractions have different boiling points.

2. Crude oil is a mixture of hydrocarbons. Explain how fractional distillation is used to separate crude oil into useful fractions. **[4 marks]**

   Crude oil is heated to evaporate the hydrocarbons. The column is cooler at the top and hotter at the bottom. The gaseous fractions travel up the column until they reach a level just below their boiling point, where they condense and can be collected.

3. Give **two** ways in which the substances in a fraction are similar to each other. **[2 marks]**

   Their molecules contain a similar number of carbon atoms, and they have similar boiling points.

Exam-style practice — Grade 4

Heavy fuel oil has many uses. It is separated from crude oil by fractional distillation. **Figure 2** shows a laboratory experiment used to separate crude oil.

Name the processes happening at **X** and **Z**.

[2 marks]

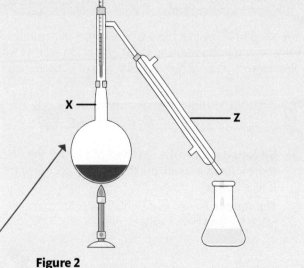

Figure 2

Process **X** is the reverse of process **Z**.

 Made a start 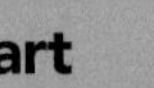  Feeling confident 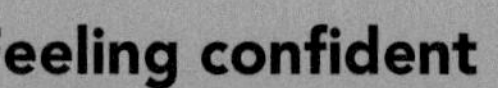  Exam ready

Hydrocarbons

You need to know how the size of hydrocarbon molecules affects their properties.

Properties of hydrocarbons

As the hydrocarbon chain increases in length, hydrocarbons become less flammable and more viscous. Their boiling points also increase.

When a hydrocarbon burns in plenty of oxygen, **complete combustion** takes place. The hydrocarbon fuel is oxidised. This process releases thermal energy.

When complete combustion of hydrocarbon fuel occurs, the same products are always produced.

hydrocarbon fuel + oxygen → carbon dioxide + water

Worked example — Grade 4

The term **complete combustion** means there is enough oxygen available for the fuel to completely react.

1. Petrol is a fuel produced from crude oil. Petrol can be used to produce energy through combustion. Write a word equation to show the complete combustion of petrol. **[2 marks]**

   petrol + oxygen → water + carbon dioxide

The type of hydrocarbon given is not important. If complete combustion of a hydrocarbon is taking place, the products will always be **water** and **carbon dioxide**.

2. The properties of methane, CH_4, and decane, $C_{10}H_{22}$, were compared. Complete the sentences to show how the properties of methane and decane differ. **[3 marks]**

   Methane is more flammable than decane.

   Decane is more viscous than methane.

   Methane has a lower boiling point than decane.

You need to consider the length of the hydrocarbon chain to determine how the properties will change from one hydrocarbon to another. Decane molecules are longer than methane molecules.

3. Balance the equation for the complete combustion of methane. **[2 marks]**

   $CH_4 + 2O_2 \rightarrow CO_2 + 2H_2O$

Balance the number of each type of atom on either side of the arrow.

Working scientifically

You need to know that there is a vast array of natural carbon compounds, including alcohols, esters (which are used as solvents and perfumes) and carboxylic acids, such as vinegar. There are also synthetic carbon compounds, including plastics, such as polystyrene, nylon and PTFE used in non-stick saucepans.

Key terms

- **Viscous** describes the thickness of a liquid: the more viscous a liquid, the thicker and less runny it is (like treacle).
- **Flammable** is used to describe materials that will catch fire and burn easily.

Exam focus

When balancing an equation in the exam, check your answer. There should be the same number of atoms of each element on both sides of the equation.

Exam-style practice — Grade 5

1. Name the products of the complete combustion of a hydrocarbon. **[1 mark]**
2. Balance the following equation for the complete combustion of ethane. **[1 mark]**

   $\_\_ C_2H_6 + \_\_ O_2 \rightarrow \_\_ CO_2 + \_\_ H_2O$

3. Describe how the viscosity of hydrocarbons changes with increasing molecular size. **[1 mark]**
4. Give **one** reason that explains why combustion is classified as an oxidation reaction. **[1 mark]**

Cracking and alkenes

You need to understand how hydrocarbons can be cracked to produce smaller, more useful alkane and alkene molecules.

Cracking

Cracking is a method used to break down longer hydrocarbons into shorter, more useful ones.

Cracking produces shorter alkane molecules and alkenes. Both of these are in much higher demand than long hydrocarbon molecules. Shorter alkanes can be used to produce fuels, such as petrol. Alkenes can be used to make polymers, such as poly(ethene), the plastic used in carrier bags, which is formed from ethene.

Catalytic cracking

A catalyst, such as aluminium oxide (Al_2O_3), is used to crack long hydrocarbons. The hydrocarbon is vaporised and then passed over the hot catalyst; this breaks the long hydrocarbon chain into at least two shorter hydrocarbon chains.

Steam cracking

The hydrocarbon is vaporised, steam is added and the mixture is heated to about 800 °C.

Alkenes

Alkenes have a double bond between two carbon atoms, shown as C=C. Alkenes share the general formula C_nH_{2n}.

The total number of C and H atoms in the products should equal the total number of C and H atoms in the hydrocarbon (on the left) being cracked. So, there should be a total of 12 C and 26 H each side of the arrow.

Bromine test

Bromine water can be used to identify alkenes and distinguish them from alkanes.

Alkanes do not decolourise bromine water. The bromine water stays orange.

Alkenes decolourise bromine water. The bromine water changes from orange to colourless.

Worked example

Grade 5

1 Long-chain hydrocarbons can be cracked to produce shorter hydrocarbons. Complete the equation to show the cracking of dodecane ($C_{12}H_{26}$). **[1 mark]**

$C_{12}H_{26} \rightarrow C_5H_{12} + C_4H_8 + C_3H_6$

2 **Figure 1** shows how cracking can be performed in the laboratory.

(a) Give **one** reason why aluminium oxide is used. **[1 mark]**

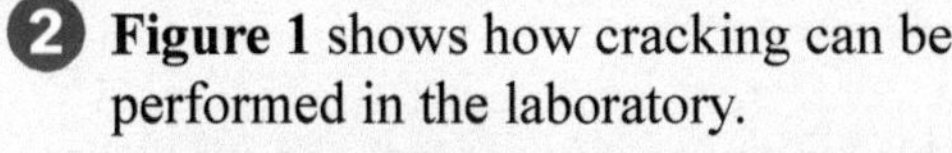

To speed up the reaction (it is a catalyst).

(b) Explain why cracking is classed as a thermal decomposition reaction. **[2 marks]**

It uses thermal energy to break something down.

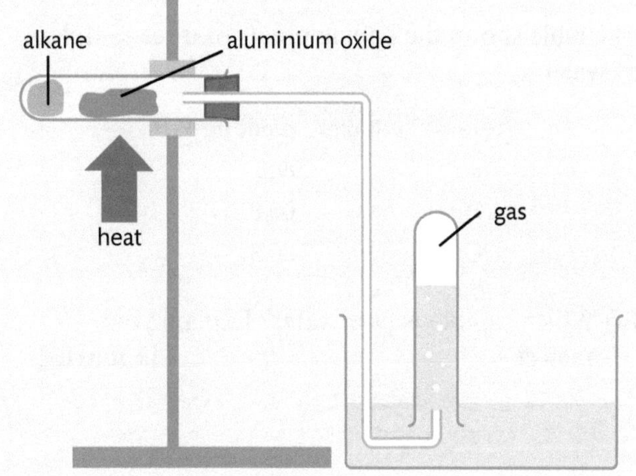

Figure 1

Exam-style practice

Grade 5

1 Give **two** reasons why cracking is used in the oil industry. **[2 marks]**

2 Complete the equation below to show the products of cracking. **[1 mark]**

$C_{28}H_{58} \rightarrow C_{20}H_{40}$ + ________

Pure substances

You need to be able to distinguish pure from impure substances using melting and boiling points.

5 What is a pure substance?

In everyday language, a pure substance is a substance that has had nothing added to it, for example, pure milk. In chemistry, a pure substance contains only atoms or molecules of that particular substance. For example, pure water contains only H_2O molecules.

Impure substances can be mixtures of elements, of compounds, or of elements and compounds. Unlike pure substances, mixtures can be separated by physical methods, such as filtration.

Impurities in a substance will affect its properties. The values for melting point, boiling point and density obtained for a sample can be compared with known data to identify its purity.

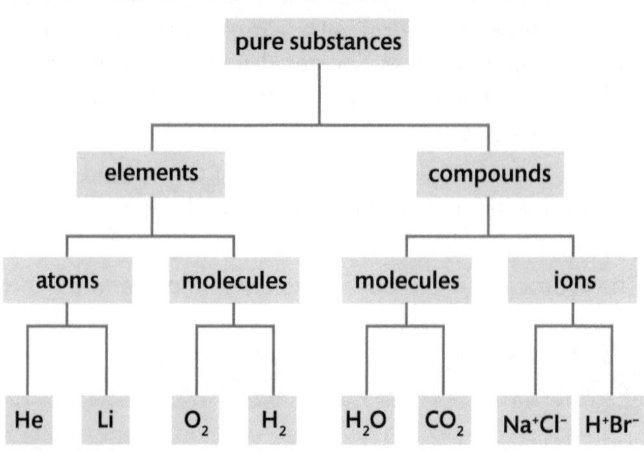

Figure 1 Examples of pure substances

1 Working scientifically

It is important to manufacture drugs to be as pure as possible. This reduces the risk of side effects and helps to ensure an accurate dose.

5 Worked example Grade 5

The table shows the boiling points of three samples of water.

Results	Boiling point in °C
A	99.8
B	100.0
C	100.3

(a) Which sample is pure water? Explain your answer. **[2 marks]**

Sample B is pure water because it boils at exactly 100.0 °C, which is the boiling point of water

(b) Suggest why the other two samples do not boil at the expected temperature. **[1 mark]**

They contain impurities.

(c) In the manufacture of pharmaceutical drugs, the drugs must be as pure as possible to reduce the chance of side effects.

Suggest **one** method that could be used to check the purity of a sample of aspirin. **[2 marks]**

Measure the melting point of the sample and compare it with the known melting point of pure aspirin.

If a substance is pure, every sample of that substance will have the same properties, including:

- melting point
- boiling point
- density.

Other possible methods involve measuring the boiling point or the density, and then comparing the measured values with known data.

5 Exam-style practice Grades 4–5

1. Describe how you could prove that a sample of liquid hexane (a solvent) is pure. **[2 marks]**
2. Purity is important when developing pharmaceutical drugs. Describe what is meant by the term 'pure'. **[2 marks]**
3. The boiling point of pure ethanol is 78.4 °C. A student measures the boiling point of a sample of ethanol and records a value of 78.9 °C. State whether the sample is pure or impure. Give a reason for your answer. **[2 marks]**

Formulations

Formulations are mixtures designed to be useful products. They contain a combination of components with specific purposes.

5 What is a formulation?

A formulation is a product that contains a mixture of useful components. The components are added in carefully measured quantities to give the product its required properties.

The table shows a typical soap formulation:

Ingredients	Percentage by weight
surfactants	30–70
plasticisers and binders	20–50
lather enhancers	0–5
fillers	5–30
water	5–12
fragrance	0–3.0
opacifying agents	0–0.3
dyes and pigments	<1

2 Examples of formulations

Soap is an example of a formulation. An acid, such as coconut oil, is reacted with an alkali, such as potassium hydroxide. This formulation creates a salt, which is the basic soap. Preservatives are then added with any further additives for skin care or fragrance. Other examples of formulations include:

- medicines
- food
- fertilisers
- alloys
- paints
- cleaning agents
- fuels.

Maths skills

1. Divide the total volume by 100 to get 1% volume.
2. Multiply the answer to step **1** by the percentage by volume.

Worked example

Grades 3–4

The table shows the typical formulations for gloss and emulsion paint.

Component	Emulsion paint (percentage by volume)	Gloss paint (percentage by volume)
binder	20	54
pigment	20	25
extenders	25	0
solvent		17
additives	5	4

A **solvent** is the liquid in which other substances are dissolved.

(a) Use the table to calculate the percentage by volume of solvent in emulsion paint. **[2 marks]**

Sum of percentages must equal 100%.

% solvent = 100 – (20 + 20 + 25 + 5)

= 100 – 70 = 30% solvent

(b) A consumer purchases 200 litres of emulsion paint. What volume of solvent will it contain? **[2 marks]**

1% of 200 = 2,
so 30% of 200 = 30 × 2 = 60.

There will be 60 litres of solvent in 200 litres of emulsion paint.

Exam-style practice

Grades 4–5

1 Paint is a mixture of liquids that has been designed as a useful product.

(a) Give the name of this type of mixture. **[1 mark]**

(b) Suggest the use of the pigment in a paint formulation. **[1 mark]**

2 Give **two** types of formulation, other than soap or paint. **[2 marks]**

Chromatography

Chromatography is a technique used to separate the components of a mixture so they can be identified. You need to understand how chromatography works and be able to calculate R_f values using chromatograms.

Paper chromatography

Chromatography is usually used to separate coloured substances, such as inks, food colourings and dyes. Chromatography is important in the manufacture of pharmaceutical drugs. The process can be used to assess the purity of drugs and medicines, enabling scientists to reduce the risk of unnecessary side effects. Go to page 137 to revise how to set up chromatography apparatus to produce a chromatogram.

Paper chromatography involves two phases:

- The chromatography paper, which contains a spot of the unknown mixture, is the **stationary phase**.
- The liquid solvent, which moves through the chromatography paper carrying the components of the mixture, is the **mobile phase**.

Mixtures are separated because different substances travel different distances depending on their attraction to the stationary phase and the mobile phase.

R_f values

The **R_f value** is the ratio of the distance moved by a substance (from the centre of its spot at the base line) to the distance moved by the solvent.

The R_f value of a particular substance will always be the same if the same type of chromatography paper and solvent are used. This means that R_f values can be used to identify unknown substances.

The more soluble a substance, the further it will travel up the chromatography paper and the higher the R_f value will be. The less attracted the substance is to the paper, the further it will travel up the paper and the higher the R_f value will be.

Pure compounds produce a single spot on the chromatogram.

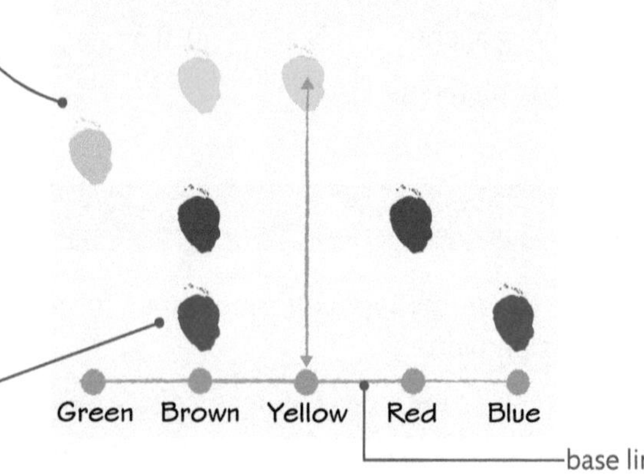

Mixtures separate into several spots in different positions on the chromatogram.

Figure 1 A chromatogram of different food colourants

Worked example — Grade 5

A substance travels 78 mm from the base line while the solvent travels 140 mm.
Calculate the R_f value for the substance. Give your answer to 2 significant figures. **[2 marks]**

$R_f = \frac{78}{140} = 0.557$

$= 0.56$ to 2 significant figures

Look at the three left-hand digits (ignoring 0 if it is there). If the third digit is 5 or more, add 1 to the second digit, otherwise remove the third digit.

Maths skills

R_f values can be worked out using the formula:

$$R_f = \frac{\text{distance moved by substance}}{\text{distance moved by solvent}}$$

Exam-style practice — Grades 5

1. A scientist uses chromatography to see what mixture of colours a brown food colourant contains. The results are shown in **Figure 1**. Identify the **three** colours that make up the brown food colourant. **[2 marks]**
2. Describe what an R_f value is. **[1 mark]**
3. Explain why R_f values are not given units. **[1 mark]**

 Made a start  Feeling confident  Exam ready

Paper chromatography

The aim of this practical is to identify an unknown substance within a mixture, using paper chromatography to find the R_f value.

2 Apparatus

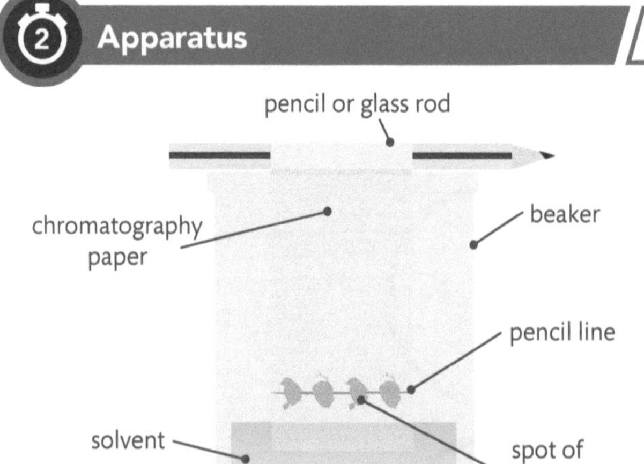

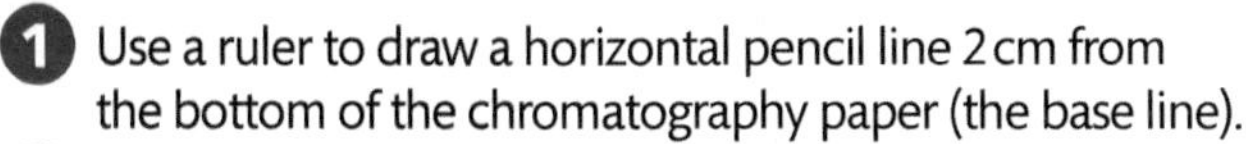

5 Investigating an unknown mixture

1. Use a ruler to draw a horizontal pencil line 2 cm from the bottom of the chromatography paper (the base line).
2. Using separate glass capillary tubes, put a small spot of each of the known colourings on the pencil line, 1 cm apart. Make sure each spot is no more than 5 mm in diameter.
3. Using another glass capillary tube, put a small spot of the unknown mixture on the paper.
4. Label each spot in **pencil**.
5. Tape the edge of the chromatography paper to the glass rod so the paper hangs with the base line at the bottom.
6. Pour water (solvent) into the beaker so that the water level is **below** the base line.
7. Rest the rod on top of the beaker so the bottom edge of the paper dips into the water.
8. Wait for the solvent to rise up the filter paper to near the top.
9. Use a ruler to measure the distance the solvent has moved up the paper (from the bottom edge of the paper) and the distance the spot has moved (from the base line).

2 Working scientifically

You need to be able to choose suitable apparatus and describe how it should be used for a particular purpose. For example, in paper chromatography:

- A pencil is used to draw the base line because ink may run and interfere with the chromatogram.
- The chromatography paper should sit above the solvent level so that the substance isn't dissolved in the solvent.
- You should wear eye protection to protect your eyes from harmful substances.

10 Worked example — Grade 5

Figure 1 shows a paper chromatogram of three food colourants and an unknown sample, **M**.

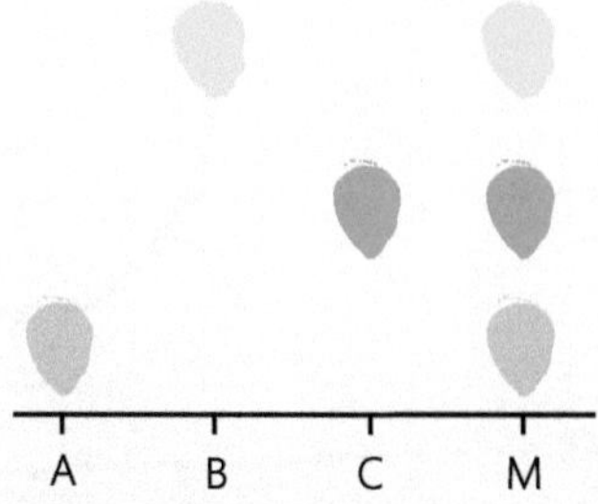

Figure 1

1 (a) How many different food colourants are present in unknown sample **M**? **[1 mark]**

Three

(b) How does the chromatogram show that food colourant **C** is present in **M**? **[1 mark]**

There is a spot in the column for M at the same point as the spot produced by sample C.

2 A student investigated the colours in inks using paper chromatography.

(a) Explain why the student used pencil to draw the base line. **[1 mark]**

Because pencil does not dissolve in the solvent

(b) Suggest **two** measurements the students must take to work out the R_f values of the inks. **[2 marks]**

The distance the inks have travelled from the base line
The distance the solvent has moved from the base line

5 Exam-style practice — Grade 5

1. Give **one** reason why the base line must be above the level of solvent at the start of the experiment. **[1 mark]**
2. Give **one** reason why the base line should be drawn using a pencil and not a pen. **[1 mark]**
3. A substance travels 23 mm from the base line while the solvent travels 74 mm. Calculate the R_f value for this substance. Give your answer to 2 significant figures. **[3 marks]**

Go to page 136 to revise how R_f values are calculated.

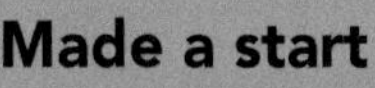

Testing for gases

When chemical reactions take place, quite often a gas is released. It is important to know which gas is being produced during a reaction so you can work out what reaction is taking place.

Identifying gases

You are expected to know how to test for the following gases.

Hydrogen
A lit splint will make a squeaky pop noise when held near a test tube of hydrogen gas.

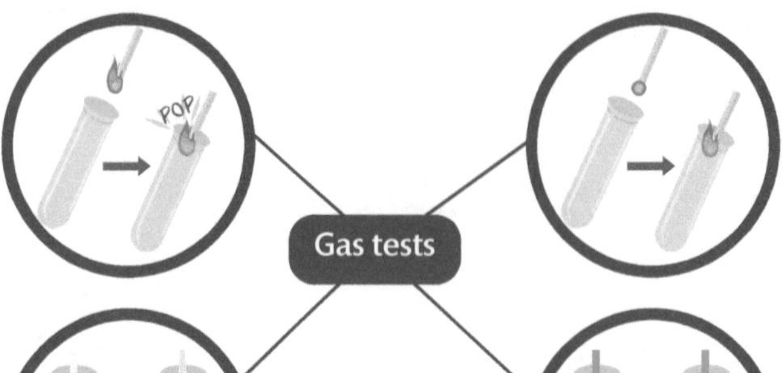

Oxygen
A glowing splint will relight if it comes into contact with a test tube of oxygen.

Carbon dioxide
Limewater (aqueous calcium hydroxide solution) will turn cloudy if carbon dioxide is passed through it.

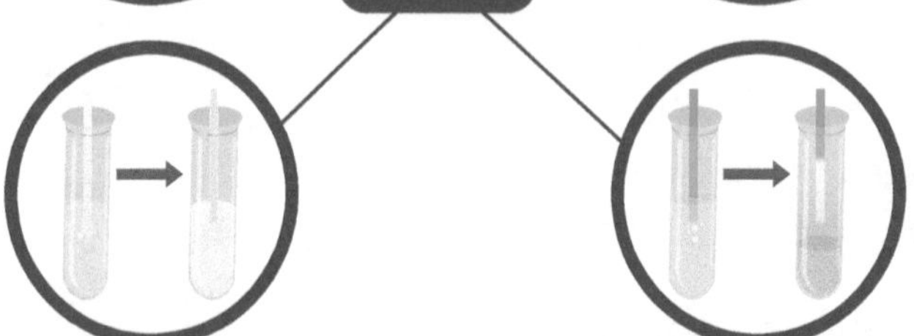

Chlorine
Damp blue litmus paper will become bleached (turn white) if held in a test tube of chlorine gas.

Worked example — Grade 5

1 A student carries out an experiment in which a gas is produced. The student collects a sample of the gas in a test tube.
Describe how to test the gas to show that it is oxygen. **[2 marks]**

Test: Place a glowing splint at the opening of the test tube.
Result: The splint will relight if the gas is oxygen.

2 The products of the combustion of ethanol are collected and tested. One of the products is bubbled through calcium hydroxide solution and the solution immediately turns cloudy.
Identify the gas being tested. **[1 mark]**

Carbon dioxide

Exam focus
Remember to answer these questions fully. For example, just stating the splint will relight will only earn half the total marks. You must show that you know how to carry out the test as well as giving the result of the test.

3 A student tested an unknown sample of gas to identify it. The results are shown in the table.

Test	Observation
bubbled through limewater	limewater stayed colourless
lit splint placed into sample of gas	flame extinguished
damp litmus held in sample of gas	colour of litmus bleached
glowing splint placed into sample of gas	flame extinguished

Identify the gas present in the unknown sample. Explain each of the observations in your answer. **[4 marks]**

The limewater didn't turn cloudy so it's not carbon dioxide.
There was no squeaky pop with the lit splint so it's not hydrogen.
It didn't relight a glowing splint so it's not oxygen.
It did bleach litmus paper so it must be chlorine gas.

5 Exam-style practice — Grades 2–3

Draw **one** line from each gas to its positive test result. **[4 marks]**

chlorine	hydrogen	oxygen	carbon dioxide

squeaky pop	limewater turns cloudy	bleaches litmus paper	relights a glowing splint

Gases in the atmosphere

You need to know the proportions of the most abundant gases in the atmosphere today.

Earth's atmosphere

The composition of Earth's atmosphere has stayed mostly the same for the past 200 million years, but the exact proportions of each gas vary continually. Scientists can use software to measure the effects humans are having on the atmosphere to develop solutions to reduce the impact.

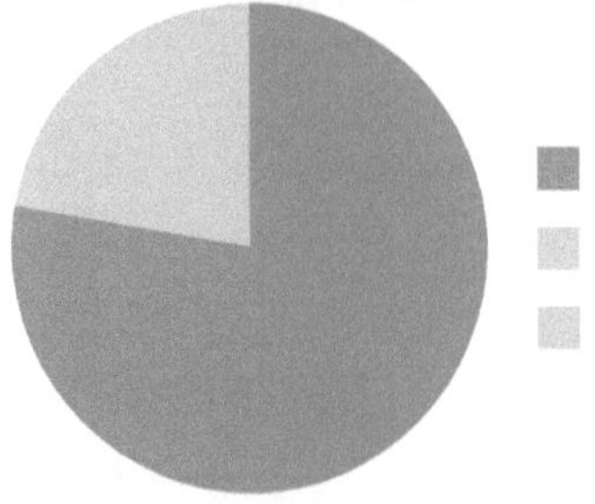

Figure 1 The proportions of gases in the atmosphere today

Maths skills

To convert from a percentage to a fraction you must divide the percentage of oxygen by the total percentage of the atmosphere.

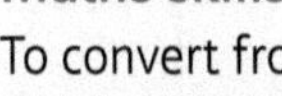

Maths skills

You are expected to be able to convert data provided as percentages, ratios and fractions. For example, the ratio of nitrogen to oxygen in the atmosphere is:

$$80 : 20 \xrightarrow{\div 20} 4 : 1$$

Ratios are a comparison of values. They are shown in their simplest form. Convert a ratio to its simplest form by dividing both values by the same factor.

Exam focus

You will need to draw graphs in the exam.

- Choose a sensible scale to work with.
- Ensure the graph covers more than half of the grid provided.
- Label the axes to identify what they are showing and give units if applicable.

Worked example — Grade 4

The table shows the approximate proportions of gases in the atmosphere today.

Gas	Percentage composition
nitrogen	80
oxygen	20
other gases	<1

(a) Using the data in the table, approximately what fraction of gas in Earth's atmosphere is oxygen? **[1 mark]**

$$\frac{20}{100} = \frac{1}{5}$$

(b) Using the grid below, draw a graph to represent the data in the table. **[3 marks]**

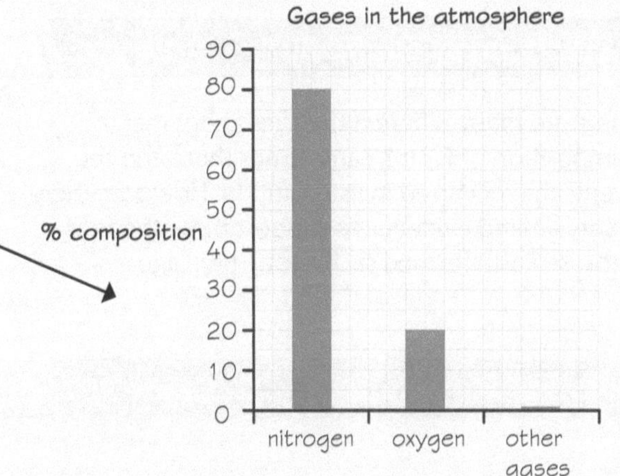

Exam-style practice — Grade 2

1 Approximately, what proportion of the Earth's atmosphere is nitrogen gas? Tick **one** box. **[1 mark]**

2% ☐ 8% ☐ 20% ☐ 80% ☐

2 Show that the fraction of nitrogen in the atmosphere is approximately four-fifths. **[1 mark]**

Earth's early atmosphere

You need to know how Earth's atmosphere has developed over time.

Evolution of Earth's atmosphere

Scientists have worked out that Earth formed about 4.6 billion years ago. To begin with, Earth was a ball of molten rock. Many scientists think that Earth's early atmosphere was formed from the gases given out by volcanoes.

Although Earth had a lot of volcanic activity, significant changes occurred within its first billion years that changed the make-up of the atmosphere, allowing life to begin and thrive.

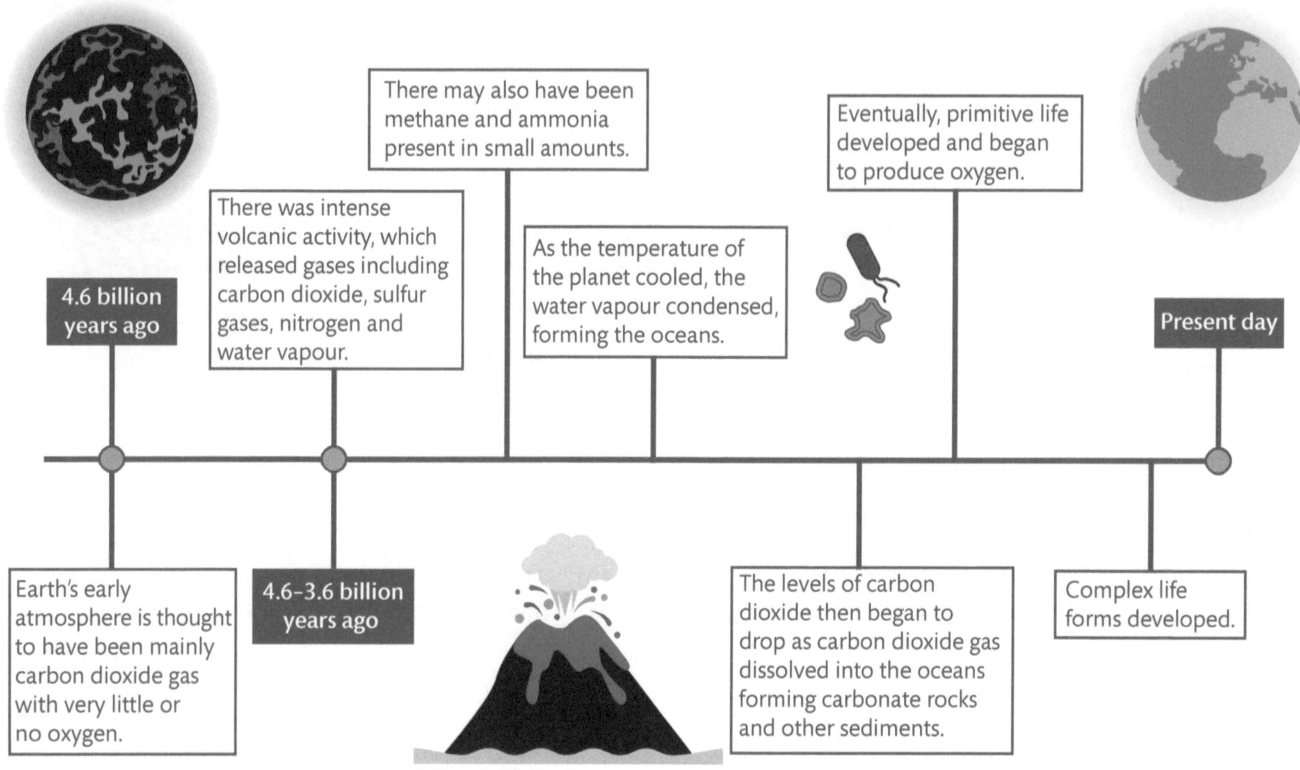

4.6 billion years ago
Earth's early atmosphere is thought to have been mainly carbon dioxide gas with very little or no oxygen.
There was intense volcanic activity, which released gases including carbon dioxide, sulfur gases, nitrogen and water vapour.
4.6–3.6 billion years ago
There may also have been methane and ammonia present in small amounts.
As the temperature of the planet cooled, the water vapour condensed, forming the oceans.
The levels of carbon dioxide then began to drop as carbon dioxide gas dissolved into the oceans forming carbonate rocks and other sediments.
Eventually, primitive life developed and began to produce oxygen.
Complex life forms developed.
Present day

Figure 1 Timeline of Earth's atmosphere

Working scientifically

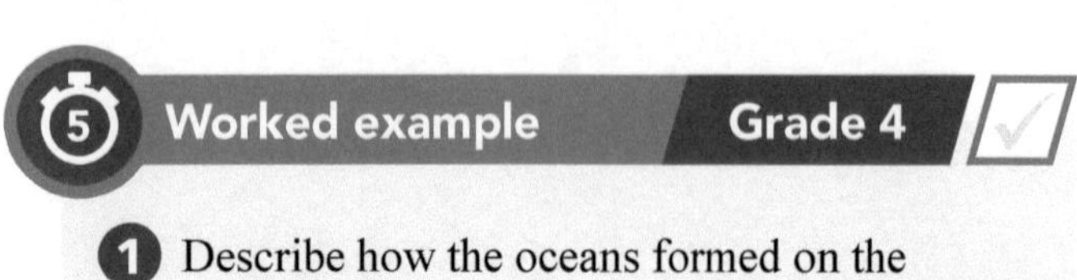

There are many different theories about the composition of Earth's early atmosphere and the events that occurred in its evolution. However, there is very limited evidence to support these theories because Earth formed such a long time ago.

Worked example — Grade 4

1. Describe how the oceans formed on the early Earth. **[2 marks]**

Water vapour in the atmosphere condensed when the Earth had cooled enough.

2. What activity is thought to have contributed to the high levels of carbon dioxide? **[1 mark]**

Volcanic activity

Exam-style practice — Grade 5

The current atmospheres of Mars and Venus are very similar to Earth's early atmosphere.

The approximate proportions of the gases in the atmosphere of Mars are given below.

Gas	Percentage composition
carbon dioxide	95
nitrogen	**X**
oxygen	0.5
argon	1

(a) Give the approximate value of **X.** **[1 mark]**

(b) Suggest why there is more oxygen on Earth than there is on Mars. **[2 marks]**

 Made a start 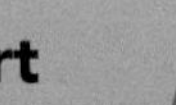  Feeling confident  Exam ready

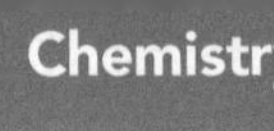

Oxygen and carbon dioxide levels

You need to know why levels of oxygen and carbon dioxide in the Earth's atmosphere changed over time.

Increasing O_2 levels

Algae and plants make their own food (glucose) by **photosynthesis**:

$$\text{carbon dioxide} + \text{water} \xrightarrow{\text{light}} \text{glucose} + \text{oxygen}$$

$$6CO_2 + 6H_2O \longrightarrow C_6H_{12}O_6 + 6O_2$$

During this process, carbon dioxide is absorbed from the air and oxygen is released.

Cyanobacteria are bacteria that photosynthesise. They evolved around 3.9 billion years ago. To begin with, the oxygen they released reacted with iron in rocks. This meant that free oxygen did not appear in the atmosphere until later.

Plants evolved over the next billion years, gradually increasing the oxygen in the atmosphere. Animals evolved when there was enough oxygen for them.

You can find out about photosynthesis on page 33.

Decreasing CO_2 levels

The percentage of carbon dioxide in the atmosphere decreased over billions of years because of photosynthesis.

Other processes also caused carbon dioxide levels to decrease, including the formation of:

- fossil fuels such as coal, crude oil and natural gas
- sedimentary rocks, such as limestone.

Fossil fuels contain carbon. Methane, CH_4, is the main compound found in natural gas for example. Limestone is mostly calcium carbonate, $CaCO_3$, so it also contains carbon.

One carbon dioxide molecule is absorbed for every oxygen molecule released.

Worked example — Grade 3

1 Crude oil and natural gas were formed from the ancient remains of tiny plants and animals.

Use words from the box to complete the sentences. **[3 marks]**

air	cooled	heated	hundreds
millions	mud	thousands	water

The remains became buried under mud.

They were put under pressure there and heated.

Their remains became crude oil and natural gas over millions of years.

2 Describe how limestone formed. **[3 marks]**

Dead sea creatures sank and formed layers of broken seashells. The weight of these layers squeezed the water out. It squashed the bits of shell together, gradually forming limestone.

Coal formed differently. About 300 million years ago there were many large swamps. When trees and other plants there died, they were buried by layers of soil. They were squashed and heated underground, and gradually became coal.

Exam focus

Make sure you can describe how deposits of coal, crude oil and natural gas formed.

The layers are called sediments. Limestone is an example of a type of rock called sedimentary rock. Calcium carbonate is found in seashells, which is why limestone is mostly calcium carbonate.

Exam-style practice — Grade 3

1 Name the process that releases oxygen into the air and removes carbon dioxide from it. **[1 mark]**

2 Name **two** fossil fuels that contain carbon. **[2 marks]**

3 Give **one** reason why limestone contains carbon. **[1 mark]**

4 Describe the main changes in the levels of oxygen and carbon dioxide in the Earth's atmosphere over time. **[2 marks]**

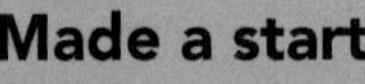
Made a start

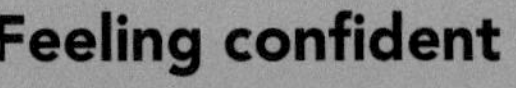
Feeling confident

Exam ready

Greenhouse gases

You need to know about the effects of greenhouse gases on the temperature of the Earth.

Production of greenhouse gases

Greenhouse gases in the atmosphere, such as carbon dioxide, water vapour and methane, maintain the temperature of Earth by trapping solar energy from the Sun. Theories suggest that greenhouse gases were originally produced by volcanic activity as Earth formed. Today, greenhouse gases are mainly produced by burning fossil fuels, such as coal, oil and gas.

Trapping solar energy

Greenhouse gases trap solar energy from the Sun in Earth's atmosphere, keeping it warm enough to support life.

Some of the solar energy is absorbed by rocks and Earth's crust, causing the planet to warm up.

Some of the solar energy is emitted from the Earth's surface as infrared (IR). Some of the IR radiation is absorbed by the greenhouse gases in the atmosphere and re-emitted back towards Earth. This heats up the surface of the planet, including the oceans.

Go to page 141 for more about carbon dioxide levels.

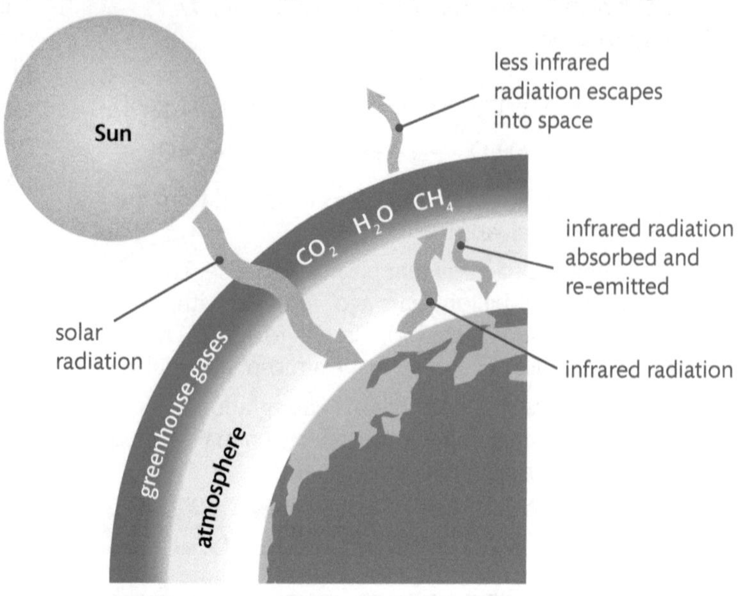

Figure 1 Trapping solar energy

Worked example — Grade 5

1. Describe what is meant by a greenhouse gas. **[2 marks]**

It is a gas that traps solar energy in the atmosphere, which maintains the temperature of Earth's surface.

2. Water vapour is a greenhouse gas found in Earth's atmosphere. Explain how the greenhouse effect increases the amount of water vapour in the atmosphere. **[2 marks]**

Water vapour traps the radiation that is being reflected from Earth's surface, causing Earth to warm up. As Earth warms up more water will evaporate, which will result in the formation of more water vapour.

3. The greenhouse gases methane, water vapour and carbon dioxide are all produced by natural and artificial processes. For each gas, suggest a natural source and an artificial source. **[6 marks]**

Methane: Natural source – produced when organic material such as plants rots
Artificial source – rotting of waste in landfill, and agriculture, e.g. cattle and rice fields

Water vapour: Natural source – evaporation from water bodies, e.g. lakes and rivers
Artificial source – burning fossil fuels

Carbon dioxide: Natural source – respiration of plants and animals, forest fires
Artificial source – combustion of fossil fuels

Exam-style practice — Grade 5

1. Name **three** greenhouse gases. **[3 marks]**
2. The Earth's surface emits thermal energy as infrared (IR) radiation. Describe the effect of greenhouse gases on this radiation in the Earth's atmosphere. **[2 marks]**

Made a start

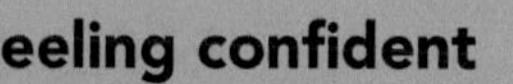

Exam ready

Human contribution to greenhouse gases

You need to know how some human activities increase the amount of greenhouse gases in the atmosphere.

Greenhouse gases

Carbon dioxide levels are increasing as a result of:

- increasing combustion of fossil fuels
- increasing population
- increasing waste and landfill
- deforestation.

Methane levels are increasing due to:

- increasing livestock farming
- decomposition of waste in landfill sites
- release of natural gas during its production at gas fields and biogas generators.

Worked example Grade 5

1 Fossil fuels release carbon dioxide when they are burned. Give a reason why many scientists are concerned about the use of fossil fuels in cars. **[1 mark]**

The combustion engine in cars produces carbon dioxide from petrol or diesel, which contributes to global warming.

2 Over the past 250 years, carbon dioxide levels in the atmosphere have increased from 0.03% to 0.04%. Give **two** human activities that may be causing this change. **[2 marks]**

Burning fossil fuels increases carbon dioxide in the atmosphere.

Deforestation reduces the amount of carbon dioxide used by trees for photosynthesis.

3 Give **one** reason why scientists cannot produce accurate models for future global climate change. **[1 mark]**

There are many different variables involved so models may not accurately predict what will happen.

It is very difficult to model global climate change because it is very complicated with many different factors to consider.

Exam focus

Make sure you can recall at least two human activities that are increasing the level of carbon dioxide in the atmosphere, and two that are increasing the level of methane.

Working scientifically

Some people believe that global warming is part of a natural cycle of climate change. However, scientists believe that human activity is causing global temperatures to rise and that this is causing global climate change. This idea is based on peer-reviewed evidence.

Peer review is a process where scientists evaluate the reliability of other scientists' investigations and results in order to help validate the research.

Most people are worried about the effects of global warming. It is important that the media, such as websites, newspapers, TV and radio news, helps to inform the public. Sometimes, through trying to explain the research findings simply, articles can become inaccurate and/or biased.

When reading articles about science you should consider:

- Who are the researchers? Are they honest and likely to produce valid results?
- What methods were used? Are they reliable?
- Who funded the research? Is it likely to be biased?
- Who is reporting the research? Are they likely to be accurate and unbiased?

Exam-style practice Grade 3

1 Give **one** reason why peer review is an important step in the development of theories. **[1 mark]**

2 Many scientists are concerned about the increasing levels of greenhouse gases. Name the effect caused by increased levels of greenhouse gases. **[1 mark]**

3 Why is it important that scientists' results are made available to a wide audience? Tick **two** boxes. **[2 marks]**

- Other scientists can use their results to inform their own work. ☐
- To frighten people unnecessarily and stop them having comfortable lives such as, using their cars and having very warm houses. ☐
- Results which have an impact on the wider population can be communicated to as many people as possible. ☐
- Scientists can be recognised for their scientific achievements. ☐

Global climate change

You need to be able to describe the possible effects of global climate change, and discuss what these effects may mean for us in the future.

Climate change

Climate is the weather over a long time, rather than the weather in one day. The **global climate** is the average climate across the whole world.

The average global temperature is increasing. Climate scientists think this is due to human activities. Rising global temperatures are a major cause of climate change.

Increasing levels of carbon dioxide and other greenhouse gases are leading to an increasing average global temperature.

Go to pages 142 and 143 to find out more about the greenhouse effect and human activities that affect it.

Impacts of climate change

Agriculture

Crop yields may decrease for all major world crops. Agricultural land on the edge of deserts will also become desert. Crops could be wiped out in low-lying areas because of flooding. With fewer crops available, food prices are likely to increase. The growing season in some areas, such as the UK, will increase. This is a benefit as more crops could be grown.

Water and ice

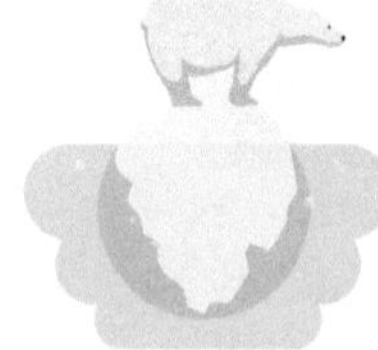

As glaciers melt, there could be avalanches and habitats will be destroyed or flooded, which may destroy entire species. Some parts of the world use meltwater from glaciers as a water source. They may become short of water. Economically, areas that rely on winter tourism may suffer from a lack of snow.

Sea level increases

Low-lying land is at risk of flooding, so the lives of 80 million people across the globe will be threatened.

Population

People will migrate from areas suffering drought. Any that remain will die from starvation and lack of water.

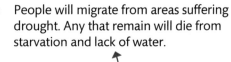

Worked example — Grade 4

The average sea level rose by 18 cm in the 20th century. It is predicted to rise 1 m this century.

(a) Suggest **two** groups of people who are most likely to be affected by rising sea levels. **[2 marks]**

People all over the world will be affected, but particularly people who live near coasts and the mouths of rivers, or on low-lying islands.

(b) Describe **one** risk of rising sea levels. **[2 marks]**

Homes and businesses near the sea may become flooded, and so may have to be abandoned.

(c) Describe **one** way in which the environment might be harmed by rising sea levels. **[2 marks]**

Fields and forests could become contaminated by salt water, so crops and other plants would be unable to grow there anymore.

Exam focus

Make sure you can describe briefly four possible effects of climate change (see above).

People living inland will also be affected as people are forced to leave affected towns, cities and farms.

Exam-style practice — Grade 3

1. Give **two** environmental impacts of climate change. **[2 marks]**
2. Identify **one** major cause of climate change. **[1 mark]**
3. Suggest **one** reason why changes in agriculture due to climate change will not just affect farmers. **[1 mark]**
4. Describe the meaning of the term 'climate'. **[1 mark]**

The carbon footprint

You need to know what the carbon footprint is and how it can be reduced.

5 What is the carbon footprint?

Whenever you use electricity generated from fossil fuels, carbon dioxide is released into the atmosphere. Carbon dioxide and other greenhouse gases contribute to the carbon footprint.

The **carbon footprint** is the total amount of greenhouse gases emitted in a full life cycle by:

- a person
- a country
- a company
- a product, such as a kettle
- a service, such as street lighting
- an event, such as a concert.

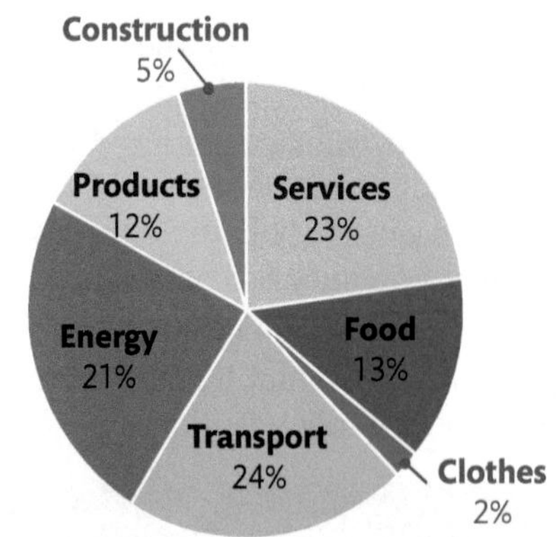

Figure 1 Sources of carbon emissions in the UK

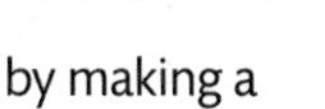

10 Reducing the footprint

Individuals, countries and industrial companies, such as steel producers, can reduce their carbon footprints by making a variety of changes which reduce carbon dioxide and methane emissions.

Individuals and companies

- **Recycle and reuse** – processing waste and decomposing waste release methane.
- **Use energy-efficient appliances** – the more energy-efficient the appliance, the lower its carbon footprint.
- **Switch things off** – leaving lights on and appliances on standby uses electricity.
- **Buy local produce** – travelling to shops far away or buying food that has been transported from other countries increases the carbon footprint.
- **Share cars, catch a bus, cycle or walk** – motor vehicle emissions significantly increase the carbon footprint. Some companies encourage employees to reduce their carbon footprint with the Cycle to Work scheme.

Countries

- **Use renewable energy** – renewable energy sources, such as solar and wind, don't produce carbon dioxide.
- **Use nuclear fuel** – nuclear fuel does not release greenhouse gases and can be used as a replacement for fossil fuels.
- **Use carbon-neutral fuels** – biofuels and biodiesel are classed as carbon neutral: the carbon dioxide they release when burned is equivalent to the carbon dioxide they absorb during photosynthesis.
- **Develop carbon capture and storage** – carbon dioxide could be pumped underground into porous rocks.
- **Tax high greenhouse gas emitters** – to encourage a reduction in car usage and transportation.

If a product is carbon neutral, it gives off no net carbon dioxide in its life cycle. This means that it has no carbon footprint.

Exam focus

In your exam, you could be asked to give reasons why actions to reduce our carbon footprint may be limited. Make sure you think about both individuals and countries in your answer.

5 Worked example — Grade 5

Suggest **three** reasons why it is difficult to reduce carbon emissions. **[3 marks]**

It is expensive to convert industries from fossil fuels to alternative energies. Not all countries agree to reduce their carbon emissions and individuals don't want to change their lifestyles.

5 Exam-style practice — Grade 5

1. Give **two** ways individuals can reduce their carbon footprint. **[2 marks]**
2. Give **two** ways industrial companies can reduce their carbon footprint. **[2 marks]**

Atmospheric pollutants

You need to know how pollutants are produced and what effects they may have.

Pollutants

Many fuels, such as coal, contain some sulfur as well as carbon and/or hydrogen.

When fuels are burned, gases are produced. Carbon dioxide, carbon monoxide, sulfur dioxide and oxides of nitrogen can all be produced when fuels burn. These gases are all pollutants. Water vapour may also be produced.

Carbon particles (soot) and unburnt hydrocarbons form solid particulates that may be released into the atmosphere, causing further pollution.

Incomplete combustion

When a fuel burns with a limited supply of oxygen **incomplete combustion** occurs.

The chemical reaction that takes place when oxygen supplies are limited is as follows:

fuel + oxygen → carbon monoxide + carbon (soot) + water

Go to page 145 to revise the carbon footprint.

Effects of atmospheric pollutants

Effects of atmospheric pollutants

Oxides of nitrogen, NO_x
- high temperatures in engines cause nitrogen from the air to react with oxygen from the air
- cause respiratory problems in humans and can lead to acid rain

Particulates
- small solid particles released into the atmosphere
- cause global dimming as they block the light from the Sun
- may also cause health issues, such as cancer, in humans

Sulfur dioxide, SO_2
- produced when sulfur from fuels is burned
- reacts with water vapour to produce acid rain
- can cause respiratory problems in humans

Carbon dioxide, CO_2
- produced when a fuel burns
- contributes to the greenhouse effect (global warming)

Carbon monoxide, CO
- a poisonous gas
- not easily detected as it is colourless and odourless

Worked example — Grade 3

1 Write the word equation for the reaction when methane burns in a plentiful supply of oxygen. **[2 marks]**

methane + oxygen → carbon dioxide + water

2 Name **three** products formed when a hydrocarbon fuel burns in a limited supply of oxygen. **[3 marks]**

Carbon monoxide, soot and water

Exam-style practice — Grade 5

1 When a fuel burns, it produces atmospheric pollutants that can cause environmental issues. Draw a straight line to link each pollutant to its corresponding environmental issue. **[3 marks]**

Pollutant	Environmental issue
carbon dioxide	global dimming
sulfur dioxide	toxic gas
solid particulates	acid rain
carbon monoxide	global warming

2 Give **one** environmental problem if sulfur dioxide gas is released into the atmosphere. **[1 mark]**

3 Describe how each of the following is produced by burning fuels.

(a) carbon monoxide and soot **[2 marks]**

(b) sulfur dioxide **[2 marks]**

(c) oxides of nitrogen **[2 marks]**

 Made a start  Feeling confident Exam ready

Earth's resources

People use the Earth's resources to keep them warm, to provide shelter and food, and for transport.

Natural resources

Natural resources are materials, fuels and sources of energy that are found in the Earth's crust, oceans or atmosphere.

Natural resources include:

- fuels such as coal and wood
- trees for building and making paper
- plants and animals for food
- cotton and wool for clothing.

Figure 1 Trees are cut down to provide wood.

Natural food resources can be improved by agricultural processes. These include using selective breeding and fertilisers.

Natural resources may be processed chemically to provide synthetic materials such as polymers.

Finite resources

Some resources are **finite** resources. They are made very slowly or are no longer being made at all. This means that they will run out one day if we keep using them. Finite resources include:

- coal, crude oil and natural gas
- metal **ores**.

Other resources are **renewable**. They can be replaced quickly enough so that they do not run out when we use them.

Figure 2 Cotton is a renewable resource.

Renewable resources include plants and animals, air, water, and wind or solar power.

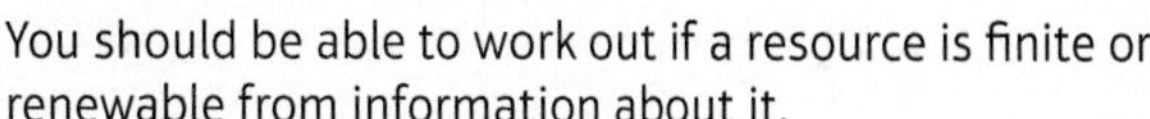

Exam focus

You should be able to work out if a resource is finite or renewable from information about it.

Worked example — Grade 3

1 Garden furniture is often made from wood. Suggest **two** other materials that could be used instead. **[2 marks]**

Plastic, or a metal such as iron.

Crude oil is the raw material for making most plastics (polymers). Iron and other suitable metals such as aluminium are made from metal ores. This means that plastics and metals are finite resources too.

2 It is estimated that there are 5600 million tonnes of copper in the world that could be mined. Every year, 20 million tonnes of copper are mined. Estimate how long it will take to mine all the copper. **[1 mark]**

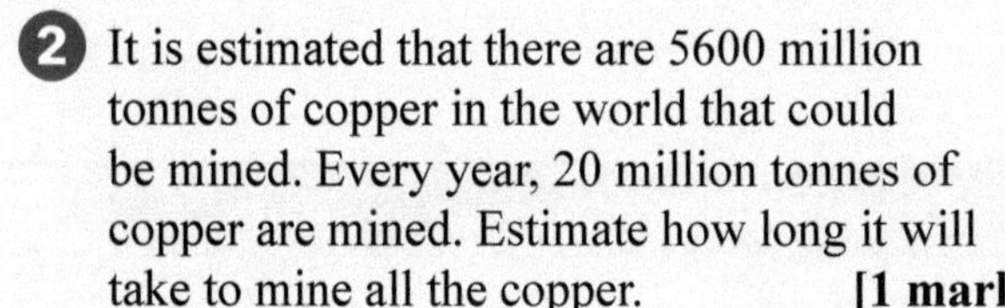

$$\text{time} = \frac{5600}{20} = 280 \text{ years}$$

The actual time taken may be different:

- New copper ores may be found in the future.
- The uses of copper may vary.

Sustainable development involves making sure that meeting our needs does not affect the ability of people in the future to meet their needs. Recycling copper or finding alternative materials will make it a more sustainable resource.

Exam-style practice — Grade 3

1. Some natural resources come from the Earth's crust. Name **two** other places where they are found. **[2 marks]**
2. Shirts may be made from cotton. Suggest **one** synthetic material that could be used instead. **[1 mark]**
3. Describe what 'sustainable development' means. **[2 marks]**
4. Give **one** reason why crude oil is a finite resource. **[1 mark]**

Potable water

You need to know how potable water (drinking water) is produced.

Pure water and potable water

Pure water only contains water molecules. **Potable**, or drinking, water is not pure as it contains dissolved substances (at safe levels), such as minerals.

Producing potable water

For water to be suitable for human consumption, it must be treated to remove microbes. The concentration of dissolved salts must be low enough to not cause harm.

The processes used to produce potable water depend on the water source and the local conditions. If supplies of fresh water are limited, desalination of salt water may be required. Desalination processes are expensive because they require large amounts of energy.

Type of water	Source	Treatment processes
fresh water	rainwater, which collects underground (the most common source of potable water in the UK) or in lakes and rivers	**Filtration** The rainwater is filtered through layers of gravel, then sand, to remove any solid waste. **Sterilisation** The final stage of water treatment is to use chlorine, ozone or ultraviolet light to kill any microbes present in the water.
salt water	from the oceans	**Distillation** The salt water is heated until it evaporates, leaving the salt behind. The water vapour is then condensed to give fresh water. **Reverse osmosis** This process involves passing water through a membrane, under pressure, to remove any ions, molecules, sediment and microbes.

Go to page 76 for more information on distillation.

Go to page 149 for more about this method of purifying water.

Worked example — Grade 4

1. There are **two** main steps involved in the treatment of rainwater to produce potable water. Name and describe each step. **[2 marks]**

Filtration removes solid particles. This is followed by sterilisation, which kills microbes.

2. Distillation of salt water is expensive due to the high amounts of energy required. Give a reason why energy is needed for distillation. **[1 mark]**

The water must be heated until it evaporates.

3. Describe how rainwater can be treated to produce potable water. **[2 marks]**

It can be filtered to remove any solid particles, then treated with chlorine, ultraviolet light or ozone to kill microbes.

Exam-style practice — Grade 4

1. Name **two** methods that can be used to produce potable water from salt water. **[2 marks]**
2. Name **one** substance that can be used to sterilise rainwater. **[1 mark]**
3. Give a reason why unprocessed seawater is not used as drinking water. **[1 mark]**
4. Name the main source of potable water in the UK. **[2 marks]**
5. Suggest **three** sources of water that can be used to produce potable water. **[3 marks]**

Made a start
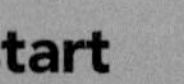

Feeling confident

Exam ready

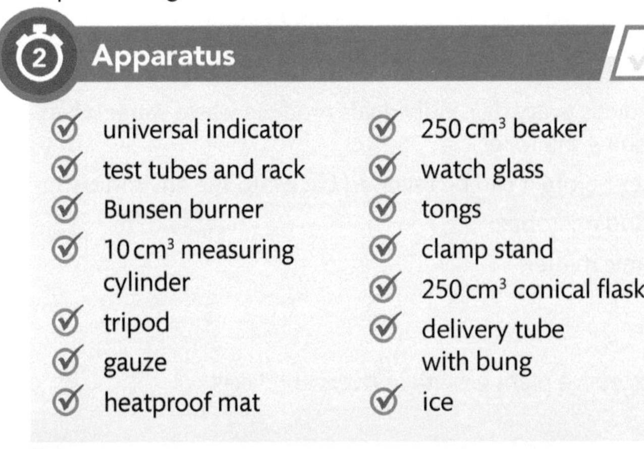

Purifying water

You will be expected to analyse and purify water samples from different sources, testing for pH and dissolved solids as well as performing a distillation.

2 Apparatus

- universal indicator
- test tubes and rack
- Bunsen burner
- $10\,cm^3$ measuring cylinder
- tripod
- gauze
- heatproof mat
- $250\,cm^3$ beaker
- watch glass
- tongs
- clamp stand
- $250\,cm^3$ conical flask
- delivery tube with bung
- ice

10 Worked example — Grade 5

Figure 1 shows how water can be separated from substances dissolved in it.

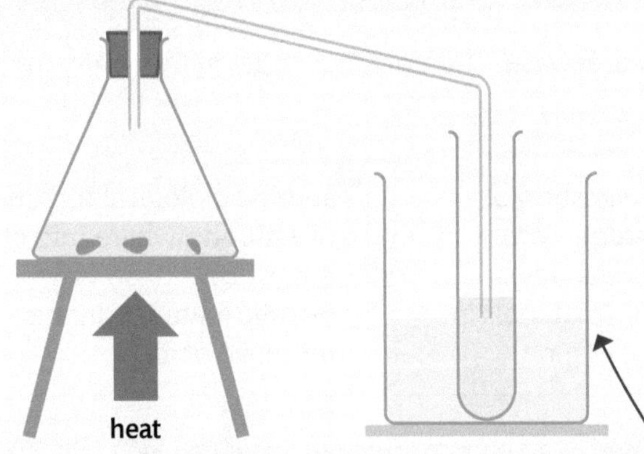

Figure 1

(a) Describe how simple distillation is used to purify seawater. **[4 marks]**

The seawater is heated to evaporate the water. Water vapour is carried through a delivery tube to a test tube. The test tube is kept cold with a mixture of ice and water. The pure water vapour cools and condenses in the test tube.

(b) Describe **two** tests you could do to show that a sample of water is pure. **[2 marks]**

Evaporate all the water and check that no solids are left behind. Boil the water and check that its boiling point is 100 °C.

10 Method

1. Using universal indicator and a pH chart, test the pH of the water samples and record the results in a table.
2. Weigh a dry watch glass. Record its mass in the table.
3. Pour a measured volume of seawater into the watch glass and place it above a beaker acting as a water bath.
4. Allow all the water to evaporate from the watch glass. The dissolved solids will remain on the watch glass.
5. Remove the watch glass with tongs and allow to cool. Dry the bottom of the watch glass.
6. Reweigh the watch glass and record the new mass.
7. Wash the watch glass, then repeat steps **2–6** for the other water samples.

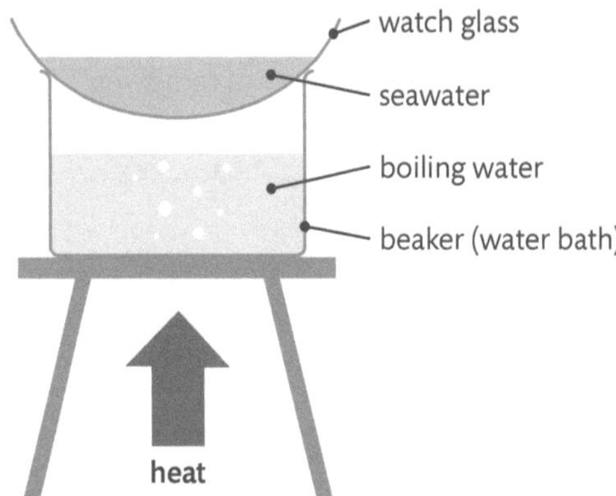

Figure 2 Apparatus for purifying water

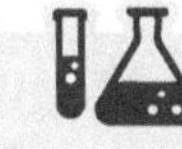

Working scientifically

In this experiment, the conical flask must be held safely on the gauze mat using a stand and clamp. The beaker contains ice and water to cool and condense the water vapour.

Pure water has a pH of 7. The pH of a sample of water can be tested using universal indicator paper or solution, or by using a pH meter. However, many solutions are also neutral, so this test on its own does not prove that a sample of water is pure.

5 Exam-style practice — Grades 2–3

1. What process is used to purify water? Tick **one** box. **[1 mark]**

   distillation ☐ neutralisation ☐ boiling ☐ filtration ☐

2. Suggest how you could test a sample of water for dissolved solids in the home. **[2 marks]**
3. Give the boiling point of pure water. **[1 mark]**

Waste water treatment

You need to know that waste water can be potentially harmful to our environment and how it can be treated to ensure it is safe.

Treating waste water

Vast volumes of waste water are produced by industries and individuals every day. Individuals produce waste water when washing clothes and dishes, bathing and showering, and when flushing the toilet.

This waste water must be treated to remove any harmful substances before it can be released back into the environment.

- Human sewage and agricultural waste contain organic matter and microbes.
- Industrial waste water contains dangerous substances and organic matter.

Processed waste water can be used for the irrigation of crops.

Effects of untreated waste water

- Eutrophication, caused by pesticides and fertilisers, results in excessive plant growth in rivers and lakes. This harms aquatic life.
- Beaches, rivers and groundwater become polluted.
- Pollutants kill fish and other aquatic organisms.
- Substances enter the food chain and cause harm to humans.

5 Sewage treatment

Sewage treatment is the process of removing contaminants from waste water. There are four stages in the treatment of sewage.

1. screening and removing grit, where large solid particles are removed →
2. sedimentation, where smaller solid particles settle out →
3. anaerobic digestion of **sewage sludge**, where microbes break down solid organic materials in the absence of air →
4. aerobic biological treatment of **effluent**, where microbes break down dissolved organic materials in the presence of air

Methane, produced by the anaerobic digestion of sludge, can be used as an energy source to generate electricity.

2 Worked example — Grade 4

(a) Name **one** gas produced by the aerobic treatment of effluent.

Carbon dioxide

(b) State which environmental issue the gas contributes to. **[2 marks]**

Carbon dioxide is a greenhouse gas which contributes to global warming when produced in excess.

Exam focus

You need to be able to make links between topics. Go to page 142 for more about greenhouse gases.

Water vapour is also produced and is also a greenhouse gas. Go to page 142 for more about greenhouse gases.

10 Exam-style practice — Grade 5

1. Name **two** sources of waste water in the home. **[2 marks]**
2. Waste water from agriculture contains pesticides and fertilisers. Suggest **two** reasons why this is potentially harmful to the environment. **[2 marks]**
3. Give the **four** stages needed to treat sewage. **[4 marks]**

Life cycle assessment

A life cycle assessment (LCA) assesses the environmental impact of a product over its lifetime, from obtaining the raw materials to disposing of it when it is no longer useful.

Stages of an LCA

An LCA looks at these four main stages:

1. Extracting the raw materials needed, and processing them into useful substances.
2. Making the product and packaging it, ready to be sold.
3. Using and repairing the product during its useful life.
4. Disposing of the product when it is no longer useful.

At each of these stages, the LCA also looks at:

- transport of materials and the product itself
- distributing the product to shops, factories and homes.

Worked example — Grade 4

Table 1 shows information from an LCA for the lifetime of four types of shopping bag.

Bag type	Energy in kJ	Waste in g
polymer **A**	22	0.42
polymer **B**	62	0.09
polymer **C**	316	5.85
paper	39	1.80

Table 1

(a) Identify the type of bag that needs the most energy during its lifetime. **[1 mark]**

Polymer C

(b) Paper bags produce more waste than bags made from polymers **A** or **B**. Explain why paper bags may be less harmful to the environment than bags made from polymers. **[2 marks]**

Paper is biodegradable but most polymers are not. This means that some waste due to paper bags may rot away, but polymer bags and some of the waste they cause will not.

Types of information used

It can be difficult to assess all the aspects of an LCA. Some factors can be quantified (given numbers or values). These include:

- the volume of water needed
- the mass of natural resources needed
- the amount of energy needed
- some of the wastes produced.

Other factors are more difficult to quantify. For example, the effects of some pollutants are difficult to work out. We may know that they harm the environment, but how much may be a subjective judgement. In other words, we may have to decide how bad something is, based on our views rather than on numbers.

All this means that producing an LCA is not a completely objective process.

Table 1 shows energy use and waste production for the whole life of the bags. However, you may be given information about one or two stages in an LCA, rather than all four together.

Bags made from polymer **C** also produce the most waste.

LCAs that are shortened, or which show only certain information, could lead to incorrect conclusions. They may even be misused in adverts that make claims about a product being 'environment-friendly'.

For example, if we only look at the amount of waste, polymer **B** seems to be best. However, this type of bag uses more energy than all the other types except for polymer **C**.

Exam-style practice — Grade 3

1. Identify the type of bag in the Worked example that uses the least amount of energy. **[1 mark]**
2. Describe what an LCA is intended to assess. **[2 marks]**
3. Give **two** factors that can be quantified fairly easily in an LCA. **[2 marks]**

Reducing the use of resources

Reusing and recycling are important because a lot of the energy used to manufacture new products comes from limited resources. Most plastics are made from crude oil, a limited raw material. Glass, metals, clay ceramics and building materials are also produced from limited raw materials. The use of resources is reduced by **recycling** materials, **reusing** products, and **reducing** the use of products.

Reusing and recycling

Some products, such as glass bottles, can be reused. Glass can also be crushed and melted to make new glass products.

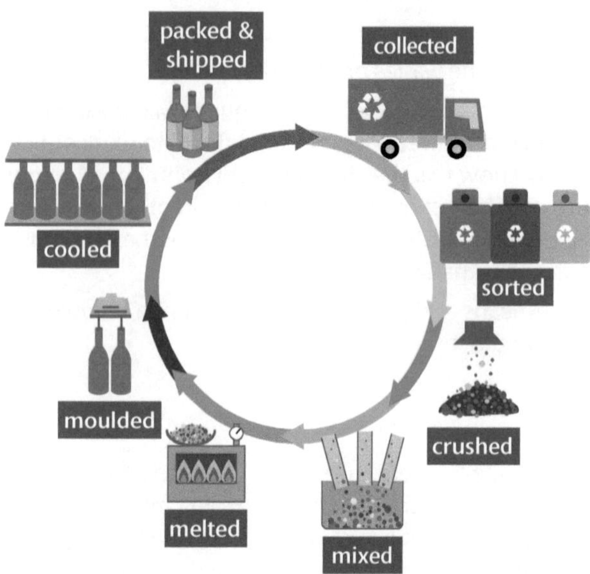

Some products cannot be reused. It is often difficult to reuse metal objects. However, metals can be melted and recast, or reformed into new products.

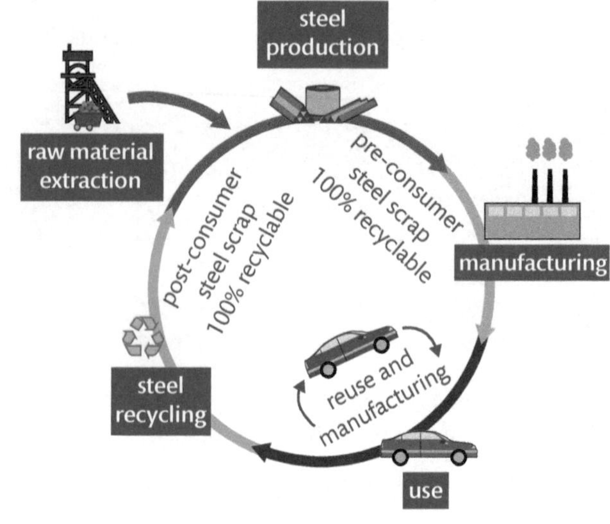

Worked example — Grades 2–3

1 (a) Explain why scrap steel is added to molten iron from a blast furnace. **[2 marks]**

It reduces the amount of iron ore needed because steel contains iron.

(b) Explain why metal recycling centres use electromagnets. **[2 marks]**

This is to separate steel from copper and aluminium. Steel is attracted to a magnet but the other two metals are not.

The different materials have to be separated from each other before they can be recycled. The amount of separation depends on:

- the material being recycled
- the properties the new product should have.

2 Which **two** of the following are reasons for reusing and recycling materials?
Tick **two** boxes. **[2 marks]**

- [ ] It increases the use of limited resources.
- [x] It reduces the production of waste.
- [ ] It increases the use of energy resources.
- [x] It reduces the impact on the environment.

Exam-style practice — Grade 4

Table 1 shows the amount of energy saved by recycling three different metals, compared to producing new metals from their ores.

Metal	% energy saved	Cost in £ per kg
aluminium	93	0.65
copper	89	4.50
steel	58	0.09

Table 1

Use information in **Table 1** to answer these questions.

(a) Identify the metal that saves the most energy by recycling. **[1 mark]**

(b) Suggest which metal is best overall for recycling. Explain your answer. **[3 marks]**

 Made a start 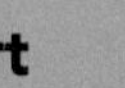  Feeling confident  Exam ready

Energy transfers in a system

A system is an object or group of objects. Systems change when energy is transferred between different energy stores.

Principle of conservation of energy

Energy is either transferred usefully, stored or dissipated. Energy cannot be created or destroyed.

This means the total amount of energy in any closed system remains constant. Where energy appears to be 'lost', it is usually being wasted. Energy can be transferred by heating, forces and an electric current.

Energy transfers
(Wasted forms of energy are underlined.)

Catching a ball
kinetic → thermal
A moving object hitting an obstacle transfers kinetic energy to thermal energy.

Archer shooting an arrow into the air
chemical store (from muscles) → strain potential (stored in the bow) → kinetic (as arrow flies) → gravitational potential energy (as arrow goes up) → kinetic (as arrow falls back down) → thermal
Some energy would be wasted as heat due to work done against air resistance as the arrow moves.

A boat constantly accelerating
chemical from fuel store → kinetic and thermal
The boat gains kinetic energy as it accelerates, and thermal energy due to more work being done against the resistance of water on the boat.

Electric kettle
electrical store → thermal store
Heat is used to boil the water.

Vehicle braking
kinetic → thermal
The friction in the brakes transfers thermal energy.

Reducing energy losses

Energy is transferred to thermal energy when work is done against friction in moving parts. Friction can be reduced by lubricating moving parts and reducing the amount of energy wasted.

Thermal energy is often a wasted energy in electrical circuits. The wasted energy can be reduced by using low currents or decreasing the resistance of the circuit.

Thermal energy is wasted in many buildings as it can be conducted through the walls. The lower the thermal conductivity and the thicker the walls, the less energy wasted. Many types of building insulation are thick and contain trapped air. Air has poor thermal conductivity, which reduces the rate of wasted thermal energy being transferred from the building.

Exam-style practice — Grade 4

A thick, wool jumper is better than a thin t-shirt for reducing energy loss from a body.

(a) Name the waste energy that is lost from the body. **[1 mark]**

(b) Compare the jumper and t-shirt and how each traps air. **[2 marks]**

(c) Explain why a jumper is better than a t-shirt at keeping you warm. **[2 marks]**

Air has poor thermal conductivity. This means it is a good insulator.

Gravitational potential energy

You need to be able to calculate gravitational potential energy (g.p.e.), a type of stored energy that an object gains when it is lifted.

2 Calculating g.p.e.

The gravitational potential energy (g.p.e.) of an object, measured in joules (J), depends on its mass, its height and the **gravitational field strength**.

It can be calculated using the equation:

g.p.e. (J) = mass (kg) × gravitational field strength (N/kg) × height (m)

$E_p = mgh$

The gravitational field strength of the Earth is 9.8 N/kg.

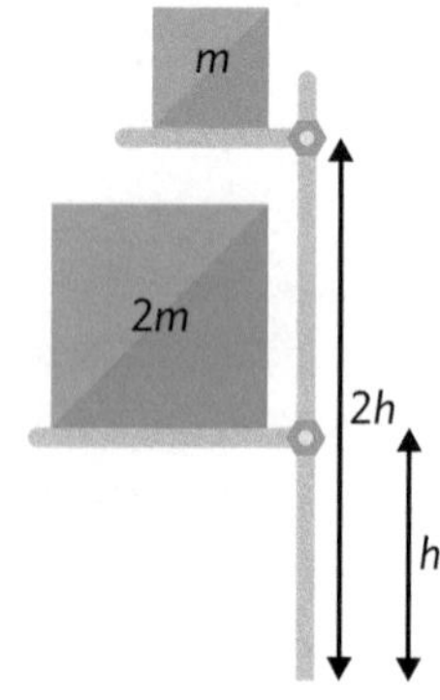

Figure 1 Both of these boxes have the same gravitational potential energy. The bottom box has twice the mass of the top box, but has only half the height. For both boxes the gravitational field strength is the same.

2 Kinetic energy

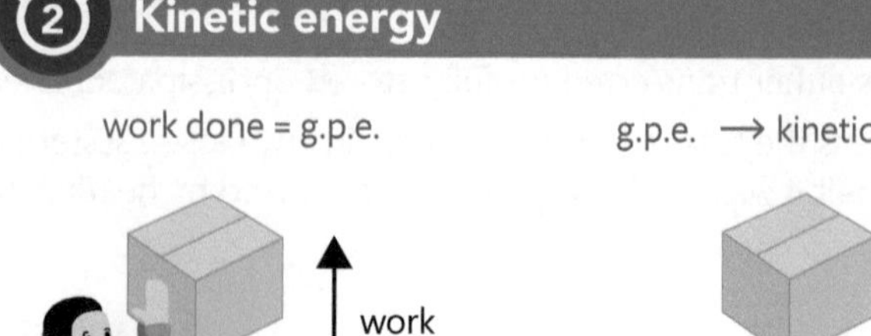

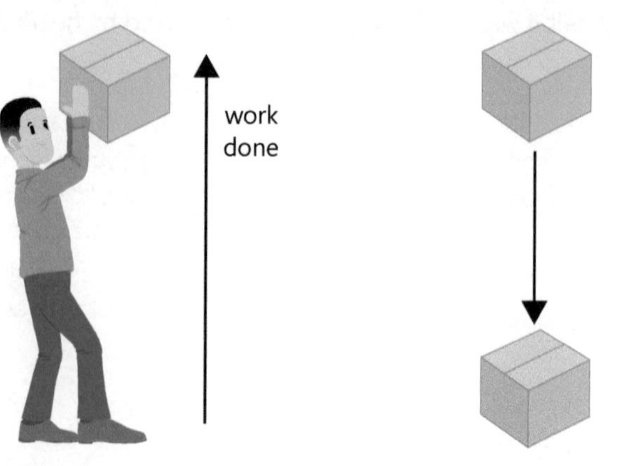

Figure 2 Lifting and dropping a box

When a box is lifted, the g.p.e. of the box is equal to the work done in lifting it. When the box is dropped, the g.p.e. will transfer into kinetic energy as it falls. The kinetic energy the box has when it hits the ground is equal to the g.p.e. it had at the highest point.

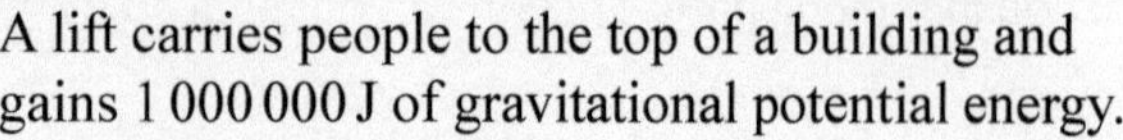

10 Worked example — Grade 5

A lift carries people to the top of a building and gains 1 000 000 J of gravitational potential energy.

(a) Explain why the lift will gain less g.p.e. if it makes this trip when empty. **[2 marks]**

It will have lower mass without the people and g.p.e. depends on mass.

> The g.p.e. depends on mass. If the lift is empty, there will be less mass and so less g.p.e.

(b) How much g.p.e. does the lift gain when it is half way up the building? **[1 mark]**

1 000 000 ÷ 2 = 500 000 J

> The height is half, therefore the g.p.e. will be half.

(c) Another lift has a mass of 550 kg and goes down 20 m. Calculate the amount of g.p.e it loses. Use g = 9.8 N/kg. **[2 marks]**

$E_p = mgh = 550 \times 9.8 \times 20 = 107\,800$ J

15 Exam-style practice — Grade 5

1 Calculate the energy in the gravitational potential energy store for a 70 kg rock climber 100 m up a cliff. ($g = 9.8$ N/kg) **[2 marks]**

2 If the same rock climber only has 50 000 J of g.p.e., calculate their height up the cliff. **[3 marks]**

3 Use the idea of energy transfer to explain why the speed of a ball increases as it falls. **[2 marks]**

4 A crane lifts a crate 20 m. The crate gains 1000 J of g.p.e.

> It might help to draw a quick sketch.

(a) Give the amount of work done by the crane. **[1 mark]**

(b) Calculate how much more g.p.e. the crate will gain if it is lifted another 40 m. **[2 marks]**

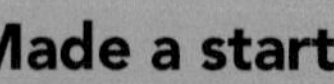
Made a start

Feeling confident

Exam ready

Kinetic energy

All moving objects have kinetic energy. You should be able to work out how much kinetic energy moving bodies have.

Calculating E_k

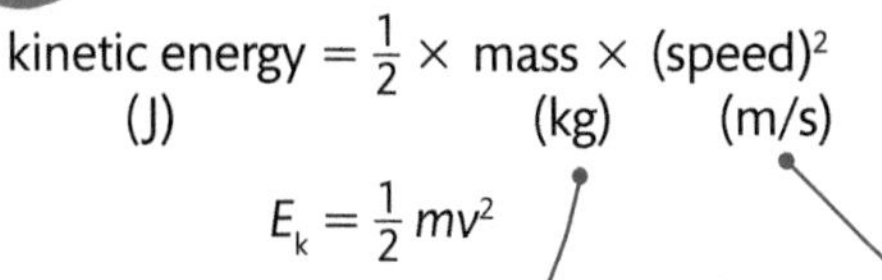

kinetic energy $= \frac{1}{2} \times$ mass $\times$ (speed)^2
(J) (kg) (m/s)

$$E_k = \frac{1}{2}mv^2$$

Doubling the mass will double the kinetic energy.

As the speed is squared, doubling the speed will make the kinetic energy four times larger.

Maths skills
Kinetic energy depends on the speed^2.

If the speed of a fixed mass is doubled, the kinetic energy increases by 2^2, which is 4 times more.

If the speed had tripled, the kinetic energy would be multiplied by 3^2, which is 9 times more.

Make sure you only square the speed.

$\frac{1}{2}$ is entered into a calculator as 0.5.

Kinetic energy depends on mass and speed. If a heavier object moves with the same speed it will have a greater kinetic energy.

Key equations

Finding mass

$$m = \frac{E_k}{\frac{1}{2}v^2} = 2\frac{E_k}{v^2}$$

Finding speed

Rearrange for v^2 first: $v^2 = \frac{E_k}{\frac{1}{2}m} = 2\frac{E_k}{m}$

then square root both sides: $v = \sqrt{2\frac{E_k}{m}}$

Worked example — Grade 5

1 A bird travelling at 10 m/s has 400 J of kinetic energy. Determine the new kinetic energy if the speed doubles. **[2 marks]**

$400 \times 2^2 = 400 \times 4 = 1600$ J

2 (a) Calculate the kinetic energy of a 1200 kg car moving at 10 m/s. **[2 marks]**

$$E_k = \frac{1}{2}mv^2 = \frac{1}{2} \times 1200 \times 10^2$$
$$= \frac{1}{2} \times 1200 \times 100$$
$$= 60000 \text{ J}$$

(b) Another car travels at 10 m/s but has a higher kinetic energy. Compare the masses of the cars. **[1 mark]**

The mass of this car is more than 1200 kg.

Energy transfers

If you do 500 J of work to move something you give it 500 J of kinetic energy.
It will also take 500 J of work to stop it from moving.
If it stops due to friction then it has done 500 J of work against friction.

Figure 1 Moving a trolley

Exam-style practice — Grade 5

1 (a) A running cat has 125 J of kinetic energy. What is the kinetic energy of a dog with twice the mass chasing at the same speed?
Tick **one** box. **[1 mark]**

62.5 J ☐ 125 J ☐ 125 J ☐ 500 J ☐

(b) If the cat runs twice as fast, what is its new kinetic energy?
Tick **one** box. **[1 mark]**

62.5 J ☐ 250 J ☐ 125 J ☐ 500 J ☐

2 An athlete with a mass of 67 kg runs at 11 m/s. Calculate the kinetic energy of the athlete. **[2 marks]**

3 A frisbee with a mass of 0.4 kg is thrown at 7 m/s. Calculate how much work is done in throwing the frisbee in joules. **[2 marks]**

Energy in a spring

When a spring is stretched or compressed, it stores energy, which is known as elastic potential energy (e.p.e.). You need to be able to calculate this, given the spring constant and extension. Anything that can be elastically deformed stores this kind of energy.

Stored energy

elastic potential energy (e.p.e) (J) = 0.5 × spring constant (N/m) × (extension)² (m)

$$E_e = \frac{1}{2}ke^2$$

This equation only works if the spring has not reached the point where it isn't extending as much. That is, the **limit of proportionality** has not been reached.

If the spring becomes inelastically deformed, the energy is used to change its shape and is not stored as elastic potential energy.

Elastic potential energy is always released as kinetic energy.

Maths skills

The energy depends on extension².

If the extension increases, the spring stores more energy.

If the extension **doubles**, the energy stored will be **four** times greater.

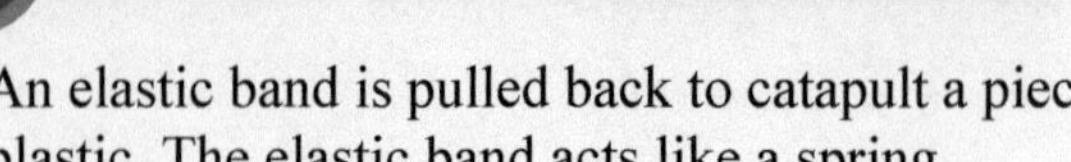

Worked example — Grade 4

An elastic band is pulled back to catapult a piece of plastic. The elastic band acts like a spring.

(a) The band stores elastic potential energy. Name the energy store this will be transferred to when the band is released. **[1 mark]**

Kinetic energy

(b) The elastic band is stretched back further. Explain how this affects the energy stored and the speed the plastic is catapulted at. **[3 marks]**

There is more elastic potential energy stored. The plastic will be catapulted faster, because it has more kinetic energy.

(c) The elastic band has a spring constant of 600 N/m. It is stretched 49 cm (0.49 m). Calculate the elastic potential energy stored. **[2 marks]**

$E = \frac{1}{2}ke^2 = 0.5 \times 600 \times 0.49^2 = 72\,J$

Make sure you use the standard units of metre and Newton/metre, to get the energy in joules.

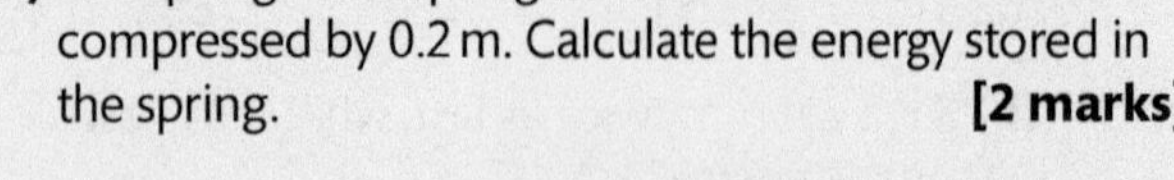

Exam-style practice — Grade 5

Figure 1 shows a compressed spring that releases a ball from the tube.

(a) Identify the energy changes that occur as the ball is released and moves upwards into the air. **[3 marks]**

(b) The spring has a spring constant of 60 N/m and is compressed by 0.2 m. Calculate the energy stored in the spring. **[2 marks]**

(c) Explain why the ball reaches a greater height when the spring is compressed by more than 0.2 m. **[3 marks]**

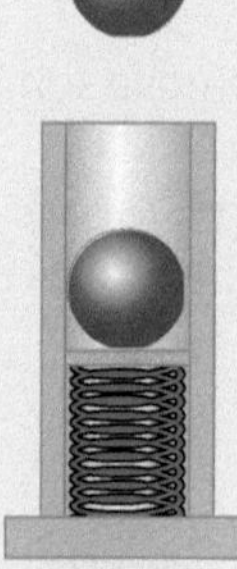

Figure 1

Made a start

Feeling confident

Exam ready

Using energy equations

In your exam, you will need to be able to recall and apply energy equations.

Worked example — Grade 5

1 **(a)** A 15 kg snow sledge is pushed until it reaches a speed of 8 m/s. Calculate the energy transferred to the sledge. **[2 marks]**

$E_k = \frac{1}{2}mv^2$

$= 0.5 \times 15 \times 8^2 = 480\,J$

Think about all the equations you might be able to use, such as kinetic energy, $E_k = \frac{1}{2}mv^2$, or work done, $W = Fs$. To decide which one to use, look at the information you have been given. In this case, mass and velocity.

(b) Write how much work is done pushing the 15 kg sledge to 8 m/s. **[1 mark]**

480 J

The work done does not need to be calculated. The kinetic energy the sledge has is the same as the amount of work done on the sledge.

2 A 0.3 kg ball is dropped from a height of 2.5 m.

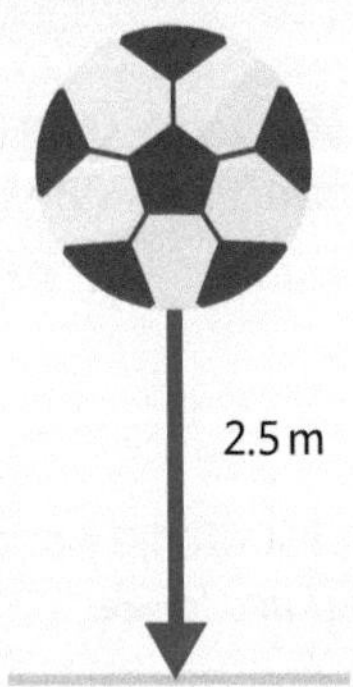

(a) Calculate the gravitational potential energy of the ball before it is dropped.

(g = 9.8 N/kg) **[3 marks]**

$E_p = mgh = 0.3 \times 9.8 \times 2.5 = 7.35\,J$

(b) The ball is lifted until it has 10 J of g.p.e. Calculate the height it has been lifted to.

(g = 9.8 N/kg) **[3 marks]**

$E_p = mgh$

$10 = 0.3 \times 9.8 \times h$

$h = \frac{10}{0.3 \times 9.8} = 3.4\,m$

$h = \frac{E_p}{mg} = \frac{10}{0.3 \times 9.8} = 3.4\,m$

You will need to be able to rearrange the equations for some questions. In this case, you have to rearrange the gravitational potential energy equation for height.

Exam focus

You need to remember k.e. and g.p.e. equations.

Exam-style practice — Grade 5

1 Write the equation used to calculate kinetic energy. **[1 mark]**

2 A brick with a mass of 1.25 kg falls off a shelf.

It hits the floor with a speed of 0.6 m/s.

Calculate the amount of kinetic energy the brick has as it hits the floor. **[2 marks]**

3 A cricket ball is thrown with 25 J of kinetic energy. How much work is done on the ball to throw it? **[1 mark]**

4 A ball has a mass of 0.35 kg. The ball is thrown upwards with 25 J of kinetic energy and reaches a maximum height.

(a) Write the equation that links the energy of a mass with height. **[1 mark]**

(b) Calculate the maximum height the ball reaches. (g = 9.8 N/kg) **[2 marks]**

5 **(a)** A van has twice the mass of a car. The van and the car travel at the same speed. How much kinetic energy does the van have compared with the car? **[1 mark]**

(b) Car A and car B are identical. Car A travels at twice the speed of car B. What is the kinetic energy of car A compared to car B? **[1 mark]**

Tick **one** box.

- double ☐
- half ☐
- quadruple ☐
- same ☐

Power

Power is a measure of the rate of energy transfer. It tells you how much energy is transferred per second. You need to know how to calculate power using two different equations.

Calculating power

You can calculate power with the equation:

$$\text{power (W)} = \frac{\text{energy transferred (J)}}{\text{time (s)}} \qquad P = \frac{E}{t}$$

or in terms of work done:

$$\text{power (W)} = \frac{\text{work done (J)}}{\text{time(s)}} \qquad P = \frac{W}{t}$$

Power is the **rate** of energy transfer. It measures how quickly energy changes or transfers.

A power of 1 watt means 1 joule is being transferred every second. A 1000 W heater will transfer 1000 J of electrical energy into heat and waste energy every second.

Worked example Grade 5

An electric heater has a power of 2 kW.

(a) It takes 20 minutes to heat a room. Calculate the energy transferred by the heater in 20 minutes. **[3 marks]**

$E = P \times t$

$= 2000 \times 1200 = 2400000$ J

(b) Give your answer in standard form. **[1 mark]**

2.4×10^6 J

(c) Another heater has a power of 500 W. How many times longer would it take this heater to heat the same room by the same amount? Assume no heat is lost. **[1 mark]**

4 times longer

Watch the units. Electrical appliances often have powers measured in kW. Remember 1 kW = 1000 W.

The time needs to be in seconds, so 1 min = 60 s.

Energies can get very large so you must be prepared to use standard form. Make sure you know how to put standard form into your calculator and how to read it.

Exam focus

Notice that the question did not ask for the *time*, it asked 'how many *times longer*'.

If it had asked for time, the answer would be 80 minutes. Make sure you read questions very carefully.

As the power is four times smaller, it will take four times longer to heat the room.

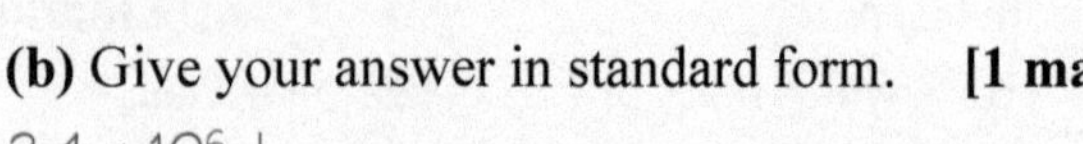

Units

$$\text{power (W)} = \frac{\text{energy transferred (J)}}{\text{time (s)}} = \frac{\text{work (J)}}{\text{time (s)}}$$

The unit for power, watts, is the same as joules per second or 1 W = 1 J/s

Many appliances have large powers which are measured in kilowatts. 1 kW = 1000 W

Likewise for energy: 1 kJ = 1000 J

If you use kilojoules in the equation, the power will be in kilowatts. The time must still be in seconds.

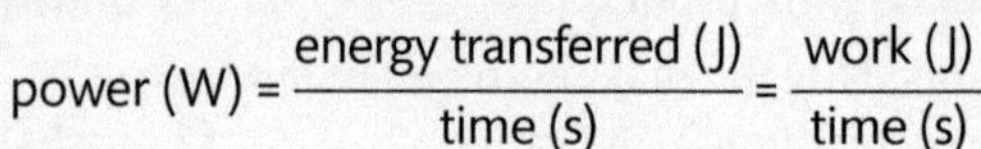

Exam-style practice Grade 4

1. Write the correct unit for each quantity.
   (a) work done **[1 mark]**
   (b) power **[1 mark]**
   (c) energy transferred. **[1 mark]**
2. Lamp **A** has power of 100 W. Lamp **B** has power of 150 W. Explain which lamp appears brighter. **[2 marks]**
3. A motor lifts a crate. The motor transfers 2000 kJ of energy in 120 s. Calculate the power of the motor in kW. **[2 marks]**

Made a start

Feeling confident

Exam ready

Efficiency

Efficiency is a measure of how much of an energy transfer is used usefully. The more efficient something is, the less energy it wastes. You need to be able to calculate efficiency and comment on how efficient something is.

2 Calculating efficiency

You can calculate efficiency using the equation:

$$\text{efficiency} = \frac{\text{useful output energy transfer (J)}}{\text{total input energy transfer (J)}}$$

Efficiency can also be calculated in terms of power:

$$\text{efficiency} = \frac{\text{useful power output (W)}}{\text{total power input (W)}}$$

Energy is normally measured in joules and power in watts. As long as the units for both output and input are the same the calculation will work; for example, both output and input energy are in MJ, or output and input power are in kW.

2 Key facts: efficiency

- The equations will give you a result between 0 and 1.
- Efficiency does not have any units.
- You could multiply the efficiency value by 100 to get it as a percentage.
- The closer to 1 (or 100%), the more efficient the process and the less energy is wasted.
- If something is 65 per cent efficient, 65 per cent of the energy is used usefully and 35 per cent is wasted.

10 Worked example — Grade 5

A power station produces 150 000 kW of electrical power and transfers chemical energy in coal at a rate of 380 000 000 W.

> Convert this to kW so the units match.
> 380 000 000 W ÷ 1000 = 380 000 kW

(a) Assuming all other energy is wasted as heat, what is the rate of heat loss? **[2 marks]**

> 'Rate of heat loss' is another way of saying 'energy loss divided by time' so it is equivalent to power (energy/time) and has the unit watts or kilowatts.

380 000 – 150 000 = 230 000 kW

> All of the 380 000 kW that is taken in must be given out. 150 000 kW comes out as electrical power so whatever is left must be the heat.

(b) Calculate the efficiency of the power station. **[2 marks]**

$$\text{efficiency} = \frac{150\,000}{380\,000} = 0.39$$

(c) A pile of coal contains 250 kJ of chemical energy. Calculate how much useful energy the pile of coal will transfer in this power station. **[2 marks]**

> You need to use the efficiency from the previous answer and rearrange the equation for useful energy output.

useful energy output
= efficiency × total energy input
= 0.39 × 250 kJ = 97.5 kJ

(d) The power station recycles some of the lost heat to heat the buildings. Explain the effect this has on the efficiency of the power station. **[2 marks]**

> Efficiency measures the proportion of energy that is used usefully. Efficiency is improved by reducing wasted energy or by making waste energy useful.

The efficiency increases because there is less waste energy.

10 Exam-style practice — Grades 2–4

1. A TV uses 400 J of energy and wastes 150 J. Calculate its efficiency. **[2 marks]**
2. A house's central heating is 85 per cent efficient. Calculate the percentage of energy that is wasted. **[1 mark]**
3. Lamp **A** and lamp **B** transfer energy at 50 W. Lamp **A** is brighter than lamp **B**. Explain which lamp is more efficient. **[2 marks]**
4. A heater has an efficiency of 0.6. It transfers 1500 J as useful energy. Calculate the input energy. **[2 marks]**

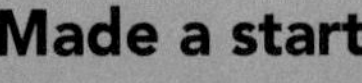

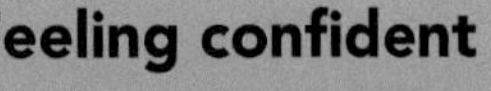
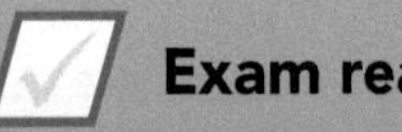

Renewable energy resources

Renewable energy resources provide alternative sources of energy that will not run out or are easy to replace. They are used for heating, transport, or to generate electricity. You need to know the advantages and disadvantages of renewable energy resources.

Advantages and disadvantages of renewable resources

Renewable resource	Advantages	Disadvantages
Sun – can directly warm buildings or sunlight can be used to generate electricity using solar panels	free energy once installed low maintenance costs (no moving parts) works anywhere	only works when the sun shines low power output
Geothermal – electricity is generated using heat from hot rocks underground	reliable high power output free energy once installed	only works in certain places expensive to drill
Biofuels – fuel for transport or electricity is made from vegetable oil, alcohol, wood, methane or waste	reliable high power output can be used to generate energy from waste	fuel crops can drive up the cost of food environmental impact if forests cleared to make room for crops releases carbon dioxide, a greenhouse gas
Wind – wind turbines turn to generate electricity	can be placed in isolated locations free energy once installed, but some maintenance costs	danger to birds noisy spoil landscape only work when it is windy cannot be used in storms
Hydro-electricity – water movement rotates turbines to generate electricity	reliable high power output small waterwheels work in some isolated locations free energy once installed, but some maintenance costs	building dams can flood valleys, which destroys habitats
Tides – the daily movement of the ocean is used to generate electricity	reliable high power output free energy once installed, but has maintenance costs	flooding river estuaries can destroy habitats
Waves – ocean waves turn turbines to generate electricity	free energy once installed, but has some maintenance costs	only works when there are waves dangerous to maintain

Worked example — Grade 3

A farmer replaces diesel generators with a wind turbine to produce electricity. Give **two** advantages and **two** disadvantages of this decision. **[4 marks]**

Advantages: The farm would not produce any chemical pollution; no fuel costs.

Disadvantages: The farm would have no electricity if there was no wind, or if it was stormy; could be a danger to birds.

Exam-style practice — Grade 3

A house in the countryside uses solar panels and rechargeable batteries to produce its electricity.

(a) Explain how the rechargeable batteries are used to get electricity at night. **[2 marks]**

(b) Suggest a reason why solar panels are useful for a house in the countryside. **[1 mark]**

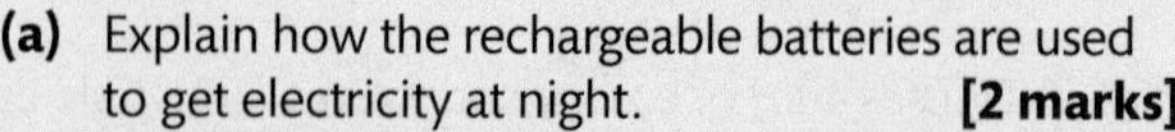

You could also write they may spoil the landscape or cause noise pollution to locals.

 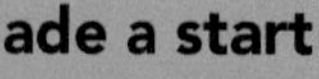 Made a start  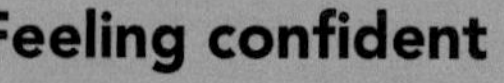 Feeling confident  Exam ready

Non-renewable energy resources

Non-renewable energy resources, such as fossil fuels and nuclear power (nuclear energy from atoms), are used to generate electricity used for heating and to power transport. You need to know the advantages and disadvantages of non-renewable energy resources.

2 Non-renewable resources

People use fossil fuels directly by:

- burning coal, oil or natural gas to heat their homes or cook food
- using petrol or diesel in their cars.

People use fossil fuels or nuclear power indirectly when using electricity. The majority of electricity in the UK is generated by burning fossil fuels, mainly natural gas.

Figure 1 Nuclear power is clean but the nuclear waste has to be disposed of correctly.

2 Three issues

1. If non-renewable energy resources run out, people will have to find other energy resources.
2. Oil has many other uses, such as producing plastics. If oil runs out, people will have to find alternatives for these other uses.
3. Resources will become more expensive as they begin to run out.

2 Worked example — Grades 4–5

Compare the environmental impact of an electric car with a diesel-powered car. **[2 marks]**

An electric car needs to source its electricity from somewhere. If this source is non-renewable then it will produce greenhouse gases and smoke. However, the electric car itself will not cause pollution directly. A diesel car contributes to air pollution every time it is used.

5 Comparing nuclear and fossil fuels

	Nuclear power	Fossil fuels
Advantages	• Other than steam, no gases are emitted. There is less effect on global warming and no effect on health. • A little fuel produces a lot of energy. • Nuclear fuel will last much longer than fossil fuels and nuclear power stations do not release carbon dioxide.	• The fuels are relatively low cost. • Fossil fuel power stations can be started up very quickly (especially gas). It is easy to adapt to changing power demands.
Disadvantages	• The nuclear waste stays radioactive for thousands of years and has to be safely stored. • Transport of radioactive fuel and waste is dangerous and costly. • Nuclear power plants are costly to decommission. • Accidents can release radioactive substances into the environment. • Nuclear power stations take a very long time to start up and shut down.	• Carbon dioxide, a greenhouse gas, is produced. Carbon dioxide contributes to global warming. • Sulfur dioxide and smoke can cause breathing problems. • A large amount of fuel needs to be transported with coal. Coal is much less efficient. • Burning fossil fuels produces more pollution, not just carbon dioxide but sulfur dioxide, carbon soot and smoke.

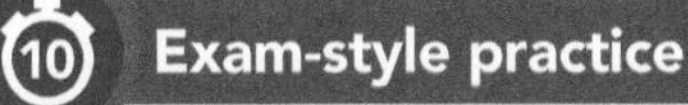

10 Exam-style practice — Grade 4

1. Name **three** types of fossil fuels. **[1 mark]**
2. Compare the advantages and disadvantages of using a nuclear power station instead of a coal-fired power station. **[4 marks]**
3. Coal power stations require a lot of fuel. Give **two** reasons why this is a problem. **[2 marks]**

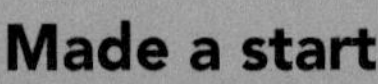

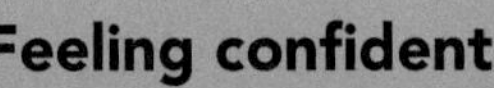

Made a start Feeling confident Exam ready

Circuit diagrams

You need to be able to recognise and draw the universal symbols used to represent the components of a circuit.

5 Circuit symbols

Make sure you know all the symbols by name as well as their uses.

switch (open)
breaks a circuit

switch (closed)
closes a circuit

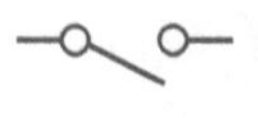

cell
provides energy to the circuit

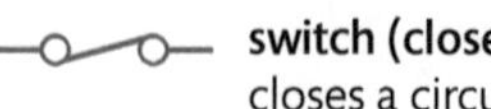

battery
more than one cell in series

diode
only lets current flow in one direction

variable resistor
a resistor you can change

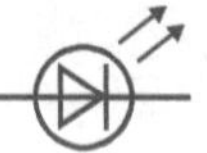

LED (light-emitting diode)
lights up when current flows in the direction of the arrow

thermistor
resistance decreases as temperature increases; used to control devices such as thermostats in central heating systems or electronic thermometers

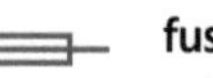

fuse
melts and breaks the circuit if the current gets too high

resistor
resists the flow of current

lamp
lights up when current flows

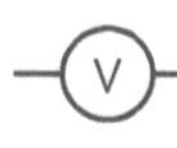

voltmeter
connected to a circuit in parallel, measures the potential difference

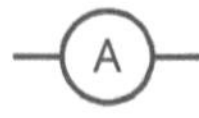

ammeter
connected to a circuit in series, measures the current

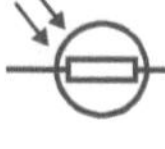

LDR (light-dependent resistor)
resistance decreases as light intensity increases; can be used to control light-sensitive devices such as street lights that come on when it's dark

5 Circuits

For a current, there must be a complete circuit. Conventional current is from positive to negative. This is particularly important when dealing with diodes and LEDs.

Test circuits

A **test circuit** allows the current and potential difference of a component to be measured. You could replace the lamp in this circuit with any other component to test. Any circuit powered by a battery carries **direct current** (dc). The **resistance** of a component can be found using a test circuit and the equation:

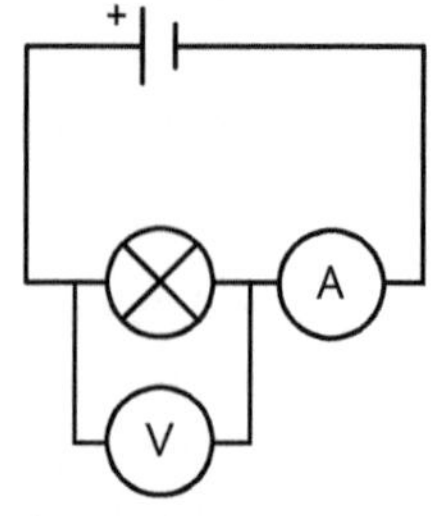

Figure 1 A test circuit

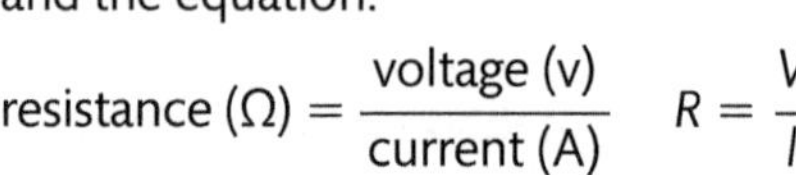

$$\text{resistance } (\Omega) = \frac{\text{voltage (v)}}{\text{current (A)}} \qquad R = \frac{V}{I}$$

5 Worked example — Grade 5

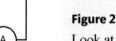

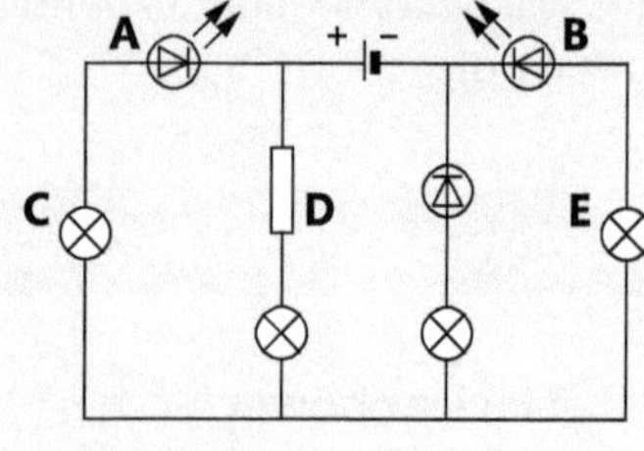

Figure 2

Look at the circuit diagram in **Figure 2**.

(a) Name component **D**. **[1 mark]**

Resistor

(b) **A** and **B** are LEDs. Which LED will allow a current to flow in this circuit? **[1 mark]**

B is the only one pointing the right way.

(c) Determine which of the lamps **C** and **E** will light. **[1 mark]**

Only E (LED A stops current flowing to C)

15 Exam-style practice — Grade 3

1. Give the direction of conventional current flow. **[1 mark]**
2. Look at the circuit diagram in **Figure 3**.
   (a) Explain why lamp **A** will not light. **[1 mark]**
   (b) Give **two** things that need to happen to make lamps **B** and **C** light up. **[1 mark]**
3. A street light turns on when it gets dark. What component could be used to control the circuit to switch on the light? **[1 mark]**

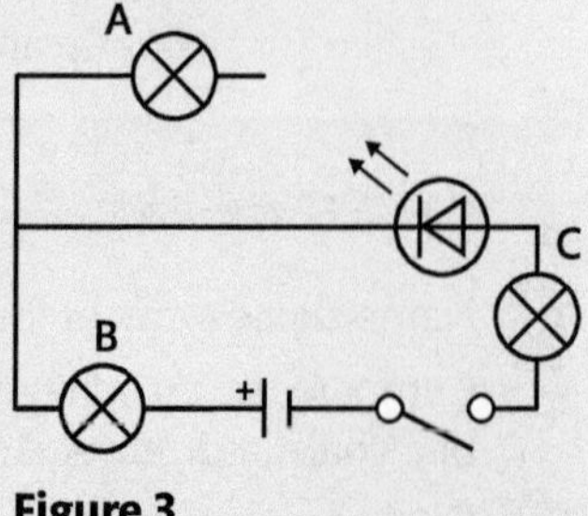

Figure 3

Current, resistance and potential difference

You need to understand current, resistance and potential difference to understand the basics of electrical circuits.

Key definitions

Current is the flow of charge. In wires, this is carried by electrons. The greater the current, the greater the rate of flow of electrical charge.

Potential difference (pd), measured in volts, is the energy transferred to or from the charge as it flows around the circuit. You will sometimes hear this referred to as *'voltage'*, but potential difference is the proper name.

Resistance opposes the flow of charge. It is measured in ohms or Ω (for example, 10 Ω or 10 ohms). Resistance is caused by electrons colliding with the metal ions inside a wire.

$V = IR$

The current in a circuit depends on the resistance and the potential difference.

potential difference (V) = current (A) × resistance (Ω)

$$V = IR$$

When the potential difference is increased, more energy is given to the charge, increasing the current.

Maths skills

For ohmic conductors where R is constant, potential difference is proportional to current.

$V \propto I$

If you double V you also double I for the same resistance.

Current is inversely proportional to resistance.

$V \propto \frac{1}{R}$

If you double the resistance you halve the current.

Worked example — Grade 3

The circuit in **Figure 1** contains a 15 Ω resistor.

(a) The ammeter reads 0.8 A. Calculate the potential difference across the resistor. **[2 marks]**

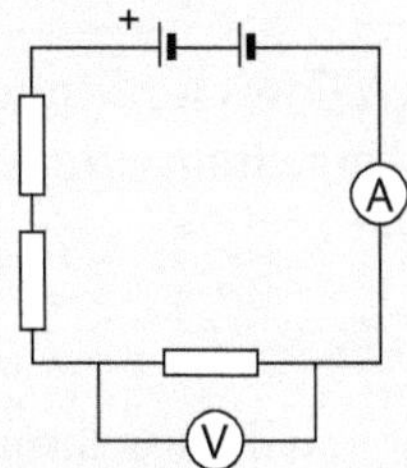

Figure 1

$V = 0.8 \times 15 = 12\,V$

(b) The cell is replaced by one with a smaller output voltage. State if each of the following will increase, decrease, or stay the same:

(i) resistance **[1 mark]**

Resistance stays the same.

(ii) current. **[1 mark]**

Current decreases.

(c) A 1.5 V cell is used in the circuit. What is the reading on the voltmeter? Tick **one** box. **[1 mark]**

15 V  22.5 V  1.5 V  ✓

Exam-style practice — Grades 2–4

1. Calculate the resistance of the lamp in **Figure 2**. **[3 marks]**
2. A second identical lamp is added in series with the first.
   (a) Describe how this affects the resistance in the circuit. **[1 mark]**
   (b) Calculate the potential difference across each lamp. **[2 marks]**
3. **(a)** Another circuit is set up as in **Figure 2** but with an 80 Ω resistor instead of a lamp. Calculate the current through the resistor. **[2 marks]**
   (b) How will doubling the battery pd to 12 V change the current in the circuit? Tick **one** box. **[1 mark]**

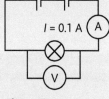

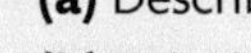

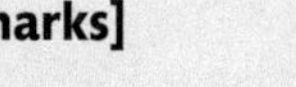

Figure 2

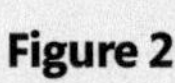

makes the current 0 A	☐	does not change the current	☐
halves the current	☐	doubles the current	☐

Electrical charge

Electrical current is a flow of charge, usually carried by electrons in wires. You need to be able to calculate charge, given the current and length of time the charge has been flowing.

5 Charge and current

The size of the electrical current (I) is the rate of flow of the electrical charge (Q). Charge is measured in coulombs (C) and current is measured in amps (A), which is the coulombs of charge per second.

The equation to work out these quantities is

$Q = It$

An ammeter can be used to measure the current over a period of time, and this equation can be used to work out the electrical charge.

Using the charge and the potential difference in a circuit, you can use the equation $E = QV$ to find out how much energy is transferred. This can then be used to work out the work done or the power of an electrical circuit.

2 Calculations

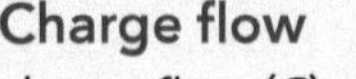

Charge flow

charge flow (C) = current (A) × time (s)

$$Q = It$$

Energy

energy transferred (J) = charge flow (C) × potential difference (V)

$$E = QV$$

You can also calculate the energy if you know the power.

Go to page 171 to revise this.

1 Exam focus

The equations on this page won't be on your exam sheet, so you need to be able to remember them. Make sure you know how to rearrange the equations as well. Equation triangles can help you to do this, but always write out the equation.

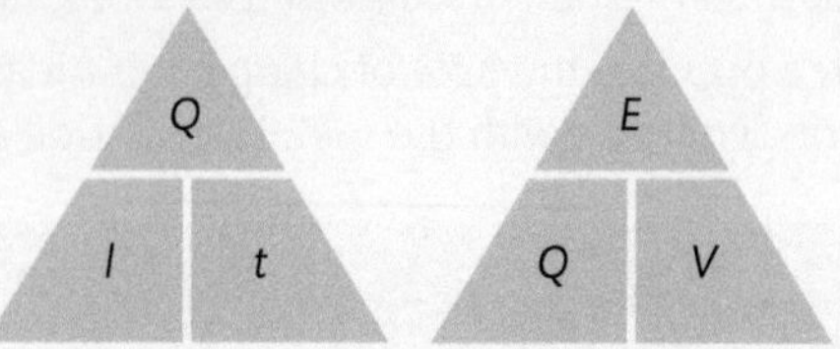

5 Worked example — Grade 4

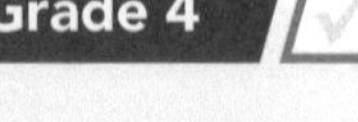

Figure 1 is a circuit diagram showing two lamps in series.

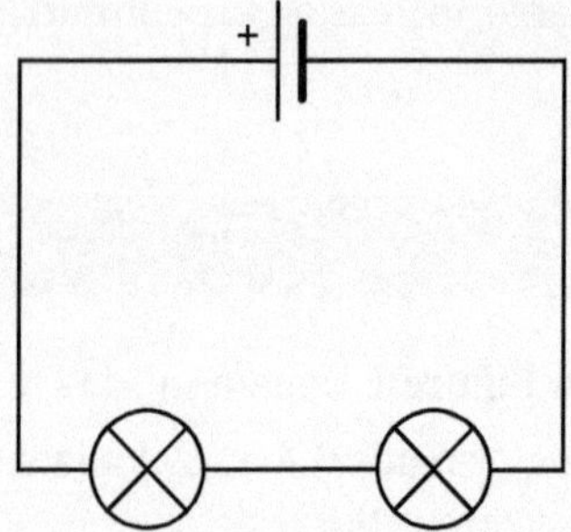

Figure 1

(a) A current of 1.2 A flows for 5 minutes. Calculate the amount of charge transferred. **[3 marks]**

$t = 5 \times 60 = 300$ s

$Q = It = 1.2 \times 300 = 360$ C

Always use the time in seconds.

(b) How much charge will pass through each lamp in this time? **[1 mark]**

360 C

Remember that the current is the same in all places in a series circuit. This means that the amount of charge flowing through each lamp is also the same.

(c) Calculate the current if 30 C of charge flows in 20 s. **[3 marks]**

$Q = It$

$30 = I \times 20$

$I = \frac{30}{20} = 1.5$ A

10 Exam-style practice — Grades 2–4

1. Give the electrical charge transferred each second by a 2 A current. **[1 mark]**
2. A starter motor needs a current of 6 A to start a car. A charge of 30 C is transferred. Calculate how long it takes the starter motor to do this. **[3 marks]**
3. Calculate the charge transferred by a 0.6 A current in 15 s. **[2 marks]**

 Made a start  Feeling confident 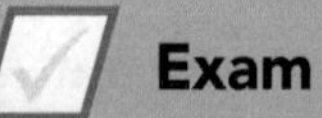 Exam ready

Resistance

This practical investigates the factors affecting the resistance of electrical circuits. You need to be familiar with the method and results.

Wire length and resistance

Set up a circuit with a cell, an ammeter connected in series and a voltmeter connected in parallel across a variable length of wire. Once the potential difference and current have been measured, the resistance can be calculated.

$$\text{resistance} = \frac{\text{potential difference}}{\text{current}} \qquad R = \frac{V}{I}$$

As length increases, the resistance increases proportionally.

Resistance is caused when electrons collide with metal ions. The longer a wire is, the more metal ions there are for electrons to collide with, so the greater the resistance.

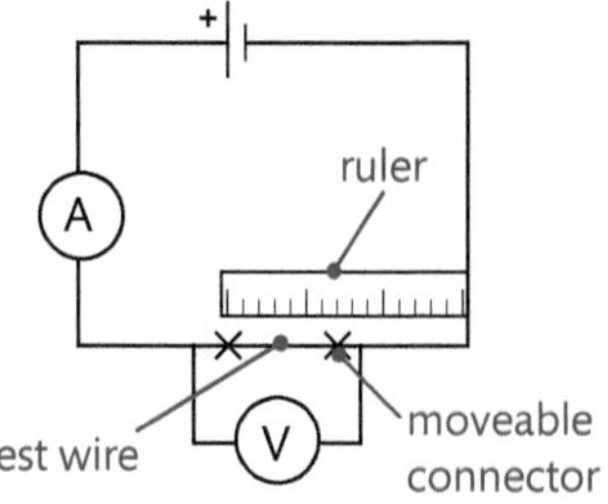

Figure 1 The effect of wire length on resistance is investigated by measuring the current and potential difference over different lengths of wire and seeing how the resistance changes.

Resistors in series and parallel

Instead of varying the length of wire, you can insert any number of resistors in series or parallel into the circuit. You have to be able to measure the potential difference across the whole set and the total current in the circuit. The voltmeter should be connected across all the resistors, or across the power supply to get the total potential difference. The ammeter should be connected so it measures the total current from the power supply.

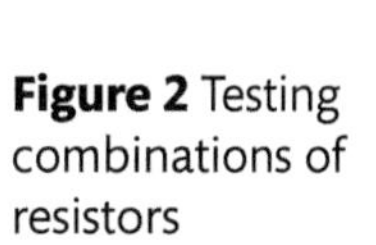

Figure 2 Testing combinations of resistors

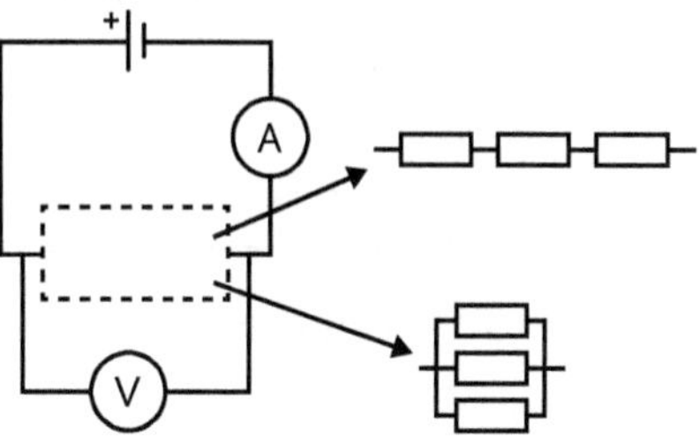

Reducing errors

- Keep the length long and the current low to limit how hot the wire will get. Resistance is increased by high temperature.
- Clean the wire with wire wool to remove any dirt or oxide that might increase the resistance in the connections.
- Tape the wire to a wooden metre rule to help keep it straight and make the length measurements more accurate.
- Switch off between tests to allow cooling.

Worked example

Grade 3

A student measures the current and potential difference for different lengths of a piece of wire to determine the resistance.

(a) Name the equipment needed to measure:

(i) current **[1 mark]**

ammeter

(ii) potential difference **[1 mark]**

voltmeter

(iii) length. **[1 mark]**

ruler

(b) The wire is cleaned as dirt may increase the resistance.

Give a reason why it is necessary to:

(i) keep the wire straight **[1 mark]**

To ensure the length measurement is accurate

(ii) keep the current as low as possible. **[2 marks]**

If the current gets too high the wire can get hot which can increase the resistance of the wire.

Exam-style practice

Grade 5

Describe a method to investigate the resistance of a filament lamp. Include a circuit diagram in your answer. **[6 marks]**

 Made a start  Feeling confident  Exam ready

Resistors

Some components have constant resistance. These are called ohmic conductors. The resistance of other components, such as lamps, diodes, thermistors and LDRs, changes. The resistance of a thermistor changes with temperature and the resistance of an LDR changes with light intensity. You need to be able to interpret an I-V graph to study the resistance of a component.

Ohmic conductors

I-V graphs for resistors

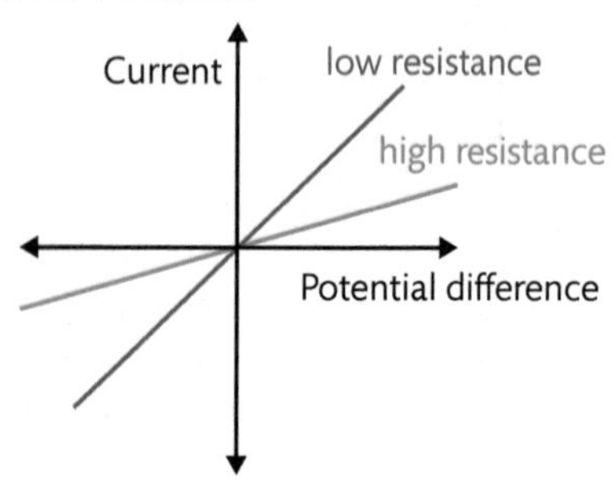

Figure 1 An I-V graph

The gradient of the I-V graph indicates the resistance. The **higher** the gradient, the **lower** the resistance.

If the resistance is constant then the graph will be a straight line.

For ohmic conductors (at constant temperature) potential difference ∝ current, $V \propto I$.

You can calculate the resistance using

$$R = \frac{V}{I}$$

Read the values for pd and current off the graph at the desired point.

Resistance and temperature

When the temperature of a conductor increases, the resistance of the conductor increases.

Worked example — Grade 4

(a) Sketch the I-V graph for a filament lamp. **[3 marks]**

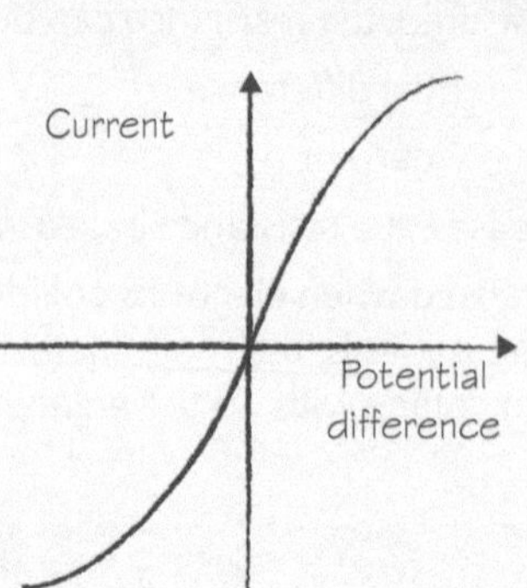

(b) The resistance of the lamp increases at higher potential differences. Explain how the graph shows this. **[1 mark]**

The gradient decreases at higher potential differences.

(c) What is the relationship between the resistance and the temperature of the lamp? **[1 mark]**

The resistance of the lamp increases as the temperature increases.

Diodes

Diodes are like electrical valves. They only let current flow one way. Above a low threshold pd the gradient is very high, meaning they have virtually no resistance. If the current is reversed, the graph is flat and shows a very high resistance, so there is no current (see page 163).

The I-V graph for a diode is non-linear. The I-V graphs for ohmic conductors are linear.

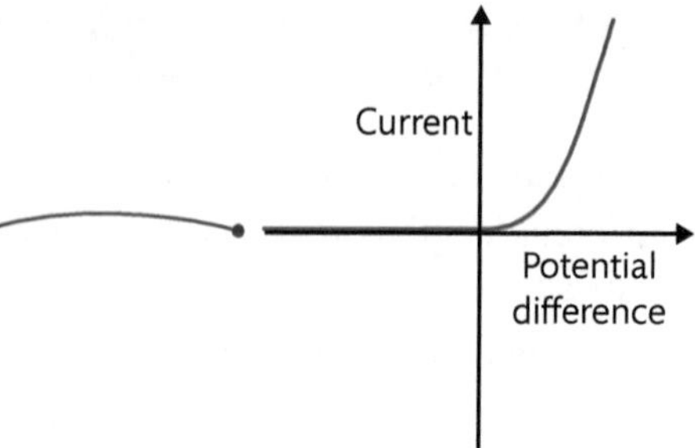

Figure 2 An I-V graph for a diode

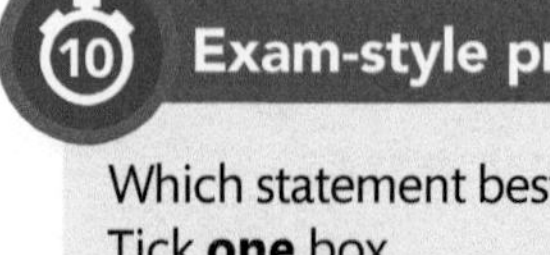

Exam-style practice — Grade 4

Which statement best describes the resistance of a diode?
Tick **one** box. **[1 mark]**

- Diodes have very high resistance. ☐
- Diodes have very low resistance. ☐
- A diode's resistance changes with temperature. ☐
- A diode's resistance is high when current flows in one direction but low when it flows in the other. ☐

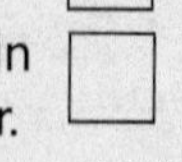

 Made a start  Feeling confident Exam ready

Series and parallel circuits

Electrical components can be joined either in series or in parallel. You need to know the differences between series and parallel circuits.

Series and parallel circuits

Potential difference and current behave differently in series and parallel circuits.

	Series circuit	Parallel circuit
Current	same through all components	sum of the current through each component
Potential difference (pd)	split across components	same across each component
Total resistance	sum of all resistances (equivalent to a single resistor with the same value)	less than the smallest resistance

Total resistance

In series

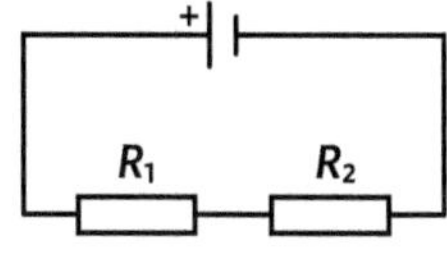

Figure 1

Any components connected in the same loop are in series. The resistances can be added together to give a total resistance.

$R_{total} = R_1 + R_2$

In series, each added component increases the resistance and decreases the current. This is because every additional component makes it more difficult for current to flow.

In parallel

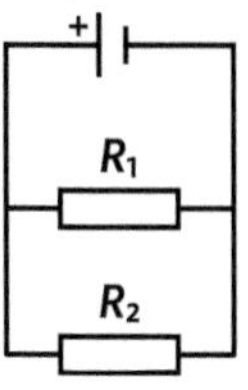

Figure 2

Components connected in different loops are in parallel. The total resistance of the two resistors is less than the resistance of the smallest individual resistor.

In parallel circuits, every new loop gives the current a new route to get around the circuit. Even though each route contains a component, it is easier overall for the current to flow, so the overall resistance decreases. The total resistance of two resistors in parallel is always less than the resistance of the smaller of the two resistors.

Worked example

Grade 3

Two lamps are connected together in two different circuits as shown in **Figure 3**.

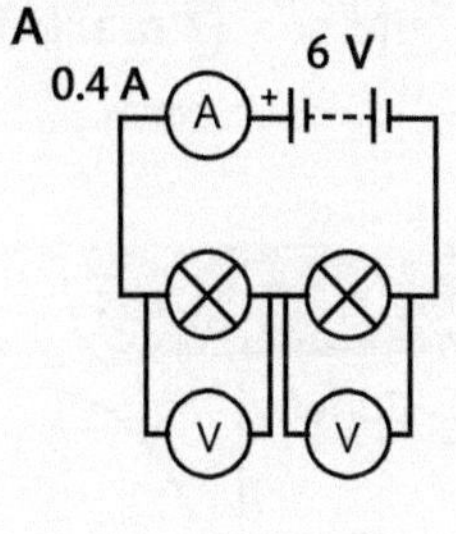

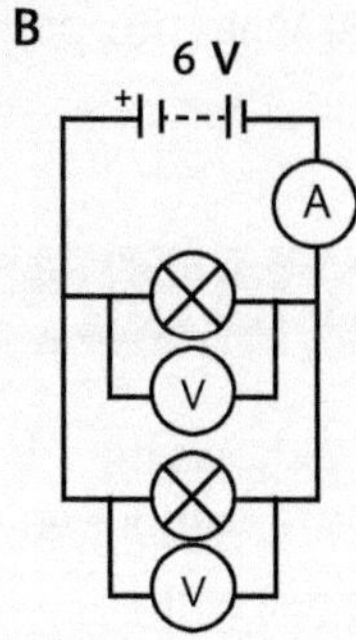

Figure 3

(a) Name each type of circuit. **[2 marks]**

A is series, B is parallel

(b) (i) The readings on each voltmeter in circuit **A** are identical. Give the value of this reading. **[1 mark]**

3 V

(ii) The readings on each voltmeter in circuit **B** are also identical. Give the value of this reading. **[1 mark]**

6 V

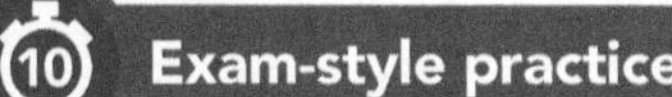

Exam-style practice

Grades 4–5

1. A series circuit has two resistors, $R_1 = 12\,\Omega$ and $R_2 = 4\,\Omega$. Calculate the total resistance. **[1 mark]**
2. Two lamps are connected in series. Explain why the brightness of the lamps decreases when another lamp is connected in series with them. **[3 marks]**
3. Describe what happens to the brightness of a lamp when another lamp is connected in parallel. **[2 marks]**

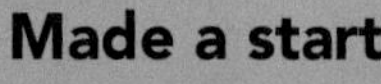

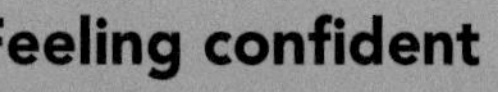

Made a start | Feeling confident | Exam ready

I–V characteristics

You need to be able to plot an I–V graph for a lamp, a diode and a resistor.

5 Plotting an I–V graph

To plot a graph of current against pd:

- Change the potential difference across the component and measure the current passing through it.
- Switch the direction by changing the pd from positive to negative. The current and potential difference will be negative numbers in this direction. Diodes do not behave in the same way in both directions, although most other components do.
- Plot potential difference on the x-axis and current on the y-axis.

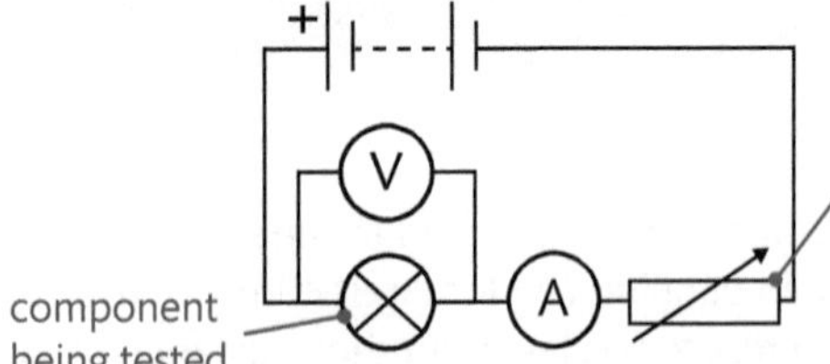

Figure 1 This circuit is a bit more complex than the circuit used to find the resistance of components as you need to be able to change the pd across the component.

2 Resistor and diode

Resistor

Allow the resistor to cool between readings to keep the temperature constant. An I–V graph for a resistor should give a straight line showing constant resistance.

Diode

In one direction the resistance will be tiny, meaning there is a large current. A large current will damage the diode. Use an extra resistor in series to keep the current low and protect the diode.

2 Gradient and resistance

A general straight-line equation is $y = mx + c$, where:

- m is the gradient
- c is the y-intercept.

Rearrange the equation $V = IR$ to give:

$$I = \frac{1}{R} V$$
$$y = m \; x + c$$

The gradient is $\frac{1}{\text{resistance}}$ so resistance is $\frac{1}{\text{gradient}}$.

Even for curves, the gradient **indicates** the resistance. Where the gradient is lower at larger potential differences, the current increases more slowly as potential difference increases, showing that the resistance increases.

2 Reducing errors

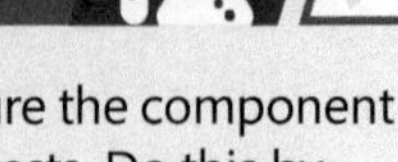

- If taking repeat readings, make sure the component has time to cool down between tests. Do this by switching off the circuit between readings.
- For wires and resistors, keep the potential difference low to reduce heating from large currents.

1 Exam focus

- Make sure you know the shape of the graph for each component and understand what this tells you about the resistance (see page 165).
- A constant gradient means constant resistance.
- For curves, link the change in gradient to the pd.

3 Worked example — Grades 3–4

Current	Potential difference
0.25	7.5
0.50	15.0
0.75	22.5
1.00	30.0

The table shows the current and potential difference for a component.

(a) Give the units that go in the headings. **[2 marks]**

Current: A or amps; Potential difference: V or volts

(b) A student concludes that current increases as potential difference increases. Another student says they can give a more specific pattern. Suggest what this pattern could be. **[2 marks]**

As potential difference doubles, current doubles.

10 Exam-style practice — Grade 5

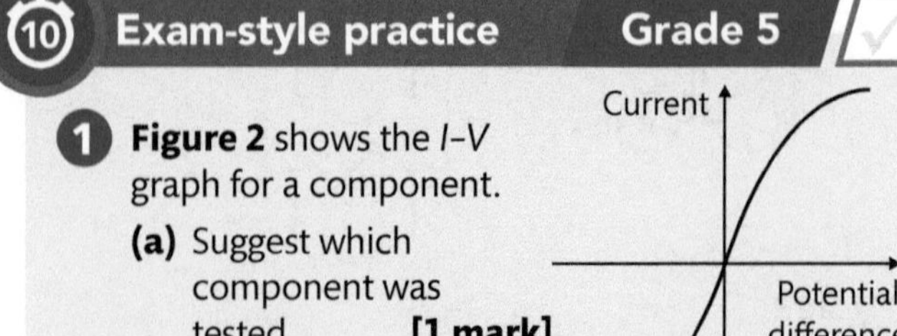

1 **Figure 2** shows the I–V graph for a component.

(a) Suggest which component was tested. **[1 mark]**

(b) Describe how the gradient changes at higher potential differences. **[1 mark]**

Figure 2

(c) What does a decreasing gradient indicate on an I–V graph? **[1 mark]**

2 When producing the I–V graph for a wire, it is important to prevent the wire from heating up. Suggest **two** ways to do this. **[2 marks]**

 Made a start 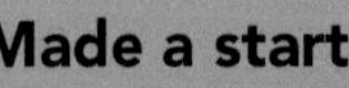  Feeling confident   Exam ready

Mains electricity

Mains electricity is alternating current and uses three colour-coded wires.

2 Alternating and direct current

- **Alternating current (ac)** changes direction from positive to negative and back very quickly.
- **Direct current (dc)** only flows in one direction.

Mains electricity in the UK uses ac with a frequency of 50 Hz. It changes direction between +230 V and –230 V 50 times a second.

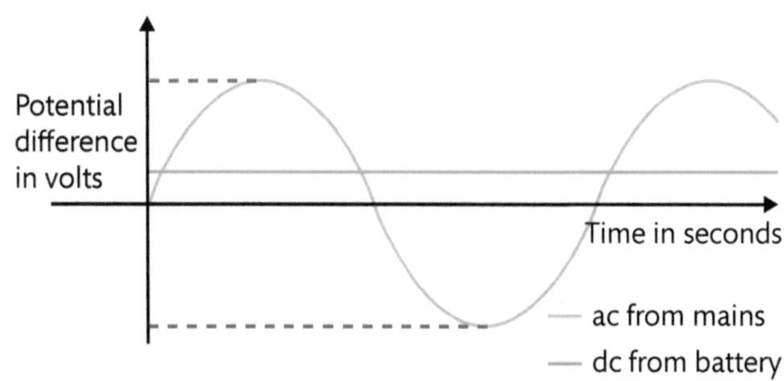

Figure 1 Batteries provide dc while mains electricity uses ac.

5 Three wires in a plug

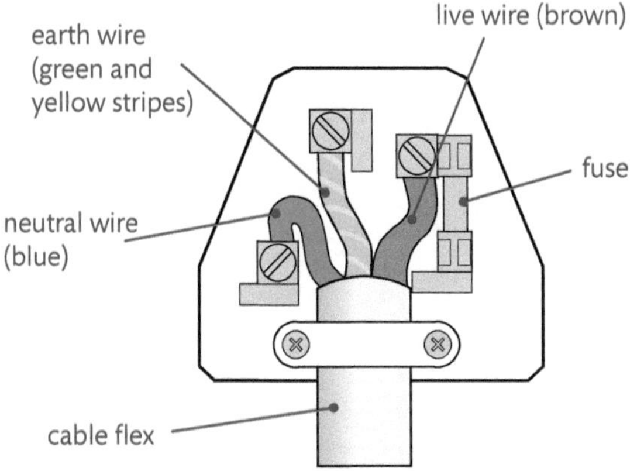

Figure 2 In the UK, appliances are connected to the mains using a three-core cable and a plug.

The **live wire** carries the ac pd at +/–230 V.

The **neutral wire** has a pd of 0 V. It completes the circuit.

The **earth wire** is at 0 V. It only carries a current if there is a fault. It 'earths' a casing that has become live, reducing the risk of an electric shock. The earth wire is only required to earth a metal casing.

The earth wire connects the outer case to the ground. If the case becomes live, the current flows through the earth wire rather than shocking a person who touches it.

5 Electrical safety

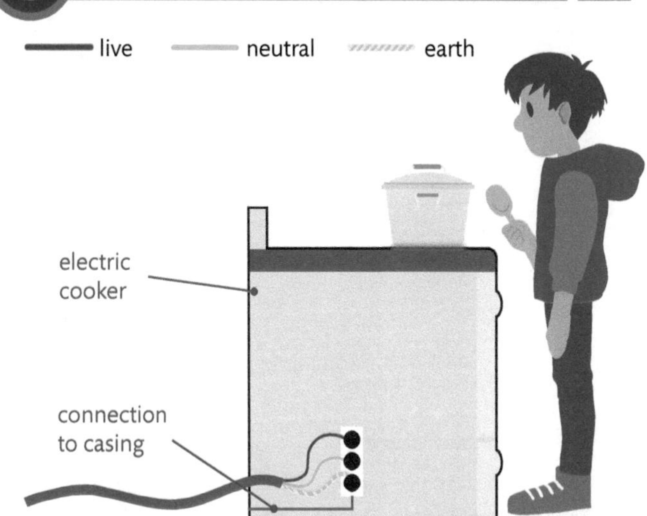

Figure 3 Take care when handling electrical equipment.

Even if the socket switch is in the off position, touching the live wire can give you a shock. This is because you are completing a new circuit between the live wire and the ground.

If the live wire touches the earth wire it causes a short circuit. In a short circuit, very large currents can flow. This breaks the fuse and disconnects the appliance. It can also cause a fire.

If there is a fault, the metal outer casing might become live. If someone touches the casing, they will receive an electric shock as the current flows through them to the ground.

2 Worked example — Grade 2

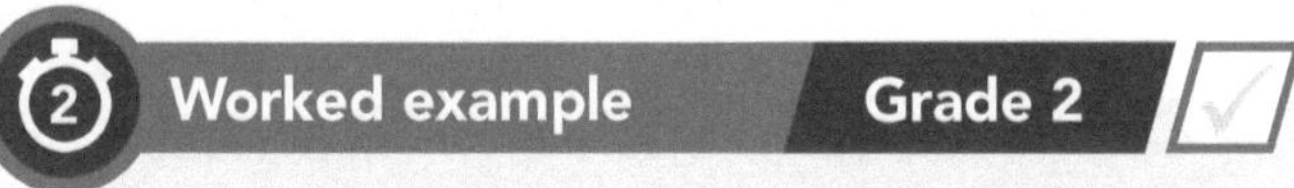

Name **two** safety features used in mains electricity. **[2 marks]**

Fuse and earth wire

10 Exam-style practice — Grade 2

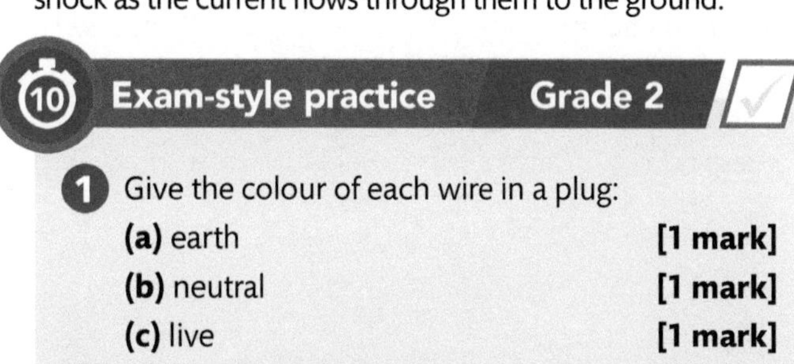

1. Give the colour of each wire in a plug:
   (a) earth **[1 mark]**
   (b) neutral **[1 mark]**
   (c) live **[1 mark]**
2. What do dc and ac stand for? **[1 mark]**
3. Give the voltage of mains ac in the UK. **[1 mark]**

Energy transfers in appliances

All electrical appliances transfer electrical energy into other useful forms; however, some energy is always wasted.

Energy stores

Energy cannot be created or destroyed, only transferred. All the energy going into an appliance has to go somewhere.

- Mains appliances transfer electrical energy into other **energy stores**.
- Battery-powered appliances transfer chemical energy to electrical energy, then into other energy stores.

Work is done when charge flows in a circuit.

Energy transfers

The appliances shown in **Figure 1** transfer electrical energy into other useful types of energy. The amount of energy transferred depends on the power of the appliance and how long it is switched on for.

The useful energy outputs are in blue, and wasted energy outputs are in red.

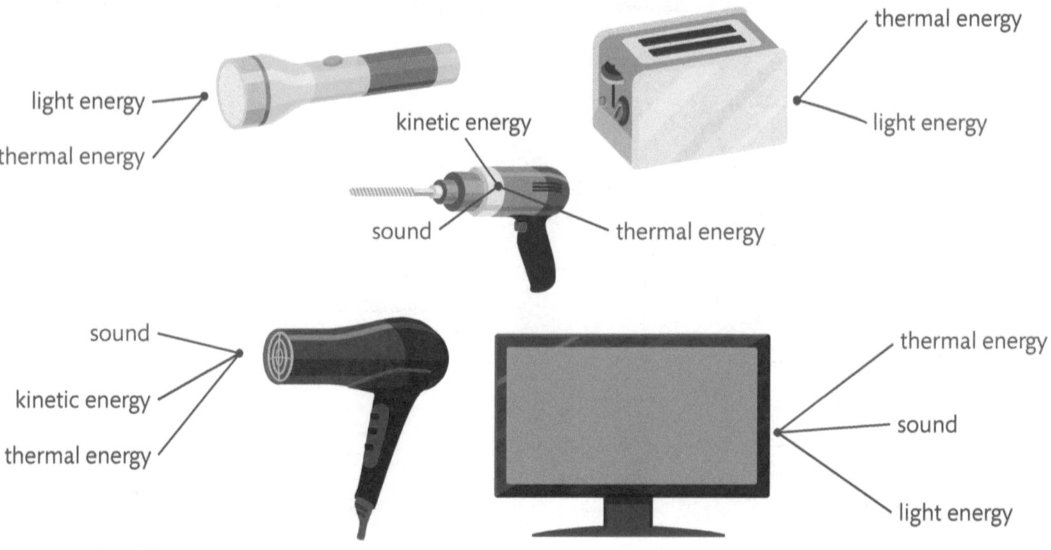

Figure 1 Energy outputs for different appliances

Wasted energy

It is important to identify all the types of energy that are transferred, whether they are useful or not. The most common forms of wasted energy are heat (often caused by friction) and sound. Some devices are meant to produce these forms of energy, in which case they are not wasted.

Worked example — Grade 2

Explain why most wasted energy is in the form of thermal energy. **[2 marks]**

Any machine with moving parts will have some friction that transfers kinetic energy to heat. Electrical appliances transfer electrical energy to thermal energy in the wires.

Exam-style practice — Grade 3

1. An electric kettle transfers energy to heat water. Explain why not all of the energy is transferred usefully. **[1 mark]**
2. A light transfers 1000 J of energy. It transfers 600 J of useful energy. How much energy is wasted? Tick **one** box. **[1 mark]**

   1600 J ☐ 600 J ☐

   400 J ☐ 1000 J ☐

Electrical power

Electricity transfers energy from a source to its components via an electrical circuit. Power is a measure of how quickly the energy is transferred. You need to be able to calculate power from several different equations.

Power

energy transferred (J) = power (W) × time (s)

$$E = Pt$$

$$1\,W = 1\,J/s$$

1 joule of energy is transferred per second.

Many electrical appliances have power ratings measured in kilowatts.

1 kW = 1000 W

Electrical power equations

power (W) = potential difference (V) × current (A)

$$P = VI$$

power (W) = current^2 (A) × resistance (Ω)

$$P = I^2R$$

The larger the potential difference across a component, or the higher the current through it, the more power it uses.

The power of a circuit tells us how quickly it transfers energy.

Worked example — Grade 5

Two kettles boil 1 litre of water each. The kettles are compared to see which is more efficient.

Kettle	Power	Time to boil
A	2.4 kW	3 min 50 s
B	6.0 kW	70 s

Note the units are kW. You need to convert these to W.

This must be changed to seconds.
3 × 60 = 180 s
180 + 50 = 230 s

Remember, kilo means '1000' so you need to multiply by 1000.

(a) Give the power of each kettle in watts. **[1 mark]**

A: 2.4 kW × 1000 = 2400 W

B: 6.0 kW × 1000 = 6000 W

(b) Which kettle boils 1 litre of water more quickly? **[1 mark]**

Kettle B

(c) Calculate how much energy is transferred by kettle B when it boils 1 litre of water. **[2 marks]**

$E = Pt$

$E = 6000 \times 70$

$E = 420\,000$ J or 420 kJ

(d) Kettle A uses 230 V. Calculate the current passing through it. **[2 marks]**

$P = VI$

$2400 = 230 \times I$

$I = \frac{2400}{230} = 10.4$ A

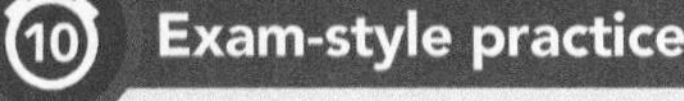

Exam-style practice — Grade 5

1. Heater **A** has a power output of 2 kW. Heater **B** has a power output of 3.5 kW. Which heater will heat up a room more quickly? **[1 mark]**
2. A television uses 230 V and a current of 5 A. Calculate its power rating. **[2 marks]**
3. A lamp has a resistance of 60 ohms and uses a current of 0.1 A. Calculate its power rating. **[2 marks]**
4. Two lamps are run for one hour. Explain why the 40 W lamp is more expensive to run than the 20 W lamp. **[1 mark]**

Transformers and the National Grid

You need to know how the National Grid transports electrical energy around the country.

The National Grid

The National Grid uses a system of cables and transformers to transfer electrical energy from power stations to consumers. When a current flows through a wire some energy is lost as heat. The National Grid transmits electricity at a low current to minimise heat loss. This requires a high voltage.

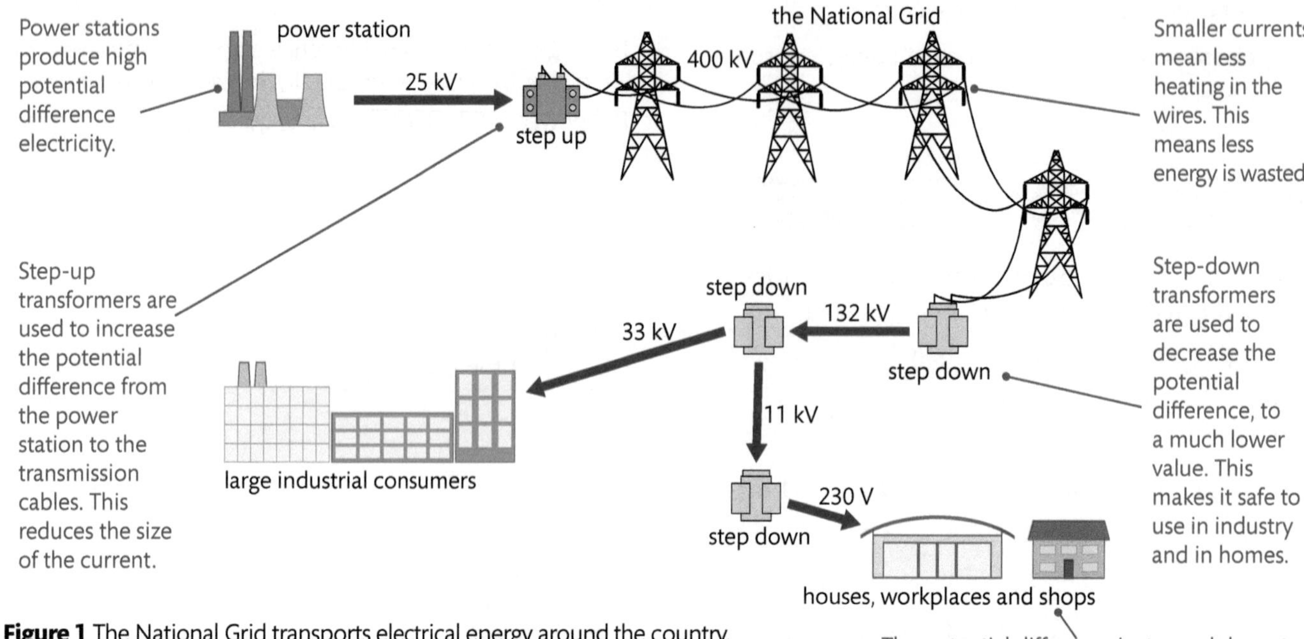

Figure 1 The National Grid transports electrical energy around the country. Energy is wasted when high currents cause the cables to heat up.

Why high pd wastes less energy

Energy = power × time

$E = Pt$ (page 171)

Power = current × pd

$P = IV$ (page 171)

Therefore $E = IVt$

So in a given time, the same amount of electrical energy can be transmitted either at low pd V and high current I, or at high pd V and low current I.

Step-up transformers enable the transmission of electricity at high pd and low current.

If the current stays low then the cables do not heat up much, and little energy is wasted as heat.

Worked example — Grade 5

Transformers in the National Grid are used to keep the current very low.

(a) Explain how a higher current would increase the amount of energy being lost. **[1 mark]**

Higher currents cause wires to heat up more.

(b) Suggest a consequence of losing a lot of energy from the National Grid. **[1 mark]**

Price of electricity might increase. More electricity might need to be generated. If this is done by burning fossil fuels this may also increase greenhouse gases and global warming.

Exam-style practice — Grade 4

1. Heating in wires is caused by high current and large resistances in the wires. Describe **one** way in which transformers help to reduce heat loss caused by current. **[1 mark]**

2. A transformer is used in a mobile phone charger to turn 230 V mains pd into 12 V to charge a battery. Give the name of this type of transformer. **[1 mark]**

 Made a start  Feeling confident  Exam ready

Density

You need to know how to calculate density, the amount of mass per unit volume.

Calculating density

Density is a property of a substance. You can work out the density of a substance using the equation:

$$\text{density (kg/m}^3) = \frac{\text{mass (kg)}}{\text{volume (m}^3)}$$

$$\rho = \frac{m}{V}$$

Having a high density does not mean that an object will be heavy or have a large mass. The mass of an object also depends on the volume.

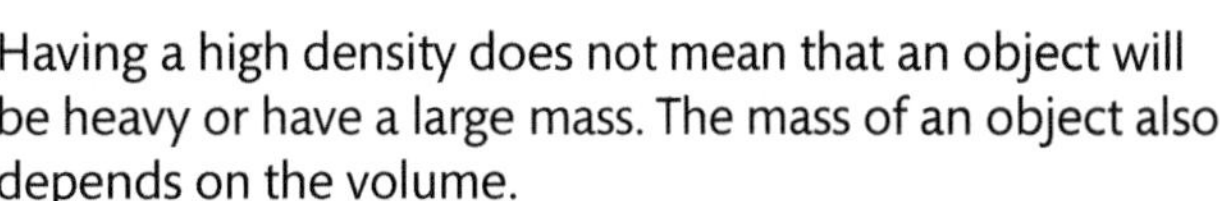

Worked example — Grade 5

Always convert lengths to metres before working out the volume; it is more complicated to do so later.

Figure 1 shows a copper cube with a mass of 140 kg. The length of each side is 0.25 m.

Figure 1

The volume of a cube is the (length of a side)³.

(a) Calculate the volume of the cube in m³. **[2 marks]**

$V = 0.25\,\text{m} \times 0.25\,\text{m} \times 0.25\,\text{m} = 0.0156\,\text{m}^3$

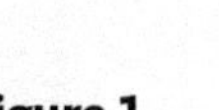

Maths skills

You can calculate the volume of a cuboid using $V = abc$

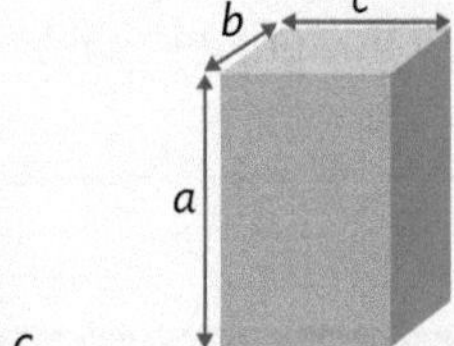

Figure 2
Cuboid with sides a, b and c

(b) Calculate the density of copper. **[2 marks]**

$\rho = \frac{m}{V} = \frac{140}{0.0156} = 8974\,\text{kg/m}^3$

As the density is a property of the material, any size piece of copper will have the same density.

(c) Calculate the volume of a copper cube of mass 2.2 kg. **[2 marks]**

$V = \frac{m}{\rho} = \frac{2.2}{8794} = 2.5 \times 10^{-4}\,\text{m}^3\ (= 0.00025\,\text{m}^3)$

Small volumes measured in m³ will be very small numbers and are best expressed in standard form. Make sure you can enter standard form into your calculator and read it off.

You will need to calculate the densities of all the objects.

Exam-style practice — Grades 2–4

1 A bucket contains twice as much water as a bottle. Which word completes the sentence correctly? **[1 mark]**

Tick **one** box.

The water in the bucket and the water in the bottle have the same:

density ☐ mass ☐ volume ☐ weight ☐

2 The density of water is 1000 kg/m³. An object will float in water if its density is lower than that of water. **Table 1** shows some data about some objects.

Object	apple	steel box	plastic toy	human
Mass (kg)	0.074	1.3	0.5	70
Volume (m³)	1.04×10^{-4}	1.6×10^{-4}	5.3×10^{-4}	0.071

Table 1

(a) Calculate the density of the apple in **Table 1**. **[2 marks]**

(b) Give the objects that will float in water. **[3 marks]**

(c) Calculate the mass of an apple with a volume of $1.5 \times 10^{-4}\,\text{m}^3$. Use the density you calculated in **(a)**. **[3 marks]**

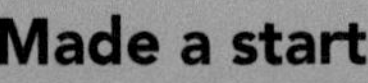

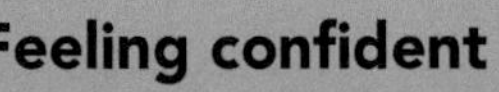

Made a start | Feeling confident | Exam ready

Density of materials

You need to know how to accurately measure the mass and volume of an object so that you can calculate its density.

Measuring density

$$\text{density (kg/m}^3\text{)} = \frac{\text{mass (kg)}}{\text{volume (m}^3\text{)}}$$

Go to page 173 to practise calculating density.

The mass of the object can be found using a digital balance. Using a mass balance with a higher level of precision will improve the precision of the answer.

Measuring the volume of an object depends on the size and shape of the object.

Volume of regular objects

To get an accurate volume, you need to measure the dimensions of a regular object to as high a precision as possible.

Large objects can be measured using a ruler or tape measure. Smaller objects can be measured using Vernier callipers, which will measure to 0.01 mm.

volume of a cuboid = length × width × depth

Remember to convert the lengths to metres to get the volume in m^3.

Volume of irregular objects

Find the volume of an irregular object by measuring the volume of water the object displaces.

1. Fill a displacement can to the spout.
2. Place the object in the can.
3. Collect the water that runs off in a measuring cylinder.

Figure 1 Apparatus

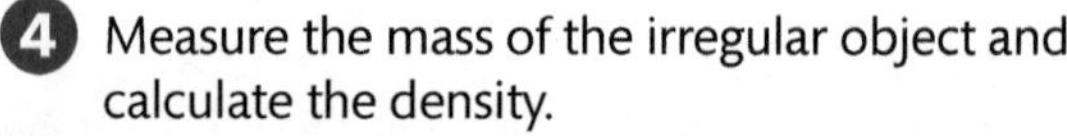

4. Measure the mass of the irregular object and calculate the density.

Density of liquid

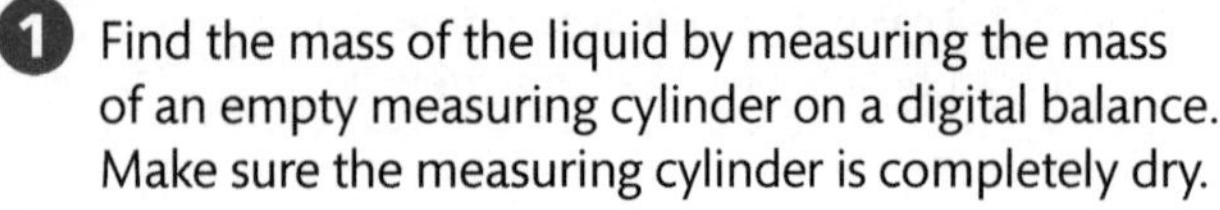

1. Find the mass of the liquid by measuring the mass of an empty measuring cylinder on a digital balance. Make sure the measuring cylinder is completely dry.
2. Measure the volume of liquid using the measuring cylinder.
3. Measure the mass of the measuring cylinder again with the liquid inside. The mass of the liquid will be the difference between the two measurements.

Reducing errors

- Suspend the object from a piece of string so it can be lowered carefully into the water without making a splash.
- Stand the measuring cylinder on a flat surface.
- Make sure your eyes are at the same level as the water when reading the measuring cylinder scale.
- Read the level of the water, ignoring the meniscus created at the edge.

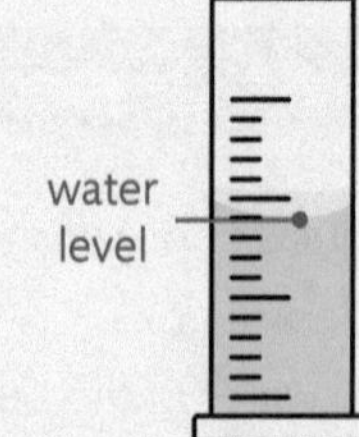

Figure 2 Taking a reading from a measuring cylinder

Worked example — Grade 4

Describe a method to find the volume of an irregularly shaped rock. **[3 marks]**

Fill a displacement can to the spout with water. Put the spout over a measuring cylinder. Lower the rock in to the water carefully. Collect the water displaced from the can. Measure the volume of water in the measuring cylinder. This is the volume of the rock.

Exam-style practice — Grade 4

1. An empty beaker has a mass of 80 g. The beaker has a mass of 420 g when it contains water. What is the mass of water in the beaker? **[1 mark]**
2. **(a)** Name the equipment needed to measure the mass and volume of a metal cuboid. **[2 marks]**

   (b) Write the equation that links density, mass and volume. **[1 mark]**

 Made a start  Feeling confident  Exam ready

State changes

You need to know about the three states of matter: solid, liquid and gas.

States and state changes

Freezing – stronger bonds are reformed and heat energy is given out.

Condensing – weak bonds are reformed and heat energy is given out.

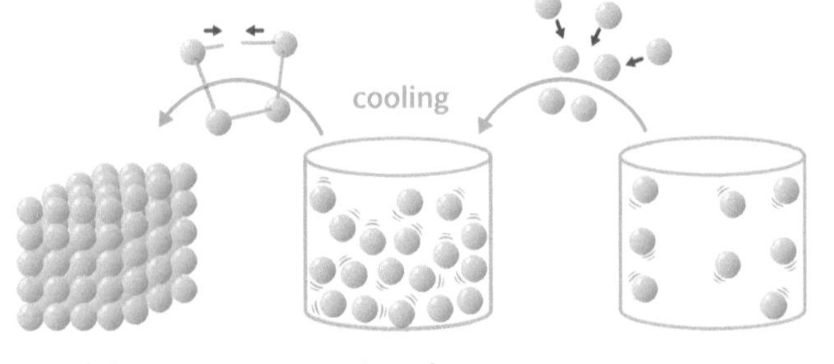

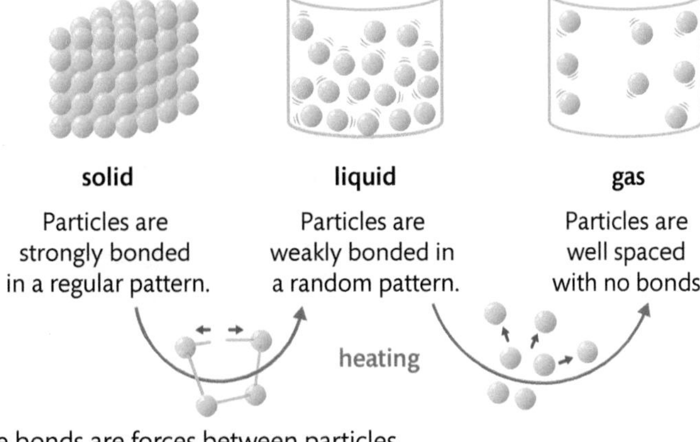

Melting – energy breaks stronger bonds. This allows particles to move freely as a liquid.

Boiling – energy breaks weak bonds. This allows particles to escape from the liquid.

Figure 1 The particle model. The bonds are forces between particles.

State changes: key facts

- The temperature at which a substance both melts and freezes is called the **melting point**.
- The temperature at which a substance both condenses and boils is called the **boiling point**.
- Changes of state are physical and reversible.
- Particles in a solid are arranged more closely than in a liquid, so solids tend to have higher density.
- Particles in gases are very far apart, so gases have very low densities.
- The properties of a substance may change when it changes state. Its density and volume may alter, but the mass will stay the same. This is because the number of particles does not change.

Heating and cooling curves

Thermal energy is transferred to kinetic energy in the particles, raising the temperature.

At the melting and boiling points, thermal energy is absorbed and causes the bonds between particles to break. The temperature remains constant and the state changes.

Heating curve

Temperature in °C; Time in minutes; melting; boiling

Cooling curve

Temperature in °C; Time in minutes; condensing; freezing

Thermal energy is given out. Particles lose kinetic energy and temperature decreases.

Thermal energy is given out as bonds reform. Temperature does not decrease until the state has finished changing.

Exam-style practice — Grade 4

1. Complete the sentence. Tick **one** box. Changes of state: **[1 mark]**

   always release energy ☐ are chemical changes ☐

   are reversible ☐ change the mass of the substance ☐

2. Describe the difference between the movement of particles in a solid and a liquid. **[2 marks]**

3. Explain how the density of a substance changes as it condenses. **[1 mark]**

 **Made a start**  **Feeling confident**  **Exam ready**

Specific heat capacity

The specific heat capacity, c, is the energy needed to change the temperature of 1 kg of a substance by 1 °C. It is measured in joules per kilogram per degree Celsius.

Calculating specific heat capacity

change in thermal energy (J) = mass (kg) × specific heat capacity (J/kg°C) × temperature change (°C)

$$\Delta E = mc\Delta\theta$$

Δ (delta) means 'change in' and θ (theta) means temperature.

The higher the specific heat capacity, the more energy it takes to warm up the same mass of substance.

Energy is stored in a system as internal energy, which is the total of all the kinetic and potential energy of the particles.

Some substances are easy to heat up, whereas others warm up only slowly. Imagine a saucepan with a metal handle and one with a ceramic handle both placed on a hob for the same length of time. The metal handle will be hot while the ceramic handle is still cool; the ceramic handle has a higher specific heat capacity, or needs more thermal energy to raise its temperature than the metal.

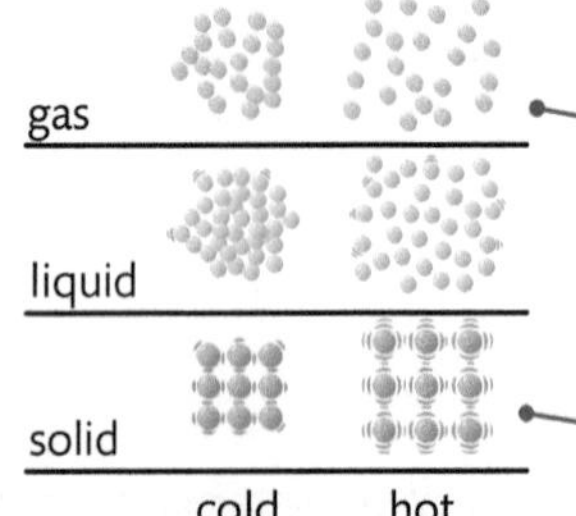

Figure 1 Arrangement and movement of particles in hot and cold solids, liquids and gases.

A higher temperature means the particles in a substance have greater kinetic energy.

Thermal energy added to a system is either used to break bonds and change the 'state' or increase the energy of the particles and raise the temperature.

Worked example — Grade 4

Liquid	Melting point in °C	Boiling point in °C	Specific heat capacity in J/kg°C
A	15	80	200
B	0	100	4200
C	−12	15	2150

Table 1

Look carefully at the headings in a table of data so you are familiar with all the information it gives before you read the question.

(a) Give the liquid, **A**, **B** or **C**, which has the smallest temperature range as a liquid. **[1 mark]**

C

(b) 100g of each liquid **A**, **B** and **C** is heated separately. Explain which liquid would warm up the fastest. **[2 marks]**

A, because it has the lowest specific heat capacity

Liquid **A** has the lowest specific heat capacity. This means it takes very little energy to increase the temperature, so it would warm up the fastest.

(c) 3 kg of liquid **B** is heated from 20 °C to 30 °C. Calculate the change in thermal energy. **[3 marks]**

$\Delta E = mc\Delta\theta = 3 \times 4200 \times 10 = 126000$ J

Work out the temperature change 20 °C–30 °C – first. Then use this temperature change $\Delta\theta$ in the equation.

Finding units

Use this equation to help you remember the unit for specific heat capacity:

$$c = \frac{\Delta E}{m\Delta\theta} \rightarrow \frac{J}{kg\,°C} = J/kg\,°C$$

Exam-style practice — Grade 4

1 Use the information from **Table 1**.

2 kg of liquid **B** was heated from its melting point to its boiling point.

(a) Calculate the temperature change. **[1 mark]**

(b) Calculate the change in thermal energy. **[2 marks]**

2 Liquid **B** is used as a coolant to take heat away from an engine. Why is having a high specific heat capacity an advantage for a coolant? **[2 marks]**

 Made a start  Feeling confident Exam ready

Specific heat capacity

You need to know how to investigate ways to determine the specific heat capacity of materials. This practical investigates two methods of finding a material's specific heat capacity: by electrical heating, or by placing in hot water.

Experiment 1: An electric heater

1. Measure the start temperature of 1 litre of water or 1 kilogram of metal.
2. Heat the water or metal for approximately 5 minutes (300 seconds).
3. Measure the highest temperature reached after the heater is switched off.

energy input = power rating of heater × time

$$c\ (\text{J/kg °C}) = \frac{\text{energy (J)}}{\text{mass (kg)} \times \text{temperature change (°C)}}$$

This method works well for solid blocks or liquids. It does not work as well for insulating solids.

c stands for 'specific heat capacity'.

Experiment 2: Warm water

An alternative method involves finding the specific heat capacity of a metal by adding it to warm water.

- Measure the starting temperature of 1 kg of room temperature metal and 1 l of warm water.
- Place the metal into the warm water. Heat energy flows from the water to the metal, cooling the water until both the metal and the water reach the same temperature.
- Measure the temperature of the metal and the water. The temperature change of the metal is the difference between its starting temperature and the final temperature of the water.

$$\text{energy lost by water} = m_{\text{water}}\, c_{\text{water}}\, \Delta\theta_{\text{water}}$$

$$c_{\text{metal}}\ (\text{J/kg °C}) = \frac{\text{energy lost by water (J)}}{\text{mass of metal (kg)} \times \text{temperature change (°C)}}$$

Worked example — Grades 3–5

Describe the safety factors you must consider when measuring specific heat capacities using the two methods above. [4 marks]

Finding specific heat capacity using an electric heater:

- Do not touch the heating element directly.
- Check equipment has cooled before moving it after the experiment.
- If heating water, take care when moving the container of hot water.
- Do not overfill the container, wait until it has cooled before moving it.
- Mop up any spills immediately and keep the water away from electrical equipment (apart from the heater).
- Do not lean the thermometer in a beaker of water in case it pulls it over.

Using warm water to find the specific heat capacity of an object:

- All the above apply.
- Place the object gently into the water to avoid splashing or breaking the beaker.
- Move the metal using tongs or attach a piece of string to avoid having to touch it and to make it easier to remove from the hot water.

Reducing errors

- Stir gently and measure the temperature of water in the middle, as hot water rises to the top. Make sure not to touch the heater.
- Insulate the block or water. A lid on the water will also reduce energy loss and mass loss by evaporation.
- Check the actual mass of the 1 kg block using a digital balance. Measure the mass of water before and after and calculate an average.
- Limit heat loss to the environment by keeping heating time short.
- The hotter the block gets, the more energy it will lose to the environment.

Exam-style practice — Grade 5

1. Consider Experiment **1**. Suggest why the maximum temperature reached, rather than the end temperature, is recorded after 5 minutes. **[2 marks]**
2. Identify **one** way to minimise the errors in Experiment **2** above. **[1 mark]**

Specific latent heat

Specific latent heat, L, is the energy required to change the state of 1 kg of a substance with no change in temperature.

2 Calculating L

energy for a change of state = mass × specific latent heat
(J) (kg) (J/kg)

$$E = mL$$

The **specific latent heat of fusion** is the energy required to melt or freeze 1 kg of a substance.

The **specific latent heat of vaporisation** is the energy required to condense or evaporate 1 kg of a substance.

10 Worked example — Grade 4

(a) A substance is heated and changes state. Explain why the temperature stays constant during the change of state. **[1 mark]**

The energy is used to break the bonds between the particles.

(b) What is specific latent heat? **[1 mark]**

Tick **one** box.

- [ ] The energy used to heat 1 kg of a substance.
- [ ] The energy used to raise the temperature of a substance by 1°C.
- [x] The energy used to change the state of 1 kg of a substance.
- [ ] The energy used to change the state of 1 m^3 of a substance.

(c) Calculate the energy needed to melt 20 kg of a metal with a specific latent heat of fusion of 250 J/kg. **[2 marks]**

$E = mL$

$E = 20 \times 250$

$E = 5000$ J

2 Latent heat and particles

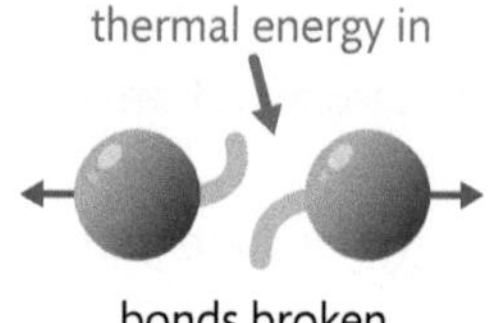

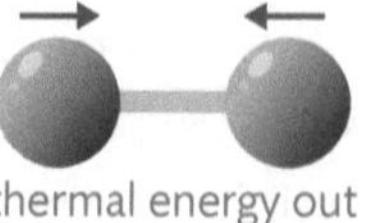

Figure 1 When a substance changes state, energy is used to break bonds or is given out as the bonds reform.

As something cools down, thermal energy is released from it. When it condenses or freezes, the temperature stays constant because the heat energy is transferred to form bonds between the particles.

Exam focus

The units for specific latent heat are J/kg.

You can use the equation to help you remember the unit:

$$L = \frac{E\text{ (J)}}{m\text{ (kg)}} \rightarrow \text{J/kg}$$

10 Exam-style practice — Grade 5

1. **(a)** Define 'specific latent heat of vaporisation'. **[1 mark]**
   (b) Give the units for specific latent heat. **[1 mark]**
2. The specific latent heat of fusion for copper is 207 J/kg. Calculate the energy needed to melt 15 kg of copper. **[2 marks]**
3. 162.5 J of energy is released when 2.5 kg of molten gold solidifies. Calculate the specific latent heat of fusion of gold. Include the unit. **[4 marks]**

 Made a start  Feeling confident  Exam ready

Particle motion in gases

Gas particles are in constant random motion. You need to be able to explain the effect of temperature and type of container on particle motion in gases.

Heating gases

When a gas is heated, the particles gain kinetic energy. This means they move faster than in liquids and solids. As there are very weak forces between the particles they spread out as far as possible. This means the volume of the gas can increase.

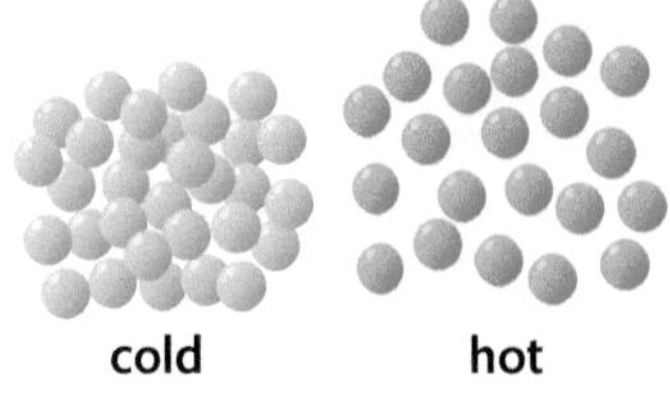

Figure 1 Heating a gas

Gas in containers

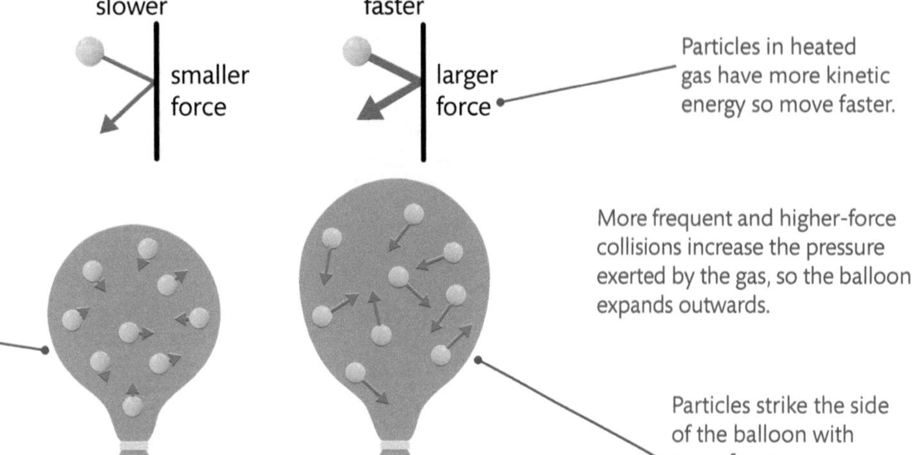

slower
smaller force
faster
larger force
Particles in heated gas have more kinetic energy so move faster.
More frequent and higher-force collisions increase the pressure exerted by the gas, so the balloon expands outwards.
Particles in cooler gases move more slowly and exert lower pressures.
Particles strike the side of the balloon with more force.
cold
hot

Figure 2 A container of gas

Worked example — Grade 4

Heating a balloon causes the gas particles to move faster. Explain how this makes the balloon expand. **[2 marks]**

The particles hit the inside of the balloon harder and more often. This increases the force (and pressure) which pushes the side of the balloon outwards.

The particles hitting the side will increase the force and pressure on the inside of the balloon. The balloon is not rigid and will expand until the pressure inside is the same as the air pressure outside.

Exam-style practice — Grade 5

1. State the effect of heating a gas at a constant volume on the:
   (a) temperature of the gas **[1 mark]**
   (b) pressure of the gas. **[1 mark]**
2. A bottle has a stopper in it. When the bottle is heated the stopper is pushed out. Explain how this happens. **[2 marks]**
3. Explain why a hot air balloon rises when the gas inside is heated. Use ideas about particles and how they move. **[3 marks]**

The structure of an atom

All atoms are made of protons, neutrons and electrons. You need to know the structure of an atom, in terms of electrons, protons and neutrons.

Structure

Electrons have a negative charge and occupy energy levels (electron shells) around the nucleus. Electrons are very small and have a tiny mass, but occupy most of the volume of the atom. This means the atom is mostly empty space.

Atoms contain equal numbers of electrons and protons. The charges balance, so atoms are neutral.

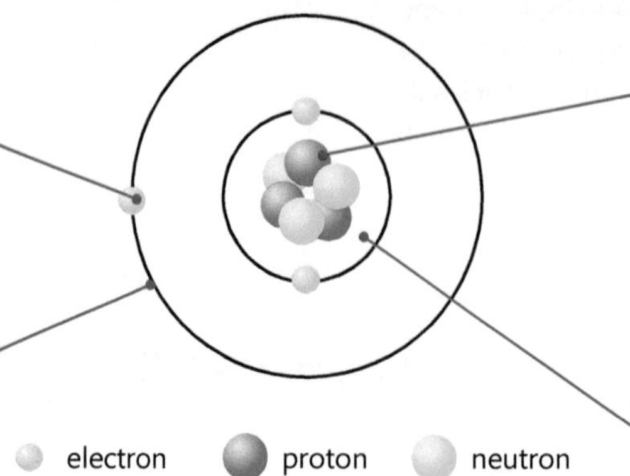

The number of protons in an atom determines what element it is. An atom is carbon if it has six protons. If it had seven, it would be nitrogen.

The **nucleus** contains positive protons and neutral neutrons. It contains most of the mass, but its radius is one ten-thousandth of the radius of the atom. Protons and neutrons have similar masses.

Figure 1 Atoms are made up of protons, neutrons and electrons.

Absorption and emission of electromagnetic radiation

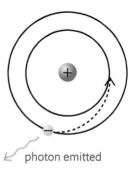

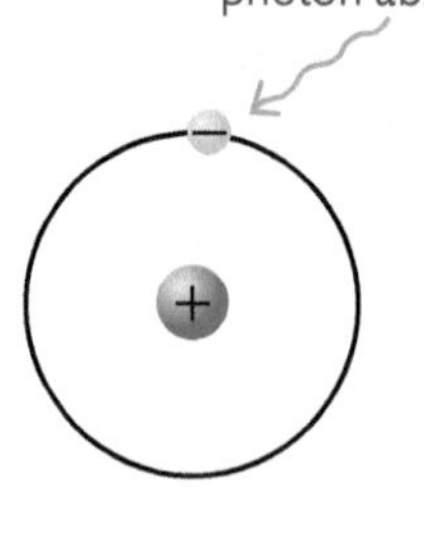

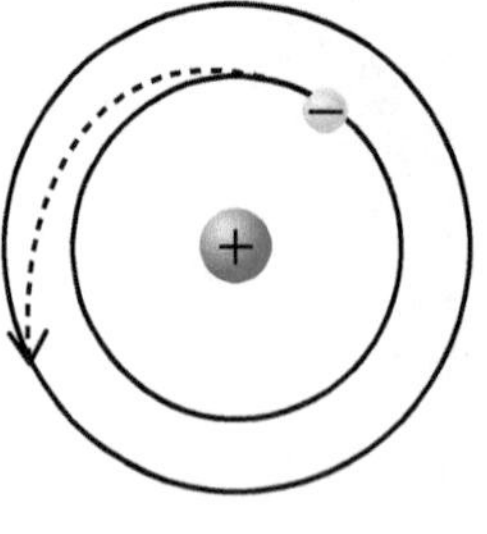

Figure 2 Atoms are around 1×10^{-10} m in radius. When electrons absorb electromagnetic radiation, they absorb the energy and move to a higher energy level further away from the nucleus.

photon emitted

Figure 3 As the electron drops back down to its ground state, its original energy level, it emits electromagnetic radiation.

Worked example — Grade 2

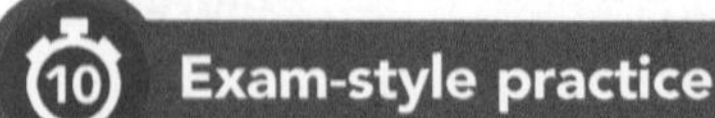

(a) Name the part of an atom that contains most of the mass of the atom. **[1 mark]**

The nucleus

(b) Name the particles that carry the negative charge in an atom. **[1 mark]**

Electrons

Exam-style practice — Grade 3

1. Name the **two** particles found in the nucleus of an atom. **[2 marks]**
2. Give the charge on a neutron. **[1 mark]**
3. Give **two** differences between a proton and an electron. **[2 marks]**
4. Describe what happens in an atom when it absorbs electromagnetic radiation. **[2 marks]**

Made a start

Feeling confident

Exam ready

Mass number, atomic number and isotopes

Every element has a mass number and an atomic number. You can use these numbers to work out how many protons and neutrons are in an element's nucleus.

Particles in an atom

number of protons = number of electrons in a neutral atom

number of neutrons = mass number − atomic number

$^{7}_{3}$Li has 3 protons, 3 electrons and 4 neutrons (7 − 3).

$^{14}_{7}$N has 7 protons, 7 electrons and 7 neutrons (14 − 7).

$^{19}_{9}$F has 9 protons, 9 electrons and 10 neutrons (19 − 9).

The mass number is equal to the total number of protons and neutrons.

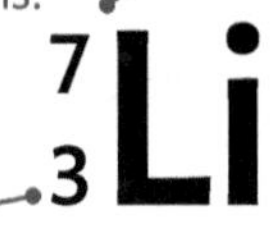

The atomic number is equal to the number of protons.

Figure 1 An atomic symbol

Isotopes

Isotopes are atoms with the same atomic number (number of protons) but different mass numbers (protons + neutrons). As the number of protons is the same, this means that isotopes have different numbers of neutrons.

Carbon $^{12}_{6}$C has six protons and six neutrons. An atom is carbon only if it has six protons. Carbon $^{14}_{6}$C is an isotope of carbon. It has six protons and eight neutrons. As $^{14}_{6}$C has six protons, it is still carbon, but it is heavier because of the extra neutrons.

Ionisation

If an atom loses or gains electrons, it becomes charged. Charged atoms are called **ions**.

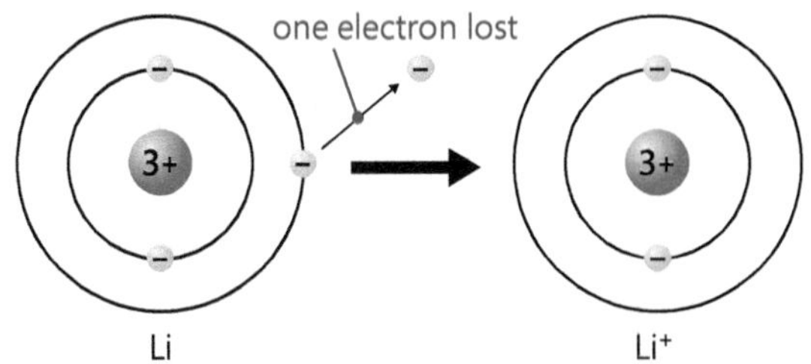

Figure 2 If an atom loses one or more electrons, it becomes a positive ion.

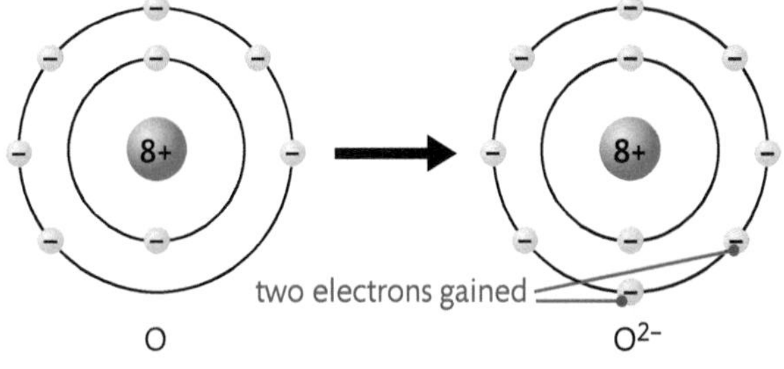

Figure 3 When an atom gains electrons, it becomes a negative ion.

Worked example — Grade 4

An atom has six protons and six neutrons.

(a) Give the atomic number of the atom. **[1 mark]**

6

(b) Give the mass number of the atom. **[1 mark]**

12

Exam-style practice — Grades 4–5

1 Lithium has three protons and four neutrons. Give its:

(a) mass number **[1 mark]**

(b) atomic number. **[1 mark]**

2 The atomic symbol for magnesium is $^{24}_{12}$Mg.

(a) Give the number of neutrons in a magnesium atom. **[1 mark]**

(b) A magnesium atom forms an ion with a +2 charge. Give the number of electrons in a magnesium ion. **[1 mark]**

3 Describe the difference between an atom and an ion. **[1 mark]**

4 Define an 'isotope' of an element. **[1 mark]**

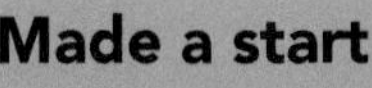

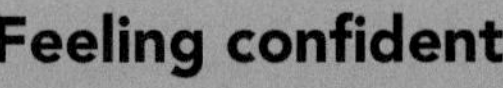

Development of the atomic model

Scientists' theories about the atom changed as new experimental evidence was discovered. You need to know how the model of the atom has developed over time.

Developing the model of the atom

1. Before electrons were discovered, it was thought that atoms were tiny spheres that could not be divided into anything else.

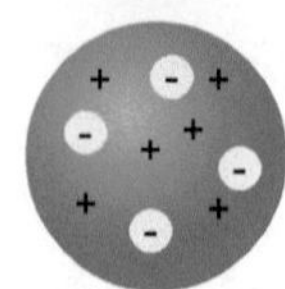

2. The **plum pudding model** was proposed by scientists who thought the atom was like a positively charged 'pudding', with electrons like 'plums' embedded in it.

3. Ernest Rutherford tested the plum pudding model by aiming a beam of positively charged alpha particles at a very thin sheet of gold foil (scattering experiment). Some of the alpha particles were repelled by positively charged particles that were concentrated in the centre of the atom (the nucleus). Most alpha particles passed through unaffected, showing that the nucleus was only a very small part of the atom. This evidence gave rise to the **nuclear model**.

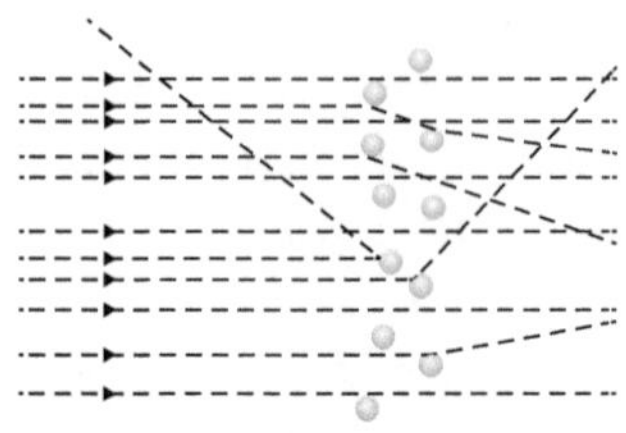

Rutherford's scattering experiment

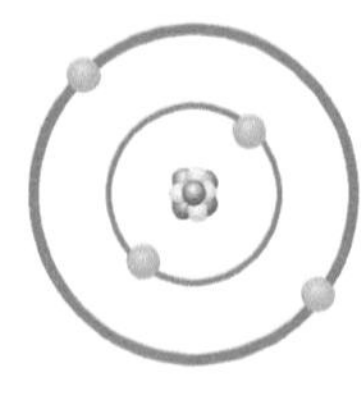

4. Niels Bohr adapted the nuclear model. Using theoretical calculations alongside experimental observations, Bohr suggested that electrons travel in circular orbits around the nucleus. Further research showed that the nucleus was actually composed of smaller particles with equal amounts of positive charge. These became known as protons. Approximately 20 years after the nuclear model became accepted, James Chadwick discovered that neutrons also existed in the nucleus.

Worked example — Grade 4

Explain how the alpha particle scattering experiment showed that the mass of an atom is concentrated at the centre and that atoms are mostly empty space. **[2 marks]**

Most of the alpha particles passed straight through without hitting anything, showing that atoms are mostly empty space.
Some of the alpha particles deflected or bounced back, showing they were repelled by the positive nucleus.

Exam-style practice — Grades 4–5

1. Describe the plum pudding model of the atom. **[3 marks]**
2. Give the differences between the plum pudding model and the nuclear model. **[2 marks]**
3. A student suggests that the plum pudding model of the atom is wrong and that the nuclear model is correct. Do you agree? Explain your answer. **[2 marks]**

Radioactive decay and nuclear radiation

Radioactive decay can result in atoms emitting alpha or beta particles, neutrons, or gamma rays.

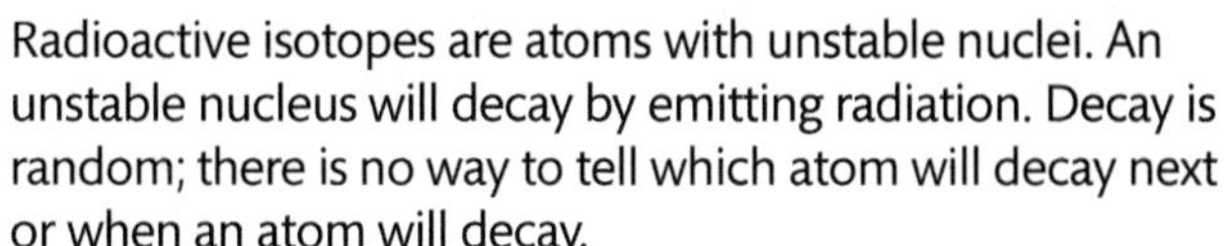

5 Radioactive decay

Radioactive isotopes are atoms with unstable nuclei. An unstable nucleus will decay by emitting radiation. Decay is random; there is no way to tell which atom will decay next or when an atom will decay.

Activity and count rate

The activity is the rate at which atoms in a radioactive source decay. Activity is measured in becquerels (Bq). 10 Bq means 10 decays per second.

The count rate is the number of decays recorded per second by a detector such as a **Geiger-Müller** (G-M) tube.

3 Three uses of radiation

1. **Smoke detector**: Alpha radiation cannot penetrate smoke particles so can be used to detect smoke.
2. **Paper mill**: Beta radiation is used to monitor the thickness of paper. If the paper gets thicker, less beta radiation can penetrate. Detectors monitor the beta intensity to keep the thickness uniform.
3. **Treatment of cancer**: Gamma radiation can pass easily into the body to kill cancerous cells.

2 Worked example — Grade 5

Suggest why the count rate measured by a G-M tube may be different to the activity of the source. **[2 marks]**

The activity is the number of decays per second in a sample but the count rate is the number of decays detected. The radiation from the decays might not all go into the detector, because it goes in all directions, so the count rate will be less than the activity.

10 Properties of radiation

Radiation	Particle	Charge	Ionisation power	Penetrative power
alpha (α)	2 protons and 2 neutrons (a helium nucleus)	+2	high	low
beta (β)	fast-moving electron	−1	medium	medium
gamma (γ)	electromagnetic wave	0	low	high

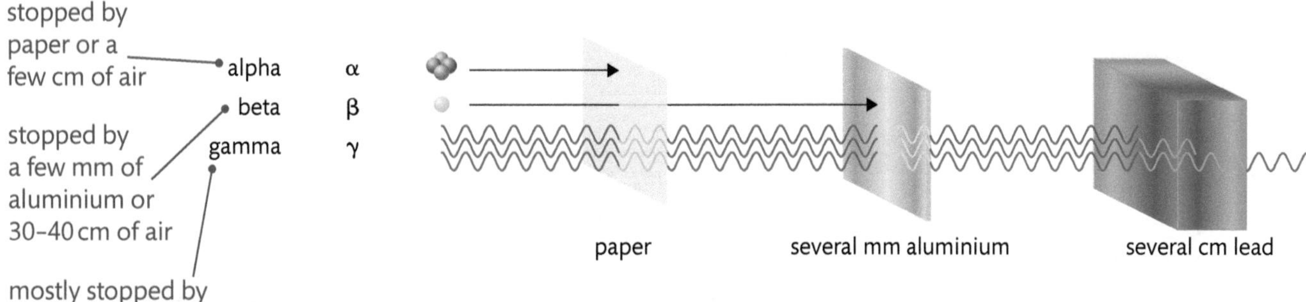

Figure 1 Radiation with a higher ionisation power is more harmful to living cells.

10 Exam-style practice — Grade 5

1. Give **one** reason why alpha or gamma radiation could not be used to monitor the thickness of paper. **[2 marks]**
2. A tracer is a radioactive source injected into the blood. It can be detected from outside the body and used in diagnosis. Evaluate which type of radioactive source would be most suitable for use as a tracer. **[6 marks]**

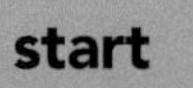

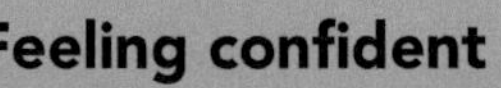

Made a start | Feeling confident | Exam ready

Half-lives

Half-life is a measure of how radioactive a source is. It can be anything from a fraction of a second to many thousands of years. You need to be able to determine a substance's half-life from a graph or table of data.

Half-life

The half-life of a radioactive source is the time taken for either:

- the **count rate** (activity) to fall to half its initial value *or*
- half the radioactive nuclei in a sample to decay.

Half-life is an average time, resulting from the random nature of radioactive decay.

Half-life from data

Time in minutes	Number of radioactive nuclei
0	1000
2	842
4	681
6	540
8	428
10	353

The number of nuclei halves to 500 between 6 and 8 minutes. This means the half-life is between 6 and 8 minutes. You can use a graph to find a more accurate answer.

Worked example — Grades 4–5

The activity after a nuclear accident is 600 Bq. It takes 60 years for the activity to drop to a safe level of 75 Bq. Calculate the half-life of the radioactive source. **[4 marks]**

$\frac{600}{2} = 300$

$\frac{300}{2} = 150$

$\frac{150}{2} = 75$

Three half-lives have passed in 60 years. $\frac{60}{3} = 20$

One half-life is 20 years.

Half-life graphs

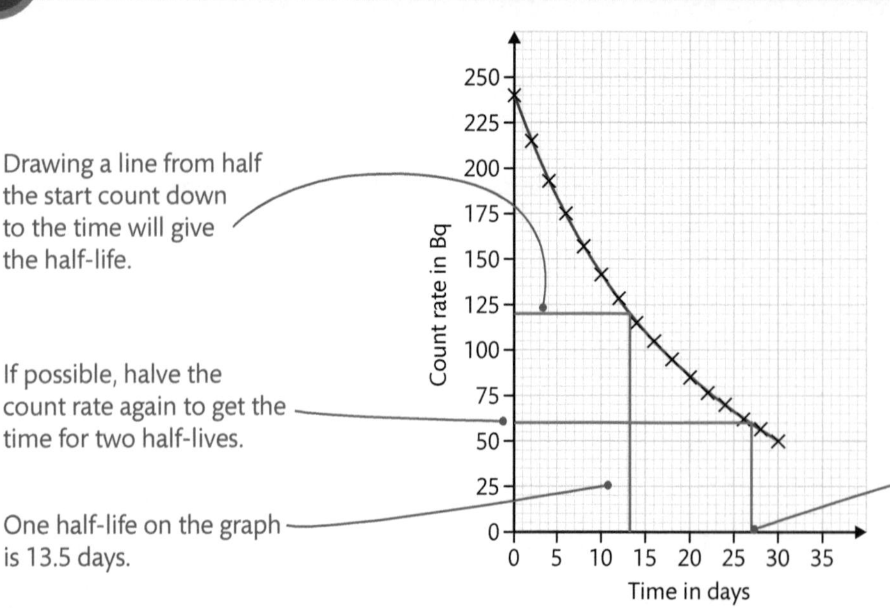

Figure 1 Finding a half-life from a graph

Exam-style practice — Grade 4

1. A sample with a half-life of 10 mins has an activity of 45 Bq. If the sample started at 1440 Bq, calculate how old it is. **[1 mark]**

   Tick **one** box.

   20 minutes ☐ 30 minutes ☐ 50 minutes ☐ 100 minutes ☐

2. The activity of a sample drops from 640 Bq to 160 Bq in 12 years. Calculate its half-life. **[1 mark]**

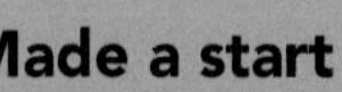 Made a start  Feeling confident  Exam ready

Nuclear equations

Nuclear equations for alpha and beta decay are similar to chemical equations, except the elements can change and particles are included. You need to be able to complete nuclear equations for alpha, beta and gamma decay.

Make-up of radiating particles

Nuclear equations are easier when you know the make-up of the radiating particles. An alpha particle (α) is made from two protons and two neutrons, the same as a helium nucleus. It has an atomic number of two and a mass number of four. You can write this as $^{4}_{2}He$ or $^{4}_{2}\alpha$. A beta particle (β) is a fast-moving electron. It is very small, with a mass number of 0 and an atomic number of −1. You can write this as $^{0}_{-1}e$ or $^{0}_{-1}\beta$.

Go to page 181 to revise mass number and atomic number.

Types of decay

Alpha decay

When a nucleus undergoes **alpha decay**, it loses two protons and two neutrons. The mass number of the nucleus decreases by four and the atomic number and the charge on the nucleus decrease by two. The nucleus becomes a new element.

> For example, when a radium (Ra) nucleus alpha decays it becomes a radon (Rn) nucleus.
> $^{226}_{88}Ra \rightarrow ^{222}_{86}Rn + ^{4}_{2}\alpha$

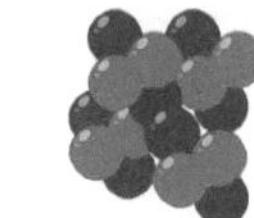

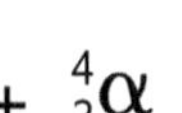

$^{\text{mass number}}_{\text{atomic number}}X \rightarrow ^{\text{mass number} -4}_{\text{atomic number} -2}Y + ^{4}_{2}\alpha$

Figure 1 Alpha decay

Remember that these decays happen randomly. The products, or **daughter nuclei**, created may be radioactive isotopes that decay again.

Beta decay

During **beta decay**, a neutron changes into a proton and a high-speed electron. The electron is ejected from the nucleus. The mass doesn't change, but the charge increases.

> For example, when the carbon isotope, $^{14}_{6}C$ decays it forms nitrogen.
> $^{14}_{6}C \rightarrow ^{14}_{7}N + ^{0}_{-1}\beta$

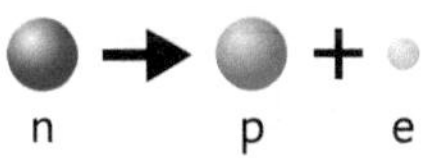

Figure 2 Beta decay

> There is still the same number of protons and neutrons in the nucleus overall, so the mass number and the charge do not change. As there is an extra proton, the atomic number increases by one. This makes a new element.

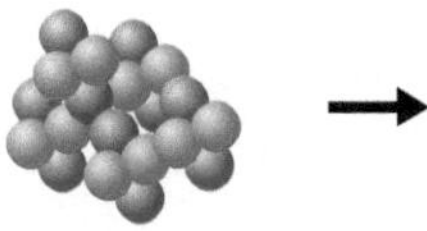

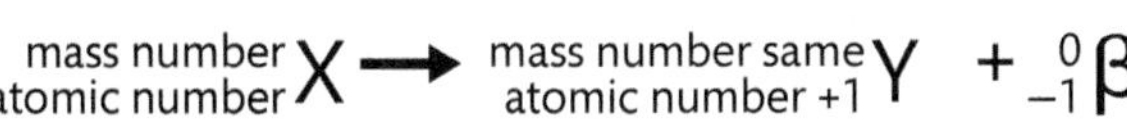

$^{\text{mass number}}_{\text{atomic number}}X \rightarrow ^{\text{mass number same}}_{\text{atomic number} +1}Y + ^{0}_{-1}\beta$

Figure 3 Equation for beta decay

Gamma decay

Gamma decay occurs when a nucleus has excess energy after a nuclear process. The energy is given off as a high energy electromagnetic wave. It does not contain any particles so the nucleus does not change.

Worked example — Grade 5

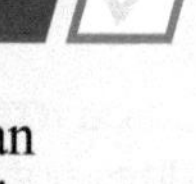

$^{230}_{92}U$ decays to an isotope of Th by emitting an alpha particle, $^{4}_{2}He$. Write the equation for this decay. **[2 marks]**

$^{230}_{92}U \rightarrow ^{226}_{90}Th + ^{4}_{2}He$

The equation is balanced because the total mass number on each side is the same and the total atomic number is the same.

The mass number (top row) on the left of the arrow must equal the sum of the mass numbers on the right. The atomic number (bottom row) on the left must equal the sum of the atomic numbers on the right.

Exam-style practice — Grade 4

1 Complete these equations.

(a) $^{239}_{94}Pu \rightarrow$ ____ U + $^{4}_{2}$____ **[2 marks]**

(b) ____ Na → $^{25}_{12}Mg$ + ____ ⊠ **[2 marks]**

2 Historically, alchemists tried to make gold from lead. Nuclear decays make it possible to change from one element to another. Use the periodic table to find out what element would be created if an isotope of lead:

(a) alpha decayed **[2 marks]**

(b) beta decayed. **[2 marks]**

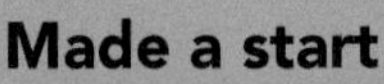

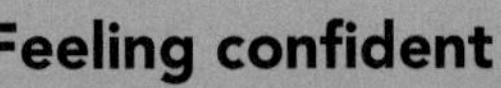

Made a start | Feeling confident | Exam ready

Radioactive contamination

Contamination and irradiation are both harmful to living organisms. You need to know about the measures taken to avoid radioactive contamination.

Irradiation

To be **irradiated** means to be exposed to a source of radiation, be it alpha, beta or gamma radiation. The irradiated object does not become radioactive. Irradiation can damage cells, alter genes and cause mutations that can lead to cancer.

The amount of radiation to which an object is exposed is called the **dose**. Doses are measured in sieverts or millisieverts. For small doses, such as radiation treatment in hospitals, the risks are much less than the benefit from the treatment.

A dose can be increased by:

- increased exposure time
- higher activity of the radioactive source
- being closer to the source.

A dose can be reduced by:

- wearing protective clothing and/or staying behind a screen
- keeping your distance from sources, for example, using long tweezers, tongs or robotic arms.

Ultraviolet rays and X-rays can have a similar hazardous effect on the body as gamma rays, although they are less powerful and less penetrating. UV can cause premature ageing of the skin and increase the risk of skin cancer.

Contamination

Touching a source can leave traces of radioactive material on you or an object. If this radioactive material is unwanted, it is called **contamination**. Contamination is dangerous, especially for living things, as the contaminating material decays right next to the body. The level of hazard depends on the type of radiation. Contamination should be cleaned off immediately, but removing it from skin can be difficult.

Avoid contamination by avoiding direct contact with sources. Precautions for reducing irradiation will reduce the risk of contamination. Liquid and powdery sources are particularly risky and should be kept in sealed containers.

Worked example — Grades 4–5

A radioactive source is stored in a box in a hospital. Explain a choice of material for the box. **[3 marks]**

It depends on the type of radiation being emitted. Alpha, beta and gamma radiation are all stopped by lead, so a thick-walled lead box would be a good container for any source.
A beta source could safely be held in a box of aluminium a few mm thick, and an alpha source needs less shielding than that. Whatever material is used, the box should be strong and secure.

Peer review and radiation research

Before a scientist publishes their research, their work is checked and evaluated by other scientists. This process is known as **peer review**. In peer review, scientists check the findings, improve the methods and repeat the experiments to check the results. This process makes scientists more confident about each other's findings.

It is important to understand the effects of radiation on humans so that people who work with radiation are better able to protect themselves. Anyone who has been contaminated, or received a high dose of radiation, can also be treated.

Exam-style practice — Grade 5

1. Explain the differences and similarities between 'irradiation' and 'contamination'. **[5 marks]**
2. Workers in a nuclear power station measure their exposure to ionising radiation. Suggest **two** reasons why one person receives a higher dose than another. **[2 marks]**
3. A geologist studies radioactive rocks. Explain what the geologist can do to reduce the risk of irradiation and contamination. **[6 marks]**

Made a start  Feeling confident  Exam ready

Scalar and vector quantities

You need to know the difference between a scalar quantity and a vector quantity.

Definitions

Scalars are quantities that have only a **magnitude** (a size).

Vectors are quantities with both a magnitude and a **direction**.

Scalar quantities can be added and subtracted as they are just numerical values. For vector quantities, you must also consider the direction.

Vector quantities

- velocity (m/s)
- displacement (m)
- acceleration (m/s^2)
- force (N)
- weight (N)
- gravitational field strength (N/kg)

Scalar quantities

- distance (m)
- speed (m/s)
- charge (C)
- density (kg/m^3)
- efficiency
- energy (J)
- frequency (Hz)
- mass (kg)
- power (W)
- pressure (Pa)
- temperature (°C)
- time (s)
- wavelength (m)
- volume (m^3)
- area (m^2)

Efficiency does not have a unit. It is usually given as a decimal or percentage.

The SI unit is the pascal (Pa). 1 Pa = 1 N/m^2

Adding vectors

Vector quantities can be represented by arrows. The length of the arrow represents the magnitude. The direction of the arrow represents the direction of the vector quantity.

If two vectors act in a straight line they can be added (same direction) or subtracted (opposite directions) to find the resultant vector.

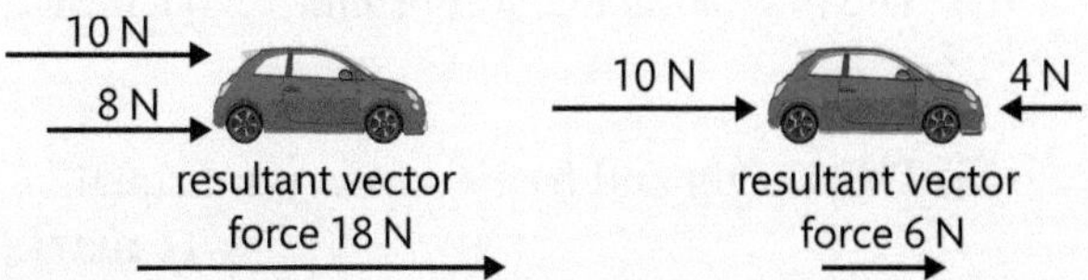

Figure 1 Finding the resultant vector

Worked example — Grades 4–5

Write down **one** similarity and **one** difference between speed and velocity. **[2 marks]**

Similarity: they both measure how fast something is moving

Difference: only velocity is in a particular direction.

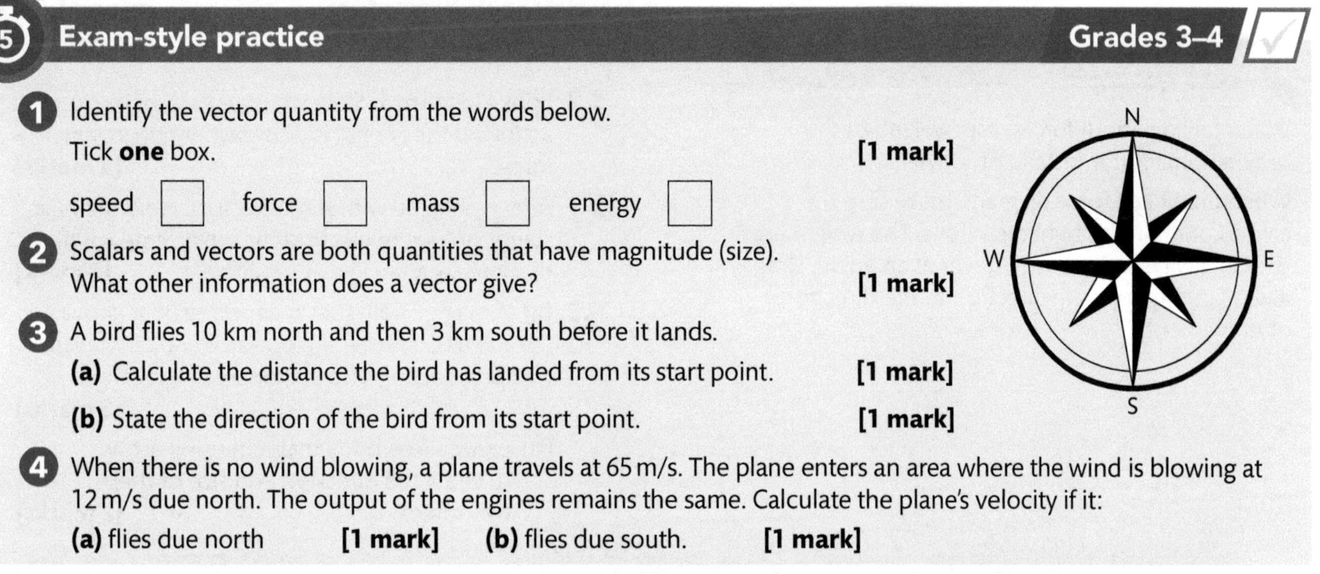

Exam-style practice — Grades 3–4

1. Identify the vector quantity from the words below. Tick **one** box. **[1 mark]**

   speed ☐ force ☐ mass ☐ energy ☐

2. Scalars and vectors are both quantities that have magnitude (size). What other information does a vector give? **[1 mark]**

3. A bird flies 10 km north and then 3 km south before it lands.

   (a) Calculate the distance the bird has landed from its start point. **[1 mark]**

   (b) State the direction of the bird from its start point. **[1 mark]**

4. When there is no wind blowing, a plane travels at 65 m/s. The plane enters an area where the wind is blowing at 12 m/s due north. The output of the engines remains the same. Calculate the plane's velocity if it:

   (a) flies due north **[1 mark]** **(b)** flies due south. **[1 mark]**

Forces

A force is a push or pull that acts on an object due to its interactions with another object. You need to know about forces that require contact to exert the force and forces that can act at a distance (non-contact).

2 Contact forces

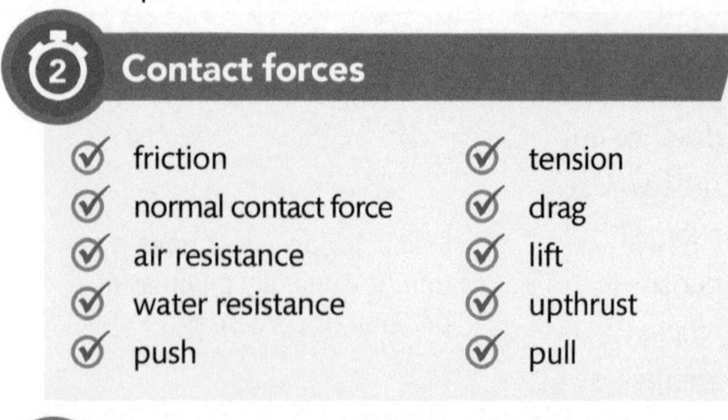

- friction
- normal contact force
- air resistance
- water resistance
- push
- tension
- drag
- lift
- upthrust
- pull

1 Non-contact forces

- gravitational force (weight)
- electrostatic force
- magnetic force

10 Free body diagrams

Free body diagrams show a simplified version of the forces acting on the centre of mass of an object, usually just shown as a dot. The forces can be labelled with their name or the magnitude of the force.

Remember, forces are vectors so the direction of the arrow shows the direction of the force and the length of the arrow shows the magnitude. Larger forces have longer arrows.

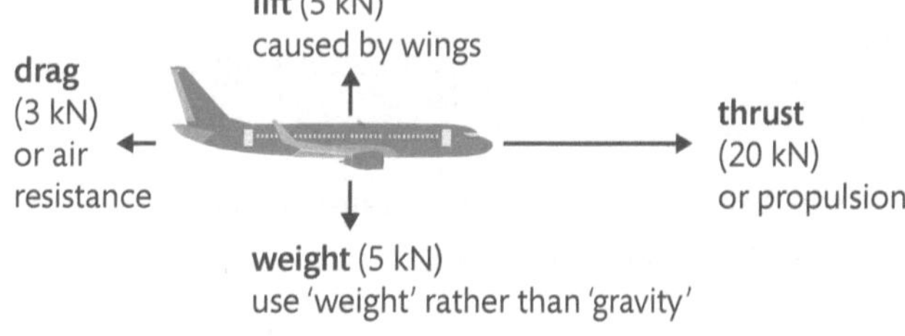

Figure 1 Forces on an aeroplane

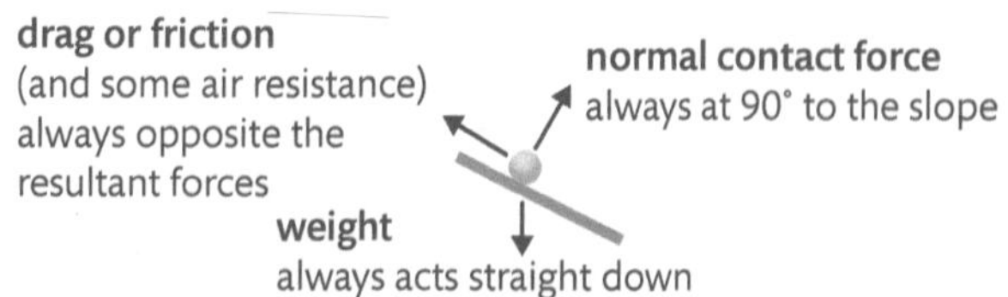

Figure 2 Forces on a ball rolling down a slope

2 Exam focus

When talking about forces, use 'weight' or 'gravitational force' instead of 'gravity'.

When drawing a force diagram, make sure the arrows point in the right directions. The weight arrow should always point down, never at an angle. Drag is always in the opposite direction to the direction of movement.

5 Worked example — Grade 4

(a) Draw and label a free body diagram to show the forces acting on a magnet stuck to a fridge. **[2 marks]**

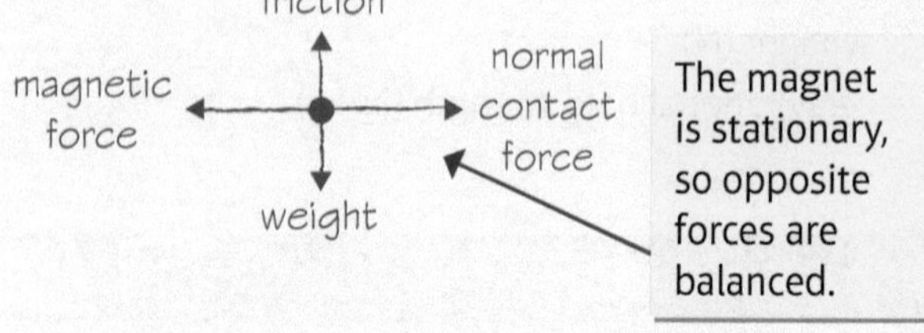

(b) Indicate which of the following statements are true or false.

(i) The forces on the magnet are all the same size. **[1 mark]**

false

(ii) The magnet is in equilibrium. **[1 mark]**

true

(iii) The weight and friction forces are equal. **[1 mark]**

true

10 Exam-style practice — Grade 3

1. Look at **Figure 1**. State whether each of the forces acting on the aircraft is a contact or non-contact force. **[3 marks]**
2. Amy is charged with static electricity and her hair stands up due to electrostatic force. State whether this force is attractive or repulsive. **[1 mark]**
3. **(a)** A maglev train uses magnets to float above the track. Name the upwards and downwards forces acting on a stationary maglev train. **[2 marks]**

   (b) Draw a free body diagram using arrows to show the direction and size of these two forces. **[2 marks]**

Gravity

You need to know the relationship between gravity, weight and mass.

Mass, weight and gravity

The weight of an object is dependent on its mass and the strength of gravity. The weight of an object may change but its mass remains constant.

Mass (m)

- the amount of matter in an object
- measured in kilograms, kg

Weight (W)

- the force acting on an object due to gravity
- the force acts downwards, towards the centre of the body causing the gravitational field, for example the planet
- measured in newtons, N
- measured using a calibrated spring-balance (newtonmeter)

Gravitational field strength (g)

- the strength of gravity at any one point
- measured in N/kg or m/s^2
- also called acceleration due to gravity (they are the same thing)

You need to know the equation:
weight (N) = mass (kg) × gravitational field strength (N/kg)

$$W = mg$$

Worked example — Grade 5

A Mars rover has a mass of 68.4 kg.
Gravitational field strength g on Earth = 9.8 N/kg

(a) Calculate the weight of the rover on Earth. **[2 marks]**

weight = mass × g = 68.4 × 9.8 = 670 N

(b) Explain what the mass of the rover is on Mars. **[2 marks]**

It is 68.4 kg because mass does not change with location.

(c) Calculate the weight of the rover on Mars. **[2 marks]**

68.4 × 3.7 = 253 N

(d) A second rover is tested for use on a planet where the gravity is exactly half the strength it is on Earth. How would the rover's mass and weight on this new planet compare to when it is on Earth? **[2 marks]**

Its mass would be the same on the new planet, but its weight would be half what it is on Earth.

Centre of mass

The weight of all the parts of an object act in the same way as a single force acting from a point called the **centre of mass**. For regular, symmetrical objects, the centre of mass usually lies in the middle. For irregularly shaped objects the centre of mass is not always so obvious. You can use the method shown in **Figure 1** to find the centre of mass of any object.

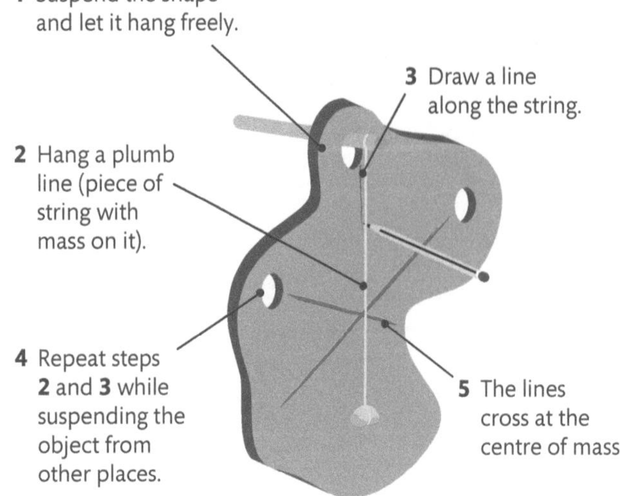

1 Suspend the shape and let it hang freely.
2 Hang a plumb line (piece of string with mass on it).
3 Draw a line along the string.
4 Repeat steps 2 and 3 while suspending the object from other places.
5 The lines cross at the centre of mass.

Figure 1 Finding the centre of mass of an irregular shape

Weight and mass

Weight and mass are directly proportional.

weight ∝ mass

If one object has twice the mass of another, it will also have twice the weight for the same gravitational field strength. Mass is constant. Weight depends on the gravitational field strength at the point where the object is.

Exam-style practice — Grade 5

1. State where the centre of mass would be on a ring donut. **[1 mark]**
2. Suggest how to measure the weight of an object. **[1 mark]**
3. In what direction does the weight of an object act on Earth? **[1 mark]**
4. Explain why astronauts have difficulty walking on the Moon. **[2 marks]**

 Made a start  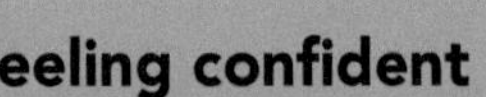 Feeling confident  Exam ready

Resultant forces

If multiple forces are acting on an object, they can be represented as one **resultant force**, which has the same effect as all the original forces acting together. You should be able to find the resultant force on a given object.

Forces on a skydiver

As a skydiver falls, their weight (the downward force) stays constant, but the drag (air resistance) will increase as they fall faster. This changes the resultant force and therefore the acceleration.

skydiver mass = 75 kg

individual forces ↓ resultant force ↓

drag = 0 N

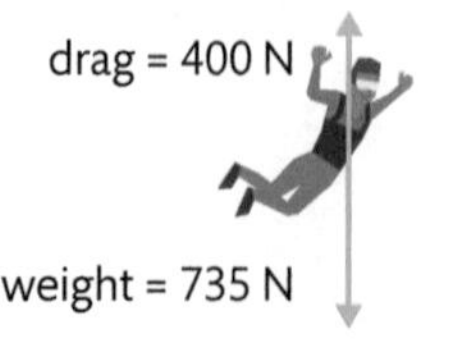

weight = 735 N

$F = 735\text{ N}$

$a = \frac{F}{m} = \frac{735\text{ N}}{75\text{ kg}} = 9.8\text{ m/s}^2$

When the skydiver jumps, they are not yet falling. They have no air resistance (drag). The only force acting on them is their weight, so they accelerate downwards at 9.8 m/s². This is the acceleration due to gravity.

drag = 400 N

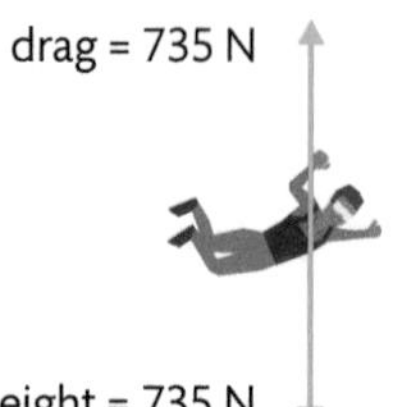

weight = 735 N

$F = 735 - 400 = 335\text{ N}$

$a = \frac{F}{m} = \frac{335\text{ N}}{75\text{ kg}} = 4.5\text{ m/s}^2$

As they accelerate (speed increases), drag increases. This upward force cancels part of the downward force (weight). The resultant force, which causes the acceleration (Newton's Second Law, page 199), is a lot smaller. The skydiver's speed is still increasing, but at a reduced acceleration.

drag = 735 N

weight = 735 N

$F = 735 - 735 = 0\text{ N}$

$a = \frac{F}{m} = 0\text{ m/s}^2$

When weight and drag are equal in magnitude, they cancel out: the resultant force and the acceleration are zero. We know from Newton's First Law (page 199) that a moving object continues to move at constant velocity if there is no resultant force on it. So the skydiver has reached maximum speed. This is called terminal velocity.

Figure 1 The forces change as a skydiver falls.

Worked example — Grade 5

A plane is flying in a straight line with a thrust of 800 000 N applied by the engines. The air resistance is 450 000 N.

(a) What is the resultant force acting on the plane? **[1 mark]**

$F_{resultant} = F_{thrust} - F_{drag} = 800000 - 450000 = 350000\text{ N forward}$

(b) The mass of the plane is 275 000 kg. What is its acceleration? **[2 marks]**

$F = ma \text{ so } a = \frac{F}{m} = \frac{350000}{275000} = 1.3\text{ m/s}^2\text{ forward}$

(c) The plane flies into a headwind and continues at a steady velocity. What is the resultant force acting on the plane now? Explain. **[2 marks]**

There is no resultant force acting on the plane, because it is not accelerating.

Remember to include the direction.

Maths skills

When two forces both act in the same direction (for example the forces on a plane flying with the wind also pushing it forward), the resultant of these two forces is their sum.

$F_1 + F_2 = F_{resultant}$

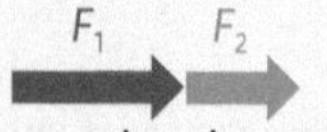

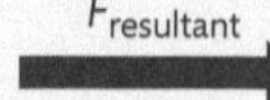

Since forces are vectors – they have size and direction – two forces acting in opposite directions have opposite signs, that is, one is $+F_1$ and one is $-F_2$. So the resultant is still their sum:

$F_1 - F_2 = F_{resultant}$

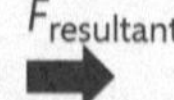

Exam-style practice — Grade 3

1. A car has no resultant force on it. Describe the speed of the car. **[1 mark]**
2. A car of mass 1200 kg is accelerating at 1.4 m/s². Calculate the resultant force acting on the car. **[2 marks]**

 Made a start  Feeling confident  Exam ready

Work done and energy transfer

Work done is energy used when a force moves an object through a distance. You need to be able to calculate work done, given the force and distance.

Calculating *W*

work done (J) = force (N) × distance (m)

$$W = Fs$$

Distance is measured along the line of action of the force.

One joule of work is done when a force of one newton is applied over a distance of one metre.

When calculating work done, the force is measured along the same line of action as the displacement. You may need to resolve forces to calculate work done.

Energy transfer

If you do work pushing an object, it will gain kinetic energy. If you do work lifting an object, it gains gravitational potential energy.

Force × distance has the unit newton metres, Nm, which is equal to work done measured in joules. So one newton metre is equal to one joule.

When a potential difference makes a current flow by 'pushing' charge around a circuit, it is doing work.

Work done against friction heats up the moving object.

Worked example — Grade 5

1 **Figure 1** shows a person carrying a box by applying an upwards force while they move forwards. Using the definition of work done, explain why this person does no work. **[2 marks]**

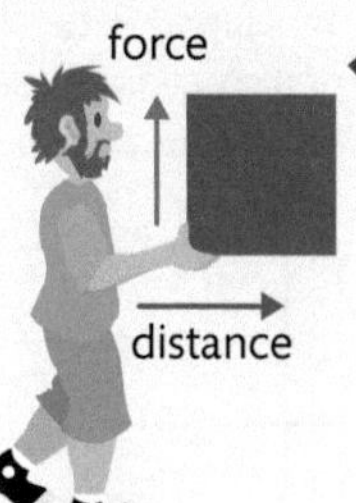

Figure 1

The person will transfer energy and their arms will get tired from holding the box, but we do not call this energy *work*. Work would only be done when they lifted or put down the box as it is moving in the line of action of the force (up or down).

Work done is force × distance moved, in direction of the force. If the force is up and the distance moved is forwards, they are not in the same direction, so the work done is zero.

2 Look at **Figure 2**. A person of weight 650 N walks up a staircase.

Figure 2

(a) What force does the person need to apply to lift themselves up each step? **[1 mark]**

650 N upwards

(b) Calculate the work done to reach the top of the staircase. **[2 marks]**

$W = Fs = 650 \times 1.4 = 910$ J

As they are applying an upward force, you are only interested in the upwards motion; the 1.1 m is not used in the calculation.

The person has weight 650 N, so the force they must use to climb the stairs must match their weight: 650 N.

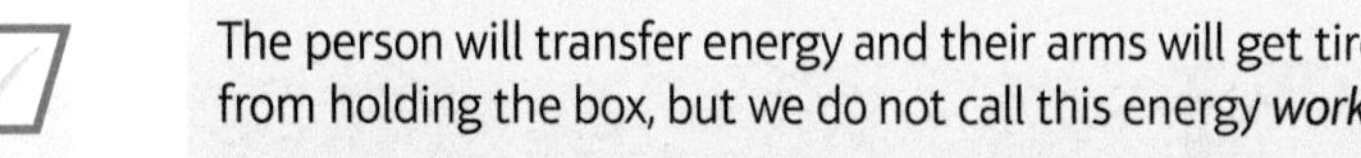

Exam-style practice — Grades 3–4

1 Calculate how much work is done against gravity by:

(a) a person of weight 500 N walking 12 m on a horizontal surface **[1 mark]**

(b) a person of weight 500 N walking up a hill 35 m high **[2 marks]**

(c) a ball of weight 20 N being lifted 1.5 m. **[2 marks]**

2 A footballer slides across the grass and comes to a stop. Work is done to stop them.

(a) What is the force that stops the footballer? **[1 mark]**

(b) Give the energy change. **[1 mark]**

(c) The footballer slides 5 m against a force of 50 N. Calculate the work done. **[2 marks]**

3 A cyclist, starting from rest, pedals up a hill. Describe the energy transfers taking place. **[3 marks]**

Forces and elasticity

Forces can cause objects to change shape permanently or temporarily, by bending, stretching or compressing them. You need to know the effects of forces on elastic objects such as springs.

Types of deformation

Deformation is the term used to describe an object changing shape. Deformation can be elastic or inelastic:

- **elastic deformation** – an object changes shape when a force is applied but returns to its original shape when the force is removed.
- **inelastic deformation** – an object changes shape when a force is applied but does not return to its original shape when the force is removed.

The amount an object changes shape is the **extension** or **compression**. To cause an object to compress, stretch or bend, you usually need two forces working against each other. If you try to squash a rubber ball, you have to push from both sides or the ball will simply move.

Hooke's Law

Hooke's Law states that the extension of an elastic object is directly proportional to the force applied to it. This can be written as:

force (N) = spring constant (N/m) × extension (m)

$$F = ke$$

- The force, F, is the load or weight applied to the object being deformed.
- The spring constant, k, is a measure of how stiff the spring or object is.
- Extension or compression, e, is the amount the object changes shape.

This equation works as long as the elastic limit (the limit of proportionality) is not exceeded.

Springs

Force against extension of a spring

An object that obeys Hooke's Law has a straight line up to the elastic limit on a force-extension graph. Beyond the elastic limit the object is being permanently deformed.

The gradient gives you the spring constant, but be careful to use only the straight line section.

Energy in a spring

Anything that stretches, compresses or bends stores elastic potential energy.

elastic potential energy (J) = 0.5 × spring constant (N/m) × extension² (m)

$$E_e = \frac{1}{2} ke^2$$

When released, the stored energy usually converts into kinetic energy.

This is true up to the elastic limit. Above the elastic limit, work is being done in permanently deforming the object.

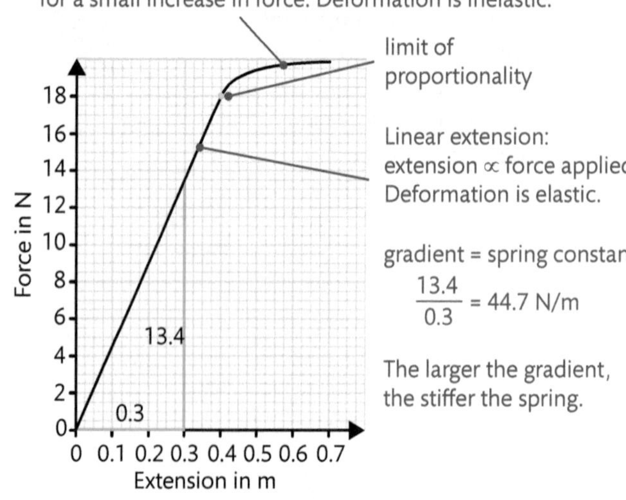

Non-linear extension: there is a large increase in extension for a small increase in force. Deformation is inelastic.
limit of proportionality
Linear extension: extension ∝ force applied. Deformation is elastic.
gradient = spring constant
13.4 / 0.3 = 44.7 N/m
The larger the gradient, the stiffer the spring.
Force in N
18
16
14
12
10
8
6
4
2
0
13.4
0.3
0 0.1 0.2 0.3 0.4 0.5 0.6 0.7
Extension in m

Figure 1 A graph showing how the extension of a spring changes when a force is applied

Worked example Grade 5

A force is applied to a spring so that it is deformed elastically. 18 N of weight is added to make the spring 0.36 m longer.

(a) Calculate the spring constant of the spring. **[4 marks]**

$F = k \times e \qquad 18 = k \times 0.36$

$k = \frac{18}{0.36} = 50\,\text{N/m}$

(b) Calculate the total elastic potential energy stored in the spring. Use the formula sheet. **[2 marks]**

$E_e = \frac{1}{2}ke^2 = 0.5 \times 50 \times 0.36^2 = 3.24\,\text{J}$

Exam-style practice Grade 5

Look at **Figure 1**.

(a) Give the maximum force that the spring can take before being damaged. **[1 mark]**

(b) Explain how the graph shows the limit of proportionality has been reached. **[1 mark]**

(c) Use the graph to find the extension of the spring when it supports a 10 N weight. **[1 mark]**

(d) The original length of the spring is 0.09 m. Calculate the spring length with a weight of 10 N attached. **[2 marks]**

(e) Calculate the energy stored in the spring at the limit of proportionality; $k = 44.7$ N/m. **[3 marks]**

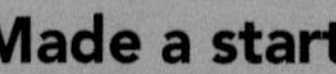

Made a start

Feeling confident

Exam ready

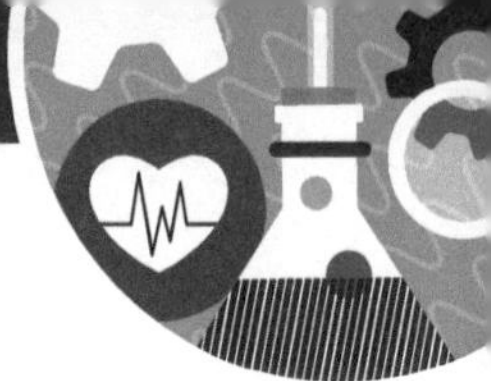

Force and extension

You need to know how to investigate the relationship between force and extension with a spring.

5 Method

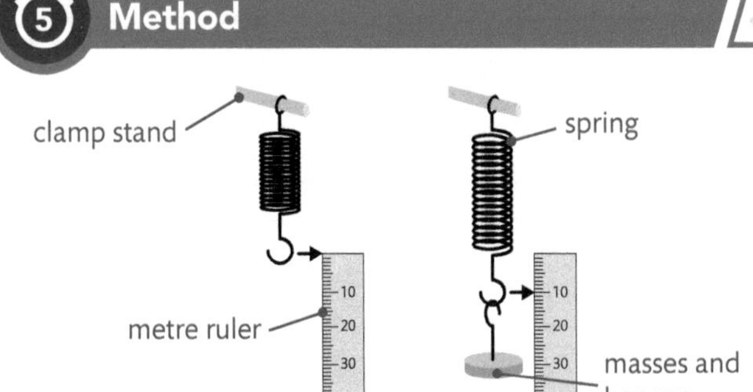

Figure 1 Apparatus

1. Clamp a ruler so that the zero mark is next to the end of the spring hook.
2. Hang a range of masses from the spring.
3. Record the force, which is the weight of each mass.
4. Record the extension of the spring for each force.
5. Plot a graph of force (*y*-axis) against extension (*x*-axis).
6. You can then use the graph to estimate the weight of another object that is hung from the spring by measuring the extension.

If the plotted points are not close to the line of best fit, it might mean that errors need reducing in the experiment.

Maths skills

The force is in newtons and the extension (e) in m, so the gradient is N/m. The gradient is also the spring constant, calculated from $F = ke$.

2 Reducing errors

- Measure the spring length from the same point on the spring each time.
- Make sure the spring is at eye level when measuring it.
- Repeat each extension by removing and rehanging the mass in case larger masses deform the spring inelastically.

5 Worked example — Grade 4

Figure 2 is a graph showing the force and extension of springs A and B.

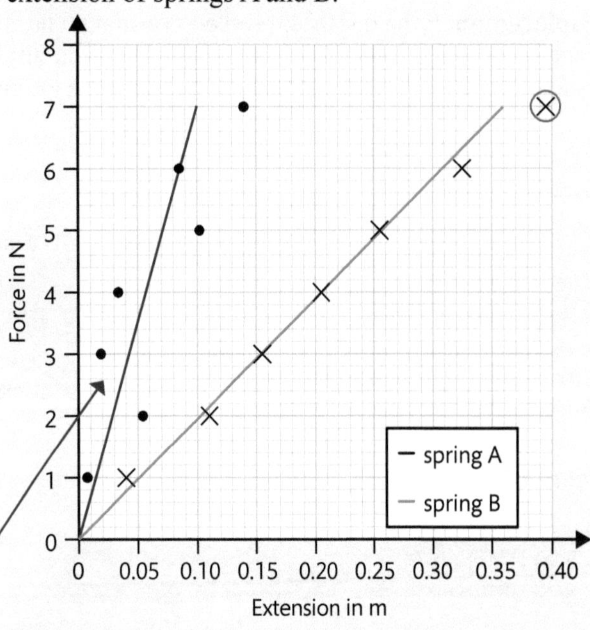

Figure 2

(a) An outlier in the results of spring **B** has been circled in red. Suggest why this point may not fit the pattern. **[2 marks]**

The spring may have exceeded the elastic limit, so force is no longer proportional to extension. Therefore, the line would start to curve and the gradient decrease.

(b) The gradient of the line for spring **A** is 70. Give the unit for the gradient. **[1 mark]**

N/m

(c) Explain whether spring **A** or spring **B** has the higher spring constant. **[2 marks]**

Spring A as it has the higher gradient, or extends less for the same force than spring B.

10 Exam-style practice — Grade 4

Look at **Figure 2**.

(a) Use the graph to find the spring constant of spring **B**. **[2 marks]**

(b) Explain whether the results for spring **A** or spring **B** are more reliable. **[2 marks]**

Distance and displacement

Distance and displacement mean different things in physics. You need to understand the difference between them.

5 Distance and displacement

Distance is how far an object has travelled. Distance only has a magnitude. It is a scalar quantity (page 187).

Displacement is the distance travelled in a straight line, in a particular direction. Displacement has direction as well as magnitude, so it is a vector quantity (page 187). The displacement at the end of a journey is usually less than the total distance travelled because of turns or bends in the journey.

This example shows a person going for a walk.

The person walks a distance of 110 m but has a displacement of 50 m from where they started. The magnitude of the displacement is less than the distance.

distance 110 metres

end

start

displacement 50 metres

The arrow shows the direction of the displacement.

Directions can be given as positive and negative, compass bearings (north, south, east or west), or simple descriptions like 'to the right' or 'up'.

Figure 1 Going for a walk

5 Worked example — Grade 4

A student leaves her house and walks 250 m due north to a postbox. She then walks 300 m east to a shop. She then walks 390 m directly back to her house.

Give the distance and displacement for:

(a) the house to the postbox

(b) the house to the shop

(c) the whole trip. **[4 marks]**

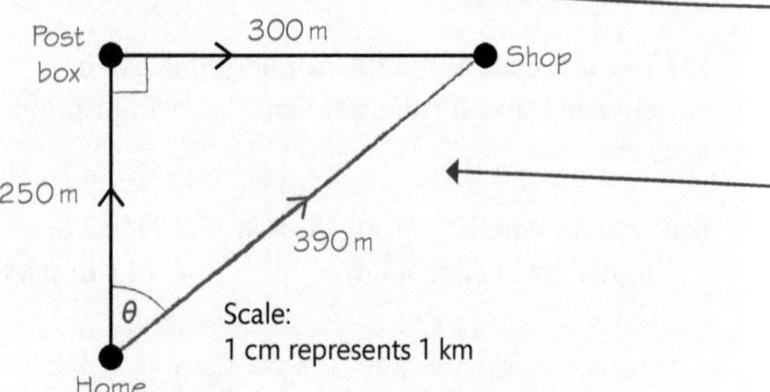

(a) Both distance and displacement are 250 m.

(b) The displacement is 390 m, but the distance is 250 + 300 = 550 m.

(c) Displacement = 0 m. The distance is 250 + 300 + 390 = 940 m.

The displacement is the distance in a straight line from the start to the finish, which in this case is the hypotenuse. Use Pythagoras' theorem:

hypotenuse^2 = $a^2 + b^2$

Displacement is the distance from the house, whereas the distance is how far she actually walked altogether.

Remember that displacements are negative when moving in the opposite direction.

Exam focus

You need to give a length and a distance. Make sure you apply the scale to your measurement.

Displacement is zero if you end up back where you started.

10 Exam-style practice — Grades 4–5

For each of the journeys given below, find the total distance travelled and the displacement.

(a) travel 200 km north, 200 km east and 200 km south **[2 marks]**

(b) run 350 m to the shops, then the same distance back to your home **[2 marks]**

(c) run once around a circle with a diameter of 10 m **[2 marks]**

(d) go up 180 m in a lift, then walk 50 m along the corridor **[3 marks]**

The circumference of a circle is given by $2\pi r$, where r is the radius and $\pi = 3.14$.

 Made a start 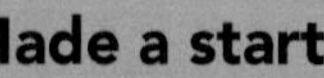  Feeling confident  Exam ready

Speed and velocity

You need to know the difference between speed and velocity. Speed is how fast an object is moving. Speed only has magnitude so is a scalar quantity. Velocity is the speed of an object in a particular direction. Velocity has magnitude and direction so is a vector quantity.

Speed

Speed is a measure of the distance an object has moved in a specific amount of time.

distance travelled (m) = speed (m/s) × time (s) $s = vt$

As most moving objects do not have a constant speed, this equation gives the average speed over time.

You need to know typical examples of everyday speeds.

Activity	walking	running	cycling	cars on a motorway	sound waves
Approximate speed in m/s	1.5	3	6	15–30	330

The speed of sound can vary.

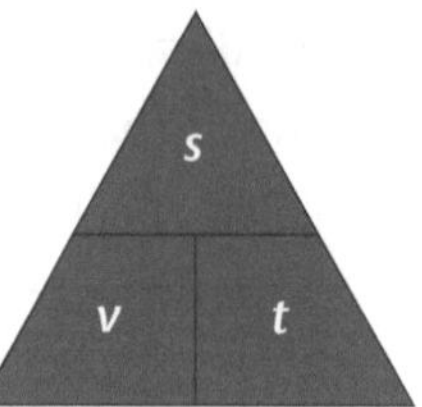

Figure 1 You can use this formula triangle to help you to rearrange the equation and calculate an unknown value.

Velocity

Velocity is speed in a particular direction.

Unlike speed, velocity has a direction. This can be shown as:

- a word, such as 'north' or 'left'
- a positive (+) or negative (−)
- an arrow.

Even at constant speed, the velocity changes if an object changes direction. A car driving around a roundabout at 20 km/h will have constant speed but its velocity changes as it changes direction. If the car drives in one full circle, the displacement is zero, which means the car's average velocity will be zero but the average speed will be 20 km/h.

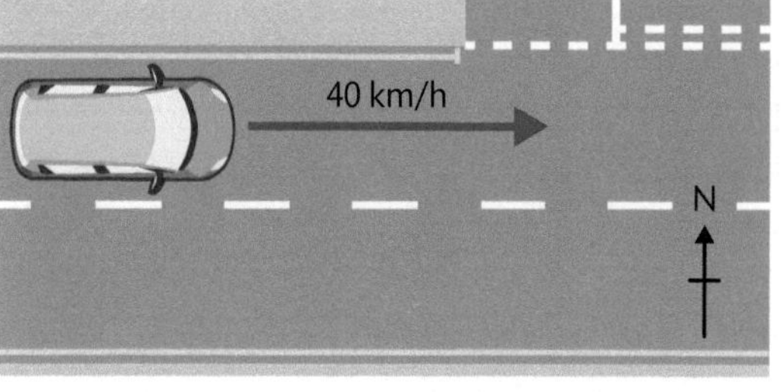

Figure 2 A car has a velocity of 40 km/h east

Maths skills

Convert km to m by multiplying by 1000.
Convert hours to minutes by multiplying by 60.
Convert minutes to seconds by multiplying by 60.

Worked example — Grade 3

Train **A** travels in a straight line due east and covers 4.5 km in 2 minutes.

(a) Convert the time into seconds and distance into metres, then calculate its average speed. **[2 marks]**

$v = \frac{s}{t} = \frac{4500}{120} = 37.5$ m/s

Write down the equation and check the units as you put the numbers in.

(b) What is the difference between the average speed and the speed shown on the speedometer? **[1 mark]**

The speedometer speed changes while the average speed is based on the whole journey over a period of time.

Train **B** travels at twice the speed of train **A**.

(c) After an hour, train **A** has travelled 75 km. How far has train **B** travelled? **[2 marks]**

75 × 2 = 150 km

Look out for things that halve or double. It could be in tables of data or mentioned in questions like this. Be specific: either give a number or say 'twice as far'.

Exam-style practice — Grades 4–5

1. A runner travels 22 m at an average speed of 3 m/s. Calculate the time he takes. Give your answer in seconds. **[2 marks]**
2. The table shows the distances travelled in certain amounts of time by four cars. Which car has the fastest average speed? **[5 marks]**

Car	A	B	C	D
Distance	600 m	200 km	20 m	3000 km
Time	24 s	90 minutes	0.5 s	24 hours

Distance–time relationships

Distance-time graphs show the distance an object travels over a period of time. You need to be able to interpret these types of graph to work out the speed of an object moving in a straight line.

5 Distance–time graphs

A **distance-time graph** shows how far an object moves over time.

The gradient of a distance-time graph represents the **speed** of an object (the distance divided by the time).

- When the line on the graph becomes steeper, the gradient increases. This means the object is **accelerating**.
- When the line on the graph becomes less steep, the gradient decreases. This means the object is **decelerating**.
- When the line on the graph is horizontal, it has a gradient of zero. This means the object is **stationary**.

10 Worked example

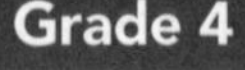

Grade 4

1 **Figure 1** shows the journey of a horse rider.

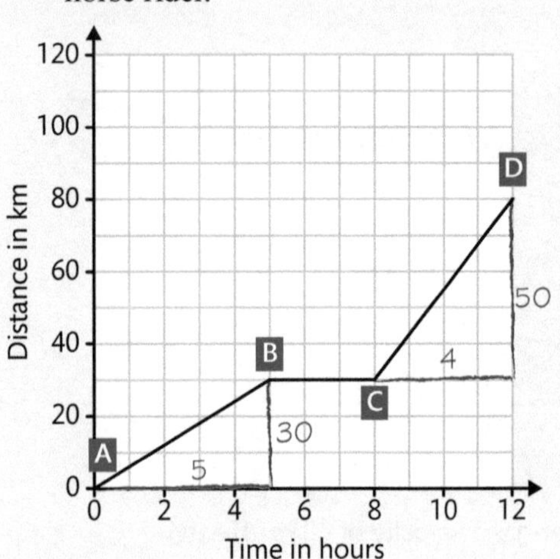

Figure 1

Describe the journey in as much detail as possible. **[4 marks]**

A–B: The rider travels 30 km in 5 hours

The speed (gradient) = 30 ÷ 5 = 6 km/h

B–C: The rider is stationary for 3 hours

C–D: The rider moves a further 50 km in 4 hours

The speed is 50 ÷ 4 = 12.5 km/h

When asked to describe a graph in detail, you should describe the different sections of the graph, giving the times for each section, the distance travelled and the speed.

Working scientifically

Use the scale when you read numbers from a graph. Don't just count squares.

Maths skills

Look carefully at the gradient and notice it is increasing. This means the speed is also increasing.

2 **Figure 2** shows the journey of a cyclist.

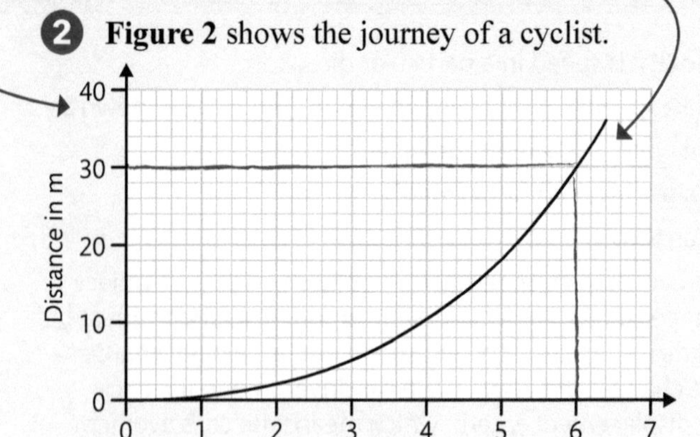

Figure 2

(a) Describe the motion of the cyclist. **[1 mark]**

The cyclist is accelerating.

(b) Use the graph to find how long it takes the cyclist to travel 30 m. **[2 marks]**

6 seconds

(c) What is the average speed of the cyclist over this time? **[1 mark]**

$$\text{speed} = \frac{\text{distance}}{\text{time}} = \frac{30}{6} = 5 \text{ m/s}$$

Exam-style practice

Grades 2–3

1 Describe the motion shown by each graph. **[4 marks]**

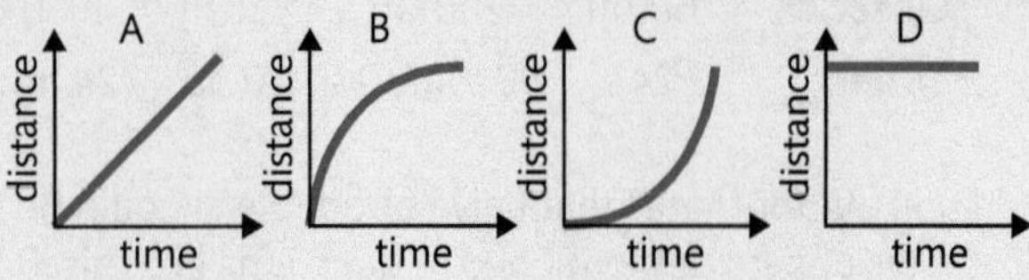

2 Which of the graphs best describes:

(a) a rolling ball that slows down and stops **[1 mark]**

(b) a jogger running at a steady speed **[1 mark]**

(c) a plane accelerating along a runway? **[1 mark]**

 Made a start  Feeling confident  Exam ready

Uniform acceleration

Acceleration is the measure of how quickly an object's velocity changes. Acceleration is a vector quantity. **Uniform** means the acceleration is constant. You need to know how to calculate acceleration for the exam.

Calculating acceleration

The **average acceleration** of an object can be worked out using this equation:

$$\text{acceleration (m/s}^2) = \frac{\text{change in velocity (m/s)}}{\text{time taken (s)}}$$

$$a = \frac{\Delta v}{t}$$

For uniform acceleration:

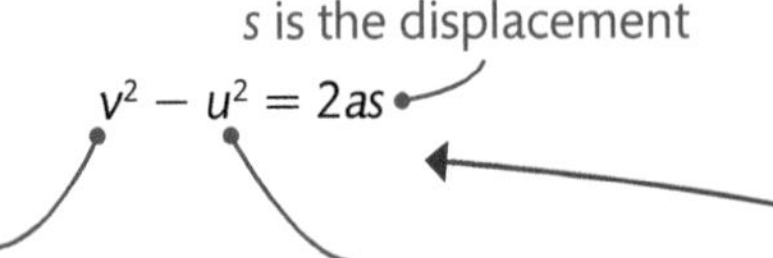

$$v^2 - u^2 = 2as$$

s is the displacement

v is the end velocity in m/s

u is the start velocity in m/s

Acceleration examples

You need to know some typical accelerations and the forces needed to achieve them.

Action	Acceleration in m/s²	Force needed in N
Train starting to move	0.5	50 000
Person starting to run	1	70
Car starting to move	1–5	1000–5000
Object in free fall	9.8	equal to the weight of the object

Exam focus

This equation appears on your formula sheet. You need to be able to rearrange it.

Worked example — Grades 4–5

1 A train travelling at 20 m/s takes 90 s to accelerate to 50 m/s.

(a) Calculate the acceleration of the train. **[2 marks]**

$$a = \frac{\Delta v}{t} = \frac{50 - 20}{90} = 0.33 \text{ m/s}^2$$

(b) Calculate how far the train travels during this time. **[3 marks]**

$$s = \frac{v^2 - u^2}{2a} = \frac{50^2 - 20^2}{2 \times 0.33} = 3182 \text{ m}$$

Write s, u, v, a and t in the margin and make a note of what numbers you know as you read the question.

Ensure you get the start and end velocities the right way around.

2 A ball is dropped and hits the floor at 6 m/s. Calculate how long it takes to fall. Acceleration due to gravity = 9.8 m/s² **[2 marks]**

$$t = \frac{\Delta v}{a} = \frac{6 - 0}{9.8} = 0.61 \text{ s}$$

3 Each lorry in **Figure 1** is accelerating at a constant rate of -2 m/s². The initial velocity of each lorry is shown. Calculate the velocity of each lorry after 5 seconds.
Change in velocity (Δv) = $a \times t$ **[2 marks]**

Negative acceleration can cause an object to speed up if the object is moving in the negative direction. Calculate the end velocity first. Then add it to the initial velocity.

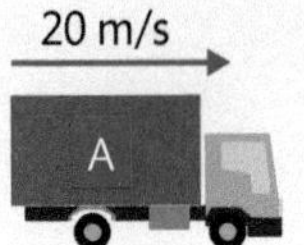

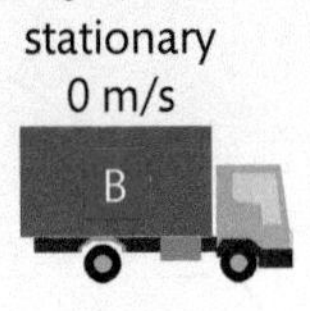

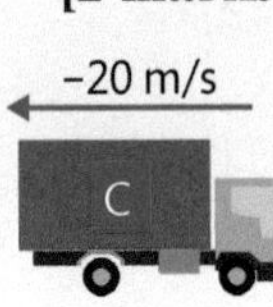

Figure 1

$\Delta v = a \times t = -2 \times 5 = -10$ m/s

A: $20 + -10 = 10$ m/s

B: $0 + -10 = -10$ m/s

C: $-20 + -10 = -30$ m/s

Exam-style practice — Grade 5

1 An apple falls from a branch onto the ground. The time taken for the apple to fall is 1.5 s. Calculate the speed of the apple when it hits the ground. (g = 9.8 m/s²) **[2 marks]**

2 (a) A jet lands at 65 m/s and comes to a stop. What is its change in velocity? **[2 marks]**

(b) The jet has an acceleration of –5 m/s². Calculate how long it takes to come to a stop. **[2 marks]**

3 Describe how the speed of an object travelling at 40 m/s is changing if its acceleration is:

(a) 2 m/s² **[1 mark]**

(b) –2 m/s². **[1 mark]**

Velocity–time graphs

Velocity–time graphs show how the velocity of an object changes over time. You need to know how to calculate acceleration from the gradient of a velocity–time graph and distance travelled from the area under the velocity–time graph.

5 Acceleration

- The acceleration for a given section of the graph is equal to the gradient of the line. If the line is straight, the acceleration is constant.
- The steeper the slope, the higher the acceleration. If the slope goes down, the velocity is decreasing. This is negative acceleration, or deceleration.

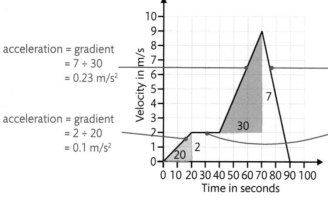

acceleration = gradient
= 7 ÷ 30
= 0.23 m/s²

acceleration = gradient
= 2 ÷ 20
= 0.1 m/s²

Here, gradient is negative, giving a deceleration.

A horizontal line (gradient = 0) indicates a constant speed.

Velocity in m/s: 0 1 2 3 4 5 6 7 8 9 10

Time in seconds: 0 10 20 30 40 50 60 70 80 90 100

20 | 2 | 30 | 7

Figure 1 A velocity–time graph

10 Interpreting graphs

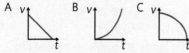

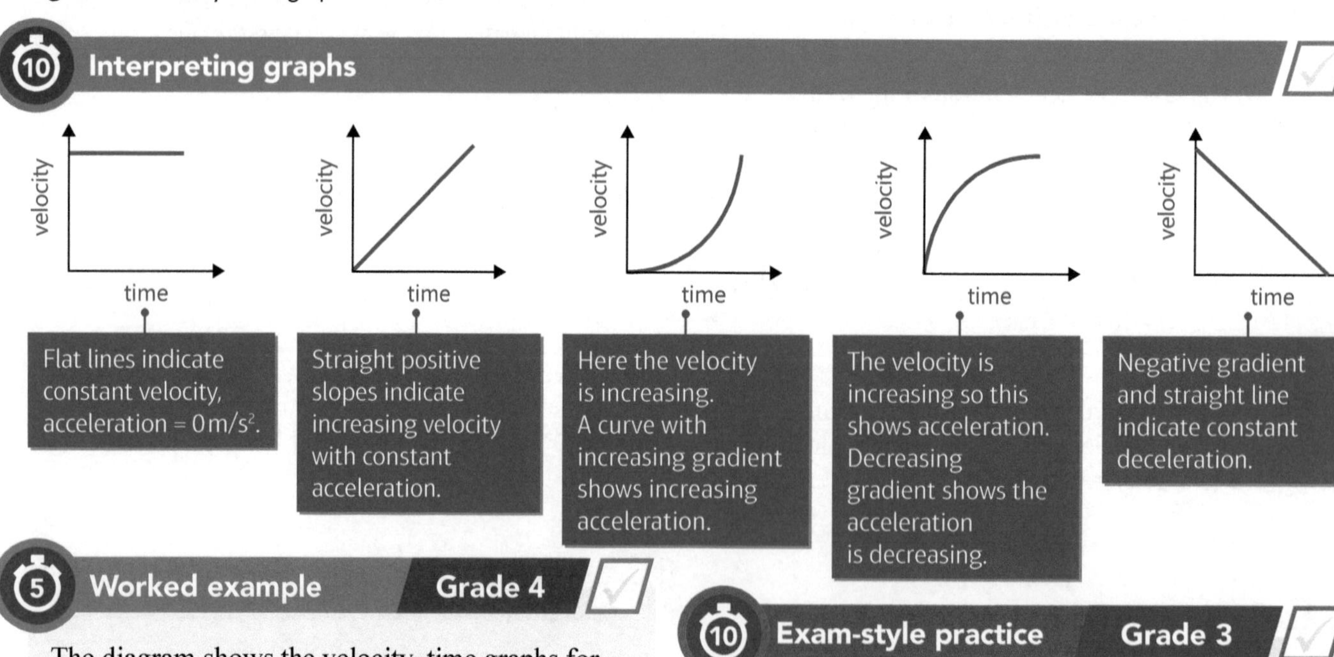

velocity
time
Flat lines indicate constant velocity, acceleration = 0 m/s².
Straight positive slopes indicate increasing velocity with constant acceleration.
Here the velocity is increasing. A curve with increasing gradient shows increasing acceleration.
The velocity is increasing so this shows acceleration. Decreasing gradient shows the acceleration is decreasing.
Negative gradient and straight line indicate constant deceleration.

5 Worked example — Grade 4

The diagram shows the velocity–time graphs for the motion of three different objects

A v t | B v t | C v t

Read the statements. State if each is true or false.

(a) Graph **A** shows acceleration. **[1 mark]**

False – it shows constant deceleration

(b) Graph **B** shows acceleration at a constant rate. **[1 mark]**

False – it shows acceleration that is increasing

(c) Graph **C** shows deceleration. **[1 mark]**

True – the velocity is decreasing non-uniformly

10 Exam-style practice — Grade 3

The graph shows the velocity of a golf cart over 35 seconds.

Velocity in m/s: 0 2 4 6 8 10 12

Time in seconds: 0 5 10 15 20 25 30 35

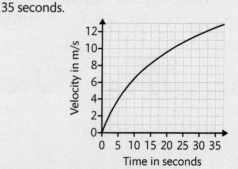

(a) Give the velocity of the cart at 5 s. **[1 mark]**

(b) Explain how we can tell the acceleration of the golf cart decreases with time. **[2 marks]**

Newton's laws of motion

Newton's three laws of motion explain how forces affect the motion of objects. You need to consider resultant forces when using Newton's laws. There is more about calculating resultant forces on page 190.

Newton's first law

If all the forces acting on an object are balanced (the resultant force = 0), the object will remain at a constant velocity or at rest.

What does it mean?

This means that once an object is moving, it will keep moving at the same velocity as long as no overall (resultant) force acts upon it.

To make the object speed up, slow down, or change direction, you need to apply a resultant force.

If an object has no resultant force then all the forces are balanced. It will continue to move with constant velocity, or remain stationary.

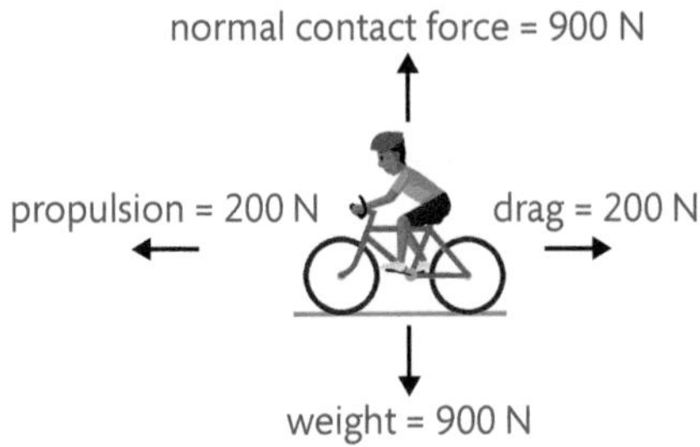

Figure 1 Balanced forces acting on a cyclist

In **Figure 1**, the vertical and horizontal forces add up to zero. We cannot say all the forces are equal; instead, we say they are balanced or in equilibrium.

The cyclist will continue at a constant speed and direction because the resistive force (drag) balances the driving force (propulsion). If the cyclist stops pedalling, the forces become unbalanced and the cyclist slows down.

Most moving objects that are not being moved by another force will eventually stop because of the force of friction.

Newton's third law

When two objects interact, they exert an equal and opposite force on each other.

What does it mean?

When one object applies a force to another, it experiences the same force itself but in the opposite direction. Note that the two forces:

- are the same size
- act in exactly opposite directions
- act on different objects, so they do not cancel out.

A bat hits a ball with a force of 200 N. The ball exerts a force of 200 N on the bat in the opposite direction.

The force has a greater effect on the ball's speed because the ball has a smaller mass.

Newton's second law

If the forces acting on an object are unbalanced, the object's acceleration will be:

- in the direction of the resultant force
- directly proportional to the resultant force: force $\propto$ acceleration
- inversely proportional to the mass of the object: acceleration $\propto \frac{1}{\text{mass}}$

What does it mean?

An unbalanced force makes an object speed up, slow down or change direction.

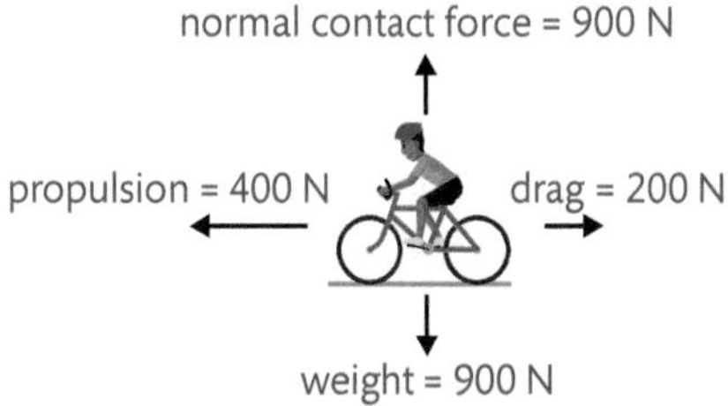

Figure 2 Unbalanced forces acting on a cyclist. There is a resultant force in the forwards direction so the cyclist will accelerate.

If you double the resultant force, the acceleration will also double.

If something is slowing down and stopping, it is decelerating. This means there must be a resultant force acting in the opposite direction to its motion.

Worked example — Grade 5

Explain what happens to the acceleration of a lorry if its mass doubles. **[2 marks]**

Acceleration is inversely proportional to an object's mass. So for the same force, if its mass doubles, its acceleration will halve.

Exam-style practice — Grade 4

For each of the following, state the opposite force described by Newton's third law. In each case give the direction of this force:

(a) a cricket bat applying a force to a ball forwards **[1 mark]**

(b) gravity pulling a person down towards Earth **[1 mark]**

(c) a cup applying a contact force downwards onto a table **[1 mark]**

Newton's second law

Newton's second law shows the relationship between force, mass and acceleration.

$F = ma$

Newton's second law tells you how much force is required to accelerate a mass.

force (N) = mass (kg) × acceleration (m/s²)

The force that causes the acceleration must be the resultant (overall) force.

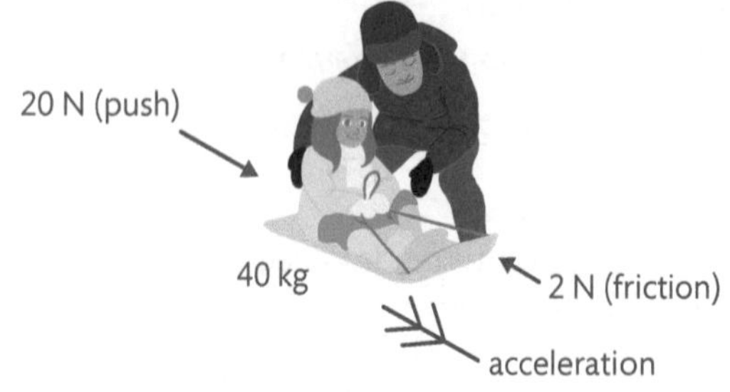

Figure 1 The sledge and passenger have a combined mass of 40 kg. The resultant force is 18 N.
(20 N forwards force − 2 N frictional force)
$a = \frac{F}{m} = 18 \div 40 = 0.45$ m/s²

Changing the values

An object will tend to remain at rest or carry on with uniform motion. For both trolleys to accelerate at the same rate, the force applied to trolley B must be greater than the force applied to trolley A.

Figure 2 Trolley **B** has a larger mass, therefore it needs a greater force to accelerate at the same rate as Trolley **A**.

Worked example — Grade 4

A firework has a mass of 0.4 kg. It is launched vertically upwards with a thrust of 45 N.

(a) Calculate the resultant upward force. **[2 marks]**

Resultant upwards force, F = thrust − weight:

45 − (0.4 × 9.8) = 41.08 N

(b) Calculate the acceleration of the firework as it is launched. Use $g = 9.8$ m/s².

$a = F \div m$

$= 41.08 \div 0.4 = 102.7$ m/s²

(c) A second firework has a smaller mass but the same thrust as the first firework. Describe how the acceleration of the second firework compares with the acceleration of the first firework. **[2 marks]**

$a \propto \frac{1}{m}$ so if mass is smaller, acceleration is greater. The mass of the second firework is less, so the acceleration is greater for the same thrust.

Maths skills

Use the resultant force to calculate the new acceleration. You don't need to write down the formula again.

Consider the proportionality between mass and acceleration:

$a = \frac{F}{m}$ so $a \propto \frac{1}{m}$

Exam focus

Be specific when talking about how something changes. Explain which quantity decreases and which increases.

Exam-style practice — Grade 4

(a) A rider accelerates on a scooter at 1.67 m/s². The forward force is 300 N and there is 50 N of drag. Calculate the resultant force on the scooter. **[1 mark]**

(b) Calculate the total mass of the scooter and rider. **[2 marks]**

(c) Carrying a passenger and luggage doubles the total mass. Calculate the acceleration if the other forces remain the same. **[2 marks]**

Investigating acceleration

You need to know how to investigate the effect of force and mass on acceleration.

Two experiments

Experiment 1

1. Increase the hanging masses (**Figure 1**).
2. The interrupt card passes through the light gate. A data logger calculates the acceleration.

Experiment 2

1. Increase the mass of the trolley by fixing masses to it.
2. Measure the acceleration. Keep the force (hanging mass) the same.

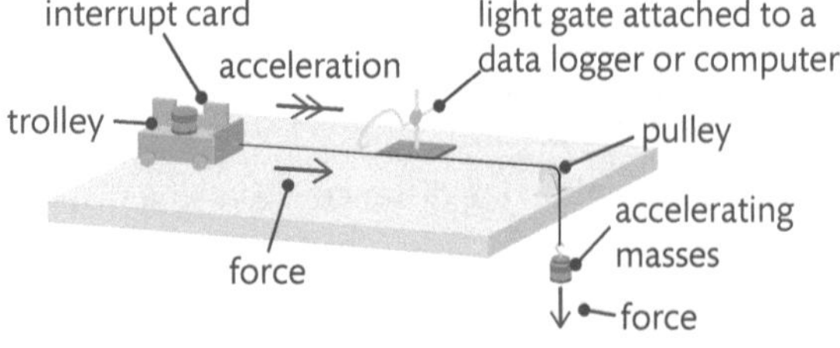

Figure 1 Apparatus for measuring acceleration

Worked example — Grade 5

(a) Give the expected findings of Experiment **1**. **[2 marks]**

Increasing the force on the trolley would increase its acceleration. Force and acceleration are proportional.

> They are proportional (written $F \propto a$) because if you double the force, the acceleration doubles.

(b) State **one** other force acting on the trolley. Explain what could be done to reduce the effect it has on the results. **[2 marks]**

Friction – lift the ramp so the trolley runs slightly downhill to counteract friction.

> Doing the experiment on an air track would be ideal, but there will still be friction in the pulley. Drag is another force that acts on the trolley. You could make the trolley more streamlined to minimise the effects of drag.

(c) A graph is plotted using the results from Experiment **1**. What would be plotted on each axis? **[2 marks]**

Force (N) on the x-axis and acceleration (m/s^2) on the y-axis

(d) For Experiment **2**, give **one** variable you would need to control and explain why. **[2 marks]**

The force used to accelerate the trolley would need to be the same. If a different force was used when the trolley mass was increased, you would not be able to tell what caused the change in acceleration.

Interrupt card

The two sections of card break the light beam for a period of time. The data logger calculates the speed for each side:

$$\text{speed} = \frac{\text{card length}}{\text{time}}$$

It also measures the time between interruptions:

$$\text{acceleration} = \frac{\text{difference in speeds}}{\text{time between interruptions}}$$

Maths skills

By convention, the independent variable (the thing being changed) is plotted on the x-axis, and the thing you measure as a result (the dependent variable) goes on the y-axis.

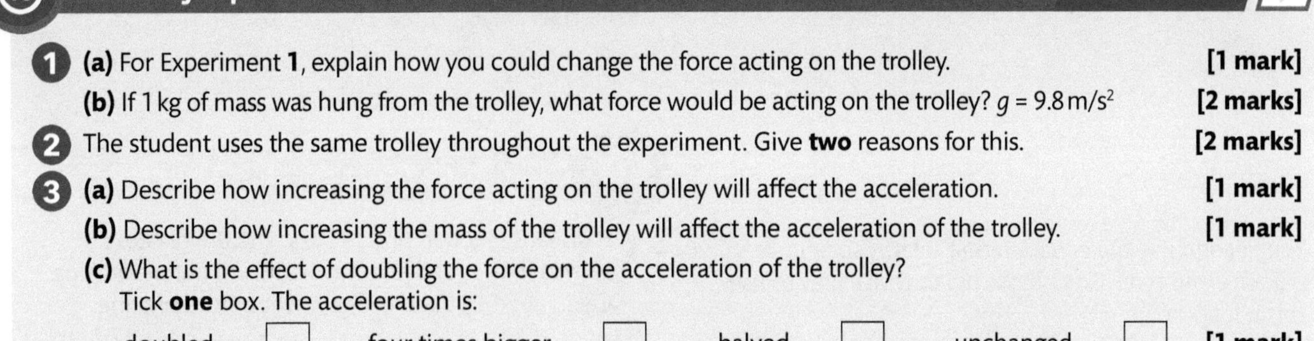

Exam-style practice — Grade 4

1. **(a)** For Experiment **1**, explain how you could change the force acting on the trolley. **[1 mark]**

   (b) If 1 kg of mass was hung from the trolley, what force would be acting on the trolley? $g = 9.8\,\text{m/s}^2$ **[2 marks]**

2. The student uses the same trolley throughout the experiment. Give **two** reasons for this. **[2 marks]**

3. **(a)** Describe how increasing the force acting on the trolley will affect the acceleration. **[1 mark]**

   (b) Describe how increasing the mass of the trolley will affect the acceleration of the trolley. **[1 mark]**

   (c) What is the effect of doubling the force on the acceleration of the trolley?
   Tick **one** box. The acceleration is:

   doubled ☐ four times bigger ☐ halved ☐ unchanged ☐ **[1 mark]**

 Made a start 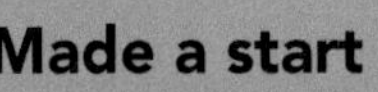  Feeling confident  Exam ready

Stopping distance

Stopping distance refers to the distance over which a vehicle stops. It is the total of the thinking distance and the braking distance. You need to know the factors that affect the stopping distance of a vehicle.

Calculating stopping distance

To calculate the stopping distance of a car, you need to account for the driver's **reaction time** (thinking distance) and the braking distance.

stopping distance = thinking distance + braking distance

- **Thinking distance** – the distance travelled while the driver is reacting. This occurs before they start to brake.
- **Braking distance** – the distance it takes the car to stop once the brakes have been applied.

Revise the factors affecting braking on page 203.

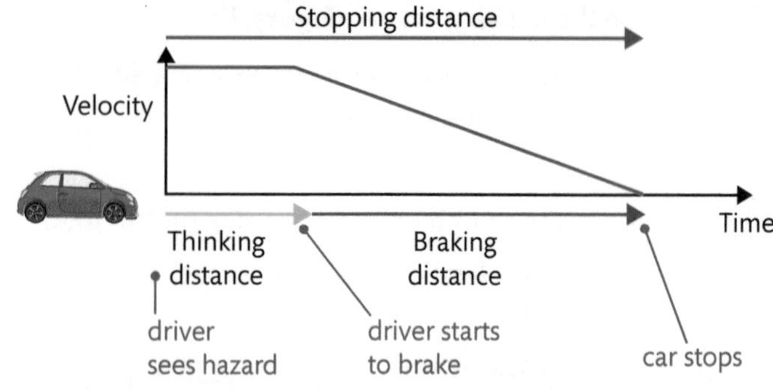

Figure 1 A graph showing the stopping distance of a car

Factors affecting thinking distance

Thinking distance increases at higher speeds, when visibility is poor, for example due to fog, and when reaction time is slowed. Typical reaction times vary from 0.2 s to 0.9 s. Factors that can slow reaction time include:

- alcohol
- drugs/medicine
- being tired
- distraction, e.g. using a mobile phone.

Measuring reactions

Method 1

Reaction times can be measured using a stop clock. One person presses start and the other has to hit the stop button as quickly as possible.

Method 2

One person holds a ruler vertically while the other holds their finger and thumb at the bottom of the ruler. When the ruler is dropped they have to catch it. The slower their reactions, the more of the ruler passes through their fingers.

Worked example — Grade 5

A student's reaction time is measured using the two methods described above. Measurements are taken with the student concentrating and then being distracted. Each measurement is repeated and recorded in a table.

	Reading 1	Reading 2
Method A concentrating	0.31 s	0.35 s
Method A distracted	0.60 s	0.64 s
Method B concentrating	10 cm	15 cm
Method B distracted	24 cm	28 cm

(a) Introducing a distraction affected the reaction time in method **A**. Suggest what effect the distraction had on reaction time. **[1 mark]**

Reaction time was increased, almost doubled.

(b) For method **B**, a student says that the person needs to keep their fingers the same distance from the ruler. Describe how holding their fingers closer to the ruler could affect the distance the ruler falls. **[2 marks]**

If the fingers are closer, it won't take as much time to close them so the ruler will not fall as far.

Exam-style practice — Grade 4

You need to use the equation that relates speed, distance and time. Go to page 195 to revise how to use this equation.

A driver's reaction time is 0.6 s. The driver sees an animal in the road and travels 18.6 m before braking. Calculate the speed of the driver before braking. **[2 marks]**

 Made a start  Feeling confident  Exam ready

Braking distance

You need to know how to calculate braking distance and the factors that affect it.

Factors affecting braking distance

Factors such as greater speed and greater mass increase the kinetic energy, which means there is more work for the brakes to do. The car therefore travels further before it stops.

Go to page 202 to revise stopping distances.

The following factors reduce friction and brake force:

- worn brakes
- worn tyres
- adverse weather conditions such as rain or snow
- adverse road conditions such as loose road surface or wet/icy roads.

As the work done by brakes = force × distance, a smaller force means the car will travel further before it stops. Go to page 191 to revise work done.

Braking distances vary from 6 m at 20 mph (32 km/h) up to 96 m at 70 mph (112 km/h). That is why when travelling faster or in conditions that make the braking distance longer, drivers need to leave larger gaps between them and the vehicle in front. In emergencies, cars decelerate at approximately 3–5 m/s^2. Rapid deceleration can cause the car to skid and the driver to lose control.

The energy of braking

Brakes use friction to do work and stop the car.

The work done is equal to the kinetic energy.

This energy is transferred to thermal energy in the brakes.

If the brakes overheat they may not function as well.

You can use the following equations for braking calculations:

work done by brakes = kinetic energy of car

force (N) × distance (m) = 0.5 × mass (kg) × velocity^2 (m/s)

$$Fs = \frac{1}{2}mv^2$$

This can be rearranged, for example, to find the braking force if the mass, speed and braking distance are known.

$$F = \frac{mv^2}{2s}$$

Worked example — Grade 4

Figure 1 is a graph showing the effect of speed on thinking distance and braking distance.

Look at **Figure 1**.

1 **(a)** Give the thinking distance when the car is travelling at 25 m/s. **[1 mark]**

17 m

2 Decide if each statement is true or false.

When the speed doubles:

(a) the braking distance doubles **[1 mark]**

False – the line curves and the braking distance more than doubles

(b) the thinking distance doubles. **[1 mark]**

True – the line is straight and would go through the origin

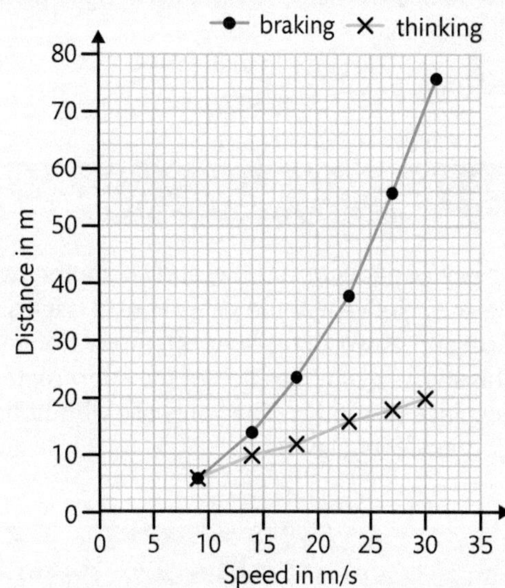

Figure 1

Exam-style practice — Grade 5

What effect does doubling the speed have on braking distance? Explain your answer. **[4 marks]**

 Made a start  Feeling confident  Exam ready

Types of waves

All waves are either transverse or longitudinal. You need to know the differences between these two types of wave.

5 Longitudinal waves

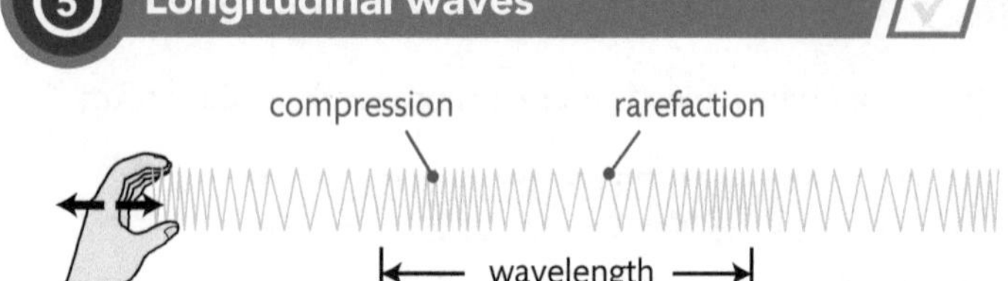

Figure 1 Longitudinal waves

For **longitudinal waves**, the vibrations are parallel to the direction of the wave (the direction of energy transfer).

There are no **peaks** or **troughs**. Instead, the wave has **compressions** (for sound, this means regions of high pressure) where particles are close together and **rarefactions** (regions of low pressure), where the particles are more spread out.

A **wavelength** is measured from the centre of one compression to the next. You could use rarefactions, but the centre of a compression is easier to find.

Examples:

- sound (in any medium)
- a slinky being pushed and pulled.

Measuring the speed of sound in air

Measure the distance to a large wall that reflects sound.

Clap and ask someone else to time how long it takes for the echo to be heard. The wave has travelled the distance to the wall twice so:

$$\text{wave speed (m/s)} = \frac{\text{distance to wall (m)} \times 2}{\text{time (s)}}$$

5 Transverse waves

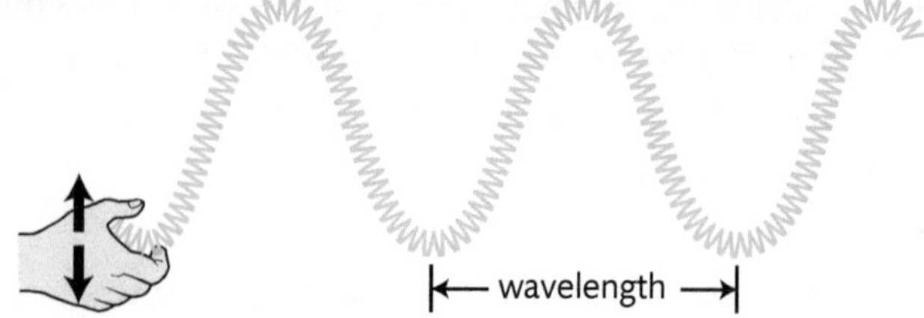

Figure 2 Transverse waves

For **transverse waves**, the vibrations are perpendicular to the direction of the wave (the direction of energy transfer).

Examples:

- ripples on water
- a slinky being shaken
- light (and all electromagnetic waves).

Measuring the speed of ripples on water

Lay a ruler flat on the bottom of a ripple tank so the ripples pass over it.

Measure the time it takes for a ripple to travel the length of the ruler.

$$\text{wave speed (m/s)} = \frac{\text{distance (m)}}{\text{time (s)}}$$

Alternatively, set the frequency of the ripples using a signal generator attached to the motor and measure the distance between the ripples.

$$\text{wave speed (m/s)} = \text{frequency (Hz)} \times \text{wavelength (m)}$$

2 Waves transfer energy

Place a piece of paper on a slinky and create the two types of wave. Notice that the paper moves back and forth or up and down, but it does not move along the wave. This shows that waves do not transport material from one place to another. They only use vibrations in matter to transfer energy.

2 Worked example — Grades 4–5

Describe the motion of the air particles in a sound wave. Refer to the direction of the vibration. **[2 marks]**

Air particles vibrate in the direction the wave is travelling. This creates a pattern of compressions (where the particles are close together and the pressure is high) and rarefactions (where the particles are further apart and the pressure is lower).

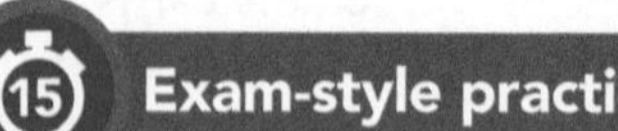

15 Exam-style practice — Grade 4

1. A student stands 200 m away from a large building. The student claps and an echo is heard. The sound is recorded by a sound meter which also measures the time between the clap and the echo. Describe how the student can determine the speed of sound using this information. **[3 marks]**
2. A gull floats on the ocean. As the waves pass, the gull bobs up and down but does not move forwards. Explain how this shows that ocean waves are transverse. **[2 marks]**
3. Explain why sound cannot pass through a vacuum. **[1 mark]**

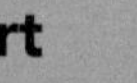
Made a start

Feeling confident

Exam ready

Properties of waves

A wave transports energy through a medium using vibrations. You need to understand the properties of waves.

Parts of a wave

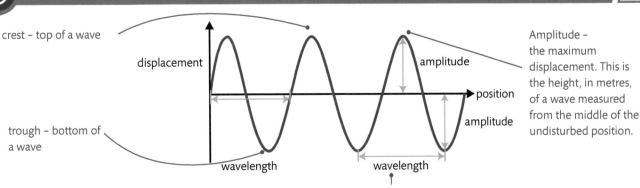

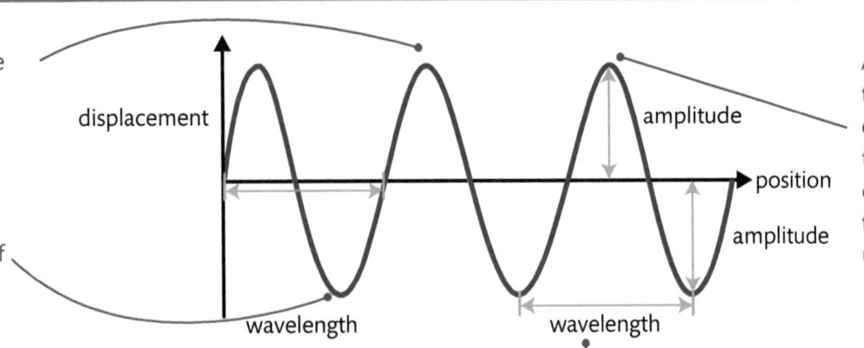

crest – top of a wave
displacement
amplitude
position
amplitude
trough – bottom of a wave
wavelength
wavelength
Amplitude – the maximum displacement. This is the height, in metres, of a wave measured from the middle of the undisturbed position.
Wavelength, λ – the length of one complete wave. It can be measured from anywhere on the wave to the next equivalent point, but crest to crest or trough to trough is easiest to find and measure.

Figure 1 A wave

- **Wavelength**, λ, is measured in metres, but may be given in centimetres depending on the type and size of wave.
- Time period, or just **period**, T, is the time to complete one full cycle or wave, measured in seconds, s.
- **Wave speed**, v, is the speed at which energy is transferred (or the wave moves) through the medium.
- **Frequency**, f, is the number of waves passing a point per second, measured in hertz, Hz.

Key equations

- time period (s) $= \frac{1}{\text{frequency (Hz)}}$ $\quad T = \frac{1}{f}$
- frequency (Hz) $= \frac{1}{\text{period (s)}}$ $\quad f = \frac{1}{T}$
- wave speed (m/s) = frequency (Hz) × wavelength (m) $\quad v = f\lambda$
- speed (m/s) $= \frac{\text{distance (m)}}{\text{time (s)}}$ $\quad v = \frac{s}{t}$

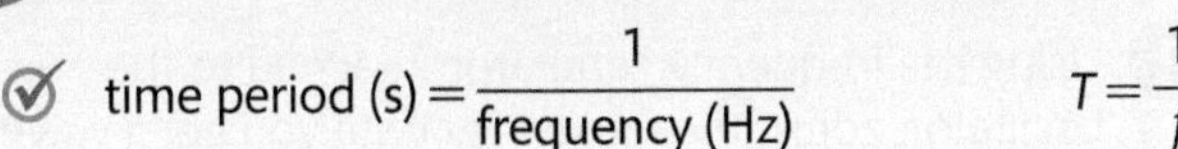

Displacement graphs

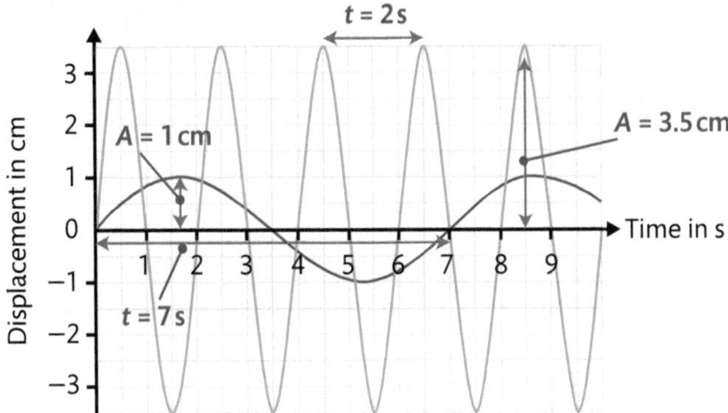

Figure 2 A displacement graph

The **amplitude** is read off as the maximum **displacement**.

If the *x*-axis shows time, the period can be read off.

If the *x*-axis shows position, the wavelength can be read off instead of the period.

Worked example — Grades 3–4

It takes 1.51 s for a sound to travel 500 m. Calculate the speed of sound. **[2 marks]**

$$\text{speed} = \frac{\text{distance}}{\text{time}}$$

$$= \frac{500}{1.51} = 331\text{ m/s}$$

Exam-style practice — Grade 4

1. Write the units for the following:
   (a) frequency **[1 mark]**
   (b) wavelength **[1 mark]**
   (c) time period **[1 mark]**
2. Fill in the missing words in these sentences. **[2 marks]**
   The speed of a wave does not change. If the frequency increases the wavelength ________.
   If the frequency increases the time period ______.
3. The period of a water wave is 2 s. What is the correct frequency of the wave? Tick **one** box. **[1 mark]**
   0.5 Hz ☐ 2 Hz ☐ 5 Hz ☐ 20 Hz ☐
4. A water wave travels 10 m in 4 s. Calculate the speed of this water wave. **[2 marks]**

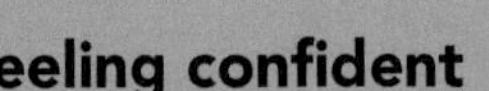

Investigating waves

These practicals investigate the speed, frequency and wavelength of waves in a ripple tank and in solids.

10 Speed of waves in a ripple tank

1. Time how long it takes for one wave to travel from the paddle to the edge of the ripple tank.
2. Measure the distance.
3. Calculate the wave speed.

$$\text{wave speed (m/s)} = \frac{\text{distance (m)}}{\text{time (s)}}$$

4. Time 10 rotations of the motor and divide by 10 to get the period. Calculate the frequency.

$$\text{frequency (Hz)} = \frac{1}{\text{period (s)}}$$

5. Calculate the wavelength.

$$\text{wavelength (m)} = \frac{\text{wave speed (m/s)}}{\text{frequency (Hz)}}$$

6. Alternatively, hold a ruler next to the water and try to estimate the distance from one ripple to the next.

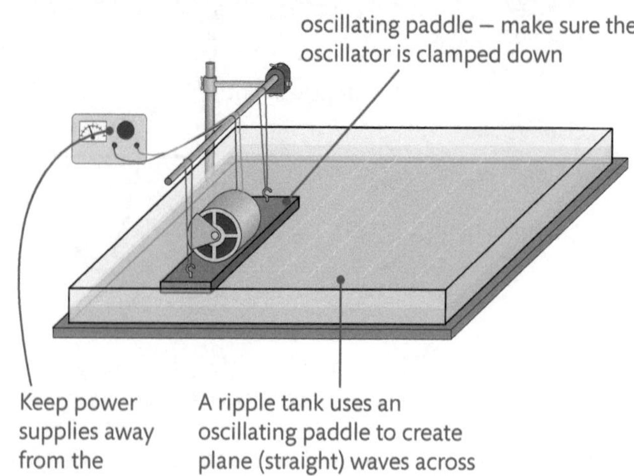

oscillating paddle – make sure the oscillator is clamped down
Keep power supplies away from the ripple tank.
A ripple tank uses an oscillating paddle to create plane (straight) waves across shallow water.

Figure 1 Using a ripple tank to measure the speed of waves

10 Studying waves on a string

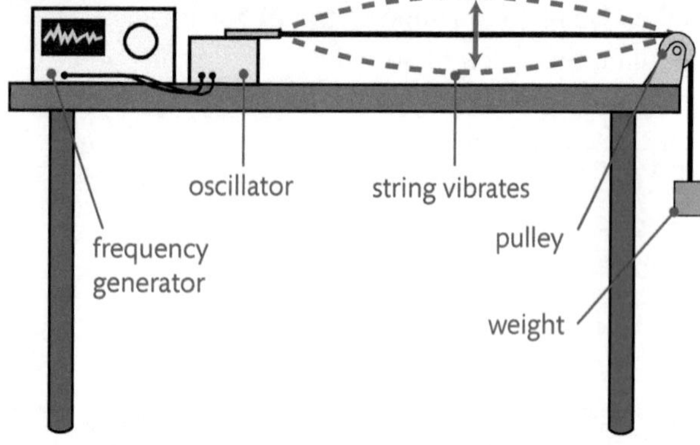

Figure 2 Using a string to measure the speed of waves

You could use a wire instead of string.

1. Using the frequency generator attached to the oscillator, adjust the frequency until you get a wave on the string as shown.
2. Read the frequency from the frequency generator.
3. Measure the length, L, of the string from oscillator to pulley. This is half a wavelength, so $\lambda = 2L$.
4. Calculate wave speed using:

wave speed (m/s) = frequency (Hz) × wavelength (m)

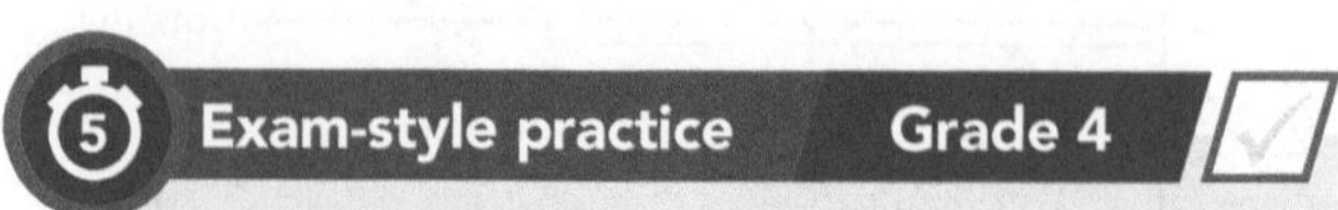

1 Working scientifically

- Wear goggles if you use wire.
- Keep clear of hanging weights.

2 Worked example — Grade 4

Describe a method to measure the speed of a sea wave. **[2 marks]**

From a safe place, find two fixed points and measure the time it takes for a wave to travel between them. Measure the distance between the points. Calculate the wave speed using:

$$\text{wave speed} = \frac{\text{distance}}{\text{time}}$$

5 Exam-style practice — Grade 4

1. It takes an oscillating motor 3.6 seconds to produce 10 vibrations. Calculate the frequency. **[3 marks]**
2. Look at **Figure 2**. Give **one** way the tension in the string can be increased. **[1 mark]**

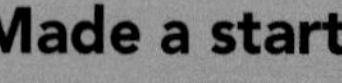 Made a start  Feeling confident  Exam ready

Types of electromagnetic wave

Waves on the electromagnetic spectrum are continuous but are grouped according to their wavelength and frequency. You need to know the properties of electromagnetic waves.

Properties of electromagnetic waves

Electromagnetic (EM) waves have properties that depend on their wavelength. All waves on the electromagnetic spectrum are transverse and transfer energy from the source to an absorber. All electromagnetic waves travel at the same velocity through a vacuum or air.

Radio waves are produced by vibrations of electrons in electrical circuits. They have low energy so are harmless.

Microwaves have slightly higher energy than radio waves. They can cause a heating effect in water.

Infrared radiation is thermal energy travelling as a wave. It is emitted from hot objects.

Visible light is seen as different colours by the human eye depending on its wavelength.

Ultraviolet (UV) light is present in sunlight. It is linked to premature ageing and skin cancer.

X-rays pass through soft tissue but are absorbed by denser bones.

Gamma rays are produced by changes to the nucleus of an atom.

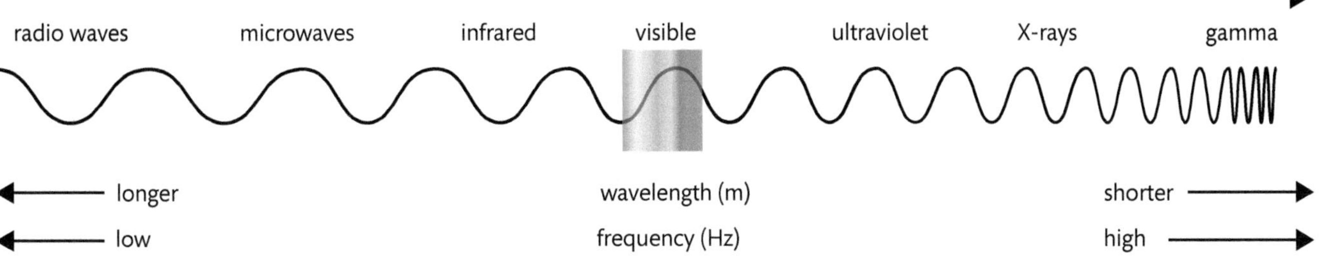

Figure 1 Electromagnetic waves

The harmful effects of radiation depend on the type of radiation and the dose. X-rays and gamma rays are ionising radiation. Ionising radiation can change genes, which can cause cancers and kill cells. Radiation dose is measured in millisieverts. 1000 millisieverts (mSv) = 1 sievert (Sv).

EM waves are often produced over a large range of frequencies by changes to atoms, such as nuclear processes or electrons moving. When EM waves are absorbed, they can cause changes, for example, they can cause electrons to move, or even be lost from, an atom.

The speed of light is 3×10^8 m/s (300 000 000 m/s)
You can use the wave equation $v = f\lambda$.
wave speed (m/s) = frequency (Hz) × wavelength (m)

Maths skills
Use the $\times 10^x$ key on your calculator to enter standard form numbers.

Worked example — Grade 4

Red light has a wavelength of 7×10^{-7} m.

(a) State the speed of red light. **[1 mark]**

speed of light = 3×10^8 m/s

(b) Calculate the frequency of red light. **[2 marks]**

$$f = \frac{v}{\lambda} = \frac{3 \times 10^8}{7 \times 10^{-7}} = 4.3 \times 10^{14}\ \text{Hz}$$

Exam-style practice — Grade 4

1. Give **two** risks of sunbathing. **[2 marks]**
2. Give **two** effects that both X-rays and gamma rays can have on the human body. **[2 marks]**
3. State **four** comparisons between microwaves and visible light. **[4 marks]**

 Made a start 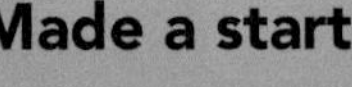  Feeling confident  Exam ready

Properties of electromagnetic waves

When electromagnetic waves are incident on a surface they can be reflected, refracted, absorbed or transmitted.

Properties of visible light

Reflection

When light hits an object, the light may be reflected or absorbed, depending on the properties of the object.

Refraction

When light enters a substance, like water or glass, it can change direction and bend closer to the normal line. This is refraction. The angle of refraction will be smaller than the angle of incidence.

When leaving a substance, the waves bend away from the normal.

Refraction occurs with all types of electromagnetic waves.

Transmission

If a substance is transparent, light may be transmitted and pass through it.

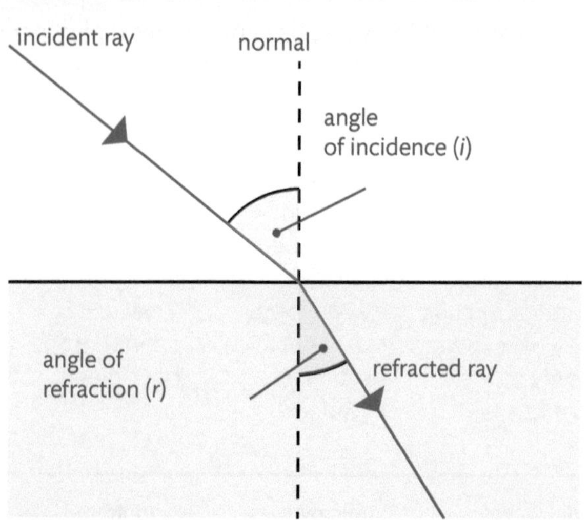

Figure 1 Refraction

Example of the effect of refraction

When an object is under water it appears to be closer to the surface than it actually is. This is because light is refracted when it enters the water.

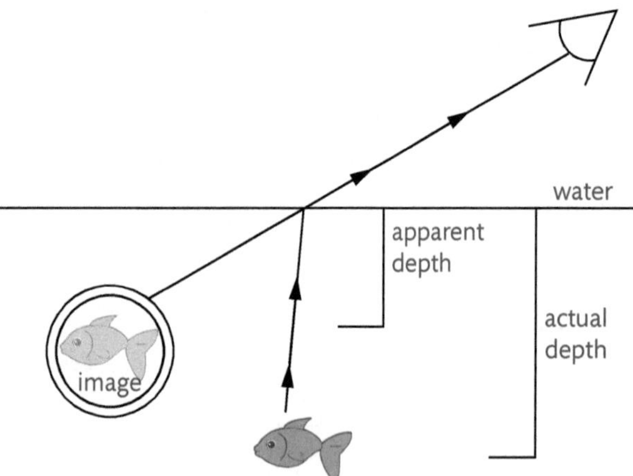

Figure 2 Effect of refraction

Worked example — Grade 4

Explain why a stone in water looks closer than it really is. **[2 marks]**

The light reflected off the stone to your eye is refracted at the boundary between water and air, so the stone seems to be closer than it really is.

Exam-style practice — Grades 2–4

1. To what type of energy is light transferred when it is absorbed by a surface? **[1 mark]**

   Tick **one** box.

   gravitational potential energy ☐

   kinetic energy ☐

   sound energy ☐

   thermal energy ☐

2. White light contains all the colours in the spectrum. When white light shines through a glass prism, the colours refract by different amounts. What would you expect to see if the light was shone onto a screen? **[1 mark]**

3. A student shines a ray of light onto a Perspex™ block with an incident angle of 10°. Estimate a value for the refracted angle inside the Perspex™ block. **[1 mark]**

 Made a start  Feeling confident Exam ready

Infrared radiation

Infrared radiation (IR) is a type of electromagnetic wave emitted from hot objects. The amount of IR absorbed or radiated by a surface depends on the nature of the surface. You need to know how to investigate how the nature of a surface affects how much infrared radiation it absorbs or radiates.

5 Experiment 1: Absorption of infrared

1. Fill the cans with hot water and measure the start temperature of each can.
2. Measure the temperature after five minutes.
3. Calculate the difference.

Black, dark or matt colours absorb radiation more quickly than white, shiny or silver colours. You can prove this by showing that the temperature of the darker object increases more rapidly.

The silver (or lighter) colours reflect radiation more than they absorb it, so they do not heat up as quickly.

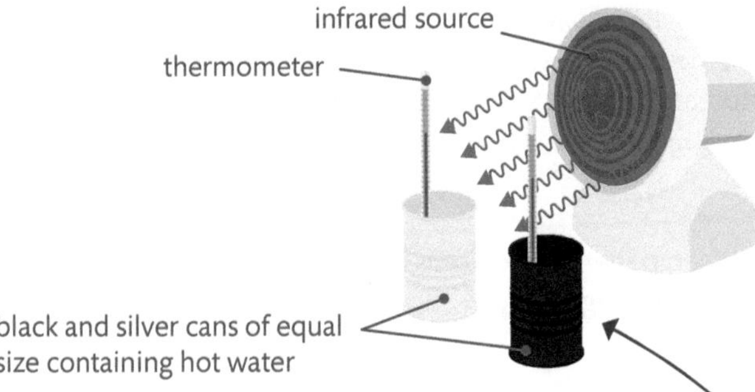

Figure 1 Apparatus for measuring infrared absorption

Working scientifically

Be careful when working with high temperatures. Allow equipment to cool before handling.

5 Experiment 2: Emission of infrared

1. Use a funnel to fill the **Leslie's cube** with hot water. Once it is full do not try to move it.
2. Use the infrared detector to measure the IR being emitted from the white side of the Leslie cube.
3. Repeat step **2** with the black and silver sides.

Darker colours emit more IR radiation than light or shiny colours.

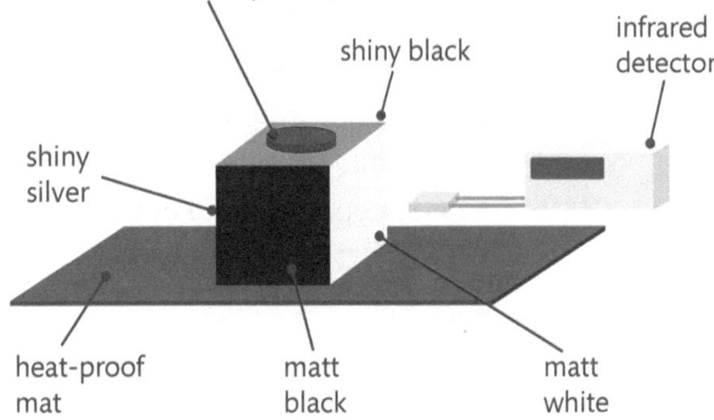

Figure 2 Apparatus for measuring infrared emission

2 Reducing errors

Experiment 1

- Each can must contain the same volume of water.
- The cans need to be an equal distance from the IR source.
- You must heat them for the same amount of time.
- You must record the start temperature.

Experiment 2

- Hold the detector at the same distance from each surface and at the same height on all sides.
- Minimise time delay between measurements so the water does not cool too much.

2 Worked example — Grade 3

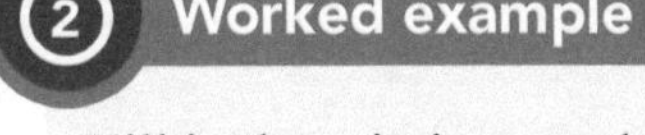

Fill in the missing words:

You can stay cool in hot sunny weather by wearing a white t-shirt because white reflects infrared. You will feel hotter in a black t-shirt because dark colours absorb infrared more than light colours. **[2 marks]**

10 Exam-style practice — Grade 4

1. Discuss how the findings of Experiments **1** and **2** above might be useful when designing energy-efficient housing. **[3 marks]**
2. A café wants to use take away cups for hot drinks. They have a choice between black and white cups. Explain which colour would help keep the drinks hotter for longer. **[2 marks]**
3. A student changes the second experiment by covering one side in tin foil and another in black paper. Identify **one** additional source of error with this method. **[2 marks]**

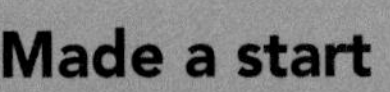

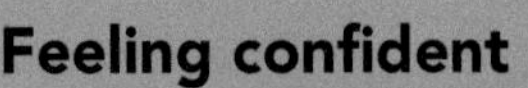

Made a start | Feeling confident | Exam ready

Applications of EM waves

Electromagnetic waves have many different uses.

Electromagnetic wave applications

Type of wave	Applications	How does it work?
radio waves	• radio and TV communications • walkie-talkies	The frequency of radio waves allows them to be transformed into electrical signals when received by aerials, and these are easily picked up by electronic circuits.
microwaves	• cooking • satellite communication, such as mobile phones	Microwaves are absorbed by water, so can be used to heat most food. They penetrate food up to about 1 cm, which means they cook food faster than infrared.
infrared	• cooking and heating • thermal imaging is used to 'see' infrared radiation	When an object absorbs infrared radiation, its temperature increases.
visible light	• lasers (pointers, etching and eye surgery) • fibre optic cables use light to carry telecommunication signals • endoscopes use fibre optics to see inside the body	Visible light waves have a frequency that interacts with the rods and cones in the eyes, causing the retina to detect light. Fibre optic cables transmit information through internal refraction.
ultraviolet (UV)	• tanning • invisible markings (money) • strip lights	UV can penetrate skin cells and interact with pigments to cause tanning.
X-ray	• medical scans • security scanners at airports	X-rays can penetrate through soft materials like skin and suitcases. They are absorbed by dense materials like bones and metal. This makes them ideal for seeing inside bodies and luggage.
gamma	• treatment of cancer • medical tracers (body scan) • sterilisation of medical equipment	Gamma radiation is very high energy and can kill cells easily, including bacteria. As it can penetrate through most materials, a weak source can be used for medical scans and large doses can target cancer cells deep within the body.

Worked example — Grade 5

Suggest why the police use thermal imaging cameras to find people. **[2 marks]**

Thermal imaging cameras can pick up IR radiation from people when no visible light is reflected from them, for example, in the dark, or if they are hidden or trapped.

Exam-style practice — Grade 3

1 **(a)** Name **two** electromagnetic waves that are used for communication. **[2 marks]**

(b) Give an example of how each type of wave is used for communicating. **[2 marks]**

2 Give **two** uses for invisible markings that show up under ultraviolet light. **[2 marks]**

 Made a start  Feeling confident  Exam ready

BBC

Magnetic fields

A magnetic field is the region around a magnet where forces are exerted on another magnet or on materials with magnetic properties. A magnet can attract or repel another magnet, but always attracts magnetic materials.

10

Magnetic fields and forces

Magnets do not have to touch to exert forces. Magnetism is a non-contact force. The closer the magnets, the stronger the force. The magnetism gets weaker as the magnets get further apart. Compasses point in the direction of a **magnetic field**.

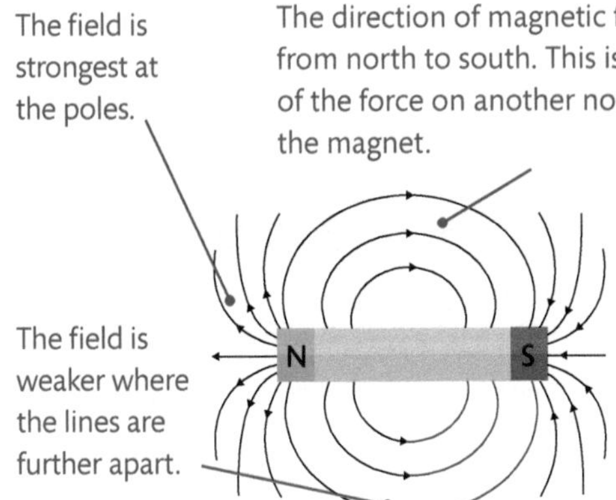
The field is strongest at the poles.
The direction of magnetic field lines is from north to south. This is the direction of the force on another north pole near the magnet.
The field is weaker where the lines are further apart.
N
S

Figure 1 A magnetic field

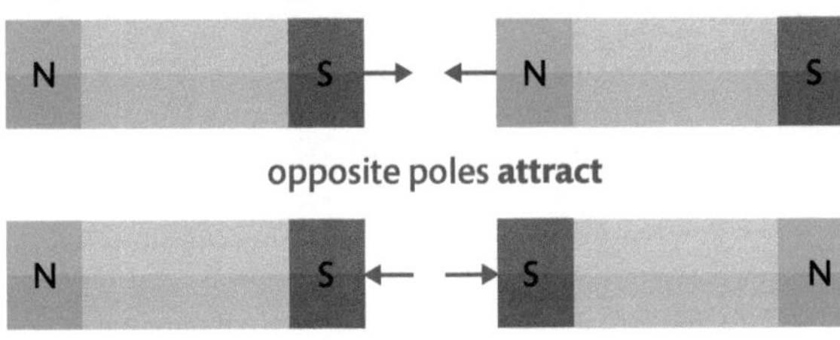
N
S
N
S
opposite poles attract
N
S
S
N
same poles repel

Figure 2 Magnetic forces

Mapping field lines

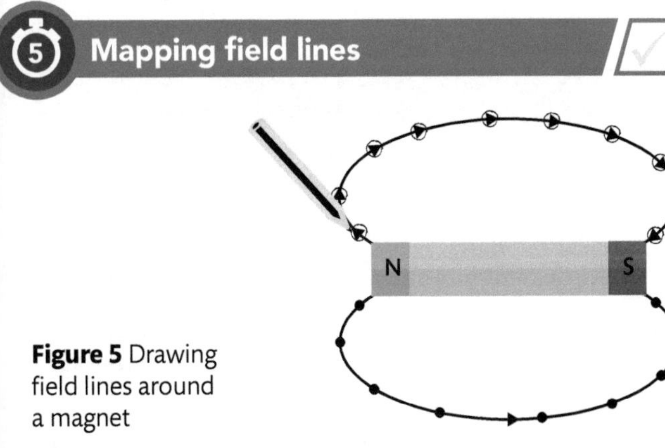
N
S

Figure 5 Drawing field lines around a magnet

1. Place a plotting compass at the north pole of a magnet. It will point away in the direction of the field. Draw a dot where it points.
2. Move the compass so the back of the needle is on the dot and draw another dot where it now points.
3. Repeat until the compass reaches the other side of the magnet.
4. Join all the dots together. Draw an arrow showing the direction of the field, north to south. This is the direction in which the compass is pointed.

Because compasses point in the direction of magnetic fields, they can be used as evidence of Earth's magnetic field.

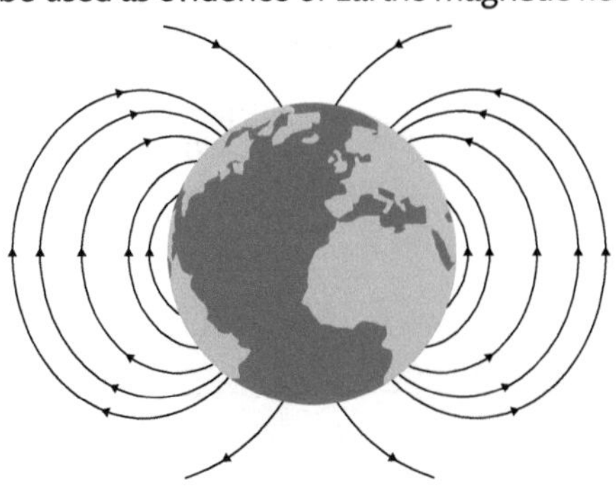

Figure 3 Earth's magnetic field is the same shape as the field around a bar magnet. It is produced by the rotating iron core.

Permanent magnets (like bar magnets) produce their own magnetic field. They can cause objects made from magnetic materials such as cobalt, iron, nickel and steel (remember CoINS) to become **induced magnets**.

N
S

Figure 4 Induced magnets do not stay magnetic. The magnetic force is always attractive.

Worked example — Grade 3

Look at **Figure 1**. The field lines are closer together near the poles. What is the relationship between the distance between field lines and magnetic field strength? **[1 mark]**

The closer the lines, the stronger the field.

Exam-style practice — Grade 4

1. Describe how you could use a compass to find the north pole of an unmarked bar magnet. **[2 marks]**
2. Describe how you could use two magnets to show that the magnetic force of attraction is non-contact. **[2 marks]**
3. **(a)** A bar magnet is a permanent magnet. Give the difference between a permanent magnet and an induced magnet. **[1 mark]**

   (b) Give **one** example of an induced magnet. **[1 mark]**

Electromagnetism

Electromagnets are made from coils of wire. You need to know how to use electric currents to make a magnetic field that is the same shape as the magnetic field around a bar magnet.

5 Electrical wires

Wires carrying an electrical current generate a magnetic field. The strength of the magnetic field depends on the current through the wire and the distance from the wire.

The magnetic field around a wire is circular.

Using your right hand, if your thumb shows the direction of the current, your fingers wrap around the wire in the direction of the magnetic field.

magnetic field

current

Figure 1 A magnetic field around a wire

2 Advantages and disadvantages

- 👍 Electromagnets can be switched off.
- 👍 Their strength can be altered easily by controlling the current.
- 👍 Their strength can be altered by increasing the number of coils.
- 👎 Electromagnets use electricity, so cost money to run.
- 👎 They can get hot, as electrical energy is transferred to thermal energy.

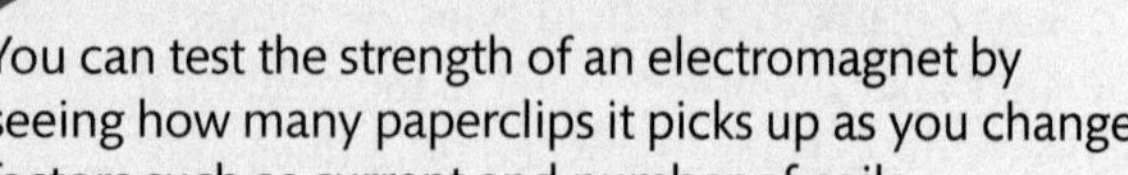

5 Electromagnetic fields

You can test the strength of an electromagnet by seeing how many paperclips it picks up as you change factors such as current and number of coils.

Direction

The current will flow from positive to negative. Curl the fingers of your right hand as shown in **Figure 1**, with your fingers pointing in the direction of the current. Your thumb will point in the direction of the north pole of the magnet. You could also use a compass which will point towards the south pole.

2 Worked example — Grade 3

An electromagnet is used to pick up paperclips.

(a) Describe how increasing the current will affect the number of paperclips picked up. **[1 mark]**

More paperclips can be picked up.

(b) Describe how increasing the current changes the magnetic field strength. **[1 mark]**

The magnetic field strength increases.

5 Solenoids

A **solenoid** is a coil of wire carrying a current that generates a magnetic field like the field around a bar magnet. When you add an iron core, the field is strengthened and the solenoid becomes an electromagnet.

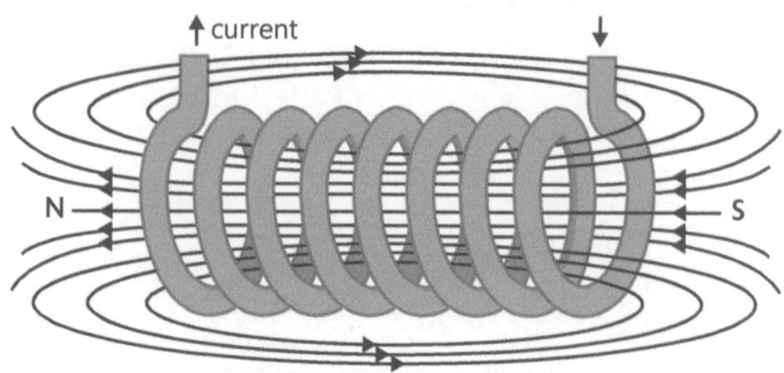

Figure 2 Coiling the wire into a solenoid increases the strength of the magnetic field. The magnetic field inside a solenoid is strong and uniform.

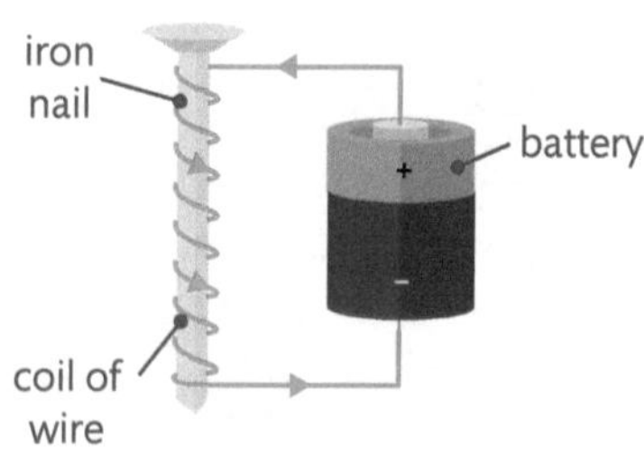

Figure 3 You can make an electromagnet by coiling wire around an iron nail and passing an electrical current through the wire.

10 Exam-style practice — Grades 2–4

1 An electromagnet is used to move cars in a scrap yard. Give **two** reasons why an electromagnet is used rather than a permanent magnet. **[2 marks]**

2 Sketch a labelled diagram of an electromagnet including the magnetic field. **[3 marks]**

3 How can the direction of the magnetic field be changed in an electromagnet? **[1 mark]**

Tick **one** box.

- ☐ Add an iron coil to the solenoid.
- ☐ Change the direction of the electric current.
- ☐ Coil more wire around the solenoid.
- ☐ Increase the electric current.

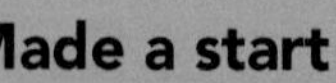
Made a start

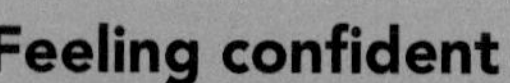
Feeling confident

Exam ready

Equations

You need to know which equations to use and how to rearrange them to answer questions in the exam. You will be given a formulae sheet with some equations on.

Three rules for rearranging

1. Decide what you want to work out. Get this on one side of the equation and everything else on the other.
2. Make sure the value you want to find is not on the bottom of a fraction.
3. When you move something across the equals sign, the operation needs to be reversed on both sides of the equation. To move $-x$, add x to each side of the equation. To move $\frac{1}{x}$, multiply each side by x.

Maths skills

Equations with three quantities

If you needed to calculate the mass, m:

$F = ma \rightarrow \frac{F}{a} = m \rightarrow m = \frac{F}{a}$

Equations with four or more quantities

$E_p = mgh \rightarrow \frac{E_p}{mg} = h \rightarrow h = \frac{E_p}{mg}$

Divide both sides of the equation by mg.

Equations with squares

$E_k = \frac{1}{2}mv^2 \rightarrow v^2 = \frac{E_k}{\frac{1}{2}m} \rightarrow v = \sqrt{\frac{E_k}{\frac{1}{2}m}}$

First rearrange for v^2, then move the $\frac{1}{2}$ and m as normal, then square root both sides.

$v^2 - u^2 = 2as$

To find v, first rearrange so that v^2 is on its own:

$v^2 = u^2 + 2as \rightarrow v = \sqrt{u^2 + 2as}$

To find a, rearrange so that a is on its own:

$v^2 - u^2 = 2as \rightarrow \frac{v^2 - u^2}{2s} = a \rightarrow a = \frac{v^2 - u^2}{2s}$

Exam focus

In the exam, you can save time by using the correct symbols rather than words. For example, use:

$F = ma$ rather than force = mass × acceleration as it is quicker to write and rearrange.

Take your time when rearranging equations and allow time to check your calculations to ensure you have written the correct answer.

1. Find out what you are being asked to find.
2. Identify which values you have been given in the question and what their units are.
3. Think of the equation that includes the thing you want to find and the numbers that you have.
4. Rearrange the equation isolating the unknown value on one side and replace the symbols with the known values.
5. Check whether you need to convert the unit.

Worked example — Grades 4–5

A 12 V motor has a power of 30 W. Calculate the current in the motor.

$P = IV$ **[2 marks]**

power = potential difference × current

$P = IV \rightarrow 30 = I \times 12 \rightarrow I = \frac{30}{12} = 2.5\,\text{A}$

Alternatively, rearrange the equation first, then put the numbers in.

$P = IV \rightarrow I = \frac{P}{V} = \frac{30}{12} = 2.5\,\text{A}$

Exam-style practice — Grades 4–5

1 Rearrange the following for each of the other quantities in the equation:

(a) $\rho = \frac{m}{V}$ **[1 mark]**

(b) $P = I^2R$ **[1 mark]**

(c) $\Delta E = mc\Delta\theta$ **[1 mark]**

(d) $a = \frac{\Delta v}{t}$ **[1 mark]**

2 Give the unit of for each quantity, choosing your answers from the list below.

kg, kilograms J, joules N, newtons m, metres

(a) force **[1 mark]**

(b) kinetic energy **[1 mark]**

(c) weight **[1 mark]**

(d) wavelength **[1 mark]**

(e) mass **[1 mark]**

Converting units

You need to know how to convert quantities to the standard unit.

Prefixes

Prefix	nano	micro	milli	centi	kilo	mega	giga
Example unit	nm	μm	mm	cm	km	Mm	Gm
Standard form	1×10^{-9}	1×10^{-6}	1×10^{-3}	1×10^{-2}	1×10^{3}	1×10^{6}	1×10^{9}
Factor	0.000 000 001	0.000 001	0.001	0.01	1000	1 000 000	1 000 000 000
Example	atom 0.1 nm	cells 1–100 μm	ball bearing few mm	pencil 15 cm	Mount Everest 9 km	Earth 13 Mm	Moon orbit 0.4 Gm

Standard form is written in terms of powers of 10. Negative numbers mean you divide by 10 that many times and positive numbers mean you multiply by 10 that many times. For example: $1 \times 10^9 = 1000000000$.

Converting units

To convert 30 mm to m, first work out what the conversion factor is between mm and m. There are 1000 mm in a m.

Then decide if you need to multiply or divide.

30 mm is much smaller than a metre so should be a very small number:

$30 \div 1000 = 0.03$

Complex units

To convert spring constant 4.5 N/cm to N/m, first work out what the conversion factor is between cm and m. This is 100.

$4.5 \times 100 = 450$ N/m

Now, check logically: if it takes 4.5 N to stretch the spring 1 cm, you would expect a lot more force to stretch it 1 m, so 450 N makes sense.

Time

Remember, that when dealing with time you need to multiply or divide by 60, not 100.

1 hour = 60 minutes, 1 minute = 60 seconds

Areas

When converting areas, take the normal conversion factor and square it.

Convert cm^2 to m^2

$250 \div 100^2 = 0.025\ m^2$

For volumes, cube the usual factor:

Convert m^3 to mm^3

$1.2 \times 1000^3 = 1\ 200\ 000\ 000\ mm^3$

or $1.2\times10^9\ mm^3$

Worked example Grades 4–5

Convert:

(a) 0.56 kg to g **[1 mark]**

$0.56 \times 1000 = 560$ g

(b) 12 mm to m **[1 mark]**

$12 \div 1000 = 0.012$ m

(c) 25 MJ to J **[1 mark]**

$25 \times 10^6 = 25\ 000\ 000$ J or 2.5×10^7 J

(d) 0.037 mm to μm **[1 mark]**

$0.037 \times 10^3 = 37$ μm

Matching units

$$\text{speed} = \frac{\text{distance}}{\text{time}}$$

Normally, the speed is in m/s, so the distance and time need to be converted into metres and seconds to match.

However, if the distance is in kilometres and the time in hours, the speed will be in km/h. Check which units you should use in your calculation and answer.

Exam-style practice Grades 2–4

1 Convert:

(a) 200 μg to g **[1 mark]**

(b) 10 N/kg to N/g **[1 mark]**

(c) 330 kJ/s to J/s. **[1 mark]**

2 Convert 4.5 minutes into seconds. **[1 mark]**

 Made a start  Feeling confident  Exam ready

Making estimations

You need to know how to estimate the results of simple calculations.

Estimating speeds and masses

Speeds

You need to have an idea of how fast some objects move.

- Cars move at around 10 m/s up to 30 m/s at motorway speeds.
- People walk at around 1–2 m/s and run at around 3–10 m/s.
- People cycle at about 6 m/s.
- Jet planes can fly up to around 250 m/s.

Try to picture an object moving and estimate how far you think it would get in 1 second. Use this to estimate its speed.

Masses

You need to have an idea of the masses of certain objects.

The following are rough estimates and vary with size:

- a person has a mass of around 50–80 kg
- a car has a mass of around 1000 kg
- 1 litre of water has a mass of 1 kg
- a dog has a mass of 5–35 kg
- a mobile phone has a mass of between about 100–200 g.

You can estimate the mass of an object by comparing it with objects of a similar mass.

Worked example — Grades 4–5

1 Estimate the kinetic energy of a person sprinting in a race. **[3 marks]**

kinetic energy $= \frac{1}{2} \times \text{mass} \times \text{speed}^2$

mass ~ 60 kg and speed ~ 10 m/s

Kinetic energy $= \frac{1}{2} \times 60\,\text{kg} \times (10\,\text{m/s})^2 = 3000\,\text{J}$

2 Calculate the increase in potential energy of a 1.45 kg mass lifted 9.5 m ($g = 9.8$ N/kg). **[3 marks]**

$E_p = mgh = 1.45 \times 9.8 \times 9.5 = 135\,\text{J}$

Check the answer is correct by rounding the numbers and working out an approximate answer.
$1.5 \times 10 \times 10 = 150$, so this answer is about right.

Maths skills

If you are asked to estimate the area under a curve, you do not need to try to calculate the area. First, work out the value of each square, then count roughly how many squares there are on the graph and then multiply these two numbers together.

Worked example — Grade 5

The time it takes a beaker of hot water wrapped in different thicknesses of insulation to cool down by 5 °C is recorded in the table below.

Thickness of insulation in mm	2	4	6	8
Time to cool by 5 °C in s	250	569	603	798

(a) Another beaker of hot water with 3 mm thick insulation is cooled by 5 °C. Use the table to estimate the time this took. **[1 mark]**

400 seconds (between 251 and 569 seconds)

(b) Use the line of best fit on the graph in **Figure 1**. Estimate the time taken for a beaker with 7 mm of insulation to cool by 5 °C. **[1 mark]**

700 seconds

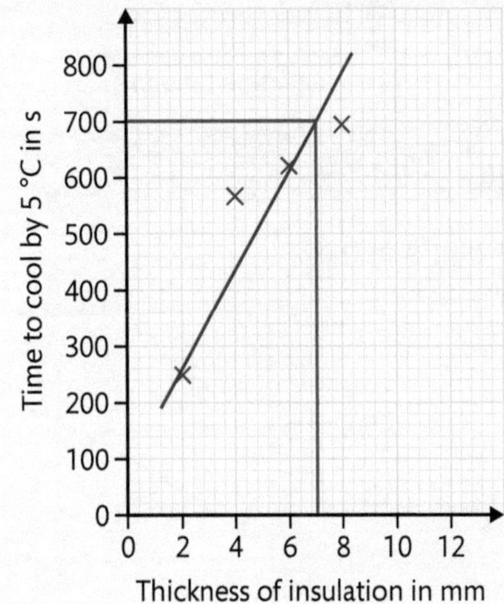

Figure 1

Exam focus

If a question instructs you to 'calculate', you should work out the answer exactly, usually using a calculator. It is good practice to then estimate the answer to check it is correct.

Exam-style practice — Grade 4

Use **Figure 1** to estimate the time it takes for the beaker to cool by 5 °C with 5 mm of insulation. **[2 marks]**

Interpreting data

In the exam, you will need to demonstrate that you can interpret data from a range of equipment, tables, charts and graphs.

2 Correlations

Scatter graphs show patterns, outliers and anomalies in numerical data. **Anomalies** do not fit the pattern at all, and **outliers** fit poorly. You may need to discount these results when finding an average for your data.

A **correlation** is a relationship between two variables that can easily be seen by drawing a line of best fit on a scatter graph. If the line is straight then the relationship is linear. If it also goes through the origin (0,0), you can say that the measurements are proportional. A lot of scatter can indicate random error affecting your experiment. Think about how you can reduce this.

Positive correlation

Acceleration in m/s²

Force in N

If the line of best fit should go through (0,0) and does not, this indicates a systematic error. All of your readings are likely to be too high or too low by the same amount.

Negative correlation

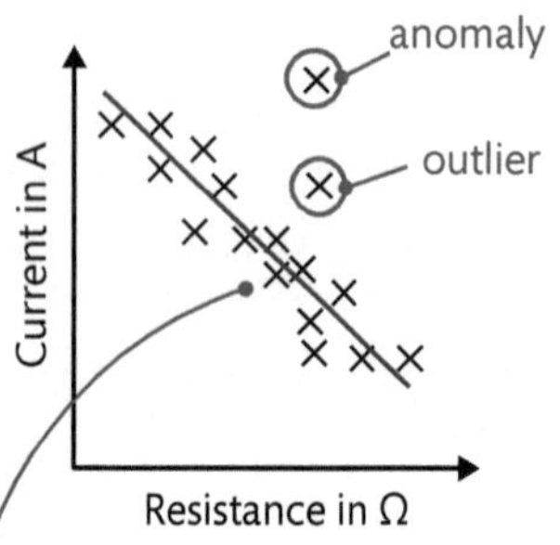

The closer together the results are, the more precise they are.

No correlation

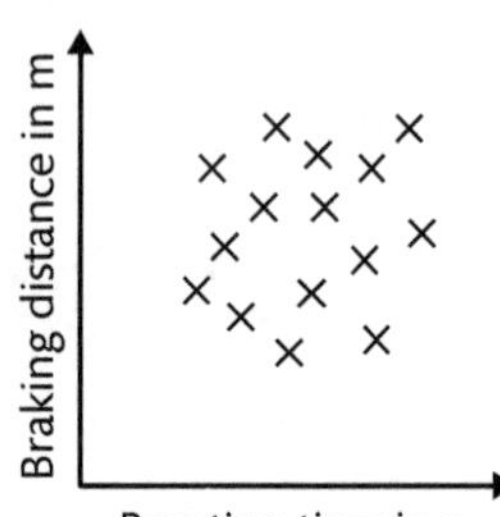

10 Worked example — Grades 4–5

Give the volume of liquid in the measuring cylinder.

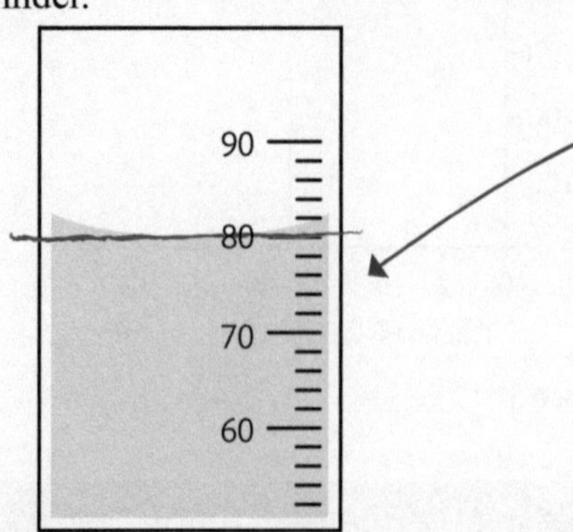

80 ml or 80 cm³

Make sure to use the correct units. If measuring volume, you can use ml or cm³. Remember that areas will use squared units.

When measuring a volume of liquid, make sure you take your reading from the **bottom** of the meniscus (the curved line that the skin of the water makes). You can draw a line across the bottom of the meniscus to help you find the right value.

5 Data in tables

If you are given data in a table, first of all look for a pattern to work out the relationship between the variables. In the table below, as speed increases, braking distance increases.

Speed in m/s	5	10	15	20	25	30
Braking distance in m	4	16	36	64	100	144

Now, look for further patterns. What happens when one of the quantities is doubled? As you double any speed the distance gets 4 times bigger.

You can make estimates for other speeds based on the values in the table. For example, the braking distance at a speed of 12 m/s would be between 16 m and 36 m.

As one measurement doubles, if the other:

- doubles, they are **directly proportional**
- halves, they **inversely proportional**.

2 Averages

$$\text{mean} = \frac{\text{sum of numbers}}{\text{amount of numbers}}$$

Use the **mean** for repeat readings. This is the most commonly used average in science. However, it should not be used where the range includes extremely large or small numbers which would affect the mean.

The **mode** is the number or measurement that occurs most often. It could be used with measurements that are not numbers, like average eye colour.

The **median** is the middle number when values are placed in order of increasing size.

10 Exam-style practice — Grades 4–5

Puppies in a litter weigh 1.1 kg, 1.2 kg, 1.2 kg, 1.3 kg, 3.3 kg.

(a) Give the mean, mode and median for the mass of these puppies. **[3 marks]**

(b) Explain why the mean gives the least accurate idea of the mass of the majority of the puppies. **[2 marks]**

 Made a start  Feeling confident  Exam ready

Using charts and graphs

Graphs are commonly used in science, particularly line and scatter graphs. You need to know how to interpret and draw a graph.

Types of graphs and charts

Pie charts

Pie charts show the proportional measurements that make up a total. For example, percentage use of energy resource.

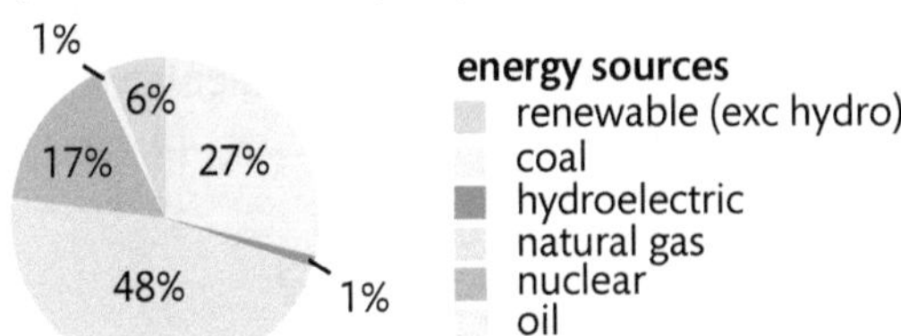

Bar charts

Bar charts should only be used to show information about discrete data. For example, the strength of the gravitational field on different planets. They are not to be confused with histograms, which show continuous data.

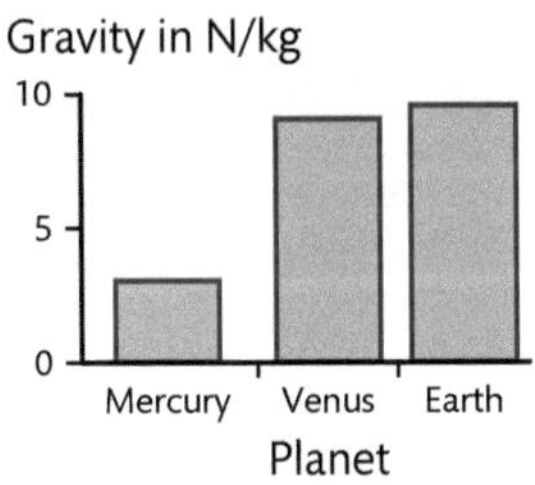

Graphs

Graphs, such as scatter graphs, show the relationship between two variables. For example, length of wire and resistance, weight and mass.

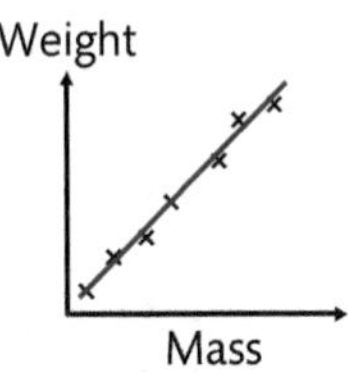

Worked example — Grade 5

Table 1 shows a student's results for an investigation.

Time in s	0	10	20	30	40	50	60
Temperature in °C	5	6	11	17	35	72	180

Table 1

(a) Use these results to draw a line graph. **[3 marks]**

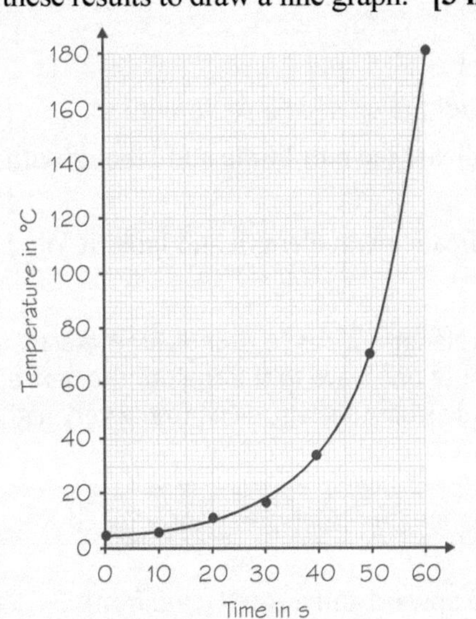

(b) Determine how long it took to reach 100 °C. **[1 mark]**

53 seconds

Interpreting graphs

Gradients

To calculate the gradient of a straight line draw on a triangle. Make it as large as you can. Read off the rise (height) and run (length of the bottom). If it helps to keep track of the numbers write them by the triangle.

$$\text{gradient} = \frac{\text{rise}}{\text{run}}$$

Straight line graphs

The general equation of a straight line is $y = mx + c$, where:

- x and y are values on the x and y axes
- m is the gradient
- c is where the line meets the y-axis.

A straight line represents a linear relationship. The equation for the line in the graph in **Figure 1** is $y = 0.5x + 2.5$. You can replace x and y with the quantities you have plotted.

The meaning of the gradient depends on the quantities being divided. For example, with speed on the y-axis and time on the x-axis the gradient is speed ÷ time = acceleration.

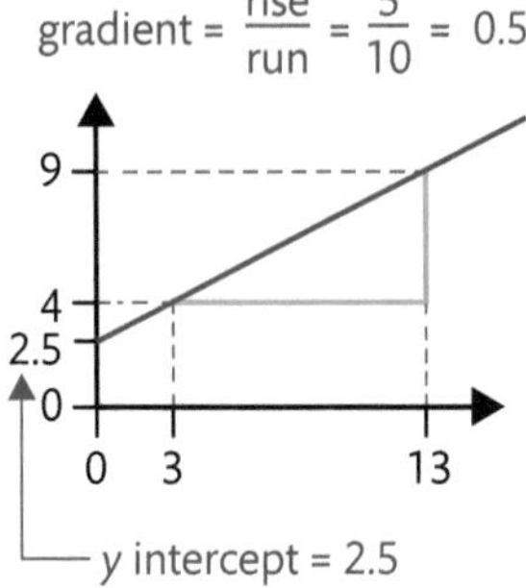

Figure 1 Find the gradient

Curved graphs

For curved graphs you can talk about how the gradient changes from left to right. In **Figure 2** the gradient is increasing.

The gradient can indicate a quantity, such as acceleration. The gradient then matches what the quantity is doing, so if the gradient is increasing this means the acceleration is increasing.

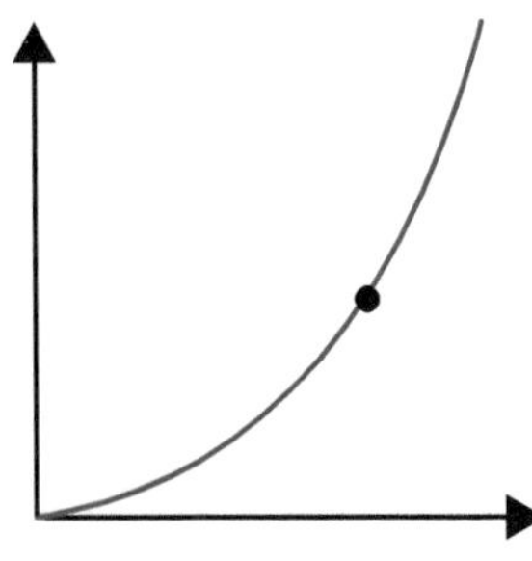

Figure 2 Curved graph

Exam-style practice — Grades 4–5

1 Name a suitable type of graph to show:

(a) the braking distances of different cars at 10 m/s **[1 mark]**

(b) the mass of salt that dissolves in water at different temperatures **[1 mark]**

(c) the percentage of energy lost from the windows, doors, walls and floors in a house. **[1 mark]**

2 A straight line graph has the equation distance = 4 × time + 10 in the form $y = mx + c$. Give the gradient and y intercept of the line. **[1 mark]**

Using diagrams

You could be asked to draw or label a diagram in the exam. Diagrams can also help you to organise information to answer a question.

Key questions

- Do you need to use a ruler?
- Do you need to label any parts?
- Should you add arrows to show direction?
- Should you draw anything to scale?
- Do you need to use symbols (like circuit symbols)?
- Do you need to use a particular shape or position?

This sketch isn't part of the answer but it helps to organise all the numbers in the question.

Worked example — Grades 4–5

A car has a mass of 1200 kg. The engine force on the car is 1000 N. The car experiences 350 N of air resistance and 200 N of friction. Calculate the acceleration of the car. **[4 marks]**

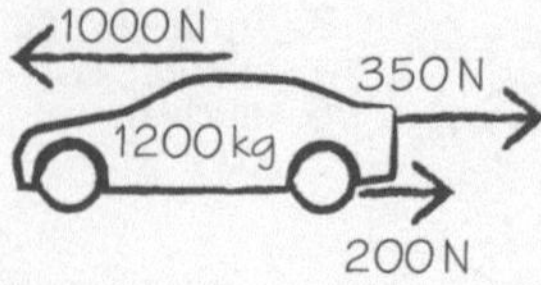

Resultant force = 1000 − 350 − 200 = 450 N

$$\text{acceleration} = \frac{\text{force}}{\text{mass}} = \frac{450}{1200} = 0.375\ \text{m/s}^2$$

Worked example — Grades 4–5

Draw a diagram of an animal cell and label the following features:

- nucleus
- ribosomes
- mitochondria
- cell membrane.

[4 marks]

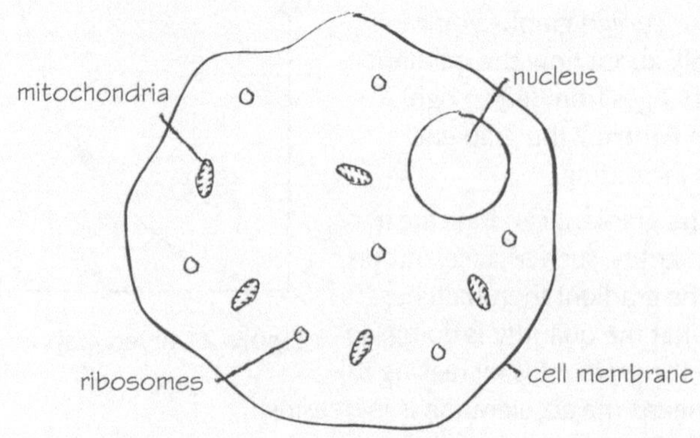

Exam focus

When asked to add a label to a diagram, make sure you think carefully about the position and draw your labels in exactly the right place. Consider using arrows or lines to clearly show the position.

The crest is just one position, but amplitude and wavelength must indicate between two positions.

Worked example — Grades 4–5

Look at the wave shown in **Figure 1**.

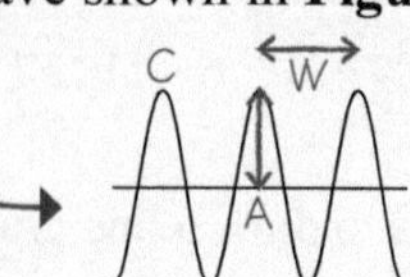

Figure 1

(a) Label the crest of a wave with **C**. **[1 mark]**

(b) Indicate the amplitude and label it with an **A**. **[1 mark]**

(c) Indicate a wavelength and label it **W**. **[1 mark]**

The wavelength needs to be indicated exactly from the crest of one wave to the crest of the next and the amplitude from the centre line to the very highest point.

Exam-style practice — Grades 4–5

1. Sketch a skydiver of weight 600 N experiencing 300 N air resistance upward and a 200 N wind from the west. **[3 marks]**
2. Draw a circuit diagram that could be used to find the resistance of a lamp. **[3 marks]**

Planning practicals

You need to know how to write a plan for a practical, including an equipment list, a method and details about control and safety measures.

Worked example

Grades 4–5 

A student makes the hypothesis that the average speed of a trolley rolling down a ramp increases with the height of the ramp.

(a) Identify the variables to compare the speed of the trolley with the height of the ramp. **[3 marks]**

Change the height of the ramp and measure the distance the trolley moves and the time it takes to reach the bottom.

$$\text{average speed} = \frac{\text{distance down ramp}}{\text{time}}$$

The variables are speed and height. You either have to measure speed directly or measure distance and time for it to be calculated.

Your equipment needs to reflect the variables you are going to measure.

You could suggest using two light gates and a data logger set up for timing here instead. A sonic distance sensor and data logger could measure the speed of the trolley directly so no need to measure time and distance individually. This would also be a way to remove reaction time uncertainty mentioned in **(c)**.

(b) Draw a diagram to show the equipment needed. List any other items not shown. **[3 marks]**

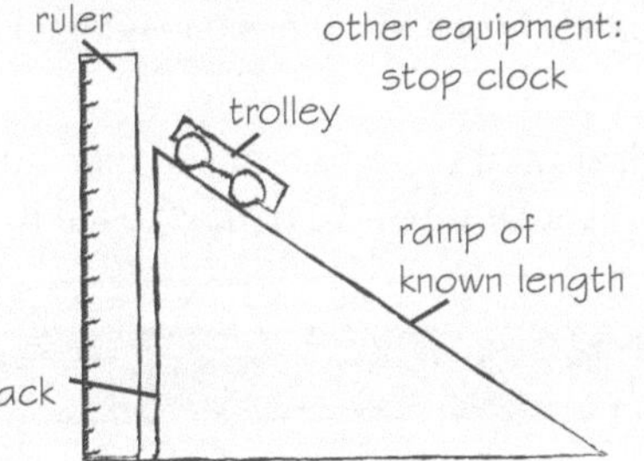

The diagram is meant to save you wasting space in a method describing the layout of equipment. Not every single piece needs to be shown, but every piece needs mentioning in an equipment list.

It can be useful to label some of the variables on your diagram like height of ramp and distance.

(c) Why is there an uncertainty involved in using a stop clock in this experiment? **[1 mark]**

The reaction time of the person who judges when the trolley reaches the bottom will affect the measurement of time.

There would also be an issue starting the stop clock at the same time as the trolley is released.

(d) Suggest how the uncertainty in **(c)** could be reduced. **[2 marks]**

Use two light gates at a set distance and a data logger to measure the time.

Using a longer ramp and small heights would increase the time. This would make the uncertainty in reaction time less significant.

(e) Identify **one** hazard. Suggest how this hazard could be reduced. **[2 marks]**

This is a low-risk experiment. The trolley may roll onto the floor and become a trip hazard. Someone should catch it at the end of the ramp.

This is a low-risk experiment, but even experiments without acid or fire have a small hazard. Keep your experiments simple, avoid getting too inventive.

Exam-style practice

Grades 4–5 

A student carries out an experiment:

Experiment: This experiment tests how the thickness of insulation around a beaker of hot water affects the temperature change.

For the experiment:

(a) Identify the variables that need measuring and controlling. **[2 marks]**

(b) List the equipment needed to take the measurements. **[2 marks]**

(c) Give **two** safety factors. **[2 marks]**

 Made a start 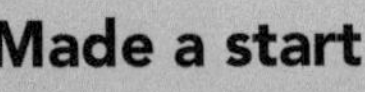  Feeling confident  Exam ready

Comparing data

You need to know how to compare data and be able to discuss the advantages and disadvantages of different ideas.

Worked example — Grades 4–5

Table 1 shows the estimated figures for the percentage of electricity produced from different resources in Spain and the UK.

Resource	Electricity production	
	UK	**Spain**
wind turbine	2.3%	26.4%
solar	0.2%	2.6%
hydroelectric	0.6%	23.9%
biomass	1.7%	0.2%
fossil fuel	87.4%	17.9%
nuclear	7.8%	29.0%

Table 1

(a) Compare the percentage of non-renewable resources in each country. **[2 marks]**

4.8% of electricity in UK comes from renewable resources compared to 53.1% in Spain, which is over 10 times higher.

(b) Suggest a reason for the difference in solar electricity production by each country. **[2 marks]**

Spain may have more hours of sunshine, or less clouds, making solar power a more useful resource.

(c) The percentage of electricity produced by nuclear power in Spain is just over three times the percentage in the UK. A student says that this means Spain has three times more nuclear power stations than the UK. Explain whether you agree with this statement or not. **[4 marks]**

No. The percentage just means that a larger fraction of Spain's energy comes from nuclear power, but a percentage does not tell us how much energy is actually used in each case. Also, power stations can produce different amounts of energy so number of power stations does not necessarily indicate power output.

Percentages just tell us how much of the total something makes up. It does not tell us how much energy is actually used.

If the two countries used different amounts of energy in total then one resource having the same percentage in both countries does not mean they actually produce the same amount of energy. Therefore, having three times the percentage does not mean you have three times the energy.

Comparing data

- Look for patterns in the data.
- Identify any similarities or differences, and what they mean.
- Consider the advantages and disadvantages of different variables.

Exam focus

When comparing data, look at the table's headings. Make sure you know exactly what the data is before answering the question.

When comparing, make sure you refer to both values and clearly state which is greater. Look for any patterns, e.g. approximately how many times one is larger than another.

First, look at what the difference is, then apply what you know about solar power to try to explain it.

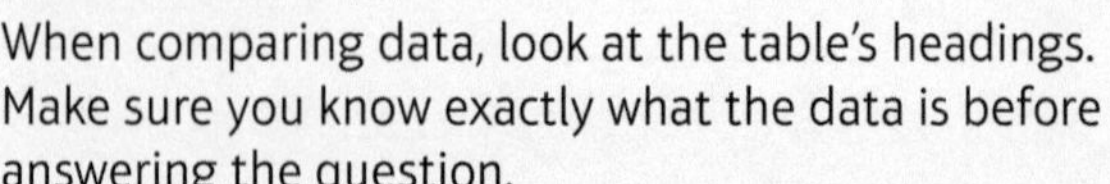

Exam-style practice — Grades 4–5

A tyre manufacturer wants to compare the performance of two tyres. Using the same car and driver, they perform emergency stops at different speeds with each set of tyres, **A** and **B**.

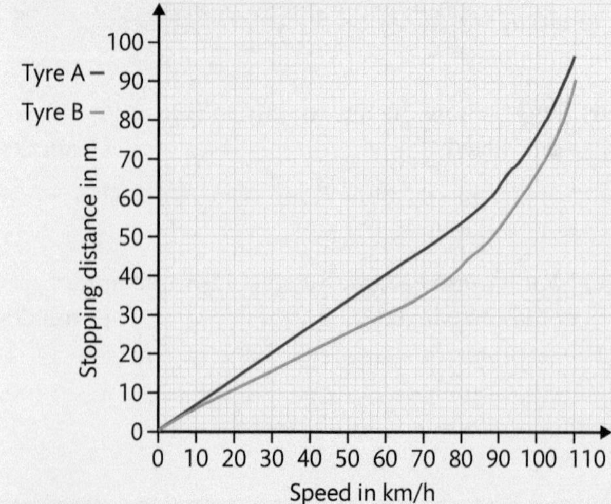

Figure 1

(a) Give **one** similarity and **one** difference between the two graphs. **[2 marks]**

(b) Describe how the stopping distances would change if the tyres were tested on a wet road. **[2 marks]**

(c) Which tyre had the best performance in this test? Explain your answer. **[3 marks]**

Made a start  Feeling confident Exam ready

Evaluating data

To evaluate an experiment, you need to look carefully at the data in tables and graphs and look critically at the method, and suggest improvements.

Evaluating data

Comment on how close the points are to the line of best fit. A lot of scatter can indicate random error affecting your experiment.

If your line should go through the origin (0,0) and does not, this indicates a systematic error. All your readings might be too high or too low by the same amount.

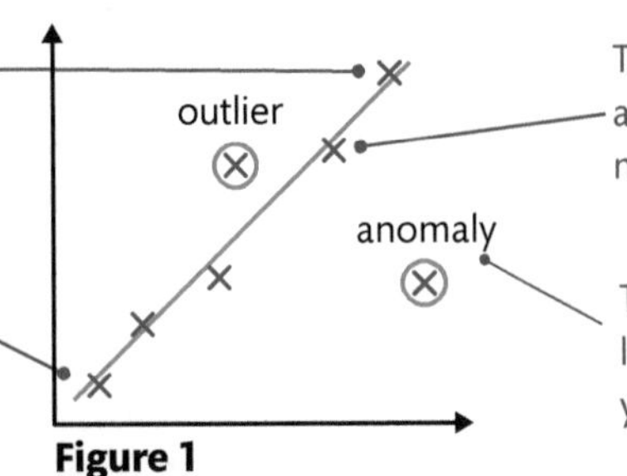

Figure 1

To be sure of the line of best fit you need at least four points to follow the pattern, or more for a curve.

The greater the number of anomalies, the less certain you can be about the position of your line of best fit.

Worked example

Grades 4–5

Potential difference in V	Current in A		
	Test 1	Test 2	Test 3
2.0	0.12	0.13	0.12
4.0	0.24	0.22	0.23

range 0.01 A
range 0.02 A

Table 1

Potential difference in V	Current in A		
	Test 1	Test 2	Test 3
2.0	0.12	0.18	0.13
4.0	0.30	0.22	0.25

range 0.06 A
range 0.08 A

Table 2

1 Study the two sets of results in the extracts in **Tables 1** and **2**.

(a) Use **Table 1** to say if these results are repeatable. **[2 marks]**

The repeat readings in Table 1 are similar, with a range of 0.01 A and 0.02 A making the results repeatable.

(b) Use both **Table 1** and **Table 2** to say if these results are reproducible. **[2 marks]**

The readings in Table 2 are more spread out, with ranges of 0.06 A and 0.08 A, which means that the results are not reproducible.

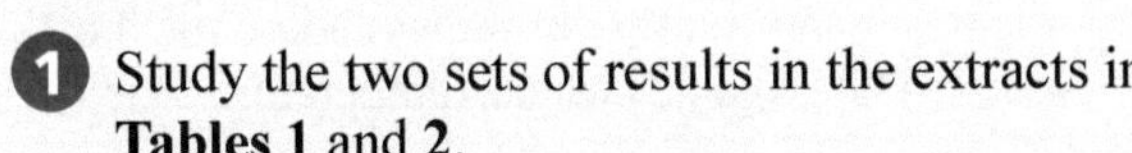

Exam focus

When there are several possible sources of uncertainty, write about the most significant sources. Always assume that someone has been careful while taking measurements – mistakes are not a source of uncertainty.

2 A student compares the insulating properties of two materials by wrapping them around two beakers. They boil a kettle and pour some hot water into the first beaker, recording the temperature of the water after 5 minutes. They boil a kettle and pour hot water into both beakers. They record the temperature of the water in both beakers after 5 minutes.

(a) Identify **two** sources of uncertainty. **[2 marks]**

Different thicknesses of material used.
Different start temperatures would affect the end temperature.

(b) Suggest **two** ways that the student could improve the method. **[2 marks]**

They could use the same thickness of material and use a cover to reduce heat loss by evaporation.

Measurements are **repeatable** if the same experiment by the same investigator gives a similar set of results (as in **Table 1**). They are **reproducible** if the same experiment by a different investigator, with different equipment, produces a similar set of results.

The more spread out the repeats, the less reproducible the results will be. To help you comment on the repeats, calculate the range of each set. The range is the difference between the highest and lowest value.

Exam-style practice

Grades 4–5

A graph shows the average speed of a ball rolling down a ramp at different heights. The speed is calculated using the time measured by a student with a stop clock.

(a) What is the source of uncertainty? **[1 mark]**
(b) What can be done to reduce it? **[2 marks]**

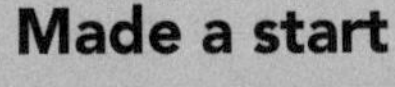
Made a start

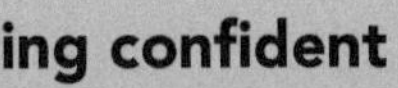
Feeling confident
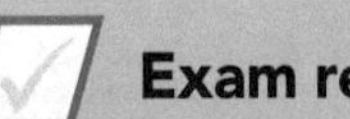
Exam ready

Working scientifically

You need to demonstrate the ability to work scientifically through your experimental skills, analysis and evaluation of data.

Experimental skills

Experiments are designed to test a hypothesis (an idea or explanation).

Scientists use experiments to find data, such as the specific heat capacity of a material. They are also used to test how one measured quantity affects another: one variable (the independent variable) is changed and another variable (the dependent variable) is measured.

Planning

Being able to choose the correct equipment and method to carry out a practical is an important skill for scientists. A plan should include an equipment list and a step-by-step method, as well as details about any control or safety measures.

Evaluation and analysis

After making and recording their observations, scientists process and present data in a way that enables them to evaluate the validity of a hypothesis.

It is important to use scientific theories and explanations to explain data and reflect on whether patterns and observations support the original hypothesis. The evaluation should also include suggestions on how the practical could be improved.

Development of scientific ideas

As new evidence comes to light, scientists change and develop their theories and knowledge. These changes may have ethical, social, environmental or economic implications.

Experimental results are published for peer review. This means other scientists can check the findings and carry out further experiments based on the original results.

15 Worked example — Grades 4–5

1 A student makes a hypothesis that the higher the light intensity, the taller a plant will grow.

(a) Identify the dependent and independent variables. **[2 marks]**

The independent variable is the level of light intensity, which needs changing. The height of the plant needs to be measured. This is the dependent variable.

> The variables need to come from the hypothesis. In this case light intensity and height can be measured directly. However, for variables like speed, you might need to measure distance and time and then calculate the variable you are investigating.

(b) Give **three** factors that need to be controlled. **[3 marks]**

Type of plant, time and growing conditions (water and carbon dioxide)

> There are lots of other factors, but these three are the most important and you should always choose the most obvious first. Others could include: temperature or soil pH.

(c) Describe the best graph to plot the data on. **[3 marks]**

A scatter graph of light intensity on the *x*-axis and height of plant on the *y*-axis with a line of best fit.

> A scatter or line graph is best for any experiment that tests the relationship between two numerical variables.

2 Scientists are researching a cure for Parkinson's disease using embryonic stem cells. Compare the advantages and disadvantages of this method of stem cell treatment. **[4 marks]**

The advantages are that it will replace the patient's damaged cell with a healthy cell, which may help them to recover. It is also easier to extract cells from an embryo, which saves time and money. One disadvantage is that some people have ethical issues with the use of embryos in stem cell research, as embryos cannot consent to being used. Another disadvantage is that stem cell treatment can cause viral infections.

> Consider the ethical, social, environmental and economic aspects. They may not all be relevant.

10 Exam-style practice — Grades 4–5

1 A student wants to find out which metal is the best conductor of electricity. Describe a method to find out which of four different metals has the highest resistance. **[6 marks]**

2 Discuss the possible effects of developing more efficient cars powered by solar cells. **[3 marks]**

 Made a start  Feeling confident Exam ready

Answers

Page 1 Levels of organisation

1. A group of organs that collectively perform specific functions within a system, such as the respiratory system.
2. The respiratory system is an organ system made up of several organs, including the lungs and heart, working together. The organs consist of different types of tissues, epithelial, muscle, nervous or connective tissues. The tissues are made up of cells, such as red blood cells.

Page 2 Prokaryotic and eukaryotic cells

1. cell membrane, cytoplasm
2. The DNA is found in a small ring called a plasmid and loops of chromosomal DNA

Page 3 Animal and plant cells

(a) cell wall, chloroplasts, (permanent) vacuole

(b) Unlike animal cells, plant cells have a cell wall. Plant cells also contain chloroplasts and a permanent vacuole, whereas animal cells do not.

Page 4 Microscopy

1. $\frac{20\,000}{100} = 200 = 2 \times 10^2$

   2×10^3
2. 3.578×10^5

Page 5 Using microscopes

1. To produce an image that the eye can see, light needs to be able to pass through the tissue.
2. Different tissues stain different colours with different dyes. This makes it easier to tell the tissues apart.

Page 6 Specialised cells

Muscle cells contain many mitochondria, which provide energy for muscle contraction. Muscle cells are composed of protein fibres that slide over each other to cause the muscle to contract.

Sperm cells have a tail which enables them to move towards an egg cell. They also have an acrosome containing enzymes that digest the outer layers of the egg, enabling fertilisation to take place.

Phloem cells consist of sieve plates which allow solutions to move easily from cell to cell and companion cells which contain many mitochondria. These mitochondria provide the energy that is required for active transport.

Page 7 Cell differentiation

1. Answers will vary, e.g.
   - hair growing
   - fingernails growing
   - healing cut skin.
2. Any two from: palisade cell, root hair cell, guard cell, xylem, phloem or any other specialised cell found in plants.

Page 8 Chromosomes, mitosis and the cell cycle

1. The cell needs to grow and increase its sub-cellular structures, such as ribosomes and mitochondria.
2. Firstly, the DNA is replicated, then the pairs of chromosomes are separated. Finally, the cells divide to produce two identical copies.

Page 9 Stem cells

1. Any one advantage from:
   - Farmers can grow a whole field of disease-resistant crops.
   - Farmers can grow crops with a large yield.
2. Arguments against embryo use:
   - the embryo's right to life
   - the embryo is destroyed in the process.

Page 10 Diffusion

1. The net movement of particles (of gas or particles in solution), down a concentration gradient, from an area of high concentration to an area of low concentration.
2. The larger the surface area, the more space there is for carbon dioxide to diffuse through the membrane from the blood into the lungs.

Page 11 Osmosis

1. Only small molecules, like water can diffuse through the partially permeable membrane.
2. **(a)** Increase

   (b) Water moves from a diluted solution to a more concentrated solution. The more concentrated the sugar solution becomes, the faster the water molecules will diffuse through the partially permeable membrane.

Page 12 Investigating osmosis

1. Independent variable: concentration of solution

   Dependent variable: size of potato chips
2. The hypothesis is correct for concentrations of sugar between 80 and 320 g/dm^3 (from –2 to 121%), however between 0 and 80 g/dm^3 the percentage change in mass becomes smaller (from 18 to –2%).

Page 13 Active transport

1. Diffusion is the movement of molecules from a high concentration to a low concentration, whereas active transport is the movement of molecules against the concentration gradient, from a low concentration to a high concentration. Active transport requires energy, whereas diffusion does not.

2. Answers will vary, e.g.
   - Plants absorbing mineral ions through their root hair cells.
   - Animals absorbing glucose through the cells of the intestine.

Page 14 Plant tissues

1. Palisade layer
2. To enable carbon dioxide to diffuse into the leaf easily.

Page 15 Plant transport

1. root hair → root → xylem → leaf vein → stomata
2. Thin cell walls, large surface area

Page 16 Digestion in humans

Bile neutralises stomach acid to create an alkaline environment for enzymes in the small intestine.
Bile emulsifies fats so they are easier to digest.

Page 17 Food tests

(a) lipids

(b) Milky white emulsion forms

Page 18 Investigating enzymes

1. Changes in temperature affect the activity of the enzyme, amylase. Higher temperatures will cause the amylase to break down the starch more quickly than lower temperatures. If the temperature is too high, the enzymes will become denatured and no more starch will be broken down.
2. Repeat the experiment several more times and take an average of the results.

Page 19 The blood

1. red blood cells, white blood cells, plasma and platelets
2. rate of blood flow = $\frac{1560}{5}$ = 312 ml/min

Page 20 The heart and lungs

Alveoli have a large surface area to absorb oxygen and remove carbon dioxide. They also have thin, moist membranes to allow gases to diffuse easily.

Page 21 Health issues

1. Pathogens are microorganisms that cause disease.
2. bacteria; virus
3. If the infected person coughed or sneezed, the infection could be carried in the water droplets expelled at high speed from them to the other person.

Page 22 Coronary heart disease

(a) Statins can reduce the risk of coronary heart disease and reduce blood pressure which can reduce risk of other diseases.

(b) Statins may cause unwanted side effects such as liver damage and are a long-term drug that must be taken regularly.

Page 23 Risk factors in disease

1. Either of lung disease or coronary heart disease
2. Obesity
3. Personal cost is ill health and a national cost is cost of treatment.

Page 24 Cancer

(a) People aged 29 or less

(b) People who have never smoked can still get lung cancer. The older you are when you stop smoking, the more likely you are to get lung cancer.

(c) inhaling smoke from their environment

Page 25 Communicable diseases

1. A disease that can be spread from person to person.
2. Avoid being in close proximity to an infected person or avoid contact with an infected person.

Page 26 Viral diseases

1. Vaccination
2. Tomato

Page 27 Bacterial and fungal diseases

1. They produce toxins, which make people ill.
2. The spread of gonorrhoea can be prevented by abstaining from sex, using a condom and regular screening followed by treatment if necessary.

Page 28 Protist diseases

1. Protists
2. an organism that carries an infectious pathogen into another living organism
3. Preventing mosquitoes breeding and preventing mosquitoes from biting people (by using a net and/or insect repellent)

Page 29 Human defence systems

1. The nose is lined with hairs and mucus to trap pathogens to stop them getting to the lungs.
2. Some white blood cells are phagocytes engulfing and destroying pathogens. Some white blood cells produce antibodies that target specific antigens and destroy the pathogen. Some white blood cells produce antitoxins, which neutralise toxins produced by pathogens.

Page 30 Vaccination

1. Dead or inactive pathogens are injected into the body, so that the body develops immunity against that disease.
2. White blood cells produce antibodies specific to the pathogen as well as memory cells.
3. One each of:

   Advantage – Controls the spread of the disease / prevents the student becoming infected.

   Disadvantage – It is expensive / might cause a bad reaction.

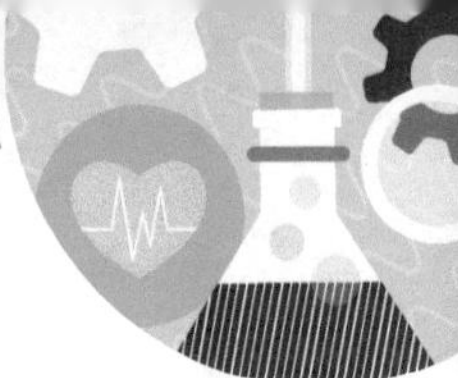

Page 31 Antibiotics and painkillers

1. Fever and headache
2. Painkillers
3. Antibiotics can only kill bacteria.

Page 32 Development of drugs

1. The work of one scientist is checked by others to make sure that it is verified.
2. cells and tissue samples and live animals

Page 33 Photosynthesis

glucose and oxygen

Page 34 Rate of photosynthesis

1. water, sunlight, carbon dioxide and temperature
2. The more chlorophyll the plant contains, the more photosynthesis can occur.

Page 35 Uses of photosynthesis

1. It is important that plants can store the glucose they make during the day to allow them to respire at night when there is no light for photosynthesis.
2. Either of: fats or oils
3. Potato tuber

Page 36 Investigating photosynthesis

1. As the distance from the lamp increases, the number of bubbles produced decreases, increasing the light intensity increases the rate of photosynthesis.
2. Light is needed for photosynthesis to occur because chlorophyll needs the energy from light to be able to convert carbon dioxide and water into glucose and oxygen.

Page 37 Aerobic and anaerobic respiration

They both produce energy.

They both use glucose.

Aerobic requires oxygen. Anaerobic doesn't.

Aerobic produces carbon dioxide and water as waste products. Anaerobic produces lactic acid.

Page 38 Response to exercise

1. Anaerobic respiration
2. So that the lungs can take in more oxygen to meet the increased oxygen demand of the muscles during exercise.

Page 39 Metabolism

1. enyzmes
2. From the breakdown of glucose in respiration

Page 40 The human nervous system

(a) For example, light receptors in the retina or touch receptors in the skin

(b) For example, a muscle or a gland.

Page 41 Reaction times

(a) $\frac{(103 + 110 + 113 + 101 + 121 + 113)}{6} = 110.166 = 110\,\text{mm}$

(b) Predict the results would be slower because the students would be tired at the end of the day.

Page 42 Homeostasis

1. Homeostasis is the regulation of conditions inside the body to maintain optimum conditions for all cell functions.
2. The body needs to maintain a constant temperature of about 37 °C to create the optimum conditions for enzymes to work.

Page 43 Human endocrine system

Line 1: thyroxine; Line 2: adrenal;

Line 3: controls glucose concentration in the blood.

Page 44 Control of blood glucose

1. Type 1 diabetes is where the pancreas does not produce sufficient insulin. Whereas, Type 2 is where the cells in the body no longer respond to insulin.

   Type 1 diabetes is controlled by injections of insulin. Whereas, Type 2 is controlled by diet.

   Obesity is a risk factor for Type 2 diabetes but not for Type 1.
2. Controlled diet (with a low sugar content) prevents glucose concentration in the blood rising too high. Exercise helps to reduce blood glucose level. Also helps weight reduction to avoid obesity - another risk factor for diabetes.
3. Insulin would be denatured by the digestive process if taken by mouth, therefore it has to be injected into the blood to reduce the glucose levels in the blood.

Page 45 Hormones in reproduction

FSH causes an egg to mature.

Page 46 Contraception

Hormonal: oral contraceptive pill and contraceptive implant;

Non-hormonal: diaphragm and condom

Page 47 Asexual and sexual reproduction

1. A gamete is a sex cell which contains genetic information.
2. Sexual reproduction involves the fusion of male and female gametes. Asexual reproduction does not.

Page 48 Meiosis

1. egg and sperm cells
2. **(a)** 23 chromosomes (unpaired)

   (b) There are two division stages. In the first stage chromosomes make copies and divide, so have pairs of chromosomes, in the second division the chromosomes do not make copies but do divide, so only one chromosome in each gamete.

Page 49 DNA and the genome

1. The genome is the total genetic material of an organism.
2. By identifying which disease Ali might get in the future, his doctor can advise him on lifestyle choices and potential preventative treatments that might prevent the disease occurring or reduce its impact. The knowledge can also inform other life choices such as having children.
3. It can be used to identify genetic diseases, trace human migration and identify disease-causing genes.

Page 50 Genetic inheritance

(a) Mother

		D	D
Father	d	Dd	Dd
	d	Dd	Dd

(b) 100%

Page 51 Inherited disorders

(a) Mother

		F	f
Father	F	FF	Ff
	f	Ff	ff

(b) i Normal, no cystic fibrosis

ii Normal, no cystic fibrosis

(c) They will have cystic fibrosis.

(d) production of a thick, sticky mucus which affects the lungs and other organs

(e) Any one advantage from the following:

- prevents having a child with the disorder who could suffer
- reduces the chance of the disease being passed on
- embryo cells could be used in stem cell treatment
- saves long term cost of treating a child with a disorder.

Page 52 Variation and mutation

1. Answers will vary, e.g.:
   - genetic – tongue rolling, Down's syndrome, blood group, eye colour, hair colour
   - environmental – weight, language spoken, religion.
2. Mutation could change the phenotype so that it is better suited to the environment.

Page 53 Sex determination

(a) XX

(b) 0.5 / $\frac{1}{2}$ / 50% / 1:1 / 50:50 / 1 in 2

Half of the sperm contain a Y chromosome, so half will be male.

(c) The sexes of the previous children do not affect whether an X or a Y sperm fertilises the egg. So the probability is still 1:1.

Page 54 Evolution

Mice with the mutated gene for lighter fur colour are more likely to survive and reproduce because the lighter fur colour provides camouflage from prey and predators in the sand. The offspring of the light fur coloured mice are likely to inherit the mutated gene causing changes to the fur colour of the population of deer mice over time.

Page 55 Selective breeding

1. 1, 4, 2, 3
2. Any one from: to produce pigs that have a lot of meat/grow fast/have a good temperament.

Page 56 Genetic engineering

1. **(a)** A change in the genetic material of an organism by insertion of a gene from another species

   (b) diabetes
2. Two from: Farmers may use more herbicide.
   The herbicides may harm people who eat the crops.
   It may also cause a herbicide-resistant weed to develop.

Page 57 Fossils

1. The remains of an organism from many years ago, found in rocks.
2. The teeth and bones of the reptile became replaced by minerals as it decayed, leaving behind a rock-like substance shaped like the skeleton of the reptile.

Page 58 Extinction

1. Any two of, for example:
   - breeding programmes
   - protection orders to prevent hunting
   - protected habitats.
2. It destroys habitats, wiping out food sources.
   Some species are unable to survive the change in temperature or are not adapted to cold temperatures.

Page 59 Resistant bacteria

1. Bacteria that are not killed by antibiotics.
2. Bacteria develop resistance to antibiotics by evolution and natural selection. Some bacteria have mutations which make them resistant to a particular antibiotic. These resistant bacteria will survive and reproduce rapidly. The bacteria that are susceptible to the antibiotic will be destroyed. Eventually, only bacteria that are resistant to the antibiotic will exist.

Page 60 Classification

Pongo albelii

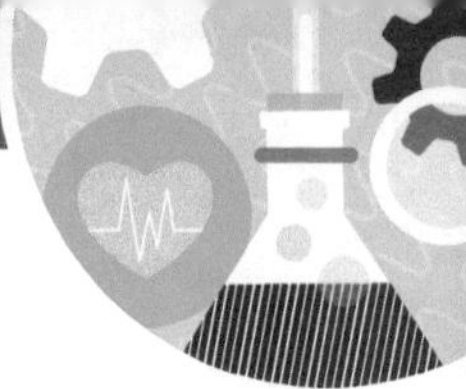

Page 61 Communities

(a) If the algae population fell then the snails would have limited food and so the population of snails would drop.

(b) The population of algae would increase as there would be fewer snails to feed off the algae.

Page 62 Abiotic factors

Any three: temperature, pH of soil and mineral content, wind intensity and direction, light intensity, carbon dioxide levels (plants), oxygen levels for aquatic animals, moisture levels

Page 63 Biotic factors

(a) $\frac{190-1110}{1110} \times 100\% = -83\%$

(b) hunting by humans and competition for territory

Page 64 Adaptations

Behavioural

Page 65 Organisation of an ecosystem

1. one which makes its own food by photosynthesis
2. The first organism in a food chain must be a producer to transfer energy into the food chain.
3. The third consumer (producer → primary consumer → secondary consumer → tertiary consumer)

Page 66 Investigating population size

(a) $3 + 5 + 3 + 1 + 3 + 5 + 2 + 2 = 24$

$24 \div 8 = 3$

(b) $2000 \div 1 = 2000$

$2000 \times 3 = 6000$

Page 67 Using a transect

Lay a tape/marked rope/transect along the grass going from the edge of the woodland to the middle of the grassy area.

Place a quadrat next to the 0 m mark on the line. Record the number of buttercups inside the quadrat.

Move the quadrat a set distance along the tape and count and record the number of buttercups.

Continue this method until the end of the line is reached.

Compare the numbers of buttercups at different distances from the woodland.

Page 68 Cycling materials

1. The sun heats the surface of the ocean causing water to evaporate, this rises and then cools, condensing to become a cloud.
2. Photosynthesis

Page 69 Biodiversity

(a) The number of cod decreased from 300 thousand to about 20 thousand.

(b) A larger human population means an increased demand for food including fish and therefore there has been more fishing of cod to meet this supply.

(c) using nets with bigger holes and limiting how many fish can be caught in any given period of time

Page 70 Waste management

1. Landfill is destroying habitats and causing pollution.
2. **(a)** 31%

   (b) One from: To reduce waste/landfill, reduce plastics in ocean/reduced air pollution from burning plastics/reduce GH gas emission.

Page 71 Land use

(a) To produce compost

(b) Destroying peat bogs would reduce biodiversity.

(c) Carbon dioxide levels are increasing (decomposers complete the decomposition of organic matter, during this process they are respiring and releasing carbon dioxide into the atmosphere).

Page 72 Deforestation

(a) Slash and burn

(b) The ash produced is full of nutrients which support the growth of the crops.

(c) carbon dioxide

(d) Without trees to hold it in place, the soil can blow or wash away.

Page 73 Global warming

The butterfly species has moved northwards as global warming has caused the warmer weather conditions that the butterfly needs to survive to spread further north.

Page 74 Maintaining biodiversity

1. They might lose jobs working for tree felling companies. They won't be able to grow food crops and cattle to sell to earn money/eat.
2. **(a)** An area of rainforest that is protected

   (b) Because it provides more habitats, shelter and food sources so it can support more species.

Page 75 Atoms, elements and compounds

1. Atom
2. Al
3. **(a)** Sodium

   (b) (i) Hydrogen, H

   (ii) hydrogen + chlorine → hydrogen chloride

Page 76 Mixtures

1. Ink and water - simple distillation

   Sand and water - filtration

   Crude oil - fractional distillation

   Sugar and water - evaporation
2. W - conical flask; X - filter paper; Y - filter funnel

Page 77 The model of the atom

The plum pudding model said that the atom was a positively charged 'pudding', with negative electrons ('plums') embedded in it.

The nuclear model was different:

- Positively charged part of the atom (protons) found in the centre
- Positive centre was small rather than the whole 'pudding' / atom
- Electrons were not embedded in the atom but orbiting the nucleus / centre of the atom

Page 78 Subatomic particles

1. **(a)** 0.1 nm
   (b) 10 000
2. Positive
3. Protons and neutrons
4. **(a)** 2
   (b) There are the two positive protons and two negative electrons so the charges are balanced.

Page 79 Size and mass of atoms

(a) The atomic number is the number of protons.

The mass number is the number of protons plus the number of neutrons.

(b)

Subatomic particle	Relative mass	Relative charge
electron	$\frac{1}{1840}$	–1
neutron	1	0
proton	1	+1

(c) 9 protons; 19 – 9 = 10 neutrons; 9 electrons

Page 80 Isotopes and relative atomic mass

1. They have the same number of protons / atomic number.
   They have a different number of neutrons / mass number.
2. atomic; average; isotopes

Page 81 Electronic structure

(a) C **(b)** B **(c)** C

Page 82 The periodic table

1. **(a)** Group 5; **(b)** Period 3; **(c)** nitrogen / N
2. In order of atomic number; in vertical groups of similar elements; and in horizontal periods where the atomic number increases one in each successive element across the period.
3. Their atoms all have the same number of electrons in their outer shells; 7 electrons.

Page 83 Developing the periodic table

1. One from: boron; aluminium
2. **(a)** atomic mass
   (b) For elements that he thought had not been discovered.

Page 84 Metals and non-metals

Any one of:

- resistant to corrosion so won't react with food
- low density so practical as a lightweight wrapping.

Page 85 Group 0

1. **(a)** 0
   (b) Unreactive
2. **(a)** The number of protons increases. The number of neutrons increases.
   (b) They have full outer shells of electrons.
3. 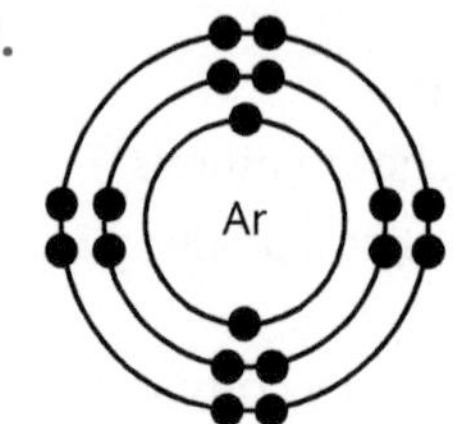

Page 86 Group 1

1. As you move down the group the elements gain an electron shell, so the outer electron is further away from the positively charged nucleus. This means that the outer electrons are held less strongly and are lost more easily, making the elements more reactive.
2. Lithium and water produce hydrogen gas (and lithium hydroxide). The bubbles are the gas being produced.

Page 87 Group 7

1. Chlorine is more reactive than iodine.
2. Chlorine or fluorine
3. Melting and boiling points increase down the group, fluorine is at the top of the group and iodine is at the bottom.

Page 88 Chemical bonds

(a) They are electrons that are free to move.

(b) Metallic bonding

Page 89 Ionic bonding

1. Group 0/noble gases
2. 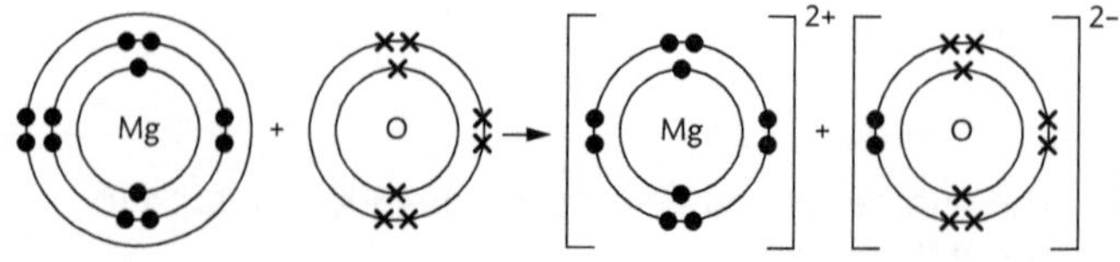

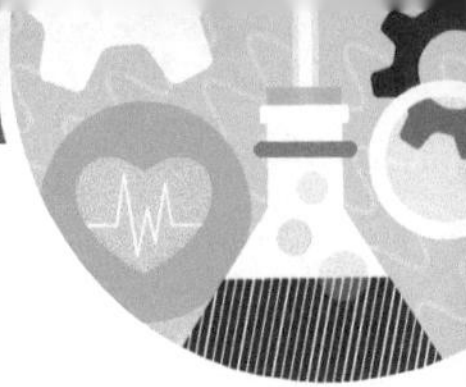

Page 90 Ionic compounds

1. Sodium chloride forms a giant **ionic** lattice, with strong **electrostatic** forces of attraction.
2. **(a)** Calcium fluoride (giant ionic) lattice
   (b) CaF_2

Page 91 Covalent bonding

1. A bond between non-metal atoms sharing a pair of electrons
2. 3
3. 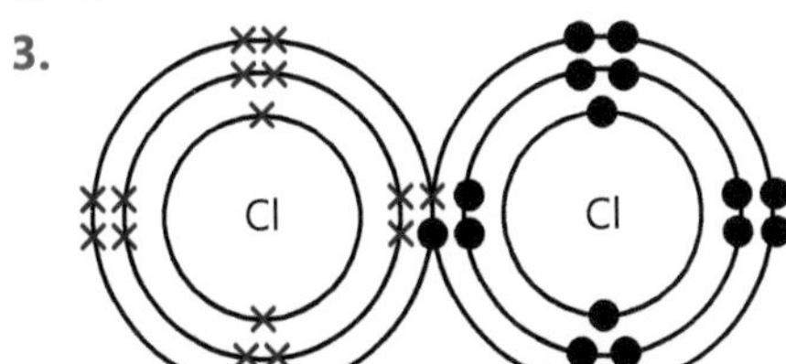

Page 92 Metallic bonding

1. attraction between positive nuclei and electrons
2. electrons; move; attraction; metallic

Page 93 States of matter

1. carbon dioxide = (g)
   water = (l)
   lead = (s)
2. boiling
3. energy; decreases

Page 94 Properties of ionic compounds

1. high; high; conduct
2. **(a)** Magnesium oxide is an ionic compound formed by the transfer of two electrons from a magnesium atom to an oxygen atom, forming Mg^{2+} and O^{2-}. It has a giant lattice structure.
   (b) When molten, the ions are free to move, which allows electrical charge to flow.
   (c) Ionic bonds are very strong. There are many bonds in an ionic lattice and they must all be broken to melt magnesium oxide.

Page 95 Properties of small molecules

1. do not conduct electricity; low melting points
2. There are only weak intermolecular forces of attraction between small molecules. These forces are easy to overcome so they are easily boiled.

Page 96 Polymers

1. 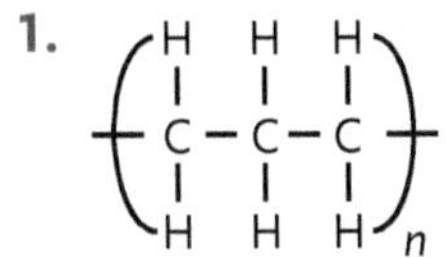

2. Covalent bonds

Page 97 Giant covalent structures

1. Three
2. Four
3. Covalent
4. **(a)** Giant covalent
   (b) It has many (strong) covalent bonds which take a lot of energy to break.

Page 98 Properties of metals and alloys

(a) a mixture of two or more metals / a metal with one or more other elements

(b) The alloy has different sized atoms / the lattice is distorted / the layers of atoms cannot slide over each other so easily.

Page 99 Metals as conductors

1. A conductor
2. Metals have delocalised electrons that carry thermal energy.
3. When a metal is heated, its delocalised electrons gain energy and vibrate more vigorously. These particles bump into nearby particles causing them to vibrate more and transferring thermal energy through the metal by conduction.

Page 100 Diamond

1. giant covalent lattice
2. carbon
3. four
4. **(a)** shiny/reflect light/lustrous
   (b) it does not conduct electricity

Page 101 Graphite

(a) high melting point; conducts electricity

(b) covalent

(c) It is made of layers.

Page 102 Graphene and fullerenes

1. Carbon
2. Similarities:
   - In both, each carbon atom is bonded to three others.
   - They both conduct electricity.

   Difference:
   - Graphite is soft because it consists of layers, whereas nanotubes are strong.

Page 103 Conservation of mass

1. 5 g
2. **(a)** magnesium carbonate → magnesium oxide + carbon dioxide
   (b) 84 g = 40 + ?
   84 - 40 = 44 g of carbon dioxide

Page 104 Relative formula mass

1. **(a)** 32 **(b)** 18 **(c)** 17 **(d)** 80
2. $2 \times 27 = 54$
   $3 \times 32 = 96$
   $12 \times 16 = 192$
   $54 + 96 + 192 = 342$

Page 105 Balancing equations

1. A balanced equation shows how many atoms or molecules of each substance are reacting OR A balanced equation shows the formula for each reactant and product involved.
2. $4K + O_2 \rightarrow 2K_2O$
   $NaOH + HCl \rightarrow NaCl + H_2O$

Page 106 Mass changes

1. **(a)** zinc carbonate → zinc oxide + carbon dioxide
   (b) Carbon dioxide gas produced in the reaction escaped.
   (c) The zinc carbonate could be heated with oxygen in a test tube and the gases collected, which would allow the products to be measured more accurately.
2. **(a)** $C_2H_5OH + \mathbf{3}O_2 \rightarrow \mathbf{2}CO_2 + \mathbf{3}H_2O$
   (b) The mass appears to decrease because carbon dioxide gas (and water vapour) will escape during the reaction.

Page 107 Chemical measurements

(a) Ignoring trial 3: $(62 + 75 + 68)/3 = 195/3 = 65$ s
(b) $68 - 62 = 6$ s
(c) $6/2 = 3$ s

Page 108 Concentrations of solutions

1. 40 g/dm^3
2. 50 g
3. The concentration will increase as the mass of solute used increases.

Page 109 Metal oxides

zinc + oxygen → zinc oxide

Page 110 The reactivity series

1. One from: copper, gold, platinum
2. A - magnesium
   B - iron
   C - copper
   D - calcium
3. The more easily a metal forms a positive ion, the more reactive it will be.

Page 111 Extraction of metals and reduction

1. **(a)** lead oxide + carbon → lead + carbon dioxide
   (b) Oxidation
   (c) $PbO_2 + C \rightarrow Pb + CO_2$
2. Calcium is above carbon in the reactivity series. Metals can only be extracted by elements that are more reactive than them.

Page 112 Reactions of acids with metals

(a) The metal would fizz and dissolve, because the zinc would react with the acid to release hydrogen and form zinc chloride solution.
(b) Hydrogen is flammable, so people in the workshop should not smoke.

Page 113 Salt production

1. Potassium nitrate
2. Neutralisation
3. Hydrochloric acid
4. **(a)** Li_2SO_4
   (b) $MgCl_2$
   (c) $Ca(NO_3)_2$

Page 114 Soluble salts

1. Filtration
2. sodium hydroxide and sulfuric acid
3. copper nitrate
4. The substance will dissolve in water.

Page 115 Making salts

3 Warm dilute sulfuric acid and add excess zinc hydroxide.
5 Filter the solution.
2 Heat the solution until most of the water has evaporated and crystals start to form.
1 Leave to cool so more crystals will form.
4 Dry the crystals obtained.

Page 116 The pH scale and neutralisation

1. hydrochloric acid + sodium hydroxide → sodium chloride + water
2. **(a)** alkali/base
   (b) OH^-
3. By using a pH probe

Page 117 Electrolysis

1. electrolyte - liquid that conducts electricity
   electrode - solid electrical conductor
   anode - positively charged electrode
   cathode - negatively charged electrode
2. To conduct electricity into the electrolyte.
3. Metal ions will move towards the negatively charged cathode, because opposite charges attract.

Page 118 Electrolysis to extract metals

1. Large amounts of energy are needed to melt the magnesium chloride to break the strong ionic bonds.
2. cryolite

3. **(a)** The reactivity of the metal (whether it is more or less reactive than carbon)
   (b) They are more reactive than carbon.
   (c) It uses a lot of energy/electricity for electrolysis
   (d) molten/liquid

Page 119 Electrolysis of aqueous solutions

(a) Negative electrode: hydrogen (1); positive electrode: iodine (1)

(b) Negative electrode: silver (1); positive electrode: oxygen (1)

Page 120 Electrolysis of copper(II) chloride

(a) Chlorine, hydrogen and sodium hydroxide

(b) Chloride ions are negative, so are attracted to the anode. Chlorine gas forms at the anode.

Hydrogen ions are positive, so are attracted to the cathode. Hydrogen gas forms at the cathode.

Page 121 Exothermic and endothermic reactions

Exothermic

Page 122 Temperature changes

–6 °C (1)

The reaction was endothermic (1) because the temperature decreased (1).

Page 123 Reaction profiles

(a) Exothermic, because the products have less energy than the reactants (as heat has been lost to the surroundings).

(b)

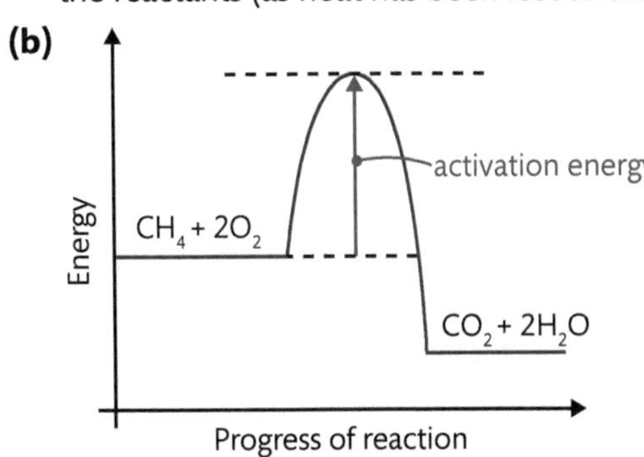

Page 124 Calculating rate of reaction

(a) B

(b) any value between 65 and 80 seconds

(c) B, because a catalyst speeds up the rate of a reaction

Page 125 Factors affecting rate of reaction

(a) No more bubbles/gas were produced.

(b)

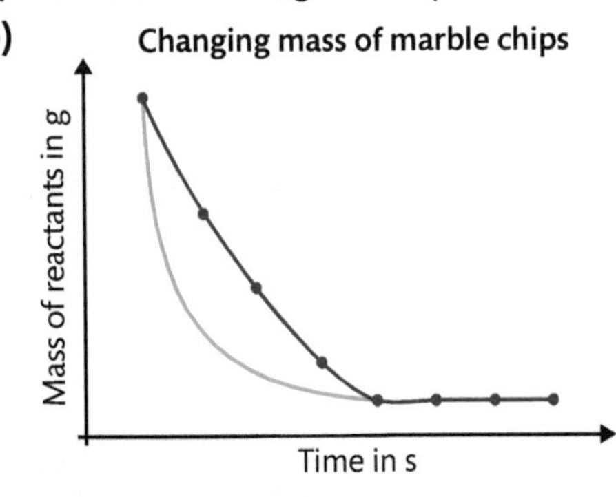

(c) One from:
- Increase the concentration of hydrochloric acid.
- Increase the surface area of the marble chips.

Page 126 Rate of reaction

(a) When the concentration of a solution is increased, there are more reactant particles in the same volume. This increases the number of collisions that occur in any given time and therefore increases the number of particles that react.

(b) Independent variable – the concentration of the acid
Dependent variable – the time taken for the cross to disappear

Control variables – the volume of acid, the volume and concentration of thiosulfate and the temperature of the reaction

Page 127 Catalysts

1.

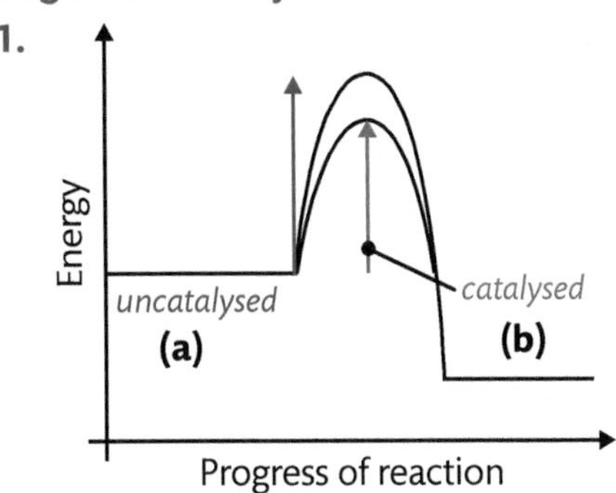

2. Enzymes

Page 128 Reversible reactions

1. The products of the reaction can react to form the original reactants.
2. **(a)** By reversing the reaction (adding water) the original substance (hydrated copper sulfate) is formed.
   (b) hydrated copper sulfate $\rightleftharpoons$ anhydrous copper sulfate + water

Page 129 Energy changes in reversible reactions

1. Energy is transferred from the surroundings.
2. The same amount of energy is transferred.
3. 256 kJ/g

Page 130 Crude oil, hydrocarbons and alkanes

1. A limited supply that will eventually run out.
2. If C = 6
   $H = (6 \times 2) + 2 = 12 + 2 = 14$

Page 131 Fractional distillation

1. X – evaporation
   Z – condensation

Page 132 Hydrocarbons

1. Water and carbon dioxide
2. $\mathbf{2}C_2H_6 + \mathbf{7}O_2 \rightarrow \mathbf{4}CO_2 + \mathbf{6}H_2O$

3. As molecular size increases, viscosity increases too.
4. In the combustion of a hydrocarbon, both the carbon and the hydrogen atoms gain oxygen.

Page 133 Cracking and alkenes

1. **Two** from: cracking produces smaller alkanes; cracking produces alkenes; smaller alkanes are in high demand / are useful as fuels; alkenes are used to make polymers.
2 C_8H_{18}

Page 134 Pure substances

1. Compare the boiling point, melting point and density of the sample with known data.
2. All the atoms or molecules within the substance are the same.
3. Impure; because it boils at a different temperature from pure ethanol

Page 135 Formulations

1. **(a)** Formulation

   (b) It is used to give the paint its colour.
2. Any two of the following: medicine, food, fertiliser, alloy, cleaning agent, fuel

Page 136 Chromatography

1. The brown food colourant contains yellow, red and blue pigments.
2. R_f values tell you the ratio of the distance moved by the dye to the distance moved by the solvent.
3. For example: $R_f = \frac{78\,mm}{150\,mm}$

   The two lots of mm cancel out.

   R_f values are not given units because they are a ratio.

Page 137 Paper chromatography

1. If the base line is below the level of solvent, the spots of dye will dissolve into the solvent.
2. Pencil will not dissolve in the solvent, but pen might.
3. 0.31

Page 138 Testing for gases

Chlorine – bleaches litmus paper

Hydrogen – squeaky pop

Oxygen – relights a glowing splint

Carbon dioxide – limewater turns cloudy

Page 139 Gases in the atmosphere

1. 80%
2. Percentage is 80% which is $\frac{80}{100}$

   Divide by a common factor (20)

   $\frac{80}{20} = 4$

   $\frac{100}{20} = 5$

   So nitrogen is $\frac{4}{5}$

Page 140 Earth's early atmosphere

(a) 3.5%

(b) There are no plants on Mars to carry out photosynthesis and produce oxygen.

Page 141 Oxygen and carbon dioxide levels

1. Photosynthesis
2. Two from: coal, crude oil, natural gas
3. It is mostly calcium carbonate / it contains $CaCO_3$
4. Oxygen increased; carbon dioxide decreased

Page 142 Greenhouse gases

1. Methane, carbon dioxide and water vapour
2. Some of the IR radiation is absorbed by the greenhouse gases in the atmosphere and re-emitted back towards Earth.

Page 143 Human contribution to greenhouse gases

1. It ensures that the evidence used to support a theory is reliable.
2. Global climate change / global warming
3. Other scientists can use their results to inform their own work.

   Results which have an impact on the wider population can be communicated to as many people as possible.

Page 144 Global climate change

1. Any two of:
   - rising sea levels / melting ice / flooding
   - increasing temperatures / heat waves
   - changing rainfall patterns
   - more / larger deserts.
2. Rising global temperatures
3. There may not be enough food for people; food prices will increase
4. The weather over a long time

Page 145 The carbon footprint

1. Any two of:
   - use energy-efficient appliances
   - switch off appliances when not in use
   - walk or use public transport
   - buy local produce
   - recycle and reuse.
2. Any two of:
   - use local resources
   - use renewable energy
   - use energy-efficient appliances
   - encourage employees to reduce their carbon footprint.

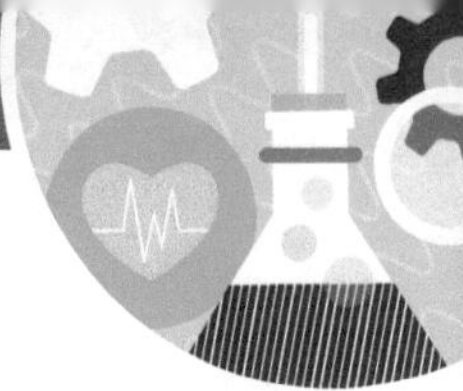

Page 146 Atmospheric pollutants

1. carbon dioxide - global warming
   sulfur dioxide - acid rain
   solid particulates - global dimming
   carbon monoxide - toxic gas
2. Sulfur dioxide causes acid rain.
3. **(a)** Carbon monoxide and soot are produced when a fuel burns in a limited supply of oxygen.
   (b) Sulfur dioxide is produced when a fuel containing sulfur is burned, such as coal.
   (c) Oxides of nitrogen are produced when the heat from car engines causes nitrogen and oxygen in the air to react together.

Page 147 Earth's resources

1. Oceans; atmosphere
2. Plastic / polymer, or a named plastic such as nylon
3. Meeting our needs without affecting the ability of people in the future to meet their needs.
4. One from: it is made very slowly; it is no longer being made

Page 148 Potable water

1. Distillation and reverse osmosis
2. One of: chlorine or ozone
3. It contains large amounts of dissolved solids/salt.
4. Rainwater
5. Any three from: rainwater, groundwater, rivers, lakes or oceans

Page 149 Purifying water

1. Distillation
2. Leave a small sample of water out to evaporate; any dissolved solids will be left behind after the water has evaporated.
3. 100 °C

Page 150 Waste water treatment

1. Any two of: dishwasher, toilet, shower, bath, washing machine or tumble dryer
2. If it enters the waterways, pesticides and fertilisers could harm aquatic life.
   If it is absorbed by aquatic life, substances that are harmful to animals and humans could enter the human food chain.
3. Screening / grit removal; sedimentation; anaerobic digestion; aerobic treatment

Page 151 Life cycle assessment

1. Polymer A
2. The environmental impact of a product; over its lifetime
3. Two from: volume of water; mass of natural resources needed; amount of energy needed; (some of) the wastes produced

Page 152 Reducing the use of resources

(a) Aluminium

(b) Copper; because it is the most valuable metal; and saves almost as much energy when recycled as aluminium does / it saves the second most energy when recycled

Page 153 Energy transfers in a system

(a) The energy lost from the body is thermal energy.

(b) The jumper is thick and the wool traps air. In contrast, a t-shirt is thin and traps little air.

(c) The thick jumper with many holes (air pockets) traps a lot of air and has poor thermal conductivity, so reduces the body's rate of heat loss. The thin t-shirt traps little air, so has higher thermal conductivity and the body loses heat more quickly.

Page 154 Gravitational potential energy

1. $70 \times 9.8 \times 100 = 68\,600$ J
2. $50\,000 = 70 \times 9.8 \times h$
   $$h = \frac{50\,000}{(70 \times 9.8)}$$
   $$= 72.9 \text{ m}$$
3. As the ball falls, its height decreases, which means its g.p.e. decreases. The g.p.e. is transferred to kinetic energy, which increases. Kinetic energy $= \frac{1}{2}mv^2$ therefore if its k.e. increases, the speed of the ball increases.
4. **(a)** The work done by the crane is equal to the g.p.e. gained, so 1000 J.
   (b) Twice the change in height, so twice the increase in g.p.e. $1000 \times 2 = 2000$ J.

Page 155 Kinetic energy

1. **(a)** 250 J
   (b) 500 J
2. $0.5 \times 67 \times 11^2 = 4054$ J
3. Kinetic energy $= 0.5 \times 0.4 \times 7^2 = 9.8$ J. Therefore, 9.8 J of work is done to throw the frisbee.

Page 156 Energy in a spring

(a) The energy is stored as elastic potential, transfers to kinetic as the ball starts to move and then transfers to gravitational potential as the ball moves upwards.

(b) $0.5 \times 60 \times 0.2^2 = 1.2$ J

(c) If the spring is compressed further, it stores more elastic potential energy, meaning there is more energy to be transferred to gravitational potential energy so the ball can go higher.

Page 157 Using energy equations

1. kinetic energy $= 0.5 \times m \times v^2$
2. $0.5 \times 1.25 \times (0.6)^2 = 0.23$ J
3. 25 J

4. **(a)** $E = m \times g \times h$

   (b) $25 = 0.35 \times 9.8 \times h$

   $h = \frac{25}{(0.35 \times 9.8)} = 7.3\,\text{m}$

5. **(a)** Double

   (b) Quadruple (×4)

Page 158 Power

1. **(a)** joules; **(b)** watts; **(c)** joules
2. Lamp B transfers more energy per second so appears brighter.
3. 2000 ÷ 120 = 16.7 kW

Page 159 Efficiency

1. Useful energy = 400 – 150 = 250J
   Efficiency = 250 ÷ 400 = 0.625
2. 15 per cent of the energy is lost or wasted.
3. Lamp A has the higher efficiency because it uses a greater proportion of the input power usefully (shown by more thermal energy being transferred as light).
4. input energy = useful output energy ÷ efficiency

   1500 ÷ 0.6 = 2500J

Page 160 Renewable energy resources

(a) The solar cells charge the batteries when there is sunlight. The batteries provide electricity at night.

(b) Solar panels can be set up almost anywhere (so there is no need for cables to the National Grid).

Page 161 Non-renewable energy resources

1. Coal, oil/diesel/petrol, natural gas
2. Advantages of nuclear power:

   Any one from:

   It produces no harmful gases that can damage people's health, such as sulfur dioxide or smoke particles

   No CO_2 produced, so less greenhouse gases

   Disadvantages of nuclear power:

   Any one from:

   They produce radioactive waste which has to be stored and remains toxic and radioactive for thousands of years

   Any accidents can release radioactive substances into the environment

   They are expensive to decommission
3. Any two from: coal is getting more expensive to buy; coal needs to be transported; coal is running out.

Page 162 Circuit diagrams

1. Positive to negative

2 **(a)** The circuit where A is connected is incomplete.

   (b) Close the switch; reverse the LED or cell

3. LDR (light-dependent resistor)

Page 163 Current, resistance and potential difference

1. $R = \frac{V}{I} = \frac{6}{0.1} = 60\,\Omega$
2. **(a)** Resistance is doubled

   (b) 3 V
3. **(a)** $I = \frac{V}{R} = \frac{6}{80} = 0.075\,\text{A}$

   (b) doubles the current

Page 164 Electrical charge

1. 2 A means 2 C are transferred every second.
2. $30 = 6 \times t$

   $t = \frac{30}{6} = 5\,\text{s}$
3. $Q = 0.6 \times 15 = 9\,\text{C}$

Page 165 Resistance

Set up this series circuit.

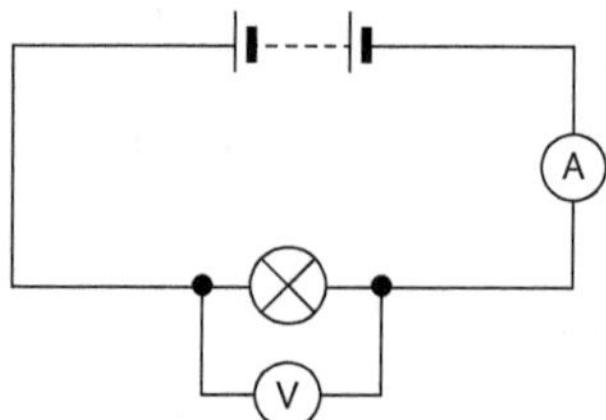

Vary the potential difference of the power supply. In a table, record the values of pd and current measured.

Plot a graph of current against pd. Calculate the resistance of the lamp at different pds using $R = \frac{V}{I}$.

Allow the lamp to cool between readings.
Take repeat readings.

Page 166 Resistors

A diode's resistance is high when current flows in one direction but low when it flows in the other.

Page 167 Series and parallel circuits

1. $12 + 4 = 16\,\Omega$
2. When another lamp is added, the overall resistance increases and the current through each lamp decreases. The pd is shared between more lamps so each lamp receives fewer volts.
3. The brightness of the lamp stays the same as all the lamps have the same pd across them when they are connected in parallel.

Page 168 *I-V* characteristics

1. **(a)** filament lamp

   (b) The gradient decreases at higher potential differences.

   (c) Increasing resistance
2. Two from: Keep the current or potential difference low. Switch off the circuit between measurements or do not leave it on for long periods of time. Use a cooling unit, or dry ice, to keep the component cool.

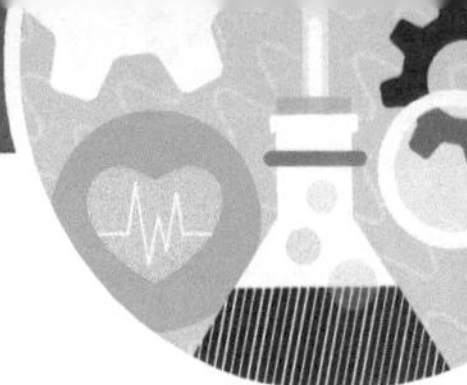

Page 169 Mains electricity

1. **(a)** green and yellow
   (b) blue
   (c) brown
2. dc = direct current; ac = alternating current
3. 230 V

Page 170 Energy transfers in appliances

1. Energy is transferred as sound and to heat up the kettle and the surroundings and this is not useful.
2. 400 J

Page 171 Electrical power

1. Heater B as it gives out heat more rapidly.
2. $P = VI = 230 \times 5 = 1150\,W$
3. $P = I^2R = 0.1 \times 0.1 \times 60 = 0.6\,W$
4. The 40 W lamp would transfer more energy in the hour (twice as much).

Page 172 Transformers and the National Grid

1. Transformers (step up the voltage and) decrease the current in the wires so they heat up less and lose less energy.
2. step down transformer

Page 173 Density

1. density
2. **(a)** apple: $0.074 \div (1.04 \times 10^{-4}) = 712\,kg/m^3$
   (b) apple – floats; steel box – floats; plastic – sinks; human – floats
   (c) $712 = \dfrac{m}{1.5 \times 10^{-4}}$
   $m = 712 \times 1.5 \times 10^{-4} = 0.107\,kg$

Page 174 Density of materials

1. $420 - 80 = 340\,g$
2. **(a)** For mass, you need a balance; for the volume, you could use a ruler to measure the lengths of the sides.
   (b) Density = mass ÷ volume; $\rho = m / V$

Page 175 State changes

1. are reversible
2. solid: vibrate around a fixed place;
   liquid: move around freely but still touching each other
3. The density of the substance increases because the particles move closer together so have the same mass in a smaller volume.

Page 176 Specific heat capacity

1. **(a)** 100 °C
   (b) $2 \times 4200 \times 100 = 840\,000\,J$
2. Having a high specific heat capacity means the liquid heats up slowly and can remove more thermal energy from the system to cool it.

Page 177 Specific heat capacity

1. There is still energy in the heater that needs to conduct into the metal or water and be detected by the thermometer. It may take some time for the thermal energy to conduct to the thermometer.
2. Stir then measure the temperature of water in the middle, as hot water rises to the top.

Page 178 Specific latent heat

1. **(a)** The energy needed to change the state of 1 kg of a substance from a liquid to a vapour
   (b) J/kg
2. $15 \times 207 = 3105\,J$
3. $162.5 = 2.5 \times L$
   $L = \dfrac{162.5}{2.5} = 65\,J/kg$

Page 179 Particle motion in gases

1. **(a)** increases; **(b)** increases
2. As the temperature of the particles inside the bottle increases, the pressure of the gas increases because the particles move more quickly. This applies a greater force to push the stopper out.
3. The gas particles inside the balloon move faster and spread out. This reduces the density of the gas. As the density of the gas is lower than the density of the air outside the balloon, the balloon will rise up.

Page 180 The structure of an atom

1. Protons and neutrons
2. Neutral or 0
3. Protons are larger and positively charged; electrons are smaller and negatively charged.
4. Electron(s) move to a higher energy level further away from the nucleus.

Page 181 Mass number, atomic number and isotopes

1. **(a)** 7; **(b)** 3
2. **(a)** 12
   (b) 10 (it has lost 2 electrons)
3. An atom has neutral charge; an ion is charged having lost or gained electrons.
4. An atom of the same element with a different number of neutrons

Page 182 Development of the atomic model

1. The atom is a positively charged sphere with tiny negatively charged electrons embedded in it.
2. Unlike the plum pudding model, the nuclear model puts the majority of the mass and the positive charge at the centre; the outside carries the negative charge and the rest is empty space.

3. No model is considered correct, just the best idea based on the evidence. As more evidence is found the models will change, including the nuclear model.

Page 183 Radioactive decay and nuclear radiation

1. Alpha would not get through the paper regardless of how thick or thin it was. Gamma would get through the paper and would not be reduced if the paper thickness increased.
2. Gamma would be the most suitable: it can be easily detected as it can pass out of the body easily and is also the least harmful to living cells. Alpha would not penetrate the skin and could not be detected outside the body. It is also most ionising and therefore would be damaging to the cells in the body. Beta radiation would not be detected if it was too deep inside the body and would also be quite harmful.

Page 184 Half-lives

1. 50 minutes
2. $640 \div 2 = 320$ Bq
   $320 \div 2 = 160$ Bq
   2 half-lives
   $12 \div 2 = 6$ years

Page 185 Nuclear equations

1. **(a)** ${}^{239}_{94}\mathrm{Pu} \rightarrow {}^{235}_{92}\mathrm{U} + {}^{4}_{2}\mathrm{He}$
   (b) ${}^{25}_{11}\mathrm{Na} \rightarrow {}^{25}_{12}\mathrm{Mg} + {}^{0}_{-1}\beta$
2. **(a)** Mercury
   (b) Bismuth

Page 186 Radioactive contamination

1. Irradiation is when radiation from a source is absorbed by something. Contamination is when something gets the radioactive material on it. They can both damage cells, change genes and possibly cause cancer. If you are being irradiated, you can stop or reduce this by moving away from the source or moving behind a screen.
   If you are contaminated, the source is already on you so you cannot move away from it and will be irradiated constantly until it is cleaned off.
2. Any two from:
   Has more exposure to / may work more closely with a source
   Works with a source with a higher activity
   Wears less protective clothing
3. They are at risk of irradiation because they are quite close to the rocks. They are at risk of contamination because the rocks may produce dust particles that could stick to their skin if they come into contact with it.
   They should not touch the rocks and should keep them in a sealed container to avoid contamination.
   They should also wear protective clothing. To reduce their dose they should keep their distance from the sources, hold them at arm's length by using long tongs or tweezers and only be near them when actually using them.

Page 187 Scalar and vector quantities

1. Force
2. Direction
3. **(a)** 7 km
   (b) North
4. **(a)** 77 m/s due north
   (b) 53 m/s due south

Page 188 Forces

1. Contact forces are lift, thrust and drag (all these are being touched by the air).
   Non-contact force is weight.
2. Repulsive
3. **(a)** Upwards: Magnetic force / magnetic repulsion
   Downwards: weight
   (b)

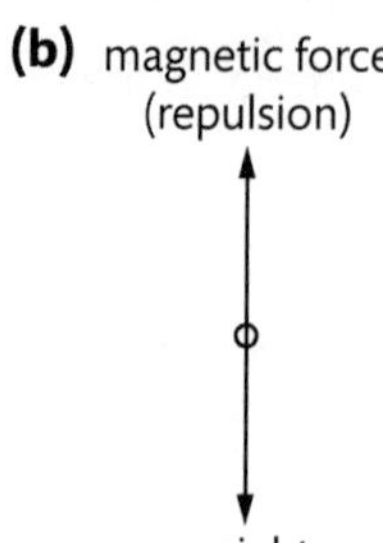

Arrows should be the same length.

Page 189 Gravity

1. In the centre of the hole of the ring donut
2. Zero the balance and place the object on it, then record the mass in kg. Weight = mass × gravitational field strength (9.81 N/kg).
3. Towards the centre of the Earth
4. The Moon has less gravity than Earth because it has less mass. The astronaut would experience less downwards force on the Moon, which would make them feel lighter and more bouncy. This could make it more difficult to move.

Page 190 Resultant forces

1. Constant speed or stationary
2. $F = ma = 1200 \times 1.4 = 1680$ N

Page 191 Work done and energy transfer

1. **(a)** 0 J, the force and distance are in different directions so no work is done.
   (b) Work = force × distance = 500 N × 35 m = 17 500 J
   (c) Work = force × distance = 20 N × 1.5 m = 30 J
2. **(a)** Friction
   (b) Kinetic to thermal
   (c) Work = force × distance = 50 N × 5 m = 250 J

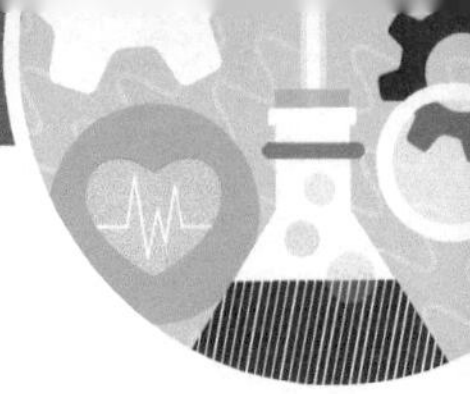

3. They are doing work as the bicycle is moving in the direction of the force. Chemical energy is partially transferred to kinetic energy as the bike speeds up and then to gravitational potential energy as the bike moves up the hill. (In actual fact, the cyclist pushes down on the pedal which moves down, so they start by doing work with their legs.)

Page 192 Forces and elasticity

(a) 18 N

(b) The graph is not a straight line / the graph curves beyond the limit of proportionality.

(c) 0.25 m

(d) $0.09 + 0.25 = 0.34$ m

(e) $e = 0.4$ (from Figure 1)
Energy stored $= 0.5 \times 44.7 \times 0.4^2 = 3.576$ J

Page 193 Force and extension

(a) $k =$ gradient $= 5 / 2.55 = 19.6$ N/m

(b) The results for spring B are more reliable as the points are closer to the line of best fit / there is less scatter.

Page 194 Distance and displacement

(a) Distance = 600 km
Displacement = 200 km east

(b) Distance = 700 m
Displacement = 0 m

(c) Distance $= 2 \times \pi \times 5 = 31.42$ m
Displacement = 0 m

(d) Distance = 230 m
Displacement = 187 m at 16° to the vertical (or 74° to the floor)

Page 195 Speed and velocity

1. $\frac{22}{3} = 7.3$ s
2. A: $600 \div 24 = 25$ m/s
B: $200\,000 \div (90 \times 60) = 37$ m/s
C: $20 \div 0.5 = 40$ m/s
D: $3\,000\,000 \div (24 \times 60 \times 60) = 35$ m/s
C is fastest on average

Page 196 Distance-time relationships

1. A - constant speed
B - decreasing speed (decelerating) and stopping
C - increasing speed (accelerating)
D - stationary
2. **(a)** B **(b)** A **(c)** C

Page 197 Uniform acceleration

1. $1.5 \times 9.8 = 14.7$ m/s
2. **(a)** -65 m/s
(b) $t = \frac{\Delta v}{a} = \frac{-65}{-5} = 13$ s
3. **(a)** The object is getting faster.
(b) The object is getting slower (decelerating).

Page 198 Velocity-time graphs

(a) Read up from 5 s; the velocity is 4 m/s

(b) The gradient of the graph is getting smaller (less steep) with time.

Page 199 Newton's laws of motion

(a) The ball applies a force to the cricket bat backwards.

(b) Gravity pulls the Earth up towards the person.

(c) The table applies a contact force upwards onto the cup.

Page 200 Newton's second law

(a) 250 N

(b) $m = F \div a = (300 - 50) \div 1.67 = 150$ kg

(c) It would be half as much:
$1.67 \div 2 = 0.835$ m/s^2

Page 201 Investigating acceleration

1. **(a)** Change the mass hanging from the pulley
(b) force = weight = mass × gravitational field strength $= 1 \times 9.8 = 9.8$ N
2. To ensure the mass of the trolley is constant; to keep the friction / drag constant
3. **(a)** Increasing the force will increase the acceleration.
(b) Increasing the mass will decrease the acceleration.
(c) doubled

Page 202 Stopping distance

1. speed = distance ÷ time = 18.6 m ÷ 0.6 s = 31 m/s

Page 203 Braking distance

Kinetic energy $= \frac{1}{2} \times$ mass $\times$ velocity^2. Doubling the speed increases the kinetic energy by four times. The brakes have to do four times the work to stop the car, so the car travels four times further when braking. Therefore, the braking distance is four times longer.

Page 204 Types of wave

1. Using speed = distance/time the student can use distance = 400 m (distance to the wall and back) and time = time taken between clap and echo. Inputting these into the equation will give the speed of sound.
2. Ocean waves are transverse as they transfer mass perpendicular to the direction of the wave. This also demonstrates that the water itself is not travelling as the wave travels.
3. There are no particles for sound to transfer through.

Page 205 Properties of waves

1. **(a)** hertz, Hz; **(b)** metres, m; **(c)** seconds, s
2. decreases; decreases
3. 0.5 Hz
4. $\frac{10}{4} = 2.5$ m/s

Page 206 Investigating waves

1. 1 vibration takes 0.36 seconds

   $\text{frequency} = \frac{1}{\text{period}} = \frac{1}{0.36} = 2.8\,\text{Hz}$

2. Either of:

   Increase the weight

   Increase distance between oscillator and pulley

Page 207 Types of electromagnetic wave

1. Any two of the following:
   - premature ageing of the skin
   - skin cancer (caused by UV light)
   - sunburn.
2. Any two from: kill cells, damage DNA, cause mutations, cause cancer, damage tissue.
3. Any four from:

   Both travel at same speed in a vacuum.

   Both transfer energy.

   Both are transverse waves.

   Both can be reflected, refracted, transmitted, absorbed.

   Visible light has shorter wavelength / higher frequency OR microwaves have longer wavelength / lower frequency.

Page 208 Properties of electromagnetic waves

1. thermal energy
2. You would expect to see the colours separately / a spectrum / a rainbow.
3. 1–9°

Page 209 Infrared radiation

1. It would help the house designers to decide what colours to paint the walls to trap heat inside the house. Making the inside light or shiny would reflect radiated heat back into the rooms. Painting the outside black would absorb heat from the environment, or painting the inside silver would reduce the heat emitted.
2. White would be better, because it would emit less infrared when hot, causing the drink to lose energy more slowly.
3. Tin foil would conduct heat relatively easily, but paper would insulate, making the test unfair.

Page 210 Applications of EM waves

1. **(a)** Any two from: radio waves, microwaves, infrared, visible light

   (b) Radio: TV, radio, two-way radio

   Microwaves: mobile phones, satellites, satellite TV

   Infrared: remote controls, wireless links between computers

   Visible light: car indicators, warning lights, flashing torches, optical fibres

2. Any two of the following:
   - to make documents such as passports, driving licenses and bank cards harder to counterfeit
   - to make it easier for the police to identify the owner of stolen items
   - to write secret messages
   - to stamp the hands of event attendees without leaving an unsightly mark.

Page 211 Magnetic fields

1. Place a compass near one of the poles. If the north arrow on the compass points towards the pole, it is the south pole. If it points away, it is the north pole.
2. Use a magnet to repel or attract another without touching it.

   Or:

   Show how a magnet moves a compass arrow without touching it.

3. **(a)** A permanent magnet always has a magnetic field. An induced magnet only has a magnetic field when placed near another magnet.

   (b) An induced magnet is an object made of cobalt, iron, nickel or steel that is being attracted to a magnet, for example, a fridge door with a magnet stuck to it.

Page 212 Electromagnetism

1. It can be switched off to put objects down, and its strength can be increased to pick up heavier objects.
2. 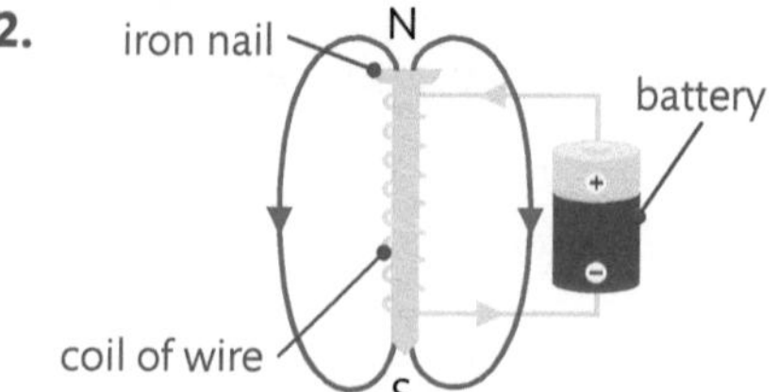

   North is at the top.

3. Change the direction of the electric current.

Page 213 Equations

1. **(a)** $m = \rho V, V = \frac{m}{\rho}$

   (b) $I = \sqrt{\frac{P}{R}}, R = \frac{P}{I^2}$

   (c) $m = \frac{\Delta E}{c\Delta\theta}, c = \frac{\Delta E}{m\Delta\theta}, \Delta\theta = \frac{\Delta E}{mc}$.

   (d) $\Delta v = at, t = \frac{\Delta v}{a}$.

2. **(a)** force: newtons

   (b) kinetic energy: joules

   (c) weight: newtons

   (d) wavelength: metres

   (e) mass: kilograms

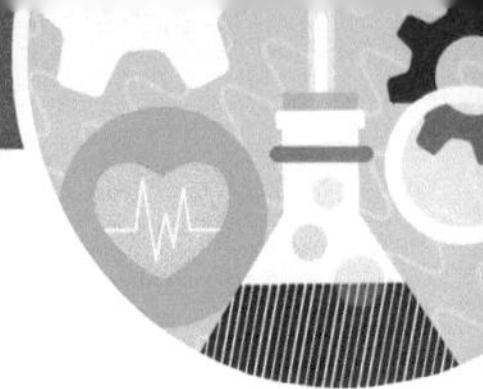

Page 214 Converting units

1. **(a)** $200\,\mu g \div 10^6 = 2\times10^{-4}$ g or 0.0002 g
   (b) $10 \div 1000 = 0.01$ N/g
   (c) $330 \times 1000 = 330\,000$ J/s $= 3.3 \times 10^5$ J/s
2. $4.5 \times 60 = 270$ s

Page 215 Making estimations

From **Figure 1**, around 500 s.

Page 216 Interpreting data

(a) mean = 1.62 kg ((1.1 kg + 1.2 kg + 1.2 kg + 1.3 kg + 3.3 kg)/5 = 1.62 kg)
mode = 1.2 kg
median = 1.2 kg

(b) There is one large puppy and this makes the mean larger than all of the other puppies.

Page 217 Using charts and graphs

1. **(a)** Bar chart - different cars are a discrete variable.
   (b) Line graph (or scatter graph with line of best fit) - they best show the relationship between two quantities.
   (c) Pie chart - they are best for showing the proportions of something that can be compared.
2. gradient = 4, *y* intercept = 10

Page 218 Using diagrams

1.

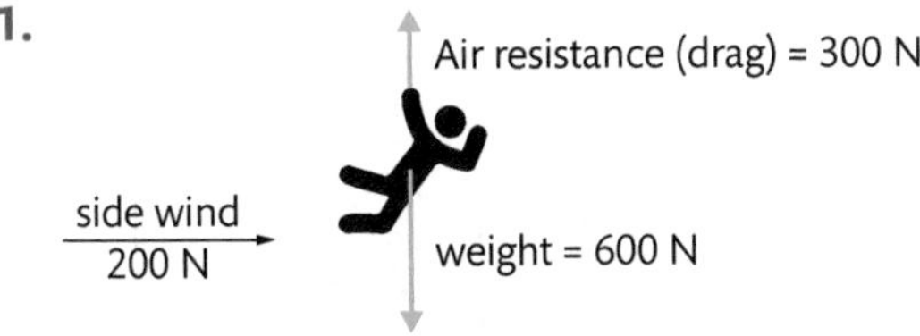

2.

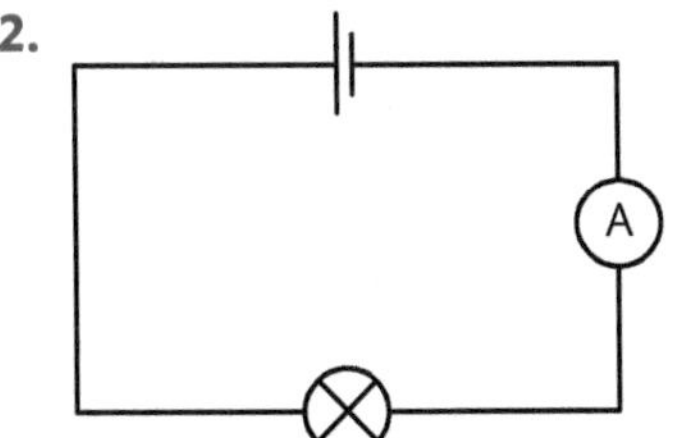

Page 219 Planning practicals

(a) Measuring: thickness of insulation; temperature change
Controlling: volume of water, size and material of beaker; insulating material

(b) Thermometer; ruler

(c) Care with hot water; wipe up spills

Page 220 Comparing data

(a) Similarities: Both show that stopping distance increases with speed,
The stopping distances of both tyres increases more rapidly at higher speeds.
Differences: Tyre A has a greater stopping distance for any speed,
Speed and stopping distance stays proportional for tyre A much longer.

(b) We would expect that the wet road would make the stopping distances much longer. Water on the road means there is less friction and therefore a lower braking force, meaning the car has to travel further to stop.

(c) Tyre B has the best performance as the stopping distances are shorter which means it is safer or stops over shorter distances. (Even though tyre A was more consistent, the stopping distances were greater making it a worse tyre).

Page 221 Evaluating data

(a) The human reaction time of the student will affect the time.

(b) The run can be timed multiple times and an average taken. Light gates could be placed at the top and bottom of the ramp attached to a timer that would start and stop as the ball passed through.

Page 222 Working scientifically

1. The best conductor would have the lowest resistance. To measure the resistance, you would need to measure the potential difference across the sample with a voltmeter and current through the sample of metal with an ammeter after connecting it to a power supply. Resistance = potential difference ÷ current.

   To reduce errors, keep the current low to avoid heating, repeat the readings several times and take an average. Use a ruler to keep the length of each sample the same and a calliper to check the width of each sample is the same.
2. More people would be able to use solar powered rather than fossil fuel powered or rechargeable electric cars, which would reduce carbon emissions and reduce the effect of global warming. Countries with variable day lengths or poor daylight through frequent poor weather would be better able to use the technology where previously they did not generate enough power to operate the cars.

Periodic table

Key

relative atomic mass atomic symbol name atomic (proton) number

1	2											3	4	5	6	7	0
							1 H Hydrogen 1										4 He Helium 2
7 Li Lithium 3	9 Be Beryllium 4											11 B Boron 5	12 C Carbon 6	14 N Nitrogen 7	16 O Oxygen 8	19 F Fluorine 9	20 Ne Neon 10
23 Na Sodium 11	24 Mg Magnesium 12											27 Al Aluminium 13	28 Si Silicon 14	31 P Phosphorus 15	32 S Sulfur 16	35.5 Cl Chlorine 17	40 Ar Argon 18
39 K Potassium 19	40 Ca Calcium 20	45 Sc Scandium 21	48 Ti Titanium 22	51 V Vanadium 23	52 Cr Chromium 24	55 Mn Manganese 25	56 Fe Iron 26	59 Co Cobalt 27	59 Ni Nickel 28	63.5 Cu Copper 29	65 Zn Zinc 30	70 Ga Gallium 31	73 Ge Germanium 32	75 As Arsenic 33	79 Se Selenium 34	80 Br Bromine 35	84 Kr Krypton 36
85 Rb Rubidium 37	88 Sr Strontium 38	89 Y Yttrium 39	91 Zr Zirconium 40	93 Nb Niobium 41	96 Mo Molybdenum 42	98 Tc Technetium 43	101 Ru Ruthenium 44	103 Rh Rhodium 45	106 Pd Palladium 46	108 Ag Silver 47	112 Cd Cadmium 48	115 In Indium 49	119 Sn Tin 50	122 Sb Antimony 51	128 Te Tellurium 52	127 I Iodine 53	131 Xe Xenon 54
133 Cs Caesium 55	137 Ba Barium 56	139 La Lanthanum 57	178 Hf Hafnium 72	181 Ta Tantalum 73	184 W Tungsten 74	186 Re Rhenium 75	190 Os Osmium 76	192 Ir Iridium 77	195 Pt Platinum 78	197 Au Gold 79	201 Hg Mercury	204 Tl Thallium	207 Pb Lead	209 Bi Bismuth 83	[210] Po Polonium 84	[210] At Astatine 85	[222] Rn Radon 86
[223] Fr Francium 87	[226] Ra Radium 88	[227] Ac Actinium 89	[261] Rf Rutherfordium 104	[262] Db Dubnium 105	[266] Sg Seaborgium 106	[264] Bh Bohrium 107	[277] Hs Hassium 108	[268] Mt Meitnerium 109	[271] Ds Darmstadtium 110	[272] Rg Roentgenium 111	[285] Cn Copernicium 112	[286] Uut Ununtrium 113	[289] Fl Flerovium 114	[289] Uup Ununpentium 115	[293] Lv Livermorium 116	[294] Uus Ununseptium 117	[294] Uuo Ununoctium 118

* The Lanthandies (atomic numbers 58 – 71) and the Actinides (atomic numbers 90 – 103) have been omitted.
Relative atomic massses for Cu and Cl have not been rounded to the nearest whole number.

Formulae for Physics

In the exam, you could be asked about any of the equations on this page. Make sure you know how to rearrange each of the equations and learn the units that match each quantity.

Formulae to learn

Word equation	Symbol equation
weight = mass × gravitational field strength	$W = mg$
work done = force × distance (along the line of action of the force)	$W = Fs$
force applied to a spring = spring constant × extension	$F = ke$
distance travelled = speed × time	$s = vt$
acceleration = change in velocity ÷ time taken	$a = \frac{\Delta v}{t}$
resultant force = mass × acceleration	$F = ma$
kinetic energy = 0.5 × mass × (speed)^2	$E_k = \frac{1}{2}mv^2$
gravitational potential energy = mass × gravitational field strength × height	$E_p = mgh$
power = energy transferred ÷ time	$P = \frac{E}{t}$
power = work done ÷ time	$P = \frac{W}{t}$
efficiency = useful output energy transfer ÷ total input energy transfer	
efficiency = useful power output ÷ total power input	
wave speed = frequency × wavelength	$v = f\lambda$
charge flow = current × time	$Q = It$
potential difference = current × resistance	$V = IR$
power = potential difference × current	$P = VI$
power = (current)^2 × resistance	$P = I^2R$
energy transferred = power × time	$E = Pt$
energy transferred = charge flow × potential difference	$E = QV$
density = mass ÷ volume	$\rho = \frac{m}{V}$

Physics equation sheet

You will be given a list of some of the more complicated equations in the exam.

Word equation	Symbol equation
(final velocity)^2 - (initial velocity)^2 = 2 × acceleration × distance	$v^2 - u^2 = 2as$
elastic potential energy = 0.5 × spring constant × (extension)^2	$E_e = \frac{1}{2}ke^2$
change in thermal energy = mass × specific heat capacity × temperature change	$\Delta E = mc\Delta\theta$
period = $\frac{1}{\text{frequency}}$	
thermal energy for a change of state = mass × specific latent heat	$E = mL$

Published by BBC Active, an imprint of Educational Publishers LLP, part of the Pearson Education Group, 80 Strand, London, WC2R 0RL.

www.pearsonschools.co.uk/BBCBitesize

Typeset by Newgen KnowledgeWorks Pvt. Ltd., Chennai, India

Produced and illustrated by Newgen Publishing UK

Cover design by Andrew Magee & Pearson Education Limited 2019

Cover illustration by Darren Lingard / Oxford Designers & Illustrators

First published 2019

24
10 9 8 7 6 5 4

British Library Cataloguing in Publication Data

A catalogue record for this book is available from the British Library

ISBN 978 1 406 68616 6

Printed and bound by CPI Group (UK) Ltd, Croydon CR0 4YY

The Publisher's policy is to use paper manufactured from sustainable forests.

Acknowledgements

Content written by Byron Dawson is included.

The authors and publisher would like to thank the following individuals and organisations for their kind permission to reproduce copyright material.

Text:

P 1-21, 23-24, 31-40, 42-49, 51-58, 60-70, 72-73, 75-134, 136, 138-214: © 2019, BBC.

P 63 The Wildlife Trust for Lancashire, Manchester & North Merseyside: Red and grey squirrels distribution in the British Isles in 1945 and 2010, The Wildlife Trust for Lancashire, Manchester & North Merseyside. Used with permission.

Photographs

(Key: T-top; B-bottom; C-centre; L-left; R-right)

123RF: Jarun Ontakrai 19, **Alamy Stock Photo:** Norbert Michalke/Imagebroker 04, Mediscan 26t, Nigel Cattlin 27, Chronicle 31, Nigel Cattlin 33, Avico Ltd 57, Premaphotos 58, Wayne Lynch/All Canada Photos 62, Doug McCutcheon/LGPL 66, Xue Yubin/Xinhua 74, Studio/PhotoCuisine RM 92, **Getty Images:** Hero Images 38, Rancho_runner/iStock 64, **Science Photo Library:** Andre Labbe ISM 07l, James King-Holmes 09, Martyn F.Chillmaid 67, **Shutterstock:** D.Kucharski K.Kucharska 05, Pistolseven 07r, Cliparea/Custom media 22b, ChaNaWiT 22t, Plant Pathology 26b, Kateryna Kon 53, DrimaFilm 71, Guentermanaus 72, Demarcomedia 99, TFoxFoto 147r, Jerry Horbert 147l, Daniel Prudek 161.

All other images © Pearson Education

Note from the publisher

Pearson has robust editorial processes, including answer and fact checks, to ensure the accuracy of the content in this publication, and every effort is made to ensure this publication is free of errors. We are, however, only human, and occasionally errors do occur. Pearson is not liable for any misunderstandings that arise as a result of errors in this publication, but it is our priority to ensure that the content is accurate. If you spot an error, please do contact us at resourcescorrections@pearson.com so we can make sure it is corrected.

Notes

Notes

Notes

Notes

Notes

Notes